W9-DJJ-832

European Foreign Policy

This book brings together for the first time all the key documents relevant to the idea of European foreign policy, tracing its development from the late 1940s right up to the present day. This idea represents the European Union's efforts to ensure that its Member States speak with one voice in international politics. The book's unparalleled comprehensive coverage includes:

* all the important documents on European foreign policy from 1948 to the Kosovo crisis;
* material from major treaties such as the North Atlantic Treaty, the Treaty of Rome and the Treaty of Amsterdam;
* European responses to major world events such as the Middle East peace process, the Falklands War and the Balkans crisis;
* detailed commentary and analysis of the documents providing a valuable political and historical context.

European Foreign Policy is a collection of basic official documents which are otherwise inaccessible; it is a vital, practical handbook for anyone interested in European foreign policy, from student to scholar or practitioner.

Christopher Hill is Montague Burton Professor of International Relations at the London School of Economics. He is a well-known authority in the field and among other works has edited *The Actors in Europe's Foreign Policy* and co-edited *Two Worlds of International Relations: Academics, Practitioners and Trade in Ideas*, both published by Routledge. **Karen E. Smith** is lecturer in international relations at the LSE, and the author of *The Making of EU Foreign Policy: The Case of Eastern Europe*.

This book is the first output of the European Foreign Policy Unit (EFPU) of the LSE's Department of International Relations.

European Foreign Policy

Key documents

Christopher Hill and Karen E. Smith

London and New York

In association with the
Secretariat of the
European Parliament

First published 2000 by Routledge
11 New Fetter Lane, London EC4P 4EE

Simultaneously published in the USA and Canada
by Routledge
29 West 35th Street, New York, NY 10001

Routledge is an imprint of the Taylor & Francis Group

Typeset in Baskerville and Helvetica by
Florence Production Ltd, Stoodleigh, Devon
Printed and bound in Great Britain by
TJ International Ltd, Padstow, Cornwall

British Library Cataloguing in Publication Data
A catalogue record for this book is available from the British Library

Library of Congress Cataloging in Publication Data
European foreign policy : key documents / [edited by] Christopher Hill
& Karen E. Smith.
      p.   cm.
  Includes bibliographical references and index.
  1. Europe—Foreign relations—1945– Sources.   I. Hill, Christopher,
1948–.   II. Smith, Karen Elizabeth.
D1060 .E887 2000–03–02
327.4–dc21   00–020256

ISBN 0–415–15822–2 (hbk)
ISBN 0–415–15823–0 (pbk)

Contents

Section 3 The revival of the WEU and the evolution of a European security identity   185

The reactivation of the WEU

The Cold War ends

The war in the former Yugoslavia
(a) Mediation

        10 April 1982   428

Central America
4c/28   Conclusions by the European Council on Central America,
        Brussels, 29–30 March 1982   429
4c/29   Conclusions by the European Council on Central America,
        Stuttgart, 17–19 June 1983   430
4c/30   Joint Communiqué of the Conference of Foreign Ministers
        of the European Community and its Member States, Portugal
        and Spain, the States of Central America and the Contadora
        States, San José, Costa Rica, 28–29 September 1984   430

ASEAN
4c/31   Joint Declaration of the Community–ASEAN Foreign
        Ministers' Conference, Brussels, 20–21 November 1978   435
4c/32   Joint Statement, EC–ASEAN Ministerial Meeting, Kuala
        Lumpur, 7–8 March 1980   436

Burma/Myanmar
4c/33   Common Position Defined by the Council of the European
        Union on the Basis of Article J.2 of the Treaty on European
        Union on Burma/Myanmar, 28 October 1996
        (96/635/CFSP)   438
4c/34   Conclusions by the General Affairs Council on Burma/
        Myanmar, Luxembourg, 26 June 1997   439

Relations with Japan
4c/35   Joint Declaration on EC–Japan Relations, The Hague,
        18 July 1991   440

Human rights
4c/36   Resolution of the Council and of the Member States
        Meeting in the Council on Human Rights, Democracy
        and Development, 28 November 1991   443
4c/37   EU Code of Conduct on Arms Exports, Council Statement,
        25 May 1998, Brussels (in Appendix)   460
4c/38   Declaration of the European Union on the Occasion of the
        Fiftieth Anniversary of the Universal Declaration on Human
        Rights, Vienna, 10 December 1998   447

Appendix

3/19   Conclusions of the European Council in Helsinki, 11 December
        1999, on the European Security and Defence Policy   450
46/60   Conclusions of the European Council in Helsinki, 11 December
        1999, on Enlargement   458
43/37   EU Code of Conduct on Arms Exports, Council Statement,
        25 May 1998, Brussels   460

        List of commonly used abbreviations   466
        Index   469

Preface

This book is designed to fill a void long noticed by students of European foreign policy, the lack of a collection of the key documents produced by European Political Cooperation (EPC) and its successor, the Common Foreign and Security Policy (CFSP). The government of the Federal Republic of Germany helpfully produced a pocket-book of selected materials which ran into five editions in the 1970s and 1980s, but although free on demand this was not readily available, and it is now, indeed, out of print. More conventionally published was Professor J.A.S. Grenville's *The Major International Treaties 1914–73*, but this first-class work has only limited space for the pre-history of EPC. Individual works of commentary such as de Schoutheete (1986) or Pijpers, Regelsberger and Wessels (1988) also contain some useful documentary annexes, but they are not systematic – or easy to find. The *European Political Cooperation Documentation Bulletin*, published from Florence and Bonn intermittently since 1987, was a useful reference source but too unwieldy and expensive for everyday purposes. It has now moved online, and is an indispensable tool for rapidly tracing CFSP and related documents (*The European Foreign Policy Bulletin*). The Council of Ministers website also now contains CFSP documents.

The editors therefore hope that the audience for this work will be twofold: on the one hand, we aim to provide a collection of documents that the specialist on European international relations would find useful because it does not exist elsewhere and because he or she would otherwise have to do a lot of time-consuming work in tracking down documents such as the Fouchet Plans or the Stuttgart Solemn Declaration that are often hard to come by. On the other hand, we intend to furnish the person coming new to the subject with the basic texts on the subject, which can be used for documents-based coursework or dissertations. To this end we have provided a linking commentary (and cross-references) which should help the reader to understand the origins and context of each document, but we have not written long essays which would repeat the excellent material already available – a bibliography of which is given at the end of this Preface.

Selection is always difficult in an exercise of this kind, and there is a choice to be made between keeping the book manageable and ensuring that the treatment is professional and comprehensive. Our preference is for the latter. The criterion used is whether or not a given document enables a reader to understand why the European Community (EC)/European Union (EU) developed a foreign policy system in the way that it did, even if some documents are more indispensable than others to such an understanding. We have also taken an eclectic view of 'European foreign policy', not restricting ourselves wholly to EPC or CFSP texts. On occasions we have wished to illustrate the transatlantic dimension, as with the Harmel Report of 1967, or that of security cooperation outside the EC, as with the foundations of the Western European Union (WEU), or even bilateral relations, as with the Elysée Treaty of 1963, which cemented the crucial Franco-German relationship. We trust that readers will regard the aesthetic losses of this strategy as being compensated for by the practical gains of being able to make connections with the wider environment in which the EC was working and of having access to some documents which are often referred to but rarely reproduced. This is particularly the case in the 1990s, when the EU, WEU and NATO all drew much closer together as part of the ongoing transformation of Europe's security architecture.

The book is organized on the basis of four sections. The four vary in terms of the commentary supplied on the documents themselves. At times the emphasis is more on an overview of a particular phase of events or linked series of documents. At others, detailed commentary is supplied for an individual document. Space constraints have been important, but the basic criterion has always been the needs of a reader conceived as being not completely unfamiliar with the history of European foreign policy but in need of contextual detail and narrative thread. No attempt has been made, however, to provide a blow-by-blow history of EPC/CFSP, and Section 4 on policy has accordingly been left largely to speak for itself.

The first section of the book deals with the origins of EPC and with various abortive attempts to create a mechanism for generating European foreign policy before the actual emergence of EPC in 1969. The second deals with the mainstream institutional developments of EPC from 1969 to 1997, and contains all the basic texts that have governed its procedure, from the Luxembourg Report to the Treaty of Amsterdam. The third covers the specialized area of security and the at first parallel then converging evolution of the WEU. The fourth and last deals with matters of policy substance. This is the most abbreviated of all – although it does not seem so – given the vast amount of declarations, statements and answers to parliamentary questions that EPC/CFSP have produced over the years. The section is itself broken down into subsections, largely on geographical lines. Not included in the book, by and large, are early drafts or position papers for eventual treaties and material relating to third country reactions.

Documents are reproduced in full where we think they are foundational or where the reader needs to see all the material to make an effective judgement. Where this is not so, and it is particularly the case where a document contains much extraneous material beyond that on foreign policy (as with the Treaty of Rome) we have made our selections transparent both by indicating which sections have been included and which not, and by using dots to show cuts within sections. In these cases the reader who wishes to see more should always be able to find the omitted material easily in the original. Texts have been reproduced, with minor exceptions, exactly as in the originals, thus illustrating the variability of terms and infelicities of English, inevitable in multinational drafting.

In putting this collection together we have become indebted to those who have gone before us: the archivists of the Auswärtiges Amt in Bonn, Professor J.A.S. Grenville, and colleagues such as Panayiotis Ifestos, Alfred Pijpers, Elfriede Regelsberger, Wolfgang Wessels, Philippe de Schoutheete de Tervarent and William Wallace. In particular the classic history of EPC written by Simon Nuttall (1992) has been an invaluable guide to the nuances and the contexts of the texts. On the practical side, we are indebted to Jürgen Haacke of the London School of Economics and Political Science (LSE) for his assistance and advice in assembling the manuscript, and to the Staff Research Fund of the LSE for financial support. John Christian Maguire did a great deal of photocopying. We are also most grateful to Jennifer Chapa of the LSE, for her highly competent secretarial assistance, and to Emir Lawless, the EU Documents Librarian at the European University Institute in Florence for her considerable assistance. The advice and assistance of the European Parliament's Secretariat, and in particular of Mr Dirk Toornstra of the Research Division, and Mr Christopher Piening, the head of the Parliament's London Office, have been indispensable, not least in enabling us to reach an interested readership. The staff of the Chatham House library, as always, have been most helpful.

All the documents are in the official realm, and copyright problems do not apply. We hope that this collection will go some way towards dispelling the mystique that still surrounds foreign policy in general and European foreign policy in particular. All states, indeed the world, need an intelligent discussion of foreign policy problems. Without basic primary information, that will remain a forlorn hope.

Sources

Readers seeking the original texts of the documents we have cited, or other related documents, will in some cases have to be prepared to put in hard labour in a first-class library, preferably one containing a European Documentation Centre. We have used the *Official Journal* of the European Communities, together with the monthly *Bulletin*, a great deal. The *European Political Cooperation Documentation Bulletin* (now *European Foreign Policy Bulletin* online) and the *European Political Cooperation* handbooks produced by the Press and Information Service of the Federal Republic of Germany have also been basic sources. The NATO and WEU Secretariats provide helpful versions of key texts gratis, which today are to be found on the Internet at their respective websites (the same is true for some EU texts, although for the original Treaty of Rome readers will need to go elsewhere – for example Tufts University's site in the United States!). For the rest, various sources have been used. The principal works containing or explaining documents are listed below.

Council of Ministers website:
   http://www.europa.eu.int

Andrew Duff (ed.) *The Treaty of Amsterdam: Text and Commentary*, London, Federal Trust, 1997.

European Foreign Policy Bulletin:
   http://www.iue.it/EFPB/Welcome.html

European Political Cooperation Documentation Bulletin, Florence, European University Institute, and Bonn, Institut für Europäische Politik, 1987 on (documents surveyed start from 1985).

European Political Cooperation, Bonn, Press and Information Service of the Government of the Federal Republic of Germany, five editions, 1977–86.

European Political Cooperation: Documents of the Irish Presidency, Dublin, Department of Foreign Affairs, 1990.

J.A.S. Grenville and Bernard Wasserstein, *The Major International Treaties since 1945: A History and Guide with Texts*, London, Methuen, 1987.

Panayiotis Ifestos, *European Political Cooperation: Towards a Framework of Supranational Diplomacy?*, Aldershot, Avebury, 1987.

Journal of Common Market Studies, 'The European Community (Union): annual review of activities', 1992–, edited by Neill Nugent, contains sections on 'External policy developments', written first by Christopher Brewin and then by David Allen and Michael Smith.

I. Macleod, I.D. Hendry and Stephen Hyett, *The External Relations of the European Communities*, Oxford, Clarendon Press, 1996.

Simon Nuttall, *European Political Cooperation*, Oxford, Clarendon Press, 1992.

Alfred Pijpers, Elfriede Regelsberger and Wolfgang Wessels (eds, in collaboration with Geoffrey Edwards) *European Political Cooperation in the 1980s: A Common Foreign Policy for Western Europe?* Dordrecht, Martinus Nijhoff, 1988.

Elfriede Regelsberger, Philippe de Schoutheete de Tervarent and Wolfgang Wessels (eds) *Foreign Policy of the European Union: From EPC to CFSP and Beyond*, Boulder, CO, Lynne Rienner, 1997.

Philippe de Schoutheete de Tervarent, *La Cooperation politique européenne*, 2nd edition, Brussels, Editions Labor, 1986.

Yearbook of European Law (eds D. Wyatt and A. Barav), Oxford, Clarendon Press (contains commentaries on European Political Cooperation for most years from 1981 on).

Section 1 The beginnings

The origins of change often turn out to have been working away by stealth with hardly anyone noticing, even those who will ultimately be awarded the historical credit. In the case of European foreign policy, or the collective diplomacy of the European Union, there are roots to be traced back well beyond the formal act of creation in 1970, when the Luxembourg Report gave birth to European Political Cooperation. Right from the beginning of the post-war period it had been evident to the leaders of the democratic states of western Europe, albeit in very different ways, that the traditional emphasis on flexible national diplomacy, and no permanent entanglements, was not going to be sufficient to cope with a world in which the two emerging superpowers were taking a close interest in Europe's fate, and where national defence seemed likely to be forever compromised by the arrival of nuclear weapons. Looking back, the broad historical conditions were in place for the eventual emergence of a form of foreign policy cooperation among some European states, and the emergence of these conditions can be traced back over the period 1945–70.

At first, however, the vision was much more myopic and specific: how to deal with Germany. France, emerging from four years of Nazi occupation, felt itself intensely vulnerable to a German revival, while Britain, once again exhausted by the effort of victory, was sent into shock by the rapidity with which the United States distanced itself from its erstwhile ally, ending both lend-lease and nuclear cooperation in 1946, and forcing sterling into a damaging convertibility in 1947. It was, then, hardly surprising that Paris and London, which had engaged in early forms of military integration from 1905 to 1918, and had considered even political union amid the hysteria of May–June 1940, should turn again to the possibility of an alliance.

Alliances are not, in fact, at all the same thing as foreign policy cooperation. Their traditional concern is to establish a *casus foederis* in the event of a military attack. However, such a commitment always implies a diplomatic alignment, and in modern conditions of detailed contingency planning and transnational bureaucracies, it produces pressures for the harmonization of policies across a much wider range than that deriving from the mutual defence obligation. Thus the alliances formed in the aftermath of the Second World War turned out to have great significance for the overall pattern of international politics, not least in terms of the permanent division between the states of eastern and western Europe.

The latter group was primarily organized around the powerful outside force of the United States, which certainly acted as Europe's external pacifier. But this did not rule out the development of a foreign policy system among the West Europeans themselves which was in large part the product of a need to cope with the consequences of American world power. Nor did the United States itself shrink from promoting a phenomenon which theoretically at least could have produced a serious rival to its own dominance. It fostered the European Defence Community (EDC) initiative of 1952 (document 1/6) and the Political Community of 1953 (document 1/7). Even American support was not sufficient to prevent the failure of these over-ambitious schemes, but the very attempt helped to prepare the ground for future, more practical developments. Furthermore smaller building blocks were also being put in place, such as the Anglo-French Dunkirk Treaty of 1947, and the Treaty of Brussels of 1948 (document 1/1).

The shipwreck of the EDC was salvaged by the British-inspired WEU deal of 1954. This built on the Brussels Treaty between Britain and what were soon to become the Six of the European Economic Community (EEC) to create a mutual defence pact which contained (in Article V) the automatic assistance clause that the North Atlantic Treaty Organization (NATO) lacked (its own Article V provides only for an individual member to take 'such action as it deems necessary' in the event of an armed attack on a partner) and the means for Germany to rearm within the context of a 'normal' alliance not solely aimed at protecting its partners from itself, even if their troops were increasingly to be based on German soil (document 1/8). Thus the Atlanticism of NATO (document 1/2) began to be paralleled by more discrete European arrangements.

On the West European front, however, foreign policy cooperation would have to wait for the foundations of functional cooperation to be laid down and consolidated. Extracts from the Schuman Plan (document 1/4) are included here both because they represent the beginnings of European integration and because they show the whole integration process was launched for reasons of international relations – to prevent a recurrence of the Franco-German conflicts which had brought Europe and the world to catastrophe twice in a generation. The same applies to the Treaty of Rome in 1957 (document 1/9) which gave birth to the European Economic Community, with its own consequential external economic relations – perhaps the *sine qua non* of the eventual development of European Political Cooperation. The relevant sections of the treaty are included – that is, those on the common commercial policy (CCP) and agreements with third countries, as the possibility of a common foreign policy is not mentioned – together with those articles from the Single European Act of 1987 (document 2/15), the Treaty of European Union (the Treaty of Maastricht) of 1993 (document 2/20) and the Treaty of Amsterdam of 1997 (document 2/22) which have modified the CCP. These relate, in particular, to Articles 113, 228 (the Commission's negotiating powers), 235 (sanctions), 237 (membership) and 238 (association agreements).

The creation of a system of diplomatic coordination did not, however, depend on linear progress in the supranational realm. It could, indeed, be proposed as an alternative to supranationalism, as General de Gaulle did with the Fouchet Plans of 1961–2 (documents 1/10 and 1/11). This attempt to refashion the whole EEC in the image of an inter-state, foreign policy-led association foundered on the opposition of the other five, but it undoubtedly provided an impetus and a blueprint for the eventual emergence of EPC. There were other important foundations being laid for foreign policy coordination, too, in the 1960s. The 1963 Elysée Treaty between France and Germany (document 1/12) began the system of bilateral consultations which has turned out to be one of the key locomotive forces in European integration, while the Harmel Report of 1967 on the Atlantic Alliance (document 1/13) was most influential in its insistence that relations with the eastern bloc had to be based on detente as well as deterrence. This concern for balance was increasingly a distinguishing mark of an emerging European perspective on the Cold War, and it was, in a very short time, to take on an institutional form.

The Brussels Treaty

Reflecting the increasing western preoccupation with the Soviet Union over 1947–8, the Brussels Treaty, committing Britain, France and the Benelux countries to each others' defence, had a more universal orientation than the Treaty of Dunkirk, of 1947 although it too referred explicitly to a possible German threat. Article IV provided for automatic assistance in the event of attack and was therefore a much stronger commitment than the NATO Treaty (see document 1/2) which was to follow a year later. The Brussels Treaty, due to expire in 1998, but with the same possibilities of renewal as that of Dunkirk, was the basis of the Paris Agreements of 1954, which set up the WEU and the eventual moving together of the EU and the WEU via the treaties of Maastricht and Amsterdam (see documents 1/8, 2/18 and 2/22).

Document 1/1   Treaty of Economic, Social and Cultural Collaboration and Collective Self-Defence between the United Kingdom of Great Britain and Northern Ireland, Belgium, France, Luxembourg and the Netherlands (The Brussels Treaty), Brussels, 17 March 1948

[The Signatories]

Resolved

To reaffirm their faith in fundamental human rights, in the dignity and worth of the human person and in the other ideals proclaimed in the Charter of the United Nations;

To fortify and preserve the principles of democracy, personal freedom and political liberty, the constitutional traditions and the rule of law, which are their common heritage;

To strengthen, with these aims in view, the economic, social and cultural ties by which they are already united;

To co-operate loyally and to co-ordinate their efforts to create in Western Europe a firm basis for European economic recovery;

To afford assistance to each other, in accordance with the Charter of the United Nations, in maintaining international peace and security and in resisting any policy of aggression;

To take such steps as may be held to be necessary in the event of a renewal by Germany of a policy of aggression;

To associate progressively in the pursuance of these aims other States inspired by the same ideals and animated by the like determination;

Desiring for these purposes to conclude a treaty for collaboration in economic, social and cultural matters and for collective self-defence;

. . .

have agreed as follows:—

ARTICLE I

Convinced of the close community of their interests and of the necessity of uniting in order to promote the economic recovery of Europe, the High Contracting Parties will so organise and co-ordinate their economic activities as to produce the best possible results, by the elimination of conflict in their economic policies, the co-ordination of production and the development of commercial exchanges.

The co-operation provided for in the preceding paragraph, which will be effected through the Consultative Council referred to in Article VII as well as through other bodies, shall not involve any duplication of, or prejudice to, the work of other economic organisations in which the High Contracting Parties are or may be represented but shall on the contrary assist the work of those organisations.

ARTICLE II

The High Contracting Parties will make every effort in common, both by direct consultation and in specialised agencies, to promote the attainment of a higher standard of living by their peoples and to develop on corresponding lines the social and other related services of their countries.

The High Contracting Parties will consult with the object of achieving the earliest possible application of recommendations of immediate practical interest, relating to social matters, adopted with their approval in the specialised agencies.

They will endeavour to conclude as soon as possible conventions with each other in the sphere of social security.

ARTICLE III

The High Contracting Parties will make every effort in common to lead their peoples towards a better understanding of the principles which form the basis of their common civilisation and to promote cultural exchanges by conventions between themselves or by other means.

ARTICLE IV

If any of the High Contracting Parties should be the object of an armed attack in Europe, the other High Contracting Parties will, in accordance with the provisions of Article 51 of the Charter of the United Nations, afford the Party so attacked all the military and other aid and assistance in their power.

ARTICLE V

All measures taken as a result of the preceding Article shall be immediately reported to the Security Council. They shall be terminated as soon as the Security Council has taken the measures necessary to maintain or restore international peace and security.

The present Treaty does not prejudice in any way the obligations of the High Contracting Parties under the provisions of the Charter of the United Nations. It shall not be interpreted as affecting in any way the authority and responsibility of the Security Council under the Charter to take at any time such action as it deems necessary in order to maintain or restore international peace and security.

ARTICLE VI

The High Contracting Parties declare, each so far as he is concerned, that none of the international engagements now in force between him and any other of the High Contracting Parties or any third State is in conflict with the provisions of the present Treaty.

None of the High Contracting Parties will conclude any alliance or participate in any coalition directed against any other of the High Contracting Parties.

ARTICLE VII

For the purpose of consulting together on all the questions dealt with in the present Treaty, the High Contracting Parties will create a Consultative Council, which shall be so organised as to be able to exercise its functions continuously. The Council shall meet at such times as it shall deem fit.

At the request of any of the High Contracting Parties, the Council shall be immediately convened in order to permit the High Contracting Parties to consult with regard to any situation which may constitute a threat to peace, in whatever area this threat should arise; with regard to the attitude to be adopted and the steps to be taken in case of a renewal by Germany of an aggressive policy; or with regard to any situation constituting a danger to economic stability.

ARTICLE VIII

In pursuance of their determination to settle disputes only by peaceful means, the High Contracting Parties will apply to disputes between themselves the following provisions:

The High Contracting Parties will, while the present Treaty remains in force, settle all disputes falling within the scope of Article 36, paragraph 2, of the Statute of the International Court of Justice by referring them to the Court, subject only, in the case of each of them, to any reservation already made by that Party when accepting this clause for compulsory jurisdiction to the extent that that Party may maintain the reservation.

In addition, the High Contracting Parties will submit to conciliation all disputes outside the scope of Article 36, paragraph 2, of the Statute of the International Court of Justice.

In the case of a mixed dispute involving both questions for which conciliation is appropriate and other questions for which judicial settlement is appropriate, any Party to the dispute shall have the right to insist that the judicial settlement of the legal questions shall precede conciliation.

The preceding provisions of this Article in no way affect the application of relevant provisions or agreements prescribing some other method of pacific settlement.

ARTICLE IX

The High Contracting Parties may, by agreement, invite any other State to accede to the present Treaty on conditions to be agreed between them and the State so invited.

Any State so invited may become a Party to the Treaty by depositing an instrument of accession with the Belgian Government. . . .

ARTICLE X

The present Treaty shall be ratified and the instruments of ratification shall be deposited as soon as possible with the Belgian Government.

It shall enter into force on the date of the deposit of the last instrument of ratification and shall thereafter remain in force for fifty years.

After the expiry of the period of fifty years, each of the High Contracting Parties shall have the right to cease to be a party thereto provided that he shall have previously given one year's notice of denunciation to the Belgian Government. . . .

The North Atlantic Treaty

NATO's Treaty of Washington represents both the foundations of European security in the second half of the twentieth century and an alternative model of cooperation to that which was to be initiated by European Political Cooperation twenty years later. It is essentially a mutual defence pact, with in Article 5 a commitment for the parties to provide assistance to each other in the event of attack in less strong language than that of Article IV of the Brussels Treaty. Still, on a strict reading the wording of Article 5 optimistically allows the attacked party to decide on what kind of assistance it is due from its partners. The subsequent apparatus of a multilateral bureaucratic alliance and policy-making system, which is what NATO has become, is only prefigured in Article 9 of the original Treaty, which sets up a Council and subsidiary bodies. There are twelve original signatories: the five Brussels Treaty members, plus the United States, Canada, Denmark, Iceland, Italy, Norway and Portugal. Article 6 defined the scope of the treaty as being effectively the north Atlantic area north of the Tropic of Cancer.

Document 1/2   The North Atlantic Treaty, Washington DC, 4 April 1949

The Parties to this Treaty reaffirm their faith in the purposes and principles of the Charter of the United Nations and their desire to live in peace with all peoples and all governments.

They are determined to safeguard the freedom, common heritage and civilisation of their peoples, founded on the principles of democracy, individual liberty and the rule of law. They seek to promote stability and well-being in the North Atlantic area.

They are resolved to unite their efforts for collective defence and for the preservation of peace and security. They therefore agree to this North Atlantic Treaty:

Article 1

The Parties undertake, as set forth in the Charter of the United Nations, to settle any international dispute in which they may be involved by peaceful means in such a manner that international peace and security and justice are not endangered, and to refrain in their international relations from the threat or use of force in any manner inconsistent with the purposes of the United Nations.

Article 2

The Parties will contribute towards the further development of peaceful and friendly international relations by strengthening their free institutions, by bringing about a better understanding of the principles upon which these institutions are founded, and by promoting conditions of stability and well-being. They will seek to eliminate conflict in their international economic policies and will encourage economic collaboration between any or all of them.

Article 3

In order more effectively to achieve the objectives of this Treaty, the Parties, separately and jointly, by means of continuous and effective self-help and mutual aid, will maintain and develop their individual and collective capacity to resist armed attack.

Article 4

The Parties will consult together whenever, in the opinion of any of them, the territorial integrity, political independence or security of any of the Parties is threatened.

Article 5

The Parties agree that an armed attack against one or more of them in Europe or North America shall be considered an attack against them all and consequently they agree that, if such an armed attack occurs, each of them, in exercise of the right of individual or collective self-defence recognised by Article 51 of the Charter of the United Nations, will assist the Party or Parties so attacked by taking forthwith, individually and in concert with the other Parties, such action as it deems necessary, including the use of armed force, to restore and maintain the security of the North Atlantic area.

Any such armed attack and all measures taken as a result thereof shall immediately be reported to the Security Council. Such measures shall be terminated when the Security Council has taken the measures necessary to restore and maintain international peace and security.*

---

*   The definition of the territories to which Article 5 applies was revised by Article 2 of the Protocol of the North Atlantic Treaty on the accession of Greece and Turkey (October 1951) and by the Protocols signed on the accession of the Federal Republic of Germany (October 1953) and of Spain (December 1981). In December 1997, Protocols were published for future entry into force with respect to Hungary, Poland and the Czech Republic.

Article 6

For the purpose of Article 5, an armed attack on one or more of the Parties is deemed to include an armed attack:

- on the territory of any of the Parties in Europe or North America, on the Algerian Departments of France,* on the territory of Turkey or on the Islands under the jurisdiction of any of the Parties in the North Atlantic area north of the Tropic of Cancer;
- on the forces, vessels, or aircraft of any of the Parties, when in or over these territories or any other area in Europe in which occupation forces of any of the Parties were stationed on the date when the Treaty entered into force or the Mediterranean Sea or the North Atlantic area north of the Tropic of Cancer.

Article 7

This Treaty does not affect, and shall not be interpreted as affecting in any way the rights and obligations under the Charter of the Parties which are members of the United Nations, or the primary responsibility of the Security Council for the maintenance of international peace and security.

Article 8

Each Party declares that none of the international engagements now in force between it and any other of the Parties or any third State is in conflict with the provisions of this Treaty, and undertakes not to enter into any international engagement in conflict with this Treaty.

Article 9

The Parties hereby establish a Council, on which each of them shall be represented, to consider matters concerning the implementation of this Treaty. The Council shall be so organised as to be able to meet promptly at any time. The Council shall set up such subsidiary bodies as may be necessary, in particular it shall establish immediately a defence committee which shall recommend measures for the implementation of Articles 3 and 5.

Article 10

The Parties may, by unanimous agreement, invite any other European State in a position to further the principles of this Treaty and to contribute to the security of the North Atlantic area to accede to this Treaty. Any state so invited may become a Party to the Treaty by depositing its instrument of accession with the Government of the United States of America. The Government of the United States of America will inform each of the Parties of the deposit of each such instrument of accession.

---

*   On January 16, 1963, the North Atlantic Council noted that insofar as the former Algerian Departments of France were concerned, the relevant clauses of this Treaty had become inapplicable as from July 3, 1962.

Article 11

This Treaty shall be ratified and its provisions carried out by the Parties in accordance with their respective constitutional processes. The instruments of ratification shall be deposited as soon as possible with the Government of the United States of America, which will notify all the other signatories of each deposit. The Treaty shall enter into force between the States which have ratified it as soon as the ratifications of the majority of the signatories, including the ratifications of Belgium, Canada, France, Luxembourg, the Netherlands, the United Kingdom and the United States, have been deposited and shall come into effect with respect to other States on the date of the deposit of their ratifications.

Article 12

After the Treaty has been in force for ten years, or at any time thereafter, the Parties shall, if any of them so requests, consult together for the purpose of reviewing the Treaty, having regard for the factors then affecting peace and security in the North Atlantic area, including the development of universal as well as regional arrangements under the Charter of the United Nations for the maintenance of international peace and security.

Article 13

After the Treaty has been in force for twenty years, any Party may cease to be a Party one year after its notice of denunciation has been given to the Government of the United States of America, which will inform the Governments of the other Parties of the deposit of each notice of denunciation.

. . .

The Council of Europe

On the face of things the Council of Europe has no relevance even to the idea of a European foreign policy. This is a mistaken view not only because the Council represents the intergovernmentalist principle which was to characterize EPC, in contrast to the supranationality of some elements of the EEC, but also because it began the whole process by which the notion slowly gained acceptance that democratic states, and especially those sharing a geographical region such as Europe, should be able to build a zone of peace *inter se* and pursue the same broadly similar principles of foreign policy. Academics have subsequently begun to discuss such attempts under the heading of 'the democratic peace' hypothesis, while decision-makers themselves have talked from the early 1970s of creating a 'communauté de vue' out of which a 'communauté d'action' might then grow.* This convergence of policies around common values, to the extent that it has taken place, has

---

*   See Philippe de Schoutheete, *La Coopération politique européenne*, Brussels, Editions Labor, 1986 (2nd edn), p. 49.

certainly been fostered by the existence of the Council of Europe, and its gradual widening of membership to include all European democracies (stretching a point in the case of Croatia). Furthermore the Council gave birth to the European Convention for the protection of Human Rights (4 November 1950) which in turn has made possible the emergence of a Commission and then a Court of Human Rights (1954 and 1959). These bodies and their associated conventions have been the most important source of human rights agreements in international politics. Although their existence has complicated the institutional architecture of Europe, in the long run it may be seen to have promoted a deeper unity, and a distinctive European identity.

The Council of Europe had ten founding members, and had grown to fifteen by 1956 (new entrants in order of joining being Turkey, Greece, Iceland, the Federal Republic of Germany and Austria). By 1983 the membership was twenty-one (Cyprus, Switzerland, Malta, Portugal, Spain and Liechtenstein – although Greece withdrew between 1969 and 1974). Since the end of the Cold War it has grown to a total of forty members. The Ministerial Committee of the Council was to meet in private and the Consultative Assembly to meet in public. Initially the members of the latter were to be appointed by governments but by 1951 it had become established that national parliaments were to decide on representatives. In April 2000 the Assembly voted to suspend Russia over its actions in Chechnyn – a form of collective foreign policy action.

Document 1/3   The Statute of the Council of Europe, 5 May 1949

The Governments of the Kingdom of Belgium, the Kingdom of Denmark, the French Republic, the Irish Republic, the Italian Republic, the Grand Duchy of Luxembourg, the Kingdom of the Netherlands, the Kingdom of Norway, the Kingdom of Sweden and the United Kingdom of Great Britain and Northern Ireland;

Convinced that the pursuit of peace based upon justice and international co-operation is vital for the preservation of human society and civilisation;

Reaffirming their devotion to the spiritual and moral values which are the common heritage of their peoples and the true source of individual freedom, political liberty and the rule of law, principles which form the basis of all genuine democracy;

Believing that, for the maintenance and further realisation of these ideals and in the interests of economic and social progress, there is need of a closer unity between all like-minded countries of Europe;

Considering that, to respond to this need and to the expressed aspirations of their peoples in this regard, it is necessary forthwith to create an organisation which will bring European States into closer association;

Have in consequence decided to set up a Council of Europe consisting of a Committee of representatives of Governments and of a Consultative Assembly, and have for this purpose adopted the following Statute:—

CHAPTER I.—AIM OF THE COUNCIL OF EUROPE

Article I

(*a*)   The aim of the Council of Europe is to achieve a greater unity between its Members for the purpose of safeguarding and realising the ideals and principles which are their common heritage and facilitating their economic and social progress.

(*b*)   This aim shall be pursued through the organs of the Council by discussion of questions of common concern and by agreements and common action in economic, social, cultural, scientific, legal and administrative matters and in the maintenance and further realisation of human rights and fundamental freedoms.

(*c*)   Participation in the Council of Europe shall not affect the collaboration of its Members in the work of the United Nations and of other international organisations or unions to which they are parties.

(*d*)   Matters relating to National Defence do not fall within the scope of the Council of Europe.

CHAPTER II.—MEMBERSHIP

Article 2

The Members of the Council of Europe are the Parties to this Statute.

Article 3

Every Member of the Council of Europe must accept the principles of the rule of law and of the enjoyment by all persons within its jurisdiction of human rights and fundamental freedoms, and collaborate sincerely and effectively in the realisation of the aim of the Council as specified in Chapter I.

Article 4

Any European State, which is deemed to be able and willing to fulfil the provisions of Article 3, may be invited to become a Member of the Council of Europe by the Committee of Ministers. Any State so invited shall become a Member on the deposit on its behalf with the Secretary-General of an instrument of accession to the present Statute.

. . .

Article 8

Any Member of the Council of Europe, which has seriously violated Article 3, may be suspended from its rights of representation and requested by the Committee of Ministers to withdraw under Article 7. If such Member does not comply with this request, the Committee may decide that it has ceased to be a Member of the Council as from such date as the Committee may determine.

(v)   STATEMENT ISSUED BY THE SIGNATORIES OF THE STATUTE OF THE COUNCIL OF EUROPE, 5 MAY 1949

The Ministers of Foreign Affairs of Denmark, France, the Irish Republic, Italy, Luxembourg, the Netherlands, Norway, Sweden, and the United Kingdom, and the Belgian Ambassador in London to-day signed the statute of the Council of Europe and an agreement concerning the establishment of a preparatory commission of the Council of Europe.

The main feature of the statute is the establishment of a Committee of Ministers and of a Consultative Assembly, which together will form the Council of Europe. Of these two bodies, the Committee of Ministers will provide for the development of cooperation between Governments, while the Consultative Assembly will provide a means through which the aspirations of the European peoples may be formulated and expressed, the Governments thus being kept continuously in touch with European public opinion.

It should be noted that questions of national defence are excluded from the scope of the Council of Europe. This is because there is no question here of any military alliance but rather, as the preamble to the statute says, of a general desire to achieve peace and to bring about a greater unity for the purpose of safeguarding and realizing those ideals which are the common heritage of the members.

The inaugural meeting of the Council of Europe will take place in Strasbourg, it is hoped during the month of August, and that first session will consequently be an event of profound significance in European history.

The conference took note of the requests received from the Hellenic and Turkish Governments to be admitted as members of the Council of Europe. It was the general view that the accession of these two States would be acceptable, and it was agreed that the matter should be dealt with under the statute by the Committee of Ministers as soon as it comes into being. The possibility of accession to the statute by other European States will be considered by the Committee of Ministers at the same time.

The Schuman Plan

Robert Schuman, French Foreign Minister, held a press conference on 9 May 1950 at which he announced a plan designed to bury Franco-German rivalry and to carry forward the federalist hopes disappointed by the intergovernmentalism of the Council of Europe. The aim was to initiate both functional and supranational cooperation, and in an area – coal and steel – which was crucial to national armaments policies. War between France and Germany would become 'not merely unthinkable, but materially impossible' through the creation of a 'common higher authority'. This was the beginning of European integration proper. Its origins were in international politics and the path it opened up made it possible to think about Europe also producing a common foreign policy. The members of the European Coal and Steel Community which followed, set up by the Paris Treaty of 18 April 1951, were France, Italy, the Federal Republic of Germany and the Benelux states. Britain was notable through its absence, determined not to enter into any sovereignty-relinquishing treaty, and this posed problems for those who wished to rush ahead with federal schemes for the high politics of defence and foreign policy. Only the Preamble to the

Treaty is included here, containing as it does the most notable statement of the international origins of European integration. By comparison, the detailed institutional arrangements of the ECSC are relatively uninteresting.

Document 1/4   The Schuman Declaration, 9 May 1950

Declaration of Mr Robert Schuman* of 9 May 1950

World peace cannot be safeguarded without the making of creative efforts proportionate to the dangers which threaten it. The contribution which an organized and living Europe can bring to civilization is indispensable to the maintenance of peaceful relations. In taking upon herself for more than 20 years the role of champion of a united Europe, France has always had as her essential aim the service of peace. A united Europe was not achieved and we had war.

Europe will not be made all at once, or according to a single plan. It will be built through concrete achievements which first create a de facto solidarity. The rassemblement of the nations of Europe requires the elimination of the age-old opposition of France and Germany. Any actions taken must in this first place concern these two countries.

With this aim in view, the French Government proposes to take action immediately on one limited but decisive point. It proposes to place Franco-German production of coal and steel as a whole under a common higher authority, within the framework of an organisation open to the participation of the other countries of Europe. The pooling of coal and steel production should immediately provide for the setting up of common foundations for economic development as a first step in the federation of Europe, and will change the destinies of those regions which have long been devoted to the manufacture of munitions of war, of which they have been the most constant victims.

The solidarity in production thus established will make it plain that any war between France and Germany becomes not merely unthinkable, but materially impossible. The setting-up of this powerful productive unit, open to all countries willing to take part and bound ultimately to provide all the member countries with the basic elements of industrial production on the same terms, will lay a true foundation for their economic unification. This production will be offered to the world as a whole without distinction or exception, with the aim of contributing to raising living standards and in promoting peaceful achievements. Europe, with new means at her disposal, will be able to pursue the realisation of one of her essential tasks: the development of the African Continent.

In this way there will be realised simply and speedily that fusion of interests which is indispensable to the establishment of a common economic system; it may be the leaven from which may grow a wider and deeper community between countries long opposed to one another by sanguinary divisions. By pooling basic production and by instituting a new higher authority, whose decisions will bind France, Germany, and other member countries, this proposal will lead to the realisation of

*   Foreign Minister of France.

the first concrete foundation of a European federation indispensable to the preservation of peace.

To promote the realisation of the objectives defined, the French Government is ready to open negotiations on the following bases:

1. that the task with which this common higher authority will be charged will be that of securing in the shortest possible time the modernization of production and the improvement of its quality;

2. the supply of coal and steel on identical terms to the French and German markets, as well as to the markets of other member countries;

3. the development in common of exports to other countries;

4. the equalization and improvement of the living conditions of workers in these industries.

To achieve these objectives, starting from the very different conditions in which the productions of member countries are at present situated, it is proposed that certain transitional measures should be instituted, such as the application of a production and investment plan, the establishment of compensation machinery for equating prices, and the creation of an amortization fund to facilitate the rationalization of production. The movement of coal and steel between member countries will immediately be freed from all Customs duty, and will not be affected by differential transport rates. Conditions will gradually be created which will spontaneously provide for the more rational distribution of production at the highest level of productivity. In contrast to international cartels, which tend to impose restrictive practices on distribution and the exploitation of national markets, and to maintain high profits, the organization will ensure the fusion of markets and the expansion of production.

The essential principles and undertakings defined above will be the subject of treaties signed between the States and submitted for the ratification of their Parliaments. The negotiations required to settle details of their application will be undertaken with the help of an arbitrator appointed by common agreement. He will be entrusted with the task of seeing that the agreements reached conform with the principles laid down, and, in the event of a deadlock, he will decide what solution is to be adopted.

The common higher authority entrusted with the management of the scheme will be composed of independent persons appointed by the Governments on an equal basis. A chairman will be chosen by common agreement between the Governments. The authority's decisions will have executive force in France, Germany, and other member countries. Appropriate measures will be provided for means of appeal against the decisions of the authority.

A representative of the United Nations will be accredited to the authority, and will be instructed to make a public report to the United Nations twice yearly, giving an account of the working of the new organisation, particularly as concerns the safeguarding of its specific objects.

The institution of the higher authority will in no way prejudge the methods of ownership of enterprises. In the exercise of its functions the common higher authority will take into account the powers conferred upon the International Ruhr Authority and the obligations of all kinds imposed upon Germany, so long as these remain in force.

Document 1/5 Treaty Establishing the European Coal and Steel Community (Preamble), Paris, 18 April 1951

THE PRESIDENT OF THE FEDERAL REPUBLIC OF GERMANY, HIS ROYAL HIGHNESS THE PRINCE ROYAL OF BELGIUM, THE PRESIDENT OF THE FRENCH REPUBLIC, THE PRESIDENT OF THE ITALIAN REPUBLIC, HER ROYAL HIGHNESS THE GRAND DUCHESS OF LUXEMBOURG, HER MAJESTY THE QUEEN OF THE NETHERLANDS,

CONSIDERING that world peace can be safeguarded only by creative efforts commensurate with the dangers that threaten it,

CONVINCED that the contribution which an organised and vital Europe can make to civilisation is indispensible to the maintenance of peaceful relations,

RECOGNISING that Europe can be built only through practical achievements which will first of all create real solidarity, and through the establishment of common bases for economic development.

ANXIOUS to help, by expanding their basic production, to raise the standard of living and further the works of peace,

RESOLVED to substitute for age-old rivalries the merging of their essential interests; to create, by establishing an economic community, the basis for a broader and deeper community among peoples long divided by bloody conflicts; and to lay the foundations for institutions which will give direction to a destiny henceforward shared,

HAVE DECIDED to create a European Coal and Steel Community . . .

European Defence Community (EDC) Treaty, Paris 1952

This treaty, of course, failed to become law once the French National Assembly refused ratification in 1954 – despite the fact that it had originally been an initiative of the French Prime Minister René Pleven in 1950. The signatories were the same Six who had agreed in 1951 to the Coal and Steel Community and who were to set up the EEC in 1957, and the aim this time was a common European army and the end of independent national forces for the six states concerned. The United States and Britain stood apart but willing to guarantee the security of the Six against aggression. Not only was this to prove an intensely ambitious federalist move – 50 years later an EDC is still far from realization – but also it put the defence horse before the foreign policy cart. Only in 1953 was a plan published for a 'European Community' to provide the political institutions which could make an EDC work on a day to day basis by relating it to other policies and organizations and to national democratic practices (this was on the basis of Article 38 of the EDC, which required the ECSC Assembly to study and report back on necessary institutional changes). The EDC provided a surprising amount of detail on the operational side of defence integration, listing weapon types exhaustively in a 'Military Protocol', and outlining the operations of an Assembly, a Council and a 'Board of Commissioners', but none of it made much sense by itself. The most important function of a national state could hardly be removed without calling into question the latter's very *raison d'être*. The EDC and the E(P)C fell together.

Document 1/6   The European Defence Community Treaty, Paris, 27 May 1952

The President of the Federal Republic of Germany, His Majesty the King of the Belgians, the President of the French Republic, the President of the Italian Republic, Her Royal Highness the Grand Duchess of Luxembourg, Her Majesty the Queen of the Netherlands,

Determined in co-operation with the free nations and in the spirit of the Charter of the United Nations to contribute to the maintenance of peace, more particularly by ensuring the defence of Western Europe against any aggression in close collaboration with organisations having the same purpose;

Considering the fullest possible integration to the extent compatible with military necessities, of the human and material elements of their Defence Forces assembled within a supra-national European organisation to be the best means for the attainment of this aim with the necessary speed and efficiency;

Convinced that such integration will lead to the most rational and economical use of their countries' resources, in particular through the establishment of a common budget and common armaments programmes;

Determined thereby to secure the expansion of their military strength without detriment to social progress;

Anxious to preserve the spiritual and moral values which are the common heritage of their peoples, and convinced that within the common force formed without discrimination between the Member States, national patriotism, far from being weakened, will be consolidated and harmonised in a broader framework;

Recognising that this is a new and essential step towards the creation of a united Europe;

Have resolved to set up a European Defence Community

. . .

PART I—FUNDAMENTAL PRINCIPLES

Chapter 1.—The European Defence Community

ARTICLE 1

The High Contracting Parties, by the present Treaty, set up among themselves a European Defence Community, supra-national in character, comprising common institutions, common Armed Forces, and a common budget.

ARTICLE 2

1. The objectives of the Community are exclusively defensive.

2. Consequently, under the conditions set forth in this Treaty, it shall ensure the security of Member States against any aggression by taking part in Western defence within the framework of the North Atlantic Treaty; by integrating the defence forces of the Member States; and by the rational and economical employment of their resources.

3. Any armed attack against any of the Member States in Europe or against the European Defence Forces shall be considered an armed attack on all Member States.

The Member States and the European Defence Forces shall afford to the State or forces so attacked all the military and other aid in their power.

ARTICLE 3

1. The Community shall act in the least onerous and most efficient manner possible. It shall only take action to the extent necessary for the fulfilment of its task, and in so doing it shall respect essential public liberties and the fundamental rights of individuals. It shall be vigilant to ensure that the interests of Member States receive all the consideration compatible with its own essential interests.

2. To enable the Community to attain its objectives, the Member States shall make available the appropriate contributions, determined according to the provisions of Articles 86 and 93 of this Treaty.

ARTICLE 4

The Community shall work in collaboration with the free nations and with any organisation having the same objectives as itself.

ARTICLE 5

The Community shall work in close co-operation with the North Atlantic Treaty Organisation.

ARTICLE 6

The present Treaty shall in no way discriminate between its Member States.

ARTICLE 7

The Community shall have juridical personality.

In international relations the Community shall have the juridical competence necessary for carrying out its functions and achieving its aims.

In each Member State, the Community shall enjoy the widest juridical competence granted to national legal entities; in particular, it shall be able to acquire and transfer real and personal property and to take judicial proceedings.

The Community shall be represented by its institutions, each acting within the framework of its competence.

ARTICLE 8

1. The institutions of the Community shall be:—
A Council of Ministers, hereinafter known as:
 The Council.
A Common Assembly, hereinafter known as:
 The Assembly.
A Board of Commissioners of the Community, hereinafter known as:
 The Board of Commissioners.
A Court of Justice, hereinafter known as:
 The Court.

2. Without prejudice to the provisions of Article 126 of the present Treaty, the organisation of these institutions as laid down in the present Treaty shall remain in force until replaced by a new organisation resulting from the establishment of the federal or confederal structure referred to in Article 38 below.

Chapter II.—European Defence Forces

ARTICLE 9

The Armed Forces of the Community, hereinafter known as the "European Defence Forces," shall be composed of units made available to the Community by its Member States, with a view to their fusion under the conditions laid down in this Treaty.

No Member State shall recruit or maintain national armed forces other than those for which provision is made in Article 10 below.

ARTICLE 10

1. Member States may recruit and maintain national armed forces intended for employment in non-European territories for whose defence they have assumed responsibility, together with home-based units necessary for the maintenance and relief of such forces.

2. Member States may also recruit and maintain national armed forces for the fulfilment of international missions accepted by them, in Berlin, in Austria or in virtue of decisions of the United Nations. On conclusion of these missions such troops shall either be dissolved or made available to the Community. The troops may be relieved, with the agreement of the competent Supreme Commander responsible to the North Atlantic Treaty Organisation, by exchanges with units composed of contingents from the Member State concerned and belonging to the European Defence Forces.

3. The troops in each State intended for the personal protection of the Head of the State shall remain national.

4. Member States may dispose of national naval forces, on the one hand for the protection of the non-European territories for which they have assumed the defence responsibilities referred to in paragraph 1 of this Article and for the protection of communications with and between these territories and, on the other hand, for fulfilling the obligations arising out of the international missions referred to in paragraph 2 of this Article and of agreements concluded within the framework of the North Atlantic Treaty prior to the entry into force of the present Treaty.

5. The total size of the national armed forces referred to in the present Article, including maintenance units, shall not be so large as to jeopardise the contribution of any Member State to the European Defence Forces, as determined by agreement between the Governments of the Member States.

Member States may carry out individual exchanges of personnel between the contingents which they place at the disposal of the European Defence Forces and the forces which do not form part thereof, provided that there is no consequent reduction in the size of the European Defence Forces.

ARTICLE 11

Police and gendarmerie forces, exclusively intended for the maintenance of internal order, may be recruited and maintained within Member States.

The national character of such forces is not affected by the present Treaty.

The size and nature of such forces on the territories of Member States shall not be such as to exceed the requirements of their mission.

ARTICLE 12

1. In the event of disorders or threatened disorders within the territory of a Member State in Europe, the portion of the contingent made available by the State concerned to the European Defence Forces and necessary for meeting this situation may, at its request and on notification to the Council, be placed at its disposal by the Board of Commissioners.

The conditions under which these units may be employed shall be as defined by the regulations in force within the territory of the Member State making the request.

2. In the event of disaster or catastrophe requiring immediate assistance, the units of the European Defence Forces in a position to take useful action shall, regardless of their country of origin, lend their assistance.

ARTICLE 13

In the event of a major crisis affecting a non-European territory for whose defence a Member State has assumed responsibility, the portion of the contingents made available by the Member State concerned to the European Defence Forces and necessary to meet the crisis shall be, at its request and with the agreement of the competent Supreme Commander responsible in the North Atlantic Treaty Organisation, placed at its disposal by the Board of Commissioners after notification to the Council. The contingents thus detached shall cease to be responsible to the Community until they are once again made available to it on being no longer needed to meet the crisis.

The military, economic and financial implications of the withdrawal provided for above shall in each case be examined and settled by the Board of Commissioners, with the approval of the Council acting on a two-thirds majority.

ARTICLE 14

In cases where an international mission outside the territory defined in Article 120, paragraph 1, is entrusted to a Member State, that part of the contingents furnished by this State to the European Defence Forces which is necessary to fulfil the mission shall, at its request and with the agreement of the competent Supreme Commander responsible to the North Atlantic Treaty Organisation, be placed at its disposal by the Board of Commissioners with the approval of the Council by a two-thirds majority. The contingents thus detached shall cease to be responsible to the Community until they are once again placed at its disposal when their employment is no longer necessary to fulfil the above-mentioned mission.

In such cases the provisions of Section 2 of Article 13 above are applicable.

ARTICLE 15

1. The European Defence Forces shall be made up of personnel recruited by conscription, of regular personnel or volunteer, long-service personnel.

2. They shall be integrated in accordance with the organic provisions of Articles 68, 69 and 70 below.

They shall wear a common uniform.

They shall be organised according to the categories laid down in the Military Protocol. This organisation may be modified by the Council, acting unanimously.

3. The contingents intended to make up the units shall be provided by Member States in accordance with a plan for their constitution to be determined by agreement among Member Governments. This plan may be revised under the conditions set forth in Article 44 below.

ARTICLE 16

The internal defence of the territories of Member States against attacks of any kind with military objectives, instigated or launched by an external enemy, shall be assured by homogeneous formations of European status, specialised for each Member State in the task of defending its territory, and depending for their employment on the authorities laid down in Article 18 below.

ARTICLE 17

Civil protection shall be the responsibility of each Member State individually.

ARTICLE 18

1. The competent Supreme Commander responsible to the North Atlantic Treaty Organisation shall, subject to the proviso in paragraph 3 below, be authorised to ensure that the European Defence Forces are organised, equipped, trained and prepared for their duties in a satisfactory manner.

As soon as they are ready for service, these Forces, subject to the proviso referred to above, shall be placed at the disposal of the competent Supreme Commander responsible to the North Atlantic Treaty Organisation who shall exercise over them such authority and responsibilities as devolve on him by virtue of his mandate and, in particular, shall submit to the Community his requirements as regards the articulation and deployment of the Forces; the corresponding plans shall be carried out as specified in Article 77 below.

The European Defence Forces shall receive technical directives from the appropriate bodies of the North Atlantic Treaty Organisation, within the framework of the military competence of the latter.

2. In time of war, the competent Supreme Commander responsible to the North Atlantic Treaty Organisation shall exercise over the Forces referred to above the full powers and responsibilities as Supreme Commander conferred upon him by his mandate.

3. In the case of units of the European Defence Forces assigned to internal defence and the protection of the sea approaches of the territories of Member States, determination of the authorities to whom they shall be subordinate for Command purposes and employment shall depend either on N.A.T.O. conventions concluded within the framework of the North Atlantic Treaty or on agreements between N.A.T.O. and the Community.

4. Should the North Atlantic Treaty terminate before the present Treaty, it shall be the responsibility of the Member States to determine, by mutual agreement, the authority to whom the Command and employment of the European Defence Forces shall be assigned.

. . .

ARTICLE 38

1. Within the period laid down in the second paragraph of this Article, the Assembly shall study—

(a) the constitution of an Assembly of the European Defence Community elected on a democratic basis:
(b) the powers which would devolve on such an Assembly:
(c) any changes which might have eventually to be made to the provisions of the present Treaty concerning the other institutions of the Community, particularly with a view to safeguarding an appropriate representation of States.

The Assembly will be particularly guided in its study by the following principles:—

The final organisation which will replace the present provisional organisation should be so conceived as to be able to constitute one of the elements in a subsequent federal or confederal structure, based on the principle of the separation of powers and having, in particular, a two-chamber system of representation.

The Assembly shall also examine problems arising from the co-existence of different agencies for European co-operation already established or which might be established, with a view to ensuring co-ordination within the framework of the federal or confederal structure.

2. The proposals of the Assembly shall be submitted to the Council within six months from the assumption of duties by the Assembly. On the advice of the Council, these proposals will thereafter be transmitted by the Chairman of the Assembly to the Governments of the Member States who will, within three months from the date on which the matter has been brought to their notice, convene a conference to consider the proposals.

. . .

PART III.   MILITARY PROVISIONS

Chapter 1.—Organisation and Administration of the European Defence Forces

ARTICLE 68

1. The basic units, in which the operational functions of the various Arms of the Land Forces will have to be combined, shall be composed of elements of the same nationality. These basic units shall be as small as is compatible with the principle of effectiveness. They shall be free, to the greatest possible extent, of logistical functions and shall depend for their support and maintenance on higher integrated echelons.

2. The Army Corps shall be composed of basic units of different nationalities, apart from exceptional cases resulting from tactical or organisational requirements determined by the Board of Commissioners on the proposal of the competent Supreme Commander responsible to the North Atlantic Treaty Organisation and with the unanimous approval of the Council. Their tactical support units and the logistical support formations shall be of the integrated type; these latter elementary units, corresponding to a regiment or a battalion, shall remain homogeneous and their division by nationalities shall be in the same proportion as that obtaining in the basic units. The command and the General Staff of the Army Corps shall be integrated; this integration shall be carried out in the method best adapted to ensure their effective use.

3. The basic units and their supporting services may from time to time be introduced into the North Atlantic Treaty Organisation Army Corps and conversely, the North Atlantic Treaty Organisation divisions may be introduced into the European Army Corps.

The Command echelons of the North Atlantic Treaty Organisation Forces to which the European units shall be organically attached shall integrate the elements coming from these units and conversely.

ARTICLE 69

1. The basic units of the Air Forces, each of which shall be supplied with homogeneous combat equipment corresponding to a single specific tactical task, shall be made up of elements of the same nationality.

These basic units shall be free to the greatest possible extent of logistical functions and shall depend for their use and maintenance on higher integrated echelons.

2. A certain number of basic units of different nationalities shall be grouped under the orders of higher echelons of an integrated type, apart from exceptional cases resulting from tactical or organisational requirements determined by the Board of Commissioners on the proposal of the competent Supreme Commander responsible to the North Atlantic Treaty Organisation and with the unanimous approval of the Council. The logistical support formations shall be of the integrated type, the elementary service units remaining of homogeneous national composition and their division by nationalities shall be in the same proportion as that obtaining in the basic units.

3. European basic units and their support units may be introduced into the North Atlantic Treaty Organisation commands and, conversely, the basic North Atlantic Treaty Organisation units may be introduced into the European Commands.

The North Atlantic Treaty Organisation Command echelons to which the European units shall be organically attached shall integrate the European elements and conversely.

ARTICLE 70

1. The European naval forces shall consist of such formations as may be required for the protection of the home waters of the European territories of Member States, as may be determined by agreement between the Governments concerned.

2. Contingents to the European naval forces shall form groups of the same nationality and European status suitable for a single tactical task.

3. These groups, in whole or in part, may from time to time be incorporated in formations responsible to the North Atlantic Treaty Organisation, whose Command shall at once integrate the elements thus supplied.

ARTICLE 71

The Board of Commissioners shall prepare plans for the organisation of the forces, with the unanimous approval of the Council. It shall ensure the implementation of the plans.

ARTICLE 72

1. Personnel recruited by conscription to serve in the European Defence Forces shall perform the same period of active service.

2. Standardisation shall be realised as quickly as possible on proposals by the Board of Commissioners and by decision of the Council acting unanimously.

ARTICLE 73

1. The recruitment of the European Defence Forces in each Member State shall be governed by the laws of that State within the framework of the common provisions on matters of principle set forth in the Military Protocol.

2. The Board of Commissioners shall follow up the recruitment operations carried out by Member States in conformity with the provisions of the present Treaty and, to ensure that conformity exists shall, when necessary, make recommendations to Member States.

3. From the date laid down by common agreement by the Governments of Member States, the Board of Commissioners shall start recruitment in accordance with the rules laid down in the above agreement within the framework of common provisions on matters of principle set forth in the Military Protocol.

ARTICLE 74

1. The Board of Commissioners shall carry out the training and preparation of the European Defence Forces in accordance with a common system and standard methods. In particular, it shall direct the staff colleges of the community.

2. At the request of a Member State, account shall be taken in applying the principles set forth in paragraph 1 of this Article, of the special position in respect of that State due to the existence, in virtue of its constitution, of several official languages.

ARTICLE 75

The Board of Commissioners shall prepare mobilisation plans for the European Defence Forces, in consultation with the Governments of Member States.

Without prejudice to the final organisation referred to in Article 38 above, the decision to begin mobilisation shall be the responsibility of Member States. The execution of mobilisation measures shall be shared between the Community and Member States, under conditions set forth in agreements between the Board of Commissioners and those States.

ARTICLE 76

The Board of Commissioners shall carry out such inspections and supervision as may be necessary.

ARTICLE 77

1. The Board of Commissioners shall determine the territorial location of the European Defence Forces within the framework of the recommendations of the competent Supreme Commander responsible to the North Atlantic Treaty Organisation. In case of differences of opinion with the latter which cannot be overcome, it can only depart from such recommendations with the approval of the Council acting unanimously.

Within the framework of the general decisions referred to in paragraph 1 above, the Board of Commissioners shall take executive decisions after consultation with the State in which the troops are to be stationed.

2. In the case of differences of opinion on essential points, the State concerned may seize the Council of the matter. The State in question shall conform with the opinion of the Board of Commissioners if the Council, by a two-thirds majority, pronounces itself in favour of that opinion.

The rights of which Member States may avail themselves under Article 56 above shall not be affected by the foregoing provisions.

ARTICLE 78

The Board of Commissioners shall administer personnel and equipment in conformity with the provisions of the present Treaty.

It shall see to it that the allocation made ensures homogeneity in the armaments and equipment of the Units composing the European Defence Forces.

ARTICLE 78 *bis*

1. The Board of Commissioners, as soon as it assumes its functions:—

shall prepare plans for the constitution and equipment of the first echelon of the Forces in conformity with the provisions adopted by agreement by the Governments of the Member States and within the framework of the plans of the North Atlantic Treaty Organisation:

shall determine and organise the help to be requested from States Parties to the North Atlantic Treaty Organisation for the training of contingents:

shall prepare brief provisional regulations covering essential points.

2. The Board of Commissioners, as soon as it assumes its duties, shall undertake the constitution of the units of the first echelon of the Forces.

3. As soon as the Treaty enters into force, units already existing and contingents to be recruited by Member States to complete this first echelon shall be subordinate to the Community and placed under the authority of the Board of Commissioners, which shall exercise in their respect the powers set forth in the present Treaty, under the conditions fixed by the Military Protocol.

4. The Board of Commissioners shall submit to the Council as soon as possible the plans and texts referred to in paragraph 1 of this article.

The Council shall draw up:

the plans for the constitution of the first echelon of the Forces, acting unanimously;

the other texts referred to, on a two-thirds majority.

The texts shall be put into force by the Board of Commissioners as soon as they have been drawn up by the Council.

ARTICLE 79

A uniform code of general military discipline applicable to the members of the European Defence Forces shall be prepared by agreement between the Governments of Member States and ratified in accordance with the constitutional laws of each of those States.

Chapter II.—Status of the European Defence Forces

ARTICLE 80

1. In the exercise of its competence under the present Treaty and without prejudice to the rights and obligations of Member States:—

the Community shall have, in respect of the European Defence Forces and their members, the same rights and obligations as the States themselves in respect of their national forces and their members, under customary international law;

the Community shall be bound to observe the provisions of the laws of war as formulated by treaty or convention and binding on one or more Member States.

2. Consequently, the European Defence Forces and their members shall enjoy, from the point of view of the law of nations, the same treatment as the national Forces of member States and their members.

ARTICLE 81

1. The Community shall ensure that the European Defence Forces and their members conform in their conduct to the rules of the law of nations. It shall ensure the punishment of any violation of such rules which may be committed by the Forces in question or their members.

2. The Community, within the limits of its competence, shall take penal and any other appropriate measures in cases where such violation has been committed by the Forces of third party States or their members.

Further, Member States shall take, on their side, within the framework of their competence, penal and any other appropriate measures against any violation of the rules of the law of nations committed against the European Defence Forces or their members.

ARTICLE 82

The status of the European Defence Forces shall be determined by a special convention.

. . .

ARTICLE 107

1. The production, import and export of war materials from or to third countries, measures directly concerning establishments intended for the production of war materials, and the manufacture of prototypes and technical research concerning war materials shall be forbidden, except as permitted in accordance with paragraph 3 below.

The present Article shall be applied with due regard to the rules of International Law relating to the prohibition of the use of certain weapons.

2. The categories of war materials forbidden under paragraph 1 above are listed in Annex I to this Article.

This list may be amended by a two-thirds majority vote of the Council, on the proposal of either the Board of Commissioners or a member of the Council.

3. The Board of Commissioners shall lay down by regulation the rules of procedure for the application of the present Article and for the granting of permits for production, import and export and for measures directly concerning establishments intended for the production of war materials, and the manufacture of prototypes and technical research concerning war materials.

4. The granting of permits by the Board of Commissioners shall be governed by the following provisions:—

(a) the Board of Commissioners shall not grant permits in respect of items listed in Annex II to present Article in strategically exposed areas, except by the unanimous decision of the Council.

(b) the Board of Commissioners shall only grant permits for the construction of new explosives factories for military purposes within an area defined by agreement between the Governments of Member States. Such permits shall be subject to the appointment of a full-time controller responsible for ensuring that the establishment in question observes the provisions of the present Article. The same procedure shall apply to short-range guided missiles for anti-aircraft defence, as defined in paragraph IV (*d*) of Annex II.

(*c*) as regards exports, the Board of Commissioners shall grant permits if it considers that they are compatible with the requirements, internal security and any international obligations of the Community.

(*d*) as regards the manufacture of prototypes and technical research concerning war materials, permits shall be granted unless the Board of Commissioners considers that such manufacture and such research might be prejudicial to the internal security of the Community or unless other directives have been given by the Council in accordance with Article 39 (2).

(*e*) the Board of Commissioners shall grant general permits for the production, import and export, of war materials required for the forces of Member States which do not form part of the European Defence Forces and for the forces of associated States for whose defence Member States have assumed responsibilities. The Board shall at the same time set up a control to ensure that these permits are not applied for in excess of requirements.

(*f*) the Board of Commissioners shall grant general permits in respect of items listed in Annex I intended for civil purposes, and at the same time shall set up a control to ensure that these permits are applied for only for such purposes.

5. The regulations envisaged in paragraph 3 above shall be drawn up by the Board of Commissioners with the concurrence of the Council, by a two-thirds majority. They may be amended with the concurrence of the Council by a two-thirds majority, on the proposal either of the Board of Commissioners, or of a member of the Council.

6. On the request of the Board of Commissioners, the Court may, in accordance with conditions laid down by the jurisdictional Agreement envisaged in Article 67, inflict the following penalties on persons or firms contravening the provisions of the present Article:—

in the case of the production, import and export of war materials, general fines and daily fines for delay, the total of which shall not exceed fifty times the value of the articles in question, but which may, in particularly serious cases or where offences have been repeated, be either doubled, or raised to the equivalent in national currency of 1 million units of account:

in the case of technical research, the manufacture of prototypes and measures leading directly to the production of war materials, fines of a maximum amount of the equivalent in national currency of 100,000 units of account, which amount may be raised to the equivalent of 1 million units of account in national currency in particularly serious cases or where offences have been repeated.

. . .

ARTICLE 121

Member States undertake not to subscribe to any international engagement in contradiction with the present Treaty.

ARTICLE 122

Member States undertake not to avail themselves of treaties, conventions or declarations at present existing among themselves in order to submit a dispute relating to the interpretation or application of the present Treaty to a method of settlement other than those set forth in this Treaty.

ARTICLE 123

1. In case of grave and urgent necessity, the Council, provisionally, shall assume or confer on the organs of the Community or on any other appropriate body, the powers necessary to meet the position, within the limits of the general mission of the Community and in order to ensure the realisation of its objectives. Such decision shall be taken unanimously.

A case of grave and urgent necessity shall result from the position provided for either in paragraph 3 of Article 2 of the Treaty, or in the Treaty between Member States and the United Kingdom dated this day or in the additional Protocol relating to the guarantees of assistance between the Member States of the European Defence Community and the States parties to the North Atlantic Treaty Organisation, or from a declaration to this effect by the Council, acting unanimously.

2. Provisional measures decided on in virtue of the above paragraph shall cease to be applicable on the date of the end of the state of necessity, to be fixed by the Council on a two-thirds majority.

The institutions normally competent shall decide under the conditions laid down in the present Treaty on the maintenance of the consequences of these measures.

3. The present Article shall not affect the engagement of the European Defence Forces to meet aggression.

. . .

PROTOCOL REGARDING THE RELATIONS BETWEEN THE EUROPEAN DEFENCE COMMUNITY AND THE NORTH ATLANTIC TREATY ORGANISATION

The Members of the European Defence Community,

Desiring that the relationships between the North Atlantic Treaty Organisation and the European Defence Community should be defined in such a way as to maintain maximum flexibility and so as to avoid duplication of responsibilities and functions wherever possible,

Agree as follows:—

1. On questions affecting the common objectives of the two Organisations, there shall be reciprocal consultations between the North Atlantic Council and the Council of the European Defence Community and, whenever either Council decides that it is desirable, combined meetings of the two Councils.

Whenever any of the Parties to the North Atlantic Treaty or any of the Parties to the Treaty establishing the European Defence Community considers that the territorial integrity, political independence or security of any of them or the continued existence or integrity of the North Atlantic Treaty Organisation or the European Defence Community is threatened, a combined meeting shall be arranged at the request of the said Party in order to consider the measures necessary to meet the situation.

2. With a view to close co-ordination on the technical level, each Organisation will communicate to the other such information as it deems appropriate and there shall be continuous contact between the staffs of the Board of Commissioners of the European Defence Community and of the civilian agencies of the North Atlantic Treaty Organisation.

3. As soon as the European Defence Forces have been placed under the Command of a Commander responsible to the North Atlantic Treaty Organisation, he will have members of the European Defence Forces as members of his own Headquarters and of the appropriate subordinate Headquarters. The Commanders responsible to the North Atlantic Treaty Organisation will ensure such liaison as may be necessary between the European Defence Forces under their command and the other military agencies of the North Atlantic Treaty Organisation.

4. The Council of the European Defence Community and the North Atlantic Council may, by common agreement, adjust the foregoing arrangements governing relationships.

5. The present Protocol shall enter into force at the same time as the Treaty setting up the European Defence Community, of which it shall form an integral part.

TREATY BETWEEN THE UNITED KINGDOM AND THE MEMBER STATES OF THE EUROPEAN DEFENCE COMMUNITY

The President of the Federal Republic of Germany, His Majesty the King of the Belgians, the President of the French Republic, the President of the Italian Republic, Her Royal Highness the Grand Duchess of Luxembourg, Her Majesty the Queen of the Netherlands and Her Majesty the Queen of Great Britain, Ireland and the British Dominions beyond the Seas,

Desiring, in the interests of the defence of Western Europe, to extend, as between the United Kingdom and the states members of the European Defence Community established by the Treaty signed at Paris on the 27th day of May 1952, the guarantees of assistance against aggression given in Article IV of the Treaty signed at Brussels on the 17th March 1948,

Have

. . .

agreed as follows:

ARTICLE I

If at any time, while the United Kingdom is party to the North Atlantic Treaty, any other party to the present Treaty which is at that time a member of the European Defence Community, or the European Defence Forces, should be the object of an armed attack in Europe, the United Kingdom will, in accordance with Article 51 of the United Nations Charter, afford the Party or the Forces so attacked all the military and other aid and assistance in its power.

ARTICLE II

If at any time while Article I remains in force the United Kingdom or its armed forces should be the object of an armed attack in Europe, the other Parties to the present Treaty which are at that time members of the European Defence Community, and the European Defence Forces, will afford the United Kingdom and its forces all the military and other aid and assistance in their power.

ARTICLE III

The present Treaty shall be ratified and its provisions carried out by the signatories in accordance with their respective constitutional processes. The instruments of ratification shall be deposited with the Government of the United Kingdom, which shall notify the Governments of the other signatories of each deposit. The Treaty shall enter into force when all the signatories have deposited their instruments of ratification and the Council of the European Defence Community has notified the Government of the United Kingdom that the Treaty establishing the European Defence Community has entered into force.

. . .

PROTOCOL ON GUARANTEES GIVEN BY THE MEMBER STATES OF THE EUROPEAN DEFENCE COMMUNITY TO THE PARTIES TO THE NORTH ATLANTIC TREATY

The Members of the European Defence Community,
Being satisfied that the creation of the European Defence Community set up under the Treaty signed at Paris on the 27th May, 1952, will strengthen the North Atlantic Community and the integrated defence of the North Atlantic area, and promote the closer association of the countries of Western Europe,
Agree as follows:—

ARTICLE 1

An armed attack—

(i) on the territory of any of the Parties to the North Atlantic Treaty in the area described in Article 6 (i) of the said Treaty, or
(ii) on the forces, vessels or aircraft of any of the Parties to the North Atlantic Treaty when in the area described in Article 6 (ii) of the said Treaty,

shall be considered an armed attack on the members of the European Defence Community and the European Defence Forces.

In the event of such an armed attack, the members of the European Defence Community, in respect of themselves and the European Defence Forces, shall have the same obligations towards the Parties to the North Atlantic Treaty as those Parties undertake towards the members of the European Defence Community and the European Defence Forces, in virtue of the Protocol between the Parties to the North Atlantic Treaty referred to in Article 2 below.

The expression "Parties to the North Atlantic Treaty" shall be taken to mean the countries adhering to the said Treaty at the date of entry into force of the present Protocol.

ARTICLE 2

The present Protocol shall enter into force at the same time as the Protocol signed by the Parties to the North Atlantic Treaty granting reciprocal guarantees to the members of the European Defence Community and the European Defence Forces.

ARTICLE 3

This Protocol shall remain in force for so long as the Treaty setting up the European Defence Community and the North Atlantic Treaty remain in force, and the Parties to the latter Treaty continue to give, in respect of themselves and their forces, guarantees to the members of the European Defence Community and the European Defence Forces equivalent to the guarantees contained in the present Protocol.

ARTICLE 4

The present Protocol shall be deposited in the Archives of the Government of the French Republic, which shall transmit duly certified copies to the Governments of all the Parties to the Treaty setting up the European Defence Community and all the Parties to the North Atlantic Treaty.

. . .

PROTOCOL OF SIGNATURE

The Governments of the States signatories of the Treaty setting up the European Defence Community, signed this day, shall consult together with a view to reaching agreement on the duration of military service to serve as a basis for the decision by the Council of Ministers of the Community, referred to in Article 12, paragraph 2, of the Military Protocol annexed to the said Treaty.

COMMON DECLARATION BY THE FOREIGN MINISTERS ON THE DURATION OF THE TREATY

The Governments represented at the Conference of Foreign Ministers in Paris,
    Aware of the essential importance of Article 5 of the Treaty establishing a European Defence Community,
    In view of Article 128 of the said Treaty, providing that the Treaty shall be concluded for a period of fifty years from the date of its entry into force,
    Express the wish that the provisions concerning the duration of the North Atlantic Treaty be adapted to those of the said Article 128,

Consider it desirable that the necessary initiative to this end be taken by the Parties to the North Atlantic Treaty participating in the present Conference.

These Governments agree to take such an initiative.

The European (Political) Community, Strasbourg, March 1953

The Ad Hoc Assembly in Strasbourg which was set up on the basis of Article 38 of the EDC Treaty went beyond the technicalities of the EDC by boldly proclaiming a supranational European Community in which Member States would clearly be relegated to a secondary position, not least in the conduct of external relations. A legislative Parliament was to be elected with directly elected deputies in the first chamber, and national representatives in the Senate. The Senate was to elect the President of the European Executive Council, who appointed the other members on the principle of not more than two from one country. A 'Council of National Ministers' would seek to ensure harmonization with the actions of Member States. A single Court would oversee the ECSC, the EDC and this new EC. Other detailed provisions were made for economic and social policy and integration with the ECSC.

The provisions for international relations, included here, are remarkably interesting for the way in which they anticipate the later procedures and problems of EPC and the CFSP. Their direct statements, such as 'the Community shall ensure that the foreign policies of Member States are co-ordinated' (Article 69) betray the theoretical nature of the exercise. Not only was there no experience of diplomatic coordination of this kind to fall back on, but also at this time, only eight years after the end of the Second World War, five of the six states in question had barely managed to develop independent foreign policies, and the sixth, France, was preoccupied with colonies in North Africa and Indo-China. In such circumstances such a statement seemed far less problematical than it does today.

The draft treaty went on to elaborate financial and institutional arrangements, and to specify the Community's ability to conclude treaties and association agreements (articles 90–92). Again, there is much here which anticipates later developments, and with hindsight it is remarkable how many of the EC's eventual characteristics had been sketched out as early as 1953.

Document 1/7   Draft Treaty embodying the Statute of the European Community, Adopted by the *Ad Hoc* Assembly in Strasbourg (European Political Community Treaty), 10 March 1953

PREAMBLE

WE, THE PEOPLES OF THE FEDERAL REPUBLIC OF GERMANY, THE KINGDOM OF BELGIUM, THE FRENCH REPUBLIC, THE ITALIAN REPUBLIC, THE GRAND DUCHY OF LUXEMBOURG AND THE KINGDOM OF THE NETHERLANDS,

CONSIDERING that world peace may be safeguarded only by creative efforts equal to the dangers which menace it;

CONVINCED that the contribution which a living, united free Europe can bring to civilization and to the preservation of our common spiritual heritage is indispensable to the maintenance of peaceful relations;

DESIROUS of assisting through the expansion of our production in improving the standard of living and furthering the works of peace;

DETERMINED to safeguard by our common action the dignity, freedom and fundamental equality of men of every condition, race or creed;

RESOLVED to substitute for our historic rivalries a fusion of our essential interests by creating institutions capable of giving guidance to our future common destiny;

DETERMINED to invite other European peoples, inspired with the same ideal, to join with us in our endeavour;

HAVE DECIDED to create a European Community.

. . .

PART I.

The European Community

ARTICLE 1

The present Treaty sets up a EUROPEAN COMMUNITY of a supra-national character.

The Community is founded upon a union of peoples and States, upon respect for their personality and upon equal rights and duties for all. It shall be indissoluble.

ARTICLE 2

The Community has the following mission and general aims:

— to contribute towards the protection of human rights and fundamental freedoms in Member States;

— to co-operate with the other free nations in ensuring the security of Member States against all aggression;

— to ensure the co-ordination of the foreign policy of Member States in questions likely to involve the existence, the security or the prosperity of the Community;

— to promote, in harmony with the general economy of Member States, the economic expansion, the development of employment and the improvement of the standard of living in Member States, by means, in particular, of the progressive establishment of a common market, transitional or other measures being taken to ensure that no fundamental and persistent disturbance is thereby caused to the economy of Member States;

— to contribute towards the endeavours of Member States to achieve the general objectives laid down in the Statute of the Council of Europe, the European

Convention for Economic Co-operation, and the North Atlantic Treaty, in co-operation with the other States parties thereto.

ARTICLE 3

The provisions of Part 1 of the Convention for the Protection of Human Rights and Fundamental Freedoms signed in Rome on 4th November 1950, together with those of the protocol signed in Paris on 20th March 1952, are an integral part of the present Statute.

ARTICLE 4

The Community shall have juridical personality.

In international relationships the Community shall enjoy the juridical personality necessary to the exercise of its functions and the attainment of its ends.

In each of the Member States the Community shall enjoy the most extensive juridical personality which is recognized for legal persons of the nationality of the country in question. Specifically, it may acquire, or transfer, immovable and movable assets and may sue and be sued in its own name.

The Community shall possess, in the territories of the Member States, such immunities and privileges as are necessary to the fulfilment of its task, under conditions determined in the Protocol appended to the present Treaty.

ARTICLE 5

The Community, together with the European Coal and Steel Community and the European Defence Community, shall constitute a single legal entity, within which certain organs may retain such administrative and financial autonomy as is necessary to the accomplishment of the tasks assigned by the treaties instituting the European Coal and Steel Community and the European Defence Community.

ARTICLE 6

The Community shall exercise all such powers and competence as are conferred upon it by the present Statute or by subsequent enactment.

The provisions defining the powers and competence conferred upon the Community by the present Treaty shall be restrictively interpreted.

ARTICLE 7

The Community shall carry out its functions in close co-operation with the national civil services, through their respective governments, and with any international organization having objectives similar to its own.

ARTICLE 8

The Community shall enact legislation defining the fundamental principles of the general status of its officials.

ARTICLE 9*

The institutions of the Community shall be:
— Parliament;
— the European Executive Council;
— the Council of National Ministers;
— the Court of Justice, hereinafter termed "the Court";
— the Economic and Social Council.

. . .

Chapter II

THE EUROPEAN EXECUTIVE COUNCIL

. . .

ARTICLE 34

The President of the European Executive Council shall represent the Community in international relations.

. . .

PART III.

Powers and Competence

Chapter I

GENERAL RIGHT OF INITIATIVE

―――――

ARTICLE 55

The Community may make proposals to the Member States with the object of attaining the general aims defined in Article 2.

Such proposals shall be made by the European Executive Council, either on its own initiative or as a result of a motion by Parliament or by one of the Chambers.

---

*   The Parliament was to consist of two chambers: one composed of deputies representing the 'peoples united in the Community' (elected directly), and the other composed of senators representing the 'people of each State' (elected by national parliaments). The President of the European Executive Council would be elected by the Senate in a majority vote; the President would then appoint the other members of the European Executive Council (though no more than two members could come from the same state). Representatives of each State would make up the Council of National Ministers. Legislation could be initiated by both the European Executive Council and the Parliament, and would require the assent of both chambers of Parliament. The European Executive Council was to assume the general administration of the Community; the Council of Ministers was to harmonize the European Executive Council's action with that of the Member States.

The European Executive Council may request Member States for information on the action which they have taken in regard to the proposals of the Community.

. . .

Chapter III

INTERNATIONAL RELATIONS

ARTICLE 67

1. Within the limits of the powers and competence conferred upon it, the Community may conclude treaties or international agreements or accede thereto.

2. The Community may conclude treaties or agreements of association with third States, under the conditions prescribed in Articles 90 to 92.

ARTICLE 68

The European Executive Council shall negotiate and conclude treaties or international agreements on behalf of the Community.

Where such treaties or agreements relate to matters in which the present Statute provides for the assent of another institution of the Community, the European Executive Council may ratify them only when authorized so to do by the other institution concerned, acting in accordance with the procedure and conditions laid down for the exercise of its competence.

ARTICLE 69

In order to achieve the general aims laid down in Article 2, the Community shall ensure that the foreign policies of Member States are co-ordinated.

For this purpose the European Executive Council may be empowered, by unanimous decision of the Council of National Ministers, to act as common representative of the Member States.

ARTICLE 70

For the purposes defined in the previous article:

1. Representatives of Member States in the Council of National Ministers shall exchange information and institute a procedure for mutual and permanent consultation on all questions which affect the interests of the Community.

2. The European Executive Council may make proposals for this purpose to the Council of National Ministers. It shall have the right to be heard at all meetings of the Council of National Ministers when these proposals are examined.

3. Parliament, acting through the European Executive Council, may address proposals to the Council of National Ministers or to the Governments of Member States on all matters affecting the interests of the Community.

The European Executive Council may, at the request of Parliament, invite the Council of National Ministers or the governments in question to make known what action has been taken on these proposals.

ARTICLE 71

The Community shall:

1. institute a procedure for consultations among the Member States, so that a common attitude may be adopted at any international conferences where the interests of the Community may be involved;

2. prepare a draft pact for the peaceful settlement of any disputes which may arise between the Member States and which do not come within the competence of the Court;

3. establish the procedure for conciliation and arbitration required for the implementation of Article 73;

4. draft other treaties or agreements among the Member States or between certain individual Member States.

The European Executive Council shall invite the Member States to implement such treaties or agreements in accordance with their usual constitutional procedure.

ARTICLE 72

Member States may not conclude treaties or international agreements which run counter to commitments entered into by the Community or adhere to such treaties or agreements.

ARTICLE 73

Member States shall inform the European Executive Council of any draft treaties or agreements which they are in process of negotiating, or of any initiative taken by them which affects the Community.

If the European Executive Council considers that any such draft or initiative is likely to impede the implementation of the present Statute or to affect the interests of the Community, and if no agreement with the State in question can be reached, the dispute shall, subject to any other procedure provided for in the present Statute, be submitted to conciliation or, if this is unsuccessful, to arbitration.

ARTICLE 74

The Community shall, to the extent required for the achievement of its aims and within the limits of its powers and competence, have the right to accredit and receive diplomatic representatives.

. . .

Chapter V

ECONOMIC POWERS

———

ARTICLE 82

The Community, while upholding the principles defined in Articles 2, 3 and 4 of the Treaty instituting the European Coal and Steel Community, shall establish progressively a common market among the Member States, based on the free movement of goods, capital and persons.

In order to achieve the aim mentioned in the preceding paragraph, the Community shall foster the co-ordination of the policy of the Member States in monetary, credit and financial matters. . . .

Chapter VI

SPECIALIZED AUTHORITIES

. . .

ARTICLE 89

The Community may represent its Member States in any Specialized Authority or Community to which all such Member States belong.

. . .

PART IV.

Association

ARTICLE 90

The Community may conclude treaties or agreements of association in order to establish, in certain fields, close co-operation, involving reciprocal rights and obligations, with such third States as guarantee the protection of the human rights and fundamental freedoms mentioned in Article 3.

Such treaties or agreements may be concluded either with a European non-member State or, in accordance with the provisions of its Constitution, with an overseas State, having constitutional links either with a Member State or with a State which is already associated with the Community.

Should such treaty or agreement of association necessitate a revision of the present Statute, such revision shall be made in accordance with the provisions of Article 116.

ARTICLE 91

A treaty of association may provide *inter alia* for:

1. Participation in the Council of National Ministers or representatives of the Governments of the associated States, and participation in the Senate of representatives of the peoples of the associated States, either with full or with partial rights;

2. the creation of permanent joint committees on the governmental or parliamentary level;

3. the obligation to exchange information and undertake mutual consultation.

ARTICLE 92

The treaty of association shall provide for procedure to uphold the rule of law in the interpretation and application of the treaty of association.

The Court of the Community may be empowered by the treaty of association to settle differences between the Community and an associated State.

The Court and the other judicial organs of the Community may also be given competence to take cognizance of certain litigation concerning nationals of an associated State.

In such cases, and in accordance with the methods defined in the treaty of association, judges appointed by the associated State may sit in the judicial organs of the Community.

. . .

PART VI.

General Provisions

. . .

ARTICLE 115

Amendments to the provisions of the Treaty instituting the European Defence Community, which might affect mutual aid agreements between the Member States of the European Defence Community and the United Kingdom, on the one hand, and the Member States of the European Defence Community and States parties to the North Atlantic Treaty, on the other hand, shall not become effective until agreement has been reached with the interested States.

ARTICLE 116

1. Accession to the Community shall be open to the Member States of the Council of Europe and to any other European State which guarantees the protection of human rights and fundamental freedoms mentioned in Article 3.

. . .

The Paris Agreements, 23 October 1954

After the failure of the EDC and the first E(P)C, it was necessary to pick up the pieces of Europe's security arrangements, not least because it was thought important to acknowledge the restoration of West German sovereignty and to enable that country to contribute to collective military defence. On a British initiative, the focus returned to intergovernmentalism and to the Brussels Treaty of 1948, which was modified so as to bring Germany and Italy on board. The Brussels Treaty Organisation became the Western European Union (WEU) of seven members, and members agreed to maximum force levels, ultimately under NATO command. Britain committed itself to maintaining a minimum of four divisions and air support on the continent, and not to withdraw them without the agreement of the majority of the WEU. Thus the chasm which had opened up between the Six and the UK was, in one respect at least, closed.

The WEU was given a full institutional structure, with a Council, a Permanent Council (of Ambassadors), an Assembly and an Agency for the Control of Armaments. German conventional rearmament was legitimized by provisions forbidding the German manufacture of atomic, chemical and biological weapons. These were important but static provisions. WEU had nothing really to make decisions about: military policy-making was increasingly focused on NATO, and on US initiatives; foreign policy remained in the hands of individual states. The hopes of some for a European foreign policy had proved distinctly premature.

Document 1/8   Protocol Modifying and Completing the Brussels Treaty (Western European Union), Paris, 23 October 1954

[The Heads of State of Belgium, France, Luxembourg, the Netherlands, and the United Kingdom, parties to the Brussels Treaty of 17 March 1948]

Inspired by a common will to strengthen peace and security;

Desirous to this end of promoting the unity and of encouraging the progressive integration of Europe;

Convinced that the accession of the Federal Republic of Germany and the Italian Republic to the Treaty will represent a new and substantial advance towards these aims;

Having taken into consideration the decisions of the London Conference as set out in the Final Act of October the 3rd, 1954, and its Annexes;

 . . .

Have agreed as follows:

Article I

The Federal Republic of Germany and the Italian Republic hereby accede to the Treaty as modified and completed by the present Protocol.

The High Contracting Parties to the present Protocol consider the Protocol on Forces of Western European Union (hereinafter referred to as Protocol No. II), the

Protocol on the Control of Armaments and its Annexes (hereinafter referred to as Protocol No. III), and the Protocol on the Agency of Western European Union for the Control of Armaments (hereinafter referred to as Protocol No. IV) to be an integral part of the present Protocol.

Article II

The sub-paragraph of the Preamble to the Treaty: "to take such steps as may be held necessary in the event of renewal by Germany of a policy of aggression" shall be modified to read: "to promote the unity and to encourage the progressive integration of Europe."

The opening words of the 2nd paragraph of Article I shall read: "The co-operation provided for in the preceding paragraph, which will be effected through the Council referred to in Article VIII. . . ."

Article III

The High Contracting Parties will make every effort in common to lead their peoples towards a better understanding of the principles which form the basis of their common civilisation and to promote cultural exchanges by conventions between themselves or by other means.

Article IV*

In the execution of the Treaty, the High Contracting Parties and any Organs established by Them under the Treaty shall work in close co-operation with the North Atlantic Treaty Organisation.

Recognising the undesirability of duplicating the military staffs of NATO, the Council and its Agency will rely on the appropriate military authorities of NATO for information and advice on military matters.

Article V**

If any of the High Contracting Parties should be the object of an armed attack in Europe, the other High Contracting Parties will, in accordance with the provisions of Article 51 of the Charter of the United Nations, afford the Party so attacked all the military and other aid and assistance in their power.

. . .

The Treaty of Rome

The setting up in 1957 of the European Economic Community (often known thereafter as the 'Common Market') through the Treaty of Rome was in itself a major development of international relations, but it was only later that its potential for influencing national foreign policies and for producing collective external strategies came to be appreciated. At the

* New Article inserted under Article III of the Protocol.
** Formerly Article IV.

time, and more particularly at the foreign ministers' meeting at Messina on 3 June 1955 which launched the project, attention focused on the economic and security benefits of extending the cooperation between the Six which had already produced the ECSC. Once again Britain stood aside. It should not, however, have been difficult to see that the creation, in time, of a customs union and a common agricultural policy were likely to have significant consequences for third parties and lead the Six into coordinated external economic relations. The more far-sighted, or idealistic, might also have predicted a spill-over into foreign policy through the need for compatibility between economic and political strategies. The Treaty of Rome has in fact turned out to be the indispensable foundation for the development of EPC and the CFSP, slow and intermittent as those processes proved to be. By contrast the Euratom Treaty, signed at the same time, failed to stimulate sufficient interests in transcending the national monopoly over nuclear power.

We include here only limited extracts from the EEC Treaty, namely those relating to the common commercial policy (articles 110–16), national security (223) and the making of agreements with other states or organizations (228, 237–38).

Document 1/9   Treaty Establishing the European Economic Community
(Treaty of Rome), Rome, 25 March 1957

HIS MAJESTY THE KING OF THE BELGIANS, THE PRESIDENT OF THE FEDERAL REPUBLIC OF GERMANY, THE PRESIDENT OF THE FRENCH REPUBLIC, THE PRESIDENT OF THE ITALIAN REPUBLIC, HER ROYAL HIGHNESS THE GRAND DUCHESS OF LUXEMBOURG, HER MAJESTY THE QUEEN OF THE NETHERLANDS,

DETERMINED to lay the foundations of an ever closer union among the peoples of Europe,

RESOLVED to ensure the economic and social progress of their countries by common action to eliminate the barriers which divide Europe,

AFFIRMING as the essential objective of their efforts the constant improvement of the living and working conditions of their peoples,

RECOGNISING that the removal of existing obstacles calls for concerted action in order to guarantee steady expansion, balanced trade and fair competition,

ANXIOUS to strengthen the unity of their economies and to ensure their harmonious development by reducing the differences existing between the various regions and the backwardness of the less favoured regions,

DESIRING to contribute, by means of a common commercial policy, to the progressive abolition of restrictions on international trade,

INTENDING to confirm the solidarity which binds Europe and the overseas countries and desiring to ensure the development of their prosperity, in accordance with the principles of the Charter of the United Nations,

RESOLVED by thus pooling their resources to preserve and strengthen peace and liberty, and calling upon the other peoples of Europe who share their ideal to join in their efforts,

Have Decided to Create a European Economic Community . . .

CHAPTER 3

COMMERCIAL POLICY

Article 110

By establishing a customs union between themselves, Member States aim to contribute, in the common interest, to the harmonious development of world trade, the progressive abolition of restrictions on international trade and the lowering of customs barriers.

The common commercial policy shall take into account the favourable effect which the abolition of customs duties between Member States may have on the increase in the competitive strength of undertakings in those States.

Article 111

The following provisions shall, without prejudice to Articles 115 and 116, apply during the transitional period:

1. Member States shall coordinate their trade relations with third countries so as to bring about, by the end of the transitional period, the conditions needed for implementing a common policy in the field of external trade.
The Commission shall submit to the Council proposals regarding the procedure for common action to be followed during the transitional period and regarding the achievement of uniformity in their commercial policies.

2. The Commission shall submit to the Council recommendations for tariff negotiations with third countries in respect of the common customs tariff.
The Council shall authorise the Commission to open such negotiations.
The Commission shall conduct these negotiations in consultation with a special committee appointed by the Council to assist the Commission in this task and within the framework of such directives as the Council may issue to it.

3. In exercising the powers conferred upon it by this Article, the Council shall act unanimously during the first two stages and by a qualified majority thereafter.

4. Member States shall, in consultation with the Commission, take all necessary measures, particularly those designed to bring about an adjustment of tariff agreements in force with third countries, in order that the entry into force of the common customs tariff shall not be delayed.

5. Member States shall aim at securing as high a level of uniformity as possible between themselves as regards their liberalisation lists in relation to third countries or groups of third countries. To this end, the Commission shall make all appropriate recommendations to Member States.

If Member States abolish or reduce quantitative restrictions in relation to third countries, they shall inform the Commission beforehand and shall accord the same treatment to other Member States.

Article 112

1. Without prejudice to obligations undertaken by them within the framework of other international organisations, Member States shall, before the end of the transitional period, progressively harmonise the systems whereby they grant aid for exports to third countries, to the extent necessary to ensure that competition between undertakings of the Community is not distorted.

On a proposal from the Commission, the Council, shall, acting unanimously until the end of the second stage and by a qualified majority thereafter, issue any directives needed for this purpose.

2. The preceding provisions shall not apply to such drawback of customs duties or charges having equivalent effect nor to such repayment of indirect taxation including turnover taxes, excise duties and other indirect taxes as is allowed when goods are exported from a Member State to a third country, in so far as such drawback or repayment does not exceed the amount imposed, directly or indirectly, on the products exported.

Article 113

1. After the transitional period has ended, the common commercial policy shall be based on uniform principles, particularly in regard to changes in tariff rates, the conclusion of tariff and trade agreements, the achievement of uniformity in measures of liberalisation, export policy and measures to protect trade such as those to be taken in case of dumping or subsidies.

2. The Commission shall submit proposals to the Council for implementing the common commercial policy.

3. Where agreements with third countries need to be negotiated, the Commission shall make recommendations to the Council, which shall authorise the Commission to open the necessary negotiations.

The Commission shall conduct these negotiations in consultation with a special committee appointed by the Council to assist the Commission in this task and within the framework of such directives as the Council may issue to it.

4. In exercising the powers conferred upon it by this Article, the Council shall act by a qualified majority.

Article 114

The agreements referred to in Article 111 (2) and in Article 113 shall be concluded by the Council on behalf of the Community, acting unanimously during the first two stages and by a qualified majority thereafter.

Article 115

In order to ensure that the execution of measures of commercial policy taken in accordance with this Treaty by any Member State is not obstructed by deflection of trade, or where differences between such measures lead to economic difficulties in one or more of the Member States, the Commission shall recommend the methods for the requisite cooperation between Member States. Failing this, the Commission shall authorise Member States to take the necessary protective measures, the conditions and details of which it shall determine.

In case of urgency during the transitional period, Member States may themselves take the necessary measures and shall notify them to the other Member States and to the Commission, which may decide that the States concerned shall amend or abolish such measures.

In the selection of such measures, priority shall be given to those which cause the least disturbance to the functioning of the common market and which take into account the need to expedite, as far as possible, the introduction of the common customs tariff.

Article 116

From the end of the transitional period onwards, Member States shall, in respect of all matters of particular interest to the common market, proceed within the framework of international organisations of an economic character only by common action. To this end, the Commission shall submit to the Council, which shall act by a qualified majority, proposals concerning the scope and implementation of such common action.

During the transitional period, Member States shall consult each other for the purpose of concerting the action they take and adopting as far as possible a uniform attitude.

. . .

Article 223

1. The provisions of this Treaty shall not preclude the application of the following rules:

(*a*)   No Member State shall be obliged to supply information the disclosure of which it considers contrary to the essential interests of its security;

(*b*)   Any Member State may take such measures as it considers necessary for the protection of the essential interests of its security which are connected with the production of or trade in arms, munitions and war material; such measures shall not adversely affect the conditions of competition in the common market regarding products which are not intended for specifically military purposes.

2. During the first year after the entry into force of this Treaty, the Council shall, acting unanimously, draw up a list of products to which the provisions of paragraph 1 (*b*) shall apply.

3. The Council may, acting unanimously on a proposal from the Commission, make changes in this list.

. . .

Article 228

Where this Treaty provides for the conclusion of agreements between the Community and one or more States or an international organisation, such agreements shall be negotiated by the Commission. Subject to the powers vested in the Commission in this field, such agreements shall be concluded by the Council, after consulting the Assembly where required by this Treaty.

The Council, the Commission or a Member State may obtain beforehand the opinion of the Court of Justice as to whether an agreement envisaged is compatible with the provisions of this Treaty. Where the opinion of the Court of Justice is adverse, the agreement may enter into force only in accordance with Article 236.

Agreements concluded under these conditions shall be binding on the institutions of the Community and on Member States.

. . .

Article 237

Any European State may apply to become a member of the Community. It shall address its application to the Council, which shall act unanimously after obtaining the opinion of the Commission.

The conditions of admission and the adjustments to this Treaty necessitated thereby shall be the subject of an agreement between the Member States and the applicant State. This agreement shall be submitted for ratification by all the Contracting States in accordance with their respective constitutional requirements.

Article 238

The Community may conclude with a third State, a union of States or an international organisation, agreements establishing an association involving reciprocal rights and obligations, common action and special procedures.

These agreements shall be concluded by the Council, acting unanimously after consulting the Assembly.

Where such agreements call for amendments to this Treaty, these amendments shall first be adopted in accordance with the procedure laid down in Article 236.

. . .

Article 240

This Treaty is concluded for an unlimited period.

The Fouchet Plans

The collapse of the EDC seemed to have ended the possibility of the Six acquiring political actorness for a generation, but a combination of the inherently political nature of European integration and new circumstances led to another attempt between 1961 and 1962 with the two Fouchet Plans. This attempt also failed, but in doing so it had cut an alternative, intergovernmentalist trail towards a system of foreign policy cooperation, one that was eventually to be navigated more successfully, and more cautiously in 1969–70.

The new circumstances which helped to produce Fouchet were the coming to power in France of General de Gaulle (1958) – as early as November 1959 the foreign ministers of the Six had agreed to meet three times a year to discuss the political repercussions of EEC activity – and the renewed possibility of British membership of the EEC (an application was actually made in July 1961). De Gaulle both preferred a 'Europe des patries' approach to the governance of the EEC and wished to create Europe as a third force in international relations, independent of the superpowers. He was also, of course, less than sympathetic to British entry, as events were soon to show, but it was clear that were Britain to join the EEC, the latter's international weight would be increased to the point where political, non-treaty-based matters could no longer be kept off the agenda.

A 'study committee' chaired by the French Ambassador in Copenhagen, Christian Fouchet, met from the spring of 1961, to discuss the principles and modalities of foreign policy cooperation and how it might be related to existing commitments. The first Fouchet Plan was the draft treaty tabled by France on 2 November 1961 (document 1/10). This envisaged an overarching Union of the states, operating on the basis of unanimity, constructive abstention and legal personality. The main aim of the Union was to achieve a common foreign and defence policy and to defend the values of European civilization, and the plan gave the impression that the supranational communities already in existence would be subordinated to its wholly intergovernmental method.

The second Fouchet Plan, tabled by France on 18 January 1962, was necessary in order to take into account the concerns of the other Five about damaging effects on supra-nationality on the one hand and relations with NATO and the UK on the other (document 1/11). In the event De Gaulle imposed a draft on the Quai d'Orsay which not only made none of the concessions expected, but actually hardened up the commitment to intergovernmentalism and to French leadership. Not surprisingly, the other states, particularly Belgium and the Netherlands, refused the *fait accompli* and countered with their own proposals. An impasse between Gaullism and the project of integration had, however, been reached, and negotiations broke down finally on 17 April. The Fouchet Plans were thus a spectacular short-term failure. Much of the structure they outlined, however, was to form the basis of European Political Cooperation when it appeared eight years later, and they must therefore be counted the most significant of all the documents which make up this phase of the 'pre-history' of European foreign policy.

Document 1/10   Draft Treaty for the Establishment of a European Political Union (Fouchet Plan I), 2 November 1961

The High Contracting Parties,

convinced that the organization of Europe in a spirit of freedom that respects its diversity will enable their civilization to develop still further, protect their common spiritual heritage from any threats to which it may be exposed and in this way contribute to the maintenance of peaceful relations in the world;

resolved jointly to safeguard the fundamental dignity, freedom and equality of men, regardless of their status, race or creed, and to work for the advent of a better world in which these values would permanently prevail;

affirming their attachment to the principles of democracy, to human rights and to justice in every sphere of social life;

desirous of welcoming to their ranks the other countries of Europe that are prepared to accept the same responsibilities and the same obligations;

resolved to pursue the task of reconciling their essential interests, already the objective, in their respective fields, of the European Coal and Steel Community, the European Economic Community and the European Atomic Energy Community, in order to lay the foundation for a destiny to be henceforth irrevocably shared;

resolved, to this end, to give statutory form to the union of their peoples, in accordance with the declaration adopted in Bonn on 18 July 1961 by the Heads of State or Government;

have appointed as their Plenipotentiaries:

. . .

who . . . have agreed as follows:

Title I — Union of the European peoples

Article 1

By the present Treaty, a union of States hereafter called "the Union", is established.

The Union is based on respect for the individuality of the peoples and of the Member States and for equality of rights and obligations. It is indissoluble.

Article 2

It shall be the aim of the Union:

— to bring about the adoption of a common foreign policy in matters that are of common interest to Member States;

— to ensure, through close co-operation between Member States in the scientific and cultural field, the continued development of their common heritage and the protection of the values on which their civilization rests;

— to contribute thus in the Member States to the defence of human rights, the fundamental freedoms and democracy;

— to strengthen, in co-operation with the other free nations, the security of Member States against any aggression by adopting a common defence policy.

Article 3

The Union shall have legal personality.

The Union shall enjoy in each of the Member States the most extensive legal capacity accorded to legal persons under their domestic law. It may, in particular, acquire or dispose of movable or immovable property and may go to law.

Title II — Institutions of the Union

Article 4

The Institutions of the Union shall be as follows:
the Council;
the European Parliament;
the European Political Commission.

Article 5

The Council shall meet every four months at Head of State or Government level, and at least once in the intervening period at Foreign Minister level. It may, moreover, at any time hold extraordinary sessions at either level at the request of one or more Member States.

At each of these meetings at Head of State or Government level, the Council shall appoint a President who shall take up his duties two months before the subsequent meeting and continue to exercise them for two months after the meeting.

Meetings of the Council held at Foreign Minister level shall be presided over by the Foreign Minister of the State whose representative presides over meetings at Head of State or Government level.

The President in office shall preside over extraordinary meetings that may be held during its term of office.

The Council shall choose the place for its meetings.

Article 6

The Council shall deliberate on all questions whose inclusion on its agenda is requested by one or more Member States. It shall adopt decisions necessary for achieving the aims of the Union unanimously. The absence or abstention of one or of two members shall not prevent a decision from being taken.

The decisions of the Council shall be binding on Member States that have participated in their adoption. Member States on which a decision is not binding, by reason of their absence or abstention, may endorse it at any time. From the moment they endorse it, the decision will be binding on them.

Article 7

The European Parliament provided for under Article 1 of the Convention relating to certain institutions common to the European Communities signed in Rome on 25 March 1957, shall deliberate on matters concerning the aims of the Union.

It may address oral or written questions to the Council.

It may submit recommendations to the Council.

Article 8

The Council on receipt of a recommendation addressed to it by the European Parliament, shall give its reply to the Parliament within a period of four months.

The Council, on receipt of a recommendation addressed to it by the European Parliament, shall inform the Parliament of the action it has taken thereon within a period of six months.

The Council shall each year submit to the European Parliament a report on its activities.

Article 9

The European Political Commission shall consist of senior officials of the Foreign Affairs departments of each Member State. Its seat shall be in Paris. It shall be presided over by the representative of the Member State that presides over the Council, and for the same period.

The European Political Commission shall set up such working bodies as it considers necessary.

The European Political Commission shall have at its disposal the staff and departments it requires to carry out its duties.

Article 10

The European Political Commission shall assist the Council. It shall prepare its deliberations and carry out its decisions. It shall perform the duties that the Council decides to entrust to it.

Title III — Obligations of Member States

Article 11

There shall be solidarity, mutual confidence and reciprocal assistance as between Member States. They undertake to abstain from any step or decision that might hinder or delay the achievement of the aims of the Union. They shall loyally co-operate in any consultations proposed to them and respond to requests for information addressed to them by the Council or, in compliance with the instructions of the Council, by the European Political Commission.

Title IV — Finances of the Union

Article 12

The budget of the Union shall be drawn up by the Council each year and shall include all revenues and expenditures.

Article 13

The revenues of the Union shall be derived from contributions by the Member States calculated according to the following scale:

Belgium	7.9
France	28
Federal Republic of Germany	28
Italy	28
Luxembourg	0.2
Netherlands	7.9
	100.0

Article 14

The budget shall be implemented by the European Political Commission which may delegate to its chairman all or part of the powers necessary for the purpose.

Title V—General provisions

Article 15

The present Treaty may be reviewed. Draft amendments shall be submitted to the Council by Member States. The Council shall pronounce on such drafts and decide whether or not they should be passed on for an opinion to the European Parliament.

Draft amendments adopted unanimously by the Council shall be submitted for ratification by the Member States, after the European Parliament, where appropriate, has expressed its opinion. They shall come into force once all the Member States have ratified them.

Article 16

Three years after this Treaty comes into force, it shall be subjected to a general review with a view to considering suitable measures for strengthening the Union in the light of the progress already made.

The main objects of such a review shall be the introduction of a unified foreign policy and the gradual establishment of an organization centralizing, within the Union, the European Communities referred to in the Preamble to the present Treaty.

The amendments arising from this review shall be adopted in accordance with the procedure outlined in Article 15 above.

Article 17

The Union shall be open for membership to Member States of the Council of Europe that accept the aims set out in Article 2 above and that have previously acceded to the European Communities referred to in the Preamble to this Treaty.

The admission of a new Member State shall be decided unanimously by the Council after an additional Act has been drawn up to this Treaty. This Act shall contain the necessary adjustments to the Treaty. It shall come into force once the State concerned has submitted its instrument of ratification.

Article 18

This treaty, drawn up in a single original in the Dutch, French, German and Italian languages, all four texts being equally authentic, shall be deposited in the archives of the Government of . . . which shall transmit a certified copy to each of the Governments of the other signatory States.

This Treaty be ratified. The instruments of ratification shall be deposited with . . . which shall notify the Governments of the other Member States that this has been done.

This Treaty shall come into force on the day when the instrument of ratification is deposited by the last signatory State to do so.

In witness whereof, the undersigned Plenipotentiaries have affixed their signatures below this Treaty under their common seal.

Document 1/11   Second Draft of the Treaty for the Establishment of a European Union (Fouchet Plan II), 18 January 1962

The High Contracting Parties.

convinced that the organization of Europe in a spirit of freedom and of respect for its diversity will enable its civilization to develop, add to the prestige of its spiritual heritage, increase its capacity to defend itself against external threats, facilitate the contribution it makes to the development of other peoples and contribute to world peace;

resolved jointly to safeguard the dignity, freedom and equality of men, regardless of their status, race or creed;

affirming their attachment to the principles of democracy, to human rights, and to social justice;

ready to welcome to their ranks other countries of Europe that are prepared to accept the same responsibilities and the same obligations;

resolved to pursue the task of reconciling their essential interests already initiated, in their respective fields, by the European Coral and Steel Community, the European Economic Community and the European Atomic Energy Community;

resolved, to this end, to give statutory form to the union of their peoples, in accordance with the declaration of 18 July 1961 by the Heads of State or Government;

. . .

have agreed as follows:

Title I—Union of the European peoples

Article 1

By the present Treaty, a union of States, hereafter called "the Union", is established.

The Union is based on respect for the individuality of the peoples and of the Member States and for equality of rights and obligations.

Article 2

It shall be the aim of the Union to reconcile, co-ordinate and unify the policy of Member States in spheres of common interest: foreign policy, economics, cultural affairs and defence.

Article 3

The Union shall have legal personality.

The Union shall enjoy in each of the Member States the legal capacity accorded to legal persons under their domestic law. It may, in particular, acquire movable or immovable property and may go to law.

Title II—Institutions of the Union

Article 4

The Institutions of the Union shall be as follows:
— the Council;
— the Committees of Ministers;
— the Political Commission;
— the European Parliament.

Article 5

The Council shall consist of the Heads of State or Government of Member States. It shall meet in principle every four months and not less than three times a year.

Article 6

The Council shall deliberate on questions whose inclusion on its agenda is requested by one or more Member States. The agenda shall be drawn up by the President. The Council shall adopt decisions necessary for achieving the aims of the Union unanimously. The absence or abstention of one or two members shall not prevent a decision from being taken.

The decisions of the Council shall be implemented by Member States that have participated in their adoption. Member States that are not bound by a decision, by reason of their absence or abstention, may endorse it at any time. From the moment they endorse it, the decision shall be binding on them.

Article 7

A Committee of Foreign Ministers and a Committee of Ministers of Education shall be set up. These Committees shall meet not less than four times a year and shall report to the Council.

Article 8

The Council may decide to set up other Committees of Ministers.

Article 9

The Political Commission shall consist of representatives appointed by each Member State. It shall prepare the deliberations of the Council and ensure that its decisions are carried out. It shall perform such other duties as the Council decides to entrust to it. It shall have at its disposal the necessary staff and departments.

Article 10

The European Parliament provided for under Article 1 of the Convention relating to certain institutions common to the European Communities, signed in Rome on 25 March 1957, shall deliberate on questions concerning foreign policy, defence and education on which the Council asks its opinion.

The Council shall each year render to the European Parliament a statement on the activities of the Union. The Council shall be represented at the debates held in the Parliament on this statement.

The Parliament may address to the Council either oral or written questions or recommendations to which a reply shall be given within a period of two months.

Title III—Obligations of Member States

Article 11

There shall be solidarity and reciprocal assistance as between Member States. They undertake to refrain from taking any step or decision that might hinder or delay the achievement of the aims of the Union.

Title IV—Finances of the Union

Article 12

The budget of the Union shall be drawn up each year. The financial year shall run from 1 January to 31 December inclusive.

The draft budget, drawn up by the Political Commission, shall be adopted by the Council which, where appropriate, may make any amendments it considers necessary.

Article 13

The administrative expenditure of the Union shall be met from contributions by the Member States calculated according the following scale:

Belgium	7.9
France	28
Federal Republic of Germany	28
Italy	28
Luxembourg	0.2
Netherlands	7.9

Article 14

The budget shall be implemented by the Political Commission.

Title V—General provisions

Article 15

The present Treaty may be reviewed. Draft amendments shall be submitted to the Council by the Governments of Member States.

Draft amendments adopted unanimously by the Council shall be submitted for ratification by the Member States, after the European Parliament, where appropriate, has expressed its opinion. They shall come into force once all the Member States have ratified them.

Article 16

Three years after this Treaty comes into force, it shall be subjected to a review in order to consider suitable measures either for strengthening the Union in general in the light of progress already made or, in particular, for simplifying, rationalizing and co-ordinating the ways in which Member States co-operate.

Article 17

The Union shall be open for membership to States that have acceded to the European Communities referred to in the Preamble to this Treaty.

The admission of a new State shall be decided unanimously by the Council after an additional Act to this Treaty has been drawn up.

Article 18

This Treaty, drawn up in a single original in the Dutch, French, German and Italian languages, all four texts being equally authentic, shall be deposited in the archives of the Government of . . . which shall transmit a certified copy to each of the Governments of the other signatory States.

This Treaty shall be ratified. The instruments of ratification shall be deposited with . . . which shall notify the Governments of the other Member States that this has been done.

This Treaty shall come into force on the day when the instrument of ratification is deposited by the last signatory State to do so.

In witness whereof, the undersigned Plenipotentiaries have affixed their signatures below this Treaty under their common seal.

Following the meeting of the Fouchet Committee on 18 January 1962, the other five delegations in turn prepared a draft of the Treaty, the text of which is reproduced below (¹):*

Article 1

By the present Treaty, a union of States and of European peoples, hereafter called "the European Union", is established.

The European Union is based on the principle of the equality of the rights and obligations of its members.

Article 2

1. It shall be the task of the European Union to promote the unity of Europe by reconciling, co-ordinating and unifying the policies of Member States.

2. For the purpose of accomplishing this task, the [main] objectives of the Union shall be:
— the adoption of a common foreign policy;
— the adoption of a common defence policy
   [within the framework of the Atlantic Alliance]
   [as a contribution towards strengthening the Atlantic Alliance];
— close co-operation in the educational, scientific and cultural fields;
— the harmonization and unification of the laws [and of the legal institutions] of Member States;
— the settlement, in a spirit of mutual understanding and constructive co-operation, of any differences that may arise in relations between Member States.

3. [Objectives other than those laid down in the preceding paragraph may be defined in accordance with the provisions of Article 16].

4. This Treaty shall not derogate from the competence of the European Communities.

Article 3

The European Union shall have legal personality.

The Union shall enjoy in each of the Member States the most extensive legal capacity accorded to legal persons under their domestic law.

(¹)   The square brackets in this draft enclose phrases regarding which the various delegations failed to agree.
*   Presented on 25 January 1962

Article 4

1. The Institutions of the Union shall be as follows:
— the Council;
— the Committees of Ministers;
— the European Parliament;
— [the Court of Justice].

2. The Council and the Committees of Ministers shall be assisted [by a Political Commission and] by a Secretary-General.

Article 5

1. The Council shall consist of the representatives of the Member States. Member States shall be represented on the Council, in accordance with the constitutional requirements and the usage prevailing in each country, by the Heads of State or Government and, where appropriate, by the Foreign Ministers.

2. The Council shall meet in ordinary session three times a year and in principle every four months. Extraordinary sessions of the Council may be convened at any time by its President on his own initiative or at the request of one or more Member States of the European Union.

3. The office of the President shall be exercised in rotation of each member of the Council for a term of [six months] [one year].

4. The Council shall lay down its own rules of procedure.

Article 6

1. The Council shall deliberate on all questions whose inclusion on the agenda is requested by one or more Member States or by the Secretary-General under the terms of Article 2. The agenda shall be drawn up by the President.

2. Decisions necessary for achieving the aims of the European Union shall be passed by the Council unanimously. The Council may, by a unanimous decision, waive the principle of unanimity in specific cases. The abstention of one or of two members shall not prevent decisions requiring unanimity from being taken.

3. [If a decision that requires unanimity cannot be adopted because it is opposed by one Member State, the Council shall adjourn the deliberation to a later date to be specified by it. If unanimity is not reached at the second deliberation of the Council because of the opposition of only one Member State, the other Member States shall have the right to refer the matter to the European Parliament with a view to securing the support of the State in question].

Article 6a

1. The Council may conclude treaties and agreements between the European Union and one or more States or an international organization. It shall lay down the methods to be followed in its rules of procedure.

2. Such treaties or agreements shall be submitted to the Parliament for an opinion. They shall not come into force until they have been approved in all Member States

by the bodies that, under the respective constitutional requirements, must approve treaties concluded by these States.

Article 7

1. The following committees shall be set up:
— a Committee of Foreign Ministers [responsible, in particular, for preparing the meetings of the Council];
— a Committee of Ministers for Defence and for the Armed Forces;
— a Committee of Ministers of Education or of Ministers responsible for international cultural relations. The competence of this Committee shall be governed [in particular] by the Convention embodying the Statute of the European Cultural Council and the annexed Conventions which as a whole are to be regarded as an integral part of this Treaty.

2. The Council may set up other Committees of Ministers.

3. The Committees enumerated above shall meet not less than four times a year and report to the Council.

Article 8

The [Political Commission] shall consist of senior officials appointed by each Member State. [It shall prepare the deliberations of the Council and ensure that its decisions are carried out]. It shall perform the duties which the Council decides to entrust to it.

Article 9

1. The Council shall appoint for a period of . . . a Secretary-General who shall be independent of the Governments of the Member States of the European Union. His term of office shall be renewable.

2. He shall be assisted in the performance of his duties by a staff appointed by him in accordance with a procedure to be laid down on his proposal, by the Council.

3. The functions of the Secretary-General and of members of the Secretariat shall be deemed to be incompatible with the exercise of any other office.

4. In the performance of their duties, the Secretary-General and the members of the Secretariat shall neither solicit nor accept instructions from any government. They shall abstain from any act that is incompatible with the nature of their functions.

5. Member States undertake to respect the independence of the Secretary-General and of his staff and to refrain from influencing these in the performance of their duties.

Article 10

1. The parliamentary institution of the European Union shall be the Parliament provided for under Article 1 of the Convention relating to certain institutions common to the European Communities signed in Rome on 25 March 1957.

2. In fields that relate to the aims of the European Union, the Parliament shall
— address oral or written questions to the Council;
— submit recommendations to the Council;
— give its opinion on questions submitted to it by the Council.

[2. In fields that relate to the aims of the European Union, the Parliament shall address the advisory and supervisory powers vested in it under this Treaty.]

3. The Parliament and its members may address oral or written questions to the Council.

4. The Parliament shall, if it thinks fit or if the Council so requests, submit recommendations or opinions to the Council.

[5. If the implementation of a decision of the Council necessitates or implies an amendment to the legal provisions of one or more Member States, the Council shall submit proposals for such a decision to the Parliament for an opinion and shall take that opinion into account when it finally adopts the decision].

[5. The Council shall submit to the Parliament for its approval:
   a) Treaties concluded by the European Union with third States or international organizations;
   b) Decisions of the Council that necessitate intervention by parliamentary organs in the Member States.]

Article 10a

1. The Council, on receipt of a question or of a recommendation from the European Parliament [or from one of its members], shall make known at its next meeting what action it has taken in respect thereof.

2. The Council shall [each year] [at least once a year] submit to the European Parliament a report on its activities.

3. The Council shall also be represented at debates of the Parliament on the objectives of the European Union.

Article 10b

Court of Justice

Reserved pending study of the articles prepared by Ambassador Ophüls.

Article 11

There shall be solidarity and reciprocal assistance as between Member States. They undertake to co-operate to the full in pursuing the objectives of the European Union and in facilitating the accomplishment of its task.

Article 12

1. The budget of the European Union shall be drawn up each year. The financial year shall run from 1 January to 31 December inclusive.

2. Estimates shall be drawn up of all revenues and expenditures relating to the objectives of the European Union and shall be shown in the draft budget.

3. The draft budget, drawn up by the Secretary-General with the assistance of the Political Commission, shall be adopted by the Council after obtaining the Parliament's opinion.

Article 13

1. The administrative expenditure of the European Union shall be met from contributions by the Member States calculated according to the following scale:

Belgium	7.9
France	28
Federal Republic of Germany	28
Italy	28
Luxembourg	0.2
Netherlands	7.9

2. At the time of the general review of the Treaty referred to in Article 10a, a study shall be made, in consultation with the Parliament of the conditions under which the contributions of Member States could be replaced or supplemented by the European Union's own resources.

Article 14

The budget shall be implemented by the Secretary-General.

Article 14a

The European Union shall enjoy on the territory of Member States such privileges and immunities as are necessary for it to accomplish its task under the conditions stipulated in a separate protocol [which forms part of this Treaty. This shall also define the contractual and non-contractual liability of the European Union and the principles that shall govern its relations with its staff.]

Article 15

1. The provisions of this Treaty may be reviewed, without prejudice to the general review referred to in Article 16.

2. Draft amendments shall be submitted to the Council either by Member States or by the Parliament. If the Council, after having consulted the Parliament where a draft is proposed by one of the Member States, unanimously adopts such a draft amendment this shall be submitted to Member States for ratification. It shall come into force when all the Member States have ratified it in accordance with their respective constitutional requirements.

Article 16

1. At the time fixed for the transition from the second to the third stage laid down in the Treaty of Rome establishing the European Economic Community, this Treaty

shall be subjected to a general review. This shall aim at determining suitable measures for strengthening the European Union in the light of the progress already made and, in particular, associating the European Parliament more closely with the work of defining and implementing the common policies.

2. With this end in view, a draft constitution of the European Union shall be drawn up by the Council before the expiry of the time-limit specified above, and submitted to the European Parliament for its opinion.

3. For this purpose, procedures and time-limits shall be laid down for the election of the European Parliament by direct universal suffrage in accordance with Article 138 of the Treaty establishing the European Economic Community.

4. At the time of the general review referred to above, procedures shall be laid down for the gradual introduction of the majority principle in decisions of the Council.

5. The general review shall be carried out together with the necessary reforms in order to simplify and rationalize the machinery provided for in the Treaties of Paris and Rome. It shall at the same time establish the conditions under which, at the end of the transition period of the Common Market, the European Union and the European Communities will be incorporated in an organic institutional framework, without prejudice to the machinery provided for in the Treaties of Paris and Rome.

6. In the course of the review, the institutional rôle of the Court of Justice shall also be defined.

[1. At the time fixed for the transition from the second to the third stage laid down in the Treaty establishing the European Economic Community, the present Treaty shall be subjected to a general review. This shall aim at determining measures for strengthening the European Union in the light of the progress already made.

The draft constitution of the European Union shall be drawn up by the Council before the expiry of the time-limit referred to above.

2. This review shall aim at developing the independence of the institutions of the Union and the powers exercised by them. In particular, it shall have the following objectives:

    a)   The election by direct universal suffrage of the European Parliament and its closer association with the work of defining the common policy and drawing up a European body of law;

    b)   The introduction of the majority principle in decisions of the Council;

    c)   The creation of an independent Executive;

    d)   The extension of the competence of the Court of Justice of the European Communities to cover any disputes that may arise in the functioning of the Union and in the mutual relations between its Member States.

3. At the end of the transition period fixed by the Treaty establishing the European Economic Community, the European Union and the European Communities shall be integrated in an organic institutional framework, without prejudice to the machinery provided for in the Treaties of Paris and Rome.]

Article 17

1. All European States that belong to the European Communities referred to in the Preamble to this Treaty shall become members of the European Union.

2. On the accession of a new Member State, the Council, after consolidating the European Parliament, shall draw up an additional Act to this Treaty embodying the necessary adjustments. Accession shall take effect once the State concerned has deposited the instrument ratifying this Act.

. . .

The Elysée Treaty

The Franco-German Treaty of Cooperation, commonly known as the Elysée Treaty, was not only one consequence of the failure of Fouchet but also a demonstration to the smaller countries of the very phenomenon they had wanted to prevent (either through supranationality or British involvement) – namely an incipient 'directoire' of the two big Member States.* However the Treaty, and the relationship it fostered, has endured remarkably well, and no understanding of European foreign policy is complete without taking it into account. The Treaty not only formalizes the most important of all the many bilateral relationships which continue to be an important dimension of European diplomacy, even in the CFSP era, but also sets up institutional mechanisms, such as the regular meetings at both official and ministerial level, which prefigure the multilateral versions of EPC (although the defence dimension remained ahead of multilateralism until the Treaty of Maastricht – document 2/18). Coordination presents the same basic problems whether between two or twelve states, and the EEC states were working on both the theory and practice of it well before the Davignon Report of 1970 (document 2/2).

In 1988 the Franco-German relationship took a further step onwards when a Protocol was added providing for intensified defence cooperation via a new Defence and Security Council. This revived a level of cooperation that had withered after 1963 and was to be the basis for the development of the Franco-German Brigade and beyond it the Eurocorps.

Document 1/12   Treaty between the French Republic and the Federal Republic of Germany Concerning Franco-German Cooperation (The Elysée Treaty), Paris, 22 January 1963

In connection with the joint declaration of the President of the French Republic and the Federal Chancellor of the Federal Republic of Germany of 22 January 1963,[†] concerning the organization and principles of cooperation between the two States, the following provisions have been agreed upon:

I. ORGANIZATION

1. The Heads of State and Government shall issue as and when necessary the requisite directives and shall regularly follow the implementation of the programme

---

* In fact the Bundestag, when ratifying the Treaty struck a small blow for wider cooperation by inserting a Preamble which insisted on the Treaty's non-exclusive character.
† in force since 2 July 1963

specified below. They shall meet as often as may be necessary for this purpose and in principle at least twice a year.

2. The Ministers for Foreign Affairs shall ensure the implementation of the programme as a whole. They shall meet at least every three months. Without prejudice to normal contacts through the Embassies, the senior officials of the two Ministries of Foreign Affairs responsible for political, economic and cultural affairs shall meet each month, alternately at Paris and at Bonn, to determine the status of current problems and to prepare for the meeting of the Ministers. In addition, the diplomatic missions and consulates of the two countries, and their permanent missions to international organizations, shall establish such contacts as may be necessary concerning problems of mutual interest.

3. There shall be regular meetings between responsible authorities of the two countries in the fields of defence, education and youth affairs. Such meetings shall in no way affect the operations of pre-existing organs – the Franco-German Cultural Commission, the Permanent Military Staff Group – whose activities shall, on the contrary, be expanded. The Ministers for Foreign Affairs shall be represented at such meetings in order to ensure the overall coordination of cooperation.

(a) The Minister of the Armed Forces and the Minister of Defence shall meet at least once every three months. The French Minister of Education shall likewise meet, at the same intervals, the person designated on the German side to follow the implementation of the programme of cooperation in the cultural field.

(b) The Chiefs of Staff of the two countries shall meet at least once every two months; if they are unable to attend a meeting, they shall be replaced by their responsible representatives.

(c) The French High Commissioner for Youth and Sport shall meet, at least once every two months, the Federal Minister for Family and Youth Affairs or his representative.

4. In each of the two countries, an interministerial commission shall be appointed to follow problems of cooperation. It shall be presided over by a senior official of the Ministry of Foreign Affairs and shall include representatives of all the departments concerned. Its function shall be to coordinate the action of the Ministries concerned and to report to its Government at regular intervals on the status of Franco-German cooperation. It shall also have the function of submitting such suggestions as may be appropriate concerning the implementation of the programme of cooperation and its possible extension to new fields.

II. PROGRAMME

A. Foreign affairs

1. The two Governments shall consult each other, prior to any decision, on all important questions of foreign policy, and particularly on questions of mutual interest, with a view to achieving as far as possible an analogous position. Such consultations shall cover, *inter alia*, the following subjects:

– Problems concerning the European communities and European political cooperation;

– East-West relations, in both the political and the economic fields;

– Matters dealt with in the North Atlantic Treaty Organization and the various international organizations which are of interest to the two Governments, particularly in the Council of Europe, the Western European Union, the Organization for Economic Cooperation and Development, the United Nations and its specialized agencies.

2. The collaboration already established in the field of information shall be continued and developed between the departments concerned in Paris and Bonn and between the missions in third countries.

3. As regards aid to developing countries, the two Governments shall systematically compare their programmes with a view to maintaining close coordination. They shall study the possibility of undertaking activities jointly. Inasmuch as several ministerial departments are competent in respect of such matters on both the French and the German sides, it shall be the responsibility of the two Ministries of Foreign Affairs to determine jointly the practical bases for such collaboration.

4. The two Governments shall study jointly the means of strengthening their cooperation in other important sectors of economic policy, such as agricultural and forestry policies, energy policies, communication and transport problems and industrial development, within the framework of the Common Market, and export credit policies.

B. Defence

1. The objectives pursued in this field shall be the following:

a) As regards strategy and tactics, the competent authorities of the two countries shall endeavour to align their theories with a view to achieving common approaches. Franco-German operational research institutes shall be established.

b) Exchanges of personnel between the armed forces shall be increased; they shall involve, in particular, instructors and students of the Staff Colleges; they may include the temporary detachment of entire units. In order to facilitate such exchanges, both sides shall endeavour to provide practical language instruction for the personnel concerned.

c) As regards armaments, the two Governments shall endeavour to organize joint teamwork as from the stage of formulation of appropriate armament projects and of preparation of the financing plans.

For this purpose, Mixed Commissions shall study, and shall undertake a comparative review of the research in progress on such projects in both countries. They shall submit proposals to the Ministers, who shall review them during their quarterly meetings and shall issue the necessary directives for the implementation thereof.

2. The Governments shall study the conditions in which Franco-German collaboration may be established in the field of civil defence.

. . .

III. FINAL PROVISIONS

1. The requisite directives shall be issued in each country for the immediate implementation of the foregoing. The Ministers for Foreign Affairs shall determine, at each of their meetings, what progress has been achieved.

2. The two Governments shall keep the Governments of the other Member States of the European communities informed of the development of Franco-German cooperation.

3. With the exception of the provisions concerning defence, this Treaty shall also apply to Land Berlin, provided that the Government of the Federal Republic of Germany has not delivered a contrary declaration to the Government of the French Republic within three months from the date of entry into force of the Treaty.

4. The two Governments may make such adjustments as may prove desirable for the implementation of this Treaty.

5. This Treaty shall enter into force as soon as each of the two Governments has notified the other that the domestic requirements for its entry into force have been fulfilled.

PREAMBLE TO THE ACT OF THE FEDERAL GERMAN GOVERNMENT RATIFYING THE FRANCO-GERMAN TREATY OF COOPERATION

(approved by the Bundestag, 16 May 1963)

CONVINCED that the treaty concluded on 22 January 1963 between the Federal Republic of Germany and the French Republic will intensify and develop the reconciliation and friendship between the German and the French peoples,

STATING that this treaty does not affect the rights and obligations resulting from multilateral treaties concluded by the Federal Republic of Germany,

RESOLVED to serve by the application of this treaty the great aims to which the Federal Republic of Germany, in concert with the other States allied to her, has aspired for years, and which determine her policy,

TO WIT the preservation and consolidation of the unity of the free nations and in particular of a close partnership between Europe and the United States of America, the realization of the right of self-determination for the German people, and the restoration of German unity, collective defense within the framework of the North Atlantic Alliance and the integration of the armed forces of the States bound together in that Alliance, the unification of Europe by following the course adopted by the establishment of the European Communities, with the inclusion of Great Britain and other States wishing to accede, and the further strengthening of those Communities, the elimination of trade barriers by negotiations between the European Economic Community, Great Britain, and the United States of America as well as other States within the framework of the General Agreement on Tariffs and Trade,

CONSCIOUS that a Franco-German cooperation inspired by such aims will benefit all nations and serve the peace of the world and will thereby also promote the welfare of the German and French peoples,

the Bundestag enacts the following Law . . .

PROTOCOL TO THE TREATY OF 22 JANUARY 1963 BETWEEN THE FEDERAL REPUBLIC OF GERMANY AND THE FRENCH REPUBLIC ON FRANCO-GERMAN COOPERATION

(Paris, 22 January 1988)

The Federal Republic of Germany and the French Republic,

– convinced that European unification will remain incomplete as long as security and defence are not included,

– determined for this purpose to expand and intensify their cooperation on the basis of the Treaty of 22 January 1963 on Franco-German cooperation, whose translation into practice was manifested in particular by the declarations of 22 October 1982 and 28 February 1986,

– convinced of the need, in conformity with the declaration issued by the ministers of the Member States of the Western European Union at The Hague on 27 October 1987, to develop a European identity in the field of defence and security which, in accordance with the obligations of solidarity assumed under the modified Brussels Treaty, effectively gives expression to the community of fate linking the two countries,

– resolved to ensure that, in consonance with Article V of the modified Brussels Treaty, their determination to defend all States parties to that treaty at their frontiers is made visible and is strengthened by the necessary means,

– convinced that the strategy of deterrence and defense, on which their security rests and which is designed to prevent any war, must continue to be based on a suitable combination of nuclear and conventional forces,

– determined to maintain, in unison with their other partners and with due regard for their own options in the North Atlantic Alliance, an adequate military contribution with a view to preventing any aggression or attempt at intimidation in Europe,

– convinced that all nations of our continent have the same right to live in peace and freedom and that strengthening both of the foregoing is the prerequisite for progress towards a just and lasting peaceful order in the whole of Europe,

– determined to ensure that their cooperation serves these goals,

– conscious of their common security interests and resolved to harmonize their views on all matters concerning the defence and security of Europe,

have to this end agreed as follows:

Article 1

To give expression to the community of fate linking the two countries and to develop their cooperation in the field of defence and security, a Franco-German Defence and Security Council shall be established in conformity with the goals and provisions of the Treaty of 22 January 1963 between the Federal Republic of Germany and the French Republic on Franco-German Cooperation.

Article 2

The Council shall consist of the Heads of State or Government and the foreign and defence ministers. The chief of staff of the Bundeswehr and the chief of staff of the French Armed Forces shall take part ex officio.

The Committee of the Council shall comprise the foreign and defence ministers. Senior civil servants and members of the military responsible for bilateral cooperation in the field of defence and security may be called upon to participate in its work.

Article 3

The Franco-German Defence and Security Council shall meet at least twice a year alternately in the Federal Republic of Germany and in France.

Its work shall be prepared by the Committee of the Council, which shall be assisted by the Franco-German Defence and Security Commission.

Article 4

The work of the Franco-German Defence and Security Council shall in particular serve the following purposes:
 – elaboration of common concepts in the field of defence and security;
 – increasing coordination between the two countries in all matters concerning Europe's security, including the sphere of arms control and disarmament;
 – decision-making in respect of the mixed military units set up through mutual agreement;
 – decision-making regarding joint maneuvers, the training of military personnel and support arrangements designed to strengthen the capacity of both countries' armed forces to cooperate with each other both in peacetime and in the event of a crisis or war;
 – improvement of the interoperability of the equipment of both countries' armed forces;
 – development and intensification of armaments cooperation with due regard for the need to maintain and strengthen an adequate industrial and technological potential in Europe for the purpose of ensuring common defence.

Article 5

The Secretariat of the Franco-German Defence and Security Council and of the Committee of the Council shall be headed by representatives of both countries. The Secretariat shall be based in Paris.

. . .

The Harmel Report

One important way in which the sense of distinctive European foreign policy interests has been fostered has, paradoxically, been through NATO. The European members of the alliance have never wanted to threaten its integrity; on the other hand they have become ever more concerned to ensure that the United States' predominant role in alliance decision-making is counterbalanced by a cohesive European response. Indeed, the need to cope with the United States and its intermittent impatience with European concerns has been a significant factor in promoting European cooperation on foreign policy. This was evident institutionally in the Eurogroup and in the Independent European Programme Group, set up in 1969 and 1976 respectively. But in terms of policy, a seminal document was the 'Report on the Future Tasks of the Alliance' authored by the Belgian foreign minister Pierre Harmel, and approved by NATO foreign ministers in December 1967 (document 1/13). It is important for two things: first, it committed the alliance to following a dual approach, accepting that military defence and deterrence must be balanced by a commitment to political detente – something of crucial importance to Europeans, only too well aware that if superpower tensions were not defused, any conflict would reduce their countries to ruins. Second, the report epitomized the growing recognition that security guarantees were not enough, and that some means of generating collective foreign policy positions would have to be found. For these two things the Harmel Report remained an important reference point for the rest of the Cold War, but its very existence helped the Europeans to realize that there were limits to the extent to which NATO could be a genuinely multilateral political forum, partly because of US domination and partly because a military alliance is an unwieldy and static organization, rarely capable of flexible or proactive policy-making. In this sense, the Harmel Report was a stage in the gradual self-realization of European foreign policy cooperation. EPC might have turned out to demonstrate some of the same sclerotic symptoms as NATO, but at least it did not contain the United States, and it seemed full of potential for development.

Document 1/13   Report on the Future Tasks of the Alliance (Harmel Report), Brussels, December 1967

Report of the Council

1. A year ago, on the initiative of the Foreign Minister of Belgium, the governments of the fifteen nations of the Alliance resolved to "study the future tasks which face the Alliance, and its procedures for fulfilling them in order to strengthen the Alliance as a factor for durable peace". The present report sets forth the general tenor and main principles emerging from this examination of the future tasks of the Alliance.

2. Studies were undertaken by Messrs. Schütz, Watson, Spaak, Kohler and Patijn.* The Council wishes to express its appreciation and thanks to these eminent personalities for their efforts and for the analyses they produced.

3. The exercise has shown that the Alliance is a dynamic and vigorous organization which is constantly adapting itself to changing conditions. It also has shown that its future tasks can be handled within the terms of the Treaty by building on the methods and procedures which have proved their value over many years.

4. Since the North Atlantic Treaty was signed in 1949 the international situation has changed significantly and the political tasks of the Alliance have assumed a new dimension. Amongst other developments, the Alliance has played a major

---

*   This reference is to K. Schütz (Federal Republic of Germany, Foreign Ministry); J.H.A. Watson (UK FCO); Paul-Henri Spaak (Minister of State, Belgium); Foy Kohler (US, Deputy Under-Secretary of State); C.L. Patijn (Professor of International Political Relations, University of Utrecht, Netherlands). It is worth noting how many Belgians have been prominent in the process of developing a European foreign policy. Apart from Messrs Harmel and Spaak above, the names of Vicomte Etienne Davignon, Philippe de Schoutheete and Léo Tindemans would also figure in any list of the dozen most influential individuals.

part in stopping Communist expansion in Europe; the USSR has become one of the two world super powers but the Communist world is no longer monolithic; the Soviet doctrine of "peaceful co-existence" has changed the nature of the confrontation with the West but not the basic problems. Although the disparity between the power of the United States and that of the European states remains, Europe has recovered and is on its way towards unity. The process of decolonisation has transformed European relations with the rest of the world; at the same time, major problems have arisen in the relations between developed and developing countries.

5. The Atlantic Alliance has two main functions. Its first function is to maintain military strength and political solidarity to deter aggression and other forms of pressure and to defend the territory of member countries if aggression should occur. Since its inception, the Alliance has successfully fulfilled this task. But the possibility of a crisis cannot be excluded as long as the central political issues in Europe, first and foremost the German question, remain unsolved. Moreover, the situation of instability and uncertainty still precludes a balanced reduction of military forces. Under these conditions, the Allies will maintain as necessary, a suitable military capability to assure the balance of forces, thereby creating a climate of stability, security and confidence.

In this climate the Alliance can carry out its second function, to pursue the search for progress towards a more stable relationship in which the underlying political issues can be solved. Military security and a policy of détente are not contradictory but complementary. Collective defence is a stabilising factor in world politics. It is the necessary condition for effective policies directed towards a greater relaxation of tensions. The way to peace and stability in Europe rests in particular on the use of the Alliance constructively in the interest of détente. The participation of the USSR and the USA will be necessary to achieve a settlement of the political problems in Europe.

6. From the beginning the Atlantic Alliance has been a co-operative grouping of states sharing the same ideals and with a high degree of common interest. Their cohesion and solidarity provide an element of stability within the Atlantic area.

7. As sovereign states the Allies are not obliged to subordinate their policies to collective decision. The Alliance affords an effective forum and clearing house for the exchange of information and views; thus, each Ally can decide its policy in the light of close knowledge of the problems and objectives of the others. To this end the practice of frank and timely consultations needs to be deepened and improved. Each Ally should play its full part in promoting an improvement in relations with the Soviet Union and the countries of Eastern Europe, bearing in mind that the pursuit of détente must not be allowed to split the Alliance. The chances of success will clearly be greatest if the Allies remain on parallel courses, especially in matters of close concern to them all; their actions will thus be all the more effective.

8. No peaceful order in Europe is possible without a major effort by all concerned. The evolution of Soviet and East European policies gives ground for hope that those governments may eventually come to recognise the advantages to them of collaborating in working towards a peaceful settlement. But no final and stable settlement in Europe is possible without a solution of the German question which lies at the heart of present tensions in Europe. Any such settlement must end the unnatural barriers between Eastern and Western Europe, which are most clearly and cruelly manifested in the division of Germany.

9. Accordingly, the Allies are resolved to direct their energies to this purpose by realistic measures designed to further a détente in East-West relations. The relaxation of tensions is not the final goal but is part of a long-term process to promote better relations and to foster a European settlement. The ultimate political purpose of the Alliance is to achieve a just and lasting peaceful order in Europe accompanied by appropriate security guarantees.

10. Currently, the development of contacts between the countries of Western and Eastern Europe is mainly on a bilateral basis. Certain subjects, of course, require by their very nature a multilateral solution.

11. The problem of German reunification and its relationship to a European settlement has normally been dealt with in exchanges between the Soviet Union and the three Western powers having special responsibilities in this field. In the preparation of such exchanges the Federal Republic of Germany has regularly joined the three Western powers in order to reach a common position. The other Allies will continue to have their views considered in timely discussions among the Allies about Western policy on this subject, without in any way impairing the special responsibilities in question.

12. The Allies will examine and review suitable policies designed to achieve a just and stable order in Europe, to overcome the division of Germany and to foster European security. This will be part of a process of active and constant preparation for the time when fruitful discussions of these complex questions may be possible bilaterally or multilaterally between Eastern and Western nations.

13. The Allies are studying disarmament and practical arms control measures, including the possibility of balanced force reductions. These studies will be intensified. Their active pursuit reflects the will of the Allies to work for an effective détente with the East.

14. The Allies will examine with particular attention the defence problems of the exposed areas e.g. the South-Eastern flank. In this respect the present situation in the Mediterranean presents special problems, bearing in mind that the current crisis in the Middle-East falls within the responsibilities of the United Nations.

15. The North Atlantic Treaty area cannot be treated in isolation from the rest of the world. Crises and conflicts arising outside the area may impair its security either directly or by affecting the global balance. Allied countries contribute individually within the United Nations and other international organisations to the maintenance of international peace and security and to the solution of important international problems. In accordance with established usage the Allies, or such of them as wish to do so, will also continue to consult on such problems without commitment and as the case may demand.

. . .

Section 2 EPC/CFSP – institutional developments

This section deals with the documents of European foreign policy proper, from the beginning of EPC in 1969 to the development of the CFSP in the 1997 Treaty of Amsterdam, and at the European Councils of Vienna and Cologne in December 1998 and June 1999. These texts are the nearest thing there is to a constitution for EPC/CFSP, and they are of more than historical interest. Decision-makers have to refer to them to ensure that proper procedures are being followed in the delicate business of multilateral consultations – although they also have the confidential 'coutumier' (collection of procedural texts) which gives the detail on internal mechanisms but has never been made available to researchers. Naturally the latest agreed text, at present Title V of the Treaty of Amsterdam, provides an authoritative definition of proper practice, but it cannot be fully understood without a knowledge both of antecedents and of the detailed provisions of past texts, many of which continue to apply in the absence of specified changes. Not all of the documents which follow fall into the category of official founding texts, but those which do not, like the European Parliament's Draft Treaty of Union of 1984, helped to set the parameters of the developments of future change and are thus crucial to a sophisticated understanding of how the CFSP has come to take the form that it has.

The Hague Summit Declaration, 2 December 1969

The departure of General de Gaulle from office as President of France in April 1969 opened up a number of new possibilities for the EEC. The way was now clear for the United Kingdom to apply for membership with the likelihood, this time, of acceptance. Furthermore it now became possible, as it had not been at the time of the Fouchet Plans (documents 1/10 and 1/11), to envisage an increased political role for Europe in the world without at the same time subordinating the Community principle to an overarching union of states. Such a development was now perceived to be overdue, given the need to reinforce detente, and the European incapacity to comment collectively on the worsening tragedy in Vietnam and the renewed crisis in the Middle East. The attainment of a Common Customs Tariff in 1968 rather than 1970 as planned was a further stimulus.

Thus the Heads of Government Conference at The Hague in December 1969 attempted to relaunch the whole project of European integration after the Gaullist interlude, but this time in a pragmatic mode which would appeal to Britain and other new members as well as to the torch-carriers for a united Europe. The new French President, Georges Pompidou, through his foreign minister Maurice Schumann, had introduced the *motif* of 'completion, development and enlargement' in July 1969, and obtained agreement at The Hague to go forward with 'progress in the matter of political unification, within the context of enlargement' (paragraph 15). By this was meant cooperation on foreign policy, and the foreign ministers were to study how it might be done.

In this low-key way, in a few lines tucked away in the final communiqué of The Hague meeting, was born European Political Cooperation and the attempt to parallel the EEC's external economic relations with a capacity to speak on the world's great political issues. Even the interested observer might have been forgiven for failing to notice.

Document 2/1   Communiqué of the Conference of the Heads of State and Government of the Member States of the European Community (The Hague Summit Declaration), The Hague, 2 December 1969

1.
On the initiative of the Government of the French Republic and at the invitation of the Netherlands Government, the Heads of State or of Government and the Ministers for Foreign Affairs of the Member States of the European Communities met at The Hague on December 1 and 2, 1969. The Commission of the European Communities was invited to participate in the work of the conference on the second day.

2.
Now that the Common Market is about to enter upon its final stage, they considered that it was the duty of those who bear the highest political responsibility in each of the Member States to draw up a balance-sheet of the work already accomplished, to show their determination to continue it and to define the broad lines for the future.

3.
Looking back on the road that has been traversed, and finding that never before have independent States pushed their co-operation further, they were unanimous in their opinion that by reason of the progress made, the Community has now arrived at a turning point in its history. Over and above the technical and legal sides of the problems involved, the expiry of the transitional period at the end of the year has, therefore, acquired major political significance. Entry upon the final stage of the Common Market not only means confirming the irreversible nature of the work accomplished by the Communities, but also means paving the way for a united Europe capable of assuming its responsibilities in the world of tomorrow and of making a contribution commensurate with its traditions and its mission.

4.
The Heads of State or of Government therefore wish to reaffirm their belief in the political objectives which give the Community its meaning and purpose, their determination to carry their undertaking through to the end, and their confidence in the final successes of their efforts. Indeed, they have a common conviction that a Europe composed of States which, while preserving their national characteristics, are united

in their essential interests, assured of internal cohesion, true to its friendly relations with outside countries, conscious of the rôle it has to play in promoting the relaxation of international tension and the rapprochement among all peoples, and first and foremost among those of the entire European continent, is indispensable if a mainspring of development, progress and culture, world equilibrium and peace is to be preserved.

The European Communities remain the original nucleus from which European unity has been developed and intensified. The entry of other countries of this continent to the Communities—in accordance with the provisions of the Treaties of Rome—would undoubtedly help the Communities to grow to dimensions more in conformity with the present state of world economy and technology.

The creation of a special relationship with other European States which have expressed a desire to that effect would also contribute to this end. A development such as this would enable Europe to remain faithful to its traditions of being open to the world and increase its efforts on behalf of developing countries.

5.

As regards the completion of the Communities, the Heads of State or of Government reaffirmed the will of their Governments to pass from the transitional period to the final stage of the European Community and, accordingly, to lay down a definitive financial arrangement for the common agricultural policy by the end of 1969.

They agreed progressively to replace, within the framework of this financial arrangement, the contributions of Member Countries by their own resources, taking into account all the interests concerned, with the object of achieving in due course the integral financing of the Communities' budgets in accordance with the procedure provided for in Article 201 of the Treaty establishing the EEC and of strengthening the budgetary powers of the European Parliament. The problem of the method of direct elections is still being studied by the Council of Ministers.

6.

They asked the Governments to continue without delay, within the Council, the efforts already made to ensure a better control of the market by a policy of agricultural production making it possible to limit budgetary charges.

7.

The acceptance of a financial arrangement for the final stage does not exclude its adaptation by unanimous vote, in particular in the light of an enlarged Community and on condition that the principles of this arrangement are not infringed.

8.

They reaffirmed their readiness to further the more rapid progress of the later development needed to strengthen the Community and promote its development into an economic union. They are of the opinion that the integration process should result in a Community of stability and growth. To this end they agreed that within the Council, on the basis of the memorandum presented by the Commission on 12 February 1969, and in close collaboration with the latter, a plan in stages should be worked out during 1970 with a view to the creation of an Economic and Monetary Union. The development of monetary co-operation should depend on the harmonization of economic policies.

They agreed to arrange for the investigation of the possibility of setting up a European Reserve Fund in which a joint economic and monetary policy would have to result.

. . .

13.

They reaffirmed their agreement on the principle of the enlargement of the Community, as provided by Article 237 of the Treaty of Rome.

In so far as the applicant States accept the treaties and their political finality, the decisions taken since the entry into force of the treaties and the options made in the sphere of development the Heads of State or of Government have indicated their agreement to the opening of negotiations between the Community on the one hand and the applicant States on the other.

They agreed that the essential preparatory work could be undertaken as soon as practically and conveniently possible. By common consent, the preparations would take place in a most positive spirit.

14.

As soon as negotiations with the applicant countries have been opened, discussion will be started with such other EFTA members as may request them on their position in relation to the EEC.

15.

They agreed to instruct the Ministers of Foreign Affairs to study the best way of achieving progress in the matter of political unification, within the context of enlargement. The Ministers would be expected to report before the end of July 1970.

16.

All the creative activities and the actions conducive to European growth decided upon here will be assured of a better future if the younger generation is closely associated with them. Communities will make provision for it.

The Davignon (Luxembourg) Report

The Belgian Political Director Vicomte Davignon was charged by the six foreign ministers in early 1970 with producing a report on which a new system of foreign policy cooperation might be based. Working with his equivalents from the other five foreign ministries – the very group which was to form the 'Political Committee' in EPC – and with the models of Fouchet and the E(P)C to provide some guidance, Davignon did not manage to complete the report by the end of the Belgian Presidency in June. It did in fact come before the Luxembourg Conference of Foreign Ministers on 27 October 1970, where it was approved and accordingly became known officially as the 'Luxembourg Report'.

   The structure set up by the Luxembourg Report is very light. Indeed, foreign ministers were enjoined only to meet 'at least every six months', unlike the quarterly heads of government meetings foreseen in Fouchet I. There was no mention of heads of government and the only other bodies envisaged were a committee of Political Directors and *ad hoc* working groups. The European Commission and the European Parliament were given the minimal involvement possible, and the process was seen as closely parallel to, but still separate from that of the Communities. There was to be no EPC secretariat.

Nonetheless, this simple model was to be the basis of everything that followed in EPC up until the Treaty of Maastricht (document 2/18), in that it relied on the principle of official collegiality to build up the consensus in preparation for foreign ministers' intergovernmental decisions. More detail and more frequent meetings were easy to add on to this base without compromising its principles. Indeed, the report made provision for progress along these lines by proposing a second report within two years. The 'ratchet mechanism' was thus present right from the start of EPC.

Document 2/2 First Report of the Foreign Ministers to the Heads of State and Government of the Member States of the European Community (The Davignon or Luxembourg Report), Luxembourg, 27 October 1970

Under the chairmanship of the Federal Minister for Foreign Affairs, Walter Scheel, the Foreign Ministers of the six European Community countries, on 27 October 1970, in Luxembourg, finally approved, on behalf of their Governments, the report made pursuant to para. 15 of the Communiqué of The Hague on 20 July 1970. The Foreign Ministers agreed to publish the report on October 30, 1970. The following is the text of the report:

Part One

1.
The Ministers for Foreign Affairs of the Member States of the European Communities were instructed by the Heads of State or Government who met at The Hague on 1 and 2 December 1969 "to study the best way of achieving progress in the matter of political unification, within the context of enlargement" of the European Communities.

2.
In carrying out this mandate, the Ministers were anxious to preserve the spirit of The Hague Communiqué. In it the Heads of State or Government noted in particular that with the entry into the final phase of the Common Market the building of Europe had reached "a turning point in its history"; they affirmed that "the European Communities remain the original nucleus from which European unity has been developed and intensified"; finally, they expressed their determination "to pave the way for a united Europe capable of assuming its responsibilities in the world of tomorrow and of making a contribution commensurate with its traditions and its mission".

3.
The Heads of State or Government expressed their "common conviction that a Europe composed of States which, while preserving their national characteristics, are united in their essential interests, assured of internal cohesion, true to its friendly relations with outside countries, conscious of the rôle it has to play in promoting the relaxation of international tension and the rapprochement among all peoples, and first and foremost among those of the entire European continent, is indispensable if a mainspring of development, progress and culture, world equilibrium and peace is to be preserved".

4.

A united Europe conscious of the responsibilities incumbent upon it by reason of its economic development, its industrial potential and its standard of living, intends to increase its efforts for the benefit of the developing countries with a view to establishing trustful relations among nations.

5.

A united Europe must be founded upon the common heritage of respect for the liberty and the rights of men, and must assemble democratic States having freely elected parliaments. This united Europe remains the fundamental aim which should be achieved as soon as possible through the political will of its peoples and the decisions of their Governments.

6.

Consequently, the Ministers held the view that for the sake of continuity and in order to meet the ultimate goal of political union in Europe, so strongly underlined by the Hague Conference, their proposals had to proceed from three considerations.

7.

First, shape ought to be given, in the spirit of the preambles to the Treaties of Paris and Rome, to the will for political union which has not ceased to further the progress of the European Communities.

8.

Second, the implementation of common policies already adopted or about to be adopted requires corresponding developments in the political sphere as such so that the time will come nearer when Europe will be able to speak with one voice. It is therefore important that the construction of Europe should proceed in successive stages and that the most appropriate method of, and instruments for, joint political action should gradually develop.

9.

Third, Europe must prepare itself to exercise the responsibilities which to assume in the world is both its duty and a necessity on account of its greater cohesion and its increasingly important rôle.

10.

The present development of the European Communities requires Member States to intensify their political co-operation and provide in an initial phase the mechanism for harmonizing their views regarding international affairs.

Thus, the Ministers felt that efforts ought first to concentrate specifically on the coordination of foreign policies in order to show the whole world that Europe has a political mission. For they are convinced that progress in this direction would favour the development of the Communities and make the Europeans more conscious of their common responsibility.

Part Two

The Ministers propose the following:
Desirous of making progress in the field of political unification, the Governments, decide to co-operate in the sphere of foreign policy.

I. Objectives

The objectives of this co-operation are as follows:
— to ensure, through regular exchanges of information and consultations, a better mutual understanding on the great international problems;
— to strengthen their solidarity by promoting the harmonization of their views, the co-ordination of their positions, and, where it appears possible and desirable,
— common actions.

II. Ministerial Meetings

1.
On the initiative of the Chairman, the Ministers for Foreign Affairs will meet at least every six months.
If they feel that the gravity of the circumstances or the importance of the subjects in question so justify, their meeting may be replaced by a conference of Heads of State or Government.
Should a grave crisis or a matter of particular urgency arise, extraordinary consultations will be arranged between the Governments of Member States. The Chairman will get in touch with his colleagues in order to determine the best way of ensuring such consultation.

2.
The Minister for Foreign Affairs of the country having the chair in the Council of the European Communities will chair the meetings.

3.
The ministerial meetings will be prepared by a committee composed of the Directors of political affairs.

III. Political Committee

1.
A committee composed of the Directors of political affairs will meet at least four times a year to prepare the ministerial meetings and carry out any tasks delegated to them by the Ministers.
Further, the Chairman may, in exceptional cases, and after having consulted his colleagues, convene the Committee either on his own initiative or at the request of one of the members.

2.
The chairmanship of the Committee will be subject to the same rules as those which apply to ministerial meetings.

3.
The Committee may set up working groups to deal with special matters.

It may appoint a group of experts to collect material relating to a specific problem and to present the possible alternatives.

4.

Any other form of consultation may be envisaged where necessary.

IV. Subjects for Consultation

Governments will consult on all important questions of foreign policy.
Member States may propose any question of their choice for political consultation.

V. Commission of the European Communities

Should the work of the Ministers affect the activities of the European Communities, the Commission will be invited to make known its views.

VI. European Parliamentary Assembly

In order to give a democratic character to political unification, it will be necessary to associate public opinion and its representatives with it.
The Ministers and members of the Political Commission of the European Parliamentary Assembly will meet for a biannual colloquy to discuss questions that are the subject of consultation within the framework of co-operation on foreign affairs. This colloquy will be held in an informal way to give parliamentarians and Ministers an opportunity freely to express their opinions.

VII. General Provisions

1.

The meetings will as a general rule be held in the country whose representative is in the chair.

2.

The host country will make the necessary arrangements to provide the secretariat and the material organization of the meetings.

3.

Each country will designate an official of its Ministry of Foreign Affairs who will liaise with his counterparts in the other countries.

Part Three

1.

In order to ensure continuity in the task undertaken, the Ministers propose to pursue their study on the best way of achieving progress in the field of political unification, and to present a second report.

2.

This study will also deal with the improvement of co-operation in foreign policy matters and with the search for other fields where progress might be achieved. This study must take into account work undertaken within the European Communities especially with a view to reinforcing their structures and thus, if need be, to enable them to live up to their increasing and developing tasks.

3.

To this end, the Ministers instruct the Political Committee to arrange its activities in such a way that it will be able to fulfil this task, and to present a summary report at each biannual ministerial meeting.

4.

The Chairman of the Council will once a year address a communication to the European Parliamentary Assembly on progress in that work.

5.

Notwithstanding any interim reports which they may consider worth submitting if their deliberations so permit, the Ministers for Foreign Affairs will present their second full report not later than two years after the commencement of consultations on foreign policy. That report must contain an assessment of the results obtained by those consultations.

Part Four

Proposals concerning association of the applicant countries with the work envisaged in parts II and III of the Report.

1.

The Ministers emphasize that there is a correlation between membership in the European Communities and participation in the activities designed to help achieve progress in the field of political unification.

2.

Since the applicant countries must be consulted on the objectives and procedures described in the present Report, and since they must adhere to them once they have become members of the European Communities, it is necessary to keep those countries informed of progress in the work of the Six.

3.

In view of those different objectives the following procedures for informing the applicant countries are suggested:

(a) Meetings of the Ministers

At each of their biannual meetings the Ministers will fix the date of their next meeting.

They will at the same time propose a date for a ministerial meeting of the Ten. That date shall be as close as possible to that of the meeting of the Six and shall normally be after it; in fixing that date such occasions shall be borne in mind when the ten Ministers or some of them meet anyhow.

After the ministerial meeting of the Six the Chairman shall inform the applicant countries of the questions which the Ministers propose to put on the agenda of the ministerial meeting of the Ten, and shall furnish them all other information likely to make the exchange of views of the Ten as fruitful as possible.

In view of the fact that the information and the exchange of views must be marked by a certain flexibility, it is understood that they will be intensified once the agreements on the applicant countries' accession to the European Communities have been signed.

(b) Meetings of the Political Committee
This Committee will furnish the applicant countries the information likely to be of interest to them. The information shall be transmitted by the Chair to whom those countries shall address their response, if any. The Chair will report on it to the Political Committee.

The Paris Declaration

In line with the provisions of the Luxembourg Report, governments were active in discussing the next stage of the development of EPC from late in 1970. In the next eighteen months papers were tabled by the Federal Republic, the Netherlands and Belgium. Another round of jousting, similar to that over the Fouchet Plans, took place over whether a new political secretariat should be created which might provide direction for the whole Community, and where it should be situated, Brussels – or Paris. This time, however, there was no De Gaulle to polarize matters, and the confederal/federal argument was put on hold in favour of letting EPC develop in its own way, without permanent institutions. The revolving Presidency, it was becoming clear, would be carrying the burden.

  Given the need to discuss institutional developments in the light of the forthcoming round of enlargement, but also substantive matters like the CSCE and relations with the United States, another summit was convened in Paris in October 1972. This meeting called for the transformation of 'the whole complex' of EEC and Member States' relations into a political union before the end of the 1970s, and requested a report to this end from the Community institutions. For their part foreign ministers were asked to report by 30 June 1973 on how to improve EPC. EPC was beginning to emerge as a practical, and discrete, form of diplomatic harmonization, rather than an alternative model to the supranational Communities. The next report was anticipated by the announcement that foreign ministers would now meet four times a year.

Document 2/3   Statement of the Conference of the Heads of State and Government of the Member States of the European Union, Paris, 21 October 1972

The Heads of State or of Government of the Countries of the enlarged community, meeting for the first time on 19 and 20 October in Paris, at the invitation of the President of the French Republic,
solemnly declare:
at the moment when enlargement, decided in accordance with the rules in the Treaties and with respect for what the six original Member States have already achieved, is to become a reality and to give a new dimension to the Community;
at a time when world events are profoundly changing the international situation;
now that there is a general desire for détente and co-operation in response to the interest and the wishes of all peoples;
now that serious monetary and trade problems require a search for lasting solutions that will favour growth with stability;
now that many developing countries see the gap widening between themselves and the industrial nations and claim with justification an increase in aid and a fairer use of wealth;

now that the tasks of the Community are growing, and fresh responsibilities are being laid upon it, the time has come for Europe to recognize clearly the unity of its interests, the extent of its capacities and the magnitude of its duties; Europe must be able to make its voice heard in world affairs, and to make an original contribution commensurate with its human, intellectual and material resources. It must affirm its own views in international relations, as befits its mission to be open to the world and for progress, peace and co-operation.

. . .

*To this End:**

. . .

7.
The construction of Europe will allow it, in conformity with its ultimate political objectives, to affirm its personality while remaining faithful to its traditional friendships and to the alliances of the Member States, and to establish its position in world affairs as a distinct entity determined to promote a better international equilibrium, respecting the principles of the Charter of the United Nations. The Member States of the Community, the driving force of the construction of Europe, affirm their intention to transform before the end of the present decade the whole complex of their relations into a European Union.

. . .

External Relations

10.
The Heads of State or of Government affirm that their efforts to construct their Community attain their full meaning only in so far as Member States succeed in acting together to cope with the growing world responsibilities incumbent on Europe.

11.
The Heads of State or of Government are convinced that the Community must, without detracting from the advantages enjoyed by countries with which it has special relations, respond even more than in the past to the expectations of all the developing countries.
With this in view, it attaches essential importance to the policy of association as confirmed by the Treaties of Accession and to the fulfilment of its commitments to the countries of the Mediterranean Basin with which agreements have been or will be concluded, agreements which should be the subject of an overall and balanced approach. In the same perspective, in the light of the results of the UNCTAD Conference and in the context of the Development Strategy adopted by the United Nations, the Institutions of the Community and Member States are invited progressively to adopt an overall policy of development co-operation on a world-wide scale, comprising, in particular, the following elements:

---

* Paragraphs 1–6, omitted, assert the Community's democratic values, the aim of an Economic and Monetary Union, and the importance of help to developing countries, of international trade, and of détente.

— the promotion in appropriate cases of agreement concerning the primary products of the developing countries with a view to arriving at market stabilization
and an increase in their exports;
— the improvement of generalized preferences with the aim of achieving a steady
increase in imports of manufactures from the developing countries.

In this connection the Community Institutions will study from the beginning of
1973 the conditions which will permit the achievement of a substantial growth
target:
— an increase in the volume of official financial aid;
— an improvement in the financial conditions of this aid, particularly in favour of
the least developed countries, bearing in mind the recommendations of the
OECD Development Assistance Committee.

These questions will be the subject of studies and decisions in good time during
1973.

12.
With regard to the industrial countries, the Community is determined, in order to
ensure the harmonious development of world trade:
— to contribute, while respecting what has been achieved by the Community, to
a progressive liberalization of international trade by measures based on reciprocity and relating to both tariffs and non-tariff barriers;
— to maintain a constructive dialogue with the United States, Japan, Canada and
its other industrialized trade partners in a forthcoming spirit, using the most
appropriate methods.

In this context the Community attaches major importance to the multilateral negotiations in the context of GATT in which it will participate in accordance with its
earlier statement.

To this end, the Community Institutions are invited to decide not later than 1 July,
1973, on a global approach covering all aspects affecting trade.

The Community hopes that an effort on the part of all partners will allow these
negotiations to be completed in 1975.

It confirms its desire for the full participation of the developing countries in the
preparation and progress of these negotiations which should take due account of
the interests of those countries.

Furthermore, having regard to the agreements concluded with the EFTA countries
which are not members, the Community declares its readiness to seek with Norway
a speedy solution to the trade problems facing that country in its relations with the
enlarged Community.

13.
In order to promote *détente* in Europe, the Conference reaffirmed its determination
to follow a common commercial policy towards the countries of Eastern Europe
with effect from 1 January, 1973; Member States declared their determination to
promote a policy of co-operation, founded on reciprocity, with these countries.

This policy of co-operation is, at the present stage, closely linked with the preparation and progress of the Conference on Security and Co-operation in Europe to
which the enlarged Community and its Member States are called upon to make a
concerted and constructive contribution.

Political Co-operation

14.

The Heads of State or of Government agreed that political co-operation between the Member States of the Community on foreign policy matters had begun well and should be still further improved. They agreed that consultations should be intensified at all levels and that the Foreign Ministers should in future meet four times a year instead of twice for this purpose. They considered that the aim of their co-operation was to deal with problems of current interest and, where possible, to formulate common medium and long-term positions, keeping in mind, inter alia, the international political implications for and effects of Community policies under construction. On matters which have a direct bearing on Community activities, close contact will be maintained with the Institutions of the Community. They agreed that the Foreign Ministers should produce, not later than 30. June, 1973, a second report on methods of improving political co-operation in accordance with the Luxembourg report.

. . .

The Copenhagen Report

The Copenhagen Report was, like its forerunner, the product in particular of the commitment of Vicomte Davignon. It still betrays some signs of the tension between those who hoped that EPC would transcend its own limitations and carry the whole integrationist project forward, and those (like the British) who saw it as a pragmatic form of assistance to national foreign policy. In effect, it was less than the first and more than the second. In building on the foundations of Luxembourg by increasing the frequency of meetings, by codifying the cooperation which was growing up in third country capitals and by introducing both the Correspondents group and the COREU telex network, the decisions taken at Copenhagen were setting up a working system of collective diplomacy on what was to become a daily basis. This had the potential to transform the attitudes of the states participating in it and to draw them closer together regardless of the lack of formal supranationality. At the same time, a great deal hung on the ability of the Presidency country to take initiatives and to sustain consensus, and these were still very early days for EPC. The question of the resources to support diplomacy had not yet been addressed, for all the growing awareness of the need for consistency with Community external relations. And this neophyte quality of EPC was about to be cruelly exposed by the coming war in the Middle East (see Section 4b).

Document 2/4   Second Report of the Foreign Ministers to the Heads of State and Government of the Member States of the European Community (The Copenhagen Report), Copenhagen, 23 July 1973

The Foreign Ministers of the nine Member States of the European Communities, in carrying out the instruction given them in para. 14 of the Declaration of the Paris Summit Conference of 21 October 1972, have submitted the second report on the European Political Co-operation. The Heads of State and Government have approved the report.

The following is the text of the report:

Part I.

The Heads of State or of Government of the Member States of the European Communities approved on 27 October 1970 the Report of the Foreign Ministers drawn up in implementation of paragraph 15 of the Communiqué of The Hague Conference of 1 and 2 December 1969. The document reflected the belief that progress towards concerted action in the field of foreign policy was likely to promote the development of the Communities and to help the Europeans to realize more fully their common responsibilities. The objectives of that co-operation are:

— to ensure, by means of regular consultations and exchanges of information, improved mutual understanding as regards the main problems of international relations;
— to strengthen solidarity between Governments by promoting the harmonization of their views and the alignment of their positions and, wherever it appears possible and desirable, joint action.

The Report also proposed that the Foreign Ministers should submit a second general report which would, *inter alia*, contain an assessment of the results obtained from such consultation. At the time when the enlargement of the European Communities became a fact, paragraph 14 of the Summit Declaration in Paris on 21 October 1972 required the Foreign Ministers to produce by 30 June 1973 a second report on methods of improving political co-operation in accordance with the Luxembourg Report.

The Heads of State or of Government, meeting in Paris, expressed their satisfaction at the results obtained since the political co-operation machinery was formally set up on the basis of the texts of 27 October 1970. In several fields, the Member States have been able to consider and decide matters jointly so as to make common political action possible. This habit has also led to the "reflex" of co-ordination among the Member States which has profoundly affected the relations of the Member States between each other and with third countries. This collegiate sense in Europe is becoming a real force in international relations.

The Ministers note that the characteristically pragmatic mechanisms set up by the Luxembourg Report have shown their flexibility and effectiveness. What is involved in fact is a new procedure in international relations and an original European contribution to the technique of arriving at concerted action. The experience acquired so far has resulted in a strengthening of the belief in the usefulness of concerted action by means of direct contact between senior officials of Foreign Ministries and of a very thorough preparation of the matters under consideration as a basis for the decisions by Ministers.

Such concerted action has also had a positive influence in so far as it has brought a more conscious collaboration between representatives of Member States of the Communities in third countries. They have been encouraged to meet and compare the information available to them. This habit of working together has enabled the procedure for concerted action to become more widespread wherever common action or common consideration seemed desirable.

In the Luxembourg Report provision was made for the Commission to be invited to make known its views when the work of the Ministers affected the activities of the European Communities. The Foreign Ministers express satisfaction that these contacts have now become a reality and that a constructive and continuing dialogue is in course both at the level of experts and of the Political Committee, and at ministerial meetings.

The colloquy with the Political Commission of the European Parliament and the communication by the President of the Council to the European Parliament have put into effect the desire of the Foreign Ministers to make a contribution to the democratic character of the construction of political union.

The final Declaration of the Conference of Heads of State or of Government held on 19–21 October 1972 expressed, *inter alia*, the conviction that Europe must be able to make its voice heard in world affairs and to affirm its own views in international relations.

Europe now needs to establish its position in the world as a distinct entity, especially in international negotiations which are likely to have a decisive influence on the international equilibrium and on the future of the European Community.

In the light of this it is essential that, in the spirit of the conclusions of the Paris Summit Conference, co-operation among the Nine on foreign policy should be such as to enable Europe to make an original contribution to the international equilibrium. Europe has the will to do this, in accordance with its traditionally outward-looking mission and its interest in progress, peace and co-operation. It will do so, loyal to its traditional friends and to the alliances of its Member States, in the spirit of good neighbourliness which must exist between all the countries of Europe both to the east and the west, and responding to the expectations of all the developing countries.

The results obtained by the procedure of political consultation since its inception, referred to in the preceding paragraphs, are the subject of a descriptive Annex attached to this Report.

Part II.

In implementation of the task entrusted to them by paragraph 14 of the Paris Summit Declaration, and having regard to the objective which the Heads of State or of Government set themselves, namely to transform, before the end of the present decade, the whole complex of the relations between the Member States of the European Communities into a European Union, the Foreign Ministers propose that the Heads of State or of Government approve the following measures:

1. Ministerial Meetings

Henceforth, the Foreign Ministers will meet four times a year. They may also, whenever they consider it necessary to consult each other on specific subjects between meetings, meet for that purpose when they happen to come together on other occasions.

2. The Political Committee of the Member States of the European Communities

The Political Directors of the Member States of the Community will meet in the Political Committee of the Member States of the European Communities with a view to preparing ministerial meetings and carrying out tasks entrusted to them by the Ministers. In order to attain that objective, meetings of the Committee will be held as frequently as the intensification of the work requires.

3. The Group of "Correspondents"

A group consisting of European "Correspondents" in the Foreign Ministry (called the Group of Correspondents) will be set up. That Group will be entrusted with the task of following the implementation of political co-operation and of studying problems of organization and problems of a general nature. Furthermore, for certain matters, the Group will prepare the work of the Political Committee on the basis of instructions given by that Committee.

4. Working Groups

(a) In order to ensure more thorough consultation on individual questions, working groups will be set up to bring together senior officials of the Ministries of Foreign Affairs responsible for the subject under consideration. These working groups will cease to meet as soon as they have completed the task entrusted to them. Exceptionally, and especially in order to ensure continuity if the work can be completed in the near future, the chairman of a working group may be required to continue in office beyond the usual period.
(b) The chairman in office may approach the Political Committee about the need to bring together senior officials of the major ministerial departments who have not met during the preceding six month period with a view to keeping them in contact with each other.

5. Medium and Long-Term Studies

In accordance with paragraph 14 of the Declaration of the Paris Summit Conference, which set as an objective on political co-operation the formulation, where possible, of common medium and long-term positions, several methods of work can be envisaged. According to circumstances, this will be done either by groups of experts in addition to the current matters which they normally deal with, or by entrusting the preparations of such studies to a special analysis and research group consisting normally of officials.
The Political Committee will propose to the Foreign Ministers specific subjects for study.

6. The Rôle of the Embassies of the Nine in the Capitals of the Member Countries of the Community

The Embassies of the Nine participate closely in the implementation of political co-operation. In particular, they receive information on a Community basis issued by the Foreign Ministry of their country of residence. Furthermore, they are occasionally entrusted with consultations on specific subjects:

— at the seat of the Presidency at the request of the Political Committee, the Presidency or another Member State; or
— in another Capital at the request of the Foreign Ministry.

They will appoint one of their diplomatic staff who will specifically be entrusted with ensuring the necessary contacts with the Foreign Ministry of their country of residence, within the framework of political co-operation.

7. *Rôles of the Embassies in Third Countries and of the Offices of Permanent Representatives to Major International Organizations*

With the introduction of the political co-operation machinery, it proved useful to associate Embassies and Permanent Representatives' offices with the work. In the light of the experience gained, better information on the work in progress in the field of political co-operation should be provided so as to enable them, where necessary, to put forward in an appropriate form those aspects which they consider of interest for this work, including considerations on joint action.

With this in mind, the Political Committee will notify the missions concerned when it considers it necessary to obtain a contribution on a specific item of its agenda. Where appropriate, it may require a common report to be prepared by them on specific questions.

In addition to the provisions contained in the texts in force governing reciprocal information on the occasion of important visits, the Ambassador concerned, accredited in the country where the visit takes place, should first provide information to his colleagues on the spot so as to enable any appropriate exchange of views. After the visit, such information as may interest them should be given to them in the most appropriate manner.

Finally, in application of the provisions governing the rôle of missions abroad, the permanent representatives of the Member States to the major international organizations will regularly consider matters together and, on the basis of instructions received, will seek common positions in regard to important questions dealt with by those organizations.

8. *The Presidency*

As regards the internal organization of the work of political co-operation, the Presidency:
— sees to it that the conclusions adopted at meetings of Ministers and of the Political Committee are implemented on a collegiate basis;
— proposes, on its own initiative or on that of another State, consultation at an appropriate level;
— may also, between meetings of the Political Committee, meet the Ambassadors of the Member States in order to inform them of the progress of the work of political co-operation. The meeting may take place at the request of an Ambassador of a Member State seeking consultation on a specific subject.

Experience has also shown that the Presidency's task presents a particularly heavy administrative burden. Administrative assistance may therefore be provided by other Member States for specific tasks.

9. Improvement of Contact between the Nine

The Foreign Ministers have agreed to establish a communications system with a view to facilitating direct contact between their departments.

10. Relations with the European Parliament

Having regard to the widening scope of the European Communities and the intensification of political co-operation at all levels, four colloquies will be held each year at which the Ministers will meet with members of the Political Committee of the European Parliament. For the purpose of preparing the colloquies, the Political Committee will draw to the attention of Ministers proposals adopted by the European Parliament on foreign policy questions.

In addition the Minister exercising the function of President will continue, as in the past, to submit to the European Parliament, once a year, a communication on progress made in the field of political co-operation.

11. Priorities to be set in respect of the Matters to be dealt with within the framework of Political Co-operation

Governments will consult each other on all important foreign policy questions and will work out priorities, observing the following criteria:
— the purpose of the consultation is to seek common policies on practical problems;
— the subject dealt with must concern European interests whether in Europe itself or elsewhere where the adoption of a common position is necessary or desirable.

On these questions each State undertakes as a general rule not to take up final positions without prior consultation with its partners within the framework of the political co-operation machinery.

The Political Committee will submit to the meetings of Foreign Ministers subjects among which the Ministers may select those to be given priority in the course of political co-operation. This is without prejudice to the examination of additional subjects either at the suggestion of a Member State or as a result of recent developments.

12. Relationship between the Work of the Political Co-operation Machinery and that carried out within the framework of the European Communities

(a) The Political Co-operation machinery, which deals on the intergovernmental level with problems of international politics, is distinct from and additional to the activities of the institutions of the Community which are based on the juridical commitments undertaken by the Member States in the Treaty of Rome. Both sets of machinery have the aim of contributing to the development of European unification. The relationship between them is discussed below.

(b) The Political Co-operation machinery, which is responsible for dealing with questions of current interest and where possible for formulating common medium and long-term positions, must do this keeping in mind, *inter alia*, the implications for and the effects of, in the field of international politics, Community policies under construction.

For matters which have an incidence on Community activities close contact will be maintained with the institutions of the Community.

(c) The last section of the previous paragraph is implemented in the following way:
— the Commission is invited to make known its views in accordance with current practice;
— the Council, through the President of the Committee of Permanent Representatives, is informed by the Presidency of the agreed conclusions which result from the work of the Political Co-operation machinery, to the extent that these conclusions have an interest for the work of the Community;
— the Ministers will similarly be able, if it is so desired, to instruct the Political Co-operation machinery to prepare studies on certain political aspects of problems under examination in the framework of the Community. These reports will be transmitted to the Council through the President of the Committee of Permanent Representatives.

In drawing up this Report, the Ministers have demonstrated their belief that even more important than the contents of their proposals is the spirit in which these are put into effect.

That spirit is the one that emerges from the decisions taken at the Paris Summit meeting.

The Ministers consider that co-operation on foreign policy must be placed in the perspective of European Union.

From now on, it is of the greatest importance to seek common positions on major international problems.

ANNEX

Results obtained from European Political Co-operation on Foreign Policy

1. Ministerial Meetings

(Luxembourg Report—Second Part, II)

As from the second half of 1970, the Ministers for Foreign Affairs of Member States of the European Communities have met regularly twice a year.

In pursuance of the decision taken by the Conference of Heads of State or of Government in Paris on 19–21 October 1972, the number of these meetings has, from 1973, been increased from two to four.

2. Political Committee

(Luxembourg Report—Second Part, III)

(a) The Luxembourg Report provided for at least four meetings a year. From the outset, the Political Committee met more often than had been foreseen; in fact, during the last twelve months, it has held nine meetings.

(b) The Political Committee has noted that the aims defined in the Luxembourg Report could only be achieved by adequate preparation. To this effect and without thereby discarding other possible formulas, it has established, within the framework of its activities, working parties entrusted with particular tasks:

— a Sub-Committee was set up to study problems relating to the Conference on Security and Co-operation in Europe (CSCE), and an *ad hoc* Group, in which the Commission of the European Communities takes part, was set up to examine the economic aspects. In view of the need for such studies, it was decided that the Sub-Committee and the *ad hoc* Group should meet on a permanent basis in Helsinki in order to work, on the spot, for agreed positions in response to developments in the negotiations;

— three working groups were set up with a view to following and studying problems relating, respectively, to the situation in the Middle East, the Mediterranean area and Asia; senior officials in the Foreign Ministries with responsibility for those questions usually participate in this work;

— there were also meetings of experts dealing with various questions as, for example, co-operation in the event of natural disasters;

— consultations also took place between the Presidency and the Embassies of Member States on the situation in the Indian sub-continent and in the Middle East.

(c) Furthermore, it was decided to place within the framework of political co-operation the consultations which used to take place within the WEU before sessions of the General Assembly of the United Nations, of the Economic and Social Council and of the FAO. For this purpose, alongside the co-ordination meetings of the Permanent Representatives, senior officials responsible for the different sectors within each of the national Administrations get together to discuss certain items placed on the Agendas of these sessions; they report to the Political Committee.

3. Group of "Correspondants"

(Luxembourg Report—Second Part, VII-3)

In order to facilitate the internal organization of political co-operation, the Luxembourg Report provided that each State should appoint from within its Ministry of Foreign Affairs an official who should act as the "correspondant" of his opposite numbers in other States. These officials were established as a "Group of Correspondants"; this Group, in addition to the task of drafting summaries of the conclusions reached at ministerial meetings and meetings of the Political Committee, was entrusted with the duty of closely following the implementation of political co-operation and of studying the problems of organization and those of a general nature, as well as particular problems the Political Committee gave it to examine, in particular for the purpose of preparing their meetings.

4. Activities of Embassies of the Nine in the Capitals of Member States of the Communities

The rôle of Ambassadors of the Nine in the capitals of Member States has proved important for the implementation of political co-operation in particular with respect to the exchange of information. In order to facilitate contacts with the Ministries of Foreign Affairs in the countries of their residence with respect to matters of political co-operation, each of these Embassies has appointed a diplomat on its staff whose special duty is to ensure contact with the Ministry of Foreign Affairs in its country of residence on matters of political co-operation.

Since the Ambassadors receive information concerning the Community from the Ministry of Foreign Affairs of their country of residence and, in particular, since they are expected by the Political Committee to engage in discussions from time to time, in the capital of the Presidency, it is important that they should be fully informed of the progress of political co-operation with the implementation of which their missions are associated.

5. Association of Ambassadors in Third Countries and of Permanent Representatives to International Organizations with the Political Co-operation

It has been judged necessary and in line with the Luxembourg Report to associate Heads of the diplomatic missions of the Nine with political co-operation. For that purpose, it has been arranged that the Political Committee can ask Ambassadors accredited to a particular country to provide it with reports and thus to encourage co-operation among the diplomatic representatives of Member States.

It had also been arranged that regular discussions can take place between Ambassadors accredited to countries other than those of the Community, on problems of common interest concerning the country to which they are accredited, in accordance with such procedures as the Ambassadors themselves would find appropriate.

These provisions were put into operation and developed during the first two years of political co-operation.

Heads of diplomatic missions in many posts, or their representatives, while taking account of local conditions, take part increasingly in political co-operation, especially through exchanges of view and in certain cases by means of joint reports.

6. Commission of the European Communities

(Luxembourg Report—Second Part, V)

The Luxembourg Report provides that:

"should the work of the Ministers affect the activities of the European Communities, the Commission will be invited to make known its views."

In accordance with this the Commission of the Communities has been invited to participate in ministerial discussions and in sessions of the Political Committee and of groups of experts when the agenda of the meeting provides for the examination of questions affecting the activities of the Communities; for example the examination of problems relating to the economic aspects of the CSCE and to the future rôle of the Council of Europe.

7. European Parliament

(Luxembourg Report—Second Part, VI, and Third Part, 4)

In accordance with the Luxembourg Report which provided for two methods of associating public opinion and its representatives with the development of political co-operation, Ministers for Foreign Affairs and members of the Political Commission of the European Parliament held a colloquy every six months and the President in office of the Council reported every year to the Parliament on the progress of work concerning the best means of advancing towards political union.

At the last two colloquies, a new procedure, consisting essentially of the notification in advance to the Political Commission of the European Parliament of the main subjects for discussion, was adopted in order to make the exchange of views more fruitful.

8. Participation of New Members

Political co-operation was started when the European Communities consisted of only six members—the applicant States being associated with their activities in accordance with the procedure specified in the fourth part of the Luxembourg Report. The procedure provided that the Ministers of the Six would meet their colleagues from acceding States at a time as near as possible to their meetings in order to ensure necessary consultation for keeping those States informed of the progress of the work of the Six.

Similarly, it was arranged for the President in office of the Political Committee to communicate to applicant States information likely to interest them and for him to obtain any reactions they had. This rule was adopted to take account of the essential connection between membership of the European Communities and participation in activities enabling further progress to be made towards political union.

After signature of the Act of Accession on 22 January, 1972 these States have fully participated in meetings at every level.

The Declaration on European Identity

The Declaration on European Identity which came out of the foreign ministers' meeting in Copenhagen on 14 December 1973 seemed an act of desperation. The brief but dangerous 'Yom Kippur' war of October 1973 had created a febrile atmosphere in which even the biggest EC state felt suddenly conscious of its own weakness, and there was every excuse for the Europeans to cast around in search of a foreign policy. The far-reaching attempt of this Declaration to define Europe's place in the world and to look forward (once again) to the construction of a united Europe was a not illogical response to a situation in which the United States appeared bent on pursuing global policies with barely a nod in its allies' direction, while the newly powerful oil-producing states were willing to embargo their European customers for political reasons.

Yet this is only half the story. The Declaration of December 1973 had in fact been commissioned in July, partly in response to Henry Kissinger's 'Year of Europe' speech and partly as a natural development from the processes initiated in 1970. What is more the term 'identity' is a misleadingly rhetorical title for what is little more than a list of worthy objectives tacked on to a fragment of collective autobiography. Identity is simply to be discovered by the process of developing relations with other countries. Still, the tone of the declaration is noticeably urgent and indicates a recognition that, somehow, EPC would have to advance rapidly from procedure to substance if it was to serve the distinctive European interests (and values) which now seemed so starkly exposed. With this, however, began the divergence between ambition and capability which has dogged the attempt to operationalize European foreign policy to this day.

Document 2/5   Declaration on European Identity by the Nine Foreign Ministers, Copenhagen, 14 December 1973

The Nine Member Countries of the European Communities have decided that the time has come to draw up a document on the European identity. This will enable them to achieve a better definition of their relations with other countries and of their responsibilities and the place which they occupy in world affairs. They have decided to define the European Identity with the dynamic nature of the Community in mind. They have the intention of carrying the work further in the future in the light of the progress made in the construction of a United Europe.

Defining the European Identity involves:
— reviewing the common heritage, interests and special obligations of the Nine, as well as the degree of unity so far achieved within the Community,
— assessing the extent to which the Nine are already acting together in relation to the rest of the world and the responsibilities which result from this,
— taking into consideration the dynamic nature of European unification.

I. The Unity of the Nine Member Countries of the Community

1.

The Nine European states might have been pushed towards disunity by their history and by selfishly defending misjudged interests. But they have overcome their past enmities and have decided that unity is a basic European necessity to ensure the survival of the civilization which they have in common.

The Nine wish to ensure that the cherished values of their legal, political and moral order are respected, and to preserve the rich variety of their national cultures. Sharing as they do the same attitudes to life, based on a determination to build a society which measures up to the needs of the individual, they are determined to defend the principles of representative democracy, of the rule of law, of social justice—which is the ultimate goal of economic progress—and of respect for human rights. All of these are fundamental elements of the European Identity. The Nine believe that this enterprise corresponds to the deepest aspirations of their peoples who should participate in its realization, particularly through their elected representatives.

2.

The Nine have the political will to succeed in the construction of a United Europe. On the basis of the Treaties of Paris and Rome setting up the European Communities and of subsequent decisions, they have created a common market, based on a customs union, and have established institutions, common policies and machinery for co-operation. All these are an essential part of the European Identity. The Nine are determined to safeguard the elements which make up the unity they have achieved so far and the fundamental objectives laid down for future development at the Summit Conferences in The Hague and Paris. On the basis of the Luxembourg and Copenhagen reports, the Nine Governments have established a system of political co-operation with a view to determining common attitudes and, where possible and desirable, common action. They propose to develop this further. In accordance with the decision taken at the Paris conference, the Nine reaffirm their intention of transforming the whole complex of their relations into a European Union before the end of the present decade.

3.

The diversity of cultures within the framework of a common European civilization, the attachment to common values and principles, the increasing convergence of attitudes to life, the awareness of having specific interests in common and the determination to take part in the construction of a United Europe, all give the European Identity its originality and its own dynamism.

4.

The construction of a United Europe, which the Nine Member Countries of the Community are undertaking, is open to other European nations who share the same ideals and objectives.

5.

The European countries have, in the course of their history, developed close ties with many other parts of the world. These relationships, which will continue to evolve, constitute an assurance of progress and international equilibrium.

6.

Although in the past the European countries were individually able to play a major rôle on the international scene, present international problems are difficult for any of the Nine to solve alone. International developments and the growing concentration of power and responsibility in the hands of a very small number of great powers mean that Europe must unite and speak increasingly with one voice if it wants to make itself heard and play its proper rôle in the world.

7.

The Community, the world's largest trading group, could not be a closed economic entity. It has close links with the rest of the world as regards its supplies and market outlets. For this reason the Community, while remaining in control of its own trading policies, intends to exert a positive influence on world economic relations with a view to the greater well-being of all.

8.

The Nine, one of whose essential aims is to maintain peace, will never succeed in doing so if they neglect their own security. Those of them who are members of the Atlantic Alliance consider that in present circumstances there is no alternative to the security provided by the nuclear weapons of the United States and by the presence of North American forces in Europe: and they agree that in the light of the relative military vulnerability of Europe, the Europeans should, if they wish to preserve their independence, hold to their commitments and make constant efforts to ensure that they have adequate means of defence at their disposal.

II. The European Identity in Relation to the World

9.

The Europe of the Nine is aware that, as it unites, it takes on new international obligations. European unification is not directed against anyone, nor is it inspired by a desire for power. On the contrary, the Nine are convinced that their union will benefit the whole international community since it will constitute an element of equilibrium and a basis of co-operation with all countries, whatever their size, culture or social system. The Nine intend to play an active rôle in world affairs and thus to contribute, in accordance with the purposes and principles of the United Nations Charter, to ensuring that international relations have a more just basis; that the independence and equality of States are better preserved; that prosperity is more equitably shared; and that the security of each country is more effectively guaranteed. In pursuit of these objectives the Nine should progressively define common positions in the sphere of foreign policy.

10.
As the Community progresses towards a common policy in relation to third countries, it will act in accordance with the following principles:
(a) The Nine, acting as a single entity, will strive to promote harmonious and constructive relations with these countries. This should not however jeopardize, hold back or affect the will of the Nine to progress towards European Union within the time limits laid down.
(b) In future when the Nine negotiate collectively with other countries; the institutions and procedures chosen should enable the distinct character of the European entity to be respected.
(c) In bilateral contacts with other countries, the Member States of the Community will increasingly act on the basis of agreed common positions.

11.
The Nine intend to strengthen their links, in the present institutional framework, with the Member Countries of the Council of Europe, and with other European countries with whom they already have friendly relations and close co-operation.

12.
The Nine attach essential importance to the Community's policy of association. Without diminishing the advantages enjoyed by the countries with which it has special relations, the Community intends progressively to put into operation a policy for development aid on a worldwide scale in accordance with the principles and aims set out in the Paris Summit Declaration.

13.
The Community will implement its undertakings towards the Mediterranean and African countries in order to reinforce its long-standing links with these countries. The Nine intend to preserve their historical links with the countries of the Middle East and to co-operate over the establishment and maintenance of peace, stability and progress in the region.

14.
The close ties between the United States and Europe of the Nine—we share values and aspirations based on a common heritage—are mutually beneficial and must be preserved. These ties do not conflict with the determination of the Nine to establish themselves as a distinct and original entity. The Nine intend to maintain their constructive dialogue and to develop their co-operation with the United States on the basis of equality and in a spirit of friendship.

15.

The Nine also remain determined to engage in close co-operation and to pursue a constructive dialogue with the other industrialized countries, such as Japan and Canada, which have an essential rôle in maintaining an open and balanced world economic system. They appreciate the existing fruitful co-operation with these countries, particularly within the OECD.

16.

The Nine have contributed, both individually and collectively to the first results of a policy of détente and co-operation with the USSR and the East European countries. They are determined to carry this policy further forward on a reciprocal basis.

17.

Conscious of the major rôle played by China in international affairs, the Nine intend to intensify their relations with the Chinese Government and to promote exchanges in various fields as well as contacts between European and Chinese leaders.

18.

The Nine are also aware of the important rôle played by other Asian countries. They are determined to develop their relations with these countries as is demonstrated, as far as commercial relations are concerned, by the Declaration of Intent made by the Community at the time of its enlargement.

19.

The Nine are traditionally bound to the Latin American countries by friendly links and many other contacts; they intend to develop these. In this context they attach great importance to the agreements concluded between the European Community and certain Latin American countries.

20.

There can be no real peace if the developed countries do not pay more heed to the less favoured nations. Convinced of this fact, and, conscious of their responsibilities and particular obligations, the Nine attach very great importance to the struggle against under-development. They are, therefore, resolved to intensify their efforts in the fields of trade and development aid and to strengthen international co-operation to these ends.

21.

The Nine will participate in international negotiations in an outward-looking spirit, while preserving the fundamental elements of their unity and their basic aims. They are also resolved to contribute to international progress, both through their relations with third countries and by adopting common positions wherever possible in international organizations, notably the United Nations and the Specialized Agencies.

III. The Dynamic Nature of the Construction of a United Europe

22.

The European Identity will evolve as a function of the dynamic construction of a United Europe. In their external relations, the Nine propose progressively to undertake the definition of their identity in relation to other countries or groups of countries. They believe that in so doing they will strengthen their own cohesion and contribute to the framing of a genuinely European foreign policy. They are convinced that building up this policy will help them to tackle with confidence and realism further stages in the construction of a United Europe thus making easier the proposed transformation of the whole complex of their relations into a European Union.

The Gymnich Agreement

US–European relations deteriorated badly during 1973 and the first part of 1974, partly as a result of Dr Kissinger's tactless talk of the 'Year of Europe' and a 'new Atlantic Charter', and partly because of sharp political differences over the Middle East war and the subsequent conflict with OPEC. The United States tended simultaneously to underestimate EPC and to insist on a seat at its tables. It regarded the 'tendency to justify European Identity as facilitating separateness from the United States'.* The Europeans, for their part, had no intention of allowing the United States to be present at all levels of their policy-making.

   Both sides had, while barely realizing it, acknowledged the theoretical truth of the fact that European foreign policy had little rationale except as a way of differing from the United States. But neither was ready to force the issue, and a compromise was reached relatively quickly, probably fostered by the sense of common external threat from OPEC, in what has become known as the 'Gymnich formula'. This was drafted during an informal European foreign ministers meeting at the Schloss Gymnich in the Rhineland – the first of the informal meetings without officials which have taken place ever since at the rate of one per Presidency. It was never written down, and announced only at the next foreign ministers' meeting in June. The basis of the 'gentlemen's agreement' reached was that the United States should be treated as a special case among the third countries who would inevitably want consultations with EPC, but that even it, of course, had no right to a seat at the EPC table. Instead, and to limit Washington's ability to divide and rule via bilateral relations, it was agreed that the Presidency should consult the United States on behalf of its partners in time for the latter to influence outcomes. This arrangement was accepted by the United States, and has no doubt helped to avoid a number of unnecessary transatlantic disputes. It would be naive, however, to believe that actual practice always follows the Gymnich formula, particularly on contentious or urgent issues. When the Presidency is held by a small country, or one out of favour in Washington, other channels are always available.

Document 2/6   Text of the Gymnich Formula, 10–11 June 1974

(German Foreign Minister Hans-Dietrich Genscher speaking, announcing the results of a foreign ministers' meeting)

---

*   Henry Kissinger, speech to the Pilgrims of Great Britain, 12 December 1973, cited in Panayiotis Ifestos, *European Political Cooperation: Towards a Framework of Supranational Diplomacy*, Aldershot, Avebury, 1987, p. 182.

'The second point is the question of consultations. The Ministers were agreed that in elaborating common positions on foreign policy there arises the question of consultations with allied or friendly countries. Such consultations are a matter of course in any modern foreign policy. We decided on a pragmatic approach in each individual case, which means that the country holding the Presidency will be authorized by the other eight partners to hold consultations on behalf of the Nine.

In practice, therefore, if any member of the EPC raises within the framework of EPC the question of informing and consulting an ally or friendly state, the Nine will discuss the matter and, upon reaching agreement, authorize the Presidency to proceed on that basis.

The Ministers trust that this gentlemen's agreement will also lead to smooth and pragmatic consultations with the United States which will take into account the interest of both sides.'

The Paris Summit, 10 December 1974

The pragmatic, low-key start to EPC, which allowed foreign ministers and political directors to take the lead, was in part out of deference to the view that the involvement of heads of government would be too reminiscent of the Fouchet Plans' attempt to subordinate the whole Community process to an overarching intergovernmental Union. Nonetheless, by 1974 *ad hoc* summits had already played a key part in moving the process on – as at Paris in 1972 – and it was becoming clear both that EPC needed to carry greater weight internationally, and to be brought into some more systematic relationship with Community external relations (until the Single European Act of 1986 [document 2/15] EPC had no legal basis of any kind).

Thus by the end of 1974 the Member States were ready to set up the European Council, consisting of three heads of government meetings per year (later reduced to one per Presidency plus special meetings). It will be seen from the following that foreign policy was to be central to the activities of the European Council. The decision also permitted EPC meetings (the Conference of Foreign Ministers) to take place at the same time as normal Council meetings, thus blurring the difference between the two bodies further, which were already attended by the same ministers (if not officials). In practice the problems of institutional liaison and identity did not disappear, and the European Council was to play a distinctly fitful part in the evolution of European foreign policy, not least because it too was to lack a clear legal basis in Community affairs for more than another decade.

Document 2/7   Communiqué of the Meeting of the Heads of State and Government of the European Community, Paris, 10 December 1974

1.
The Heads of Government of the nine States of the Community, the Ministers of Foreign Affairs and the President of the Commission, meeting in Paris at the invitation of the French President, examined the various problems confronting Europe. They took note of the reports drawn up by the Ministers of Foreign Affairs and

recorded the agreement reached by these Ministers on various points raised in the reports.

2.

Recognizing the need for an overall approach to the internal problems involved in achieving European unity and the external problems facing Europe, the Heads of Government consider it essential to ensure progress and overall consistency in the activities of the Communities and in the work on political co-operation.

3.

The Heads of Government have therefore decided to meet, accompanied by the Ministers of Foreign Affairs, three times a year and, whenever necessary, in the Council of the Communities and in the context of political co-operation.

The administrative secretariat will be provided for in an appropriate manner with due regard for existing practices and procedures.

In order to ensure consistency in Community activities and continuity of work, the Ministers of Foreign Affairs, meeting in the Council of the Community, will act as initiators and co-ordinators. They may hold political co-operation meetings at the same time.

These arrangements do not in any way affect the rules and procedures laid down in the Treaties or the provisions on political co-operation in the Luxembourg and Copenhagen Reports. At the various meetings referred to in the preceding paragraphs the Commission will exercise the powers vested in it and play the part assigned to it by the above texts.

4.

With a view to progress towards European unity, the Heads of Government reaffirm their determination gradually to adopt common positions and co-ordinate their diplomatic action in all areas of international affairs which affect the interests of the European Community. The President-in-Office will be the spokesman for the Nine and will set out their views in international diplomacy. He will ensure that the necessary concertation always takes place in good time.

In view of the increasing rôle of political co-operation in the construction of Europe, the European Assembly must be more closely associated with the work of the Presidency, for example through replies to questions on political co-operation put to him by its Members.

. . .

The Tindemans Report

The lengthy report of Léo Tindemans, the Belgian Prime Minister, on European Union had been commissioned at the Paris Summit of December 1974 which set up the European Council, but its origin can be traced back to the Summit in the same city of June 1972, which had asked the Community institutions to produce such a document by the end of 1975. Various reports had indeed been forthcoming from the individual institutions, but it was thought necessary to pull them all together, and a European enthusiast like Tindemans was eager to use the opportunity to help the Community take a *saut qualitatif* into the next stage of integration.

In the event Tindemans reined himself in and the report attempted to practise politics as the art of the possible. It did not seek to rebuild the whole European enterprise on federalist lines, but confined itself to a limited number of proposals which would, if followed, nonetheless have represented a biggish leap forward. It began with foreign policy, as if a 'voice in the world' was Europe's greatest need (in fact the report's General Conclusions are careful to subordinate foreign policy to decisions about what kind of Community the peoples of Europe might want). It also called for 'a single decision-making centre' whereby EPC would be given legal status and effectively merged with EC external relations. It was implied that unity and decisiveness could be ensured only by an extension of majority voting to foreign policy questions. There was also a good deal of rhetoric on matters of substance, such as the need for Europe to play a major role in the 'new world economic order', but none of this required any immediate decisions, with the exception of defence and arms manufactures, where Tindemans proposed breaching the taboo on the Community's right to involve itself in NATO's traditional province.

The Tindemans Report caused a certain amount of embarrassment among European leaders in 1976. It had caught the downslope, not the crest, of the wave of enthusiasm which had characterized the EC in the early 1970s. There was no general will either for a rapid move forward or for the inevitable political battles which would follow the attempt of some states to force the pace against the wishes of others. The report was therefore quietly shelved at the European Council meeting at The Hague in December 1976 (see document 2/9). In retrospect the Tindemans Report can either be seen as the first attempt to yoke EPC to integration proper, and therefore to promote supranationality by demonstrating how much the international system needed a united Europe, or it can be seen as the last throw of the dice by those who had seen EPC as a means of promoting general 'political union'.

What is clear is that for the next ten years EPC was confined to developing its procedures in a down to earth and non-doctrinal way, and both theorists of integration and political federalists lost interest in it accordingly.

Document 2/8   Report on European Union, by Leo Tindemans (The Tindemans Report), 29 December 1975

I. A common vision of Europe

A. Europe today

Why has the European concept lost a lot of its force and initial impetus? I believe that over the years the European public has lost a guiding light, namely the political consensus between our countries on our reasons for undertaking this joint task and the characteristics with which we wish to endow it. We must first of all restore this common vision if we wish to have European Union.

In 1975 the European citizen does not view the reasons for the construction of Europe in exactly the same way as in 1950. The European idea is partly a victim of its own successes: the reconciliation between formerly hostile countries, the economic prosperity due to the enlarged market, the *détente* which has taken the place of the Cold War, thanks particularly to our cohesion, all this seems to have been achieved and consequently not to require any more effort. Europe today is part of the general run of things; it seems to have lost its air of adventure.

Our peoples are concerned with new problems and values scarcely mentioned by the Treaties. They realize that political union does not automatically follow from economic integration; too many fruitless discussions cast doubt on the credibility and topicality of our joint endeavour: to this extent the European idea is also a victim of its failures.

In this state of mind we plunged into a crisis and are experiencing rates of inflation and unemployment the likes of which have never been seen by the present generation. It is therefore hardly surprising if the Community is crumbling beneath the resurgence, which is felt everywhere, of purely national preoccupations. Especially as the Community, in its present state, is unbalanced: in some fields it has been given far-reaching powers, in others nothing, or practically nothing, has been done, very often because our States were too weak to undertake anything new: the fragile nature of Europe in some ways also reflects the powerlessness of our States.

An unfinished structure does not weather well: it must be completed, otherwise it collapses. Today Community attainments are being challenged.

Basically, however, Europeans are still in favour of closer links between our peoples as laid down in the Treaties of Paris and Rome, first between the Six, later between the Nine. They even take this *rapprochement* as a matter of course and regret not having more evidence of it in their daily lives. A return to selfish national attitudes, to national barriers, and to the antagonisms which they have frequently engendered would be seen as a historic defeat, the collapse of the efforts of a whole generation of Europeans.

If this extensive will for *rapprochement* is to take on a political dimension vital to ensure that action is taken, Europe must find its place again among the major concerns of public opinion thus ensuring that it will be the focal point of the political discussions of tomorrow. We must listen to our people. What do the Europeans want? What do they expect from a united Europe?

1. A voice in the world

During my visits I was struck by the widespread feeling that we are vulnerable and powerless. This is a new experience for our peoples in recent history. Inequality in the distribution of wealth threatens the stability of the world economic system; exhaustion of resources weighs heavily on the future of industrial society; the internationalization of economic life makes our system of production ever more dependent. Our States seem very weak to face these challenges alone. What weight do isolated voices have unless they are those of the super powers?

And yet the will to make an active contribution is still very strong as we can see from the 100 000 young Europeans who are working in cooperation programmes throughout the world. Our peoples are conscious that they embody certain values which have had an inestimable influence on the development of civilization. Why should we cease to spread our ideas abroad when we have always done so? Which of us has not been surprised to see the extent to which the European identity is an accepted fact by so many of the foreigners to whom we speak? It is not only from within that there is a call to the countries of Europe to unite.

Our peoples expect the European Union to be, where and when appropriate, the voice of Europe. Our joint action must be the means of effectively defending our legitimate interests, it must provide the basis for real security in a fairer world, and enable us to take part in this dialogue between groups which clearly characterizes international life. How can we reconcile these requirements in today's world if we do not unite?

Europe must guard against isolation, against turning inwards on itself which would reduce it to a footnote in history, and also against the subjection and narrow dependence which would prevent it from making its voice heard. It must recover some control over its destiny. It must build a type of society which is ours alone and which reflects the values which are the heritage and the common creation of our peoples.

. . .

B. European Union

The basic choice made by the Founding Fathers of Europe and embodied in the Treaties of Rome and Paris was to bring about an ever closer union between our peoples. This option is still ours. In the face of the internal and external challenges of our society, felt by the whole of Europe, six countries initially and then nine decided to fight back by joining forces.

The 1972 and 1974 Paris Conferences decided that European Union was the best means of doing this at the present stage of the construction of Europe.

As the aims and nature of European Union are not today clearly understood the first task of our governments is to decide within the European Council what precisely are the scope and consequences of these choices. It is now up to the European Council to decide in which general perspective the joint endeavour will be pursued during the Union phase. The time to enshrine in a legal text all the changes which have been gradually made to the European structure will be when the process of building the Union has acquired its own momentum.

As a result of my consultations in all our countries, *I propose that the European Council should define the different components of European Union as follows:*

(1) *European Union implies that we present a united front to the outside world. We must tend to act in common in all the main fields of our external relations whether in foreign policy, security, economic relations or development aid. Our action is aimed at defending our interests but also at using our collective strength in support of law and justice in world discussions.*

(2) *European Union recognizes the interdependence of the economic prosperity of our States and accepts the consequences of this: a common economic and monetary policy to manage this prosperity, common policies in the industrial and agricultural sectors and on energy and research to safeguard the future.*

(3) *European Union requires the solidarity of our peoples to be effective and adequate. Regional policy will correct inequalities in development and counteract the centralizing effects of industrial societies. Social action will mitigate inequalities of income and encourage society to organize itself in a fairer and more humane fashion.*

(4) *European Union makes itself felt in people's daily lives. It helps to protect their rights and to improve their life style.*

(5) *In order to achieve these tasks European Union is given institutions with the necessary powers to determine a common, coherent and all-inclusive political view, the efficiency needed for action, the legitimacy needed for democratic control. The principle of the equality of all our States continues to be respected within the Union by each State's right to participate in political decision making.*

(6) *Like the Community whose objectives it pursues and whose attainments it protects European Union will be built gradually. So as to restart the construction of Europe straight away and increase its credibility its initial basis is the political commitment of the States to carry out in different fields specific actions selected according to their importance and the chances of success.*

The different facets of European Union described above are closely connected. The development of the Union's external relations cannot occur without a parallel development of common policies internally. Neither can be achieved without consolidating the authority and effectiveness of common institutions. In this vast scheme everything goes together and it is the sum of the progress achieved in parallel which constitutes the qualitative change which is European Union. The rest of this report will examine in each of the fields referred to the aim and the first positive actions which need to be and can be taken.

The general framework which I propose should be adopted by the European Council must serve as guidelines for our efforts to build Europe. The will of our States, expressed in this way, is based on the deep-seated motivations of public opinion and can convey to it the guiding light of our common action.

The political consequences of these choices must be carefully assessed. They cannot occur without a transfer of competences to common institutions. They cannot occur without a transfer of resources from prosperous to less prosperous regions. They cannot occur without constraints, freely accepted certainly, but then enforced unreservedly. This is the price of Union. But what price would we pay for inaction? The crumbling away of the Community, voices isolated and often going unheard on the world stage, less and less control over our destiny, an unconvincing Europe without a future.

II. Europe in the world

Our States' reasons for presenting a united front in world discussions are convincing from an objective point of view: they stem from power relationships and the size of the problems. From a subjective point of view they are felt very strongly by our peoples: our vulnerability and our relative impotence are in the thoughts of everyone. The convergence of these two factors means that external relations are one of the main reasons for building Europe, and make it essential for the European Union to have an external policy.

A. A single decision-making centre

The examination of our possibilities for action in the world should be based on one obvious fact: the increasing intermeshing of different sectors of international activity.

In the framework described in the preceding chapter the European Union should not only be concerned with foreign policy in the traditional sense, including security aspects, nor solely with tariff and trade policies which are already common policies by virtue of the Treaty of Rome, but also with all external economic relations. The traditional distinctions maintained by diplomatic chancelleries in this field make increasingly less sense in the modern world. Recent developments of international life show that economic, industrial, financial and commercial questions will all in the future be the subject of negotiations, the significance of which will be highly political. If the European Union did not have the means to cover all aspects of our external relations it would not be equal to its task. The Union must have a comprehensive and coherent outlook, and act accordingly. *I propose that the European Council should now decide:*

(a) *to put an end to the distinction which still exists today between ministerial meetings which deal with political cooperation and those which deal with the subjects covered by the Treaties: in order to decide on a policy the Ministers must be able to consider all aspects of the problems within the Council.*

(b) *that the institutions of the Union can discuss all problems if they are relevant to European interests and consequently come within the ambit of the Union.*

The existence of a single decision-making centre does not mean that there will be confusion between those activities which today are the responsibility of the Community and those which lie in the field of political cooperation. The nature of the problems is not such that they must all be dealt with in the same way. But coherence of activity, which is essential, does require that the different aspects of the often complex problems which the European Union will have to examine be dealt with together, at least at ministerial level, by the same people and in the same place.

With this in mind *I propose changing the political commitment of the Member States which is the basis of political cooperation into a legal obligation.* A very short protocol taking up paragraph 11* of the Copenhagen Report ought to give competence to the Council and thus clarify the legal framework in which it is to operate.

The development of new policies on the basis of the Treaties does not cause any particular problem: the provisions binding us are clear and there are numerous precedents. The same thing does not apply in fields not covered by the Treaties. The way in which future developments are to take place must be specified here.

B. Towards a common foreign policy

In those fields of foreign relations not covered by the Treaties the Nine nowadays

---

*   This paragraph reads as follows:
    'Governments will consult each other on all important foreign policy questions and will work out priorities, observing the following criteria:
    — the purpose of the consultation is to seek common policies on practical problems;
    — the subjects dealt with must concern European interests whether in Europe itself or elsewhere where the adoption of a common position is necessary or desirable.
    On these questions each State undertakes as a general rule not to take up final positions without prior consultation with its partners within the framework of the political cooperation machinery.'

coordinate their policies, and in recent years this arrangement has been extended and has met with considerable success. Such an arrangement would not, however, be adequate within the framework of the European Union. It explicitly incorporates within its structure the possibility of failure: the pursuit of different policies whenever coordination has not been achieved. The European identity will not be accepted by the outside world so long as the European States appear sometimes united, sometimes disunited.

European Union obviously implies that, within the fields covered by the Union, the European States should always present a united front, otherwise the term would be meaningless. The coordination of policies, which is important during a transitional period, must therefore gradually make way for common policies, which means that within the framework of the European Union, our States must be able together to draw up a policy and to enact it.

Chapter V of this report gives details on the respective roles of the European institutions in the formulation and implementation of a common foreign policy. Here suffice it to say that the European Council has a vital role to play in stating general policy guidelines based on a global political analysis, without which there can be no common policy. The political decision, which is the application of agreed general policy guidelines to the realities of everyday life, is the responsibility of the Council.

The main difference between the coordination of policies, as practised at present, and a common external policy, which distinguishes the Union, does not arise from the kind of procedure adopted or the nature of the relevant institution. It lies in the obligation to reach a common point of view. The State will undertake to define the broad guidelines for their policy within the European Council. On this basis, the Council then has the obligation to reach a common decision on specific questions. This obviously means that the minority must rally to the views of the majority at the conclusion of a debate.

In order to provide the necessary impetus to the dynamic process of European Union, our States must now undertake the political commitment to pursue a common foreign policy within a given number of specific fields, selected in relation to their importance and the prospects of practical results. During the gradual evolution of the Union this political commitment will have to be extended to all essential aspects of our external relations.

C. Immediate positive action

When defining its foreign relations, the European Union must approach both the major world problems and the problems arising in its own regional area. Owing to their basic importance, four problems must be of foremost concern to us:
— a new world economic order;
— relations between Europe and the United States;
— security;
— the crises occurring within Europe's immediate geographical surroundings.

When dealing with such complex problems it is unavoidable that certain decisions should be subject to provisions of the Treaties while others are not. In these cases of joint responsibility, common policies will have to apply concurrently to both the procedures of the Treaties and on the procedure arising from Member States' political commitment mentioned above.

1. A new world economic order

Our external relations with countries of the Third World are, and will continue to be, dominated by the problem of sharing the world's economic resources and, to a lesser extent, by the after effects of the colonial era. These questions affect our economic relations, our supplies, our development cooperation effort and, finally, the solidarity of mankind and world stability. This is therefore one of those complex situations in which the voice of Europe must make itself heard.

Furthermore, there is every indication that this is a field in which the Nine can and must formulate a common external policy without delay since:
— the main negotiations have not yet really begun;
— they will take place between groups of countries, and, in such circumstances, bilateral diplomatic relations, however close they may be, solve nothing, whereas the EEC has acquired valuable experience through the Yaoundé and Lomé Agreements;
— the divergences of opinions and interests among the Nine, which are unavoidable when dealing with so vast a subject, are not insuperable, as has been shown recently by the common stand adopted at the seventh special session of the UN General Assembly, and in the preparations for the Conference on International Economic Cooperation;
— even without a new political commitment, the respect for Community authority, the requirements of political action and the defence of our common interests, call for a very high degree of cooperation and common action on our part.

The Nine are already making serious efforts to present a united front at major negotiations ahead, and the European Council meeting held in Rome in December 1975 has, in this respect, produced some encouraging results. Our countries have taken the initiative on joint negotiations in the Lomé Agreement, the Euro-Arab dialogue and in Mediterranean policies.

I propose, first, that we should decide:
— *that come what may we present a united front at multilateral negotiations relating to a new world economic order, at the various gatherings where these take place, and in the implementation of their conclusions. This means that we shall, in every case, place the primary interest of joint action above our divergent opinions and interests;*
— *that we shall designate, as the need arises, the delegates responsible for pursuing such policies on our collective behalf.*

I propose that decisions should then be taken:
— *to strengthen the instrument of our common action by gradually transferring to the Community a substantial part of national appropriations intended for development cooperation (major development projects, food aid, financial aid), and in coordinating the remainder of our activities in this field.*
— *to complement this approach by adopting a common stand on general political problems which could arise in our relations with the Third World.*

If these decisions are taken, we shall *de facto* be pursuing a common external policy in the essential elements of our relations with the Third World.

2. Relations between Europe and the United States

Relations with the United States, who are at one and the same time our allies, our partners and occasionally our competitors, raise problems of vast proportions for the European Union. They are of prime importance in the political field, in defence, in economic affairs, not only on account of the interdependence of United States and European economies, but also because of the joint responsibility of these two industrial centres for the world economy, a responsibility which the Rambouillet meeting of November 1975 has once again underlined.

The need for Europe to speak with one voice in its relations with the United States is one of the main underlying reasons for the construction of Europe. A constructive dialogue between the European Union, conscious of its identity, and the leading Western political, economic and military power, is necessary without delay. Its usefulness has been recognized by the document on the European Identity adopted at the Conference of Heads of Government at Copenhagen in December 1973. Only in this manner, and in accordance with the development of the Union, shall we be able to establish relations with the United States based on the principle of equality, free of any sense of dependence, which reflects at the same time both what is common in our basic values, interests and responsibilities, and the differences in the destinies of our two regions.

It is doubtful whether the European States can have a strictly identical appreciation of relations between the United States and Europe so long as their respective analyses of the problems of defence are noticeably divergent. This question must however be examined frankly and thoroughly with the object of laying down certain principles and rules determining the content of and procedures for cooperation between Europe and the United States.

In this context *I propose that the European Council should take the initiative to delegate one of its members to hold talks with the United States in view of initiating a common reflection of the character and scope of relations between that major power and the European Union.*

3. Security

By virtue of the Atlantic Alliance we in Europe enjoy a measure of security and stability which has enabled us to undertake the construction of Europe. Since our States recognize the existence of a common destiny, the security of one member necessarily affects the security of others. No foreign policy can disregard threats, whether actual or potential, and the ability to meet them. Security cannot therefore be left outside the scope of the European Union.

On the other hand, the Conference on Security and Cooperation in Europe has shown, if that was necessary, that in matters of security, political, military, economic factors and those affecting human relations, closely overlap.

During the gradual development of the European Union, the Member States will therefore have to solve the problems of maintaining their external security. European Union will not be complete until it has drawn up a common defence policy.

Meanwhile, I note that our States are not really at present in a position to determine the general policy guidelines without which no common defence policy is possible, and are unlikely to be able to do so in the near future. But this does not mean that nothing should be done, and *I therefore propose that we should decide:*

— *regularly to hold* exchanges of views *on our specific problems in defence matters and on European aspects of multilateral negotiations on security. Exchanges of views of this kind will one day enable Member States to reach a common analysis of defence problems and, meanwhile, to take account of their respective positions in any action they take;*

— *to cooperate in the* manufacture of armaments *with a view to reducing defence costs, and increasing European independence and the competitiveness of its industry. The efforts undertaken at present to provide the European countries of the Alliance with an organization for the standardization of armaments, on the basis of joint programmes, will have important consequences for industrial production. This strengthens the need to initiate a common industrial policy on the manufacture of armaments within the framework of the European Union. Setting up a European armaments agency for that purpose must be given consideration.*

On the question of *détente* the Nine have already succeeded, through political cooperation, in outlining joint positions that have enabled them, during the Conference on Security and Cooperation in Europe, to defend identical points of view. This practice must obviously be pursued and generalized. It will also have to include that element of obligation which distinguishes a common policy from mere coordination. It will have to be extended, during the gradual development of the Union, to all the problems which play an important role in the general field of *détente*, including agreements on economic cooperation and the increase of human contacts.

The development of a *détente* policy in Europe presupposes that all those with whom we negotiate recognize the European Union as an entity. Our resolve to act together in the field of external relations is a reality in Europe today; it will be even more so in the future and all States, including those which today still hesitate to do so, will then have to recognize that fact.

4. Crises in the European region

The political problems which arise within our immediate geographical surroundings, that is to say in Europe and in the Mediterranean area, have a particular significance for the European Union. The credibility of our undertaking requires that in this field, where our interests are greatest, we should from now on be united, that is to say, that we should accept the constraints imposed by a common policy.

In the last two years, political cooperation has enabled the Nine to adopt common positions on questions such as the crises in the Middle East, Cyprus and Portugal and their political action has often been expressed through the Community. In effect, our States tend to prefer common action. Indeed, the increasing political weight of the Nine, when they are united, and their common interests in lessening potential sources of conflict in their immediate surroundings, tend to induce our countries to act together, and will do so increasingly.

I therefore propose that we decide to make what has been the constant practice in recent years into a general rule, that is to say, to lay down a common policy and to act together within this framework, with the constraints that this entails, wherever important political problems or crises arise in Europe or in the Mediterranean area.

In the strictly political field of external relations the European Union must, independently of the specific situations mentioned above, carry on the kind of cooperation begun in 1970 until the natural evolution of their undertaking leads Member States to accept the more compelling formula of a common policy.

We must assert the European Identity in all international political discussions, as the Nine have been doing with increasing success at the United Nations. We must define our relations with countries belonging to other continents some of which, such as China, Canada and Japan show increasing sympathy for the task of European unification.

In Europe, we must pay particular attention to those European countries which have a democratic system similar to ours. We should establish relations with them which make it possible to take account of their interests and their points of view when formulating the Union's political decisions, and also to obtain their understanding and their support for our actions. The habit of such informal cooperation will, in due course, facilitate the accession of those States wishing to join.

We should give greater joint consideration than in the past to those problems of our external relations which bear upon the European Union in the medium term. *I propose that the Ministers for Foreign Affairs should submit suggestions to the European Council on how joint consideration of such problems can be undertaken.*

Conclusion

Our common action with regard to the outside world cannot, obviously, be considered in isolation. In some fields the practical opportunities for progress will depend on parallel progress being made in building the Union's internal structure: as in the case, for example, of monetary and financial questions. The implementation of common policies in our external relations presupposes increased efficiency in the institutional system. These questions are examined elsewhere in this report, and it is the progress of the whole which will enable Union to be achieved.

Subject to that reservation, the proposals set out in this chapter constitute a qualitative change in the nature and intensity of our relations, which is what the Union seeks to achieve.

In order to ensure such a common front and such common action in relation to the outside world, our States will gradually wish to submit the greater part of their external relations problems to a common policy, and they will accept the constraints imposed in consequence. In order to give the necessary new impulse to the dynamic process of Union, they should now take, in a number of selected sections, certain binding political commitments. During the gradual development of the European Union, these will have to be enshrined in legal obligations which will confirm the qualitative changes which the Union seeks to achieve. In the very important field of our external relations the European Union will then have become a living reality.

. . .

V. Strengthening the institutions

. . .

C. The Council

The Treaties lay down the powers and the procedures of the Council in the Community field. When it acts in fields of Union activity not covered by the Treaties, the competence of the Council will derive for the present from the political commitment of the Member States and will later be confirmed by a juridical instrument.

To reinforce the authority and efficiency of the Council its activity must become more coherent, speedier and more continuous.

To this end I formulate the following proposals.

1. Coherence

(a) *The Council of Ministers (Foreign Affairs) should be entrusted by a decision of the European Council with coordinating in the most appropriate manner the activities of the specialist Councils.*
(b) *The distinction between ministerial meetings devoted to political cooperation and meetings of the Council should be abolished. The abolition of this distinction would not however affect the current procedures for preparing the diplomatic discussions of the Ministers.*

2. Speed

Speeding up the decision-making process requires greater use of majority mechanisms.
(a) *Recourse to majority voting in the Council should become normal practice in the Community field.*
(b) *In those sectors of external relations where the Member States have undertaken to pursue a common policy, they must be able speedily to reach decisions and to act when faced with a crisis. This implies that by analogy with the institutional mechanism of the Treaties, minority opinion should, in these sectors, rally to the view of the majority at the end of the discussion.*

3. Continuity

(a) *A Treaty amendment should extend to a whole year the term of the Presidency of the European Council and the Council in order to:*
— *strengthen the authority of the Presidency,*
— *permit a more coherent dialogue between the Parliament and the Council,*
— *lend more continuity to its activity.*
(b) *The European Council and the Council should entrust special or temporary tasks, like a negotiation or study, to the Commission, to a single country or to one or more persons independently of changes in the Presidency. This should in no way diminish the powers which the Commission derives from the Treaties.*

F. Other Community bodies

. . .

4. The *Political Committee* has proved how effective it is in preparing the diplomatic discussions of Ministers. The creation of the single decision-making centre in the form of the Council must not change either its powers or its composition.

I find however that the pragmatic development of the organs of political cooperation has chiefly been designed to work out common positions on topical problems.
We are equipped to react rather than to act. In order to adapt to a situation where
there will be much scope for joint action on external policy the Ministers of Foreign
Affairs will have to see that the existing machinery is improved.

. . .

The Hague Summit Statement, 29–30 November 1976

The Hague Summit Statement on the Tindemans Report is notable for its blandness even
by the standards of EC communiqués. EMU and other economic goals are privileged over
foreign policy, where the only injunction is that cooperation must lead 'to the search for a
common external policy'. In the context of the hopes for the report, and the care taken
by its author not to overreach himself, this amounted to a clear signal that even limited
moves towards political union were off the agenda for the foreseeable future.

Document 2/9   Statement by the European Council on European Union, The
Hague, 29–30 November 1976

1.
The European Council examined the report on European Union submitted to it
by Mr. Tindemans at its request. It heard an account given by the Chairman of
the work carried out, and approved the general lines of the comments by the
Ministers for Foreign Affairs on the various Chapters of the report.

2.
The European Council indicated its very great interest in the analyses and proposals
put forward by Mr. Tindemans. It shared the views expressed by the Belgian
Prime Minister on the need to build European Union by strengthening the practical solidarity of the nine Member States and their peoples, both internally and in
their relations with the outside world, and gradually to provide the Union with the
instruments and institutions necessary for its operation. It considered that European Union should make itself felt effectively in the daily life of individuals by
assisting in the protection of their rights and the improvement of the circumstances
of their life.

3.
On this occasion the European Council had a wide-ranging discussion of the principles which must underlie the construction of European Union over the coming
years. European Union will be built progressively by consolidating and developing
what has been achieved within the Community, with the existing Treaties forming
a basis for new policies. The achievement of Economic and Monetary Union is
basic to the consolidation of Community solidarity and the establishment of
European Union. Priority importance must be given to combating inflation and
unemployment and to drawing up common energy and research policies and a
genuine regional and social policy for the Community.

4.

The construction of Europe must also make the best use of possibilities for co-operation between the nine Governments in those areas where the Member States are prepared to exercise their sovereignty in a progressively convergent manner.
This form of co-operation in the field of foreign policy must lead to the search for a common external policy.

5.

In the light of future developments as defined by the report on European Union, the Heads of Government, with the intention of establishing a comprehensive and coherent common political approach, reaffirm their desire to increase the authority and efficiency of the Community institutions, as well as the support of the peoples for then, and confirm the role of the European Council as a driving force.

6.

On the basis of the conclusions reached by the Ministers for Foreign Affairs, the European Council invites them, and the Commission, in the sectors for which it is competent, to report to it once a year on the results obtained and the progress which can be achieved in the short term in the various sectors of the Union, thus translating into reality the common conception of European Union.

Report on European Union to the Brussels European Council, 5–6 December 1977

Virtually the only practical response of the European Council of The Hague to the Tindemans Report was the decision to require foreign ministers to make a yearly report on progress with respect to 'European Union' – that is, political cooperation of various kinds. This first report, made a year later, is surprisingly concrete and free of overblown rhetoric. It chronicles modest but real achievements such as improved common voting at the UN and the Code of Conduct for European firms operating in South Africa. It seemed that the pragmatic, 'step by step' approach to speaking with a single voice might after all be working.

Document 2/10   Report by the Foreign Ministers to the European Council on European Union, Brussels, 5–6 December 1977

External solidarity

Member States' solidarity in practical terms towards the outside world is finding expression both in matters covered by the Treaties and in matters outside their scope. Accordingly, the Nine are showing an increasing tendency to speak with one voice on foreign policy.

In matters covered by the Treaties, this is reflected in increasingly frequent representation of the Community as such in international fora dealing with problems coming under the Community's responsibilities.

The Council has decided that, as in the case of the decision of the European Council in Rome (25 and 26 March 1977) on the Downing Street meeting which was held on 7 May 1977, whenever any Western economic summit meetings were held thenceforth, the Presidency and the President of the Commission would be invited to attend any meetings in the course of which matters of immediate concern to the Community were discussed. The same arrangement would apply to preparatory meetings and follow-up meetings.

Moreover the Community's presence and role in international life are gaining increasing understanding from our partners, including those States which at first refused to have any dealings with the Community. This has been shown this year 1977, by the fisheries negotiations between the Community and certain East European countries and by initial contacts between the EEC and the CMEA at ministerial level. Moreover, as in the case of Latin America, a dialogue has been entered into with the ASEAN countries too. Lastly, a trade arrangement is being negotiated with the People's Republic of China.

In foreign policy, the practice of political cooperation between the nine Governments often results in their stating a joint or coordinated position in the international arena. The Nine put forward joint positions at the Lagos Conference on apartheid. They have established constant consultation at the General Assembly of the United Nations and in so doing have managed to make themselves an important party to all the debates there.

For the purposes of the Belgrade meeting on security and cooperation, they continued their practice, as successfully introduced at the CSCE, of putting forward joint positions and carrying out close coordination of their statements and whatever steps they took.

They have voiced their joint views on the burning international issues of the day, particularly in the European Council's statement on the Middle East on 29 June 1977.

They have agreed on the need to lay down and follow a firmer, concerted attitude towards South Africa, with the emphasis on practical steps, so as to bring about the discontinuation of the apartheid policy there. They have adopted to that end a code of conduct for their firms operating in South Africa.

By means of a considerable number of joint approaches, the Nine have been able to make known their positions to third country governments.

Regular contact has been kept up with the United States through the approved procedures. Contacts are also maintained with a number of other industrialized countries.

The Euro-Arab dialogue has continued and has made progress in recent months.

Both in Community matters and elsewhere, then, the Member States are gradually acquiring the habit of acting as one and speaking with one voice. In that respect 1977 has been a satisfactory year. This trend is by no means a completed development and must be actively pursued over the years ahead; but, as the European Council in The Hague desired, it is leading step by step to the seeking of a common external policy, which will form a constituent part of European Union.

The London Report, 13 October 1981

The London Report was the third of the reports which established and codified EPC, after Luxembourg in 1970 and Copenhagen in 1973. It arose out of the growing perception in the late 1970s that the procedures of EPC needed extending and refining, so as to cope with the weight of work and to respond more effectively to the unforeseen contingencies of international politics. More specifically it was the product of British concerns, articulated forcibly by Lord Carrington as Foreign Secretary in 1980–1, that EPC had made a mess of reacting to the Soviet invasion of Afghanistan in December 1979, and to the Iranian hostage crisis which dragged on through 1980.

Accordingly, foreign ministers agreed to a number of practical changes which both pulled together developments which had already begun and introduced new measures. Among the former were the acceptance of the troika principle as the way of supporting the Presidency in speaking to third countries, and the full association of the Commission with the work of EPC. Among the latter was the introduction of a crisis consultation mechanism, whereby any three foreign ministers could convene an emergency meeting of the whole group within 48 hours, and the agreement in principle (almost revolutionary in the context of Irish and NATO sensitivities at the time) that EPC could discuss 'the political aspects of security' (in practice the Europeans had been discussing such matters in the CSCE context since 1972). The setting up of an embryonic EPC secretariat in the form of a small team of officials seconded from preceding and succeeding presidencies to help the incumbent foreign ministry, is also noteworthy. It meant that foreign ministries would henceforth have to cope with a few foreign nationals working in their buildings. Out of small acorns would great oaks grow?

Document 2/11   Report Issued by the Foreign Ministers of the Ten on European Political Co-operation (The London Report), London, 13 October 1981

Part I

The Foreign Ministers of the Ten Member States of the European Community have examined the development of European Political Co-operation. It is their constant concern that this should be improved and to this end they have considered how it might be further strengthened.

Political Co-operation, which is based on membership of the European Community, has developed to become a central element in the foreign policies of all Member States. The Community and its Member States are increasingly seen by third countries as a coherent force in international relations. The Foreign Ministers of the Ten note that in the years since the foundations of European Political Co-operation were laid in the Luxembourg Report (approved by Heads of State and Government on 27 October 1970) and the Copenhagen Report (approved by Foreign Ministers on 23 July 1973 and subsequently agreed by Heads of State and Government) significant progress has been achieved towards the objectives set out in those reports.

The development of European Political Co-operation over these years has shown that it answers a real need felt by the Member States of the European Community for a closer unity in this field. It is a mark of its proven value that European Political Co-operation has steadily intensified and its scope continually broadened. This development has contributed to the ultimate objective of European Union.

The Foreign Ministers agree that further European integration, and the maintenance and development of Community policies in accordance with the Treaties, will be beneficial to a more effective co-ordination in the field of foreign policy, and will expand the range of instruments at the disposal of the Ten.

The Foreign Ministers believe that in a period of increased world tension and uncertainty the need for a coherent and united approach to international affairs by the members of the European Community is greater than ever. They note that, in spite of what has been achieved, the Ten are still far from playing a rôle in the world appropriate to their combined influence. It is their conviction that the Ten should seek increasingly to shape events and not merely to react to them.

As regards the scope of European Political Co-operation, and having regard to the different situations of the Member States, the Foreign Ministers agree to maintain the flexible and pragmatic approach which has made it possible to discuss in Political Co-operation certain important foreign policy questions bearing on the political aspects of security.

The Ten Foreign Ministers also consider it timely to renew their commitment to implement fully the undertakings in the Luxembourg and Copenhagen Reports. In particular they underline the importance of consultation among the Ten, which lies at the heart of European Political Co-operation. They emphasise their commitment to consult partners before adopting final positions or launching national initiatives on all important questions of foreign policy which are of concern to the Ten as a whole. They undertake that in these consultations each member state will take full account of the position of other partners and will give due weight to the desirability of achieving a common position. They note that such consultations will be particularly relevant for important international conferences where one or more of the Ten are to participate, and where the agenda will include matters under discussion in European Political Co-operation or on which the Ten have a common position.

The Foreign Ministers note that it is increasingly possible for the Ten to speak with one voice in international affairs. Where substantial common positions have been achieved, they undertake to give due prominence to these by means of appropriate references in national statements on foreign policy questions. At the same time they emphasise that not merely a common attitude but joint action, which has always been an objective of European Political Co-operation, should be increasingly within the capacity of the Ten.

The Foreign Ministers have also examined the machinery and procedures of Political Co-operation and have agreed on certain practical improvements which are set out in Part II of this document.

Part II

1. Ministerial Meetings

A. Formal Meetings

The agenda for meetings at Ministerial level will include only items of major importance. The agenda will, where possible, also be annotated in such a way that the discussion will concentrate on matters for decision.

The analyses and draft texts submitted to Ministers should contain either precise recommendations or clearly defined options, so that the Ministers can make decisions for future action.

When declarations are issued by Ministerial meetings and the European Council, they should as a rule be accompanied by a list of posts in third countries where the local representative of the Ten will draw the declaration to the attention of the host government. In the absence of such a list the Presidency has discretion to take action on its own initiative.

B. Gymnich Type Meetings

In order to protect the informal character of these meetings the following guidelines should be observed:

Consultations are confidential;

There will be no formal agenda, official interpretation or officials present (except for a Presidency notetaker);

The Presidency will summarise for the attention of partners any guidelines of an operational nature that emerged from the meeting.

The press will only be briefed on subjects authorised by the Ten. The Presidency will be responsible in the first instance for such briefing, the lines of which will be agreed in advance with partners.

2. The Political Committee

The Political Committee is one of the central organs of European Political Co-operation. It is responsible for directing the work of the Working Groups and for the preparation of discussions at Ministerial level.

The Political Committee will ensure the effective operation of Working Groups by giving them a clear mandate to report on matters of current interest. The Presidency will make the proposals necessary to achieve this. The Working Groups will, however, remain free to suggest topics for reports to the Political Committee.

3. The Correspondents' Group

In order to permit the Political Committee to focus on the more important items on its agenda the European Correspondents will identify those Working Group reports which are not likely to require substantive discussion in the Political Committee.

4. Working Groups

Working Groups, Reports will include a summary drawing the attention of the Political Committee to points which will require decisions for future action, or on which the Political Committee should concentrate.

In general, partners' comments via the COREU system on the oral reports of Working Groups should concentrate on points of substance and not of drafting.

If the Presidency considers a partner to be particularly well qualified on an agenda point at a Working Group meeting, it may request that partner to introduce the discussion on that topic.

5. Studies

Even when partners do not hold the Presidency, they should be encouraged to offer proposals and ideas for consideration by the Working Groups.

At present most of the efforts of political co-operation are devoted to reacting to world events as they occur. In future the Political Committee may wish to take a longer term approach to certain problems, and to institute studies to that end. Such studies are already mentioned in the Copenhagen Report (part II, paragraph 15) and should wherever possible be undertaken by existing Working Groups.

The Ten may also prepare studies on areas where their positions diverge (eg subjects on which they do not vote unanimously at the United Nations).

It is particularly important that the confidentiality of these studies should be maintained.

6. Confidentiality

The success of the process of Political Co-operation depends to a large degree on its confidentiality; certain particularly delicate matters need to be handled in a way which guarantees that the required level of confidentiality is maintained. In such cases papers will be transmitted to the Foreign Ministers via Embassies, and distributed within Foreign Ministries by the European Correspondent.

7. Procedures for EPC/Third Country Contacts

As European Political Co-operation intensifies and broadens the Ten as such will appear as significant interlocutors. Third countries will increasingly express the desire to enter into more or less regular contact with them. It is important that the Ten should be able to respond effectively to these demands, in particular vis-à-vis countries of special interest to them, and that they should speak with one voice in dealings with them.

The Presidency may meet individual representatives of third countries in order to discuss certain matters of particular interest to the country in question.

The Presidency may respond to a request for contacts by a group of Ambassadors of Member States of organisations with which the Ten maintain special links.

The Heads of Mission of the Ten in a country which expresses the desire for closer contacts with EPC may meet representatives of that country in order to hear its views and to explain the position of the Ten.

If necessary, and if the Ten so agree, the Presidency, accompanied by representatives of the preceding and succeeding Presidencies, may meet with representatives of third countries.

If necessary, and if the Ten so agree, the Presidency may meet the representative of a third country in the margins of a Ministerial level meeting of the Ten.

8. Procedure for Political Co-operation in Third Countries

In view of the increasing activities of the Ten in third countries it is important that the Heads of Mission of the Ten maintain the practice of meeting regularly in order to exchange information and co-ordinate views. In considering their response to significant developments in the country to which they are accredited their first instinct should be to co-ordinate with their colleagues of the Ten.

The participation of the Head of Mission at Political Co-operation meetings should remain the rule. When this is impossible he may be represented by a member of his Mission.

The Political Committee welcomes joint reports from Heads of Mission of the Ten. These may be prepared in response to a request from the Political Committee, or, exceptionally on the Heads of Missions' own initiative, when the situation requires it. Recommendations for joint action are particularly valuable.

Where reports are made on the Heads of Missions' own initiative, it is for them to decide whether to draft a joint report, or to report separately on the basis of their joint discussions. An equally acceptable alternative is for the Presidency to draft an oral report on its own authority reflecting the views expressed.

9. Contacts in the Capitals of the Ten

In certain capitals of the Ten the practice has developed of regular meetings between the nine Heads of Mission and the Political Director of the host government. This has proved useful and is to be encouraged.

10. The Presidency

As Political Co-operation has developed, the areas of agreement among the Ten have enlarged and the range of subjects handled has become more extensive. The workload of the Presidency in its rôle as spokesman in the European Parliament, and in contacts with third countries, has also increased. These trends may be expected to continue, particularly in the light of the enlargement of the Community. As a result it has become desirable to strengthen the organisation and assure the continuity of Political Co-operation and to provide operational support for the Presidency without, however, reducing the direct contact, pragmatism and economy which are among the chief virtues of the present arrangements.

Henceforth the Presidency will be assisted by a small team of officials seconded from preceding and succeeding Presidencies. These officials will remain in the employment of their national Foreign Ministries, and will be on the staff of their Embassy in the Presidency capital. They will be at the disposition of the Presidency and will work under its direction.

The burden of work during the Presidency falls particularly heavily on the Foreign Minister who is President-in-office. The Ten note that should he wish to do so the

President may delegate certain tasks to his successor; he may also request his predecessor to finish tasks which are close to completion when the Presidency is handed over.

11. Relations with the European Parliament

In accordance with the Luxembourg and Copenhagen reports, which underline the importance of associating the European Parliament with Political Co-operation, there are frequent contacts between the European Parliament and the Presidency. These take the form of four annual colloquies with the Political Affairs Committee, answers to Questions on Political Co-operation, the Annual Report on Political Co-operation, and the Presidency Speeches at the beginning and end of its term of office which now usually include Political Co-operation subjects.

The contacts between the Council of Ministers and the European Parliament have been extended to include informal meetings between Ministers and the leaders of the different political groups represented in the Parliament; these informal meetings provide a further opportunity for informal exchanges on Political Co-operation.

Taking account of the need further to strengthen ties with the directly elected Parliament the Ten envisage the possibility of more frequent reference to resolutions adopted by the Parliament in the deliberations, communiqués and declarations of the Ten, and in Ministers' opening statements at colloquies with the Political Affairs Committee of the Parliament.

The Ten note that after a meeting of the European Council the President of the European Council will make a statement to the Parliament. This statement will include Political Co-operation subjects discussed at the meeting.

12. Relations between the Activities of Political Co-operation and those of the European Community

The Ten will provide, as appropriate, for Political Co-operation meetings on the occasion of Foreign Affairs Councils. The Presidency will ensure that the discussion of the Community and Political Co-operation aspects of certain questions is co-ordinated if the subject matter requires this.

Within the framework of the established rules and procedures the Ten attach importance to the Commission of the European Communities being fully associated with Political Co-operation at all levels.

13. Crisis Procedures

The Political Committee or, if necessary, a Ministerial meeting will convene within 48 hours at the request of three Member States.

The same procedure will apply in third countries at the level of Heads of Mission. In order to improve the capacity of the Ten to react in an emergency Working Groups are encouraged to analyse areas of potential crisis and to prepare a range of possible reactions by the Ten.

The Genscher-Colombo Plan

What is generally known as the Genscher-Colombo Plan was the attempt by the German and Italian foreign ministers in 1981 to carry EPC much further forward than the procedural innovations envisaged by the British at the time could possibly do. The aim was at the least to raise the eyes of Europeans from mundane matters like money and institutions, and at the most to ensure that the previously taboo area of defence was opened up for discussion by Europeans outside the NATO context. Originally it was hoped that a parallel council of defence ministers might be set up, but this soon proved excessively optimistic (see the cautious formulation of Part Two, 4(1)). Cultural cooperation and cultural identity was another area seen as important, and the idea of common action in the areas of law and order, foreshadowing the eventual third pillar of the 1993 Treaty of European Union, was floated. Tindemans' proposal to merge the external relations of the Communities with EPC was put up again – with the same negative result. The European Parliament was to be given more opportunities to influence external policy. An 'expandable' EPC secretariat was to be set up, and the idea of constructive abstention, first mentioned in Fouchet I twenty years before, was also flagged.

Hans-Dietrich Genscher and Emilio Colombo wanted to get the agreement of the Ten to a 'European Act' (i.e. a treaty) which would advance the 'establishment of European Union'. The term 'Act', with its legislative overtones, set alarm bells ringing in London, Copenhagen and elsewhere and proved impossible to use – although only five years later concerns had subsided sufficiently to allow the Single European Act to be launched. It is significant that in attempting to show vision rather than pragmatism in the area of foreign policy, the German government chose Italy as its partner. France, after 1985 to become the habitual choice, had not yet elected François Mitterand to power and transformed its approach to the EC. Rome was, by contrast, reliably progressive in its attitudes towards integration, although the Italian emphasis on economic rather than political progress held up the presentation of a formal draft to the foreign ministers of the Ten until November 1981 (a 'Draft statement on questions of economic integration' tacked onto the end of the German–Italian Initiative reveals Italian priorities: completing the common market; the European Monetary System (EMS); the accession of Spain and Portugal).

A number of Member States had problems with the Genscher-Colombo proposals, such as Ireland with security and defence, and Denmark with cultural cooperation. This meant that the impetus of the attempt to raise the question of European Union again was soon lost, and discussions on the proposals dragged on until the anticlimax of the Stuttgart 'Solemn Declaration' on 19 June 1983 (document 2/13).

Document 2/12   Draft European Act Proposal by the German and Italian Foreign Ministers (The Genscher-Colombo Plan), 12 November 1981

Draft European Act

The Heads of State or Government of the Member States of the European Communities, meeting within the European Council,

Resolved to continue the work begun with the Treaties of Paris and Rome and to create a united Europe capable of assuming its responsibilities in the world and of making an international contribution commensurate with its traditions and its mission,

Considering what has already been achieved in the construction of economic integration and political cooperation, and the political objectives of the Community, which enjoy the broad support of all democratic forces in Europe,

convinced that the unification of Europe in freedom and respect for its diversity will enable it to make progress and develop its culture and thus contribute to the maintenance of equilibrium in the world and to the preservation of peace,

proceeding from the respect for fundamental rights expressed in the laws of the Community and its Member States and in the European Convention for the Protection of Human Rights and Fundamental Freedoms,

determined to work together for democracy and fundamental human rights, notably the dignity, freedom and equality of man, and for social justice,

aware of the international responsibility incumbent upon Europe by virtue of its level of civilization, its economic strength and its manifold links with the States and nations of other continents,

convinced that the security of Europe must be guaranteed by joint action on security policy, which would also help to preserve the common security of the members of the Atlantic Alliance,

having regard to the decisions taken by the Heads of State or Government of the Member States of the European Communities in Paris on 21 October 1972 and the Document on the European Identity published by the Foreign Ministers on 14 December 1973,

mindful of the statement made by the European Council in The Hague on 29/30 November 1976 concerning the progressive construction of European Union, and in particular the goal, set by the Heads of State or Government, of establishing a comprehensive and coherent common political approach,

reaffirm their political will to develop the whole complex of relations between their States and create a European Union. To this end they have formulated the following principles in a European Act as a further contribution to the establishment of European Union.

Part One: Principles

1. Our peoples expect the process of European unification to continue and to bring increasing solidarity and joint action. To this end the construction of a united Europe must be more clearly oriented towards its political objective; there must be more effective decision-making structures and a comprehensive political and legal framework which is capable of developing. The European Union to be created step by step will be an ever closer union of the European peoples and States based on genuine, effective solidarity and common interest, and on equal rights and obligations for all its members.

2. Desiring to consolidate the political and economic progress already made towards European Union, the Heads of State or Government reaffirm the following aims:

(i) to strengthen and further develop the European Communities as the foundation of European unification, in accordance with the Treaties of Paris and Rome,

(ii) to enable Member States, through a common foreign policy, to act in concert in world affairs so that Europe will be increasingly able to assume the international role incumbent upon it by virtue of its economic and political importance,

(iii) the coordination of security policy and the adoption of common European positions in this sphere in order to safeguard Europe's independence, protect its vital interest and strengthen its security,

(iv) close cultural cooperation between the Member States in order to promote an awareness of common cultural origins as a facet of the European identity, while at the same time drawing on the existing variety of individual traditions and intensifying the mutual exchange of experience, particularly between young people,

(v) harmonization and standardization in further areas of the legislation of the Member States in order to strengthen the common European legal consciousness and create a legal union,

(vi) the strengthening and expansion of joint activities by the Member States to cope, through coordinated action, with the international problems of public order, major acts of violence, terrorism and transnational crime in general.

3. The European Communities, which continue to be based on the Treaties of Paris and Rome, European political cooperation, the rules and procedures of which are governed by the Report adopted in Luxembourg (1970), Copenhagen (1973) and London (1981), and the European Parliament shall cooperate in the pursuit of the above aims.

4. Measures to further the development of European political cooperation shall include the following:

(i) intensified, regular and timely consultation among the Ten with a view to united action on all international questions of common interest,

(ii) the adoption of final positions only after consultation with the other Member States,

(iii) acceptance of statements by the Ten as a binding common basis,

(iv) closer worldwide contacts with other countries of particular interest to the Ten,

(v) greater respect for resolutions of the European Parliament when the Ten come to decisions.

Part Two: Institutions

The following measures shall serve to amalgamate the existing structures of the European Communities, European political cooperation and the European Parliament and to strengthen the political orientation of the work of European unification:

1. The decision-making structures of the European Communities and European political cooperation shall be brought together under the responsibility of the European Council. The European Council shall be the source of political guidance of the European Community and of European political cooperation. It shall be

composed of the Heads of State or Government and of the Foreign Ministers of the Member States.

2. The European Council shall deliberate upon all matters concerning the European Community and European political cooperation. Preparations for its meetings shall be the special responsibility of the Foreign Ministers. The European Council may take decisions and lay down guidelines.

Matters concerning the European Communities shall continue to be governed by the provisions and procedures of the Treaties of Paris and Rome and agreements supplementary thereto.

3. The Heads of State or Government reaffirm the central importance of the European Parliament in the development of European Union, an importance which must be reflected in its direct involvement in the decision-making process and by its review function. They therefore envisage the following improvements for the Community within the scope of the Treaties of Paris and Rome:

(1) The European Parliament shall debate all matters relating to the European Community and European political cooperation.

(2) The European Council shall report to Parliament every six months. It shall also submit an annual report to Parliament on progress towards European Union. In the debate on these reports the European Council shall be represented by its President (or by one of its members).

(3) the European Parliament may submit oral or written questions concerning all aspects of European Union to the Council and the Commission. It may make recommendations to the European Council, the Council and the Commission. Resolutions of the European Parliament shall be notified to the Council (foreign affairs) for discussion by it. If Parliament asks for the Council's comments, the Council shall comply with the request. The President of the Council shall keep Parliament informed through its Political Affairs Committee of the subjects of international policy dealt with in European political cooperation.

. . .

(6) Before the accession or association of further States and before the conclusion of international treaties by the European Communities, Parliament shall be consulted: its appropriate committees shall be briefed regularly on such matters. In formulating the expanding consultation procedure, due regard shall be given to the requirements of confidentiality and urgency.

(7) In the further development of fundamental human rights, special legitimacy attaches to the deliberations and decisions of the European Parliament.

. . .

4. (1) The Council (foreign affairs) shall be responsible for European political cooperation.

This shall not affect the powers of the Council of the European Communities pursuant to the Treaties of Paris and Rome.

Coordination in matters of security should promote common action with a view to safeguarding the independence of Europe, protecting its vital interests and strengthening its security. For these discussions the Council may convene in a different composition if there is a need to deal with matters of common interest in more detail.

(2) In addition, a Council of Ministers responsible for cultural cooperation and a Council of Ministers of Justice shall be established.

(3) The European Council may decide on the establishment of further councils to coordinate the policy of the Member States in areas are not covered by the Treaties of Paris and Rome.

(4) The Council (foreign affairs) may appoint committees to deal with specific questions; they shall report to the Council. Both the Council and the committees may avail themselves of the services of experts.

(5) The role of the Presidency in European political cooperation will be strengthened by both expanding its powers as regards initiatives and coordination and enhancing its operative capabilities.

. . .

7. The European Council and the councils shall, where matters pertaining to the European Communities are concerned, be assisted by the Secretariat of the Council and, in the fields of foreign policy, security policy and cultural cooperation, by an expandable Secretariat of European political cooperation.

8. (1) In view of the need to improve the decision-making processes and hence the European Communities' capacity for action, decisive importance attaches to the voting procedures provided in the Treaties of Paris and Rome. The Member States will utilize every opportunity to facilitate decision-making.

(2) To this end greater use should be made of the possibility of abstaining from voting so as not to obstruct decisions. A Member State which considers it necessary to prevent a decision by invoking its 'vital interests' in exceptional circumstances will be required to state in writing its specific reasons for doing so.

(3) The Council will take note of the reasons stated and defer its decision until its next meeting. If on that occasion the Member State concerned once more invokes its 'vital interest' by the same procedure, a decision will again not be taken.

(4) Within the scope of European political cooperation, the Member States shall likewise utilize every opportunity to facilitate decision-making, in order to arrive more quickly at a common position.

9. The Heads of State or Government stress the particular importance attaching to the Commission as guardian of the Treaties of Paris and Rome and as a driving force in the process of European integration. In addition to its tasks and powers under the Treaties of Paris and Rome, the Commission shall advise and support the European Council, whose meetings it shall attend, by making proposals and comments. It shall be associated closely with European political cooperation.

. . .

Part Three: Perspectives

1. All other European States which share the values and aims embodied in this Act and accede to the European Communities may accede to the 'European Act' so as to participate in the achievement of European Union.

On acceding to the European Communities they undertake to accede to this 'European Act'.

2. The Heads of State or Government shall subject this 'European Act' to a general review five years after its signing with a view to incorporating the progress achieved in European unification in a Treaty on European Union. To this end a draft shall be submitted to the European Council by the Foreign Ministers before the end of the said period and presented to the European Parliament for comment.

. . .

The Stuttgart Declaration

The Stuttgart 'Solemn Declaration on European Union' has been given a bad press by commentators disappointed by its bland generalities, anti-climactic after the ambitions of the Genscher-Colombo Plan. It is true both that this was the best the German Presidency could do after the foot-dragging of 1982, and that the text consists wholly of earnest injunctions to better performance unsupported by actual reforms. Nonetheless, there are certain features that are worth noting for the way in which they anticipate future developments. Although the Declaration deals with the general functioning of the Community (including the Luxembourg Compromise), only the references relevant to foreign policy are discussed here.

The Declaration does, for example, push forward the frontier of what EPC can cover in the sensitive area of security, marginally but significantly. Whereas the London Report said that 'the political aspects' of security could be discussed, Stuttgart (1.4.2 and 3.2) expanded the definition to 'the political and economic aspects of security'. This was part of the slow process of edging the Community towards defence matters and the extension of the common commercial policy to cover the arms trade (still to happen). Even so, both Denmark and Greece entered formal reservations as footnotes, thus initiating the concept of 'footnote countries'. Second, the Stuttgart Declaration talked of the importance of 'consistent action' between EPC and the Communities, thus anticipating the provisions of the Single European Act four years later (document 2/15). Third, following Genscher-Colombo there was a reference to the need for concerted action on 'international problems of law and order', thus preparing the ground for an eventual incorporation of political cooperation over internal affairs into the legal structure of the Union, as it was indeed to become in the 1990s. Finally, the ratchet mechanism which was an integral part of the Monnet method and which had been present in EPC from the outset, notwithstanding its wholly intergovernmental character, was manifest in the decision to review the Declaration not later than five years from its signature.

Document 2/13   Solemn Declaration on European Union by the European
Council (The Stuttgart Declaration), Stuttgart, 19 June 1983

Preamble

'The Heads of State or Government of the Member States of the European
Communities, meeting within the European Council,

resolved to continue the work begun on the basis of the Treaties of Paris and Rome
and to create a united Europe, which is more than ever necessary in order to meet
the dangers of the world situation, capable of assuming the responsibilities incumbent on it by virtue of its political role, its economic potential and its manifold links
with other peoples,

considering that the European idea, the results achieved in the fields of economic
integration and political cooperation, and the need for new developments correspond to the wishes of the democratic peoples of Europe, for whom the European
Parliament, elected by universal suffrage, is an indispensable means of expression,

determined to work together to promote democracy on the basis of the fundamental
rights recognized in the constitutions and laws of the Member States, in the
European Convention for the Protection of Human Rights and the European Social
Charter, notably freedom, equality and social justice,

convinced that, in order to resolve the serious economic problems facing the
Member States, the Community must strengthen its cohesion, regain its dynamism
and intensify its action in areas hitherto insufficiently explored,

resolved to accord a high priority to the Community's social progress and in particular to the problem of employment by the development of a European social policy,

convinced that, by speaking with a single voice in foreign policy, including political aspects of security, Europe can contribute to the preservation of peace,

recalling their decisions taken in Paris on 21 October 1972 and 10 December 1974,
the Document on the European Identity of 14 December 1973 and the statement
made by the European Council in The Hague on 30 November 1976 concerning
the progressive construction of European Union,

determined to achieve a comprehensive and coherent common political approach
and reaffirming their will to transform the whole complex of relations between their
States into a European Union,

have adopted the following:

1 Objectives

1.1 The Heads of State or Government, on the basis of an awareness of a common
destiny and the wish to affirm the European identity, confirm their commitment to
progress towards an ever closer union among the peoples and Member States of
the European Community.

1.2 The Heads of State or Government reaffirm the Declaration on Democracy
adopted by the European Council on 8 April 1978 which stated that respect for

and maintenance of representative democracy and human rights in each Member State are essential elements of membership of the European Communities.

1.3 In order to achieve ever increasing solidarity and joint action, the construction of Europe must be more clearly oriented towards its general political objectives, more efficient decision-making procedures, greater coherence and close coordination between the different branches of activity, and the search for common policies in all areas of common interest, both within the Community and in relation to third countries.

1.4 Desiring to consolidate the progress already made towards European Union in both the economic and political fields, the Heads of State or Government reaffirm the following objectives:

1.4.1 to strengthen and continue the development of the Communities, which are the nucleus of European Union, by reinforcing existing policies and elaborating new policies within the framework of the Treaties of Paris and Rome;

1.4.2* to strengthen and develop European Political Cooperation through the elaboration and adoption of joint positions and joint action, on the basis of intensified consultations, in the area of foreign policy, including the coordination of the positions of Member States on the political and economic aspects of security, so as to promote and facilitate the progressive development of such positions and actions in a growing number of foreign policy fields.

1.4.3 to promote, to the extent that these activities cannot be carried out within the framework of the Treaties:

• closer co-operation on cultural matters, in order to affirm the awareness of a common cultural heritage as an element in the European identity;

• approximation of certain areas of the legislation of the Member States in order to facilitate relationships between their nationals;

• a common analysis and concerted action to deal with international problems of law and order, serious acts of violence, organized international crime and international lawlessness generally.

2 Institutions

The Heads of State or Government emphasize the importance of greater coherence and close coordination between the existing structures of the European Communities and European Political Cooperation at all levels so that comprehensive and consistent action can be taken to achieve European Union.

Matters within the scope of the European Communities are governed by provisions and procedures laid down in or pursuant to the Treaties of Paris and Rome and in agreements supplementing them. In matters of Political Cooperation, procedures which were agreed on in the Luxembourg (1970), Copenhagen (1973) and London (1981) reports will apply, together with other procedures to be agreed on if necessary.

---

*   Danish reservation—see end of document

2.1 The European Council

2.1.1 The European Council brings together the Heads of State or Government and the President of the Commission assisted by the Foreign Ministers of the Member States and a member of the Commission.

2.1.2 In the perspective of European Union, the European Council

• provides a general political impetus to the construction of Europe;

• defines approaches to further the construction of Europe and issues general political guidelines for the European Communities and European Political Cooperation;

• deliberates upon matters concerning European Union in its different aspects with due regard to consistency among them;

• initiates cooperation in new areas of activity;

• solemnly expresses the common position in questions of external relations.

2.1.3 When the European Council acts in matters within the scope of the European Communities, it does so in its capacity as the Council within the meaning of the Treaties.

2.1.4 The European Council will address a report to the European Parliament after each of its meetings. This report will be presented at least once during each Presidency by the President of the European Council.

The European Council will also address a written annual report to the European Parliament on progress towards European Union.

In the debates to which these reports give rise, the European Council will normally be represented by its President or one of its members.

2.2 The Council and its members

2.2.1 The consistency and continuity of the work needed for the further construction of European Union as well as the preparation of meetings of the European Council are the responsibility of the Council (General Affairs) and its members.

With a view to bringing the institutional apparatus of the Community and that of Political Cooperation closer together, the Council deals with matters for which it is competent under the Treaties in accordance with the procedures laid down by the latter, and its members will deal also, in accordance with the appropriate procedures, with all other areas of European Union, particularly matters coming within the scope of Political Cooperation.

The Member States will arrange their representation as provided for in their respective constitutions.

2.2.2 The application of the decision-making procedures laid down in the Treaties of Paris and Rome is of vital importance in order to improve the European Communities' capacity to act.

Within the Council every possible means of facilitating the decision-making process will be used, including, in cases where unanimity is required, the possibility of abstaining from voting.

2.2.3 To promote the objective of a Europe speaking with a single voice and acting in common in the field of foreign policy, the Governments of the Member States will make a constant effort to increase the effectiveness of Political Cooperation and will seek, in particular, to facilitate the decision-making process, in order to reach common positions more rapidly.

They recently adopted new arrangements in the London report of 13 October 1981.

In the light of experience they will continue in this direction, in particular by:

• strengthening the Presidency's powers of initiative, of coordination and of representation in relations with third countries;

• appropriately strengthening operational support for successive Presidencies, corresponding to the increasing tasks which they have to perform.

2.3 The Parliament

2.3.1 The Assembly of the European Communities has an essential role to play in the development of European Union.

2.2.2 The European Parliament debates all matters relating to European Union, including European Political Cooperation. In matters relating to the European Communities, it deliberates in accordance with the provisions and procedures laid down in the Treaties establishing the European Communities and in agreements supplementing them.

2.3.3 In addition to the consultation procedures provided for in the Treaties, the Council, its members and the Commission will, in keeping with their respective powers, respond to:

• oral or written questions from Parliament;
• resolutions concerning matters of major importance and general concern, on which Parliament seeks their comments.

2.3.4 The Presidency will address the European Parliament at the beginning of its term of office and present its programme. It will report to the European Parliament at the end of its term on the progress achieved.

The Presidency keeps the European Parliament regularly informed through the Political Affairs Committee of the subjects of foreign policy examined in the context of European Political Cooperation.

Once a year the Presidency reports to the European Parliament in plenary session on progress in the field of Political Cooperation.

2.3.5(*) Before the appointment of the President of the Commission, the President of the Representatives of the Governments of the Member States seeks the Opinion of the enlarged Bureau of the European Parliament.

After the appointment of the members of the Commission by the Governments of the Member States, the Commission presents its programme to the European Parliament to debate and to vote on that programme.

* Danish reservation—see end of document

2.3.6(*) The Council will enter into talks with the European Parliament and the Commission with the aim, within the framework of a new agreement, of improving and extending the scope of the conciliation procedure provided for in the Joint Declaration of 4 March 1975.

2.3.7 In addition to the consultations provided for in the Treaties with respect to certain international agreements, the Opinion of the European Parliament will be sought before:

• the conclusions of other significant international agreements by the Community,

• the accession of a State to the European Community.

The existing procedures for providing the European Parliament with confidential and unofficial information on progress in negotiations will be extended, taking into account the requirements of urgency, to all significant international agreements concluded by the Communities.

2.4 The Commission

The Heads of State or Government underline the particular importance of the Commission as guardian of the Treaties of Paris and Rome and as a driving force in the process of European integration. They confirm the value of making more frequent use of the possibility of delegating powers to the Commission within the framework of the Treaties. In addition to the tasks and powers laid down in those Treaties, the Commission is fully associated with the work of European Political Cooperation and, where appropriate, with other activities within the framework of European Union.

2.5 The Court of Justice

The Court of Justice of the European Communities has an essential role to play in progress towards European Union, by securing compliance with, and development of, Community law. Taking account of the respective constitutional provisions in their States, the Heads of State or Government agree to consider, on a case-by-case basis, the inclusion, as appropriate, in international conventions between Member States, of a clause conferring on the Court of Justice appropriate jurisdiction with regard to the interpretation of the texts.

3 Scope

3.1 European Communities

. . .

3.1.5 Given the importance of the Community's external relations, strengthening of the common commercial policy and development of its external economic policy on the basis of common positions; the Community will, in this way, give effect to its special responsibility as the principal world trader and to its commitment to a free and open trading system.

In this context, improvement and coordination of national and Community development cooperation policies are needed in order to reflect more fully the needs of the developing countries and the interdependence between them and Europe, and so that Europe plays a stronger and more stimulating role in relations between the industrialized and developing countries.

. . .

3.2 Foreign policy

In order to cope with the increasing problems of international politics, the necessary reinforcement of European Political Cooperation must be ensured, in particular by the following measures:

• intensified consultations with a view to permitting timely joint action on all major foreign policy questions of interest to the Ten as a whole;

• prior consultation with the other Member States in advance of the adoption of final positions on these questions. The Heads of State or Government underline their undertaking that each Member State will take full account of the positions of its partners and give due weight to the adoption and implementation of common European positions when working out national positions and taking national action;

• development and extension of the practice by which the views of the Ten are defined and consolidated in the form of common positions which then constitute a central point of reference for Member States' policies;

• progressive development and definition of common principles and objectives as well as the identification of common interests in order to strengthen the possibilities of joint action in the field of foreign policy;

• coordination of positions of Member States on the political and economic aspects of security;

• increased contracts with third countries in order to give the Ten greater weight as an interlocutor in the foreign policy field;

• closer cooperation in diplomatic and administrative matters between the missions of the Ten in third countries;

• the search for common positions at major international conferences attended by one or more of the Ten and covering questions dealt with in Political Cooperation;

• increasing recognition of the contribution which the European Parliament makes to the development of a coordinated foreign policy of the Ten.

3.3 Cultural cooperation

With a view to complementing Community action and stressing that, in consideration of the membership of their States of the Council of Europe, they maintain their firm support for an involvement in its cultural activities, the Heads of State or Government agree to promote, encourage or facilitate the following, taking account of respective constitutional provisions:

. . .

• closer coordination of cultural activities in third countries, within the framework of Political Cooperation.

3.4 Approximation of laws

. . .

4 Final provisions

4.1 The Heads of State or Government stress the link between membership of the European Communities and participation in the activities described above.

4.2 European Union is being achieved by deepening and broadening the scope of European activities so that they coherently cover, albeit on a variety of legal bases, a growing proportion of Member States' mutual relations and of their external relations.

4.3(*) The Heads of State or Government will subject this Declaration to a general review as soon as the progress achieved towards European unification justifies such action, but not later than five years from signature of the Declaration.

In the light of the results of this review they will decide whether the progress achieved should be incorporated in a Treaty on European Union.

The Opinion of the European Parliament will be sought on this subject.

Statement by the Commission and the Member States

The President of the Commission, to avoid any misunderstanding which could arise from the words 'the political and *economic* aspects of security' appearing in 1.4.2 and 3.2, is anxious to point out that these words should not be seen as undermining the competences of the Community. The Ministers support this view.

Statement by the Greek delegation on the subject of paragraphs 2 and 3

In signing this declaration Greece declares that nothing can restrain its right to determine its own foreign policy on the basis of its national interests.

(*) Danish reservations on paragraphs 1.4.2, 2.3.5, 2.3.6, 3.1.1, 3.4.3 and 4.3.

The Draft Treaty on European Union, February 1984

Despite its generally elitist character it should not be thought that EPC has developed in a vacuum, the result of intergovernmental bargains without reference to wider political forces. Although it was true that in its first decade few outsiders were even aware of the existence of a system for coordinating national foreign policies, thereafter voices began to be raised on a regular basis calling for more effective and/or unified actions by Europe in international relations. The European Parliament, that much maligned institution, was one of the main sources of this pressure and indeed of specialized knowledge about EPC, particularly after the first direct elections in 1979 and among the members of its Political Affairs Committee.

The EP itself has slowly managed over the years to squeeze a greater involvement for itself in EPC – and particularly in EC external relations – out of the Member States, but until the 1990s this was largely a matter of consultations rather than powers. Nonetheless, MEPs have realized that the use of what Kant called 'publicity', or what we might now think of as consciousness-raising by high-profile events, can increase their influence in the long term by using public opinion to pressurize decision-makers. One of the most effective operators in this sense was the Italian communist and federalist Altiero Spinelli, who was the prime mover in 1983–4 behind the European Parliament's 'Draft Treaty establishing European Union', to the extent that the document is sometimes known as the 'Spinelli Plan'. Spinelli and his colleagues worked, of course, closely with those governments which themselves felt frustrated by the failure to get consensus on another great leap forward in integration, such as those in Bonn and Rome.

The Draft Treaty, adopted by 237 votes to 31 with 43 abstentions, derived from the setting-up of a Committee on Institutional Affairs as far back as July 1981, i.e. in the midst of the Genscher-Colombo initiative. It attempts to relight the torch of European Union virtually extinguished after the failure of the Tindemans Report, and only a small proportion deals with foreign policy and external relations – although the stated purposes of the Treaty highlight the need for a civilized international society in which a European Community clear about its own values and identity could play a full part.

The Draft Treaty provided for a European Union with legal personality, and aimed to increase the amount of work done by 'common action' (the supranational method) as opposed to (intergovernmental) cooperation. The legislative and other powers of the Parliament were naturally to be sharply increased. So far as policies were concerned, a 'homogeneous judicial area' was to be created, and the internal market to be liberalized in the areas of what later were to be known as the 'four freedoms', of persons, services, goods and capital. All states were to participate in a developing European Monetary System, while an ambitious range of other policies for industry, energy and 'society' were outlined.

In the area of the 'international relations of the Union', the Draft Treaty had been firmed up during the last months before the Parliament's vote, to allow for the Member States to delegate certain EPC matters for implementation to the Commission and the Council of Ministers, thus encouraging greater coordination of EPC and external relations. It allowed for the approval of guidelines and international agreements by absolute majorities in the Council, except on security questions and other foreign policy areas, where the European Council would hold responsibility for coordinating Member States' national policies. The European Council would be able to extend this 'cooperation' to include defence and arms trade questions. Commission representations in third countries would coordinate European positions in conjunction with the Ambassador (or other agent) of the country holding the Presidency.

It was perhaps not surprising that most of those proved too much for most Member States to swallow at the time, although some of it has become accepted practice in the course of time. Spinelli and his colleagues had made a considerable effort to be realistic but at bottom they believed ardently in the historical destiny of a federal Europe. They were therefore not content with the kind of empirical gradualism on European foreign policy represented by the London Report and indeed by EPC in general. In this they made common cause with certain governments, so that although the EP lost a battle when the Draft Treaty, which had been submitted to the governments and national parliaments of Member States, came to nothing, it was beginning to shape the outcome of the longer war.

Document 2/14   Draft Treaty Establishing the European Union, approved by the European Parliament, 14 February 1984

Preamble

With a view to continuing and reviving the democratic unification of Europe, of which the European Communities, the European Monetary System and European Political Cooperation represent the first achievements, and convinced that it is increasingly important for Europe to assert its identity;

Welcoming the positive results achieved so far, but aware of the present need to redefine the objectives of European integration, and to confer on more efficient and more democratic institutions the means of attaining them;

Basing their actions on their commitment to the principles of pluralist democracy, respect for human rights and the rule of law;

Reaffirming their desire to contribute to the construction of an international society based on cooperation between peoples and between States, the peaceful settlement of disputes, security and the strengthening of international organizations;

Resolved to strengthen and preserve peace and liberty by an ever closer union, and calling on the other peoples of Europe who share their ideal to join in their efforts;

Determined to increase solidarity between the peoples of Europe, while respecting their historical identity, their dignity and their freedom within the framework of freely accepted common institutions;

Convinced of the need to enable local and regional authorities to participate by appropriate methods in the unification of Europe;

Desirous of attaining their common objectives progressively, accepting the requisite transitional periods and submitting all further development for the approval of their peoples and States;

Intending to entrust common institutions, in accordance with the principle of subsidiarity, only with those powers required to complete successfully the tasks they may carry out more satisfactorily than the States acting independently;

The High Contracting Parties, Member States of the European Communities, have decided to create a European Union.

The Union

Creation of the Union

I, By this Treaty, the High Contracting Parties establish among themselves a European Union.

. . .

Legal personality of the Union

6. The Union shall have legal personality. In each of the Member States, the Union shall enjoy the most extensive legal capacity accorded to legal persons under national legislation. It may, in particular, acquire or dispose of movable and immovable property and may be a party to legal proceedings. In international relations, the Union shall enjoy the legal capacity it requires to perform its functions and attain its objectives.

. . .

International relations of the Union

Principles and methods of action

1. The Union shall direct its efforts in international relations towards the achievement of peace through the peaceful settlement of conflicts and towards security, the deterrence of aggression, détente, the mutual balanced and verifiable reduction of military forces and armaments, respect for human rights, the raising of living standards in the Third World, the expansion and improvement of international economic and monetary relations in general and trade in particular and the strengthening of international organization.

2. In the international sphere, the Union shall endeavour to attain the objectives set out in Article 9 of this Treaty. It shall act either by common action or by cooperation.

Common action

64. 1. In its international relations, the Union shall act by common action in the fields referred to in this Treaty where it has exclusive or concurrent competence.

2. In the field of commercial policy, the Union shall have exclusive competence.

3. The Union shall pursue a development aid policy. During a transitional period of 10 years, this policy as a whole shall progressively become the subject of common action by the Union. In so far as the Member States continue to pursue independent programmes, the Union shall define the framework within which it will ensure the coordination of such programmes with its own policy, whilst observing current international commitments.

4. Where certain external policies fall within the exclusive competence of the European Communities pursuant to the Treaties establishing them, but where that competence has not been fully exercised, a law shall [lay] down the procedures required for it to be fully exercised within a period which may not exceed five years.

Conduct of common action

65. 1. In the exercise of its competences, the Union shall be represented by the Commission in its relations with non-member States and international organizations. In particular, the Commission shall negotiate international agreements on behalf of the Union. It shall be responsible for liaison with all international organizations and shall cooperate with the Council of Europe, in particular in the cultural sector.

2. The Council of the Union may issue the Commission with guidelines for the conduct of international action; it must issue such guidelines, after approving them by an absolute majority, where the Commission is involved in drafting acts and negotiating agreements which will create international obligations for the Union.

3. The Parliament shall be informed, in good time, and in accordance with appropriate procedures, of every action of the institutions competent in the field of international policy.

4. The Parliament and the Council of the Union, both acting by an absolute majority shall approve international agreements and instruct the President of the Commission to deposit the instruments of ratification.

Cooperation

66. The Union shall conduct its international relations by the method of cooperation where Article 64 of this Treaty is not applicable and where they involve:

matters directly concerning the interests of several Member States of the Union,

or fields in which the Member States acting individually cannot act as efficiently as the Union,

or fields where a policy of the Union appears necessary to supplement the foreign policies pursued on the responsibility of the Member States,

or matters relating to the political and economic aspects of security.

Conduct of cooperation

67. In the fields referred to in Article 66 of this Treaty:

1. The European Council shall be responsible for cooperation; the Council of the Union shall be responsible for its conduct; the Commission may propose policies and actions which shall be implemented, at the request of the European Council or the Council of the Union, either by the Commission or by the Member States.

2. The Union shall ensure that the international policy guidelines of the Member States are consistent.

3. The Union shall coordinate the positions of the Member States during the negotiation of international agreements and within the framework of international organizations.

4. In an emergency, where immediate action is necessary, a Member State particularly concerned may act individually after informing the European Council and the Commission.

5. The European Council may call on its President, on the President of the Council of the Union or on the Commission to act as spokesman of the Union.

Extension of the field of cooperation and transfer from cooperation
to common action

68. 1. The European Council may extend the field of cooperation, in particular as regards armaments, sales of arms to non-Member States, defence policy and disarmament.

2. Under the conditions laid down in Article 11 of this Treaty, the European Council may decide to transfer a particular field of cooperation to common action in external policy. In that event the provisions laid down in Article 23(3) of this Treaty shall apply without any time-limit. Bearing in mind the principle laid down in Article 35 of this Treaty, the Council of the Union, acting unanimously, may exceptionally authorize one or more Member States to derogate from some of the measures taken within the context of common action.

3. By way of derogation from Article 11(2) of this Treaty, the European Council may decide to restore the fields transferred to common action in accordance with paragraph 2 above, either to cooperation or to the competence of the Member States.

4. Under the conditions laid down in paragraph 2 above, the European Council may decide to transfer a specific problem to common action for the period required for its solution. In that event, paragraph 3 above shall not apply.

Right of representation abroad

69. 1. The Commission may, with the approval of the Council of the Union, establish representations in non-member States and international organizations.

2. Such representatives shall be responsible for representing the Union in all matters subject to common action. They may also, in collaboration with the diplomatic agent of the Member States holding the presidency of the European Council, coordinate the diplomatic activity of the Member States in the fields subject to cooperation.

3. In non-member States and international organizations where there is no representation of the Union, it shall be represented by the diplomatic agent of the Member State currently holding the presidency of the European Council or else by the diplomatic agent of another Member State.

. . .

The Single European Act

The Single European Act (SEA) is largely remembered for its introduction of the idea of the Single European Market (to be completed by 1992, with the aid of qualified majority voting in more areas) and of the 'cooperation procedure' between the European Parliament and the other Community institutions. Nonetheless it is also important for innovations in the area of foreign policy, and will probably be recalled by historians as representing a half-way house in the long-term struggle between those wishing for a relatively static process of coordination between independent national foreign policies, and those seeking to bring the latter within the Community stockade so that they might be integrated with treaty-based external relations.

The SEA was effectively agreed in December 1985, but not ratified until 1 July 1987, after the Irish government had been subject to a legal challenge and then a referendum on the grounds that the country's commitment to international neutrality had been infringed. It was entitled the 'Single' Act to convey the way it brought EPC and the Communities under the same legal umbrella for the first time. As Simon Nuttall has said, the Community now had a second pillar (and would at Maastricht gain a third).* EPC was now codified and brought into a formal relationship with the Communities, by references in Title I of the SEA to the Luxembourg, Copenhagen and London reports, and to the Stuttgart Solemn Declaration. Title III, however, is where the main material on EPC resides, set apart from the rest of the Act to emphasize its strongly intergovernmental character, as in the wholly separate 'Decision of the Foreign Ministers of 28 February 1986', which contains the detail on EPC's procedures. The legal obligations contained in these documents are very arguable, not least because their language is mostly that of exhortation and rarely that of prescription.

Essentially the EPC aspects of the SEA were the result of myriad compromises, necessitated by the battles of 1981–4 on whether foreign policy could be the vehicle for another leap forward towards political union. The new French President, François Mitterand, had talked of the possibility of a high-profile political secretariat, answering to the European Council itself, which would have made EPC seem rather small-scale and bureaucratic. The Germans, the Italians and the Benelux states, to say nothing of the European Parliament, wished to revive the federalist project. As a result, after the solution of the EC's financial problems at Fontainebleau in June 1984, Britain agreed to the setting up of an *ad hoc* committee to make suggestions for improving European cooperation across the board. This became the 'Dooge Committee', after its Irish chairman, and it reported in March 1985 with some very modest proposals due to the innumerable reservations by Member States such as Denmark and Greece.

The British then tabled a detailed but unimaginative series of proposals on how to refine EPC procedures, only to be trumped at the Milan summit of June 1985 by a Franco–German counter-draft in the more high-flown language of European union and reasserting the proposal for a Secretary-General to answer to the European Council. In consequence Mrs Thatcher, furious at being out-manoeuvred by Bettino Craxi of Italy in the chair, had little choice (because such decisions are by majority vote) but to agree to an inter-governmental conference with two tracks, one on decision-making in the EC and one working towards an EPC treaty. The latter had to reconcile the existing competing drafts, as well as other national documents which were to be laid before it. In the circumstances it is remarkable that broad agreement was reached (at Luxembourg) on a single, if ramshackle structure as early as December 1985.

Title III's innovations are modest but real. Security is brought formally into the Community ambit for the first time, and although the formulation ('the political and economic aspects') is basically the same as that of the Stuttgart Declaration, there is an additional reference to the 'High Contracting Parties' (the Member States) being 'determined to maintain the technological and industrial conditions necessary for their security' (Article 30, paragraphs 6a and 6b). Other changes are the insistence that EC external relations and EPC 'must be consistent' (Article 30, paragraphs 5), and the replacement of the travelling troika of officials by a new secretariat for EPC, to be based in Brussels but with the main function of helping the presidency and (as it turned out) of keeping a low profile.

*   Simon Nuttall, *European Political Cooperation*, Oxford, Clarendon Press, 1992, p. 249.

Less important, but still notable, is the absence from Title III of provisions for cooperation on internal security, despite the fact that EPC had actually been fostering technical liaisons on anti-terrorism under the 'Trevi' arrangements since the mid-1970s. Less predictably, the 'Decision' (paragraph 2) contains the first public reference to the mysterious 'coutumier' which summarized the internal workings of EPC for the practitioners themselves. This reference was said by some to be the result of a slip in drafting. Lastly, Denmark insisted on appending a Declaration, the whole text of which reads:

> The Danish Government states that the conclusion of Title III on European Political Cooperation in the sphere of foreign policy does not affect Denmark's participation in Nordic cooperation in the sphere of foreign policy.

In general Title III codified EPC and linked it explicitly to the Communities. In so doing it constructed a cross-roads at which Member States could make choices for their future direction in foreign policy. As the product of political bargaining, it contained both inter-governmental and communautaire elements which did, however, sit uneasily together in a single framework. It is, for example, sometimes forgotten that the SEA gave the European Parliament what became known as a new 'assent power' over enlargement and over association agreements. This was a rather more important form of foreign policy accountability than anything the Parliament had achieved with respect to EPC. But EPC was not yet capable by itself of generating agreements or treaties to be assented to, and the two forms of activity remained in their separate compartments.

Document 2/15   The Single European Act, Luxembourg, 17 February 1986, and The Hague, 28 February 1986

[The Heads of State or Government of the Twelve Member States]

MOVED by the will to continue the work undertaken on the basis of the Treaties establishing the European Communities and to transform relations as a whole among their States into a European Union, in accordance with the Solemn Declaration of Stuttgart of 19 June 1983,
RESOLVED to implement this European Union on the basis, firstly, of the Communities operating in accordance with their own rules and, secondly, of European Cooperation among the Signatory States in the sphere of foreign policy and to invest this union with the necessary means of action,
DETERMINED to work together to promote democracy on the basis of the fundamental rights recognized in the constitutions and laws of the Member States, in the Convention for the Protection of Human Rights and Fundamental Freedoms and the European Social Charter, notably freedom, equality and social justice,
CONVINCED that the European idea, the results achieved in the fields of economic integration and political co-operation, and the need for new developments correspond to the wishes of the democratic peoples of Europe, for whom the European Parliament, elected by universal suffrage, is an indispensable means of expression,
AWARE of the responsibility incumbent upon Europe to aim at speaking ever increasingly with one voice and to act with consistency and solidarity in order more effectively to protect its common interests and independence, in particular to display

the principles of democracy and compliance with the law and with human rights to which they are attached, so that together they may make their own contribution to the preservation of international peace and security in accordance with the undertaking entered into by them within the framework of the United Nations Charter,

DETERMINED to improve the economic and social situation by extending common policies and pursuing new objectives, and to ensure a smoother functioning of the Communities by enabling the Institutions to exercise their powers under conditions most in keeping with Community interests,

. . .

HAVE AGREED AS FOLLOWS:

Title I

Common Provisions

Article 1

The European Communities and European Political Cooperation shall have as their objective to contribute together to making concrete progress towards European unity.

The European Communities shall be founded on the Treaties establishing the European Coal and Steel Community, the European Economic Community, the European Atomic Energy Community, and on the subsequent Treaties and Acts modifying or supplementing them.

Political Co-operation shall be governed by Title III. The provisions of that Title shall confirm and supplement the procedures agreed in the reports of Luxembourg (1970), Copenhagen (1973), London (1981), the Solemn Declaration on European Union (1983) and the practices gradually established among the Member States.

Article 2

The European Council shall bring together the Heads of State or of Government of the Member States and the President of the Commission of the European Communities. They shall be assisted by the Ministers for Foreign Affairs and by a Member of the Commission.

The European Council shall meet at least twice a year.

Article 3

1. The institutions of the European Communities, henceforth designated as referred to hereafter, shall exercise their powers and jurisdiction under the conditions and for the purposes provided for by the Treaties establishing the Communities and by the subsequent Treaties and Acts modifying or supplementing them and by the provisions of Title II.

2. The institutions and bodies responsible for European Political Co-operation shall exercise their powers and jurisdiction under the conditions and for the purposes laid down in Title III and in the documents referred to in the third paragraph of Article 1.

. . .

Title II

Provisions amending the Treaties establishing the European Communities

CHAPTER 4—COMMERCIAL POLICY

. . .

Article 110

By establishing a customs union between themselves Member States aim to contribute, in the common interest, to the harmonious development of world trade, the progressive abolition of restrictions on international trade and the lowering of customs barriers.

The common commercial policy shall take into account the favourable effect which the abolition of customs duties between Member States may have on the increase in the competitive strength of undertakings in those States.

Article 111

. . .

Member States shall aim at securing as high a level of uniformity as possible between themselves as regards their liberalisation lists in relation to third countries or groups of third countries. To this end, the Commission shall make all appropriate recommendations to Member States.

If Member States abolish or reduce quantitative restrictions in relation to third countries, they shall inform the Commission beforehand and shall accord the same treatment to other Member States.

Article 112

1. Without prejudice to obligations undertaken by them within the framework of other international organisations, Member States shall, before the end of the transitional period, progressively harmonise the systems whereby they grant aid for exports to third countries, to the extent necessary to ensure that competition between undertakings of the Community is not distorted.

On a proposal from the Commission, the Council, shall, acting unanimously until the end of the second stage and by a qualified majority thereafter, issue any directives needed for this purpose.

2. The preceding provisions shall not apply to such drawback of customs duties or charges having equivalent effect nor to such repayment of indirect taxation including turnover taxes, excise duties and other indirect taxes as is allowed when goods are

exported from a Member State to a third country, in so far as such drawback or repayment does not exceed the amount imposed, directly or indirectly, on the products exported.

Article 113

1. After the transitional period has ended, the common commercial policy shall be based on uniform principles, particularly in regard to changes in tariff rates, the conclusion of tariff and trade agreements, the achievement of uniformity in measures of liberalisation, export policy and measures to protect trade such as those to be taken in case of dumping or subsidies.

2. The Commission shall submit proposals to the Council for implementing the common commercial policy.

3. Where agreements with third countries need to be negotiated, the Commission shall make recommendations to the Council, which shall authorise the Commission to open the necessary negotiations.

The Commission shall conduct these negotiations in consultation with a special committee appointed by the Council to assist the Commission in this task and within the framework of such directives as the Council may issue to it.

4. In exercising the powers conferred upon it by this Article, the Council shall act by a qualified majority.

Article 114

The agreements referred to in Article 111 (2) and in Article 113 shall be concluded by the Council on behalf of the Community, acting unanimously during the first two stages and by a qualified majority thereafter.

Article 115

In order to ensure that the execution of measures of commercial policy taken in accordance with this Treaty by any Member State is not obstructed by deflection of trade, or where differences between such measures lead to economic difficulties in one or more of the Member States, the Commission shall recommend the methods for the requisite co-operation between Member States. Failing this, the Commission shall authorise Member States to take the necessary protective measures, the conditions and details of which it shall determine.

In case of urgency during the transitional period, Member States may themselves take the necessary measures and shall notify them to the other Member States and to the Commission, which may decide that the States concerned shall amend or abolish such measures.

In the selection of such measures, priority shall be given to those which cause the least disturbance to the functioning of the common market and which take into account the need to expedite, as far as possible, the introduction of the common customs tariff.

Article 116

From the end of the transitional period onwards, Member States shall, in respect of all matters of particular interest to the common market, proceed within the framework of international organisations of an economic character only by common action. To this end, the Commission shall submit to the Council, which shall act by a qualified majority, proposals concerning the scope and implementation of such common action.

During the transitional period, Member States shall consult each other for the purpose of concerting the action they take and adopting as far as possible a uniform attitude.

. . .

Article 237

Any European State may apply to become a member of the Community. It shall address its application to the Council, which shall act unanimously after consulting the Commission and after receiving the assent of the European Parliament which shall act by an absolute majority of its component members.

The conditions of admission and the adjustments to this Treaty necessitated thereby shall be the subject of an agreement between the Member States and the applicant State. This agreement shall be submitted for ratification by all the Contracting States in accordance with their respective constitutional requirements.

Article 238

The Community may conclude with a third State, a union of States or an international organisation agreements establishing an association involving reciprocal rights and obligations, common action and special procedures.

These agreements shall be concluded by the Council, acting unanimously and after receiving the assent of the European Parliament which shall act by an absolute majority of its component members.

Where such agreements call for amendments to this Treaty, these amendments shall first be adopted in accordance with the procedure laid down in Article 236.

Title III

Treaty Provisions on European Co-operation in the Sphere of Foreign Policy

Article 30

European Co-operation in the sphere of foreign policy shall be governed by the following provisions:
1. The High Contracting Parties, being members of the European Communities, shall endeavour jointly to formulate and implement a European foreign policy.

2.   (a) The High Contracting Parties undertake to inform and consult each
      other on any foreign policy matters of general interest so as to ensure that
      their combined influence is exercised as effectively as possible through co-
      ordination, the convergence of their positions and the implementation of joint
      action.
      (b) Consultations shall take place before the High Contracting Parties decide
      on their final position.
      (c) In adopting its positions and in its national measures each High Contracting
      Party shall take full account of the positions of the other partners and shall
      give due consideration to the desirability of adopting and implementing
      common European positions.
      In order to increase their capacity for joint action in the foreign policy field,
      the High Contracting Parties shall ensure that common principles and objec-
      tives are gradually developed and defined.
      The determination of common positions shall constitute a point of reference
      for the policies of the High Contracting Parties.
      (d) The High Contracting Parties shall endeavour to avoid any action or posi-
      tion which impairs their effectiveness as a cohesive force in international
      relations or within international organizations.

3.   (a) The Ministers for Foreign Affairs and a member of the Commission shall
      meet at least four times a year within the framework of European Political
      Co-operation. They may also discuss foreign policy matters within the frame-
      work of Political Co-operation on the occasion of meetings of the Council of
      the European Communities.
      (b) The Commission shall be fully associated with the proceedings of Political
      Co-operation.
      (c) In order to ensure the swift adoption of common positions and the imple-
      mentation of joint action, the High Contracting Parties shall, as far as possible,
      refrain from impeding the formation of a consensus and the joint action which
      this could produce.

4.   The High Contracting Parties shall ensure that the European Parliament is
      closely associated with European Political Co-operation. To that end the
      Presidency shall regularly inform the European Parliament of the foreign policy
      issues which are being examined within the framework of Political Co-oper-
      ation and shall ensure that the views of the European Parliament are duly
      taken into consideration.

5.   The external policies of the European Community and the policies agreed in
      European Political Co-operation must be consistent.
      The Presidency and the Commission, each within its own sphere of compe-
      tence, shall have special responsibility for ensuring that such consistency is
      sought and maintained.

6.   (a) The High Contracting Parties consider that closer co-operation on ques-
      tions of European security would contribute in an essential way to the
      development of a European identity in external policy matters. They are ready
      to co-ordinate their positions more closely on the political and economic
      aspects of security.
      (b) The High Contracting Parties are determined to maintain the techno-
      logical and industrial conditions necessary for their security. They shall work

to that end both at national level and, where appropriate, within the framework of the competent institutions and bodies.

(c) Nothing in this Title shall impede closer co-operation in the field of security between certain of the High Contracting Parties within the framework of the Western European Union or the Atlantic Alliance.

7.   (a) In international institutions and at international conferences which they attend, the High Contracting Parties shall endeavour to adopt common positions on the subjects covered by this Title.

(b) In international institutions and at international conferences in which not all the High Contracting Parties participate, those who do participate shall take full account of positions agreed in European Political co-operation.

8.   The High Contracting Parties shall organize a political dialogue with third countries and regional groupings whenever they deem it necessary.

9.   The High Contracting Parties and the Commission, through mutual assistance and information, shall intensify co-operation between their representations accredited to third countries and to international organizations.

10.   (a) The Presidency of European Political Co-operation shall be held by the High Contracting Party which holds the Presidency of the Council of the European Communities.

(b) The Presidency shall be responsible for initiating action and co-ordinating and representing the positions of the Member States in relations with third countries in respect of European Political Co-operation activities. It shall also be responsible for the management of Political Co-operation and in particular for drawing up the timetable of meetings and for convening and organizing meetings.

(c) The Political Directors shall meet regularly in the Political Committee in order to give the necessary impetus, maintain the continuity of European Political Co-operation, and prepare Ministers' discussions.

(d) The Political Committee or, if necessary, a ministerial meeting shall convene within forty-eight hours at the request of at least three Member States.

(e) The European Correspondents' Group shall be responsible, under the direction of the Political Committee, for monitoring the implementation of European Political Co-operation and for studying general organizational problems.

(f) Working Groups shall meet as directed by the Political Committee.

(g) A Secretariat based in Brussels shall assist the Presidency in preparing and implementing the activities of European Political Co-operation and in administrative matters. It shall carry out its duties under the authority of the Presidency.

11.   As regards privileges and immunities, the members of the European Political Co-operation Secretariat shall be treated in the same way as members of the diplomatic missions of the High Contracting Parties based in the same place as the Secretariat.

12.   Five years after the entry into force of this Act the High Contracting Parties shall examine whether any revision of Title III is required.

Document 2/16   Decision of the Foreign Ministers, Meeting in the Framework of European Political Co-operation, 28 February 1986

The Foreign Ministers, meeting in the framework of European Political Co-operation, hereby decide, on the occasion of the signing of the Single European Act, to adopt the provisions set out in the body of this text concerning the practical application of certain aspects of Title III of this Act. These provisions may be reviewed in accordance with the procedures in force within European Political Co-operation.

The Ministers confirm that the customary procedures which have been set up to ensure the practical working of European Political Co-operation, in particular in the Luxembourg (1970), Copenhagen (1973) and London (1981) reports and the Solemn Declaration on European Union (1983), and which are summarized in the "Coutumier", remain in force, the following provisions being supplementary to them.

I. Relations between European Political Co-operation and the European Parliament

With a view to ensuring the close association of the European Parliament with European Political Co-operation, contacts with the European Parliament shall take place as follows.

1. The Presidency shall regularly inform the European Parliament of foreign policy topics discussed in the context of European Political Co-operation.
2. The Presidency shall address the European Parliament at the start of its period in office and present its programme. At the end of this period, it shall present a report to the European Parliament on progress made.
3. Once a year, the Presidency shall send a written communication to the European Parliament on progress in the field of European Political Co-operation and take part at ministerial level in the general European Parliament debate on foreign policy.
4. The Presidency-in-Office of European Political Co-operation and the members of the Political Affairs Committee of the European Parliament shall hold an informal colloquy four times a year to discuss the most important recent developments in European Political Co-operation.

    In order to prepare these colloquies, the Political Committee shall draw the Ministers' attention to the positions adopted by the European Parliament on foreign policy matters.

    In order to make these discussions more fruitful, the Presidency and the Political Affairs Committee of the European Parliament shall communicate to each other in advance the main possible topics for discussion.
5. By joint agreement, special information sessions at ministerial level on specific European Political Co-operation topics may be organized as required.
6. The Presidency shall reply to parliamentary questions on European Political Co-operation activities and take part in European Parliament Question Time according to the approved customary procedures.
7. The Presidency shall ensure that the views of the European Parliament, as expressed in its resolutions, shall be duly taken into consideration in European Political Co-operation work.

It shall reply to resolutions on matters of major importance and general concern on which the European Parliament requests its comments.

8. The Presidency shall transmit to the European Parliament as soon as possible declarations adopted within the framework of European Political Co-operation.

II. Co-operation of Member States' missions and Commission delegations in third countries and international organizations

1. Member States' missions and Commission delegations shall intensify their co-operation in third countries and international organizations in the following areas:
   (a) exchange of political and economic information;
   (b) pooling of information on administrative and practical problems;
   (c) mutual assistance in the material and practical sphere;
   (d) communications;
   (e) exchange of information and drawing up of joint plans in case of local crises;
   (f) security measures;
   (g) consular matters;
   (h) health, particularly in the field of health and medical facilities;
   (i) educational matters (schooling);
   (j) information;
   (k) cultural affairs;
   (l) development aid. The relevant Council provisions should be noted here.

2. The Member States' Heads of Mission and the Commission's Representative in third countries shall meet regularly in order to co-ordinate their views and prepare joint reports, either at the request of the Political Committee or on their own initiative when the situation requires.

3. With a view to strengthening the co-operation of missions in third countries, this topic shall be examined periodically by the Political Committee on the basis of reports drawn up for this purpose by the missions.

4. The Member States shall examine the possibility of providing help and assistance in third countries to nationals of Member States which have no representation there.

III. European Political Cooperation Secretariat: Responsibilities and Organization

The Secretariat of European Political Co-operation shall act under the authority of the Presidency. It shall assist the Presidency in preparing and implementing European Political Co-operation activities and in administrative matters.

It shall assist the Presidency in ensuring the continuity of European Political Co-operation and its consistency with Community positions.

1. The Secretariat shall:
   (a) assist the Presidency in the organization of European Political Co-operation meetings, including the preparation and circulation of documents and the drawing up of minutes;

    (b) work with the European Correspondents Group in the preparation of conclusions and guidelines and in carrying out any other task entrusted to the Group by the Political Committee;

    (c) assist the chairmen of Working Groups as regards procedures and precedents and the drafting of oral reports and studies;

    (d) assist the Presidency in the preparation of texts to be published on behalf of the Member States, including replies to parliamentary questions and resolutions as defined in item 7, sub-paragraph 2, of Chapter I on relations between European Political Co-operation and the European Parliament;

    (e) maintain the European Co-operation archives and assist the Presidency in preparing the six-monthly compilation of European Political Co-operation texts;

    (f) keep up to date the body of European Political Co-operation working practices;

    (g) assist the Presidency, where appropriate, in contacts with third countries.

2. The Secretariat shall make the necessary arrangements to provide interpretation into all the official languages of the Community at meetings of Heads of State and Government as well as ministerial meetings. It shall ensure that all European Political Co-operation texts submitted to or adopted at these meetings are immediately translated into all the official Community languages.

3. The Secretariat shall be composed of five officials. Following on from the support team arrangement, the Presidency-in-Office of European Political Co-operation together with the two preceding and the two following Presidencies shall each second an official for a period covering five presidencies. The status of the officials of the Foreign Affairs Ministries on temporary secondment to the Secretariat shall be identical to that of members of the diplomatic missions in Brussels, to which they shall be administratively attached.

    The Head of the Secretariat shall be appointed by the Foreign Ministers under arrangements to be agreed between them.

4. Matters concerning administrative staff, infrastructure, equipment and operating expenses will be the subject of a further decision.

IV. Venues for European Political Co-operation meetings

European Political Co-operation meetings shall normally be held at the seat of the Secretariat. Ministerial level and Political Committee meetings may take place in the capital city of the Presidency.

V. Use of languages in European Political Co-operation

Use of languages shall be in accordance with the rules of the European Communities.

For meetings of officials and COREU communications, the current practice of European Political Co-operation will serve as a guide for the time being.

The Rhodes Declaration on the International Role of the European Community

The Rhodes Declaration of 1988 is not a landmark in the evolution of European foreign policy, but it is an interesting product of a particular, and unusual period.

In the year or so immediately after the ratification of the Single European Act in 1987 there was a new mood of optimism about the future of the European Community as a whole, and in particular about its foreign policy. Title III of the SEA had not been revolutionary, but it had raised the public profile of EPC. Furthermore the Single European Market (SEM) was coming to fruition and it was becoming clear that a certain natural convergence was taking place between the economic external relations of the EC and EPC whatever formal decisions might be taken to keep them apart. The Rhodes Declaration itself starts with various acknowledgements of the likely impact of the SEM on third countries, and moves fairly seamlessly into a discussion of high politics. 'Foreign policy' was clearly coming to subsume the whole range of EC external activities, now that outsiders needed reassuring about 'fortress Europe' and the possible extra leverage it might bestow on the EC.

There was also a more bullish tone to European pronouncements at this time because of movements in international relations. Mikhail Gorbachev had come to power in the USSR in 1985 and the impact of his reforms became rapidly evident. At last the Europeans' belief in detente seemed to have been vindicated and the dangers of the Second Cold War put behind them. Indeed, there was some sense of the even bigger changes which were at hand. The Declaration ends by calling on other countries to join in an 'historic effort to leave to the next generation a continent and a world more secure, and more just, and more free'.

Document 2/17   Declaration by the European Council on the International Role of the European Community (The Rhodes Declaration), Rhodes, 3 December 1988

Reaffirming its commitment to achieve concrete progress towards European unity on the basis of the European Single Act;
determined to strengthen and expand the role of the European Community and its Member States on the international political and economic stage, in cooperation with all other States and appropriate organizations;
and aware that the completion of the Internal Market in 1992, which is already inspiring a new dynamism in the Community's economic life, will equally affect the Community's political and economic role in the world;
the European Council reaffirms that the Single Market will be of benefit to Community and non-Community countries alike by ensuring economic growth. The Internal Market will not close in on itself. 1992 Europe will be a partner and not a 'fortress Europe'. The Internal Market will be a decisive factor contributing to greater liberalization in international trade on the basis of the GATT principles of reciprocal and mutually advantageous arrangements. The Community will continue to participate actively in the GATT Uruguay Round, committed as it is to strengthen the multilateral trading system. It will also continue to pursue, with

the United States, Japan and the other OECD partners, policies designed to promote sustainable non-inflationary growth in the world economy.

The Community and its Member States will continue to work closely and cooperatively with the United States to maintain and deepen the solid and comprehensive transatlantic relationship. Closer political and economic relations with Japan and the other industrialized countries will also be developed. In particular, the Community wishes to strengthen and to expand relations with EFTA countries and all other European nations which share the same ideals and objectives. Open and constructive dialogue and cooperation will be actively pursued with other countries or regional groups of the Middle East, and the Mediterranean, Africa, the Caribbean, the Pacific, Asia and Latin America, with special emphasis on interregional cooperation.

The European Council emphasizes the need to improve social and economic conditions in less-developed countries and to promote structural adjustment, both through trade and aid. It also recognizes the importance of a continuing policy to tackle the problems of the highly indebted countries on a case-by-case basis. It looks forward to the successful conclusion of the negotiations for the renewal of the convention between the European Community and its 66 African, Caribbean and Pacific partners during the coming year.

The European Community and its Member States are determined to play an active role in the preservation of international peace and security and in the solution of regional conflicts, in conformity with the United Nations Charter. Europe cannot but actively demonstrate its solidarity to the great and spreading movement for democracy and full support for the principles of the Universal Declaration of Human Rights. The Twelve will endeavour to strengthen the effectiveness of the United Nations and to actively contribute to its peace-keeping role.

Against the background of improved East-West relations, the European Council welcomes the readiness of the European Members of the CMEA to develop relations with the European community and reaffirms its willingness to further economic relations and cooperation with them, taking into account each country's specific situation, in order to use the opportunities available in a mutually beneficial way.

The European Council reaffirms its determination to act with renewed hope to overcome the division of our continent and to promote the Western values and principles which Member States have in common.

To this effect it will try to achieve:

— full respect for the provisions of the Helsinki Final Act and further progress in the CSCE process, including an early and successful conclusion of the Vienna follow-up meeting;

— the establishment of a secure and stable balance of conventional forces in Europe at a lower level, the strengthening of mutual confidence and military transparence and the conclusion of a global and verifiable ban on chemical weapons;

— promotion of human rights and fundamental freedoms, free circulation of people and ideas and the establishment of more open societies; promotion of human and cultural exchanges between East and West;

— the development of political dialogue with our Eastern neighbours.

The European Community and the Twelve are determined to make full use of the provisions of the Single European Act in order to strengthen solidarity among them, coordination on the political and economic aspects of security, and consistency between the external policies of the European Community and the policies agreed in the framework of the European political cooperation. They will strive to reach swift adoption of common positions and implementation of joint action.

The European Council invites all countries to embark with the European Community as world partner on an historic effort to leave to the next generation a continent and a world more secure, and more just, and more free.

The Treaty of European Union: (I) The CFSP

The Treaty of European Union (TEU), agreed at Maastricht in December 1991, signed in February 1992 and finally entering into force on 1 November 1993 after traumas arising from the serious doubts of the populations of Britain, Denmark and France, was the product of a wave of optimism among those who felt themselves responsible for the construction of Europe. The twin forces of, on the one hand the *rélance* of Europe after the Single European Act and on the other the liberation of Eastern Europe, created from 1988 onwards a sense of opportunity, indeed responsibility for the EC in international relations. As in the past, whether with Fouchet, Tindemans or Stuttgart, this could not be separated politically or intellectually from the general process of European integration. Progress in institution-building always seemed to imply progress towards a common foreign policy, and vice versa, although the direction of the causal process was not clear and the two halves of the equation were rarely in balance.

The Single Market timetable gave a decisive boost to the idea of economic and monetary union (EMU), and the Strasbourg summit of December 1991 talked of an Intergovernmental Conference being convened in 1991 to prepare the final stages of EMU. Originally there was no intention of revising the political aspects of the treaties, but this changed under the impact of the great events of 1989–90. After the submission of a formal memorandum from the Belgian government, and then, crucially, a joint message to the Irish Presidency from Helmut Kohl and François Mitterand in April 1990, the Dublin summit of 25–26 June decided to convene an Intergovernmental Conference (IGC) on political union to start at the end of the year and to run alongside that on EMU. The main concerns of this IGC would be the efficient functioning of the EC institutions, the 'democratic deficit' (the lack of democratic accountability at the Community level) and the need for what the French and German leaders called a 'common foreign and security policy'. This new concept met a need at the time for Europe to be seen to be capable of filling the vacuum being left in Europe by the crisis of communism, and attracted support even from previous sceptics about the idea of a European foreign policy. This did not, however, mean that it was properly thought through.

Considerable debate took place in the second half of 1990 on what the new common foreign and security policy might look like, with most Member States, plus the European Parliament and the Commission taking a hand. The Iraqi invasion of Kuwait in August and the fall of Mrs Thatcher in November further heightened expectations of a sea-change in European capabilities. The IGC began at Rome in December 1990, with already some consensus evident on bringing EPC and external relations together, on some right of initiative for the Commission and on relegating the 'lowest common denominator' image of EPC to the past.

The disagreements of 1991 in and around the IGC centred on the issues of security, majority voting and how to integrate foreign policy into the Community proper. For, going beyond the SEA, it was generally accepted that the EC needed a foreign policy and that foreign policy cooperation could not be kept at arms length from the Community. Indeed, the eventual TEU was to contain important innovations in the making of external economic policy and treaty amendments to that end.

On security the issue was not whether or not this should be part of the CFSP's brief – it had been part of EPC since the London Report – but whether the theological distinction always made between security and defence could now be abandoned. What is more, if it were to be accepted that the European Union (as it was to be called after Maastricht) might in time have a common defence policy and even a common defence, would that necessitate starting to merge the WEU with the EU? The United States and the more pro-NATO Member States were extremely worried about this possibility and what they saw as the likely damage to NATO and therefore western security as a whole.

On majority voting there was a clear division between the more integrationist states which had long believed that the Community methods should be introduced to foreign policy discussions, and those, like Britain, France, Denmark and Greece who felt that freedom of manoeuvre for national foreign policy was a matter of vital interest, and could not be surrendered. For much of the debate it seemed that there was to be no question of the latter group surrendering any ground, but the final text, as we shall see, allowed qualified majority voting (QMV) a foot in the door.

On the overall structure into which EPC was to be brought there was genuine uncertainty and much disagreement. Some wished to retain EPC's separate, informal quality alongside Community external relations but in close association with them; others wished to abolish the very distinction. Nor was it clear which solution served what value. For example while the smaller countries generally were in favour of convergence they were also anxious not to see the kind of overarching structure which would effectively introduce a directoire of the powerful states. These uncertainties led to the humiliation of the Dutch Presidency on 30 September 1991, when Foreign Minister van den Broek misread the drift of opinion and tabled a draft treaty which went well beyond his Luxembourg predecessor's notion of separate 'pillars' into an organic, integrationist model. This was summarily and publicly rejected by his colleagues. The Luxembourg paper quickly came back to centre stage and formed the basis of the agreement at Maastricht in December.

In the end the foreign policy contents of the TEU seemed substantial enough. EPC disappeared and was replaced by a CFSP, constituting pillar two of a new three pillar European Union, in Title V and its associated Declarations. Majority voting was introduced, if in the most strait-jacketed of forms, confined to implementation measures and then only when the issues had been defined already by unanimity. The CFSP was permitted to discuss the previously forbidden term of 'defence', with the possibility allowed of moving 'in time' to a common defence. The WEU was to be closely associated with the CFSP, effectively as a bridge between it and NATO, even if the idea of merger had for the time being been submerged. (Denmark, however, 'opted out' of the provisions on defence cooperation under the Edinburgh European Council agreements to ensure that the second Danish referendum would approve the Treaty; see document 2/19.) The new concepts of 'common positions' and 'joint actions' were introduced to try to ensure that the CFSP moved from talking to doing by giving concrete reference points for agreement. It was also agreed that the Community budget should pay for the CFSP's administrative expenditure and that, if the Member States agreed, it might also be used for 'operational' funds. The Commission got its (joint) right of initiative in CFSP, and the EPC Secretariat in Brussels was to be enlarged. Finally, foreign policy was at last to be discussed in the Council of Ministers with external relations, and the pedantry of separate agendas ended.

This was a significant list of innovations, and it contained a number of 'detonators', such as the financing clause and majority voting, which could conceivably be triggered at some future time to transform the construction even further. But the changes still represented only procedural change, necessary and important perhaps, but not enough in itself to change the willingness of states to work in unison and to *act* on the international scene by committing resources. If the substance of policy were to be influenced by procedural change, then it would inevitably take a long time. This was something that not all policy-makers understood at the time, and a technical point that the European public, brought by now to the view that this was 'the hour of Europe', in Luxembourg prime minister Jacques Poos' ineffable phrase just before the Bosnian crisis erupted, certainly did not appreciate. The CFSP was riding for a fall.

Document 2/18   Treaty on European Union (The Maastricht Treaty), Maastricht, 7 February 1992; Title V: Provisions on a Common Foreign and Security Policy

Signed in Maastricht in December 1991, ratified by all Member States by 1 November 1993

Article J

A common foreign and security policy is hereby established which shall be governed by the following provisions.

Article J.1

1. The Union and its Member States shall define and implement a common foreign and security policy, governed by the provisions of this Title and covering all areas of foreign and security policy.

2. The objectives of the common foreign and security policy shall be:

— to safeguard the common values, fundamental interests and independence of the Union;

— to strengthen the security of the Union and its Member States in all ways;

— to preserve peace and strengthen international security, in accordance with the principles of the United Nations Charter as well as the principles of the Helsinki Final Act and the objectives of the Paris Charter;

— to promote international cooperation;

— to develop and consolidate democracy and the rule of law, and respect for human rights and fundamental freedoms.

3. The Union shall pursue these objectives:

— by establishing systematic cooperation between Member States in the conduct of policy, in accordance with Article J.2;

— by gradually implementing, in accordance with Article J.3, joint action in the areas in which the Member States have important interests in common.

4. The Member States shall support the Union's external and security policy actively and unreservedly in a spirit of loyalty and mutual solidarity. They shall refrain from any action which is contrary to the interests of the Union or likely to impair its effectiveness as a cohesive force in international relations. The Council shall ensure that these principles are complied with.

Article J.2

1. Member States shall inform and consult one another within the Council on any matter of foreign and security policy of general interest in order to ensure that their combined influence is exerted as effectively as possible by means of concerted and convergent action.

2. Whenever it deems it necessary, the Council shall define a common position.

Member States shall ensure that their national policies conform to the common positions.

3. Member States shall coordinate their action in international organizations and at international conferences. They shall uphold the common positions in such forums.

In international organizations and at international conferences where not all the Member States participate, those which do take part shall uphold the common positions.

Article J.3

The procedure for adopting joint action in matters covered by the foreign and security policy shall be the following:

1. The Council shall decide, on the basis of general guidelines from the European Council that a matter should be the subject of joint action.

    Whenever the Council decides on the principles of joint action, it shall lay down the specific scope, the Union's general and specific objectives in carrying out such action, if necessary its duration, and the means, procedures and conditions for its implementation.

2. The Council shall, when adopting the joint action and at any stage during its development, define those matters on which decisions are to be taken by a qualified majority.

    Where the Council is required to act by a qualified majority pursuant to the preceding subparagraph, the votes of its members shall be weighted in accordance with Article 148(2) of the Treaty establishing the European Community, and for their adoption, acts of the Council shall require at least 54 votes in favour, cast by at least eight members.

3. If there is a change in circumstances having a substantial effect on a question subject to joint action, the Council shall review the principles and objectives of

that action and take the necessary decisions. As long as the Council has not acted, the joint action shall stand.

4. Joint actions shall commit the Member States in the positions they adopt and in the conduct of their activity.

5. Whenever there is any plan to adopt a national position or take national action pursuant to a joint action, information shall be provided in time to allow, if necessary, for prior consultations within the Council. The obligation to provide prior information shall not apply to measures which are merely a national transposition of Council decisions.

6. In cases of imperative need arising from changes in the situation and failing a Council decision, Member States may take the necessary measures as a matter of urgency having regard to the general objectives of the joint action. The Member State concerned shall inform the Council immediately of any such measures.

7. Should there be any major difficulties in implementing a joint action, a Member State shall refer them to the Council which shall discuss them and seek appropriate solutions. Such solutions shall not run counter to the objectives of the joint action or impair its effectiveness.

Article J.4

1. The common foreign and security policy shall include all questions related to the security of the Union, including the eventual framing of a common defence policy, which might in time lead to a common defence.

2. The Union requests the Western European Union (WEU), which is an integral part of the development of the Union, to elaborate and implement decisions and actions of the Union which have defence implications. The Council shall, in agreement with the institutions of the WEU, adopt the necessary practical arrangements.

3. Issues having defence implications dealt with under this Article shall not be subject to the procedures set out in Article J.3.

4. The policy of the Union in accordance with this Article shall not prejudice the specific character of the security and defence policy of certain Member States and shall respect the obligations of certain Member States under the North Atlantic Treaty and be compatible with the common security and defence policy established within that framework.

5. The provisions of this Article shall not prevent the development of closer cooperation between two or more Member States on a bilateral level, in the framework of the WEU and the Atlantic Alliance, provided such cooperation does not run counter to or impede that provided for in this Title.

6. With a view to furthering the objective of this Treaty, and having in view the date of 1998 in the context of Article XII of the Brussels Treaty, the provisions of this Article may be revised as provided for in Article N(2) on the basis of a report to be presented in 1996 by the Council to the European Council, which shall include an evaluation of the progress made and the experience gained until then.

Article J.5

1. The Presidency shall represent the Union in matters coming within the common foreign and security policy.

2. The Presidency shall be responsible for the implementation of common measures; in that capacity it shall in principle express the position of the Union in international organizations and international conferences.

3. In the tasks referred to in paragraphs 1 and 2, the Presidency shall be assisted if need be by the previous and next Member States to hold the Presidency. The Commission shall be fully associated in these tasks.

4. Without prejudice to Article J.2(3) and Article J.3(4), Member States represented in international organizations or international conferences where not all the Member States participate shall keep the latter informed of any matter of common interest.

Member States which are also members of the United Nations Security Council will concert and keep the other Member States fully informed. Member States which are permanent members of the Security Council will, in the execution of their functions, ensure the defence of the positions and the interests of the Union, without prejudice to their responsibilities under the provisions of the United Nations Charter.

Article J.6

The diplomatic and consular missions of the Member States and the Commission Delegations in third countries and international conferences, and their representations to international organizations, shall cooperate in ensuring that the common positions and common measures adopted by the Council are complied with and implemented.

They shall step up cooperation by exchanging information, carrying out joint assessments and contributing to the implementation of the provisions referred to in Article 8c of the Treaty establishing the European Community.

Article J.7

The Presidency shall consult the European Parliament on the main aspects and the basic choices of the common foreign and security policy and shall ensure that the views of the European Parliament are duly taken into consideration. The European Parliament shall be kept regularly informed by the Presidency and the Commission of the development of the Union's foreign and security policy.

The European Parliament may ask questions of the Council or make recommendations to it. It shall hold an annual debate on progress in implementing the common foreign and security policy.

Article J.8

1. The European Council shall define the principles of and general guidelines for the common foreign and security policy.

2. The Council shall take the decisions necessary for defining and implementing the common foreign and security policy on the basis of the general guidelines

adopted by the European Council. It shall ensure the unity, consistency and effectiveness of action by the Union.

The Council shall act unanimously, except for procedural questions and in the case referred to in Article J.3(2).

3. Any Member State or the Commission may refer to the Council any question relating to the common foreign and security policy and may submit proposals to the Council.

4. In cases requiring a rapid decision, the Presidency, of its own motion, or at the request of the Commission or a Member State, shall convene an extraordinary Council meeting within 48 hours or, in an emergency, within a shorter period.

5. Without prejudice to Article 151 of the Treaty establishing the European Community, a Political Committee consisting of Political Directors shall monitor the international situation in the areas covered by common foreign and security policy and contribute to the definition of policies by delivering opinions to the Council at the request of the Council or on its own initiative. It shall also monitor the implementation of agreed policies, without prejudice to the responsibility of the Presidency and the Commission.

Article J.9

The Commission shall be fully associated with the work carried out in the common foreign and security policy field.

Article J.10

On the occasion of any review of the security provisions under Article J.4, the Conference which is convened to that effect shall also examine whether any other amendments need to be made to provisions relating to the common foreign and security policy.

Article J.11

1. The provisions referred to in Articles 137, 138, 139 to 142, 146, 147, 150 to 153, 157 to 163 and 217 of the Treaty establishing the European Community shall apply to the provisions relating to the areas referred to in this Title.

2. Administrative expenditure which the provisions relating to the areas referred to in this Title entail for the institutions shall be charged to the budget of the European Communities.

The Council may also:

— either decide unanimously that operational expenditure to which the implementation of those provisions gives rise is to be charged to the budget of the European Communities; in that event, the budgetary procedure laid down in the Treaty establishing the European Community shall be applicable:

— or determine that such expenditure shall be charged to the Member States, where appropriate in accordance with a scale to be decided.

Document 2/19　Conclusions of the Presidency of the European Council, Edinburgh, 12 December 1992

Decision on Certain Problems Raised by Denmark

Defence Policy

The Heads of State and Government note that, in response to the invitation from the Western European Union (WEU), Denmark has become an observer to that organisation. They also note that nothing in the Treaty on European Union commits Denmark to become a member of the WEU. Accordingly, Denmark does not participate in the elaboration and the implementation of decisions and actions of the Union which have defence implications, but will not prevent the development of closer cooperation between Member States in this area.

. . .

DECLARATION ON DEFENCE

The European Council takes note that Denmark will renounce its right to exercise the Presidency of the Union in each case involving the elaboration and the implementation of decisions and actions of the Union which have defence implications. The normal rules for replacing the President, in the case of the President being indisposed, shall apply. These rules will also apply with regard to the representation of the Union in international organisations, international conferences and with third countries.

The Treaty of European Union: (II) The Common Commercial Policy

The TEU was the most wide-ranging overhaul of the Treaty of Rome in its 35-year history, and included far more than the CFSP, with provisions for monetary union and cooperation on justice and home affairs (Pillar III) among others. Given that it was also concerned to ensure more consistency between the political and the economic aspects of external policy it was not surprising that the IGC should have taken the opportunity to revise key elements of the Treaty's stipulations about the conduct of commercial policy.

To be more specific, Articles 111–16 were revised to take into account the Single Market and to link it up to the new Article on the procedure for negotiating trade agreements, Article 228, and to weaken the position of Member States *vis-à-vis* the Commission in the taking of 'protective measures' on trade deflection. Article 228 itself is wholly new and takes the procedure for concluding agreements with third parties out of Article 238, which now refers only to association agreements. For the latter, unanimity is retained, but for general trade agreements the Community method is to be employed. The European Parliament is to be consulted on trade agreements, but its assent is required for association agreements, and others with important institutional or budgetary implications.

The element of foreign policy in all this may not seem self-evident. But in the context of the increasing use of economic instruments for political purposes, and the rash of new agreements with the countries of eastern Europe in particular, it was an urgent requirement to clarify the relationship between trade policy proper and the new CFSP. It was difficult to know which economic areas should be ring-fenced and which might be legitimate tools of foreign policy. International trade rules overseen by the World Trade Organization were the ultimate arbiter but the EU also needed to get its own house in order. This was particularly the case over economic sanctions, which a 'civilian power' like the EU has had to have increasing resort to. The new Article 228a of the TEU accordingly specifies that in the event of CFSP generating the need for sanctions, the Council 'shall act on a qualified majority on a proposal from the Commission'. This puts an end to the confusion arising out of the way sanctions had cut right across the formal dividing line between EPC and Community external relations without any guidance from the Treaty of Rome as to proper procedure or legal basis.* At least now less time should be spent in wrangling between the Commission and the Member States on how to proceed in the event of the EU's resources having to be mobilized for foreign policy reasons.

Document 2/20   Treaty of European Union, Title II: Provisions on a Common Commercial Policy, 7 February 1992

COMMON COMMERCIAL POLICY

(27) Article III shall be repealed.

(28) Article 113 shall be replaced by the following:

Article 113

1. The common commercial policy shall be based on uniform principles, particularly in regard to changes in tariff rates, the conclusion of tariff and trade agreements, the achievement of uniformity in measures of liberalization, export policy and measures to protect trade such as those to be taken in the event of dumping or subsidies.

2. The Commission shall submit proposals to the Council for implementing the common commercial policy.

3. Where agreements with one or more States or international organizations need to be negotiated, the Commission shall make recommendations to the Council, which shall authorize the Commission to open the necessary negotiations.

The Commission shall conduct these negotiations in consultations with a special committee appointed by the Council to assist the Commission in this task and within the framework of such directives as the Council may issue to it.

The relevant provisions of Article 228 shall apply.

4. In exercising the powers conferred upon it by this Article, the Council shall act by a qualified majority.'

(29) Article 114 shall be repealed.

(30) Article 115 shall be replaced by the following:

---

*   These matters have many complex legal ramifications, discussed authoritatively in I. Macleod, I. D. Hendry and Stephen Hyett, *The External Relations of the European Communities*, Oxford, Clarendon Press, 1996. See in particular ch. 19 on 'Sanctions' and ch. 20 on 'Association agreements', pp. 352–85.

Article 115

In order to ensure that the execution of measures of commercial policy taken in accordance with this Treaty by any Member State is not obstructed by deflection of trade, or where differences between such measures lead to economic difficulties in one or more Member States, the Commission shall recommend the methods for the requisite cooperation between Member States. Failing this, the Commission may authorize Member States to take the necessary protective measures, the conditions and details of which it shall determine.

In case of urgency, Member States shall request authorization to take the necessary measures themselves from the Commission, which shall take a decision as soon as possible; the Member States concerned shall then notify the measures to the other Member States. The Commission may decide at any time that the Member States concerned shall amend or abolish the measures in question.

In the selection of such measures, priority shall be given to those which cause the least disturbance to the functioning of the common market.'

(31) Article 116 shall be repealed.

. . .

(80) Article 228 shall be replaced by the following:

Article 228

1. Where this Treaty provides for the conclusion of agreements between the Community and one or more States or international organizations, the Commission shall make recommendations to the Council, which shall authorize the Commission to open the necessary negotiations. The Commission shall conduct these negotiations in consultation with special committees appointed by the Council to assist it in this task and within the framework of such directives as the Council may issue to it.

In exercising the powers conferred upon it by this paragraph, the Council shall act by a qualified majority, except in the cases provided for in the second sentence of paragraph 2, for which it shall act unanimously.

2. Subject to the powers vested in the Commission in this field, the agreements shall be concluded by the Council, acting by a qualified majority on a proposal from the Commission. The Council shall act unanimously when the agreement covers a field for which unanimity is required for the adoption of internal rules, and for the agreements referred to in Article 238.

3. The Council shall conclude agreements after consulting the European Parliament, except for the agreements referred to in Article 113(3), including cases where the agreement covers a field for which the procedure referred to in Article 189b or that referred to in Article 189c is required for the adoption of internal rules. The European Parliament shall deliver its opinion within a time-limit which the Council may lay down according to the urgency of the matter. In the absence of an opinion within that time-limit, the Council may act.

By way of derogation from the previous subparagraph, agreements referred to in Article 238, other agreements establishing a specific institutional framework by organizing cooperation procedures, agreements having important budgetary implications for the Community and agreements entailing amendment of an act adopted under the procedure referred to in Article 189b shall be concluded after the assent of the European Parliament has been obtained.

The Council and the European Parliament may, in an urgent situation, agree upon a time-limit for the assent.

4. When concluding an agreement, the Council may, by way of derogation from paragraph 2, authorize the Commission to approve modifications on behalf of the Community where the agreement provides for them to be adopted by a simplified procedure or by a body set up by the agreement; it may attach specific conditions to such authorization.

5. When the Council envisages concluding an agreement which calls for amendments to this Treaty, the amendments must first be adopted in accordance with the procedure laid down in Article N of the Treaty on European Union.

6. The Council, the Commission or a Member State may obtain the opinion of the Court of Justice as to whether an agreement envisaged is compatible with the provisions of this Treaty. Where the opinion of the Court of Justice is adverse, the agreement may enter into force only in accordance with Article N of the Treaty on European Union.

7. Agreements concluded under the conditions set out in this Article shall be binding on the institutions of the Community and on Member States.

(81) The following Article shall be inserted:

Article 228a

Where it is provided, in a common position or in a joint action adopted according to the provisions of the Treaty on European Union relating to the common foreign and security policy, for an action by the Community to interrupt or to reduce, in part or completely, economic relations with one or more third countries, the Council shall take the necessary urgent measures. The Council shall act by a qualified majority on a proposal from the Commission.

. . .

(84) Article 228 shall be replaced by the following:

Article 238

The Community may conclude with one or more States or international organizations agreements establishing an association involving reciprocal rights and obligations, common action and special procedures.

The Lisbon Report

European foreign ministers were well aware that procedure by itself was not enough to generate a common policy. Accordingly after the TEU had been agreed at Maastricht they moved on to the question of how to define Europe's common interests, and the areas of priority for the CFSP. This led, at the Lisbon European Council of June 1992, to the acceptance of a report which identified the areas in which Joint Actions might be formulated and the CFSP developed. It should be noted that this took place in the hiatus before the TEU was actually ratified. It was also somewhat ironic that immediately after the summit and its emphasis on coordination, French President Mitterand flew directly and unannounced to Sarajevo in a national demonstration of solidarity with Bosnia, a public relations manoeuvre which did not go down well with his EC colleagues.

The list itself arose out of an earlier draft known as the 'Asolo list' (after the place where it had been conceived during the Italian Presidency in October 1990). This in turn had gone through various versions – and much debate – before its eventual formalization at Lisbon. It is in many respects a rather academic, even theoretical paper by the standards of EPC/CFSP documents, and contains several careful reminders about its provisional status. It identifies the CFSP as the long-looked-for *saut qualitatif* in European foreign policy, and outlines the criteria to be used in identifying where the EU could act usefully in international politics. To this end, democracy, human rights and conflict prevention are given prominence, although they had in any case been the semi-articulated values behind EPC's 'civilian power' diplomacy in the 1970s and 1980s. Encouraging regional cooperation elsewhere and contributing to international coordination on emergencies were more obviously new features of the list.

The list specified the EU's regional priorities, thereby implicitly recognizing that global power was beyond its reach (as Henry Kissinger had pointed out in 1973, to European consternation). The areas named are Central and Eastern Europe, the Mediterranean and the Middle East. Still, these three contained more than enough potential quagmires for the EU to get bogged down in, and the report could not in any case resist extra references to North–South relations, and to the special relationships with the United States, Canada and Japan, to avoid offence and misunderstanding. Thus the list was a paradigm of the diplomatic and political overload to which the CFSP was soon to be subjected. The ambition is particularly evident in Section IV, which deals with security questions. Freed from the inhibition of not being able to refer to defence matters, this lists not only the CSCE which EPC had always dealt with, but also disarmament and arms control, nuclear non-proliferation, and economic aspects such as technology transfer and arms exports. These were issues which inevitably would test the European capacity for collective meaningful action to the full.

Document 2/21   Report to the European Council on the Likely Development of the Common Foreign and Security Policy (CFSP) with a View to Identifying Areas Open to Joint Action *vis-à-vis* Particular Countries or Groups of Countries, Lisbon, 26–27 June 1992

I—Introduction: the likely development of CFSP

The Treaty establishing the European Union, which should come into force on 1 January 1993, will mark the creation of the common foreign and security policy.

The CFSP should be seen as the successor to the activities hitherto pursued by Member States in the framework of European political cooperation (EPC) under the Single European Act. With specific aims and means, the CFSP represents a *saut qualitatif* in the sense that it integrates the *acquis* of EPC and gives it greater potential principally by means of joint action, an additional instrument which implies a strict discipline among Member States and enables the Union to make full use of the means at its disposal.

With the new phase now beginning, the CFSP should contribute to ensuring that the Union's external action is less reactive to events in the outside world, and more active in the pursuit of the interests of the Union and in the creation of a more favourable international environment. This will enable the European Union to have an improved capacity to tackle problems at their roots in order to anticipate the outbreak of crises. Furthermore, the Union will be able to make clearer to third countries its own aims and interests, and to match more closely those parties' expectations of the Union.

In order to contribute to the strengthening of the Union's external activities as a whole, it will be up to the Council and to the Commission to ensure consistency between the CFSP, the Community external action and the cooperation in the fields of justice and home affairs.

The legal provisions on CFSP are to be found in Title V of the Maastricht Treaty where it is stated that the Union shall gradually implement 'joint action in the areas in which the Member States have important interests in common' (Article J.1.3).

It was specifically with a view to identifying the areas open to joint action that the Maastricht European Council issued a statement in which the Council was invited:

'to prepare a report to the European Council in Lisbon on the likely development of the CFSP with a view to identifying areas open to joint actions *vis-à-vis* particular countries or groups of countries'.

It should be noted that the proposals herein constitute only a starting point for the implementation of CFSP and more specifically for joint action. Consequently the proposals on geographical areas and horizontal domains for joint action are to be seen as a first indication and should in no way be regarded as exhaustive.

II—Framework

In accordance with the Union's Treaty, the CFSP covers all area of foreign and security policy and implies, with the aim of achieving the objectives set out in Article J.1.2:
(i)   systematic cooperation between Member States in the conduct of policy on any matter of foreign or security policy of general interest;
(ii)   the gradual implementation of joint action in the areas in which the Member States have important interests in common.

Joint action must be seen as a means for the definition and the implementation by the Union of a policy in the framework of the CFSP in a specific issue. It must necessarily:
(i)   satisfy the objectives of the Union set out in Article B and, more particularly, in Article J.1.2;
(ii)   take into account the Union's *acquis*;
(iii) remain consistent with other actions and positions adopted by the Union.

For each area, the Union should define specific objectives in order to select the issues in which joint action may be envisaged. These specific objectives might be *inter alia*:
(i)   strengthening democratic principles and institutions, and respect for human and minority rights;

(ii) promoting regional political stability and contributing to the creation of political and/or economic frameworks that encourage regional cooperation or moves towards regional or subregional integration;
(iii) contributing to the prevention and settlement of conflicts;
(iv) contributing to a more effective international coordination in dealing with emergency situations;
(v) strengthening existing cooperation in issues of international interest such as the fight against arms proliferation, terrorism and the traffic in illicit drugs;
(vi) promoting and supporting good government.

The existence of important interests in common constitute the basic criterion for adopting joint action (Article J.3). According to the principle of solidarity among Member States, this does not rule out the possibility of a given interest being of more importance to some Member States than to others.

It is possible at this stage to list certain factors determining important common interests. Account should be taken of these and other factors in defining the issues and areas for joint action:
(i)   the geographical proximity of a given region or country;
(ii) an important interest in the political and economic stability of a region or country;
(iii) the existence of threats to the security interests of the Union.

Bearing in mind that joint action should be gradually implemented, a limited number of geographical areas has been identified. For each area, a number of horizontal issues in respect of which joint action could be undertaken in the short term were selected. These areas are: Central and Eastern Europe, in particular the Commonwealth of Independent States and the Balkans, the Mediterranean, in particular the Maghreb, and the Middle East.

In addition, certain domains within the security dimension have already been identified by the European Council.

As pointed out in the introduction, the selection of areas for implementation of joint action is merely illustrative.

The European Council will review the international situation in order to establish general guidelines for joint action in the light of change in the areas already identified and in any others where appropriate.

With regard to the special importance of the North-South relations, the Union may want to develop gradually in a consistent and coordinated manner its external activities *vis-à-vis* the countries of Africa, Latin America and the Caribbean and Asia in all aspects of its relations (e.g. foreign, security, economic and development policies) in order to contribute to the development of those regions within a context of full respect for human rights, and to the strengthening of their relations with the Union. Particular account will be taken of relations, including contractual relations, which have been established with regional and other groupings.

The Union wishes also to draw attention to the high priority it continues to attribute to the relations with the United States of America, Canada and Japan, with whom the Union has adopted separate joint declarations which constitute a basis for a fruitful partnership. All sides remain aware that cooperation in a close partnership remains indispensable.

In accordance with the provisions of Title V, the Member States of the Union will coordinate their action in international organizations of which they are members and at international conferences at which they participate both in pursuing common positions and following up joint actions.

III—*Joint action* vis-à-vis *particular countries and groups of countries*

The following paragraphs identify, in accordance with the European Council's mandate areas in which joint action *vis-à-vis* selected individual countries or groups of countries would appear to be, in a first phase, particularly beneficial for the attainment of the objectives of the Union.

A—Central and Eastern Europe

The Community and its Member States have followed closely the economic and political changes in the region. They seek to respond to challenges by mobilizing the resources at their disposal to support the transformation taking place in those countries, in particular the establishment of the rule of law and the process of economic reform.

The Union will:
(i)   promote political stability and contribute to the creation of political and/or economic frameworks that encourage regional cooperation or moves towards regional or sub-regional integration:
(ii) encourage full implementation of the CSCE commitments in the framework of the CSCE itself and elsewhere, including in particular the provisions relating to:
(a)   the human dimension, notably respect for democracy, the rule of law, human rights including those of persons belonging to national minorities;
(b)   the prevention and settlement of conflicts, whilst fully respecting the inviolability of frontiers and other CSCE principles.

1. *Russia and the former Soviet Republics*

Hitherto, the action of the Community and its Member States in the political field has been dominated by the need to assure the area's stability, with particular attention to the preservation of European security. With a view to strengthening the Union's capacity for influence *vis-à-vis* this group of countries, joint action might be envisaged in the following areas:
(i)   support for the setting-up of a framework of harmonious relations between the European Union and the new States, taking into account the different interests and historical experiences of the States concerned;
(ii) reinforcing existing patterns of cooperation and trade between the new States themselves:
(iii) encouraging full compliance with all the treaties on disarmament and arms control to which they are parties, including those on non-proliferation;
(iv) opening joint facilities and missions, each case being treated on its merits.

2. *Other countries in Central and Eastern Europe including the Balkans*

These countries are engaged in the road to democracy and in the process of setting up new political and economic structures. It would be convenient to reinforce their links with the European Union and other organizations.

Progress has already been made by some of these countries in the process of democratization and integration in European institutions. Taking it into account, joint action might be envisaged in establishing the political frameworks to foster these countries' relations with each other and with the Union and the reinforcement of their ties with European organizations and structures.

3. *Former Yugoslavia*

For the present the essential aim is to promote peace among the peoples and countries of the area and to contribute to safeguarding European security.

The following issues could fall within the framework of joint action:
(i)   the Union efforts to find a peaceful and lasting solution to the Yugoslav crisis including the Peace Conference and the continuation of the various aspects of the monitoring mission;
(ii) the monitoring of a possible future solution and the promotion of cooperation between the Republics;
(iii) the promotion of cooperation in political and security issues between the Republics and the Union;
(iv) the contribution to the strengthening of democracy and the rule of law, human and minority rights, by means of legal and technical cooperation.

B—Maghreb and Middle East

The southern and eastern shores of the Mediterranean as well as the Middle East are geographical areas in relation to which the Union has strong interests both in terms of security and social stability.

The Union has therefore an interest in establishing with the countries of the area a relationship of good neighbourliness. The goal should be to avoid a deepening of the North–South gap in the region by favouring economic development and promoting full respect for human rights and fundamental freedoms and the development and consolidation of democracy and the rule of law.

1. *Maghreb*

The Maghreb is the Union's southern frontier. Its stability is of important common interest to the Union. Population growth, recurrent social crises, large-scale migration, and the growth of religious fundamentalism and integralism are problems which threaten that stability.

Without prejudice to the necessary differences in approach concerning the region's various countries, attention might be given in priority to the following:
(i)   promoting a constructive dialogue, aimed at creating an area of peace, security and prosperity, in which respect of the fundamental principles of international law is assured;

(ii) establishing a framework of cooperation in all fields, which should gradually lead to an upgraded partnership between the Union and its Member States and the Maghreb countries;

(iii) strengthening of existing cooperation measures on the foreign policy aspects of the fight against terrorism and illicit traffic in drugs;

(iv) ensuring full compliance by the countries of the region with the relevant treaties and agreements on disarmament and arms control, including those on non-proliferation;

(v) supporting the current moves towards regional integration.

2. *Middle East*

The Middle East has been one of the constant preoccupations of the Community and its Member States. The instability which has been a permanent feature of this region affects international security and the interests of the Union, the most important of which are to ensure the stability of the area and a relationship of cooperation and dialogue.

Within the framework of the objectives set by the Union, the following domains are potentially open to joint action:

(i)   development of systematic action to support the process of negotiations launched by the Middle East Conference in Madrid on the basis of the relevant resolutions of the United Nations Security Council which should lead to a just and comprehensive solution to the Arab-Israeli conflict and the Palestinian question:

(ii) ensure the Union's active involvement in the peace process;

(iii) making efforts to persuade Israel to change its policy regarding settlements in the Occupied Territories and to persuade Arab countries to renounce their trade boycott;

(iv) support moves towards regional integration;

(v) ensure the full compliance by the countries of the region with the relevant treaties and agreements on disarmament and arms control, including those on non-proliferation, and with the relevant resolutions of the United Nations Security Council;

(vi) the foreign policy aspects of the fight against terrorism and the illicit traffic in drugs.

IV—Domains within the security dimension

The Heads of State or Government at the Maastricht European Council adopted provisions for the establishment, the definition and the implementation of a common foreign and security policy. This policy shall include all questions related to the security of the Union, including the eventual framing of a common defence policy, which might in time lead to a common defence.

In this context, the European Council indicated the domains within the security dimension which may be, as from the entry into force of the Treaty, the object of joint actions, namely:

(i)   the CSCE process;

(ii) the policy of disarmament and arms control in Europe, including confidence-building measures;

(iii) nuclear non-proliferation issues;

(iv) the economic aspects of security, in particular control of the transfer of military technology to third countries and control of arms exports.

In accordance with Article J.4, the Union requests the WEU, which is an integral part of the development of the European Union, to elaborate and implement decisions and actions of the Union which have defence implications. In this context, Member States which are also members of the WEU recall the Declaration adopted at Maastricht in December 1991 and which was noted by the Intergovernmental Conference. The issues having defence implications dealt with under Article J.4. shall not be subject to the procedure of joint action.

The policy of the Union in accordance with Article J.4 shall not prejudice the specific character of the security and defence policies of certain Member States and shall respect the obligations of certain Member States under the North Atlantic Treaty and be compatible with the common security and defence policy established within that framework.

The European Council has also invited the Ministers for Foreign Affairs to begin preparatory work with a view to defining the necessary basic elements for a policy of the Union by the date of entry into force of the Treaty. This preparatory work should in particular consider the elements which will be necessary to the Union in the framework of the CFSP. To this effect an *ad hoc* working group on security will be created under the Political Committee.

The Treaty of Amsterdam

The TEU was so clearly an unsatisfactory compromise, with a good deal of unfinished business, that it was inevitable that it would contain a commitment to yet another IGC. The Maastricht Treaty's ratchet mechanism was Title V, Article N, which stated that 'A conference of representatives of the governments of the Member States shall be convened in 1996 to examine those provisions of this treaty for which revision is provided'. One of these provisions was the CFSP and it was given extra force by the knowledge that the Brussels Treaty, on which the WEU was based, was coming up for review in 1998.

The issues at stake in the CFSP were the WEU, and whether its trajectory towards merger with the EU could be maintained, an expanded use of majority voting, financing (where the TEU's open-ended Article J.11 had been a recipe for disaster) and the general and perennial question of how to improve the chances of speaking with one voice, which even during the discussions on Maastricht were being damaged by events in the Gulf and the Balkans.

This new IGC, the third attempt to revise the treaties in ten years, began in Turin on 29 March 1996 after a 'Reflection Group' had prepared the ground by reporting to the Madrid European Council three months earlier. It ended at the Amsterdam Council of 16–17 June 1997, and entered into force on 1 May 1999.

The IGC took place in a very different atmosphere from that of its predecessors in 1991. There was a distinct lack of enthusiasm in some quarters for another round of change so soon after the TEU; where the public was not sceptical, it was indifferent. Centre stage was in any case being occupied by EMU and the issue of enlargement and there was little space for a serious debate on treaty reform – although it was also true that if EMU and further enlargement were to occur and to be successful they would certainly require further institutional change sooner rather than later.

By 1996 expectations of the CFSP had clearly been lowered, by the general factors referred to above but also by the CFSP's apparent failures in its first three years of life. The track record, with the difficult problems of Iraq, Bosnia, Algeria and the Middle East, seemed to many disastrous, although reactions then differed as to whether success was inherently impossible or dependent on extending integration to the sphere of foreign policy. Those involved in the Reflection Group and the IGC probably encouraged the view that little of significance would come forth on the CFSP, forearmed by the experience of 1991–3. It is usually better to exceed expectations than to disappoint them.

And so it has proved with the Treaty of Amsterdam. Although at first sight its foreign policy provisions did not seem to amount to very much, they did in fact go beyond what conventional wisdom had predicted – namely little more than a new policy planning unit. Title V of the TEU remains but many of the 'J' articles it contains have been amended. The most important changes include

- an enlarged space for majority voting, once a 'common strategy' has been agreed and/or joint actions and common positions agreed (J.13); the onus is now on the states to stop QMV on routine foreign policy matters – a big change from the immovable double-lock imposed by Maastricht in its own J.3
- the possibility of 'constructive abstention', to allow one or more Member States to opt out of a common position without preventing the whole policy going ahead (J.13)
- the incorporation of the 'Petersberg tasks' (qv, Section 3) into the Treaty and thereby further specifying the link between the WEU and CFSP (J.7.2)
- the Secretary-General of the Council adds to his responsibilities the new function of 'High Representative' for the CFSP, with the aim of working towards a new working troika, consisting of the Presidency foreign minister, the High Representative, and a senior representative of the Commission (J.8)
- a Policy Planning and Early Warning Unit is set up under the High Representative, with personnel drawn from EU institutions, the Member States and the WEU
- the financing of CFSP is clarified, with the EC budget becoming the default setting, apart from military and defence operations and where the Council decides unanimously otherwise; as with QMV, the onus is reversed, to the disadvantage of intergovernmentalism
- the Presidency is given the power to negotiate international agreements in pursuit of the CFSP, 'assisted by the Commission as appropriate' (J.14); the agreements will be concluded unanimously by the Council and the EU still does not have 'legal personality'.

In the grey area at the margin of foreign policy, it is also important to note that the Treaty of Amsterdam incorporates the *acquis* of the Schengen agreements of 1985 and 1990 into the EU, putting asylum, immigration and border control measures under Pillar I, and police and judicial cooperation on criminal matters under Pillar III. Although there is still an element of variable geometry in that the UK, Ireland and Denmark are excluded by their own wish, this change should make it easier for the EU to discuss 'the new security agenda' without being quite so hampered by legal or bureaucratic pedantries.*

The Treaty of Amsterdam therefore marked a rather more substantial set of provisions on foreign policy in the widest sense than most observers predicted, and this may have been the result of a greater degree of canniness on the part of the decision-makers most anxious for change than we have been used to. The ratification of the Treaty, however, seemed interminably delayed (although in fact it took little longer than Maastricht), thus diluting its contemporary impact even further. Still, the Vienna Council at the end of the Austrian Presidency in the second half of 1998 (document 2/23) gave an important boost to the process of implementing Amsterdam's CFSP provisions, in three respects. It identified the first common strategies, decided that Mr/Ms CFSP had to be a high-profile politician, not a diplomat, and welcomed the unexpected Franco-British Declaration at St Malo the week before (document 3/15).

In the event the Treaty of Amsterdam entered into force on 1 May 1999. The Cologne Council of 3–4 June then immediately returned to the subject of CFSP with new proposals (document 2/24). As we shall see in Section 3 these focused mainly on the security side of the equation, where the impasse had been unblocked by St Malo, and where the German Presidency had been working assiduously, insofar as the Kosovo crisis allowed. Providing the timetable to absorb the WEU into the EU was an important decision, both practically and symbolically. Cologne thus represented yet another general attempt to relaunch the CFSP, this time with the rationale of giving it the 'necessary means and capabilities to assume its responsibilities'. In terms of implementing Amsterdam the Council finally decided, after two years of indecision, the identity of Mr CFSP. The job was given to the (retiring) Secretary-General of NATO, Javier Solana, which can be interpreted as a sign either of its inherent importance, or of the failure of the CFSP to emerge from under the shadow of the Atlantic Alliance. The Helsinki Council of December 1999 (document 3/19 in Appendix) then completed this latest phase of common foreign policy building.

One thing, however, is certain. Whatever ups and downs lie ahead for the institutional development of the CFSP, the story of Europe's attempt to construct a common foreign policy is far from being concluded. There are more documents, more treaties – and more arguments – to come.

Document 2/22   Treaty of Amsterdam, Brussels, 19 June 1997

CHAPTER 12. THE COMMON FOREIGN AND SECURITY POLICY

Amend Article C, second subparagraph, of the TEU

The Union shall in particular ensure the consistency of its external activities as a whole in the context of its external relations, security, economic and development

---

* The relevant sections of the Treaty of Amsterdam – Titles IIIa and VI – are not included here for reasons of space. A useful, brief analysis of them may be found in Gavin Barrett, 'Justice and home affairs cooperation: an overview', in Ben Tonra (ed.) *Amsterdam: What the Treaty Means*, Dublin, Institute of European Affairs, 1997, pp. 119–31.

policies. The Council and the Commission shall be responsible for ensuring such consistency and shall cooperate to this end. They shall ensure the implementation of these policies, each in accordance with its respective powers.

TITLE V

Provisions on a common foreign and security policy

Article J.1

1. The Union shall define and implement a common foreign and security policy covering all areas of foreign and security policy, the objectives of which shall be:
    –   to safeguard the common values, fundamental interests, independence and integrity of the Union in conformity with the principles of the United Nations Charter;
    –   to strengthen the security of the Union in all ways;
    –   to preserve peace and strengthen international security, in accordance with the principles of the United Nations Charter, as well as the principles of the Helsinki Final Act and the objectives of the Paris Charter, including those on external borders;
    –   to promote international cooperation;
    –   to develop and consolidate democracy and the rule of law, and respect for human rights and fundamental freedoms.

2. The Member States shall support the Union's external and security policy actively and unreservedly in a spirit of loyalty and mutual solidarity.

    The Member States shall work together to enhance and develop their mutual political solidarity. They shall refrain from any action which is contrary to the interests of the Union or likely to impair its effectiveness as a cohesive force in international relations.

    The Council shall ensure that these principles are complied with.

Article J.2 (former J.1(3))

The Union shall pursue the objectives set out in Article J.1 by:
–   defining the principles of and general guidelines for the common foreign and security policy;
–   deciding on common strategies;
–   adopting joint actions;
–   adopting common positions;
–   and strengthening systematic cooperation between Member States in the conduct of policy.

Article J.3 (former J.8(1) and (2), first subparagraph)

1. The European Council shall define the principles of and general guidelines for the common foreign and security policy, including for matters with defence implications.

2. The European Council shall decide on common strategies to be implemented by the Union in areas where the Member States have important interests in common.

    Common strategies shall set out their objectives, duration and the means to be made available by the Union and the Member States.

3. The Council shall take the decisions necessary for defining and implementing the common foreign and security policy on the basis of the general guidelines defined by the European Council.

    The Council shall recommend common strategies to the European Council and shall implement them, in particular by adopting joint actions and common positions.

    The Council shall ensure the unity, consistency and effectiveness of action by the Union.

Article J.4 (former J.3)

1. The Council shall adopt joint actions. Joint actions shall address specific situations where operational action by the Union is deemed to be required. They shall lay down their objectives, scope, the means to be made available to the Union, if necessary their duration, and the conditions for their implementation.

2. If there is a change in circumstances having a substantial effect on a question subject to joint action, the Council shall review the principles and objectives of that action and take the necessary decisions. As long as the Council has not acted, the joint action shall stand.

3. Joint actions shall commit the Member States in the positions they adopt and in the conduct of their activity.

4. The Council may request the Commission to submit to it any appropriate proposals relating to the common foreign and security policy to ensure the implementation of a joint action.

5. Whenever there is any plan to adopt a national position or take national action pursuant to a joint action, information shall be provided in time to allow, if necessary, for prior consultations within the Council. The obligation to provide prior information shall not apply to measures which are merely a national transposition of Council decisions.

6. In cases of imperative need arising from changes in the situation and failing a Council decision, Member States may take the necessary measures as a matter

of urgency having regard to the general objectives of the joint action. The Member State concerned shall inform the Council immediately of any such measures.

7. Should there be any major difficulties in implementing a joint action, a Member State shall refer them to the Council which shall discuss them and seek appropriate solutions. Such solutions shall not run counter to the objectives of the joint action or impair its effectiveness.

Article J.5 (former J.2(2))

The Council shall adopt common positions. Common positions shall define the approach of the Union to a particular matter of geographical or thematic nature. Member States shall ensure that their national policies conform to the common positions.

Article J.6 (former J.2(1))

Member States shall inform and consult one another within the Council on any matter of foreign and security policy of general interest in order to ensure that the Union's influence is exerted as effectively as possible by means of concerted and convergent action.

Article J.7 (former J.4)

1. The common foreign and security policy shall include all questions relating to the security of the Union, including the progressive framing of a common defence policy, in accordance with the second subparagraph, which might lead to a common defence, should the European Council so decide. It shall in that case recommend to the Member States the adoption of such a decision in accordance with their respective constitutional requirements.

    The Western European Union (WEU) is an integral part of the development of the Union providing the Union with access to an operational capability notably in the context of paragraph 2. It supports the Union in framing the defence aspects of the common foreign and security policy as set out in this Article. The Union shall accordingly foster closer institutional relations with the WEU with a view to the possibility of the integration of the WEU into the Union, should the European Council so decide. It shall in that case recommend to the Member States the adoption of such a decision in accordance with their respective constitutional requirements.

    The policy of the Union in accordance with this Article shall not prejudice the specific character of the security and defence policy of certain Member States and shall respect the obligations of certain Member States, which see their common defence realized in NATO, under the North Atlantic Treaty and be compatible with the common security and defence policy established within that framework.

The progressive framing of a common defence policy will be supported, as Member States consider appropriate, by cooperation between them in the field of armaments.

2.   Questions referred to in this Article shall include humanitarian and rescue tasks, peacekeeping tasks and tasks of combat forces in crisis management, including peacemaking.

3.   The Union will avail itself of the WEU to elaborate and implement decisions and actions of the Union which have defence implications.

The competence of the European Council to establish guidelines in accordance with Article J.3 shall also obtain in respect of the WEU for those matters for which the Union avails itself of the WEU.

When the Union avails itself of the WEU to elaborate and implement decisions of the Union on the tasks referred to in paragraph 2 all Member States of the Union shall be entitled to participate fully in the tasks in question. The Council, in agreement with the institutions of the WEU, shall adopt the necessary practical arrangements to allow all Member States contributing to the tasks in question to participate fully and on an equal footing in planning and decision-taking in the WEU.

Decisions having defence implications dealt with under this paragraph shall be taken without prejudice to the policies and obligations referred to in paragraph 1, third subparagraph.

4.   The provisions of this Article shall not prevent the development of closer co-operation between two or more Member States on a bilateral level, in the framework of the WEU and the Atlantic Alliance, provided such cooperation does not run counter to or impede that provided for in this Title.

5.   With a view to furthering the objectives of this Article, the provisions of this Article will be reviewed in accordance with Article N.

Protocol on Article J.7 of the Treaty on European Union

THE HIGH CONTRACTING PARTIES

BEARING IN MIND the need to implement fully the provisions of Article J.7(1), second subparagraph, and (3) of the TEU

BEARING IN MIND that the policy of the Union in accordance with Article J.7 shall not prejudice the specific character of the security and defence policy of certain Member States and shall respect the obligations of certain Member States, which see their common defence realized in NATO, under the North Atlantic Treaty, and be compatible with the common security and defence policy established within that framework

HAVE AGREED upon the following provisions, which shall be annexed to the Treaty on European Union

The European Union shall draw up, together with the WEU, arrangements for enhanced cooperation between them, within a year from the entry into force of this Protocol.

> ## Declaration on enhanced cooperation between the EU and the WEU

With a view to enhanced cooperation between the European Union and the Western European Union, the Conference invites the Council to seek the early adoption of appropriate arrangements for the security clearance of the personnel of the General Secretariat of the Council.

Article J.8 (former J.5)

1. The Presidency shall represent the Union in matters coming within the common foreign and security policy.

2. The Presidency shall be responsible for the implementation of common measures; in that capacity it shall in principle express the position of the Union in international organizations and international conferences.

3. The Presidency shall be assisted by the Secretary-General of the Council who shall exercise the function of High Representative for the common foreign and security policy. The Secretary-General, High Representative for the common foreign and security policy, shall be seconded by the deputy Secretary-General of the Council referred to in Article 151 of the TEC who shall be responsible for the running of the General-Secretariat[1].

4. The Commission shall be fully associated in the tasks referred to in paragraphs 1 and 2. The Presidency shall be assisted in those tasks if need be by the next Member State to hold the Presidency.

5. The Council may, whenever it deems it necessary, appoint a special representative with a mandate in relation to particular policy issues.

Article J.9 (former J.2(3) and J.5(4))

1. Member States shall coordinate their action in international organizations and at international conferences. They shall uphold the common positions in such fora.

   In international organizations and at international conferences where not all the Member States participate, those which do take part shall uphold the common positions.

2. Without prejudice to the previous paragraph and Article J.4(3), Member States represented in international organizations or international conferences where not all the Member States participate shall keep the latter informed of any matter of common interest.

[1]   Article 151 TEC is amended accordingly

Member States which are also members of the United Nations Security Council will concert and keep the other Member States fully informed. Member States which are permanent members of the Security Council will, in the execution of their functions, ensure the defence of the positions and the interests of the Union, without prejudice to their responsibilities under the provisions of the United Nations Charter.

Article J.10 (former J.6)

The diplomatic and consular missions of the Member States and the Commission Delegations in third countries and international conferences, and their representations to international organizations, shall cooperate in ensuring that the common positions and common measures adopted by the Council are complied with and implemented.

They shall step up cooperation by exchanging information, carrying out joint assessments and contributing to the implementation of the provisions referred to in Article 8c of the Treaty establishing the European Community.

Article J.11 (former J.7)

The Presidency shall consult the European Parliament on the main aspects and the basic choices of the common foreign and security policy and shall ensure that the views of the European Parliament are duly taken into consideration. The European Parliament shall be kept regularly informed by the Presidency and the Commission of the development of the Union's foreign and security policy.

The European Parliament may ask questions of the Council or make recommendations to it. It shall hold an annual debate on progress in implementing the common foreign and security policy.

Article J.12 (former J.8(3) and (4))

1. Any Member State or the Commission may refer to the Council any question relating to the common foreign and security policy and may submit proposals to the Council.

2. In cases requiring a rapid decision, the Presidency, of its own motion, or at the request of the Commission or a Member State, shall convene an extraordinary Council meeting within forty-eight hours or, in an emergency, within a shorter period.

Article J.13

1. Decisions under this Title shall be taken by the Council acting unanimously. Abstentions by members present in person or represented shall not prevent the adoption of such decisions.

When abstaining in a vote, any member of the Council may qualify its abstention by making a formal declaration under the present subparagraph. In that case, it shall not be obliged to apply the decision, but shall accept that the decision commits the Union. In a spirit of mutual solidarity, the Member State concerned shall refrain from any action likely to conflict with or impede Union action based on that decision and the other Member States shall respect its position. If the members of the Council qualifying their abstention in this way represent more than one third of the votes weighted in accordance with Article 148(2) of the TEC, the decision shall not be adopted.

2. By derogation from the provisions of paragraph 1, the Council shall act by qualified majority:

– when adopting joint actions, common positions or taking any other decision on the basis of a common strategy;

– when adopting any decision implementing a joint action or a common position.

If a member of the Council declares that, for important and stated reasons of national policy, it intends to oppose the adoption of a decision to be taken by qualified majority, a vote shall not be taken. The Council may, acting by a qualified majority, request that the matter be referred to the European Council for decision by unanimity.

The votes of the members of the Council shall be weighted in accordance with article 148(2) of the Treaty establishing the European Community. For their adoption, decisions shall require at least 62 votes in favour, cast by at least 10 members.

This paragraph shall not apply to decisions having military or defence implications.

3. For procedural questions, the Council shall act by a majority of its members.

New Article J.14

When it is necessary to conclude an agreement with one or more States or international organizations in implementation of this Title, the Council, acting unanimously, may authorize the Presidency, assisted by the Commission as appropriate, to open negotiations to that effect. Such agreements shall be concluded by the Council acting unanimously on a recommendation from the Presidency. No agreement shall be binding on a Member State whose representative in the Council states that it has to comply with the requirements of its own constitutional procedure; the other members of the Council may agree that the agreement shall apply provisionally to them.

The provisions of this Article shall also apply to matters falling under Title VI.*

---

* That is, 'Provisions on police and judicial cooperation in criminal matters' – the 'K' articles.

> ## Declaration to the Final Act relating to Articles J.14 and K.10

The provisions of Articles J.14 and K.10 and any agreements resulting from them shall not imply any transfer of competence from the Member States to the Union.

Article J.15 (former J.8(5))

Without prejudice to Article 151 of the Treaty establishing the European Community, a Political Committee shall monitor the international situation in the areas covered by common foreign and security policy and contribute to the definition of policies by delivering opinions to the Council at the request of the Council or on its own initiative. It shall also monitor the implementation of agreed policies, without prejudice to the responsibility of the Presidency and the Commission.

> ## Declaration to the Final Act and Article J.15

The Conference agrees that Member States shall ensure that the Political Committee referred to in Article J.15 is able to meet at any time, in the event of international crises or other urgent matters, at very short notice at Political Director or deputy level.

Article J.16

The Secretary-General of the Council, High Representative for the common foreign and security policy, shall assist the Council in matters coming within the scope of the common foreign and security policy, in particular through contributing to the formulation, preparation and implementation of policy decisions, and, when appropriate and acting on behalf of the Council at the request of the Presidency, through conducting political dialogue with third parties.

Article J.17 (former J.9)

The Commission shall be fully associated with the work carried out in the common foreign and security policy field.

Article J.18 (former J.11)

1. The provisions referred to in Articles 137, 138, 139 to 142, 146, 147, 150 to 153, 157 to 163, 191a and 217 of the Treaty establishing the European Community shall apply to the provisions relating to the areas referred to in this Title.

2. Administrative expenditure which the provisions relating to the areas referred to in this Title entail for the institutions shall be charged to the budget of the European Communities.

3. Operational expenditure to which the implementation of those provisions give rise shall also be charged to the budget of the European Communities, except for such expenditure arising from operations having military or defence implications, and cases where the Council acting unanimously decides otherwise.

    In cases where expenditure is not charged to the budget of the European Communities it shall be charged to the Member States in accordance with the GNP scale, unless the Council acting unanimously decides otherwise. As for expenditure arising from operations having military or defence implications, Member States which have made a formal declaration under Article J.13(1), second subparagraph, shall not be obliged to contribute to the financing thereof.

4. The budgetary procedure laid down in the Treaty establishing the European Community shall apply to the expenditure charged to the budget of the European Communities.

Inter Institutional Agreement between the European Parliament,
the Council and the European Commission on provisions regarding financing of
the Common Foreign and Security Policy

General Provisions

A. CFSP operational expenditure shall be charged to the budget of the European Communities, unless the Council decides otherwise, in accordance with Article J.17 of the treaty.

B. CFSP expenditure shall be treated as expenditure not necessarily resulting from the Treaty. However, the following specific modalities of implementation of the expenditure in question are hereby laid down by common agreement between the European Parliament, the Council and the Commission.

Financial Arrangements

C. On the basis of the preliminary draft budget established by the Commission, the European Parliament and the Council shall annually secure agreement on the amount of the operational CFSP expenditure to be charged to the Communities' budget and on the allocation of this amount among the articles of the CFSP budget chapter (for articles: see suggestions under G).

    In the absence of agreement, it is understood that the European Parliament and the Council shall at least agree to enter in the CFSP budget the amount contained in the previous budget, unless the Commission proposes to lower that amount.

D. The total amount of operational CFSP expenditure shall be entirely entered in one (CFSP) budget chapter, under the articles of this chapter (as suggested in G). This amount shall cover the real predictable needs and a reasonable margin for unforeseen actions. No funds will be entered into a reserve. Each article shall cover common strategies or joint actions already adopted, measures which are foreseen but not yet adopted and all future – i.e. unforeseen – actions to be adopted by the Council during the financial year concerned.

E. In conformity with the Financial Regulation, the Commission, on the basis of a Council decision, will have the authority to, autonomously, make credit-transfers between articles within one budget chapter, i.e. the CFSP envelope, the flexibility deemed necessary for a speedy implementation of CFSP actions will be assured.

F. In the event of the amount of the CFSP budget during the financial year being insufficient to cover the necessary expenses, the European Parliament and the Council shall agree to find a solution as a matter of urgency, on a proposal by the Commission.

G. Within the CFSP budget chapter, the articles into which the CFSP actions are to be entered, could read along the following lines:

  – observation and organisation of elections/participation in democratic transition processes
  – EU-envoys
  – Prevention of conflicts/peace and security processes
  – Financial assistance to disarmament processes
  – Contributions to international conferences
  – Urgent actions

The European Parliament, the Council and the Commission agree that the amount for actions entered under the article mentioned in the sixth indent cannot exceed 20 per cent of the global amount of the CFSP budget chapter.

Ad hoc concertation procedure

H. An ad hoc concertation procedure shall be set up, with a view to reaching an agreement between the two arms of the budgetary authority as far as the aforementioned amount of CFSP expenditure and the distribution of this amount over the articles of CFSP budget chapter are concerned.

I. This procedure will be applied at the request of the European Parliament or the Council, notably if either of these institutions intends to depart from the preliminary draft budget of the Commission.

J. The ad hoc concertation procedure has to be concluded before the date set by the Council for establishing its draft budget.

K. Each arm of the budgetary authority shall take whatever steps are required to ensure that the results which will be secured in the ad hoc concertation procedure, are respected throughout the budgetary procedure.

Consultation and information of the European Parliament

L. On a yearly basis the Presidency of the Council shall consult the European Parliament on a document established by the Council on the main aspects and basic choices of the CFSP, including the financial implications for the Communities budget. Furthermore, the Presidency shall on a regular basis inform the European Parliament on the development and implementation of CFSP actions.

M. The Council shall, each time it adopts a decision in the field of CFSP entailing expenses, immediately and in each case communicate to the European Parliament an estimate of the costs envisaged ("fiche financière"), in particular those regarding time-frame, staff employed, use of premises and other infra-structure, transport facilities, training requirements and security arrangements.

N. The Commission shall inform the budgetary authority on the execution of CFSP actions and the financial forecasts for the remaining period of the year on a quarterly basis.

Declaration to the Final Act on the establishment of a policy planning and early warning unit

The Conference agrees that:

1. *A policy planning and early warning unit shall be established in the General Secretariat of the Council under the responsibility of its Secretary-General. Appropriate cooperation shall be established with the Commission in order to ensure full coherence with the Union's external economic and development policies.*

2. *The tasks of the unit shall include the following:*
   (a) *monitoring and analysing developments in areas relevant to the CFSP;*
   (b) *providing assessments of the Union's foreign and security policy interests and identifying areas where the CFSP could focus in future;*
   (c) *providing timely assessments and early warning of events or situations which may have significant repercussions for the Union's foreign and security policy, including potential political crises;*
   (d) *producing, at the request of either the Council or the Presidency or on its own initiative, argued policy options papers to be presented under the responsibility of the Presidency as a contribution to policy formulation in the Council, and which may contain analyses, recommendations and strategies for the CFSP.*

3. *The unit shall consist of personnel drawn from the General Secretariat, the Member States, the Commission and the WEU.*

4. *Any Member State or the Commission may make suggestions to the unit for work to be under-taken.*

5. *Member States and the Commission shall assist the policy planning process by providing, to the fullest extent possible, relevant information, including confidential information.*

CHAPTER 13. EXTERNAL ECONOMIC RELATIONS

New Article 113(5) of the TEC

5. The Council, acting unanimously on a proposal from the Commission and after consulting the European Parliament, may extend the application of paragraphs 1 to 4 to international negotiations and agreements on services and intellectual property insofar as they are not covered by these paragraphs.

Amend Article 228(2) of the TEC

2. Subject to the powers vested in the Commission in this field, the signing, which may be accompanied by a decision on provisional application before entry into force, and the conclusion of the agreements shall be decided on by the Council, acting by a qualified majority on a proposal from the Commission. The Council shall act unanimously when the agreement covers a field for which unanimity is required for the adoption of internal rules and for the agreements referred to in Article 238.

By way of derogation from the rules laid down in paragraph 3, the same procedure shall apply for a decision to suspend the application of an international agreement, and for the purpose of establishing the position to be adopted on behalf of the Community in a body set up by an agreement based on Article 238, when that body is called upon to adopt decisions having legal effects, with the exception of decisions supplementing or amending the institutional framework of the agreement.

The European Parliament shall be immediately and fully informed on any decision under this paragraph concerning the provisional application or the suspension of agreements, or the establishment of the Community position in a body set up by an agreement.

Document 2/23   Conclusions of the European Council Meeting in Vienna, 11–12 December 1998

I. Vienna strategy for Europe

. . .

2. At Cardiff, the European Council initiated a broad debate on the future development of the European Union. The Pörtschach meeting emphasised the need for a strong and effective Union. In this spirit, the Vienna European Council has identified four issues of primary concern to European citizens where rapid and effective action is necessary. It has therefore agreed on the following 'Vienna Strategy for Europe':

. . .

– Effective application of the new Common Foreign and Security Policy (CFSP) instruments following the entry into force of the Amsterdam Treaty (High Representative, CFSP Planning and Early Warning Unit, improved decision-making mechanisms); review at the Helsinki European Council.

– Preparation of the first Common Strategies on Russia, Ukraine, the Mediterranean Region and the Western Balkans; first adoption at the Cologne European Council.

– Continuation of reflection on the development of a European security and defence policy; examination at the Cologne European Council.

Building on these elements, the European Council will, at its meeting in Helsinki, adopt a 'Millennium Declaration' on the Union's priorities for future years.

VII: Preparing the implementation of the Amsterdam Treaty

. . .

73. Regarding the Common Foreign and Security Policy, the European Council agrees that the Secretary-General of the Council and High Representative for the CFSP will be appointed as soon as possible and will be a personality with a strong political profile. The European Council takes note of the work undertaken by the Council concerning the establishment of a Policy Planning and Early Warning Unit within the General Secretariat.

74. The European Council invites the Council in accordance with the recommendations in its report to prepare common strategies on Russia, Ukraine, the Mediterranean region, taking specifically into account the Barcelona Process and the Middle East Peace Process, as well as on the Western Balkans, on the understanding that the first common strategy will be on Russia. When identifying further subjects for common strategies, thematic subjects should also be considered.

75. The European Council invites the Council to bring forward, in agreement with the WEU, the completion of arrangements for enhanced cooperation under the Protocol on Article 17 of the Treaty on European Union, as amended by the Amsterdam Treaty, so that these may come into effect on the Treaty's entry into force.

76. The European Council welcomes the new impetus given to the debate on a common European policy on security and defence. The European Council considers that in order for the European Union to be in a position to play its full role on the international stage, the CFSP must be backed by credible operational capabilities. It welcomes the Franco-British declaration made on 4 December 1998 in St Malo. The reinforcement of European solidarity must take into account the various positions of European States, including the obligations of some Member States within NATO.

77. It welcomes the intention of the WEU to conduct an audit of the assets available for European operations.

78. The European Council invites the incoming Presidency to further this debate in the wake of discussions in the WEU Ministerial in Rome on 16 November and in the General Affairs Council held on 7 December. The European Council will examine this issue in Cologne on 3 and 4 June 1999.

Document 2/24   Conclusions of the European Council Meeting in Cologne, 3–4 June 1999*

I. INTRODUCTION

1. The European Council met in Cologne on 3 and 4 June 1999 to consider major issues for the future following the entry into force of the Amsterdam Treaty ...

II. STAFFING DECISIONS

4. The European Council took several major staffing decisions. Pursuant to the Amsterdam Treaty, it designated Mr. Javier Solana Madariaga for the new post of Secretary-General of the Council and High Representative for the Common Foreign and Security Police. It designated Mr. Pierre de Boissieu as Deputy Secretary-General ...

III. FURTHER DEVELOPMENT OF THE EUROPEAN UNION

...

Common European security and defence policy

55. The European Council continued its discussion on a common European policy on security and defence and issued the annexed declaration on the further development of a common European security and defence policy [*document 3/18*]. It welcomes the work of the German Presidency and endorses the Presidency report set out in Annex III as a basis for further work. The European Council invites the incoming Presidency to continue work with a view to a further report to the European Council at its meeting in Helsinki.
56. The European Council invites the Council (General Affairs) to deal thoroughly with all discussions on aspects of security, with a view to enhancing and better coordinating the Union's and Member-States' non-military crisis response tools. Deliberations might include the possibility of a stand-by capacity to pool national civil resources and expertise complementing other initiatives within the common foreign and security policy.

---

*   [See also document 3/18.]

Section 3 The revival of the WEU and the evolution of a European security identity

The reactivation of the WEU

During the early 1980s, security and defence issues were largely kept off EPC's formal agenda. Most Community Member States, however, began to perceive a need to discuss such issues in a forum external to NATO, which was dominated by the United States. From the late 1970s on, US policy had alarmed the West European states, as the Carter Administration wavered and the Reagan Administration assumed an aggressive attitude towards the 'evil empire'. Under the 1981 London Report, the political aspects of security could be discussed in EPC. The Genscher-Colombo plan of the same year would have added defence as well to EPC's remit, but this proposal failed: the UK did not want to challenge NATO's primacy, and Denmark, Greece and Ireland – all for different reasons – saw it as outside EPC's remit.

Several Member States then turned their attention to the WEU, of which Denmark, Greece and Ireland were not members. The WEU had been dormant between 1973 and 1983: after the UK joined the Community, it was no longer needed as a forum for discussions between the Six and the UK, and its core treaty functions were handled in other fora – namely NATO and the Community. Reactivating the WEU would re-establish a forum for the discussion of defence issues among the willing West European states (including, of course, France, which was not part of NATO's military command) and would, rather usefully for the UK, help counter any possible German–French defence axis.

The WEU's reactivation was heralded in the declaration of the WEU Council of foreign and defence ministers, who met together for the first time in October 1984, in Rome (document 3/1). They agreed to meet twice a year and to set up a presidency system similar to that of the Community. In addition, the ministers agreed to increase contacts between the Council and the Assembly of parliamentary representatives from the Member States. The ministers also pledged to cooperate more on armaments.

The Single European Act (document 2/15) allowed EPC to discuss the political and economic aspects of security, but also referred to the primacy of NATO and the WEU in security matters. This satisfied those states that did not want EPC to take on security responsibilities, as well as those that did not want to challenge NATO's primacy.

In October 1986, Reagan and the new Soviet leader Mikhail Gorbachev almost agreed to eliminate medium-range nuclear missiles from Europe. The NATO decision of December 1979 to deploy Cruise and Pershing missiles, in response to a Soviet buildup, had been one of the most difficult decisions made by West European governments – and it had virtually destroyed the national consensus on defence in several countries. At the Reykjavik summit, Reagan seemed willing to eliminate them, without so much as consulting his allies. Furthermore, he was pushing forward the development of a Strategic Defence Initiative ('Star Wars') which threatened to destabilise the strategic nuclear balance and decouple American and west European defence. EPC could not respond, and the WEU was not yet developed enough as a forum to present common views to the United States. This was a powerful new incentive to take it further.

In October 1987, the WEU ministers agreed on a Platform on European Security Interests (document 3/2). They stated their willingness to develop a 'more cohesive European defence identity' (paragraph 4, preamble), which would help 'strengthen the European pillar of the Alliance' (paragraph 2, section III). The WEU Member States thus declared their desire to balance the US role, and address the at times acrimonious 'burden-sharing' debate. In addition, they would concert their policies on crises outside Europe; NATO was, by contrast, limited to acting only in case of an armed attack on its members. Nevertheless, the Platform was very careful to include balancing commitments to NATO as the primary institution of allied defence.

The WEU's tasks and membership then expanded. When Spain and Portugal joined the European Community in 1986, they were invited to join the WEU and did so in 1988. The WEU's usefulness in acting out of area, and in sharing the burden with the United States, was illustrated in the summer of 1987. As a result of the Iran–Iraq war, freedom of shipping in the Persian Gulf was threatened by mines laid by both the warring parties. In August 1987, the WEU Council discussed the matter, and France, the UK, Italy, the Netherlands and Belgium decided to strengthen their military presence in the Gulf and send minesweepers. Germany replaced some of their naval units in the Atlantic and Mediterranean, and Luxembourg helped fund the operation. For the next year and a half, the WEU Member States coordinated their actions in the Gulf. The success of the co-ordination contributed to the view that the WEU could now serve as a collective military vehicle for the west European states.

Document 3/1   Declaration by the Western European Union Council of Ministers, Rome, 27 October 1984*

1. At the invitation of the Italian Government, the Foreign and Defence Ministers of the seven member States of Western European Union met in extraordinary session in Rome on 26–27 October 1984 to mark the 30th anniversary of the modified Brussels Treaty.

2. The Ministers stressed the importance of the Treaty and their attachment to its goals:

---

*   The omitted sections are II: Relations between Council and Assembly, consisting of procedural improvements, and III: Agency for Control of Armaments and the Standing Armaments Committee, of which the main interest consists in the injunction to support the Independent European Programme Group (IEPG) within the Atlantic Alliance. A decision was taken by the IEPG to transfer its functions to the WEU on 4 December 1992. The WEAG (Western European Armaments Group) was set up in WEU.

- to strengthen peace and security;
- to promote the unity and to encourage the progressive integration of Europe;
- to cooperate more closely both among member States and with other European organisations.

3. Conscious of the continuing necessity to strengthen western security and of the specifically Western European geographical, political, psychological and military dimensions, the Ministers underlined their determination to make better use of the WEU framework in order to increase cooperation between the member States in the field of security policy and to encourage consensus. In this context, they called for continued efforts to preserve peace, strengthen deterrence and defence and thus consolidate stability through dialogue and cooperation.

4. The Ministers recalled that the Atlantic Alliance, which remains the foundation of western security, had preserved peace on the Continent for 35 years. This permitted the construction of Europe. The Ministers are convinced that a better utilisation of WEU would not only contribute to the security of Western Europe but also to an improvement in the common defence of all the countries of the Atlantic Alliance and to greater solidarity among its members.

5. The Ministers emphasised the indivisibility of security within the North Atlantic Treaty area. They recalled in particular the vital and substantial contribution of all the European allies, and underlined the crucial importance of the contribution to common security of their allies who are not members of WEU. They stressed the necessity, as a complement to their joint efforts, of the closest possible concertation with them.

6. The Ministers are convinced that increased cooperation within WEU will also contribute to the maintenance of adequate military strength and political solidarity and, on that basis, to the pursuit of a more stable relationship between the countries of East and West by fostering dialogue and cooperation.

7. The Ministers called attention to the need to make the best use of existing resources through increased cooperation, and through WEU to provide a political impetus to institutions of cooperation in the field of armaments.

8. The Ministers therefore decided to hold comprehensive discussions and to seek to harmonise their views on the specific conditions of security in Europe, in particular:

- defence questions;
- arms control and disarmament;
- the effects of developments in East-West relations on the security of Europe;
- Europe's contribution to the strengthening of the Atlantic Alliance, bearing in mind the importance of transatlantic relations;
- the development of European cooperation in the field of armaments in respect of which WEU can provide a political impetus.

They may also consider the implications for Europe of crises in other regions of the world.

9.   The Ministers recalled the importance of the WEU Assembly which, as the only European parliamentary body mandated by treaty to discuss defence matters, is called upon to play a growing role.

They stressed the major contribution which the Assembly has already made to the revitalisation of WEU and called upon it to pursue its efforts to strengthen the solidarity among the member States, and to strive to consolidate the consensus among public opinion on their security and defence needs.

10. In pursuance of these goals, the Ministers have decided on a number of specific measures with regard to the better functioning of the WEU structure and organisation, which are set out in a separate document.

INSTITUTIONAL REFORM OF WEU

At their meeting in Rome on 26 and 27 October 1984 to mark the 30th anniversary of the modified Brussels Treaty of 1954, the Foreign and Defence Ministers of the signatory States decided to make fuller use of the institutions of WEU and, accordingly, to bring the existing institutions into line with the changed tasks of the Organisation.

I. Activation of the Council

The Ministers regard activation of the Council as a central element in the efforts to make greater use of Western European Union. In conformity with Article VIII of the modified Brussels Treaty, which allows the Council to decide on the organisation of its work and to consult or set up subsidiary bodies, the Ministers decided the following:

1   The Council would in future normally meet twice a year at ministerial level. One of these sessions could take place in a small group with no formal agenda. These meetings would bring together the Foreign Ministers and Defence Ministers. Separate meetings of the Foreign Ministers and/or Defence Ministers could also take place, if the member States considered it necessary, to discuss matters lying within their respective area of responsibility.

2.   The Presidency of the Council will be held by each member State for a one year term. Meetings of the Council will in principle take place in the country holding the Presidency.

3.   The work of the Permanent Council will have to be intensified in line with the increased activities of the Council of Ministers. The Permanent Council, mandated to discuss in greater detail the views expressed by the Ministers and to follow up their decisions, will, pursuant to the second paragraph of the above-mentioned Article VIII, make the necessary arrangements for this purpose, including as appropriate the setting-up of working groups.

4.   The Secretariat-General should be adapted to take account of the enhanced activities of the Council of Ministers and the Permanent Council.

5.   The Ministers have asked the Secretariat-General to submit, as soon as possible, a report on the work done by the Secretariat and to consider what measures

might be necessary to strengthen its activities. In this connection, the Ministers stated that any reorganisation in the staffing of the Secretariat-General should take account of the adjustments made elsewhere in the other WEU institutions. They stressed that any proposed adjustments should not result in an overall increase in the Organisation's establishment.

. . .

IV. Contacts with non-member States

1. The Ministers also attached great importance to liaison with those States in the Alliance which are not members of WEU.

2. Invoking the relevant provisions of the modified Brussels Treaty, and in particular Article IV, the Ministers pointed out that it was the responsibility of the Presidency of WEU to inform those countries on either a bilateral or multilateral basis.

Document 3/2   Western European Union, Platform on European Security Interests, The Hague, 27 October 1987

1. Stressing the dedication of our countries to the principles upon which our democracies are based and resolved to preserve peace in freedom, we, the Foreign and Defence Ministers of the member States of WEU, reaffirm the common destiny which binds our countries.

2. We recall our commitment to build a European union in accordance with the Single European Act, which we all signed as members of the European Community. We are convinced that the construction of an integrated Europe will remain incomplete as long as it does not include security and defence.

3. An important means to this end is the modified Brussels Treaty. This Treaty with its far-reaching obligations to collective defence, marked one of the early steps on the road to European unification. It also envisages the progressive association of other States inspired by the same ideals and animated by the like determination. We see the revitalisation of WEU as an important contribution to the broader process of European unification.

4. We intend therefore to develop a more cohesive European defence identity which will translate more effectively into practice the obligations of solidarity to which we are committed through the modified Brussels and North Atlantic Treaties.

5. We highly value the continued involvement in this endeavour of the WEU Assembly which is the only European parliamentary body mandated by treaty to discuss all aspects of security including defence.

I

Our starting point is the present conditions of European security

1. Europe remains at the centre of East–West relations and, forty years after the end of the Second World War, a divided continent. The human consequences of this division remain unacceptable, although certain concrete improvements have been made on a bilateral level and on the basis of the Helsinki Final Act. We owe it to our people to overcome this situation and to exploit in the interest of all Europeans the opportunities for further improvements which may present themselves.

2. New developments in East-West relations, particularly in arms control and disarmament, and also other developments, for example in the sphere of technology, could have far-reaching implications for European security.

3. We have not yet witnessed any lessening of the military build-up which the Soviet Union has sustained over so many years. The geostrategic situation of Western Europe makes it particularly vulnerable to the superior conventional, chemical and nuclear forces of the Warsaw Pact. This is the fundamental problem for European security. The Warsaw Pact's superior conventional forces and its capability for surprise attack and large-scale offensive action are of special concern in this context.

4. Under these conditions the security of the Western European countries can only be ensured in close association with our North American allies. The security of the Alliance is indivisible. The partnership between the two sides of the Atlantic rests on the twin foundations of shared values and interests. Just as the commitment of the North American democracies is vital to Europe's security, a free, independent and increasingly more united Western Europe is vital to the security of North America.

5. It is our conviction that the balanced policy of the Harmel Report remains valid. Political solidarity and adequate military strength within the Atlantic Alliance, arms control, disarmament and the search for genuine détente continue to be integral parts of this policy. Military security and a policy of détente are not contradictory but complementary.

II

European security should be based on the following criteria

1. It remains our primary objective to prevent any kind of war. It is our purpose to preserve our security by maintaining defence readiness and military capabilities adequate to deter aggression and intimidation without seeking military superiority.

2. In the present circumstances and as far as we can foresee, there is no alternative to the Western strategy for the prevention of war, which has ensured peace in freedom for an unprecedented period of European history. To be credible

and effective, the strategy of deterrence and defence must continue to be based on an adequate mix of appropriate nuclear and conventional forces, only the nuclear element of which can confront a potential aggressor with an unacceptable risk.

3. The substantial presence of US conventional and nuclear forces plays an irreplaceable part in the defence of Europe. They embody the American commitment to the defence of Europe and provide the indispensable linkage with the US strategic deterrent.

4. European forces play an essential role: the overall credibility of the Western strategy of deterrence and defence cannot be maintained without a major European contribution, not least because the conventional imbalance affects the security of Western Europe in a very direct way.
   The Europeans have a major responsibility both in the field of conventional and nuclear defence. In the conventional field, the forces of the WEU member States represent an essential part of those of the Alliance. As regards nuclear forces, all of which form a part of deterrence, the cooperative arrangements that certain member States maintain with the United States are necessary for the security of Europe. The independent forces of France and the United Kingdom contribute to overall deterrence and security.

5. Arms control and disarmament are an integral part of Western security policy and not an alternative to it. They should lead to a stable balance of forces at the lowest level compatible with our security. Arms control policy should, like our defence policy, take into account the specific European security interests in an evolving situation. It must be consistent with the maintenance of the strategic unity of the Alliance and should not preclude closer European defence cooperation. Arms control agreements have to be effectively verifiable and stand the test of time. East and West have a common interest in achieving this.

III

The Member States of WEU intend to assume fully their responsibilities

a. *In the field of Western defence*

1. We recall the fundamental obligation of Article V of the modified Brussels Treaty to provide all the military and other aid and assistance in our power in the event of armed attack on any one of us. This pledge, which reflects our common destiny, reinforces our commitments under the Atlantic Alliance, to which we all belong, and which we are resolved to preserve.

2. It is our conviction that a more united Europe will make a stronger contribution to the Alliance, to the benefit of Western security as a whole. This will enhance the European role in the Alliance and ensure the basis for a balanced partnership across the Atlantic. We are resolved to strengthen the European pillar of the Alliance.

3.   We are each determined to carry our share of the common defence in both the conventional and the nuclear field, in accordance with the principles of risk- and burden-sharing which are fundamental to allied cohesion.

   –   In the conventional field, all of us will continue to play our part in the ongoing efforts to improve our defences.
   –   In the nuclear field also, we shall continue to carry our share: some of us by pursuing appropriate cooperative arrangements with the US; the UK and France by continuing to maintain independent nuclear forces, the credibility of which they are determined to preserve.

4.   We remain determined to pursue European integration including security and defence and make a more effective contribution to the common defence of the West.

   To this end we shall:

   –   ensure that our determination to defend any member country at its borders is made clearly manifest by means of appropriate arrangements;
   –   improve our consultations and extend our coordination in defence and security matters and examine all practical steps to this end;
   –   make the best possible use of the existing institutional mechanisms to involve the Defence Ministers and their representatives in the work of WEU;
   –   see to it that the level of each country's contribution to the common defence adequately reflects its capabilities;
   –   aim at a more effective use of existing resources, inter alia by expanding bilateral and regional military cooperation, pursue our efforts to maintain in Europe a technologically advanced industrial base and intensify armaments cooperation;
   –   concert our policies on crises outside Europe insofar as they may affect our security interests.

5.   Emphasising the vital contribution of the non WEU members of the Alliance to the common security and defence, we will continue to keep them informed of our activities.

b.   *In the field of arms control and disarmament*

1.   We shall pursue an active arms control and disarmament policy aimed at influencing future developments in such a way as to enhance security and to foster stability and cooperation in the whole of Europe. The steadfastness and cohesion of the Alliance and close consultations among all the Allies remain essential if concrete results are to be brought about.

2.   We are committed to elaborate further our comprehensive concept of arms control and disarmament in accordance with the Alliance's declaration of 12 June 1987 and we will work within the framework of this concept as envisaged particularly in paragraphs 7 and 8 of this declaration. An agreement between the US and the Soviet Union for the global elimination of land-based INF missiles with a range between 500 km and 5500 km will constitute an important element of such an approach.

3. In pursuing such an approach we shall exploit all opportunities to make further progress towards arms reduction, compatible with our security and with our priorities, taking into account the fact that work in this area raises complex and interrelated issues. We shall evaluate them together, bearing in mind the political and military requirements of our security and progress in the different negotiations.

c. *In the field of East-West dialogue and cooperation*

1. The common responsibility of all Europeans is not only to preserve the peace but to shape it constructively. The Helsinki Final Act continues to serve as our guide to the fulfilment of the objective of gradually overcoming the division of Europe. We shall therefore continue to make full use of the CSCE process in order to promote comprehensive cooperation among all participating states.

2. The possibilities contained in the Final Act should be fully exploited. We therefore intend:

    - to seek to increase the transparency of military potentials and activities and the calculability of behaviour in accordance with the Stockholm Document of 1986 by further confidence-building measures;
    - vigorously to pursue our efforts to provide for the full respect of human rights without which no genuine peace is possible;
    - to open new mutually beneficial possibilities in the fields of economy, technology, science and the protection of the environment;
    - to achieve more opportunities for the people in the whole of Europe to move freely and to exchange opinions and information and to intensify cultural exchanges, and thus to promote concrete improvements for the benefit of all people in Europe.

It is our objective to further European integration. In this perspective we will continue our efforts towards closer security cooperation, maintaining coupling with the United States and ensuring conditions of equal security in the Alliance as a whole.

We are conscious of the common heritage of our divided continent, all the people of which have an equal right to live in peace and freedom. That is why we are determined to do all in our power to achieve our ultimate goal of a just and lasting peaceful order in Europe.

The Cold War ends

The events of 1989–91 changed the security map not only of Europe but also of the whole international system. The collapse of communism in Eastern Europe, and then of the Warsaw Pact and the Soviet Union itself, brought the Cold War to an end and seemed to initiate an era of low-cost security, in both financial and political terms. Germany was able to unify and the unified country continued virtually seamlessly as a member of both the EU and NATO. This perception lasted only as long as it took for the Yugoslav crisis to unfold in 1991. It became clear that whereas the brutalities of a divided Europe had at least been relatively stable and predictable, there might now be many states whose viability could be in question right on the frontiers of the EC. These problems could not be ignored, and both the EC and the United States would have to consider how European order might be reconstructed.

The years since 1991 have been characterized by much discussion of and some action on 'a new European security architecture'. Although it had been widely assumed that NATO too would prove to be a Cold War institution, both American and European members soon came to regard it as an indispensable form of reassurance in a fluid environment, and indeed NATO was quicker off the mark in producing the new architecture than was the EC. In 1991 the North Atlantic Cooperation Council (NACC) was set up in order to institutionalize security consultations with the successor states to the east (document 3/3). For their part, the Europeans began to talk of a European Security and Defence Identity (ESDI), which once again alarmed a United States anxious for Europeans to bear more of the burden but not to rival NATO. The Declarations attached to the Maastricht Treaty in 1992 clearly represented a compromise between those states that wanted to make the WEU into the defence arm of the new EU, and those that put NATO first (document 3/4). For the time being it made sense to see the WEU as the bridge between the two larger institutions. The WEU also attempted at this time to clarify the complex variable geometry of diverging memberships between the EU, NATO and WEU by creating the categories of Observer and Associate Member to enable those EU members like Denmark and NATO members like Turkey, which for one reason or another were not able to become full members, to be part of the 'WEU family' and participate in what was to become an extensive network of discussions. This was extended in 1992 via a 'Forum of Consultation' (document 3/6) to nine Eastern European countries. The Forum differed from NACC in that it excluded Russia and was therefore expected to be more popular with the Central and East Europeans. In practice the latter looked for as many close ties to their western protectors as possible, and in January 1994 NATO set up the Partnership for Peace (PfP) programme to make possible close consultations at the politico-military level between all the member countries of the Conference on Security and Cooperation in Europe (CSCE), including Russia (document 3/9). A few months later, in May 1994, the Forum countries were offered the status of 'Associate Partners' by the WEU (document 3/10). These partners can attend meetings of the Permanent Council (of Ambassadors), but cannot vote. They may, if the Council agrees, participate in joint 'Petersberg' operations (document 3/5) but they are not offered the WEU's security guarantee.

It was becoming ever more clear that the only way forward in Europe was that of 'mutually reinforcing institutions' (document 3/11), in which NATO, the EU, the WEU and what in 1994 was to become the Organisation of Security and Cooperation in Europe (OSCE) attempted to cooperate and to divide labour as much as possible. This kind of pragmatism was reinforced by the growing awareness of how difficult it was to resolve conflicts like that in Yugoslavia by *any* means. Peacekeeping emerged as a central concept in European security discussions, not least because the EU and WEU's growing relationship was much better suited to such an activity than to the defence and deterrence functions of NATO. At the July 1992 Helsinki Summit the CSCE decided to launch peacekeeping and other crisis management operations, calling on the other European institutions (document 3/7). A month previously the WEU had issued the Petersberg Declaration (document 3/5) which made clear a willingness to engage in humanitarian, peacekeeping and crisis-management tasks, this despite the evident operational incapacity of the WEU thus far in former Yugoslavia (see Section 4b).

In December 1992 NATO joined the bandwagon by agreeing to participate in UN operations on a case-by-case basis, thus ending its formal ban on 'out of area' engagements (document 3/8). In fact NATO had already started to cooperate with the UN and the WEU in the Balkans; it was, of course, to play a crucial role in the eventual peace-monitoring forces of I-FOR and S-FOR from late 1995 on.

Foreign and security policy questions continued to be complicated by the questions of institutional transformation, and in particular the dual enlargement of NATO and the EU. To some extent enlargement was being used as a foreign policy instrument; to some extent it was the result of an institutional logic; and to some extent it was pulled along by external demands. What was certainly true was that it was not very well coordinated, and at times caused serious transatlantic antagonism. This was particularly true of NATO enlargement, which the United States and Germany had driven along from 1993, leading NATO to make a formal commitment to enlarge at Brussels in January 1994 (document 3/9). Sympathetic to the angry Russian complaints about encirclement, many Europeans criticized and tried to stall the process, but the United States proved immovable and the argument was lost by about mid-1996. After a further round of jockeying for position over which countries would be allowed into the alliance, the North Atlantic Council in Madrid, on 8 July 1997, invited the Czech Republic, Hungary and Poland to begin accession talks with a view to entering NATO by the latter's fiftieth anniversary in 1999 (document 3/14). Russia had been brought into the process to some degree by the signing of a Founding Act on Mutual Relations, Cooperation and Security between NATO and the Russian Federation on 27 May 1997, in Paris. The EU followed on in December of the same year (document 4a/17) by deciding to open membership negotiations with the ten Central and Eastern European States and Cyprus (see Section 4b).

Faltering progress was meanwhile being made on the ESDI, hampered by a US determination to locate any such entity firmly within the confines of Atlanticism, and by the support offered to Washington by a number of the Europeans themselves. The Franco-German brigade was metamorphosed into the Eurocorps but this in turn has been folded into an increasingly tight WEU network. The enthusiasts for a federal Europe found at this time the possibility of an EU-WEU merger increasingly remote, and had to accept that Europeans did not have the political desire, the operational resources or the money to be able to support their own defence identity on a par with NATO. From this perspective the emergence of the idea of Combined Joint Task Forces (CJTFs), first seen in the NATO decision of January 1994, and ratified in the Berlin Council of June 1996 (document 3/13), had a certain inevitability about it. This is the notion of 'separable but not separate military capabilities in operations led by the WEU', that is, NATO facilities and forces being available for the WEU when it wants to act but cannot sustain action through its own resources. The United States' permission for the use of its assets would naturally have to be obtained first, thus setting strict limits on the development of an independent European security policy.

The Treaty of Amsterdam (document 2/22) in this respect merely ratified what had already been decided, with no movement towards any EU–WEU merger, but acceptance of increased institutional and functional cooperation – the European Commission had in any case been allowed to attend WEU meetings from 1994, and the WEU had outlined a detailed statement of the 'common concept' of security shared by the 27 members of its family, at Madrid in November 1995 (document 3/12). The 'Petersberg Tasks' were now recorded as part of the EU/WEU's mission, and the bringing of the Schengen accord into the Union's ambit also promises to be important for Member

States now extremely concerned about the scrutiny implications of transitional population movement in Europe.

The autumn of 1998 saw an unexpected breakthrough on security cooperation. The Blair government had evidently been engaging in quiet diplomacy with its French counterpart to some effect, for in December the 'St Malo Declaration' was released (document 3/15). To the surprise even of expert commentators it announced in effect that the WEU would after all be folded into the EU and then disappear. It had been heralded at an informal Council under the Austrian Presidency in October, at Pörtschach, and amounted to a clear change in direction on the part of the United Kingdom (but not of France, which had long been pushing in this direction). Prime Minister Blair, Foreign Secretary Cook and Defence Minister Robertson were the key players, and they seem to have concluded during 1998 not only that the UK needed to be seen in a more positive light in the EU given the distancing from the single currency (the cynical explanation of St Malo) but also that the CFSP would fall into disrepute if it were not given at least some potential military muscle. Furthermore they appear to have been confident of their ability to persuade the United States to drop anxieties about the effects on NATO, and to see the renewed possibilities of a 'second pillar' for the alliance.

In practice the language of St Malo was studied and vague, but its drift, reinforced by off-the-record briefings, was clear. It produced a flurry of work in the capitals of the major states to draw out the implications – for the EU, for NATO, for the countries of Central and Eastern Europe, and for national foreign policy. The German Presidency carried this work forward (helped by the WEU having mandated meetings of national directors for security policy to work on the details) despite the heavy load of other commitments, not least the crisis and subsequent war in Kosovo. On 25 April 1999 the Fiftieth Anniversary Summit of NATO notably endorsed the idea of European defence cooperation and stressed its compatibility with, indeed importance to, the Alliance (document 3/16). On 13 May the Labour and Liberal Democratic parties in London issued a joint paper on the future of European defence (itself a remarkable innovation). This genuflected appropriately to Atlanticism but argued that 'structural and institutional changes [in the EU] will count for little unless they are underpinned by improvements in European military capability'. It did, however, see a common European army as 'neither necessary nor desirable', a statement which only drew attention to the issues at stake and led to a short-lived furore in the British press. Two days previously the WEU Ministerial Council had issued the 'Bremen Declaration' (document 3/17), which *inter alia* further endorsed the moves afoot to provide the EU with operational capabilities to implement the Petersberg tasks and authorized the continuing process of auditing European assets in this respect (a process already begun in NATO).

The culmination of this hectic and important diplomatic activity was the Cologne European Council (document 3/18), whose major result in fact was the announcement of the end of the WEU by the start of 2001, and the arrival of a legitimate EU defence policy system. The aim is set as the launch 'of a new step in the construction of the European Union', through creating 'more effective European military capabilities', the strengthening of the industrial and technological defence base and the emergence of an effective EU-led crisis management capacity. It is envisaged that the EU will take over WEU institutions, which means a permanent political-security committee in Brussels, an EU Military Staff, the Satellite Centre and the Institute for Security Studies. Defence ministers will need to attend some meetings of the General Affairs Council. In November 1999, Javier Solana was therefore appointed WEU Secretary-General, in addition to his role as CFSP High Representative.

By December 1999, the Helsinki European Council could agree on a 'headline goal': by 2003, the EU will be able to deploy up to 60,000 forces in Petersberg task operations (document 3/19). New permanent political and military bodies will be established under the Council, involving defence ministers, chiefs of staff and military specialists. A mere two months later, the first such bodies were already meeting – a sign of how quickly the creation of a 'European Security and Defence Policy' (EDSP) was proceeding.

There are many problems which still have to be worked out, and not just of detail. Such issues as the involvement of WEU Associate Partners and EU states that are not members of NATO, or the likely unwieldiness of the Council, will preoccupy EU decision-makers for at least the next few years. The delicate distinction between EU-led operations using NATO assets and EU-led operations using its own (or national) assets also barely conceals the fundamental question of whether EU states wish to mobilize enough resources to act militarily without the United States' participation. They have now agreed in principle that they do (including, notably, all the 'neutrals') but the practice will prove another matter altogether.

Document 3/3 Declaration Issued by the Heads of State and Government Participating in the Meeting of the North Atlantic Council, Rome, 7–8 November 1991*

1. We, the Heads of State and Government of the member countries of the North Atlantic Alliance, have gathered in Rome to open a new chapter in the history of our Alliance. The far-reaching decisions we have taken here mark an important stage in the transformation of NATO that we launched in London last year.

2. The world has changed dramatically. The Alliance has made an essential contribution. The peoples of North America and the whole of Europe can now join in a community of shared values based on freedom, democracy, human rights and the rule of law. As an agent of change, a source of stability and the indispensable guarantor of its members' security, our Alliance will continue to play a key role in building a new, lasting order of peace in Europe: a Europe of cooperation and prosperity.

A new security architecture

3. The challenges we will face in this new Europe cannot be comprehensively addressed by one institution alone, but only in a framework of interlocking institutions tying together the countries of Europe and North America.

---

* Paragraphs 14–18, omitted here, elaborate the roles of the different institutions of the CSCE and the details of arms control diplomacy. It is also worth noting that paragraph 14 draws attention to the importance of the new Conflict Prevention Centre. This is one of the first examples of the new emphasis on the concept of conflict prevention.

Consequently, we are working toward a new European security architecture in which NATO, the CSCE, the European Community, the WEU and the Council of Europe complement each other. Regional frameworks of cooperation will also be important. This interaction will be of the greatest significance in preventing instability and divisions that could result from various causes, such as economic disparities and violent nationalism.

The future role of the Alliance: our new strategic concept

4. Yesterday, we published our new Strategic Concept. Our security has substantially improved: we no longer face the old threat of a massive attack. However, prudence requires us to maintain an overall strategic balance and to remain ready to meet any potential risks to our security which may arise from instability or tension. In an environment of uncertainty and unpredictable challenges, our Alliance, which provides the essential transatlantic link as demonstrated by the significant presence of North American forces in Europe retains its enduring value. Our new strategic concept reaffirms NATO's core functions and allows us, within the radically changed situation in Europe, to realise in full our broad approach to stability and security encompassing political, economic, social and environmental aspects, along with the indispensable defence dimension. Never has the opportunity to achieve our Alliance's objectives by political means, in keeping with Articles 2 and 4 of the Washington Treaty, been greater. Consequently, our security policy can now be based on three mutually reinforcing elements: dialogue; cooperation; and the maintenance of a collective defence capability. The use, as appropriate, of these elements will be particularly important to prevent or manage crises affecting our security.

5. The military dimension of our Alliance remains an essential factor; but what is new is that, more than ever, it will serve a broad concept of security. The Alliance will maintain its purely defensive purpose, its collective arrangements based on an integrated military structure as well as cooperation and coordination agreements, and for the foreseeable future an appropriate mix of conventional and nuclear forces. Our military forces will adjust to their new tasks, becoming smaller and more flexible. Thus, our conventional forces will be substantially reduced as will, in many cases, their readiness. They will also be given increased mobility to enable them to react to a wide range of contingencies, and will be organised for flexible build-up, when necessary, for crisis management as well as defence. Multinational formations will play a greater role within the integrated military structure. Nuclear forces committed to NATO will be greatly reduced: the current NATO stockpile of sub-strategic weapons in Europe will be cut by roughly 80% in accordance with the decisions taken by the Nuclear Planning Group in Taormina. The fundamental purpose of the nuclear forces of the Allies remains political: to preserve peace, and prevent war or any kind of coercion.

European security identity and defence role

6. We reaffirm the consensus expressed by our Ministers of Foreign Affairs in Copenhagen. The development of a European security identity and defence

role, reflected in the further strengthening of the European pillar within the Alliance, will reinforce the integrity and effectiveness of the Atlantic Alliance. The enhancement of the role and responsibility of the European members is an important basis for the transformation of the Alliance. These two positive processes are mutually reinforcing. We are agreed, in parallel with the emergence and development of a European security identity and defence role, to enhance the essential transatlantic link that the Alliance guarantees and fully to maintain the strategic unity and indivisibility of security of all our members. The Alliance is the essential forum for consultation among its members and the venue for agreement on policies bearing on the security and defence commitments of Allies under the Washington Treaty. Recognising that it is for the European Allies concerned to decide what arrangements are needed for the expression of a common European foreign and security policy and defence role, we further agree that, as the two processes advance, we will develop practical arrangements to ensure the necessary transparency and complementarity between the European security and defence identity as it emerges in the Twelve and the WEU, and the Alliance.

7. We welcome the spirit in which those Allies who are also members of the Twelve and the WEU have kept the other members of the Alliance informed about the progress of their ongoing discussions on the development of the European identity and about other issues, such as their peace efforts in Yugoslavia. Appropriate links and consultation procedures between the Twelve and the WEU, and the Alliance will be developed in order to ensure that the Allies that are not currently participating in the development of a European identity in foreign and security policy and defence should be adequately involved in decisions that may affect their security. The Alliance's new Strategic Concept, being an agreed conceptual basis for the forces of all Allies, should facilitate the necessary complementarity between the Alliance and the emerging defence component of the European integration process. As the transformation of the Alliance proceeds, we intend to preserve the operational coherence we now have and on which our defence depends. We welcome the perspective of a reinforcement of the role of the WEU, both as the defence component of the process of European unification and as a means of strengthening the European pillar of the Alliance, bearing in mind the different nature of its relations with the Alliance and with the European Political Union.

8. We note the gradual convergence of views in the discussions concerning the developing European security identity and defence role compatible with the common defence policy we already have in our Alliance. We feel confident that in line with the consensus in Copenhagen, the result will contribute to a strong new transatlantic partnership by strengthening the European component in a transformed Alliance. We will help move this development forward.

Relations with the Soviet Union and the other countries of Central and Eastern Europe: a qualitative step forward

9. We have consistently encouraged the development of democracy in the Soviet Union and the other countries of Central and Eastern Europe. We therefore

applaud the commitment of these countries to political and economic reform following the rejection of totalitarian communist rule by their peoples. We salute the newly recovered independence of the Baltic States. We will support all steps in the countries of Central and Eastern Europe towards reform and will give practical assistance to help them succeed in this difficult transition. This is based on our conviction that our own security is inseparably linked to that of all other states in Europe.

10. The Alliance can aid in fostering a sense of security and confidence in these countries, thereby strengthening their ability to fulfil their CSCE commitments and make democratic change irrevocable. Wishing to enhance its contribution to the emergence of a Europe whole and free, our Alliance at its London Summit extended to the Central and Eastern European countries the hand of friendship and established regular diplomatic liaison. Together we signed the Paris Joint Declaration. In Copenhagen last June, the Alliance took further initiatives to develop partnership with these countries. Our extensive programme of high level visits, exchanges of views on security and other related issues, intensified military contacts, and exchanges of expertise in various fields has demonstrated its value and contributed greatly to building a new relationship between NATO and these countries. This is a dynamic process: the growth of democratic institutions throughout Central and Eastern Europe and encouraging cooperative experiences, as well as the desire of these countries for closer ties, now call for our relations to be broadened, intensified and raised to a qualitatively new level.

11. Therefore, as the next step, we intend to develop a more institutional relationship of consultation and cooperation on political and security issues. We invite, at this stage of the process, the Foreign Ministers of the Republic of Bulgaria, the Czech and Slovak Federal Republic, the Republic of Estonia, the Republic of Hungary, the Republic of Latvia, the Republic of Lithuania, the Republic of Poland, the Republic of Romania, and the Soviet Union to join our Foreign Ministers in December 1991 in Brussels to issue a joint political declaration to launch this new era of partnership and to define further the modalities and content of this process. In particular, we propose the following activities:

   – annual meetings with the North Atlantic Council at Ministerial level in what might be called a North Atlantic Cooperation Council;
   – periodic meetings with the North Atlantic Council at Ambassadorial level;
   – additional meetings with the North Atlantic Council at Ministerial or Ambassadorial level as circumstances warrant;
   – regular meetings, at intervals to be mutually agreed, with:
      – NATO subordinate communities, including the Political and Economic Committees;
      – the Military Committee and under its direction other NATO Military Authorities.

This process will contribute to the achievement of the objectives of the CSCE without prejudice to its competence and mechanisms. It will be carried out in accordance with the core functions of the Alliance.

12. Our consultations and cooperation will focus on security and related issues where Allies can offer their experience and expertise, such as defence planning, democratic concepts of civilian-military relations, civil/military coordination of air traffic management, and the conversion of defence production to civilian purposes. Our new initiative will enhance participation of our partners in the "Third Dimension" of scientific and environmental programmes of our Alliance. It will also allow the widest possible dissemination of information about NATO in the Central and Eastern European countries, inter alia through diplomatic liaison channels and our embassies. We will provide the appropriate resources to support our liaison activities.

The Conference on Security and Cooperation in Europe

13. We remain deeply committed to strengthening the CSCE process, which has a vital role to play in promoting stability and democracy in Europe in a period of historic change. We will intensify our efforts to enhance the CSCE's role, in the first instance by working with the other participating CSCE states to ensure that the Helsinki Follow-Up Meeting in 1992 will be another major step towards building a new Europe. The CSCE has the outstanding advantage of being the only forum that brings together all countries of Europe and Canada and the United States under a common code of human rights, fundamental freedoms, democracy, rule of law, security, and economic liberty. The new CSCE institutions and structures, which we proposed at our London Summit and which were created at the Paris Summit, must be consolidated and further developed so as to provide CSCE with the means to help ensure full implementation of the Helsinki Final Act, the Charter of Paris, and other relevant CSCE documents and thus permit the CSCE to meet the new challenges which Europe will have to face. Our consultations within the Alliance continue to be a source of initiatives for strengthening the CSCE.

. . .

Broader challengers

19. Our Strategic Concept underlines that Alliance security must take account of the global context. It points out risks of a wider nature, including proliferation of weapons of mass destruction, disruption of the flow of vital resources and actions of terrorism and sabotage, which can affect Alliance security interests. We reaffirm the importance of arrangements existing in the Alliance for consultation among the Allies under Article 4 of the Washington Treaty and, where appropriate, coordination of our efforts including our responses to such risks. We will continue to address broader challenges in our consultations and in the appropriate multilateral forums in the widest possible cooperation with other states.

. . .

20. The North Atlantic Alliance was founded with two purposes: the defence of the territory of its members, and the safeguarding and promotion of the values they share. In a still uncertain world, the need for defence remains. But in a world

where the values which we uphold are shared ever more widely, we gladly seize the opportunity to adapt our defences accordingly: to cooperate and consult with our new partners: to help consolidate a now undivided continent of Europe: and to make our Alliance's contribution to a new age of confidence, stability and peace.

Document 3/4   Declarations on the Western European Union (annexed to the Treaty on European Union on 7 February 1992) issued on the occasion of the European Council at Maastricht, 10 December 1991

I. DECLARATION

by Belgium, Germany, Spain, France, Italy, Luxembourg, the Netherlands, Portugal and the United Kingdom of Great Britain and Northern Ireland, which are members of the Western European Union and also members of the European Union on

THE ROLE OF THE WESTERN EUROPEAN UNION AND ITS RELATIONS WITH THE EUROPEAN UNION AND WITH THE ATLANTIC ALLIANCE

Introduction

1. WEU Member States agree on the need to develop a genuine European security and defence identity and a greater European responsibility on defence matters. This identity will be pursued through a gradual process involving successive phases. WEU will form an integral part of the process of the development of the European Union and will enhance its contribution to solidarity within the Atlantic Alliance. WEU Member States agree to strengthen the role of WEU, in the longer term perspective of a common defence policy within the European Union which might in time lead to a common defence, compatible with that of the Atlantic Alliance.

2. WEU will be developed as the defence component of the European Union and as a means to strengthen the European pillar of the Atlantic Alliance. To this end, it will formulate common European defence policy and carry forward its concrete implementation through the further development of its own operational role.

    WEU Member States take note of Article J.4 relating to the common foreign and security policy of the Treaty on European Union which reads as follows:

    '*1. The common foreign and security policy shall include all questions related to the security of the Union, including the eventual framing of a common defence policy, which might in time lead to a common defence.*
    2. The Union requests the Western European Union (WEU), which is an integral part of the development of the Union, to elaborate and implement decisions and actions of the Union which have defence implications. The Council shall, in agreement with the institutions of the WEU, adopt the necessary practical arrangements.

3. Issues having defence implications dealt with under this Article shall not be subject to the procedures set out in Article J.3.

4. The policy of the Union in accordance with this Article shall not prejudice the specific character of the security and defence policy of certain Member States and shall respect the obligations of certain Member States under the North Atlantic Treaty and be compatible with the common security and defence policy established within that framework.

5. The provisions of this Article shall not prevent the development of closer cooperation between two or more Member States on a bilateral level, in the framework of the WEU and the Atlantic Alliance, provided such cooperation does not run counter to or impede that provided for in this Title.

6. With a view to furthering the objective of this Treaty, and having in view the date of 1998 in the context of Article XII of the Brussels Treaty, the provisions of this Article may be revised as provided for in Article N(2) on the basis of a report to be presented in 1996 by the Council to the European Council, which shall include an evaluation of the progress made and the experience gained until then.'

A — WEU's relations with European Union

3. The objective is to build up WEU in stages as the defence component of the European Union. To this end, WEU is prepared, at the request of the European Union, to elaborate and implement decisions and actions of the Union which have defence implications.

    To this end, WEU will take the following measures to develop a close working relationship with the Union:
    – as appropriate, synchronization of the dates and venues of meetings and harmonization of working methods;
    – establishment of close cooperation between the Council and Secretariat-General of WEU on the one hand, and the Council of the Union and General Secretariat of the Council on the other;
    – consideration of the harmonization of the sequence and duration of the respective Presidencies;
    – arranging for appropriate modalities so as to ensure that the Commission of the European Communities is regularly informed and, as appropriate, consulted on WEU activities in accordance with the role of the Commission in the common foreign and security policy as defined in the Treaty on European Union;
    – encouragement of closer cooperation between the Parliamentary Assembly of WEU and the European Parliament.

    The WEU Council shall, in agreement with the competent bodies of the European Union, adopt the necessary practical arrangements.

B — WEU's relations with the Atlantic Alliance

4. The objective is to develop WEU as a means to strengthen the European pillar of the Atlantic Alliance. Accordingly WEU is prepared to develop further the close working links between WEU and the Alliance and to strengthen the role, responsibilities and contributions of WEU Member States in the Alliance. This will be undertaken on the basis of the necessary transparency and

complementarity between the emerging European security and defence identity and the Alliance. WEU will act in conformity with the positions adopted in the Atlantic Alliance.

- WEU Member States will intensify their coordination on Alliance issues which represent an important common interest with the aim of introducing joint positions agreed in WEU into the process of consultation in the Alliance which will remain the essential forum for consultation among its members and the venue for agreement on policies bearing on the security and defence commitments of Allies under the North Atlantic Treaty.
- Where necessary, dates and venues of meetings will be synchronized and working methods harmonized.
- Close cooperation will be established between the Secretariats-General of WEU and NATO.

C — Operational role of WEU

5. WEU's operational role will be strengthened by examining and defining appropriate missions, structures and means, covering in particular:

- WEU planning cell;
- closer military cooperation complementary to the Alliance in particular in the field of logistics, transport, training and strategic surveillance;
- meetings of WEU Chiefs of Defence Staff;
- military units answerable to WEU.

Other proposals will be examined further, including:

- enhanced cooperation in the field of armaments with the aim of creating a European armaments agency;
- development of the WEU Institute into a European Security and Defence Academy.

Arrangements aimed at giving WEU a stronger operational role will be fully compatible with the military dispositions necessary to ensure the collective defence of all Allies.

D — Other measures

6. As a consequence of the measures set out above, and in order to facilitate the strengthening of WEU's role, the seat of the WEU Council and Secretariat will be transferred to Brussels.

7. Representation on the WEU Council must be such that the Council is able to exercise its functions continuously in accordance with Article VIII of the modified Brussels Treaty. Member States may draw on a double-hatting formula, to be worked out, consisting of their representatives to the Alliance and to the European Union.

8. WEU notes that, in accordance with the provisions of Article J.4(6) concerning the common foreign and security policy of the Treaty on European Union, the Union will decide to review the provisions of this Article with a view to furthering

the objective to be set by it in accordance with the procedure defined. The WEU will re-examine the present provisions in 1996. The re-examination will take account of the progress and experience acquired and will extend to relations between WEU and the Atlantic Alliance.

II. DECLARATION

by Belgium, Germany, Spain, France, Italy, Luxembourg, the Netherlands, Portugal and the United Kingdom of Great Britain and Northern Ireland which are members of the Western European Union

'*The Member States of WEU welcome the development of the European security and defence identity. They are determined, taking into account the role of WEU as the defence component of the European Union and as the means to strengthen the European pillar of the Atlantic Alliance, to put the relationship between WEU and the other European States on a new basis for the sake of stability and security in Europe. In this spirit, they propose the following:*

State which are members of the European Union are invited to accede to WEU on conditions to be agreed in accordance with Article XI of the modified Brussels Treaty, or to become observers if they so wish. Simultaneously, other European Member States of NATO are invited to become associate members of WEU in a way which will give them the possibility of participating fully in the activities of WEU.

The Member States of WEU assume that treaties and agreements corresponding with the above proposals will be concluded before 31 December 1992.'

Document 3/5 Declaration by the Western European Union's Council of Ministers (The Petersberg Declaration), Bonn, 19 June 1992*

The Foreign and Defence Ministers of WEU member States met in Bonn on 19 June 1992 and issued the Petersberg Declaration consisting of the following three parts:

I. On WEU and European Security

II. On strengthening WEU's operational role

III. On relations between WEU and the other European member States of the European Union or the Atlantic Alliance

I. ON WEU AND EUROPEAN SECURITY

Developments in the security situation in Europe, disarmament and arms control.

1. Ministers reviewed the significant changes that had taken place in the security situation in Europe since their last regular meeting in November 1991. They emphasized the importance of strengthening the role and institutions of the

---

* Paragraphs 16–19 of part I on the 'Activities of Working Groups' and the 'WEU Institute for Security Studies' have been omitted, as have two inconsequential paragraphs at the end of the document.

CSCE for peace and security in Europe. They looked forward to decisions at Helsinki to start new negotiations on measures of arms control and disarmament and to enhance regular consultations and cooperation on security matters. In the light of the establishment of a new CSCE Forum for Security Cooperation, they considered that decisions to enhance the CSCE's capabilities for conflict prevention, crisis management and the peaceful settlement of disputes are of primary importance. They supported the proposal under discussion at the Helsinki Follow-up meeting for the CSCE to declare itself as a regional arrangement under Chapter VIII of the United Nations Charter. Ministers considered that the CSCE should have the authority to initiate and pursue peacekeeping operations under its own responsibility.

2. As WEU develops its operational capabilities in accordance with the Maastricht Declaration, we are prepared to support, on a case-by-case basis and in accordance with our own procedures, the effective implementation of conflict-prevention and crisis-management measures, including peacekeeping activities of the CSCE or the United Nations Security Council. This will be done without prejudice to possible contributions by other CSCE countries and other organisations to these activities.

3. Ministers welcomed the decisions taken by the CSCE Council in Berlin and Prague regarding the relationships between the CSCE and other mutually reinforcing European and transatlantic organizations including WEU. They declared that WEU together with the European Union, was ready to play a full part in building up Europe's security architecture. They likewise reaffirmed their conviction that the Atlantic Alliance is one of the indispensable foundations of Europe's security. They welcomed the ongoing reform process of NATO with a view to establishing a strong new transatlantic partnership.

4. Ministers welcomed the agreement reached at the CFE Extraordinary Conference on 5 June 1992 in Oslo which provides the basis for the entry into force of the CFE Treaty which has been and remains a major objective of their arms control agenda. Its full and effective implementation will increase stability and open the way to a new cooperative security order in Europe. They call upon the new States parties to the Treaty to ensure its ratification by the time of the CSCE Summit in Helsinki. Ministers attach great importance to the conclusion of an agreement on the limitation of personnel strengths of ground and air forces (CFE 1a) in time for the Helsinki Summit and to the implementation of the Open Skies Treaty. They reaffirmed their commitment to the early entry into force of the Open Skies agreement and invited other CSCE States to accede to the Treaty in accordance with its provisions.

5. Ministers welcomed steps recently taken by the States concerned to allow for the entry into force of the START Treaty and the important agreement on further strategic reductions reached between the United States and Russia in Washington on 17 June 1992.

6. Ministers recalled that the presence of foreign forces on the territory of a sovereign state requires the explicit consent of that state. They stressed the importance of rapidly establishing, in the negotiations under way, timetables for the withdrawal of foreign troops from the territory of the Baltic States.

7. Ministers expressed their conviction that a Chemical Weapons Convention can be reached within the next few months. They are confident that this Convention can play an important and pioneering role in worldwide multilateral arms control and call on all member States of the Conference on Disarmament to lend their support to the emerging consensus. They repeat their commitment to be among the original signatories of this Convention and ask all other nations to follow this course.

8. WEU member States reaffirmed their resolution to contribute further to the establishment of a new order of peace in Europe which, in accordance with the Charter of Paris, will be based in cooperation. Ministers underlined the valuable contribution at NACC in this connection. In the same spirit, WEU has invited the Foreign and Defence Ministers of eight States of Central Europe to a special Ministerial meeting later today. WEU and the invited countries intend to enhance consultation and cooperation in the framework of the new European security structure.

Implementation of the Maastricht Declaration

9. Ministers stressed the fundamental importance of the Treaty on European Union and they looked forward to the further elaboration of the common foreign and security policy at the Lisbon European Council. They discussed the progress made in developing the role of WEU as the defence component of the European Union and as the means to strengthen the European pillar of the Atlantic Alliance in accordance with the Declaration adopted by WEU member States at the Maastricht European Council in December 1991.

10. Ministers reaffirmed the importance for WEU to develop close working relations with the European Union and Atlantic Alliance in accordance with the Maastricht Declaration of WEU. They adopted a report on the practical measures necessary for WEU to develop these relations. They asked the Permanent Council to propose to the Council of the Twelve and to the North Atlantic Council concrete measures aimed at facilitating the development of close cooperation between the respective Secretariats.

11. Ministers heard a report from the Secretary-General on the progress made towards the transfers of the WEU Council and Secretariat-General from London to Brussels. They instructed the Permanent Council and Secretary-General to expedite the necessary arrangements so that the transfer could become effective by January 1993.

12. Ministers heard a report from the German Chief of Defence Staff on the meetings of Chiefs of Defence Staff. Ministers agreed that the Chiefs of Defence Staff should meet twice a year prior to the regular Ministerial Councils and on an ad hoc basis whenever necessary. Ministers also agreed that, following the transfer of the Council and Secretariat to Brussels, national delegations could be reinforced with military delegates to develop and provide advice for the Council, to introduce the views of the Chiefs of Defence Staff to the Planning Cell and to monitor the professional standards of the Planning Cell's work.

13. WEU Ministers welcomed the IEPG Defence Ministers' decision, at their Oslo meeting on 6 March 1992, to analyse the future role of the IEPG in the new European security architecture. This represents a positive development fully in line with the objective set by WEU member States in Maastricht further to examine enhanced cooperation in the field of armaments with the aim of creating a WEU European Armaments Agency. WEU Ministers propose that both WEU and IEPG experts analyse this issue in depth, carry out an initial examination of the role and functions of a possible European Armaments Agency and submit a report for consideration.

14. WEU Ministers welcomed the decision of Eurogroup Defence Ministers at their meeting in Brussels on 25 May 1992 to consider the possibility, among other options, and if the necessary preconditions are met, of transferring to WEU some or all of Eurogroup's present functions for which there is still a need.

15. Ministers noted with satisfaction the considerable progress which had been made in setting up the experimental WEU Satellite Centre in Torrejón (Spain), a concrete example of the strengthening of WEU's operational role, and they looked forward to the official inauguration which would take place later in the year. They also noted that the contract for the main system feasibility study had been awarded to a consortium of firms from WEU member States led by a German firm.

. . .

II. ON STRENGTHENING WEU'S OPERATIONAL ROLE

1. In accordance with the decision contained in the Declaration of the member States of WEU at Maastricht on 10 December 1991 to develop WEU as the defence component of the European Union and as the means to strengthen the European pillar of the Atlantic Alliance, WEU member States have been examining and defining appropriate missions, structures and means covering, in particular, a WEU planning cell and military units answerable to WEU, in order to strengthen WEU's operational role.

2. WEU member States declare that they are prepared to make available military units from the whole spectrum of their conventional armed forces for military tasks conducted under the authority of WEU.

3. Decisions to use military units answerable to WEU will be taken by the WEU Council in accordance with the provisions of the UN Charter. Participation in specific operations will remain a sovereign decision of member States in accordance with national constitutions.

4. Apart from contributing to the common defence in accordance with Article 5 of the Washington Treaty and Article V of the modified Brussels Treaty respectively, military units of WEU member States, acting under the authority of WEU, could be employed for:

   – humanitarian and rescue tasks;
   – peacekeeping tasks;
   – tasks of combat forces in crisis management, including peacemaking.

5. The planning and execution of these tasks will be fully compatible with the military dispositions necessary to ensure the collective defence of all Allies.

6. Military units will be drawn from the forces of WEU member States, including forces with NATO missions – in this case after consultation with NATO – and will be organized on a multinational and multi-service basis.

7. All WEU member States will soon designate which of their military units and headquarters they would be willing to make available to WEU for its various possible tasks. Where multinational formations drawn from the forces of WEU nations already exist or are planned, these units could be made available for use under the authority of WEU, with agreement of all participating nations.

8. WEU member States intend to develop and exercise the appropriate capabilities to enable the deployment of WEU military units by land, sea or air to accomplish these tasks.

9. A Planning Cell will be established on 1 October 1992, subject to practical considerations, under the authority of the Council. It will be located with the Secretariat-General in a suitable building in Brussels. The Council has today appointed Maj. Gen. Caltabiano (Italian Air Force) as its first Director. The Planning Cell will be responsible for:

   – preparing contingency plans for the employment for forces under WEU auspices;
   – preparing recommendations for the necessary command, control and communication arrangements, including standing operating procedures for headquarters which might be selected;
   – keeping an updated list of units and combinations of units which might be allocated to WEU for specific operations.

10. The Council of Ministers approved the terms of reference for the Planning Cell.

III. ON RELATIONS BETWEEN WEU AND THE OTHER EUROPEAN MEMBER STATES OF THE EUROPEAN UNION OR THE ATLANTIC ALLIANCE

A. Following the Declaration released in Maastricht on 10 December 1991 in connection with the Treaty on European Union, WEU Ministers recalled the fundamental principles on which relations between member States and associate member States should be based:

   – settlement of their mutual differences by peaceful means, in accordance with the obligations resulting from the modified Brussels Treaty, the North Atlantic Treaty and the United Nations Charter, the commitments entered into under the terms of the Helsinki Final Act and the Paris Charter, and the other generally recognized principles and rules of international law.
   – in their mutual relations, refraining from resorting to the threat or use of force, in accordance with the United Nations Charter.

They also stressed that the security guarantees and defence commitments in the Treaties which bind the member States within Western European Union and which bind them within the Atlantic Alliance are mutually reinforcing and will not be invoked by those subscribing to Part III of the Petersberg Declaration in disputes between member States of either of the two organizations.

B. In their Maastricht Declaration of 10 December 1991, the member States of WEU proposed that States which are members of the European Union be invited to accede to WEU on conditions to be agreed in accordance with Article XI of the modified Brussels Treaty, or to become observers if they so wished. Simultaneously, other European member States of NATO were invited to become associate members of WEU in a way which would give them a possibility of participating fully in the activities of WEU.

In accordance with Part III of the Petersberg Declaration, Ministers agreed that the following points should be made in extending the invitation to the countries interested in becoming members, observers or associate members:

Members

Member States of the European Union which have accepted the invitation to accede to WEU undertake

- to respect, in accordance with the principles and values adhered to by all WEU member States, the Brussels Treaty of 1948, modified on 23 October 1954, its Protocols and associated texts, and the agreements concluded among the member States pursuant to the Treaty,
- to note with approval the agreements, decisions and rules adopted in conformity with the Treaty, and the Declarations starting with the Rome Declaration of 27 October 1984,
- to develop WEU as the defence component of the European Union and as the means to strengthen the European pillar of the Atlantic Alliance in keeping with the obligation entered into on 10 December 1991 in the Declaration on the role of WEU and its relations with the European Union and with the Atlantic Alliance attached to the Treaty on European Union, and
- to accept in full the substance of Part III of the Petersberg Declaration which will form part of the Protocol of Accession.

Observers

Member States of the European Union, which have accepted the invitation to become observers,

- may, although not being a party to the MBT [Modified Brussels Treaty], attend the meetings of the WEU Council without prejudice to the provisions laid down in Article VIII of the modified Brussels Treaty; at the request of a majority of the member States, or of half of the member States including the Presidency, presence at Council meetings may be restricted to full members;
- may be invited to meetings of working groups;
- may be invited, on request, to speak;
- will have the same rights and responsibilities as the full members for functions transferred to WEU from other fora and institutions to which they already belong.

Associate members

Other European member States of the Atlantic Alliance which have accepted the invitation to become associate members of WEU, although not being parties to the modified Brussels Treaty, may participate fully in the meetings of the WEU Council – without prejudice to the provisions laid down in Article VIII of the modified Brussels Treaty – of its working groups and of the subsidiary bodies, subject to the following provisions:

– at the request of a majority of the member States, or of half of the member States including the Presidency, participation may be restricted to full members;
– they will be able to be associated to the Planning Cell through a permanent liaison arrangement;
– they will have the same rights and responsibilities as the full members for functions transferred to WEU from other fora and institutions to which they already belong;
– they will have the right to speak but may not block a decision that is the subject of consensus among the member States;
– they may associate themselves with the decisions taken by member States; they will be able to participate in their implementation unless a majority of the member States, or half of the member States including the Presidency, decide otherwise;
– they will take part on the same basis as full members in WEU military operations to which they commit forces;
– they will accept in full the substance of Section A of Part III of the Petersberg Declaration which will form part of the association document;
– they will be connected to the member States' telecommunications system (WEUCOM) for messages concerning meetings and activities in which they participate;
– They will be asked to make a financial contribution to the Organization's budgets.

Document 3/6 Declaration by the Western European Union Council of Ministers' Extraordinary Meeting with the States of Central Europe, Bonn, 19 June 1992

1. At the invitation of the German Presidency of Western European Union, the Foreign and Defence Ministers of Belgium, Bulgaria, Czechoslovakia, Estonia, France, Germany, Hungary, Italy, Latvia, Lithuania, Luxembourg, the Netherlands, Poland, Portugal, Romania, Spain and the United Kingdom met in Bonn on 19 June 1992 to demonstrate their resolve to enhance the scope of the relationship initiated by a decision of the Ministerial Council in Brussels in April 1990.

2. Ministers agreed that, in view of the profound changes in Europe of the last few years, intensifying the relations between WEU and the states of Central Europe will contribute to stability and the emergence of a new peaceful order in Europe based on partnership and cooperation, greater security and confidence, as well as disarmament.

. . .

5. The enhancement of WEU's relations with Bulgaria, Czechoslovakia, Estonia, Hungary, Latvia, Lithuania, Poland and Romania should reflect the specific relations which exist and are developing between these countries and the European Union and its member States. Other appropriate forms of cooperation could be set up as required in the light of the development of these relations.

6. Ministers had a detailed exchange of views on the development of cooperation between WEU and these states. They agreed to strengthen existing relations by structuring the dialogue, consultations and cooperation.

    The focus of consultations will be the security architecture and stability in Europe, the future development of the CSCE, arms control and disarmament, in particular the implementation of the CFE and "Open Skies" Treaties, as well as the 1992 Vienna Document. Developments in Europe and neighbouring regions will be of particular interest to the participants.

    In this way, WEU's Central European partners will be able to acquaint themselves with the future security and defence policy of the European Union and find new opportunities to cooperate with the defence component of the Union and with the European pillar of the Atlantic Alliance as these develop.

7. The Foreign and Defence Ministers adopted the following concrete measures:

    –   Foreign and Defence Ministers will meet once a year. Additional meetings at Ministerial level may be convened if circumstances require.
    –   A forum of consultation will be established between the WEU Permanent Council and the Ambassadors of the countries concerned. It will meet at the seat of the WEU Council at least twice a year.
    –   These meetings will provide an opportunity to monitor the implementation of the measures adopted and, where appropriate, to make proposals for the inclusion of other fields of cooperation.
    –   Consultations at Ministerial and WEU Permanent Council/Ambassador level on security issues may be complemented by meetings with an ad hoc WEU troika at senior official level.
    –   The following initiatives will be continued and encouraged:
        *   Regular exchanges of documents and information;
        *   Growing cooperation between the WEU Institute for Security Studies and the corresponding bodies in the countries concerned. An increased number of seminars and colloquia will be organized. The programme of scholarships will be continued.

8. Ministers advocated the development of relations between the WEU Assembly and the parliaments of the states concerned.

9. These measures, conducted in the framework of WEU with the states of Central Europe, and similar endeavours conducted in the Alliance framework, will be mutually complementary and reinforcing.

Document 3/7   Declaration of the Heads of State and Government, Conference for Security and Cooperation in Europe, Helsinki, July 1992*

Promises and problems of change

1. We, the Heads of State or Government of the States participating in the Conference on Security and Co-operation in Europe, have returned to the birthplace of the Helsinki process, to give new impetus to our common endeavour.

. . .

12. This is a time of promise but also a time of instability and insecurity. Economic decline, social tension, aggressive nationalism, intolerance, xenophobia and ethnic conflicts threaten stability in the CSCE area. Gross violations of CSCE commitments in the field of human rights and fundamental freedoms, including those related to national minorities, pose a special threat to the peaceful development of society, in particular in new democracies.

There is still much work to be done in building democratic and pluralistic societies, where diversity is fully protected and respected in practice. Consequently, we reject racial, ethnic and religious discrimination in any form. Freedom and tolerance must be taught and practiced.

13. For the first time in decades we are facing warfare in the CSCE region. New armed conflicts and massive use of force to achieve hegemony and territorial expansion continue to occur. The loss of life, human misery, involving huge numbers of refugees have been the worst since the Second World War. Damage to our cultural heritage and the destruction of property have been appalling.

Our community is deeply concerned by these developments. Individually and jointly within the CSCE and the United Nations and other international organizations, we have sought to alleviate suffering and seek long-term solutions to the crises which have arisen.

With the Helsinki decisions, we have put in place a comprehensive programme of co-ordinated action which will provide additional tools for the CSCE to address tensions before violence erupts and to manage crises which may regrettably develop. The Council and the Committee of Senior Officials have already established for the CSCE an important role in dealing with crises which have developed within our area.

No international effort can be successful if those engaged in conflicts do not reaffirm their will to seek peaceful solutions to their differences. We stress our determination to hold parties to conflicts accountable for their actions.

. . .

The CSCE and the management of change

18. The CSCE has been instrumental in promoting changes; now it must adapt to the task of managing them. Our decisions in Helsinki are making the CSCE more

---

* Extracts from this lengthy document are included to give a sense of the attempt to revitalize the CSCE and adapt it to the urgent need for mutually reinforcing European security institutions in the early 1990s. The material omitted is of a preliminary or excessively detailed nature.

operational and effective. We are determined to fully use consultations and concerted action to enable a common response to the challenges facing us.

19. In approaching these tasks, we emphasize the central role of the CSCE in fostering and managing change in our region. In this era of transition, the CSCE is crucial to our efforts to forestall aggression and violence by addressing the root causes of problems and to prevent, manage and settle conflicts peacefully by appropriate means.

20. To this end, we have further developed structures to ensure political management of crises and created new instruments of conflict prevention and crisis management. We have strengthened the Council and the Committee of Senior Officials (CSO) and devised means to assist them. The CSCE capacities in the field of early warning will be strengthened in particular by the activities of the newly established High Commissioner on National Minorities.

We have provided for CSCE peacekeeping according to agreed modalities. CSCE peacekeeping activities may be undertaken in cases of conflict within or among participating States to help maintain peace and stability in support of an ongoing effort at a political solution. In this respect, we are also prepared to seek, on a case-by-case basis, the support of international institutions and organizations, such as the EC, NATO and WEU, as well as other institutions and mechanisms, including the peacekeeping mechanism of the CIS. We welcome their readiness to support CSCE peacekeeping activities, including by making available their resources.

We are further developing our possibilities for peaceful settlement of disputes.

21. Our approach is based on our comprehensive concept of security as initiated in the Final Act. This concept relates the maintenance of peace to the respect for human rights and fundamental freedoms. It links economic and environmental solidarity and co-operation with peaceful inter-State relations. This is equally valid in managing change as it was necessary in mitigating confrontation.

22. The CSCE is a forum for dialogue, negotiation and co-operation, providing direction and giving impulse to the shaping of the new Europe. We are determined to use it to give new impetus to the process of arms control, disarmament and confidence- and security-building, to the enhancement of consultation and co-operation on security matters and to furthering the process of reducing the risk of conflict. In this context, we will also consider new steps to further strengthen norms of behaviour on politico-military aspects of security. We will ensure that our efforts in these fields are coherent, interrelated and complementary.

23. We remain convinced that security is indivisible. No State in our CSCE community will strengthen its security at the expense of the security of other States. This is our resolute message to States which resort to the threat or use of force to achieve their objectives in flagrant violation of CSCE commitments.

24. Essential to the success of our efforts to foster democratic change within the CSCE framework will be increased co-operation with other European and transatlantic organizations and institutions. Therefore, we are convinced that a lasting and peaceful order for our community of States will be built on mutually reinforcing institutions, each with its own area of action and responsibility.

25. Reaffirming the commitments to the Charter of the United Nations as subscribed to by our states, we declare our understanding that the CSCE is a regional arrangement in the sense of Chapter VIII of the Charter of the United Nations. As such, it provides an important link between European and global security. The

rights and responsibilities of the Security Council remain unaffected in their entirety. The CSCE will work together closely with the United Nations especially in preventing and settling conflicts.

Document 3/8 Communiqué Issued by the Ministerial Meeting of the North Atlantic Council, Brussels, 17 December 1992*

1. We have met today at a time of serious challenges to European security arising from regional conflicts. We have consulted on this grave situation and on the contributions that the Atlantic Alliance can make to meeting these challenges. As the Harmel Report emphasised 25 years ago, the ultimate political purpose of the Alliance is to achieve a just and lasting peaceful order in Europe. This remains our goal. In our new Strategic Concept, we have recognised the changing security environment. To meet the new risks and challenges, we will use Alliance resources and expertise in a framework of mutually reinforcing institutions, while continuing to ensure an effective collective defence.

Transatlantic Link

2. The transatlantic partnership, which is embodied in our Alliance, remains vital for European security and stability. The Alliance not only guarantees its members' security, but also remains one of the indispensable instruments for promoting stability and shaping change throughout Europe. An effective Atlantic Alliance and a continuing active, broad cooperation between Europe and North America are essential for a durable order of peace and cooperation in the Euro-Atlantic area. The substantial presence of US armed forces in Europe and the continuing political and military commitment and active engagement in European security of both the United States and Canada will remain essential. The tasks we face in supporting the process of democratic reform in Central and Eastern Europe and the republics on the territory of the former Soviet Union underscore the importance of maintaining a strong transatlantic partnership based on a community of values and purpose.

NATO's Role in Peacekeeping

3. Following the decision which we took in Oslo, we have reviewed the progress made concerning Alliance support for CSCE peacekeeping and have instructed the Council in Permanent Session to complete its work on this issue. We will further strengthen Alliance coordination in peacekeeping, and develop practical measures to enhance the Alliance's contribution in this area. The Military Committee has already advised the Council in Permanent Session of the resources available and the modalities for possible Alliance support for peace-

---

*   By the end of 1992 the United States was becoming concerned that NATO should not be under-mined, whether by the absence of its habitual threat or by the emergence of rival institutions. The Communiqué issued by the North Atlantic Council on 17 December 1992 illustrates the preoccupation with other institutions and the attempt to respond creatively to new challenges by, for example, undertaking peacekeeping missions for which the WEU and CSCE were not yet prepared. Some detailed material, especially on arms control, has been omitted here.

keeping. We are ready to share experiences in peacekeeping with our Cooperation Partners and other CSCE participating states, and to join them as required in supporting CSCE peacekeeping operations.

4.   We confirm today the preparedness of our Alliance to support, on a case-by-case basis and in accordance with our own procedures, peacekeeping operations under the authority of the UN Security Council, which has the primary responsibility for international peace and security. We are ready to respond positively to initiatives that the UN Secretary-General might take to seek Alliance assistance in the implementation of UN Security Council Resolutions. We have asked NATO's Secretary-General to maintain in this respect, under the guidance of the Council in Permanent Session, the necessary contacts with the Secretary-General of the UN regarding the assistance that the Alliance could provide.

5.   In this spirit, we are contributing individually and as an Alliance to the implementation of the UN Security Council resolutions relating to the conflict in the former Yugoslavia. For the first time in its history, the Alliance is taking part in UN peacekeeping and sanctions enforcement operations. The Alliance, together with the WEU, is supporting with its ships in the Adriatic the enforcement of the UN economic sanctions against Serbia and Montenegro and of the arms embargo against all republics of former Yugoslavia. UNPROFOR is using elements from the Alliance's NORTHAG command for its operational headquarters. NATO airborne early-warning aircraft – AWACS – are monitoring daily the UN-mandated no-fly zone over Bosnia-Hercegovina.

. . .

Practical Relationship between NATO and WEU

9.   We reaffirm our support for the development of a common European foreign and security policy and defence identity as reflected in the Declaration on Peace and Cooperation adopted by the Alliance in Rome on 8 November 1991 and in the Treaty and Declarations adopted by the European Community and the Western European Union in Maastricht on 9 and 10 December 1991. We believe that the Alliance's interests are best served by a more united Europe and that the maintenance of a strong Atlantic Alliance will be a fundamental element in any emerging European defence policy.

10. We welcome the results of the WEU Ministerial Council meeting in Rome on 20 November, which confirmed the participation of all European Allies in the activities of the WEU as full members, associate members or observers, thereby reinforcing the European pillar of the Alliance. We also welcome the progress made by the WEU in further developing its operational role and structures. These developments will facilitate close working relations and interaction between NATO and the WEU. Our cooperation in the Adriatic is a case in point. We reaffirm the importance of maintaining Allies' existing obligations and commitments of forces to NATO and we emphasise in this regard that the primary responsibility of forces answerable to the WEU will remain NATO's collective defence under the Washington Treaty.

11. We have endorsed an Alliance document proposing guidelines for the practical working relations between the two organisations. These arrangements will help to ensure that all the Allies are properly involved in decisions that may affect their security. We look forward to the transfer of the WEU Council and Secretariat to Brussels early in 1993, which will allow close practical cooperation between the two Councils and Secretariats. We welcomed the presence of the Secretary General of the WEU, Mr. Willem van Eekelen, who participated in our meeting for the first time.

We are committed to ensuring that the two organisations continue to work on the basis of transparency and complementarity, recognising that it is for each of them to take its own decisions. We reiterate our appreciation of the fact that in stating their aim of introducing joint positions into the process of consultation in the Alliance, the WEU Member States have affirmed that the Alliance will remain the essential forum for consultation among its members and the venue for agreement on policies bearing on the security and defence commitments of Allies under the Washington Treaty; and also of WEU's stated intention to strengthen the role, responsibilities and contributions of the WEU Member States in the Alliance and to act in conformity with the positions adopted in the Alliance.

12. We express our satisfaction at the initiative taken by the French and German governments in submitting to the Council their joint proposal on the relationship between the European Corps they have created and the Alliance.

This major unit, which we note is open to the other WEU partners, is a step forward in strengthening both the European security and defence identity and the European pillar of the Alliance.

We welcome the agreement between the French and German Chiefs of Staff and the Supreme Allied Commander in Europe on the conditions under which the Corps is to be used within the framework of the Atlantic Alliance.

This agreement will be considered by the Military Committee and submitted expeditiously to the Council in Permanent Session for approval.

. . .

Document 3/9   Declaration of the Heads of State and Government Participating in the Meeting of the North Atlantic Council, Brussels, 10–11 January 1994

1.   We, the Heads of State and Government of the member countries of the North Atlantic Alliance, have gathered in Brussels to renew our Alliance in light of the historic transformations affecting the entire continent of Europe. We welcome the new climate of cooperation that has emerged in Europe with the end of the period of global confrontation embodied in the Cold War. However, we must also note that other causes of instability, tension and conflict have emerged. We therefore confirm the enduring validity and indispensability of our Alliance. It is based on a strong transatlantic link, the expression of a shared destiny. It reflects a European Security and Defence

Identity gradually emerging as the expression of a mature Europe. It is reaching out to establish new patterns of cooperation throughout Europe. It rests, as also reflected in Article 2 of the Washington Treaty, upon close collaboration in all fields.

Building on our decisions in London and Rome and on our new Strategic Concept, we are undertaking initiatives designed to contribute to lasting peace, stability, and well-being in the whole of Europe, which has always been our Alliance's fundamental goal. We have agreed:

– to adapt further the Alliance's political and military structures to reflect both the full spectrum of its roles and the development of the emerging European Security and Defence Identity, and endorse the concept of Combined Joint Task Forces;
– to reaffirm that the Alliance remains open to the membership of other European countries:
– to launch a major initiative through a Partnership for Peace, in which we invite Partners to join us in new political and military efforts to work alongside the Alliance;
– to intensify our efforts against the proliferation of weapons of mass destruction and their means of delivery.

2.   We reaffirm our strong commitment to the transatlantic link, which is the bedrock of NATO. The continued substantial presence of United States forces in Europe is a fundamentally important aspect of that link. All our countries wish to continue the direct involvement of the United States and Canada in the security of Europe. We note that this is also the expressed wish of the new democracies of the East, which see in the transatlantic link an irreplaceable pledge of security and stability for Europe as a whole. The fuller integration of the countries of Central and Eastern Europe and of the former Soviet Union into a Europe whole and free cannot be successful without the strong and active participation of all Allies on both sides of the Atlantic.

3.   Today, we confirm and renew this link between North America and Europe developing a Common Foreign and Security Policy and taking on greater responsibility on defence matters. We welcome the entry into force of the Treaty of Maastricht and the launching of the European Union, which will strengthen the European pillar of the Alliance and allow it to make a more coherent contribution to the security of all the Allies. We reaffirm that the Alliance is the essential forum for consultation among its members and the venue for agreement on policies bearing on the security and defence commitments of Allies under the Washington Treaty.

4.   We give our full support to the development of a European Security and Defence Identity which, as called for in the Maastricht Treaty, in the longer term perspective of a common defence policy within the European Union, might in time lead to a common defence compatible with that of the Atlantic Alliance. The emergence of a European Security and Defence Identity will strengthen the European pillar of the Alliance while reinforcing the transatlantic link and will enable European Allies to take greater responsibility for their common security and defence. The Alliance and the European Union share common strategic interests.

5.   We support strengthening the European pillar of the Alliance through the Western European Union, which is being developed as the defence component of the European Union. The Alliance's organisation and resources will be adjusted so as to facilitate this. We welcome the close and growing cooperation between NATO and the WEU that has been achieved on the basis of agreed principles of complementarity and transparency. In future contingencies, NATO and the WEU will consult, including as necessary through joint Council meetings, on how to address such contingencies.

6.   *We therefore stand ready to make collective assets of the Alliance available, on the basis of consultations in the North Atlantic Council, for WEU operations undertaken by the European Allies in pursuit of their Common Foreign and Security Policy. We support the development of separable but not separate capabilities which could respond to European requirements and contribute to Alliance security. Better European coordination and planning will also strengthen the European pillar and the Alliance itself. Integrated and multinational European structures, as they are further developed in the context of an emerging European Security and Defence Identity, will also increasingly have a similarly important role to play in enhancing the Allies' ability to work together in the common defence and other tasks.*

7.   *In pursuit of our common transatlantic security requirements, NATO increasingly will be called upon to undertake missions in addition to the traditional and fundamental task of collective defence of its members, which remains a core function. We reaffirm our offer to support, on a case by case basis in accordance with our own procedures, peacekeeping and other operations under the authority of the UN Security Council or the responsibility of the CSCE, including by making available Alliance resources and expertise. Participation in any such operation or mission will remain subject to decisions of Member States in accordance with national constitutions.*

8.   *Against this background, NATO must continue the adaptation of its command and force structure in line with requirements for flexible and timely responses contained in the Alliance's Strategic Concept. We also will need to strengthen the European pillar of the Alliance by facilitating the use of our military capabilities for NATO and European/WEU operations, and assist participation of non-NATO partners in joint peacekeeping operations and other contingencies as envisaged under the Partnership for Peace.*

9.   *Therefore, we direct the North Atlantic Council in Permanent Session, with the advice of the NATO Military Authorities, to examine how the Alliance's political and military structures and procedures might be developed and adapted to conduct more efficiently and flexibly the Alliance's missions, including peacekeeping, as well as to improve cooperation with the WEU and to reflect the emerging European Security and Defence Identity. As part of this process, we endorse the concept of Combined Joint Task Forces as a means to facilitate contingency operations, including operations with participating nations outside the Alliance. We have directed the North Atlantic Council, with the advice of the NATO Military Authorities, to develop this concept and establish the necessary capabilities. The Council, with the advice of the NATO Military Authorities, and in coordination with the WEU, will work on implementation in a manner that provides separable but not separate military capabilities that could be employed by NATO or the WEU. The North Atlantic Council in Permanent Session will report on the implementation of these decisions to Ministers at their next regular meeting in June 1994.*

10.   *Our own security is inseparably linked to that of all other states in Europe. The consolidation and preservation throughout the continent of democratic societies and their freedom from any form of coercion or intimidation are therefore of direct and material concern to us, as they are to all other CSCE states under the communities of the Helsinki Final Act and the Charter of Paris. We remain deeply committed to further strengthening the CSCE, which is the only organisation comprising all European and North American countries, as an instrument of preventive diplomacy, conflict prevention, cooperative security, and the advancement of democracy and human rights. We actively support the efforts to enhance the operational capabilities of the CSCE for early warning, conflict prevention, and crisis management.*

11.   As part of our overall effort to promote preventive diplomacy, we welcome the European Union proposal for a Pact on Stability in Europe, will contribute to its elaboration, and look forward to the opening conference which will take place in Paris in the Spring.

12.   Building on the close and long-standing partnership among the North American and European Allies, we are committed to enhancing security and stability in the whole of Europe. We therefore wish to strengthen ties with the democratic states to our East. We reaffirm that the Alliance, as provided for in Article 10 of the Washington Treaty, remains open to membership of other European states in a position to further the principles of the Treaty and to contribute to the security of the North Atlantic area. We expect and would welcome NATO expansion that would reach to democratic states to our East, as part of an evolutionary process, taking into account political and security developments in the whole of Europe.

13.   We have decided to launch an immediate and practical programme that will transform the relationship between NATO and participating states. This new programme goes beyond dialogue and cooperation to forge a real partnership – a Partnership for Peace. We invite the other states participating in the NACC, and other CSCE countries able and willing to contribute to this programme, to join with us in this Partnership. Active participation in the Partnership for Peace will play an important role in the evolutionary process of the expansion of NATO.

14.   The Partnership for Peace, which will operate under the authority of the North Atlantic Council, will forge new security relationships between the North Atlantic Alliance and its Partners for Peace. Partner states will be invited by the North Atlantic Council to participate in political and military bodies at NATO Headquarters with respect to Partnership activities. The Partnership will expand and intensify political and military cooperation throughout Europe, increase stability, diminish threats to peace, and build strengthened relationships by promoting the spirit of practical cooperation and commitment to democratic principles that underpin our Alliance. NATO will consult with any active participant in the Partnership if that partner perceives a direct threat to its territorial integrity, political independence, or security. At a pace and scope determined by the capacity and desire of the individual participating states, we will work in concrete ways towards transparency in defence budgeting, promoting democratic control of defence ministries, joint planning, joint military exercises, and creating an ability to operate with NATO forces in such fields as peacekeeping, search and rescue and humanitarian operations, and others as may be agreed.

15.   To promote closer military cooperation and interoperability, we will propose, within the Partnership framework, peacekeeping field exercises beginning in 1994. To coordinate joint military activities within the Partnership, we will invite states participating in the Partnership to send permanent liaison officers to NATO Headquarters and a separate Partnership Coordination Cell at Mons (Belgium) that would, under the authority of the North Atlantic Council, carry out the military planning necessary to implement the Partnership programmes.

16.   Since its inception two years ago, the North Atlantic Cooperation Council has greatly expanded the depth and scope of its activities. We will continue to work with all our NACC partners to build cooperative relationships across the entire spectrum of the Alliance's activities. With the expansion of NACC activities and the establishment of the Partnership for Peace, we have decided to offer permanent facilities at NATO Headquarters for personnel from NACC countries and other Partnership for Peace participants in order to improve our working relationships and facilitate closer cooperation.

. . .

26. *The past five years have brought historic opportunities as well as new uncertainties and instabilities to Europe. Our Alliance has moved to adapt itself to the new circumstances, and today we have taken decisions in key areas. We have given our full support to the development of a European Security and Defence Identity. We have endorsed the concept of Combined Joint Task Forces as a means to adapt the Alliance to its future tasks. We have opened a new perspective of progressively closer relationships with the countries of Central and Eastern Europe and of the former Soviet Union. In doing all this, we have renewed our Alliance as a joint endeavour of a North America and Europe permanently committed to their common and indivisible security. The challenges we face are many and serious. The decisions we have taken today will better enable us to meet them.*

Document 3/10 Declaration by the Western European Union's Council of Ministers (The Kirchberg Declaration), Luxembourg, 9 May 1994*

I

COMMUNIQUÉ

Ministers devoted a substantial part of their discussions to the strengthening of relations with the nine Central European Partners and to the adoption of a status of Association with WEU, which represents the culmination of the initiative extended to them at the meeting in Luxembourg last November.

Other topics addressed at this meeting were the enhanced status offered to the future Associate Members and the strengthening of the European Security and Defence Identity and WEU's operational capabilities. Given the political and operational importance for WEU of the results of the Alliance Summit of January 1994, Ministers discussed the significant possibilities these offered for the further development of WEU. They finally addressed the development of the dialogue with the Mediterranean States and contacts with Russia and Ukraine.

1.   Further to the reflection by the Permanent Council on the basis of the mandate given in Luxembourg on 22 November 1993, Ministers warmly welcomed the agreement reached on the content and modalities of a status of Association with WEU offered to the Consultation Partners. They agreed on a Document on a status of Association which figures as Part II of this Declaration.

WEU is launching this major political initiative in the context of the developing links between these States and European institutions, notably through Europe Agreements. This will constitute a concrete contribution by WEU towards preparing these States for their integration and eventual accession to the European Union, opening up in turn the perspective of membership of WEU. This initiative is fully complementary to cooperation within the Alliance framework, in particular to the Partnership for Peace programme, and to that taking place within the framework of the Stability Pact, these processes being mutually reinforcing. Ministers considered that greater participation by these States in

---

*   Paragraphs 7–12 deal with the review of policy matters current at the time and have been omitted.

WEU activities, together with the closer consultation on security questions that will ensue, will contribute significantly to greater stability in Europe.

In this context, Ministers welcomed the positive contribution made by the WEU Assembly to the reinforcement of European security.

2. Recognising the highly valuable contribution that the Republic of Iceland, the Kingdom of Norway and the Republic of Turkey are already making to WEU's activities as future Associate Members, Ministers agreed on a Declaration which figures in Part III of the present document. By enabling WEU to draw fully on these countries' expertise and resources, this package of measures will enhance WEU's role as the defence component of the European Union and as the means to strengthen the European pillar of the Atlantic Alliance.

3. On the occasion of their first meeting following the January 1994 Summit of the Atlantic Alliance, Ministers warmly welcomed the full support expressed by the Alliance for the development of a European Security and Defence Identity. They expressed satisfaction that the relevant parts of the Luxembourg Declaration of 22 November 1993, intended as a European contribution to the Alliance Summit, had been duly taken into account. In this context, they acknowledged the importance of the decision of the Alliance to examine how to further develop and adapt its structures and procedures.

They welcomed the Summit's endorsement of the principle that collective assets and capabilities of the Alliance can be made available for WEU operations in order to strengthen WEU as the defence component of the European Union and as the means to strengthen the European pillar of the Atlantic Alliance. They underlined that the modalities for making these available should preserve WEU's own planning procedures and capabilities.

Ministers stressed the importance of work under way in WEU on the WEU-related aspects of the adaptation of the Alliance structures. In order to enhance WEU's ability to carry out the tasks defined in the Petersberg Declaration, Ministers endorsed the approach to identify the assets and capabilities required to perform the necessary military functions.

Ministers underlined the importance of coordination with the Alliance on the implementation of the CJTF concept and the definition of separable but not separate military capabilities so as to ensure their effective use where appropriate by WEU, and in that case under its command.

While recalling their commitment to strengthen the operational capabilities of WEU, they also agreed that WEU would benefit from careful management of resources as well as existing standardized procedures.

Ministers requested the Permanent Council to take discussions on these matters forward as fast as possible with a view to the timely presentation of joint positions into the process of consultation in the Alliance.

4. Ministers recalled that WEU was fully prepared to play its role in accordance with the Treaty on European Union and the Maastricht Declaration and to respond to requests from the European Union concerning its decisions and

actions having defence implications. They welcomed the fact that working relations with the European Union were now being developed. They also recalled their endorsement at their last meeting of the measures to ensure close cooperation between the European Union and WEU contained in the conclusions of the General Affairs Council of 26 October 1993 and approved by the European Council on 29 October 1993. Ministers emphasized in this context the need to improve cooperation particularly in the management of crises and looked forward to close cooperation between the two Organizations in order to respond rapidly and efficiently in the event of crises. In this context, Ministers welcomed the request by the European Union to make a contribution to a future European Union administration of Mostar and confirmed that WEU was ready to offer its support. This constituted a promising example of the close cooperation between WEU and the European Union foreseen by the Maastricht Treaty.

Ministers also welcomed the successful conclusion of the negotiations on the accession of Austria, Finland, Norway and Sweden to the European Union whereby those countries undertook, inter alia, to accept the Community "acquis" in the field of common foreign and security policy. They expressed the hope that their accession could become effective by 1 January 1995 and recalled that WEU was prepared, in the period leading up to that accession, to strengthen contacts.

5. Ministers recalled the longer term perspective of a common defence policy within the European Union, which might lead in time to a common defence, compatible with that of the Atlantic Alliance. In this spirit, they tasked the Permanent Council to begin work on the formulation of a common European defence policy with a view to presenting preliminary conclusions at their next Ministerial meeting in the Netherlands.

6. Ministers recalled the importance they attached to the continued operational development of WEU, as the defence component of the European Union and as the means to strengthen the European pillar of the Alliance.

Ministers noted the work of the Planning Cell on the Forces Answerable to WEU, and requested it to develop further an inventory of force packages which will enable WEU to carry out the tasks conferred to it, particularly in the field of humanitarian missions, peacekeeping and crisis management. They also took note of the report of the role of WEU in peacekeeping.

Ministers warmly welcomed and endorsed the adoption of the Joint Declarations setting the conditions for the use of the Belgian/German/Netherlands/UK Multinational Division (Central) and the United Kingdom/Netherlands Amphibious Force in the framework of WEU and the understandings in these regards.

Ministers noted with satisfaction Luxembourg's decision to join the European Corps.

Ministers approved a "WEU Operation Plan Combined Endeavour" for the generation of a WEU Maritime Force as presented by the Planning Cell and agreed that such an initiative should be further developed in accordance with the initial mandate.

In the same framework, Ministers looked forward to the further development of the Italian proposals currently under consideration with France and Spain, envisaging a multinational ground force answerable to WEU.

They are confident that these initiatives will significantly contribute to European capabilities for crisis management and to the development of the European security and defence identity.

Ministers confirmed the aim of further developing WEU's capability to use satellite imagery for security purposes. In this context, they envisaged establishing the WEU Satellite Centre at Torrejón as a permanent body of the Organization and would take a decision on this point in the light of the evaluation of the work undertaken by the Centre during its experimental period. They recognized the need to take appropriate decisions in November 1994 to ensure the continuity of the Centre's work until that evaluation was completed.

Ministers reaffirmed their will to set up an independent European satellite system. A decision would be taken subject to evaluation of the costs and merits of the proposed system and of other WEU alternatives and affordability. To prepare a possible decision of a launch of such a programme, Ministers tasked the Space Group to prepare, for their Spring 1995 meeting, a proposal for decision, including the preparation of a draft Memorandum of Understanding containing the detailed specifications, to be concluded between the present WEU member States.

II

DOCUMENT ON A STATUS OF ASSOCIATION WITH WEU FOR THE REPUBLIC OF BULGARIA, THE CZECH REPUBLIC, THE REPUBLIC OF ESTONIA, THE REPUBLIC OF HUNGARY, THE REPUBLIC OF LATVIA, THE REPUBLIC OF LITHUANIA, THE REPUBLIC OF POLAND, ROMANIA AND THE SLOVAK REPUBLIC

The WEU Council of Ministers and the Ministers of Foreign Affairs and Defence of the Republic of Bulgaria, the Czech Republic, the Republic of Estonia, the Republic of Hungary, the Republic of Latvia, the Republic of Lithuania, the Republic of Poland, Romania and the Slovak Republic met in Luxembourg on 9 May 1994.

Recalling:

– the Declaration of the Extraordinary Meeting of the WEU Council of Ministers with States of Central Europe in Bonn on 19 June 1992

and

– the Communiqué of the Meeting of the WEU Forum of Consultation at Ministerial level in Rome on 20 May 1993;

Recalling more particularly the Declaration of the WEU Council of Ministers in Luxembourg on 22 November 1993 which:

- underlined the need, in the interest of increased stability in Europe, for closer consultation on security issues;
- considered, particularly in the light of the entry into force of the Treaty on European Union, that these relations should be broadened and deepened in parallel to the closer cooperation of these states with the European Union;
- initiated a reflection on an enhanced status for those consultation partners who had already concluded or would conclude a Europe agreement with the European Union in order to allow those countries to participate to a larger extent in the activities of WEU and to be involved in initiatives and missions as envisaged in the Petersberg Declaration;

Recalling also the Declaration of the European Council in Copenhagen of 22–23 June 1993, which underlined the vocation of countries of Central and Eastern Europe to enter the European Union, and taking into account the developing links of these States with European institutions notably through the Europe Agreements and the desirability of preparing those States for their integration and eventual accession to the European Union;

Bearing in mind that the development of closer relations with the nine Central European nations through an enhanced status within WEU and through cooperation within the Alliance framework, in particular the Partnership for Peace programme, will be mutually reinforcing and contribute significantly to security and stability in Europe;

Emphasizing that such an enhanced status based on stability of institutions, guaranteeing democracy, the rule of law, human rights, and respect for and protection of minorities, should contribute to security and stability in Europe, and welcoming in this regard the forthcoming conference on Stability to be held in Paris;

Recognizing that the relations among WEU countries and consultation partners are based on the following criteria:

- settlement of differences by peaceful means, in accordance with the obligations from the United Nations Charter, the commitments entered into under the terms of the Helsinki Final Act and the Paris Charter and the generally recognized principles and rules of international law,
- refraining from resorting to the threat or use of force, in accordance with the United Nations Charter;

The WEU Council of Ministers and the Ministers of Foreign Affairs and Defence of Bulgaria, the Czech Republic, Estonia, Hungary, Latvia, Lithuania, Poland, Romania and Slovakia have agreed on the present status whereby the Republic of Bulgaria, the Czech Republic, the Republic of Estonia, the Republic of Hungary, the Republic of Latvia, the Republic of Lithuania, the Republic of Poland, Romania and the Slovak Republic will become Associate Partners of WEU; this status will comprise the following elements:

This status does not entail any changes to the modified Brussels Treaty.

1. They may participate in the meetings of the Council subject to the following provisions:

   – they may take part in discussions but may not block a decision that is the subject of consensus among the Member States.
   – to enable WEU to perform to the full its role as the defence component of the European Union and as the means to strengthen the European pillar of the Atlantic Alliance and also to address any other questions in an appropriate configuration, meetings of the Council according to present arrangements will be convened on the basis of the provisions agreed in Rome on 20 November 1992 in the Document on Associate Membership of WEU and the Declaration on WEU Observers.

   They will be regularly informed at the Council of the activities of its working groups and may be invited to participate in working groups on a case by case basis.

   They may have a liaison arrangements with the Planning Cell.

2. They may associate themselves with decisions taken by member States concerning the following tasks envisaged in para II.4 of the Petersberg Declaration, i.e.: "humanitarian and rescue tasks, peacekeeping tasks, tasks of combat forces in crisis management, including peacemaking".

   They will be able to participate in their implementation as well as in relevant exercises and planning unless a majority of the member States, or half of the Member States including the Presidency, decide otherwise. They will be invited to provide information on forces. They will also be able to offer forces for specific operations.

   When it is agreed that they join such WEU operations by committing forces, they will have the same obligations as other participants, as well as the right of involvement in the command structures and in the Council's subsequent decision-making process. The precise modalities of their participation, including their rights and obligations, in each such WEU operation will be agreed on a case-by-case basis.

III

DECLARATION FOLLOWING ON FROM THE "DOCUMENT ON ASSOCIATE MEMBERSHIP" OF 20 NOVEMBER 1992

The WEU Council of Ministers met in Luxembourg on 9 May 1994.

Recalling:

– the WEU Maastricht Declaration of 10 December 1991 whereby other European member States of NATO were invited to become associate members of WEU in a way which would give them the possibility to participate fully in the activities of WEU, taking into account its role as the defence component of the European Union and as the means to strengthen the European pillar of the Atlantic Alliance;

- the Petersberg Declaration "On Relations between WEU and the other European member States of the European Union or the Atlantic Alliance" of 19 June 1992;
- the "Document on Associate Membership" agreed at the WEU Ministerial Council in Rome on 20 November 1992;

Recognizing the significant contribution of the associate members of WEU to European security and stability;

Underlining the need to reinforce the relationship of the associate members with WEU in a way that would enable them to make an even stronger contribution to WEU as it faces new challenges and opportunities;

Ministers:

- reaffirmed the Council's commitment fully to take into consideration associate members' security interests;
- reiterated that the security guarantees and defence commitments binding the members states within WEU and the Atlantic Alliance are mutually reinforcing and recalled that, as members of the Atlantic Alliance, the WEU associate members fully enjoy the provisions of article 5 of the Washington Treaty;

Ministers further:

- recalled that under the document on associate membership, associate members may associate themselves with decisions taken by Member States;
- emphasized that associate members, by committing forces to WEU military operations, will, under conditions laid down by the Rome document of 20 November 1992, participate on the same basis as full members in these operations, as well as in relevant exercises and planning;
- confirmed that in all questions concerning the security of forces committed for such operations, there will be no distinction between the forces of associate members and the forces of full members.

The present Declaration does not entail any changes to the "Document on Associate Membership" adopted in Rome on 20 November 1992.

The WEU Council of Ministers agreed that:

- associate members have full rights to nominate forces answerable to WEU;
- the Republic of Iceland, the Kingdom of Norway and the Republic of Turkey may nominate officers to the Planning Cell in order to increase WEU's planning capabilities and to enable WEU to draw more easily on the Associate Members' expertise and resources for the tasks identified in the Petersberg Declaration;
- the Republic of Iceland, the Kingdom of Norway and the Republic of Turkey should be connected as soon as possible to the WEUCOM network for all communications concerning meetings and activities in which associate members participate.

Ministers confirmed that the arrangements contained in the present Declaration cannot be modified without the consent of the associate members.

Finally, the Council, while recognizing the autonomy of the WEU Assembly invited the Assembly through its national delegations, to examine further the present arrangements for the participation of parliamentarians from associate members countries.

Document 3/11   Interlocking Institutions. Source: *A Common Foreign and Security Policy for Europe: the Intergovernmental Conference of 1996*, Centre for Defence Studies, King's College, London, p. 18*

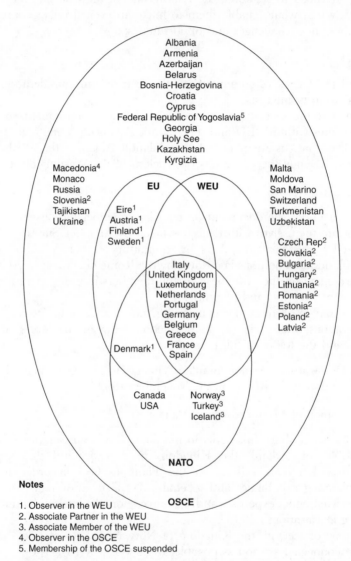

Notes

1. Observer in the WEU
2. Associate Partner in the WEU
3. Associate Member of the WEU
4. Observer in the OSCE
5. Membership of the OSCE suspended

*   This chart – included by kind permission of the Centre for Defence Studies, King's College, London – shows the complex of overlapping memberships in the European international order in the mid-1990s. The most striking features are the inclusive structure provided by the OSCE, the tight but difficult relations between the EU, the WEU and NATO, and the growth of the WEU 'family' to 28 states involved in some form or other.

Document 3/12   European Security: A Common Concept of the 27 WEU
Countries, WEU Council of Ministers, Madrid, 14 November
1995*

. . .

2.   Europe's worldwide economic interests

22.   Growing European economic integration, for which the European Union is
the driving force, has created and reinforced interdependence and solidarity among
Europeans. The political initiatives taken by the European Union towards its Central
and Eastern European partners are a logical extension of the same process.
European association agreements are designed to reinforce economic and political
stability and to increase the interdependence and solidarity of European countries.
For its part, the Pact on Stability also has an economic dimension.

23.   The European Union has reached economic agreements with a number of
European countries. Partnership agreements with Russia and Ukraine, for example,
and those concluded under the forms of cooperation now being set up with countries south of the Mediterranean, will help prevent economic imbalances from
becoming threats to the security of our continent.

24.   The maintenance of communications links within its territory is a prerequisite for
the efficient functioning of the modern state. Threats to communications systems
could turn out, depending on their scope, to be threats to the economy and security
of the state. The improvement of cross-border communications is an important
factor in promoting trade and the free exchange of ideas, thus enhancing interdependence between states and increasing the stake each has in the security of its
neighbours. By creating the conditions necessary to attract inward capital investment,
market-oriented economic reforms will play an important role in upgrading these
communication links. The European Union has also expressed its determination to
promote the development of trans-European networks. The European Council at
Essen in December 1994 also stated that the integration of associate countries
into trans-European networks is a key factor in European economic and political
integration.

25.   Access to technology is a factor vital to the security of Europe. The development of the industrial and technological capacity of Europe is vital both to its
economic prosperity and to its security.

26.   Most European countries are largely dependent for their supplies of energy
and raw materials on countries whose political and economic stability over the
medium term cannot be taken for granted. Gas and oil are conveyed, at least in
part, through pipelines crossing countries of uncertain stability. In the event of a
major crisis, the disruption of those supplies is a distinct probability and maritime

---

*   The WEU's 'Common Concept' of European Security, produced at the Madrid Council of Ministers'
meeting in November 1995, is striking for its length, comprehensiveness and detail, covering all
conceivable aspects of policy, institutions and operations. Here we include, by way of illustration,
only that section which defines the European interests at stake in the international order of the
1990s. It is particularly interesting for its global perspectives and for the way in which the EU's
economic rationale is seamlessly integrated with traditional security concerns.

transport routes could be vulnerable. The flow of gas and oil to European markets through reliable pipeline and maritime routes holds great political and strategic significance. The diversification of European energy supplies may help reduce these potential risks.

27.   The European Energy Charter has as its aim to help make available to countries of Central and Eastern Europe as well as the countries of the CIS the technologies, expertise and capital they need for prospection, and to contribute to the security of European countries' energy supplies. The International Energy Agency has agreed on an emergency oil-sharing system and other emergency response measures for use in major oil supply disruptions and other situations.

3.   The security of European citizens in the world

28.   There are large numbers of European citizens living and working abroad, many in unstable or dangerous areas. Many more travel abroad on a short-term basis. Their security over and above that provided by the countries where they are present, is the responsibility of national authorities. This applies to citizens present on European territory as well as to those outside national and European borders and who might find themselves in situations where their security is endangered. Their protection is undertaken through consulates and embassies. Many governments have negotiated agreements with other countries to extend the protection that can be provided.

29.   For example, the Treaty on European Union makes provision for European consular protection to any European Union citizen abroad not having a local consulate of his own country. Similar arrangements have been made among other European states.

30.   This system of cooperation has recently been successfully put to the test in various situations: Zaire, Angola, the Yemen and Rwanda are just a few examples of cooperation among WEU States in this field. Practical experience in these cases has underlined the usefulness of current work in WEU on evacuation planning and of coordination between WEU and the EU.

C.   The new risks

1.   Potential armed conflicts

31.   The end of the Cold War has brought to a close a period of division in Europe and made massive military confrontation a remote prospect. But dangers remain, and new security risks and uncertainties are emerging in the Continent and its neighbouring regions.

32.   Europe faces a broad spectrum of security problems, some of which may lead to armed conflict.

33.   Recent events have demonstrated the need to settle border disputes peacefully in accordance with international law. Crises may also arise from severe neglect of the rights of persons belonging to national minorities in violation of internationally agreed norms.

34.   Particular dangers arise when armed groups operate outside the law or without proper democratic control. The larger and better armed these groups, the greater the risk of conflict is likely to be. Security risks can also be associated with excessive concentrations of military forces.

35.   The conflict in the former Yugoslavia is a source of major concern and a threat to European security: the risk of its potential expansion, the level of armaments involved, the forces mobilized, the extent of human suffering and the degree of international political involvement, all underline the seriousness of this crisis.

2.   The proliferation of weapons of mass destruction and their delivery means

36.   The proliferation of all weapons of mass destruction (WMD) and their delivery means continues to constitute a threat to international and European peace and security. A European priority in this field has been to pursue universal participation in, and compliance with, multilateral disarmament and non-proliferation conventions such as the Nuclear Non-Proliferation Treaty (NPT), the Chemical Weapons Convention (CWC) and the Biological and Toxin Weapons Convention (BTWC) and, at the same time, to continue to strengthen export control regimes such as the Missile Technology Control Regime (MTCR), the Zangger Committee, the Nuclear Suppliers Group (NSG) and the Australia Group. On the other hand, European countries and defence organizations have relied on deterrence and other means in countering the threat posed by weapons of mass destruction. In addition, there may be a need to develop other aspects of defence posture to meet the specific threats from WMD proliferation.

37.   When assessing the proliferation of these weapons, a distinction should be made between nuclear, chemical and biological weapons, as the risk they pose can be of a substantially different nature.

Nuclear Weapons

38.   The entire international community faces potential risks in the field of nuclear proliferation. On the dissolution of the former Soviet Union, European states faced a potentially serious problem arising from uncertainties over the control of Soviet nuclear forces. The accession of Ukraine, Belarus and Kazakhstan as non-nuclear-weapon states to the NPT, which remains the cornerstone of the non-proliferation regime, has done much to reduce this threat. The process of removal of nuclear weapons from Belarus, Kazakhstan and Ukraine is well underway with the assistance of Western countries; and Russia, who also benefits from such assistance, is continuing with the difficult task of the safe and secure dismantlement of these weapons.

39.   One proliferation risk is the possibility that scientists previously involved with the Soviet nuclear weapons programme, but now unemployed, will offer their services to potential proliferators outside the region. The contributions of a number of countries to the creation of the International Science and Technology Centre in Moscow and the Science and Technology Centre in Ukraine, in Kiev, are specifically intended to avert this risk.

. . .

Document 3/13   Communiqué, Ministerial Meeting, North Atlantic Council, Berlin, 3 June 1996*

1. We met today in Berlin, the capital of a united Germany and the city that stood for the success of Alliance policy and transatlantic cohesion for over four decades. Its unification is now a symbol of the new era of partnership and cooperation.

2. Here in Berlin, we have taken a major step forward in shaping the new NATO, a NATO taking on new missions such as IFOR. Today, we have taken decisions to carry further the ongoing adaptation of Alliance structures so that the Alliance can more effectively carry out the full range of its missions, based on a strong transatlantic partnership; build a European Security and Defence Identity within the Alliance; continue the process of opening the Alliance to new members; and develop further strong ties of cooperation with all Partner countries, including the further enhancement of our strong relationship with Ukraine, and the development of a strong, stable and enduring partnership with Russia.

3. This new NATO has become an integral part of the emerging, broadly based, cooperative European security structure. We are in Bosnia and Herzegovina, together with many of our new Partners and other countries, contributing through the Implementation Force (IFOR) to bringing an end to war and conflict in that country and assisting the building of peace in the region. This joint endeavour, the largest military operation in the Alliance's history, points the way to our future security cooperation throughout the Euro-Atlantic area.

4. We have today given new impetus to the process of the Alliance's adaptation and reform, which began in 1990 at the NATO Summit meeting in London and was carried forward at the 1994 Brussels Summit. Taking into account the sweeping changes in the security environment in Europe as new democracies have taken root and following the adoption of our new Strategic Concept in 1991, we have reorganised and streamlined our political and military structures and procedures; reduced significantly our force and readiness levels; and reconfigured our forces to make them better able to carry out the new missions of crisis management, while preserving the capability for collective defence. In addition, we have been conducting an expanding array of outreach activities with our Partners. We want to make our adapted Alliance better able to fulfil its main purpose: peace and security in the Euro-Atlantic area.

---

*   The Berlin North Atlantic Council of June 1996 was an important occasion for the seal of approval it gave to the CJTF concept, and to the apparent end it signified of a battle over whether or not the WEU was to move further towards merger with the EU. The United States and Britain in particular had opposed the tendency in the more *communautaire* states to assume that the WEU should become the defence arm of the EU in a short order, for reasons of both principle (the need to preserve NATO) and practicality (the WEU is dependent on NATO for operational capability). Accordingly the CJTF concept became the means of satisfying honour on both sides, although in practice the Atlanticists were more satisfied by the outcome, since the USA retains an effective veto on any WEU-led operation through the need for North Atlantic Council approval for the use of NATO assets.

5. Much has been achieved, but now is the moment to take a decisive step forward in making the Alliance increasingly flexible and effective to meet new challenges. Therefore we are determined to:

- adapt Alliance structures. An essential part of this adaptation is to build a European Security and Defence Identity within NATO, which will enable all European Allies to make a more coherent and effective contribution to the missions and activities of the Alliance as an expression of our shared responsibilities; to act themselves as required; and to reinforce the transatlantic partnership;
- develop further our ability to carry out new roles and missions relating to conflict prevention and crisis management and the Alliance's efforts against the proliferation of weapons of mass destruction and their means of delivery, while maintaining our capability for collective defence; and
- enhance our contribution to security and stability throughout the Euro-Atlantic area by broadening and deepening our dialogue and cooperation with Partners, notably through PfP and NACC, and by further developing our important relations with Russia and Ukraine, as we maintain our openness to new members through our established enlargement process and strengthen our links with other organisations which contribute to European security.

6. Today we welcome the progress achieved in the internal adaptation of our Alliance, building on the decisions taken at the 1994 Brussels Summit, in particular:

- the completion of the CJTF concept. By permitting a more flexible and mobile deployment of forces, including for new missions, this concept will facilitate the mounting of NATO contingency operations, the use of separable but not separate military capabilities in operations led by the WEU, and the participation of nations outside the Alliance in operations such as IFOR. We now request the Military Committee to make recommendations to the Council for the implementation of this concept to the satisfaction of all Allies, taking into account ongoing work to adapt military structures and procedures;
- the establishment of the Policy Coordination Group (PCG), which will meet the need, especially in NATO's new missions, for closer coordination of political and military viewpoints;
- the first results of the Military Committee's Long-Term Study, which will result in recommendations for a military command structure better suited to current and future Euro-Atlantic security. We task the Military Committee to continue its work on the Long-Term Study, consistent with the decisions we have taken today;
- completion of original work plans of the Senior Politico-Military Group on Proliferation (SGP) and the Senior Defence Group on Proliferation (DGP) to address the common security concern of proliferation;
- the meeting later this month of the North Atlantic Council (Defence Ministers), in which all 16 NATO countries will take part.

7. In our adaptation efforts to improve the Alliance's capability to fulfil its roles and missions, with the participation of all Allies, we will be guided by three fundamental objectives.

The first objective is to ensure the Alliance's military effectiveness so that it is able, in the changing security environment facing Europe, to perform its traditional mission of collective defence and through flexible and agreed procedures to undertake new roles in changing circumstances, based on:

*   [The existence of a renewed structure of integrated military command which reflects the strategic] situation in Europe and enables all Allies to participate fully and which is able to undertake all missions through procedures to be defined in accordance with decisions by the Council;*
*   HQ structures which are more deployable and forces which are more mobile, both capable of being sustained for extended periods;
*   the ability to provide for increased participation of Partner countries and to integrate new members into the Alliance's military structure;
*   the ability to mount NATO non-Article 5 operations, guided by the concept of one system capable of performing multiple functions. We will further develop flexible arrangements capable of undertaking a variety of missions and taking into account national decisions on participation in each operation, building upon the strength of NATO's existing arrangements. These operations may differ from one another in contributions by Allies and, as a result of Council decision on a case-by-case basis, aspects of military command and control. The CJTF concept is central to our approach for assembling forces for contingency operations and organising their command within the Alliance. Consistent with the goal of building the European Security and Defence Identity within NATO, these arrangements should permit all European Allies to play a larger role in NATO's military and command structures and, as appropriate, in contingency operations undertaken by the Alliance;
*   increased political-military cooperation in particular through the PCG, and effective exercise of political control by the North Atlantic Council through the Military Committee;
*   the need for cost-effectiveness.

The second objective is to preserve the transatlantic link, based on:

[*inter alia*]

*   full transparency between NATO and WEU in crisis management, including as necessary through joint consultations on how to address contingencies.

The third objective is the development of the European Security and Defence Identity within the Alliance. Taking full advantage of the approved CJTF concept, this identity will be grounded on sound military principles and supported by appropriate military planning and permit the creation of militarily coherent and effective forces capable of operating under the political control and strategic direction of the WEU.

---

*   The material in brackets here was omitted from the official English version of the text. The Editors have translated the relevant lines from the French version.

As an essential element of the development of this identity, we will prepare, with the involvement of NATO and the WEU, for WEU-led operations (including planning and exercising of command elements and forces). Such preparations within the Alliance should take into account the participation, including in European command arrangements, of all European Allies if they were so to choose. It will be based on:

- identification, without the Alliance, of the types of separable but not separate capabilities, assets and support assets, as well as, in order to prepare for WEU-led operations, separable but not separate HQs, HQ elements and command positions, that would be required to command and conduct WEU-led operations and which could be made available, subject to decision by the NAC;
- elaboration of appropriate multinational European command arrangements within NATO, consistent with and taking full advantage of the CJTF concept, able to prepare, support, command and conduct the WEU-led operations. This implies double-hatting appropriate personnel within the NATO command structure to perform these functions. Such European command arrangements should be identifiable and the arrangements should be sufficiently well articulated to permit the rapid constitution of a militarily coherent and effective operational force.

Further, the Alliance will support the development of the ESDI within NATO by conducting at the request of and in coordination with the WEU, military planning and exercises for illustrative WEU missions identified by the WEU. On the basis of political guidance to be provided by the WEU Council and the NAC, such planning would, at a minimum:

- prepare relevant information on objectives, scope and participation for illustrative WEU missions;
- identify requirements for planning and exercising of command elements and forces for illustrative WEU-led operations;
- develop appropriate plans for submission through the MC and NAC to the WEU for review and approval.

NATO and the WEU should agree on arrangements for implementing such plans. The NAC will approve the release of NATO assets and capabilities for WEU-led operations, keep itself informed on their use through monitoring with the advice of the NATO Military Authorities and through regular consultations with the WEU Council, and keep their use under review.

. . .

12. As part of its overall adaptation, the Alliance has continued to adapt to the new security situation facing Europe by strengthening its relations with the Partner countries and with other international organisations playing important roles in enhancing security and stability in the Euro-Atlantic area. This pattern of growing, open and transparent cooperation has become a central feature of the Alliance's concept of cooperative security.

13. We reaffirm our commitment to open the Alliance to new members. The process of enlargement is on track and we are convinced that the overall adaptation of the Alliance will facilitate this process. As decided last December, we have a

three-fold process for advancing our preparations this year: we are conducting an intensified dialogue with interested countries; working on a further enhancement of PfP both to help possible new members to join and to provide a strong long-term partnership with NATO for others; and considering the necessary internal adaptations for enlargement. We have today reviewed progress in each of these areas and are pleased at the steady advances being made. We have received a report on the ongoing consultations in the individual, intensified dialogue with, so far, fifteen interested countries. It provides them with an opportunity to improve their understanding of the Alliance and to address implications of NATO enlargement, and provides those who aim for membership with specific and practical details of Alliance membership. The dialogue will continue actively over the coming months. We are pleased to note the national efforts of Partners complementing our work. We will ensure that considerations about enlargement are factored into our deliberations and decisions on the internal adaptation process of the Alliance. We look forward to a report by the Secretary General at our next meeting in December, at which time we will assess progress and consider the way forward.

We reaffirm our determination that the process of opening the Alliance to new members should not create dividing lines in Europe or isolate any country. Our goal remains ever-closer and deeper cooperative ties with all NACC and PfP Partners who wish to build such relations with us. The enlargement of the Alliance is consistent with a wider process of cooperation and integration already underway in today's Europe involving the EU and the WEU as well as the OSCE, the Council of Europe and other European institutions. Our strategy is to help build a broad European security architecture based on true cooperation throughout the whole of Europe.

. . .

20. We are satisfied with the growing ties between NATO and the WEU, and are determined to broaden and deepen our cooperation with the WEU, on the basis of the agreed principles of complementarity and transparency. We welcome the conclusion of a security agreement between our organisations, and the framework it provides for the exchange of information critical to the pursuit of our common security objectives. We hope that this will open the way for more intensive cooperation. We are pleased that, in response to our mandate to the Council in Permanent Session, additional areas of focussed NATO–WEU cooperation (joint meetings on their respective Mediterranean dialogues and exchanges of information in the field of relations with Russia and Ukraine) have been identified. We will explore possibilities for enhanced cooperation in other areas as well. We attach importance to our consultations, including in joint NATO–WEU Council meetings, on issues of common concern, We welcome the resumption of meetings of the WEU Permanent Council with SACEUR.

We continue to support the WEU in its efforts to enhance the development of its operational capabilities and welcome the decisions taken in this regard last month at the WEU Ministerial Council in Birmingham.

21. The Organisation for Security and Cooperation in Europe (OSCE) has an essential role to play in European security and stability. We reaffirm our commitment to support the OSCE's comprehensive approach to security and the ongoing process of developing a security model for the 21st Century. We value the OSCE's effectiveness in the prevention, management and resolution of conflicts and the work of the High Commissioner for National Minorities. These are important contributions to regional stability which we will continue to support and work to strengthen.

The OSCE is playing a vitally important role in Bosnia and Herzegovina contributing to implementing civil aspects of the Peace Agreement, particularly in supervising the preparation and conduct of the first elections, in promoting and monitoring human rights, and in overseeing implementation of confidence- and security-building measures and negotiation of arms limitations. These tasks are a major contribution to building a just and stable peace in the region. IFOR is supporting the OSCE's tasks, and in particular the preparation of the elections, by helping to create a secure environment and promoting freedom of movement. We are also pleased with the practical support that NATO has been able to provide through its Verification Coordination Section to the OSCE in helping establish measures to verify the arms control elements of the Peace Agreement. We support the continued development of such pragmatic cooperation between NATO and the OSCE.

. . .

Document 3/14 Declaration on Euro-Atlantic Security and Cooperation, Issued by the Heads of State and Government, North Atlantic Council, Madrid, 8 July 1997*

1. We, the Heads of State and Government of the member countries of the North Atlantic Alliance, have come together in Madrid to give shape to the new NATO as we move towards the 21st century. Substantial progress has been achieved in the internal adaptation of the Alliance. As a significant step in the evolutionary process of opening the Alliance, we have invited three countries to begin accession talks. We have substantially strengthened our relationship with Partners through the new Euro-Atlantic Partnership Council and enhancement of the Partnership for Peace. The signature on 27th May of the NATO–Russia Founding Act and the Charter we will sign tomorrow with Ukraine bear witness to our commitment to an undivided Europe. We are also enhancing our Mediterranean dialogue. Our aim is to reinforce peace and stability in the Euro-Atlantic area.

---

*   The main elements of the Madrid Declaration of July 1997, included here, are of historical significance for the decision they contain to invite the Czech Republic, Hungary and Poland to begin accession talks with NATO – and for the decision not to include others, such as Slovenia and Romania, whose case had been pressed by France and Italy. The Declaration also includes balancing material on Mediterranean cooperation, on Spain's entry into the full command structure and on NATO's relations with the WEU and OSCE.

A new Europe is emerging, a Europe of greater integration and cooperation. An inclusive European security architecture is evolving to which we are contributing, along with other European organisations. Our Alliance will continue to be a driving force in this process.

2. We are moving towards the realisation of our vision of a just and lasting order of peace for Europe as a whole, based on human rights, freedom and democracy. In looking forward to the 50th anniversary of the North Atlantic Treaty, we reaffirm our commitment to a strong, dynamic partnership between the European and North American Allies, which has been, and will continue to be, the bedrock of the Alliance and of a free and prosperous Europe. The vitality of the transatlantic link will benefit from the development of a true, balanced partnership in which Europe is taking on greater responsibility. In this spirit, we are building a European Security and Defence Identity within NATO. The Alliance and the European Union share common strategic interests. We welcome the agreements reached at the European Council in Amsterdam. NATO will remain the essential forum for consultation among its members and the venue for agreement on policies bearing on the security and defence commitments of Allies under the Washington Treaty.

3. While maintaining our core function of collective defence, we have adapted our political and military structures to improve our ability to meet the new challenges of regional crisis and conflict management. NATO's continued contribution to peace in Bosnia and Herzegovina, and the unprecedented scale of cooperation with other countries and international organisations there, reflect the cooperative approach which is key to building our common security. A new NATO is developing: a new NATO for a new and undivided Europe.

4. The security of NATO's members is inseparably linked to that of the whole of Europe. Improving the security and stability environment for nations in the Euro-Atlantic area where peace is fragile and instability currently prevails remains a major Alliance interest. The consolidation of democratic and free societies on the entire continent, in accordance with OSCE principles, is therefore of direct and material concern to the Alliance. NATO's policy is to build effective cooperation through its outreach activities, including the Euro-Atlantic Partnership Council, with free nations which share the values of the Alliance, including members of the European Union as well as candidates for EU membership.

5. At our last meeting in Brussels, we said that we would expect and would welcome the accession of new members, as part of an evolutionary process, taking into account political and security developments in the whole of Europe. Twelve European countries have so far requested to join the Alliance. We welcome the aspirations and efforts of these nations. The time has come to start a new phase of this process. The Study on NATO Enlargement – which stated, inter alia, that NATO's military effectiveness should be sustained as the Alliance enlarges – the results of the intensified dialogue with interested Partners, and the analyses of relevant factors associated with the admission of new members have provided a basis on which to assess the current state of preparations of the twelve countries aspiring to Alliance membership.

6. Today, we invite the Czech Republic, Hungary and Poland to begin accession talks with NATO. Our goal is to sign the Protocol of Accession at the time of the Ministerial meetings in December 1997 and to see the ratification process completed in time for membership to become effective by the 50th anniversary of the Washington Treaty in April 1999. During the period leading to accession, the Alliance will involve invited countries, to the greatest extent possible and where appropriate, in Alliance activities, to ensure that they are best prepared to undertake the responsibilities and obligations of membership in an enlarged Alliance. We direct the Council in Permanent Session to develop appropriate arrangements for this purpose.

7. Admitting new members will entail resource implications for the Alliance. It will involve the Alliance providing the resources which enlargement will necessarily require. We direct the Council in Permanent Session to bring to an early conclusion the concrete analysis of the resource implications of the forthcoming enlargement, drawing on the continuing work on military implications. We are confident that, in line with the security environment of the Europe of today, Alliance costs associated with the integration of the new members will be manageable and that the resources necessary to meet those costs will be provided.

8. We reaffirm that NATO remains open to new members under Article 10 of the North Atlantic Treaty. The Alliance will continue to welcome new members in a position to further the principles of the Treaty and contribute to security in the Euro-Atlantic area. The Alliance expects to extend further invitations in coming years to nations willing and able to assume the responsibilities and obligations of membership, and as NATO determines that the inclusion of these nations would serve the overall political and strategic interests of the Alliance and that the inclusion would enhance overall European security and stability. To give substance to this commitment, NATO will maintain an active relationship with those nations that have expressed an interest in NATO membership as well as those who may wish to seek membership in the future. Those nations that have previously expressed an interest in becoming NATO members but that were not invited to begin accession talks today will remain under consideration for future membership. The considerations set forth in our 1995 Study on NATO Enlargement will continue to apply with regard to future aspirants, regardless of their geographic location. No European democratic country whose admission would fulfil the objectives of the Treaty will be excluded from consideration. Furthermore, in order to enhance overall security and stability in Europe, further steps in the ongoing enlargement process of the Alliance should balance the security concerns of all Allies.

To support this process, we strongly encourage the active participation by aspiring members in the Euro-Atlantic Partnership Council and the Partnership for Peace, which will further deepen their political and military involvement in the work of the Alliance. We also intend to continue the Alliance's intensified dialogues with those nations that aspire to NATO membership or that otherwise wish to pursue a dialogue with NATO on membership questions. To this end, these intensified dialogues will cover the full range of political, military, financial and security issues relating to possible NATO membership, without prejudice to any eventual Alliance decision. They will include meeting within the EAPC as well as periodic meetings with the North Atlantic Council in Permanent Session and the NATO International Staff and with other NATO bodies as appropriate. In keeping with our pledge to maintain an open door to the admission of additional Alliance members in the future, we also direct that NATO Foreign Ministers keep that process under continual review and report to us.

We will review the process at our next meeting in 1999. With regard to the aspiring members, we recognise with great interest and take account of the positive developments towards democracy and the rule of law in a number of southeastern European countries, especially Romania and Slovenia.

The Alliance recognises the need to build greater stability, security and regional cooperation in the countries of southeast Europe, and in promoting their increasing integration into the Euro-Atlantic community. At the same time, we recognise the progress achieved towards greater stability and cooperation by the states in the Baltic region which are also aspiring members. As we look to the future of the Alliance, progress towards these objectives will be important for our overall goal of a free, prosperous and undivided Europe at peace.

9.   The establishment of the Euro-Atlantic Partnership Council in Sintra constitutes a new dimension in the relations with our Partners. We look forward to tomorrow's meeting with Heads of State and Government under the aegis of the EAPC.

The EAPC will be an essential element in our common endeavour to enhance security and stability in the Euro-Atlantic region. Building on the successful experience with the North Atlantic Cooperation Council and with Partnership for peace, it will provide the overarching framework for all aspects of our wide-ranging cooperation and raise it to a qualitatively new level. It will deepen and give more focus to our multilateral political and security-related discussions, enhance the scope and substance of our practical cooperation, and increase transparency and confidence in security matters among all EAPC Member States. The expanded political dimension of consultation and cooperation which the EAPC will offer will allow Partners, if they wish, to develop a direct political relationship individually or in smaller groups with the Alliance. The EAPC will increase the scope for consultation and cooperation on regional matters and activities.

. . .

16.   Against this background, the members of the Alliance's integrated military structure warmly welcome today's announcement by Spain of its readiness to participate fully in the Alliance's new command structure, once agreement has been reached upon it. Spain's full participation will enhance its overall contribution to the security of the Alliance, help develop the European Security and Defence Identity within NATO and strengthen the transatlantic link.

17.   We are pleased with the progress made in implementing the CJTF concept, including the initial designation of parent headquarters, and look forward to

the forthcoming trials. This concept will enhance our ability to command and control multinational and multiservice forces, generated and deployed at short notice, which are capable of conducting a wide range of military operations. Combined Joint Task Forces will also facilitate the possible participation of non-NATO nations in operations and, by enabling the conduct of WEU-led CJTF operations, will contribute to the development of ESDI within the Alliance.

18. We reaffirm, as stated in our 1994 Brussels Declaration, our full support for the development of the European Security and Defence Identity by making available NATO assets and capabilities for WEU operations. With this in mind, the Alliance is building ESDI, grounded on solid military principles and supported by appropriate military planning and permitting the creation of militarily coherent and effective forces capable of operating under the political control and strategic direction of the WEU. We endorse the decisions taken at last year's Ministerial meeting in Berlin in this regard which serve the interests of the Alliance as well as of the WEU.

We further endorse the considerable progress made in implementing these decisions and in developing ESDI within the Alliance. In this context we endorse the decisions taken with regard to European command arrangements within NATO to prepare, support, command and conduct WEU-led operations using NATO assets and capabilities (including provisional terms of reference for Deputy SACEUR covering his ESDI-related responsibilities both permanent and during crises and operations), the arrangements for the identification of NATO assets and capabilities that could support WEU-led operations, and arrangements for NATO–WEU consultation in the context of such operations. We welcome inclusion of the support for the conduct of WEU-led operations in the context of the ongoing implementation of the revised Alliance defence planning process for all Alliance missions. We also welcome the progress made on work regarding the planning and future exercising of WEU-led operations, and in developing the necessary practical arrangements for release, monitoring and return of NATO assets and the exchange of information between NATO and WEU within the framework of the NATO–WEU Security Agreement.

We note with satisfaction that the building of ESDI within the Alliance has much benefitted from the recent agreement in the WEU on the participation of all European Allies, if they were so to choose, in WEU-led operations using NATO assets and capabilities, as well as in planning and preparing for such operations. We also note the desire on Canada's part to participate in such operations when its interests make it desirable and under modalities to be developed. We direct the Council in Permanent Session to complete expeditiously its work on developing ESDI within NATO, in cooperation with the WEU.

19. The Alliance Strategic Concept, which we adopted at our meeting in Rome in 1991, sets out the principal aims and objectives of the Alliance. Recognising that the strategic environment has changed since then, we have decided to examine the Strategic Concept to ensure that it is fully consistent with Europe's new security situation and challenges. As recommended by our Foreign Ministers in Sintra, we have decided to direct the Council in Permanent Session to develop terms of reference for this examination, and an update as necessary,

for endorsement at the Autumn Ministerial meetings. This work will confirm our commitment to the core function of Alliance collective defence and the indispensable transatlantic link.

20. We reiterate our commitment to full transparency between NATO and WEU in crisis management, including as necessary through joint consultations on how to address contingencies. In this context, we are determined to strengthen the institutional cooperation between the two organisations. We welcome the fact that the WEU has recently undertaken to improve its capacity to plan and conduct crisis management and peacekeeping operations (the Petersberg tasks), including through setting the groundwork for possible WEU-led operations with the support of NATO assets and capabilities, and accepted the Alliance's invitation to contribute to NATO's Ministerial Guidance for defence planning. We will therefore continue to develop the arrangements and procedures necessary for the planning, preparation, conduct and exercise of WEU-led operations using NATO assets and capabilities.

21. We reaffirm our commitment to further strengthening the OSCE as a regional organisation according to Chapter VIII of the Charter of the United Nations and as a primary instrument for preventing conflict, enhancing cooperative security and advancing democracy and human rights. The OSCE, as the most inclusive European-wide security organisation, plays an essential role in securing peace, stability and security in Europe. The principles and commitments adopted by the OSCE provide a foundation for the development of a comprehensive and cooperative European security architecture. Our goal is to create in Europe, through the widest possible cooperation among OSCE states, a common space of security and stability, without dividing lines or spheres of influence limiting the sovereignty of particular states.

    We continue to support the OSCE's work on a Common and Comprehensive Security Model for Europe for the Twenty-First Century, in accordance with the decisions of the 1996 Lisbon Summit, including consideration of developing a Charter on European Security.

22. We welcome the successful holding of elections in Albania as a vital first step in providing the basis for greater stability, democratic government and law and order in the country. We stress, in this context, the importance of a firm commitment by all political forces to continue the process of national reconciliation. We also welcome the crucial role of the Italian-led Multinational Protection Force, with the participation of several Allies and Partners, in helping to create a secure environment for the re-establishment of peace and order. We value the efforts of the OSCE as the coordinating framework for international assistance in Albania, together with the important contributions made by the EU, WEU and the Council of Europe. We are following closely events in Albania and are considering measures through the Partnership for Peace to assist, as soon as the situation permits, in the reconstruction of the armed forces of Albania as an important element of the reform process. Continued international support will be essential in helping to restore stability in Albania.

. . .

26. The steps we have taken today, and tomorrow's meeting with our Partners under the aegis of the EAPC, bring us closer to our goal of building cooperative security in Europe. We remain committed to a free and undivided Euro-Atlantic community in which all can enjoy peace and prosperity. Renewed in structure and approach, strengthened in purpose and resolve, and with a growing membership, NATO will continue to play its part in achieving this goal and in meeting the security challenges in the times ahead.

Document 3/15   Franco-British Declaration on European Defence (The St Malo Declaration), St Malo, 4 December 1998

The Heads of State and Government of France and the United Kingdom are agreed that:

1.   The European Union needs to be in a position to play its full role on the international stage. This means making a reality of the Treaty of Amsterdam, which will provide the essential basis for action by the Union. It will be important to achieve full and rapid implementation of the Amsterdam provisions on CFSP. This includes the responsibility of the European Council to decide on the progressive framing of a common defence policy in the framework of CFSP. The Council must be able to take decisions on an intergovernmental basis, covering the whole range of activity set out in Title V of the Treaty of European Union.

2.   To this end, the Union must have the capacity for autonomous action, backed up by credible military forces, the means to decide to use them, and a readiness to do so, in order to respond to international crises.

In pursuing our objective, the collective defence commitments to which Member States subscribe (set out in Article 5 of the Washington Treaty, Article V of the Brussels Treaty) must be maintained. In strengthening the solidarity between the Member States of the European Union, in order that Europe can make its voice heard in world affairs, while acting in conformity with our respective obligations in NATO, we are contributing to the vitality of a modernised Atlantic Alliance which is the foundation of the collective defence of its members.

Europeans will operate within the institutional framework of the European Union (European Council, General Affairs Council, and meetings of Defence Ministers).

The reinforcement of European solidarity must take into account the various positions of European states.

The different situations of countries in relation to NATO must be respected.

3.   In order for the European Union to take decisions and approve military action where the Alliance as a whole is not engaged, the Union must be given appropriate structures and a capacity for analysis of situations, sources of intelligence, and a capability for relevant strategic planning, without unnecessary duplication, taking account of the existing assets of the WEU and the evolution of its relations with the EU. In this regard, the European Union will also need to have recourse to suitable military means (European capabilities pre-designated within NATO's European pillar or national or multinational European means outside the NATO framework).

4.   Europe needs strengthened armed forces that can react rapidly to the new risks, and which are supported by a strong and competitive European defence industry and technology.

5.   We are determined to unite in our efforts to enable the European Union to give concrete expression to these objectives.

Document 3/16   Summit Communiqué issued by the Heads of State and Government Participating in the Meeting of the North Atlantic Council, Washington DC, 24 April 1999

An Alliance for the 21st Century

. . .

4.   The NATO of the 21st century starts today – a NATO which retains the strengths of the past and has new missions, new members and new partnerships. To this end, we have:

- approved an updated Strategic Concept;
- reaffirmed our commitment to the enlargement process of the Alliance and approved a Membership Action Plan for countries wishing to join;
- completed the work on key elements of the Berlin Decisions on building the European Security and Defence Identity within the Alliance and decided to further enhance its effectiveness;
- launched the Defence Capabilities Initiative;
- intensified our relations with Partners through an enhanced and more operational Partnership for Peace and strengthened our consultations and co-operation within the Euro-Atlantic Partnership Council;
- enhanced the Mediterranean Dialogue; and
- decided to increase Alliance efforts against weapons of mass destruction and their means of delivery.

5.   As part of the Alliance's adaptation to the new security challenges, we have updated our Strategic Concept to make it fully consistent with the Alliance's new security environment. The updated Concept reaffirms our commitment to collective defence and the transatlantic link; takes account of the challenges the Alliance now faces; presents an Alliance ready and with a full range of capabilities to enhance the security and stability of the Euro-Atlantic area; reaffirms our commitment to building the ESDI within the Alliance; highlights the enhanced role of partnership and dialogue; underlines the need to develop defence capabilities to their full potential to meet the spectrum of Alliance missions including forces which are more deployable, sustainable, survivable and able to engage effectively; and provides guidance to the NATO Military Authorities to this end.

6.   To achieve its essential purpose, as an Alliance of nations committed to the Washington Treaty and the United Nations Charter, the Alliance performs the following fundamental security tasks:

Security: To provide one of the indispensable foundations for a stable Euro-Atlantic security environment, based on the growth of democratic institutions and commitment to the peaceful resolution of disputes, in which no country would be able to intimidate or coerce any other through the threat or use of force.

Consultation: To serve, as provided for in Article 4 of the North Atlantic Treaty, as an essential transatlantic forum for Allied consultations on any issues that affect their vital interests, including possible developments posing risks for members' security, and for appropriate co-ordination of their efforts in fields of common concern.

Deterrence and Defence: To deter and defend against any threat of aggression against any NATO member state as provided for in Articles 5 and 6 of the Washington Treaty.

And in order to enhance the security and stability of the Euro-Atlantic area:

- Crisis Management: To stand ready, case-by-case and by consensus, in conformity with Article 7 of the Washington Treaty, to contribute to effective conflict prevention and to engage actively in crisis management, including crisis response operations.
- Partnership: To promote wide-ranging partnership, cooperation, and dialogue with other countries in the Euro-Atlantic area, with the aim of increasing transparency, mutual confidence and the capacity for joint action with the Alliance.

. . .

8. We reaffirm our commitment to preserve the transatlantic link, including our readiness to pursue common security objectives through the Alliance wherever possible. We are pleased with the progress achieved in implementing the Berlin decisions and reaffirm our strong commitment to pursue the process of reinforcing the European pillar of the Alliance on the basis of our Brussels Declaration of 1994 and of the principles agreed at Berlin in 1996. We note with satisfaction that the key elements of the Berlin decisions are being put in place. These include flexible options for the selection of a European NATO Commander and NATO Headquarters for WEU-led operations, as well as specific terms of reference for DSACEUR and an adapted CJTF concept. Close linkages between the two organisations have been established, including planning, exercises (in particular a joint crisis management exercise in 2000) and consultation, as well as a framework for the release and return of Alliance assets and capabilities.

9. We welcome the new impetus given to the strengthening of a common European policy in security and defence by the Amsterdam Treaty and the reflections launched since then in the WEU and – following the St. Malo Declaration – in the EU, including the Vienna European Council Conclusions. This is a process which has implications for all Allies. We confirm that a stronger European role will help contribute to the vitality of our Alliance for the 21st

century, which is the foundation of the collective defence of its members. In this regard:

a. We acknowledge the resolve of the European Union to have the capacity for autonomous action so that it can take decisions and approve military action where the Alliance as a whole is not engaged;

b. As this process goes forward, NATO and the EU should ensure the development of effective mutual consultation, co-operation and transparency, building on the mechanisms existing between NATO and the WEU;

c. We applaud the determination of both EU members and other European Allies to take the necessary steps to strengthen their defence capabilities, especially for new missions, avoiding unnecessary duplication;

d. We attach the utmost importance to ensuring the fullest possible involvement of non-EU European Allies in EU-led crisis response operations, building on existing consultation arrangements within the WEU. We also note Canada's interest in participating in such operations under appropriate modalities.

e. We are determined that the decisions taken in Berlin in 1996, including the concept of using separable but not separate NATO assets and capabilities for WEU-led operations, should be further developed.

10. On the basis of the above principles and building on the Berlin decisions, we therefore stand ready to define and adopt the necessary arrangements for ready access by the European Union to the collective assets and capabilities of the Alliance, for operations in which the Alliance as a whole is not engaged militarily as an Alliance. The Council in Permanent Session will approve these arrangements, which will respect the requirements of NATO operations and the coherence of its command structure, and should address:

a. Assured EU access to NATO planning capabilities able to contribute to military planning for EU-led operations;

b. The presumption of availability to the EU of pre-identified NATO capabilities and common assets for use in EU-led operations;

c. Identification of a range of European command options for EU-led operations, further developing the role of DSACEUR in order for him to assume fully and effectively his European responsibilities;

d. The further adaptation of NATO's defence planning system to incorporate more comprehensively the availability of forces for EU-led operations.

We task the Council in Permanent Session to address these measures on an ongoing basis, taking into account the evolution of relevant arrangements in the EU. The Council will make recommendations to the next Ministerial meeting for its consideration.

11. We have launched a Defence Capabilities Initiative to improve the defence capabilities of the Alliance to ensure the effectiveness of future multinational operations across the full spectrum of Alliance missions in the present and foreseeable security environment with a special focus on improving interoperability among Alliance forces (and where applicable also between Alliance and Partner forces). Defence capabilities will be increased through improvements in the

deployability and mobility of Alliance forces, their sustainability and logistics, their survivability and effective engagement capability, and command and control and information systems. In this connection, we endorse the Council decision to begin implementing the Multinational Joint Logistics Centre concept by the end of 1999, and to develop the C3 system architecture by 2002 to form a basis for an integrated Alliance core capability allowing interoperability with national systems. We have established a temporary High-Level Steering Group to oversee the implementation of the Defence Capabilities Initiative and to meet the requirement of co-ordination and harmonisation among relevant planning disciplines, including for Allies concerned force planning, with the aim of achieving lasting effects on improvements in capabilities and interoperability. Improvements in interoperability and critical capabilities should also strengthen the European pillar in NATO.

. . .

40. The Alliance and the European Union share common strategic interests. Our respective efforts in building peace in the former Yugoslavia are complementary. Both organisations make decisive contributions to peace stability on the European continent. Co-operation between the two organisations on topics of common concern, to be decided on a case-by-case basis, could be developed when it enhances the effectiveness of action by NATO and the EU.

41. The Alliance, in order to adapt its structures to better prepare it to meet future challenges, launched a comprehensive programme including the continuing adaptation of NATO's command structure. Accordingly, Allies welcome the activation decision of the implementation phase of the Alliance's new command structure. This will ensure NATO's ability to carry out the whole range of its missions more effectively and flexibly; support an enlarged Alliance and our more operational relationship with Partners; and provide, as part of the development of the ESDI within NATO, for European command arrangements able to prepare, support, command and conduct WEU-led operations. After successful trials, we have embarked on the full implementation of the CJTF concept, giving us an important new tool for crisis management in the next century. Allies also welcome the full integration of Spain into NATO's military structure from January this year, another significant milestone for the Alliance.

Document 3/17   Declaration of the WEU Council of Ministers (The Bremen Declaration), Bremen, 10–11 May 1999

. . .

4. Ministers had an exchange of views on the question of European security and defence in light of the entry into force of the Amsterdam Treaty, of the reflections launched since the Rome Declaration in WEU and – following the St. Malo Declaration – in the EU, including the Vienna European Council conclusions, and of NATO's Washington Summit. They looked forward to the decisions to be taken in this regard by the European Council in Cologne.

Ministers stressed the importance of continuing to develop European security and defence. This development will serve the interests of all WEU nations. In this context they welcomed the informal reflection mandated in Rome and held at meetings of directors for security policy from Foreign and Defence Ministries which had confirmed:

- the willingness of European nations to strengthen European operational capabilities for Petersberg tasks based on appropriate decision-making bodies and effective military means, within NATO or national and multi-national means outside the NATO framework;
- their wish to further develop these structures and capabilities in complementarity with the Atlantic Alliance whilst avoiding unnecessary duplication;
- the need for WEU to be operationally effective with the involvement and participation of all WEU nations in accordance with their status and to continue its cooperation with the EU and NATO, in preparation for any new arrangements which may be agreed in light on ongoing developments.

Ministers decided that the informal reflection should be pursued on this basis.

Ministers took note of the oral report of the Presidency Defence Minister on the informal meeting of EU and European NATO Defence Ministers in Bremen. They welcomed the determination expressed on this occasion to contribute to the development of an effective European defence and security policy and the capability for European crisis management in the scope of Petersberg tasks.

Ministers welcomed the report of the Presidency on the audit of assets and capabilities available for European operations inter alia on the basis of the Special Report prepared in NATO. They asked the Permanent Council to continue the evaluation of the first results contained in the Report. They requested the Permanent Council to carry out phase two of the audit, on the basis of modalities proposed by the Presidency. This shall, in addition to multi-national forces, also cover the identification and evaluation of relevant national forces and force capabilities. The results shall be presented to the next Ministerial meeting in Luxembourg.

The findings of this audit should help to identify what changes need to be made to ensure that WEU's operational instruments (Military Staff, Military Committee, Satellite Centre etc) can make a more effective contribution to the mounting of crisis-management missions within the EU framework.

They should also assist nations in identifying areas where national and multi-national capabilities need to be strengthened in order to make the conduct of Petersberg operations more effective.

5.   Ministers welcomed the entry into force of the Treaty of Amsterdam.

Recalling the invitation of the European Council in Vienna to bring forward the completion of arrangements for enhanced WEU–EU cooperation under the Protocol of Art. 17 of the Treaty on European Union, so that these may come into effect on the Treaty's entry into force, Ministers endorsed the present set of arrangements which had been elaborated in WEU and EU and underlined the need for close dialogue and cooperation at all levels between the two Organisations with a view to the full application of the Amsterdam Treaty.

6.   Ministers welcomed the results of the NATO Summit in Washington.

They noted with satisfaction that the key elements for the development of the European Security and Defence Identity within the Alliance, building on the Berlin, Brussels and Birmingham ministerial decisions, are being put in place and that the Alliance reaffirmed its strong commitment to pursue the process of reinforcing its European pillar. In this context, they welcomed the agreement with NATO of a Framework Document on the release of assets to WEU, and of improved consultation arrangements in the event of a WEU-led operation using NATO assets and capabilities. They appreciated that the Alliance welcomed the new impetus given to the strengthening of a common European policy in security and defence as laid out in paragraphs 8, 9 and 10 of the Washington Summit Communique.

7.   Ministers noted with interest the report by the Presidency on the Military Committee meeting held at Berlin on 20 April 1999. In particular, they welcomed the progress made with regard to the organisational structure and functioning of the Military Staff and the decisions taken with a view to improving harmonisation of future military requirements in support of the process of force and armaments planning and subsequently for further developing European military capabilities.

Ministers endorsed the WEU proposal to NATO to incorporate the capabilities of the Associate Partner countries drawn from the PARP process into the Special Report on forces and capabilities available for WEU-led operations. This, as well as their future participation in relevant WEU discussions, would lead to a further enhancement of the role of the Associate Partner countries in the operational development of WEU.

8.   Ministers underlined Russia's key role in Europe's security and stability and looked forward towards further developing WEU's relationship with Russia based on enhanced political dialogue and practical cooperation.

Declaration on the New Associate Members of WEU: The Czech Republic, Hungary and Poland

1.   Ministers warmly welcomed the Associate Membership in WEU of the Czech Republic, Hungary and Poland as a significant contribution to the security of Europe and as an important step towards strengthening WEU in the perspective of a common European policy in security and defence. They considered, moreover, that the association of these three countries represents a significant step in the strengthening of the European pillar of the Atlantic Alliance, and thus of the transatlantic link itself.

. . .

4.   Ministers recalled the essential importance of the full participation, in accordance with their status and relevant documents, of Associate Members in all aspects of the preparation, planning and conduct of WEU Petersberg operations. They

looked forward to the part the Associate Members would play in the work and evolution of WEU.

Document 3/18   Conclusions of the European Council Meeting in Cologne, 3–4 June 1999*

. . .

ANNEX III

European Council Declaration on strengthening the Common European Policy on Security and Defence

1.   We, the members of the European council, are resolved that the European Union shall play its full role on the international stage. To that end, we intend to give the European Union the necessary means and capabilities to assume its responsibilities regarding a common European policy on security and defence. The work undertaken on the initiative of the German Presidency and the entry into force of the Treaty of Amsterdam permit us today to take a decisive step forward.

In pursuit of our Common Foreign and Security Policy objectives and the progressive framing of a common defence policy, we are convinced that the Council should have the ability to take decisions on the full range of conflict prevention and crisis management tasks defined in the Treaty on European Union, the 'Petersberg tasks'. To this end, the Union must have the capacity for autonomous action, backed up by credible military forces, the means to decide to use them, and a readiness to do so, in order to respond to international crises without prejudice to actions by NATO. The EU will thereby increase its ability to contribute to international peace and security in accordance with the principles of the UN Charter.

2.   We are convinced that to fully assume its tasks in the field of conflict prevention and crisis management the European Union must have at its disposal the appropriate capabilities and instruments. We therefore commit ourselves to further develop more effective European military capabilities from the basis of existing national, bi-national and multinational capabilities and to strengthen our own capabilities for that purpose. This requires the maintenance of a sustained defence effort, the implementation of the necessary adaptations and notably the reinforcement of our capabilities in the field of intelligence, strategic transport, command and control. This also requires efforts to adapt, exercise and bring together national and multinational European forces.

We also recognise the need to undertake sustained efforts to strengthen the industrial and technological defence base, which we want to be competitive and dynamic. We are determined to foster the restructuring of the European defence industries amongst those States involved. With industry we will therefore work towards closer and more efficient defence industry collaboration. We will seek further progress in the harmonisation of military requirements and the planning and procurement of arms, as Member States consider appropriate.

*   [See also document 2/24.]

3. We welcome the results of the NATO Washington summit as regards NATO support for the process launched by the EU and its confirmation that a more effective role for the European Union in conflict prevention and crisis management will contribute to the vitality of a renewed Alliance. In implementing this process launched by the EU, we shall ensure the development of effective mutual consultation, cooperation and transparency between the European Union and NATO.

We want to develop an effective EU-led crisis management in which NATO members, as well as neutral and non-allied members, of the EU can participate fully and on an equal footing in the EU operations.

We will put in place arrangements that allow non-EU European allies and partners to take part to the fullest possible extent in this endeavour.

4. We therefore approve and adopt the report prepared by the German Presidency, which reflects the consensus among the Member States.

5. We are now determined to launch a new step in the construction of the European Union. To this end we task the General Affairs Council to prepare the conditions and the measures necessary to achieve these objectives, including the definition of the modalities for the inclusion of those functions of the WEU which will be necessary for the EU to fulfil its new responsibilities in the area of the Petersberg tasks. In this regard, our aim is to take the necessary decisions by the end of the year 2000. In that event, the WEU as an organisation would have completed its purpose. The different status of Member States with regard to collective defence guarantees will not be affected. The Alliance remains the foundation of the collective defence of its Member States.

We therefore invite the Finnish Presidency to take the work forward within the General Affairs Council on the basis of this declaration and the report of the Presidency to the European Council meeting in Cologne. We look forward to a progress report by the Finnish Presidency to the Helsinki European Council meeting.

Presidency Report on Strengthening of the Common European Policy on Security and Defence

1. Introduction

The Treaty of Amsterdam which entered into force on 1 May provides for the enhancement of the Common Foreign and Security Policy (CFSP), including the progressive framing of a common defence policy as provided in Article 17 of the TEU. The Treaty also provides for the possibility of integrating the WEU into the EU, should the European Council so decide.

The European Council in Vienna welcomed the new impetus given to the debate on a common European policy in security and defence. It considered that in order for the EU to be in a position to play its full role on the international stage, the CFSP must be backed by credible operational capabilities. Furthermore, it welcomed

252 Europeanforeignpolicy
the Franco–British declaration made on 4 December 1998 in St. Malo. The European Council invited the German Presidency to pursue this debate and agreed to examine the question again at the European Council in Cologne. To this end Foreign Ministers discussed the subject at their informal meeting in Reinhartshausen on 13/14 March and at the General Affairs Council on 17 May.

The NATO Washington Summit welcomed the new impetus given to the strengthening of a common European policy on security and defence by the Amsterdam Treaty and confirmed that a stronger European role will help contribute to the vitality of the Alliance for the 21st century. The NATO summit furthermore stressed that the development of a CFSP, as called for in the Amsterdam Treaty, would be compatible with the common security and defence policy established within the framework of the Washington Treaty. This process will lead to more complementarity, cooperation and synergy.

At the WEU Ministerial Council on 10 and 11 May this question was also discussed on the basis of the informal reflection which was initiated at the Rome Ministerial Council. Member States will undertake efforts in line with the conclusions of the ongoing WEU Audit of European defence capabilities.

2. Guiding Principles

The aim is to strengthen the CFSP by the development of a common European policy on security and defence. This requires a capacity for autonomous action backed up by credible military capabilities and appropriate decision making bodies. Decisions to act would be taken within the framework of the CFSP according to appropriate procedures in order to reflect the specific nature of decisions in this field. The Council of the European Union would thus be able to take decisions on the whole range of political, economic and military instruments at its disposal when responding to crisis situations. The European Union is committed to preserve peace and strengthen international security in accordance with the principles of the UN Charter as well as the principles of the Helsinki Final Act and the objectives of the Charter of Paris, as provided for in Article 11 of the TEU.

The Amsterdam Treaty incorporates the Petersberg tasks ('humanitarian and rescue tasks, peace-keeping tasks and tasks of combat forces in crisis management, including peace-making') into the Treaty.

The focus of our efforts therefore would be to assure that the European Union has at its disposal the necessary capabilities (including military capabilities) and appropriate structures for effective EU decision making in crisis management within the scope of the Petersberg tasks. This is the area where a European capacity to act is required most urgently. The development of an EU military crisis management capacity is to be seen as an activity within the framework of the CFSP (Title V of the TEU) and as a part of the progressive framing of a common defence policy in accordance with Article 17 of the TEU.

The Atlantic Alliance remains the foundation of the collective defence of its Members. The commitments under Article 5 of the Washington Treaty and Article V of the Brussels Treaty will in any event be preserved for the Member States party to these Treaties. The policy of the Union shall not prejudice the specific character of the security and defence policy of certain Member States.

3. Decision Making

As regards EU decision making in the field of security and defence policy, necessary arrangements must be made in order to ensure political control and strategic direction of EU-led Petersberg operations so that the EU can decide and conduct such operations effectively.

Furthermore, the EU will need a capacity for analysis of situations, sources of intelligence, and a capability for relevant strategic planning.

This may require in particular:

- regular (or ad hoc) meetings of the General Affairs Council, as appropriate including Defence Ministers;
- a permanent body in Brussels (Political and Security Committee) consisting of representatives with pol/mil expertise;
- an EU Military Committee consisting of Military Representatives making recommendations to the Political and Security Committee;
- a EU Military Staff including a Situation Centre;
- other resources such as a Satellite Centre, Institute for Security Studies.

Further institutional questions may need to be addressed.

Decisions relating to crisis management tasks, in particular decisions having military or defence implications will be taken in accordance with Article 23 of the Treaty on European Union. Member States will retain in all circumstances the right to decide if and when their national forces are deployed.

4. Implementation

As regards military capabilities, Member States need to develop further forces (including headquarters) that are suited also to crisis management operations, without any unnecessary duplication. The main characteristics include: deployability, sustainability, interoperability, flexibility and mobility.

For the effective implementation of EU-led operations the European Union will have to determine, according to the requirements of the case, whether it will conduct:

- EU-led operations using NATO assets and capabilities or
- EU-led operations without recourse to NATO assets and capabilities.

For EU-led operations without recourse to NATO assets and capabilities, the EU could use national or multinational European means pre-identified by Member States. This will require either the use of national command structures providing multinational representation in headquarters or drawing on existing command structures within multinational forces. Further arrangements to enhance the capacity of European multinational and national forces to respond to crisis situations will be needed.

For EU-led operations having recourse to NATO assets and capabilities, including European command arrangements, the main focus should be on the following aspects:

- Implementation of the arrangements based on the Berlin decisions of 1996 and the Washington NATO summit decisions of April 1999.
- The further arrangements set out by NATO at its summit meeting in Washington should address in particular:
  - assured EU access to NATO planning capabilities able to contribute to military planning for EU-led operations;
  - the presumption of availability to the EU of pre-identified NATO capabilities and common assets for use in EU-led operations.

5. Modalities of Participation and Cooperation

The successful creation of the European policy on security and defence will require in particular:

- the possibility of all EU Member States, including non-allied members, to participate fully and on an equal footing in EU operations;
- satisfactory arrangements for European NATO members who are not EU Member States to ensure their fullest possible involvement in EU-led operations, building on existing consultation arrangements within WEU;
- arrangements to ensure that all participants in an EU-led operation will have equal rights in respect of the conduct of that operation, without prejudice to the principle of the EU's decision-making autonomy, notably the right of the Council to discuss and decide matters of principle and policy;
- the need to ensure the development of effective mutual consultation, cooperation and transparency between NATO and the EU;
- the consideration of ways to ensure the possibility for WEU Associate Partners to be involved.

. . .

Section 4 Major policy developments

(a) East–West and transatlantic relations

EPC and the CSCE

Only after Cold War tensions had diminished, in the late 1960s, did the Community begin to play a role in East–West relations. Before then, it lacked a foreign policy dimension, and US policy towards the Soviet bloc inhibited independent initiatives by the Community. Detente allowed the evolving EPC to develop common positions with respect to the Soviet Union and Eastern Europe that differed from the US stance. The EPC positions were first expressed in the forum of the Conference on Security and Cooperation in Europe (CSCE).

In 1969, the West (through NATO) accepted a long-standing Soviet proposal to convene a pan-European security conference, on the condition that talks on force reductions be held at the same time (in line with 1967 Harmel Report, document 1/13). At the first EPC meeting on 19 November 1970, in Munich, the foreign ministers discussed the proposed conference and agreed to work out a common position. While European security and detente were obviously of common interest for the EC Member States, other factors also spurred cooperation. There was room for an EPC initiative because the United States initially showed little interest in the CSCE. West Germany sought a European position to counterbalance its own *Ostpolitik*. The Six recognized that a common stance would be more effective in responding to the Soviet Union's agenda for the CSCE: legitimation of the post-war borders in Europe. The Six (later Nine) wanted to improve security and detente, encourage human rights, foster economic cooperation and avoid validating the status quo.

Because economic cooperation was to be discussed in the CSCE, the question of the Commission's participation arose, in both the 'internal' EPC preparations and the CSCE itself. At the end of 1972, the Member States were due to hand over responsibility for negotiating trade agreements with the Soviet bloc countries to the Community.* But if the Commission were to be formally represented at the CSCE, the Soviet Union might insist on CMEA participation (and thus increase its control over the East Europeans' foreign economic relations). France also resisted boosting the Commission's stature. In the end, the Commission took part in the CSCE's work (document 4a/1) and participated

---

* But since the Council for Mutual Economic Assistance (CMEA) members refused to recognize the Community, no formal EC trade agreements were concluded with the Eastern bloc until the late 1980s (although Romania broke with the official CMEA line and signed a trade agreement with the EC in 1980).

in the *ad hoc* group which prepared the EPC positions on economic cooperation. There was no separate EC delegation to the CSCE; instead, Commission representatives joined the delegation of the Member State which held the Community Presidency. The Helsinki Final Act was signed by Italian Prime Minister Aldo Moro in his dual capacity as the representative of Italy and president of the EC Council (document 4a/3).

The European Council, in July 1975, congratulated itself on the constructive role played by the Nine at the Helsinki conference (document 4a/2). The Nine had led the West, which in turn set the agenda for the East, and the Helsinki Final Act reflected this input.

By the late 1970s, however, detente was under strain and the importance of military issues increased, in the CSCE and in East–West relations generally. EPC did not formally address military subjects (such as the stationing of Cruise missiles in Western Europe) and played less and less of a role at successive CSCE review conferences. In 1978, France launched its proposal for a Conference on Disarmament in Europe (1984–6) outside the EPC framework. NATO became the forum in which the West coordinated its position in the CSCE. The United States also took much more interest in the CSCE, using it as a forum to berate the Soviet Union for not fulfilling CSCE obligations, especially on human rights issues. The CSCE review conference in Madrid (1980–3) was particularly tense and rancorous.

Document 4a/1   Statement by K.B. Andersen, Foreign Minister of Denmark, during the Conference on Security and Cooperation in Europe, Helsinki, 3 July 1973

. . .

Co-operation in the fields of economics, of science and technology and of the environment encompass matters under the competence of the European Economic Community of which nine of the States participating in the Conference on Security and Co-operation in Europe are members. It is mainly a question of commercial exchanges where the Community has a common policy.

Accordingly, the nine States have examined the instructions on commercial exchanges also in their capacity of members of the European Economic Community. In the name of the Community I am able to affirm concurrence in these instructions.

At the same time I draw the attention of the participants to the fact that, depending on the subjects, the Community may become involved according to its own competence and procedures in the future work of the Conference and that the implementation of any possible outcome of negotiations on these subjects will depend on agreement with the Community.

May I finally recall the intention of the Community and of its member States, expressed by the Heads of State or Government of these States at the Conference held in Paris in October 1972, to render a concerted and constructive contribution to the progress of the Conference.

Document 4a/2   Statement by the European Council on the Conference for Security and Cooperation in Europe, Brussels, 17 July 1975

1.

Viewing the final stage of the Conference on Security and Co-operation in Europe, the European Council is glad to find that after two years of negotiation, thirty-five countries of Europe and North America have succeeded in defining the guidelines for their future relations.

2.

The Conference was marked by the concerted contribution made by the member countries of the Community, in accordance with the intention expressed by their Heads of Government meeting in Paris on 22 October 1972, just before the consultations opened in Helsinki. The Helsinki and Geneva negotiations afforded the Nine the opportunity to take up a common task which became a shining example of constructive co-operation; they also showed that the process of growing unity in which the Community countries embarked, fully aware of their responsibilities to history, has now reached the stage of maturation.

. . .

4.

The European Council believes that the substance of the Final Act is a milestone on the road of détente, whose true significance can be gauged only in terms of the effective application, on the part of each participating State, of all the principles reaffirmed, and of the action agreed. For their part, the Nine are resolved to adhere to the principles voiced by the Conference and to take any measures in their power to ensure that as far as they are concerned, the conclusions are put into practice. Thus the climate of mutual trust could be established which would allow the barriers to be opened in order to bring the peoples more closely together.

Moved by the firm hope that implementing the conclusions of the CSCE will lead to a real improvement in relations between the States taking part in the Conference, the Nine feel that, on such a basis, continuation of the multilateral dialogue instituted by the CSCE will be of value in the future. They declare themselves already resolved to co-operate towards this in the positive spirit which inspired their contribution to the work of the Conference.

. . .

Document 4a/3   Statement by Italian Prime Minister A. Moro, during the third stage of the Conference for Security and Cooperation in Europe, Helsinki, 30 July 1975

It is within this framework of a dynamic perspective and an enrichment of the very fabric of political and human relations that, as Chairman of the Council of the European Communities, I would like to recall the declaration made in Helsinki on 3 July, 1973 by the Minister of Foreign Affairs of Denmark on behalf of the European Communities. Mr. Andersen drew the attention of his colleagues to the fact that, according to the subjects, the Communities could be involved, in conformity with their competences and internal procedures, in the work of the Conference and that the implementation of the results of the negotiations on these subjects would depend on the agreement of the Communities. The latter have considered the conclusions of the Conference on these matters and I have the honour to inform you that these have been accepted.

Consequently, I shall sign the Final Act of the Conference in my dual capacity: as representative of Italy and as President in office of the Council of the Communities respectively.

Third countries will have the assurance therefore that the conclusions of this Conference will be applied by the Communities in all matters which are within their competence, or which may come within their competence in future.

As regards these matters, the expression "Participating States", mentioned in the Final Act, is to be considered therefore as applicable also to the European Communities.

As for the implementation of the conclusions of the Conference, the points of view of the Communities will be expressed in accordance with their internal rules each time a matter within their competence is involved.

I would like to recall that in terms of economic and social development, and also with a view to greater and improved international economic relations, the European Communities have already made a significant contribution to the objectives of this Conference. The Member States of the European Communities, recalling the evolving nature of their institutions, consider that the results of the Conference will not provide an hindrance to the process of European integration which they intend freely to pursue. This process, which is a factor of peace and security, constitutes a positive contribution to the development of co-operation in Europe. The Member States intend to continue together to co-operate with all participating countries in order to achieve this objective.

The cohesion of the nine countries of the European Communities has proved useful in the work of the Conference and this is indeed a constructive contribution in trying to find points of common agreement with the participating States. In fact it is a testimony to the open spirit with which these countries intend to continue their multilateral dialogue for the purpose of détente, peace and co-operation.

The Community and the second Cold War, 1979–89

While the United States had never been convinced that detente was based on solid ground, there was much more reluctance in Western Europe to rupture relations. West European governments believed that interdependence with the Soviet Union could reduce the military threat in Europe; their economic interests in trade with the East were also much stronger than those of the United States, for obvious geographical and historical reasons. The history of East–West relations in the first half of the 1980s is also that of frequent clashes in West–West relations.

Afghanistan

On 26 December 1979, the Soviet Union invaded Afghanistan. The United States restricted exports to the Soviet Union and imposed a grain embargo. The delayed EPC reaction to the event is infamous: foreign ministers took nearly three weeks to formulate their initial collective response.* The foreign ministers were unable to agree on a joint statement via Coreu and, because of the Christmas vacation period and the reluctance of the Italian Presidency (from 1 January 1980) to call an emergency meeting, the first time they met to discuss the Soviet invasion was 'in the margins' of the General Affairs Council on 15 January (this was the first time the foreign ministers met in both EPC and EC frameworks, and both the political directors and permanent representatives were involved.)

At that meeting, the foreign ministers agreed on a declaration (document 4a/4), which called the invasion a flagrant interference in the internal affairs of a non-aligned country. But the Member States were divided over further action. On the same day, acting as the Council, the foreign ministers could agree only not to undercut US grain sanctions. They did not agree on a US proposal to boycott the 1980 Olympics in Moscow: the UK favoured a tough stand, but Germany and France were concerned not to undermine detente. The EPC/Community position provoked American dismay.

On 19 February, the Nine took more positive action, putting forward a proposal to 'neutralize' Afghanistan (document 4a/5). While the Third World response to the idea was favourable, the Soviet Union opposed it. This remained the EPC stance, as declared again by the European Council in June 1980. Over a year later, at the instigation of UK Foreign Secretary Lord Carrington, the Ten took the initiative further. The Luxembourg European Council, in June 1981, proposed convening an international conference, in two stages (document 4a/6). In the first stage, the participants would work out arrangements to end the external intervention; in the second stage, they would agree on implementing the arrangements. But the Soviet Union again considered the idea to be unacceptable and it was shelved (document 4a/7).

Document 4a/4   Declaration by the Nine Foreign Ministers on Afghanistan, Brussels, 15 January 1980

The Foreign Ministers of the Nine countries of the European Community have focused their attention on the Afghan crisis, in the light of its dramatic developments, the debate in the Security Council and the Resolution adopted by the General Assembly of the United Nations.

The nine Ministers have reaffirmed their grave concern with regard to the crisis created by the military intervention of the Soviet Union in Afghanistan, which represents a serious violation of the principles of international relations enshrined in the Charter of the United Nations. They have emphasized that the explanations given by the Soviet Union to justify its intervention in Afghanistan are unacceptable. They take the view that the Soviet intervention constitutes a flagrant interference in the internal affairs of a non-aligned country belonging to the Islamic World and constitutes furthermore a threat to peace, security and stability in the region, including

---

*   This prompted the agreement in the 1981 London Report (document 2/11) that three Member States could call an emergency EPC meeting within 48 hours.

the Indian subcontinent, the Middle East and the Arab World. It is with great concern that the Foreign Ministers of the nine countries of the European Community have noted that despite the almost universal protests against the Soviet military intervention, the Soviet Union has vetoed a Resolution of the Afghan crisis sponsored by non-aligned countries and supported by a large majority of Members of the Security Council. They urge the Soviet Union to act in conformity with the Resolution on the Afghan crisis adopted by the General Assembly of the United Nations with an overwhelming majority, which calls for the immediate and unconditional withdrawal of all foreign troops from Afghanistan.

The nine countries of the European Community have devoted continuous efforts to the cause of détente and they remain convinced that this process is in the interest of all members of the international community. They are, however, convinced that détente is indivisible and has a global dimension. They, therefore, urge the Soviet Union, in conformity with the standards and principles of the United Nations Charter, to allow the Afghan people to determine their own future without foreign interference.

In formulating their position on this important question, the Foreign Ministers of the Member Countries of the European Community have also been keenly aware of the sufferings borne by the Afghan people as a whole as a result of the crisis, including those Afghans who are being forced to leave their country.

Document 4a/5   Declaration by the Nine Foreign Ministers on Afghanistan, Rome, 19 February 1980

1.
The Nine focused their discussion mainly on the situation created by the Soviet intervention in Afghanistan.

2.
They noted their agreement on the analysis of the situation and its implications. In this connections they took the view that their declaration of 15th January is still completely valid.

3.
They stressed in particular that the withdrawal of Soviet troops from Afghanistan remains their objective and that they will endeavour to establish the conditions for this.

4.
It is also their desire to seek out ways and means of restoring a situation in line with the Resolution of the Assembly. General of the United Nations of 14th January, which appeals to all States to respect the sovereignty, territorial integrity, political independence and non-aligned character of Afghanistan and to refrain from any interference in the internal affairs of that country.

5.
They take the view that, in this spirit, the crisis could be overcome constructively through an arrangement which allows a neutral Afghanistan to be outside competition among the powers.

6.

Accordingly, they have decided to go into this point more thoroughly and to concert their position on the subject with all allied and friendly countries and with all countries having an interest in the equilibrium and stability of the region.

Document 4a/6   Declaration by the European Council on Afghanistan, Luxembourg, 29–30 June 1981

1.

The European Council notes with deep concern that the situation in Afghanistan remains an important cause of international tension, that Soviet troops remain in Afghanistan and that the sufferings of the Afghan people continue to increase.

2.

The European Council recalls its earlier statements, notably those issued at Venice on 13 June 1980, and Maastricht on 24 March 1981, which stressed the urgent need to bring about a solution which would enable Afghanistan to return to its traditional independent and non-aligned status free from external interference and with the Afghan people having the full capacity to exercise their right to self-determination. In keeping with the Resolutions voted by the United Nations, the Islamic Conference and the New Delhi Conference of the Non-Aligned Movement, the European Council has made it clear on several occasions that it will support any initiative which could lead to the desired result.

3.

The European Council considers that the time has come for a fresh attempt to open the way to a political solution to the problem of Afghanistan. They therefore propose that an international conference should be convened as soon as possible, for example in October or November 1981, and that the Conference should consist of two stages, each stage being an integral part of the conference.

4.

The purpose of Stage One would be to work out international arrangements designed to bring about the cessation of external intervention and the establishment of safeguards to prevent such intervention in the future and thus to create conditions in which Afghanistan's independence and nonalignment can be assured.

5.

The European Council proposes that in due course the Permanent Members of the United Nations Security Council, Pakistan, Iran and India and the Secretary-General of the United Nations and the Secretary-General of the Islamic Conference, or their representatives, be invited to participate in Stage One of the Conference.

6.

The purpose of Stage Two would be to reach agreement on the implementation of the international arrangements worked out in Stage One and on all other matters designed to assure Afghanistan's future as an independent and non-aligned state.

7.

Stage Two would be attended by the participants in Stage One together with representatives of the Afghan people.

8.

The member states of the European Community will be ready at a later stage to make further proposals on the detailed arrangements for the proposed conference.

9.

The European Council firmly believes that the situation in Afghanistan continues to demand the attention of the international community. It is convinced that this proposal offers a constructive way forward and therefore calls on the international community to support it fully with the aim of reducing international tension and ending human suffering in Afghanistan.

Document 4a/7   Speech by Lord Carrington on behalf of the Ten to the European Parliament, Strasbourg, 8 July 1981

. . . I have just come back from Moscow where I have been discussing this with Mr Gromyko. In explaining the proposal I made it plain that I was speaking on behalf of the Ten member states of the European Community. I emphasised that the problem with which it dealt was one of global significance and whose solution was essential in the interest of peace, stability and the development of East/West relations. I reminded the Soviet Government that the Ten—and indeed the great majority of the international community—are convinced that the complete withdrawal of Soviet troops is an essential element of any solution. Mr Gromyko took the view that the proposal by the Ten was, as he put it, "unrealistic", because the main problem was intervention by others in the affairs of Afghanistan, because it was not stated that the present Afghan regime should participate at the outset and because the proposed composition of the conference was unsatisfactory. I told him that I did not find these arguments convincing. Mr Gromyko did not say that he rejected the proposal and did not exclude further discussion. For my part I made it plain that the proposal, which has already received an encouraging degree of support in the international community, remains on the table and that a positive response from the Soviet Union was highly desirable in the interests of world peace and stability. The proposal provides the best hope of a negotiated settlement, which is wanted by the international community, and which the Soviet Union has also said that they want. It is obvious that a Soviet refusal to negotiate on Afghanistan makes it impossible to speak of normal relations and prejudices efforts to reach agreement with the Soviet Union on other matters. Ours is a serious proposal, and I hope that on reflection the Soviet Government will react in a constructive manner.*

. . .

---

*   After very little reflection, the Soviet Union let the matter drop.

Poland

A further blow to detente, and another occasion on which the Community/EPC clashed with the United States, came with the declaration of martial law in Poland on 13 December 1981. Following the emergence of Solidarnosc in Poland in August 1980, the European Council warned the Soviet Union not to interfere – in December 1980 (document 4a/8) and again in March 1981. The Polish government's decision to declare martial law thus caught the West off-balance. The United States imposed sanctions on both Poland and the Soviet Union, which it held responsible for the Polish decision, and pressed the West European countries to do the same. On 15 December, the Ten declared their concern at the imposition of martial law and warned against outside interference. Three weeks later, on 4 January 1982, the foreign ministers issued a stronger statement calling for the end of martial law and noted that they were considering economic measures (document 4a/9).

The Member States did not, however, agree on the measures to be taken. Germany was loath to endanger detente by imposing sanctions; others were not so reluctant. Greece was unhappy with the EPC stance in general, and withdrew its agreement to most of the 4 January communiqué. In February, the Council (not EPC) discussed restricting some imports from the Soviet Union; sanctions on Poland itself were out of the question. But Greece opposed the proposal, and Denmark did not like using article 113 (common commercial policy) for political purposes. The final regulation to cut imports from the Soviet Union was adopted on 15 March; Greece was excluded from its application.* This was the first time that an EC regulation was used to back up a common position decided in EPC.

This response clearly differed from that of the United States. As if to reiterate the point, the European Council in March 1982 stressed the importance of economic ties for stabilizing East–West relations (document 4a/10). The United States considered this completely inadequate. In June, it tried to block the involvement of West European companies in a project to pump natural gas from Siberia to Western Europe, by extending its sanctions to all subsidiaries and licensees of US companies. The Community protested (documents 4a/11 and 4a/12), and in November 1982, the United States lifted its 'extraterritorial' sanctions. In July 1983, martial law was lifted in Poland, and the EC measures were allowed to lapse at the end of the year.

---

* The regulation, no. 596/82 (OJ L 72, 16 March 1982), was based on article 113, and contains only a vague reference to the political reasons behind it ('Whereas the interests of the Community require that imports from the USSR be reduced'). Denmark's objections were in the future countered by referring to 'discussions in the context of EPC' in regulations implementing sanctions. Denmark, Greece and Ireland were sometimes known as the 'footnote countries' in the 1980s. They would place reservations on some sections of EPC documents, but would not block agreement among the other Member States. This anticipated the 'constructive abstention' clause of the Treaty of Amsterdam (J13.1).

Document 4a/8   Declaration by the European Council on East–West Relations, Luxembourg, 2 December 1980

The European Council expressed its sympathy for Poland and outlined the position of the Nine as follows:

1.
In their relations with Poland, the Nine conform and will conform strictly to the United Nations Charter and to the principles of the Helsinki Final Act.

2.
In this context, they would point out that in subscribing to these principles, the States signatory to the Final Act have undertaken in particular to:
– respect of the right of every country to choose and freely develop its own political, social, economic and cultural system as well as to determine its own laws and regulations,
– refrain from any direct or indirect, individual or collective intervention in internal or external affairs which fall within the national competence of another signatory State regardless of their mutual relations,
– recognize the right of all peoples to pursue their own political, economic, social and cultural development as they see fit and without external interference.

3.
The Nine accordingly call upon all the signatory States to abide by these principles with regard to Poland and the Polish people. They emphasize that any other attitude would have very serious consequences for the future of international relations in Europe and throughout the world.

4.
They state their willingness to meet, insofar as their recources allow, the requests for economic aid which have been made to them by Poland.

Document 4a/9   Communiqué Issued on the Occasion of the Informal European Political Cooperation Ministerial Discussion on Poland, Brussels, 4 January 1982

1.
The Ten utterly disapprove of the development of the situation in Poland.

2.
They have noted the declarations of the Polish leadership of its intention to maintain national independence and to reestablish in the near future liberty and the process of reform as well as resuming the dialogue with the various elements of the Polish Nation. Unhappily the Ten must note today that, contrary to these declarations, what has taken place has not been dialogue but repression bringing in its train violations of the most elementary human and citizen's rights, contrary to the Helsinki Final Act, the United Nations Charter, and the Universal Declaration of Human Rights.

3.

The Ten therefore appeal urgently to the Polish authorities to end as soon as possible the state of martial law, to release those arrested, and to restore a genuine dialogue with the Church and Solidarity.

4.

The significance of these grave events extends beyond Poland itself. The inability of totalitarian systems such as those in Eastern Europe to accept the modifications necessary to meet the legitimate aspirations of the people is such as to endanger public confidence in the possibility of cooperative links with the East, and thus seriously to affect international relations. In this context the Ten note with concern and disapproval the serious external pressure and the campaign directed by the USSR and other Eastern European Countries against the efforts for renewal in Poland.

5.

This already grave situation would be further aggravated if it led to an open intervention by the Warsaw Pact. For this reason the Ten wish to issue a solemn warning against any such intervention.

6.

The Ten are totally in sympathy with the Polish people and are willing to continue the direct humanitarian aid to them.

7.

The Ten have taken note of the economic measures taken by the United States Government with regard to the USSR. The Ten will undertake in this context close and positive consultations with the United States Government and with the Governments of other Western States in order to define what decisions will best serve their common objectives and to avoid any step which could undermine their respective actions.

8.

Developments in Poland constitute a grave violation of the principles of the Helsinki Final Act. The Ten therefore consider that the Madrid Conference should discuss them as soon as possible at ministerial level. The Ten will make approaches to the neutral and non-aligned States to propose an early resumption of the Madrid Meeting.

9.

The Ten will work in the United Nations and its specialized agencies for a denunciation of violations of human rights and acts of violence.

10.

Other measures will be considered in the light of developments of the situation in Poland, in particular measures concerning credit and economic assistance to Poland, and measures concerning the Community's commercial policy with regard to the USSR. In addition the Ten will examine the question of further food aid to Poland.

11.

The Ten have called on the Polish authorities both nationally and through the Presidency to lift the abnormal and unacceptable restrictions which have been placed on the work of embassies, representatives of the media, air services and other communications in Poland.

12.
The Ten will study what can be done to alleviate the situation of Poles outside Poland who do not wish to return to their country under present circumstances.

Document 4a/10   Declaration of the European Council on East–West Relations, Brussels, 29–30 March 1982

The Heads of State and of Government noted that the situation in Poland continued to place a strain on East–West relations, and thus to affect the relations of the Ten with Poland, and the USSR bore a clear responsibility in this situation.

(The Greek delegation has reserved its position on the section of the first sentence which indicates that the Polish situation affects the relations of the Ten with the USSR.)

The Ten recalled their earlier Statements on the grave consequences of the present situation in Poland for security and co-operation in Europe, and for East–West relations as a whole. They renewed their call to the Polish authorities with the minimum delay to end the state of martial law, release those arrested and resume a genuine dialogue with the Church and Solidarity.

The Ten also noted with concern the recent statements of the Polish authorities on the possibility of the departure of detainees from the country. The Ten rejected any attempt to place pressure to (sic) those concerned. They would interpret such a policy as a further deterioration of the situation in Poland, and a grave breach of fundamental human rights.

The Heads of State and of Government reviewed the state of economic relations between their own countries and those of Eastern Europe, particularly in the light of the significant role played by Community trade with these countries.

They recognized the role which economic and commercial contacts and co-operation have played in the stabilisation and the development of East–West relations as a whole and which they wish to see continue on the basis of a genuine mutual interest. They discussed the basis on which East–West economic and commercial relations had been conducted.

The Heads of State and Government agreed that these questions, including the important and related question of credit policy, should be the subject of careful study by the European Community and by their own and other Governments, both nationally and internationally and in close consultations with other Members of the OECD.

(The Greek delegation has reserved its position on the section of this text beginning "They discussed . . ." and ending ". . . the other members of the OECD".)

The European Council regretted that violations of the principles of the Helsinki Final Act, of which the repression in Poland constitutes a particularly grave element, had not only prevented the Madrid Meeting from achieving positive results, but also put at risk the entire CSCE process.

It noted that the adjournment of the Madrid Meeting was necessary to preserve the CSCE process, to which the Ten remained fully committed. The objective remained the adoption of a substantial and balanced Final Document.

The Ten expressed the hope that, when the Madrid Meeting resumed in November, the prevailing circumstances would be more conducive to the achievement of a positive outcome.

Document 4a/11   Declaration of the Ministers of Foreign Affairs, Meeting in the Council, 21–22 June 1982

. . .

The attention of the Council has . . . been drawn to the recent decision of the United States Administration to extend sanctions on the export of oil and gas equipment to the Soviet Union through the adoption of new regulations to include equipment produced by subsidiaries of US companies abroad as well as equipment produced abroad under licences issued by US companies. This action taken without any consultation with the Community implies an extraterritorial extension of US jurisdiction which in the circumstances is contrary to the principles of international law, unacceptable to the Community and unlikely to be recognized in courts in the EEC. . . .

Document 4a/12   Conclusions of the European Council on European Community–United States Relations, Brussels, 28–29 June 1982

The European Council had a detailed discussion of the development of economic relations between the European Community and the United States.

. . .

The European Council emphasized its view that the maintenance of the open world trade system will be seriously jeopardized by unilateral and retroactive decisions on international trade, attempts to exercise extraterritorial legal powers and measures which prevent the fulfilment of existing trade contracts.

The European Council expressed its concern at these recent developments, which could have adverse consequences for their relations with the United States.

The European Council therefore considered that it was of the highest importance:
(a) To defend vigorously the legitimate interests of the Community in the appropriate bodies, in particular the GATT;
(b) To make sure that the Community, in managing trade policy, acts with as much speed and efficiency as its trading partners;
(c) That a genuine and effective dialogue take place between those in the United States and the Community responsible for decisions in the areas of possible dispute. This dialogue should be instituted as a matter of urgency. The Community for its part is prepared to make a constructive contribution to this dialogue.

The Community and the end of the Cold War

The end of the Cold War coincided with a very dynamic period in the Community's history. When communism began to fail in Eastern Europe, the Single European Act had been signed, the single European market was under construction, economic and monetary union was under consideration, and Spain and Portugal had been admitted as new members. The Community seemed much more able to act collectively, on a wider world stage. It seemed natural that the Community would assume a leading role in transforming Europe. Certainly, the East European countries looked to the Community for leadership, and the United States encouraged the Community to provide it.

But within the space of only a few years, the European Union seemed less able to deal effectively with the end of the Cold War, which clearly was not going to be an era of worldwide peace. Enlargement to Central and Eastern Europe, which was supposed to spread stability and security eastward, seemed to depend on intergovernmental agreement on fundamental reform of the EU, yet the Member States continued to put forward different visions of the future shape of the EU. What is more, the EU was divided over how to deal with Russia in the post-Cold War period, unable to supplant the crucial US–Russian relationship.

Relations with Central and Eastern Europe

The Soviet Union portrayed the establishment of the European Coal and Steel Community as the beginning of an American–German hegemony over Europe, and remained hostile towards the Community until the mid-1980s. Yet from the early 1970s the Soviet Union also insisted that only the Council for Mutual Economic Assistance or Comecon could conclude trade agreements with the EC (although several East European states approached the Commission seeking trade concessions). For its part, the Community maintained that economic ties should be developed with the separate CMEA countries, to prevent the Soviet Union from limiting the East European states' autonomy. Relations between the two organizations thus remained blocked until after Mikhail Gorbachev assumed power, and the CMEA agreed to the Community's demands. On 25 June 1988, the two organizations established official relations. At the same time, the Community negotiated trade and cooperation agreements with several CMEA states, including the Soviet Union. These agreements were concluded on the basis of *de facto* conditionality, that is, only with countries that were proceeding with political and economic reforms.

Following the remarkable events of the autumn of 1989, the Community was very conscious of the primary role it could play in shaping the new European architecture (see document 4a/13). The trade and cooperation agreements were but one of the instruments used to encourage reforms. In 1990, the Community also set up the PHARE aid programme for the reforming East European countries (in 1991, the TACIS aid programme was set up for the former Soviet republics). The Community went further and agreed to negotiate association agreements with the fastest reformers in Eastern Europe. The first three associates were Poland, Hungary and Czechoslovakia (whose association agreements were signed in 1991); then followed Romania and Bulgaria (agreements signed in 1992), the three Baltic republics (agreements signed in 1995) and Slovenia (agreement signed in 1996). These accords were to become known as the 'European agreements'.

Although the East European countries were pushing to join the Community – supported by, among others, Germany, the UK and the Commission – the Member States could not agree on the prospect of enlargement until June 1993. In that month, the Copenhagen European Council agreed that the East European associates could eventually join the EU, provided that they met certain conditions (document 4a/14). Enlargement, it was believed, would spread stability and security eastward. The Copenhagen European Council also established a 'structured relationship' with the new associates, consisting of a multilateral dialogue (in which the Commission and the Presidency participated), an agreement to 'accelerate the Community's efforts to open up its markets', and a commitment of new finance (these sections are not reproduced here). In December 1994, the Essen European Council approved a pre-accession strategy, to help the associates prepare for EU member-ship (document 4a/15). As part of this, the associates participate in an enhanced political dialogue on CFSP matters, and can back CFSP démarches and statements, and partici-pate in certain Joint Actions. In addition, the WEU also tightened links with the associates: in May 1994, they became associate partners (see document 3/10).

Tensions between the prospective membership candidates over minority rights and borders caused anxiety, nonetheless. At French instigation, in December 1993 the EU approved a CFSP Joint Action to convene a conference on a Pact for Stability in Europe. The intentions were to encourage the East European countries to conclude bilateral agree-ments among themselves guaranteeing the protection of minority rights and sanctifying borders, and to encourage them to cooperate among themselves. The conference began in May 1994 and wound up in March 1995, with not too much substance to show for it (document 4a/16). The many agreements attached to the Final Declaration were for the most part bilateral arrangements which had already been concluded. The Pact does include an agreement between Slovakia and Hungary, but a hoped-for agreement between Romania and Hungary was signed only on 16 September 1996. It notably does not include an agreement between Estonia and Russia.

After the Essen European Council, the enlargement process was speeded up: ten East European countries had applied for EU membership and the Commission was asked to prepare its opinions on those applications and to present them as soon as possible after the conclusion of the 1996–7 intergovernmental conference (IGC). The IGC ended in June 1997, with agreement on the Amsterdam Treaty; the Commission presented its report, called 'Agenda 2000', in July 1997. Agenda 2000 also contained controversial proposals for reforming the common agricultural policy (CAP) and the structural and cohesion funds for poorer regions and countries, so as to pay for enlargement. The Commission recom-mended that the EU begin accession negotiations with five of the applicant countries: the Czech Republic, Estonia, Hungary, Poland and Slovenia (as well as Cyprus, see docu-ments 4b/55 and 4b/56). The other five were not yet considered ready, and the Commission considered that Slovakia had also failed to meet the political criteria. To minimize the potentially negative implications of excluding some of the applicant countries from the first round of enlargement, the Commission suggested revising the pre-accession strategy. The Luxembourg European Council, held in December 1997, largely approved the Commission's proposals (document 4a/17). The European Council emphasized that all ten East European countries were included in a comprehensive 'accession process', but that membership negotiations would begin only with the five front-runners, in March 1998. The remaining applicant countries could join the front-runners if they made substantial progress towards meeting the Copenhagen criteria. And to further prevent the alienation of the excluded applicant countries, the European Council established a 'European Conference' – which was also intended to appease Turkey, an applicant state which the EU conspicuously did not include in the accession process (see also document 4b/59). The European Council did not reach agreement on policy reform and a revised budget until March 1999. Then, in December 1999, the Helsinki European Council agreed to open negotiations with the remaining five East European applicant countries (as well as Malta), on the grounds that they all met the political conditions.

Document 4a/13   Statement by the European Council on Central and Eastern Europe, Strasbourg, 8–9 December 1989

Each day in Central and Eastern Europe change is asserting itself more strongly. Everywhere a powerful aspiration toward freedom, democracy, respect for human rights, prosperity, social justice and peace is being expressed. The people are clearly showing their will to take their own destiny in hand to choose the path of their development. Such a profound and rapid development would not have been possible without the policy of openness and reform led by Mr Gorbachev.

. . .

Expressing the feelings of the people of the whole Community, we are deeply gladdened by the changes taking place. These are historic events and no doubt the most important since the Second World War. The success of a strong and dynamic European Community, the vitality of the CSCE process and stability in the area of security, in which the United States and Canada participate, have contributed greatly to them.

These changes give reason to hope that the division in Europe can be overcome in accordance with the aims of the Helsinki Final Act which seeks, through a global and balanced approach and on the basis of a set of principles which retain their full value, to establish new relations between European countries whether in the area of security, economic and technical cooperation, or the human dimension.

We seek the strengthening of the state of peace in Europe in which the German people will regain its unity through free self-determination. This process should take place peacefully and democratically, in full respect of the relevant agreements and treaties and of all the principles defined by the Helsinki Final Act, in a context of dialogue and East–West cooperation. It also has to be placed in the perspective of European integration.

Already the hopes which we expressed a year ago in the Rhodes Declaration (document 2/17) have begun to take shape. The progress recorded in the negotiations on conventional and chemical disarmament, the greater freedom of movement of persons and ideas, the greater assurance of respect of human rights and fundamental freedoms, and the different agreements concluded between the Community and certain of these countries are substantially changing the climate of relations in Europe.

The European Council is convinced in the present circumstances that all must, more than ever, demonstrate their sense of responsibility. The changes and transitions which are necessary must not take place to the detriment of the stability of Europe but rather must contribute to strengthening it.

Far from wanting to derive unilateral advantages from the present situation, the Community and its Member States mean to give their support to the countries which have embarked upon the road to democratic change. They deplore all the more so that in certain countries this process is still hindered.

The Community and its Member States are fully conscious of the common responsibility which devolves on them in this decisive phase in the history of Europe. They are prepared to develop with the USSR and the other countries of Central and Eastern Europe, and with Yugoslavia in so far as they are committed to this path, closer and more substantive relations based upon an intensification of political dialogue and increased cooperation in all areas. The Community has in particular decided to support the economic reforms undertaken in these countries by contributing – in collaboration with its Western partners – to the establishment of healthy and prosperous economies within the framework of appropriate structures.

The European Council has drawn up conclusions which illustrate this intention.

For the future and in accordance with the developments taking place, the Community is willing to implement still closer forms of cooperation with these countries.

At this time of profound and rapid change, the Community is and must remain a point of reference and influence. It remains the cornerstone of a new European architecture and, in its will to openness, a mooring for a future European equilibrium. This equilibrium will be still better ensured by a parallel development of the role of the Council of Europe, EFTA and the CSCE process.

Construction of the Community must therefore go forward: the building of European union will permit the further development of a range of effective and harmonious relations with the other countries of Europe.

Document 4a/14 Conclusions of the European Council on Relations with the Countries of Central and Eastern Europe, Copenhagen, 21–22 June 1993

A. The Associated Countries

i) The European Council held a thorough discussion on the relations between the Community and the countries of Central and Eastern Europe with which the Community has concluded or plans to conclude Europe agreements ("associated countries"), on the basis of the Commission's communication prepared at the invitation of the Edinburgh European Council.

ii) The European Council welcomed the courageous efforts undertaken by the associated countries to modernize their economies, which have been weakened by 40 years of central planning, and to ensure a rapid transition to a market economy. The Community and its Member States pledge their support to this reform process. Peace and security in Europe depend on the success of those efforts.

iii) The European Council today agreed that the associated countries in Central and Eastern Europe that so desire shall become members of the European Union. Accession will take place as soon as an associated country is able to assume the obligations of membership by satisfying the economic and political conditions required.

Membership requires that the candidate country has achieved stability of institutions guaranteeing democracy, the rule of law, human rights and respect for and protection of minorities, the existence of a functioning market economy as well as the capacity to cope with competitive pressure and market forces within the Union. Membership presupposes the candidate's ability to take on the obligations of membership including adherence to the aims of political, economic and monetary union.

The Union's capacity to absorb new members, while maintaining the momentum of European integration, is also an important consideration in the general interest of both the Union and the candidate countries.

The European Council will continue to follow closely progress in each associated country towards fulfilling the conditions of accession to the Union and draw the appropriate conclusions.

. . .

Document 4a/15   Conclusions of the European Council on Relations with the Central and Eastern European Countries, Essen, 9–10 December 1994

The European Council confirms the conclusions of the European Councils in Copenhagen and Corfu that the associated States of Central and Eastern Europe can become members of the European Union if they so desire and as soon as they are able to fulfil the necessary conditions.

The European Council has decided to boost and improve the process of further preparing the associated States of Central and Eastern Europe for accession. It is doing so in the knowledge that the institutional conditions for ensuring the proper functioning of the Union must be created at the 1996 Intergovernmental Conference, which for that reason must take place before accession negotiations begin. The European Council has decided on a comprehensive strategy submitted by the Council and the Commission at the request of the European Council in Corfu for preparing these countries for accession to the European Union (see Annex IV):

That strategy is tailored to the needs of the countries with which Europe Agreements were concluded and will be applied to other countries with which such Agreements are concluded in the future.

The European Council requests the Commission and the Council to do everything necessary to ensure that Europe Agreements can be concluded with the Baltic States and Slovenia under the French Presidency, so that these States can be included in the accession preparation strategy.

The strategy adopted by the European Council is being politically implemented by the creation, between the associated States and the Institutions of the European Union, of 'structured relations' which encourage mutual trust and will provide a framework for addressing topics of common interest.

The key element in the strategy to narrow the gap is preparation of the associated States for integration into the internal market of the Union.

The European Council requests the Commission to submit a White Paper on this subject in time for its next meeting and to report annually to the General Affairs Council on the progress of implementation of the accession preparation strategy that has been adopted, in particular on the gradual adoption of the internal market rules.

. . .

The European Council further calls on the Commission to submit a study of means of developing relations between the EU and the associated countries of Central and Eastern Europe in the agricultural sector during 1995, with a view to future accession.

Preparation for the internal market is to be backed up by a variety of measures designed to promote integration through the development of infrastructure and of cooperation in fields having above all a trans-European dimension (including energy, environment, transport, science and technology, etc.), in the fields of common foreign and security policy and of justice and home affairs. The PHARE programme, appropriately funded within a multiannual financial framework in accordance with the preparatory strategy agreed upon, will provide financial support for the purpose.

Being aware of the role of regional cooperation within the Union, the Heads of State or Government emphasize the importance of similar cooperation between the associated countries for the promotion of economic development and good neighbourly relations. The Council has therefore approved a programme to promote such cooperation. That programme will also contribute to the objectives of the Stability Pact.

It is the European Council's belief that this strategy by the Union and the associated countries will help to prepare for accession and to make the associated countries better able to assume their responsibilities as future Member States.

The European Council regards the narrowing of the gap between the countries of Central and Eastern Europe and the EU and WEU as a contribution to security and stability in Europe. The European Council welcomes the intention of the WEU to initiate deliberations on the new security situation in Europe, including the suggestion that a White Paper on security in Europe should be prepared.

Annex IV

Report from the Council to the Essen European Council on a strategy to prepare for the accession of the associated countries of Central and Eastern Europe

. . .

Common foreign and security policy

The structured relationship covering common foreign and security policy is especially important as a means for overcoming the widespread sense of insecurity in Central and Eastern Europe. It can reinforce efforts in the framework of the Western European Union, NATO and the partnership for peace, the Conference on Security and Cooperation in Europe and the stability pact, to increase security and stability throughout Europe. The Union and the associated countries have a common interest in preventing conflicts related to issues such as borders and frontiers, and should consult frequently on foreign and security policy issues of mutual concern.

Achievements in this field of cooperation have been considerable. The multilateral political dialogue with the associated countries is being intensified starting with the conclusions of the Copenhagen European Council June 1993 and aiming now at acquainting the associated countries with procedures used within the EU and at the same time giving them an opportunity to be associated with Union actions.

The General Affairs Council in its 7 March 1994 meeting decided not only to further reinforce and broaden the dialogue at all levels but also to open the possibility for the associated countries to align themselves with certain CFSP activities of the Union: statements, demarches and joint actions. Practical guidelines on implementation of this were drawn up in consultation with the associated countries in October 1994.

This process can be built upon, and cooperation made more focused and substantive, by identifying priority themes at the beginning of each Presidency. . . .

Document 4a/16   Political Declaration Adopted at the Conclusion of the Final Conference on the Pact on Stability in Europe, Paris, 20–21 March 1995

1. We, ministers for foreign affairs and representatives of States and international organizations participating in the Paris Conference on Stability in Europe, met in Paris on 20 and 21 March 1995, in response to the European Union's call, to adopt the Pact on Stability in Europe.

2. Half a century after the end of the Second World War, a few years after the historic changes which now make it possible to overcome the divisions of Europe, the Stability Pact expresses our common, continuing effort to prevent and put an end to threats of tensions and crises and to create an area of lasting good-neighbourliness and cooperation in Europe, in order to promote and render irreversible

the achievements of democracy, respect for human rights, the rule of law, economic progress, social justice and peace.

3. The Stability Pact consists of the following declaration, together with a list of good-neighbourliness and cooperation agreements and arrangements. It is supplemented by a list of measures taken or planned by the European Union in support of initiatives by the interested States and in consultation with them, to contribute to the achievement of the objectives of the Pact.

I. Declaration

4. Europe is undergoing a period of change and organization. Our aim is to direct this evolution towards building a more united Europe based on greater solidarity, open to dialogue and cooperation, favouring, for this purpose, exchanges of all kinds, respectful of national identities and of the shared values of freedom and democracy. To achieve that aim, we shall continue to combat all manifestations of intolerance, and especially of aggressive nationalism, racism, chauvinism, xenophobia and anti-semitism, as well as discrimination between persons and persecution on religious or ideological grounds. We undertake to combine our efforts to ensure stability in Europe.

5. A stable Europe is one in which peoples democratically express their will, in which human rights, including those of persons belonging to national minorities, are respected, in which equal and sovereign States cooperate across frontiers and develop among themselves good-neighbourly relations. A stable Europe is necessary for peace and international security.

. . .

8. Good-neighbourly relations must promote regional economic development in order to reduce the economic and social inequalities which create tensions, as well as transborder cooperation which should enable, in the economic, cultural, administrative and human spheres, the development of free movement of persons, ideas, good and services.

9. As we had agreed at the inaugural Conference held in Paris on 26 and 27 May 1994, intensive consultations were organized and have been continuing steadily in recent months. In particular, two regional round tables have been set up, chaired by the European Union, one bringing together four States of the Baltic region – Estonia, Lativia, Lithuania and Poland – and those invited by them, the other bringing together six other States of Central and Eastern Europe – Bulgaria, Hungary, Poland, Romania, Slovakia, Czech Republic – and those invited by them, including Slovenia. The Organization for Security and Cooperation in Europe, the Council of Europe and the Council of the Baltic Sea States have also participated in the regional round tables. At the same time, the Presidency of the European Union visited several capitals to promote the objectives of the Pact. Lastly, all the States which participated in the inaugural Conference have been associated with the work in progress.

10. The States participating in the regional round tables undertook, in accordance with the concluding document of the inaugural Paris Conference of May 1994, to

list the agreements and arrangements devoted to links of friendship and cooperation between them. The Member States of the European Union, in order to
underline their interest for the region, have included in the list agreements and
arrangements and arrangements signed with the nine countries which have the
prospect of joining the Union. Also, these countries and those invited by them have
included in the list agreements and arrangements concluded between them, some
prior to the inaugural Conference in May 1994, but also others concluded since
that date. We particularly welcome the considerable progress towards stability made
in this way by several countries. We express the hope that this list will be supplemented at a later date by other agreements and arrangements, concluded or to be
concluded by the States participating in the regional round tables.

11. The States participating in the regional round tables have also devoted great
attention to the areas for cooperation identified at the inaugural Conference: in
response to the European Union's appeal, a systematic search for projects which
could strengthen good-neighbourly relations was conducted in the interested countries, which made it possible not only to list some existing projects as meeting the
Pact's objectives, but also to identify new orientations.

12. The Pact thus established becomes for us all an essential political reference for
developing relations between the nations of all of Europe. We undertake to give it,
individually and collectively, our political support.

13. Referring to the concluding document of the inaugural Conference in Paris
(Article 5.2), which was welcomed by the Budapest Summit Declaration (Article
16), and to the Budapest Summit Decision on strengthening the OSCE (Article 27),
according to which 'as a comprehensive framework for security, the OSCE will be
ready to act as the repository for freely negotiated bilateral and multilateral arrangements and agreements and to follow their application if requested by the parties',
we transmit the Pact on Stability to the OSCE and entrust it with following its
implementation.

. . .

Document 4a/17　Conclusions of the European Council on European Union
Enlargement, Luxembourg, 12–13 December 1997*

. . .

EUROPEAN UNION ENLARGEMENT

1. The Luxembourg European Council has taken the decisions necessary to launch
the overall enlargement process.

2. The task in the years ahead will be to prepare the applicant States for accession
to the Union and to see that the Union is properly prepared for enlargement. This
enlargement is a comprehensive, inclusive and ongoing process, which will take
place in stages; each of the applicant States will proceed at its own rate, depending
on its degree of preparedness.

*　See also document 4b/59.

3. As a prerequisite for enlargement of the Union, the operation of the institutions must be strengthened and improved in keeping with the institutional provisions of the Amsterdam Treaty.

The European Conference

4. The European Council decided to set up a European Conference which will bring together the Member States of the European Union and the European States aspiring to accede to it and sharing its values and internal and external objectives.

5. The members of the Conference must share a common commitment to peace, security and good neighbourliness, respect for other countries' sovereignty, the principles upon which the European Union is founded, the integrity and inviolability of external borders and the principles of international law and a commitment to the settlement of territorial disputes by peaceful means, in particular through the jurisdiction of the International Court of Justice in the Hague. Countries which endorse these principles and respect the right of any European country fulfilling the required criteria to accede to the European Union and sharing the Union's commitment to building a Europe free of the divisions and difficulties of the past will be invited to take part in the Conference.

6. The States which accept these criteria and subscribe to the above principles will be invited to take part in the Conference. Initially, the EU offer will be addressed to Cyprus, the applicant States of Central and Eastern Europe and Turkey.

7. The European Conference will be a multilateral forum for political consultation, intended to address questions of general concern to the participants and to broaden and deepen their cooperation on foreign and security policy, justice and home affairs, and other areas of common concern, particularly economic matters and regional cooperation.

8. The Conference will be chaired by the State holding the Presidency of the Council of the European Union. At the Presidency's invitation, Heads of State and Government and the President of the Commission will meet at the Conference once a year, as will the Ministers for Foreign Affairs.

9. The first meeting of the Conference will be in London in March 1998.

The process of accession and negotiation

10. The European Council has considered the current situation in each of the eleven applicant States on the basis of the Commission's opinions and the Presidency's report to the Council. In the light of its discussions, it has decided to launch an accession process comprising the ten Central and East European applicant States and Cyprus. This accession process will form part of the implementation of Article 0 of the Treaty on European Union. The European Council points out that all these States are destined to join the European Union on the basis of the same criteria and that they are participating in the accession process on an equal footing.

. . .

German unification

On 9 November 1989, perhaps the most symbolic event of the revolutions of 1989 occurred: the Berlin Wall fell. German unification became an immediate possibility. Although this clearly would affect the Community, neither the EC nor EPC had much influence over the process of unification: Kohl did not always inform his EC partners of German discussions, and the external dimension of German unity was handled in the two plus four framework (the four Second World War allies and the two Germanies, begun as the four plus two talks). After some initial hesitation (particularly on the part of France and the UK), the Member States accepted the prospect of unification, thus sending an important signal that the former German Democratic Republic (GDR) would be welcome in the Community. In early December 1989, the Strasbourg European Council, in its statement on Eastern Europe (see document 4a/13), proclaimed the right of the German people to self-determination, placing few conditions on the process.

Events moved quickly in the spring of 1990, after the March elections were won by an alliance advocating rapid unification. In April, the Dublin European Council agreed to a plan to integrate the former GDR into the Community, without revising the EC treaties (document 4a/18). By mid-September, provisional measures to 'enlarge' the Community to the former GDR were in place, just in time for unification on 3 October, which the Community and the Member States welcomed (document 4a/19).

Document 4a/18   Conclusions of the Special Meeting of the European Council on German Unification, Dublin, 28 April 1990

German unification

We are pleased that German unification is taking place under a European roof. The Community will ensure that the integration of the territory of the German Democratic Republic into the Community is accomplished in a smooth and harmonious way. The European Council is satisfied that this integration will contribute to faster economic growth in the Community, and agrees that it will take place in conditions of economic balance and monetary stability. The integration will become effective as soon as unification is legally established, subject to the necessary transitional arrangements. It will be carried out without revision of the Treaties.

During the period prior to unification, the Federal Government will keep the Community fully informed of any relevant measures discussed and agreed between the authorities of the two Germanys for the purpose of aligning their policies and their legislation. Furthermore, the Commission will be fully involved with these discussions.

In this period the German Democratic Republic will benefit from full access to the European Investment Bank, Euratom and ECSC loan facilities, in addition to Community support in the context of the coordinated action of the Group of 24 countries and participation in Eureka projects.

As regards the transitional arrangements, the Commission will as soon as possible, and in the context of an overall report, submit to the Council proposals for such measures as are deemed necessary, and the Council will take decisions on these rapidly. These measures, which will enter into force at the moment of unification, will permit a balanced integration based on the principles of cohesion and solidarity and on the need to take account of all the interests involved, including those resulting from the *acquis communautaire*. The transitional measures will be confined to what is strictly necessary and aim at full integration as rapidly and as harmoniously as possible.

Document 4a/19   Statement Concerning German Unification, 2 October 1990

Germany regains its unity today, thus ending an anomalous situation which has been for so many years the most visible sign of Europe's division, the legacy of a now long-past war. A people which has so enriched our common civilization is recovering its rightful place in Europe and in the world. It is finally witnessing the fulfilment of a yearning unswervingly supported by the Community and its Member States, which accordingly share all the more the German people's joy at this event.

This historic change has happened peacefully and democratically, in full compliance with the principles of the Helsinki Final Act. The Community and its Member States pay tribute to the steadfastness of the German people, which has nurtured through difficult years its desire for freedom and democracy today fulfilled, and to the wisdom of the governments and the statesmen who made it possible.

The restoration of German unity heralds a new age for Germany and all of Europe. It is a milestone along the road to the construction of a new framework for cooperation and stability in our continent, actively involving both sides of the Atlantic. The unification of Germany is occurring on the eve of major decisions which will mark the road that lies ahead for the European Community. Since the beginning, the FRG has made an outstanding contribution to European integration. A united Germany will continue to be a powerful factor for cohesion, which will help Europe along the path towards political union, and to achieving an even more influential role on the international scene.

Germany's regained unity facilitates the task of the Community and its Member States in consolidating, through the CSCE process and on the basis of the shared values of freedom and democracy, the climate of trust and friendly cooperation now extending throughout Europe. It will make all the sounder the framework for peace and security, solidarity, progress and democracy which we are on the point of achieving in accordance with the aspirations of all peoples of Europe.

The European Community and its Member States welcome the new citizens of the Community and express their warmest wishes to the German people and its Government for a shared future of peace and prosperity.

Relations with the Soviet Union/Russia

An indication of the turmoil that the end of the Cold War could bring came with the attempted *coup d'état* in the Soviet Union, 19–22 August 1991. The Twelve, to their credit, reacted quickly and strongly: on 20 August, an EPC statement condemned the coup and announced the suspension of Community aid to the Soviet Union (document 4a/20). Two days later, after the coup had failed, the decision was revoked.

Gorbachev was weakened by the coup, and the Soviet Union disintegrated by the end of year. This, in combination with the war in Yugoslavia, raised the tricky issue of the recognition of the constituent republics of a dissolving federation. The Maastricht European Council in December 1991 precipitated a declaration on recognition, reiterating the importance of respect for human rights and democracy (document 4a/21).

The Community's policy towards the former Soviet republics was formulated in early 1992: partnership and cooperation agreements would be concluded with them (although the three Baltic republics were granted a more exclusive relationship), but they were not considered potential EU members. In December 1993, the presidents of the EC Council, Commission, and Russia agreed to meet twice a year.

The EU's position was thrown into confusion by the war in Chechnya, a Russian republic in the Caucasus which was fighting for its independence. On 11 December 1994, Russia initiated a ground assault against the Chechen forces. The use of excessive force troubled Western governments, but they did not want to risk isolating Russia by imposing harsh sanctions on it (particularly at a time when NATO had begun to consider enlarging to Central Europe). The EU condemned the fighting in January 1995 and decided to postpone the signing of an interim trade agreement.* The EU set several conditions for signing the agreement: the conclusion of a ceasefire; progress toward a political solution; unhindered access for humanitarian assistance; and the establishment of an OSCE assistance group in Chechnya. But the June 1995 Cannes European Council decided, somewhat prematurely, that the conditions had been met (document 4a/22); the interim agreement was signed on 17 July.

In November 1995, the Council adopted a new strategy on Russia. The strategy called for closer relations with Russia in the security area – important given the sensitive issue of the enlargement of Western security institutions – and for closer political consultation. In 1997, Finland began to push for a comprehensive EU strategy on the 'northern dimension' – relations with Norway, the three Baltic republics and Russia. The Vienna European Council in December 1998 endorsed the idea. But once again, events conspired to confuse the EU's policy. The Kosovo crisis in spring 1999 not only detracted attention from the northern dimension, but also affected relations between the West and Russia. Russia's objections to the NATO bombing created serious tensions with the NATO allies. Significantly, the first CFSP 'common strategy', agreed by the Cologne European Council in June 1999, launched a new policy towards Russia (document 4a/23), a clear attempt to repair relations. The common strategy identified several laudable policy objectives – from consolidating democracy in Russia to developing a strategic partnership with Russia – but the instruments provided did not appear sufficient to reach them. Only the proposal to create a permanent EU/Russia mechanism for political and security dialogue generated much outside interest. Although the Finnish Presidency (second half of 1999) attempted to refocus the EU's sights northwards, it appeared likely that even the new common strategy would be swamped by the need to concentrate on reconstruction in the Balkans (especially as TACIS aid became an easy target for Member States seeking to redirect funds to the Balkans rather than commit new money). Another Russian offensive in Chechnya in late 1999 and early 2000 once again swept aside the EU's policy. In the meantime, Ukraine complained that the Balkans were also drawing EU attention away from it – a proposed common strategy on Ukraine was delayed until the end of 1999.

---

*   This agreement would provide a framework for trade while the partnership and cooperation agreement, signed at the June 1994 Corfu European Council, was being ratified.

Document 4a/20   Declaration of the European Political Cooperation Extraordinary Ministerial Meeting on the Situation in the Soviet
Union, The Hague, 20 August 1991

. . .

The European Community and its member States are deeply concerned at the coup
d'état in the Soviet Union. They strongly condemn the removal of President
Gorbachev from office and the seizure of all power by a "State Committee for the
state of emergency" as a clearly unconstitutional act and a flagrant violation of the
Soviet Union's obligations under the Helsinki Final Act and the Paris Charter. The
Community and its member States demand that constitutional order be re-established forthwith and that President Gorbachev be reinstated in his functions and
rights as Head of State of the Soviet Union.

The European Community and its member States believe that the continuation in
power of the new regime cannot but bring to a halt the process of democratic
reforms in the Soviet Union and the dramatic improvements in the international
climate to which President Gorbachev has made such an important contribution
and which they consider a prerequisite for fruitful cooperation between them and
the Soviet Union.

. . .

The Community and its member States hold those now in power accountable for
the possible consequences of their action for the stability, security and cooperation
in Europe and for international relations in general. They are aware of the special
concerns of the countries of Central and Eastern Europe in this respect.

As a measure of their solidarity with these countries, the Community and its member
States reaffirm their desire to conclude association agreements with Hungary, Poland
and Czechoslovakia in the near future. In the same spirit, they reiterate their full
support for the ongoing process of reform in Bulgaria and Romania. They also
underline their commitment to reinforce contacts with Albania. The Commission
will explore ways and means to further expand cooperation with Bulgaria, Romania
and Albania.

. . .

The European Community and its member States insist that the Soviet Union abide
by all its international commitments and treaties, including those concerning troop
withdrawals and disarmament. They expect it to respect the integrity and security
of all States in Europe. Until the Soviet Union returns to constitutional order and
the full observance of its international obligations under the Charter of Paris, the
Community will suspend its economic assistance in the form of credits for food
supplies and technical assistance. However, it will continue humanitarian emergency
aid provided that it reaches the population in need. The member States are invited
to consider acting likewise.

Furthermore, the Community and its member States are of the opinion that until
such time that constitutional order and democratic freedoms will have been restored,
their participation in the meeting in Moscow of the Conference on the Human
Dimension in the framework of the CSCE cannot be justified.

Document 4a/21   Declaration of the Extraordinary European Political Cooperation Ministerial Meeting on the 'Guidelines on the Recognition of New States in Eastern Europe and in the Soviet Union', Brussels, 16 December 1991

In compliance with the European Council's request, Ministers have assessed developments in Eastern Europe and in the Soviet Union with a view to elaborating an approach regarding relations with new States.

In this connection they have adopted the following guidelines on the formal recognition of new states in Eastern Europe and in the Soviet Union:

"The Community and its member States confirm their attachment to the principles of the Helsinki Final Act and the Charter of Paris, in particular the principle of self-determination. They affirm their readiness to recognise, subject to the normal standards of international practice and the political realities in each case, those new States which, following the historic changes in the region, have constituted themselves on a democratic basis, have accepted the appropriate international obligations and have committed themselves in good faith to a peaceful process and to negotiations.

Therefore, they adopt a common position on the process of recognition of these new States, which requires:
- respect for the provisions of the Charter of the United Nations and the commitments subscribed to in the Final Act of Helsinki and in the Charter of Paris, especially with regard to the rule of law, democracy and human rights;
- guarantees for the rights of ethnic and national groups and minorities in accordance with the commitments subscribed to in the framework of the CSCE;
- respect for the inviolability of all frontiers which can only be changed by peaceful means and by common agreement;
- acceptance of all relevant commitments with regard to disarmament and nuclear non-proliferation as well as to security and regional stability;
- commitment to settle by agreement, including where appropriate by recourse to arbitration, all questions concerning State succession and regional disputes.

The Community and its member States will not recognise entities which are the result of aggression. They would take account of the effects of recognition on neighbouring States.

The commitment to these principles opens the way to recognition by the Community and its member States and to the establishment of diplomatic relations. It could be laid down in agreements."

Document 4a/22   Conclusions of the European Council on the European Union's Relations with Russia, Cannes, 26–27 June 1995

. . .

The European Council takes note of the Commission communication and confirms its commitment to developing the European Union's relations with Russia, a process which is essential to the stability of the European continent. It reiterates the Union's resolve to establish a substantive partnership with Russia, on the basis of the strategy adopted in Carcassonne in March 1995. The European Union intends to contribute to the OSCE comprehensive security model for Europe in the 21st century.

With regard to security, the European Council considers that dialogue between Russia and the Atlantic Alliance should be stepped up, using the existing mechanisms. It further considers that conclusion of an agreement, perhaps in the form of a charter, should be envisaged. This process must be compatible with NATO and WEU policies and with the gradual integration of the countries of Central and Eastern Europe.

In the near term the European Council, noting that progress has been made with regard to the situation in Chechnya and relying on confirmation of that progress, has decided in favour of signing the Interim Agreement.

. . .

Document 4a/23 Common Strategy of the European Union on Russia, 4 June 1999

THE EUROPEAN COUNCIL,

Having regard to the Treaty on European Union, in particular Article 13 thereof; Whereas the Agreement on Partnership and Cooperation (PCA) between the European Communities, their Member States and the Russian Federation entered into force on 1 December 1997,

HAS ADOPTED THIS COMMON STRATEGY:

PART I
VISION OF THE EU FOR ITS PARTNERSHIP WITH RUSSIA

A stable, democratic and prosperous Russia, firmly anchored in a united Europe free of new dividing lines, is essential to lasting peace on the continent. The issues which the whole continent faces can be resolved only through ever closer cooperation between Russia and the European Union. The European Union welcomes Russia's return to its rightful place in the European family in a spirit of friendship, cooperation, fair accommodation of interests and on the foundations of shared values enshrined in the common heritage of European civilisation.

The European Union has clear strategic goals:
– a stable, open and pluralistic democracy in Russia, governed by the rule of law and underpinning a prosperous market economy benefitting alike all the people of Russia and of the European Union;
– maintaining European stability, promoting global security and responding to the common challenges of the continent through intensified cooperation with Russia.

The Union remains firmly committed to working with Russia, at federal, regional and local levels, to support a successful political and economic transformation in

Russia. The Union and its Member States offer to share with Russia their various experiences in building modern political, economic, social and administrative structures, fully recognising that the main responsibility for Russia's future lies with Russia itself.

The European Council therefore adopts this Common Strategy to strengthen the strategic partnership between the Union and Russia at the dawn of a new century. The European Council recognises that the future of Russia is an essential element in the future of the continent and constitutes a strategic interest for the European Union. The offer of a reinforced relationship, based on shared democratic values, will help Russia to assert its European identity and bring new opportunities to all the peoples of the continent. The enlargement of the Union will further increase these benefits and opportunities.

. . .

PRINCIPAL OBJECTIVES

The European Council has identified the following principal objectives:
1. Consolidation of democracy, the rule of law and public institutions in Russia:

. . .

2. Integration of Russia into a common European economic and social space:

. . .

3. Cooperation to strengthen stability and security in Europe and beyond:
Russia and the Union have strategic interests and exercise particular responsibilities in the maintenance of stability and security in Europe, and in other parts of the world.

The Union considers Russia an essential partner in achieving that objective and is determined to cooperate with her. It proposes that the strategic partnership develop within the framework of a permanent policy and security dialogue designed to bring interests closer together and to respond jointly to some of the challenges to security on the European continent. That dialogue will allow greater concertation in all the relevant fora to which both Russia and the Member States belong, particularly the UN and the OSCE.

4. Common challenges on the European continent:
Geographical proximity, as well as the deepening of relations and the development of exchanges between the Union and Russia, are leading to growing interdependence in a large number of areas. Only through common responses will it be possible to find solutions to challenges which are more and more often common to both parties.

The Union and Russia have a common interest in developing their energy policies in such a way as to improve the exploitation and management of resources and security of supplies in Russia and in Europe.

Nuclear safety is an essential issue. The Union is prepared to continue providing expertise and support in that area.

The environment is the common property of the people of Russia and the European Union. The sustainable use of natural resources, management of nuclear waste and the fight against air and water pollution, particularly across frontiers, are priorities in this area.

Russia and the Union have a common interest in stepping up their cooperation in the fight against common scourges, such as organised crime, money-laundering, illegal trafficking in human beings and drug trafficking.

The fight against illegal immigration is also a major preoccupation. The Union proposes to put increased cooperation in place in these areas by creating the necessary tools and forms of cooperation between the competent bodies and by developing exchanges of experts. It is also ready to offer its expertise, particularly in the development of legislation and competent institutions.

Regional cooperation, particularly in the framework of existing regional organisations, is a useful framework for putting practical cooperation in place which will allow a local response to these challenges.

INSTRUMENTS AND MEANS

1. General provisions:
This Common Strategy shall be implemented in accordance with the applicable procedures of the Treaties. The European Council calls on the Council and the Commission in accordance with the responsibilities defined in Articles 3 and 13 of the Treaty on European Union to ensure the unity, consistency and effectiveness of the Union's actions in implementing this Common Strategy.

The European Union will work to achieve the objectives of this Common Strategy by making appropriate use of all relevant instruments and means available to the Union, the Community and to the Member States.

The Secretary-General of the Council, High Representative for the CFSP, shall assist the Council in implementing this Common Strategy in the framework of his or her obligations under the Treaties. The Commission shall be fully associated in accordance with Articles 18 and 27 of the Treaty on European Union.

2. The Council, the Commission and Member States:
The European Council calls on the Council, the Commission and Member States:
– to review, according to their competencies and capacities, existing actions, programmes, instruments, and policies to ensure their consistency with this Strategy; and, where there are inconsistencies, to make the necessary adjustments at the earliest review date.
– to make full and appropriate use of existing instruments and means, in particular the PCA, as well as all relevant EU and Member States instruments and Member States programmes, and to develop and maintain to this end an indicative inventory of the resources of the Union, the Community and Member States through which this Common Strategy will be implemented.

3. Coordination:
Member States shall make additional efforts to coordinate their actions vis-à-vis Russia, including in regional and international organisations such as the Council of Europe, the UN, the OSCE and the IFIs, and including coordination with the Community where it has competencies.

Coordination between the Member States and the Commission must also be consolidated, including through regular consultations between their respective representatives in Russia.

. . .

4. Implementation and review:

The European Council requests the Council:

– to ensure that each incoming Presidency presents to the Council, in the framework of its general programme, a work plan for implementation of this Common Strategy, based on the areas of action in Part II and taking due account of the specific initiatives in Part III;

– to review and evaluate the Union's action under this Strategy and to report to the European Council on progress towards its objectives not less than annually;

– to review the situation in Russia and the state of Russia's cooperation in the implementation of this Strategy, including through periodic reports by the Heads of Mission, and make an assessment in its report to the European Council;

– where necessary, to submit recommendations for amendments to Part II and III of this Strategy to the European Council.

The Commission will contribute to the above within its competence.

5. Cooperation with Russia:

The European Union and its Member States will work closely together with Russia to implement this Common Strategy, in particular through the PCA and its institutions.

. . .

PART II
AREAS OF ACTION

The European Union shall focus on the following areas of action in implementing this Common Strategy:

1. Consolidation of democracy, the rule of law and public institutions in Russia.

To enhance democracy, institution-building and the rule of law in Russia, which is a prerequisite for the development of a market economy, the Union will undertake efforts to:

(a) Strengthen the rule of law and public institutions

. . .

(b) Strengthen Civic Society

. . .

2. Integration of Russia into a common European economic and social space:
The EU will:

(a) Consolidate the process of economic reform in Russia

. . .

(b) Support the integration of Russia into a wider area of economic cooperation in Europe:

. . .

(c) Lay the basis for a social market economy

. . .

3. Cooperation to strengthen stability and security in Europe and beyond:
The EU wishes to deepen and widen cooperation with Russia and identify common responses to the security challenges in Europe and beyond through:

(a) reinforcing political dialogue
– by considering ways to give more continuity to the existing political dialogue and render it more operational, including through the important role to be played by the Secretary-General of the Council, High Representative for the CFSP;
– by working with Russia to develop joint foreign policy initiatives in support of common foreign policy objectives.
(b) Russia's place in the European Security Architecture:
– by further developing cooperation with Russia in the new European Security Architecture within the framework of the OSCE, in particular in the run-up to the Istanbul Summit;
– by continuing cooperation with Russia in the elaboration of aspects of the European Security Charter;
– by considering facilitating the participation of Russia when the EU avails itself of the WEU for missions within the range of the Petersberg tasks.
(c) Preventive diplomacy:
– by enhancing EU-Russia cooperation to contribute to conflict prevention, crisis management and conflict resolution, including within the OSCE and the UN;
– by promoting arms control and disarmament and the implementation of existing agreements, reinforcing export controls, curbing the proliferation of WMD, and supporting nuclear disarmament and CW destruction.

4. Common challenges on the European continent:
The European Union will, in particular, cooperate with Russia in:

. . .

(c) fight against organised crime, money laundering and illicit traffic in human beings and drugs; judicial cooperation
– by enhancing the rule of law and offering assistance in developing the legal order, including by encouraging Russia to sign, ratify and implement key conventions, especially in the field of judicial cooperation in civil and criminal matters;
– by pursuing, on the basis of existing common positions, an appropriate dialogue with Russia in the ongoing negotiations in Vienna on the United Nations Convention against Transnational Organised Crime;
– by increasing the cooperation and exchange of experts between Member States and Russia in the context of combatting organised crime, including in the field of the treatment and rehabilitation of drug addicts as well as in the field of drug prevention. This shall be achieved in cooperation with the European Monitoring Centre for Drugs and Drug Addiction;
– by organising seminars on types and methods of money laundering;
– by developing the cooperation of Europol with the competent Russian authorities as provided for under the Europol Convention, notably for improving the fight against illicit traffic in human beings and drugs as well as immigrant smuggling;

– by intensifying cooperation between the liaison officers of the Member States in Moscow, within the limits of their respective national laws;

– by developing cooperation mechanisms in combatting transnational drug crime, and the involvement of Russia in the concertation process of the Dublin Group;

– by carrying out information campaigns in cooperation with Russian agencies in order to prevent the traffic of human beings;

– by improving the cooperation regarding the re-admission of own nationals, persons without nationality and third country nationals, including the conclusion of a re-admission agreement; by combatting illegal migration including by continuing the basic and advanced training courses for staff members of border and migration authorities;

– by intensifying dialogue with Russia on the adjustment of Russia's visa policy to the European Union through the introduction of visa requirements in accordance with the EC provisions and introduction of travel documents which are sufficiently fake-proof;

– by working together with Russia with a view to the introduction of sanctions by Russia on carriers providing transfrontier transport of inadequately documented passengers and with a view to the introduction of penal provisions for combatting immigrant-smuggling.

(d) regional and cross border cooperation and infrastructure:

– by working more effectively with Russia in the various fora for regional cooperation (CBSS, BSEC, Barents Euro-Arctic Council), and by enhancing cross-border cooperation with neighbouring Russian regions (including Kaliningrad), especially in view of the EU's enlargement and including in the framework of the Northern Dimension;

– by enhancing cooperation and technical assistance in the areas of border management and customs;

– by exploring the scope for working towards linking the Russian transportation systems (road and rail) with the Transeuropean corridors and by seeking mutually satisfactory ways to address transport issues.

PART III
SPECIFIC INITIATIVES

The following specific initiatives shall be pursued not precluding possible new initiatives:

Political and security dialogue:

The Union will consider ways to give more continuity, flexibility and substance to the existing political dialogue, as instituted under the PCA, and to render it more operational and effective:

– the Council will examine the possibility of creating a permanent EU/Russia mechanism for political and security dialogue, bearing in mind the important role to be played by the Secretary-General of the Council, High Representative for the CFSP. One of the aims would be to work with Russia to develop joint foreign policy initiatives with regard to specific third countries and regions, to conflict prevention and to crisis management especially in areas adjacent to Russia, on the Balkans and the Middle East;

– the Council will consider developing a consultation mechanism, in addition to existing troika expert level talks, with Russia, possibly involving third countries, on non-proliferation issues, as well as intensifying efforts, including through increased coordination/joint activities with third countries, in support of Russia's chemical weapons destruction;

– the Council will, in addition, examine the scope for Joint Actions and Common Positions concerning the safe management of biological, and chemical materials, as well as fissile materials in Russia under IAEA verification which are designated as no longer necessary for defence purposes, notably on the basis of international conventions. Particular consideration will be given to the International Science and Technology Centre in Moscow.

Work on these actions will begin by the end of 1999.

. . .

PART IV
DURATION

This Common Strategy shall apply from the date of its publication for an initial period of four years. It may be prolonged, reviewed and, if necessary, adapted by the European Council on the recommendation of the Council.

PUBLICATION

This Common Strategy shall be published in the Official Journal.
Done at Brussels,
For the Council
The President

European Council Declaration related to the Common Strategy on Russia

The Council acts by qualified majority when adopting joint actions, common positions or any other decisions with the scope of Title V of the Treaty on European Union (Common Foreign and Security Policy), on the basis of the Common Strategy. Acts adopted outside the scope of Title V of the Treaty on European Union shall continue to be adopted according to the appropriate decision-making procedures provided by the relevant provisions of the Treaties, including the Treaty establishing the European Community and Title VI of the Treaty on European Union.

Transatlantic relations

In November 1990, in the margins of a CSCE summit, the Community and the Member States signed similar declarations with the United States (document 4a/24) and Canada. (The EC–Canada declaration is very similar to the EC–US declaration, although it does not set up quite as intensive a schedule for future dialogue.) Both the United States and the EC had wanted to set up a new framework for consultations, to reflect the post-Cold War situation in Europe. At the time, the Community was constructing the single European market, raising fears of a 'fortress Europe' in North America and was assuming a leadership role (with US encouragement) in helping the East European countries to adopt democracy and the market economy. The two transatlantic partners appeared to be overcoming the Cold War disparity between a global superpower and a Europe dependent on the United States for defence.

The 1990 Declaration followed two previous attempts to 'institutionalize' transatlantic relations. In 1962, John Kennedy's 'Grand Design' for a transatlantic partnership never got off the ground because the Community could not agree on how much it would cooperate on foreign policy (witness the divisions over the Fouchet Plans, documents 1/10 and 1/11). In 1973, Henry Kissinger launched a 'Year of Europe', but provoked a transatlantic crisis by insisting that the United States be informed about EPC declarations and actions at a very early stage. In response, the nine foreign ministers, meeting informally in April 1974 (the Gymnich-type meetings),* worked out procedures for consulting with 'allied or friendly states' (e.g. the United States) on foreign policy issues. The need for consultations was acknowledged in the Ottawa Declaration on Atlantic Relations, approved by the heads of NATO governments in June 1974. Since 1974, there have been regular meetings at cabinet and lower levels – but provisions for these were not formally set out.

The 1990 Transatlantic Declaration provides for regular high-level meetings, but does not commit the two sides to conduct joint action, and is not a formal treaty. In practice, though, there followed a number of coordinated foreign policy declarations and actions (such as those in relation to the Soviet Union and Eastern Europe, and the war in the former Yugoslavia), although there were also several points of disagreement between the two sides (over the war in the former Yugoslavia, GATT and other trade issues, and the roles of NATO and the WEU). Whether the Declaration and its procedures made any difference to this pattern of activity is a moot point.

In December 1995, another attempt was made to strengthen the transatlantic relationship. At the biannual EU–US summit on 3 December 1995, US President Bill Clinton, Spanish Prime Minister Felipe Gonzalez (President of the Council) and Commission President Jacques Santer signed the New Transatlantic Agenda and Joint Action Plan (document 4a/25). The United States and EU are to act jointly – or at least to coordinate their actions – to promote peace, stability, democracy and development worldwide, respond to global challenges, and expand world trade and investment. Monetary and security affairs, two of the most sensitive issues in EU–US relations, are not mentioned. These two areas even proved relatively uncontroversial following the 1995 summit. The United States in fact expressed little concern over the adoption of the euro, especially as the euro did not appear to pose an imminent threat to the dollar's dominance. On the security front, the allies cooperated intensively on the response to the Kosovo crisis. It was trade that provoked the greatest strains in the transatlantic relationship, as the EU and United States clashed over the EU's banana import regime, the EU's ban on hormone-treated US beef and EU restrictions on genetically modified crops, to name only a few of the disputes of the late 1990s.

---

*   The Gymnich-type meetings began with this meeting in April 1974, at Schloss Gymnich in Germany, under the German Presidency. They are informal meetings among the foreign ministers, with few officials in attendance, which is supposed to encourage freer discussion on both EPC and Community matters. No decisions are taken at these meetings, nor is an official record of them made. Gymnich-type meetings are now held once per Presidency (see document 2/6).

Document 4a/24   Joint Declaration on EC–US Relations, 22 November 1990

The United States of America on one side and, on the other, the European Community and its Member States,

– mindful of their common heritage and of their close historical, political, economic and cultural ties;

– guided by their faith in the values of human dignity, intellectual freedom and civil liberties, and in the democratic institutions which have evolved on both sides of the Atlantic over the centuries;

– recognizing that the transatlantic solidarity has been essential for the preservation of peace and freedom and for the development of free and prosperous economies as well as for the recent developments which have restored unity in Europe;

– determined to help consolidate the new Europe, undivided and democratic;

– resolved to strengthen security, economic cooperation and human rights in Europe in the framework of the CSCE, and in other fora;

– noting the firm commitment of the United States and the EC Member States concerned to the North Atlantic Alliance and to its principles and purposes;

– acting on the basis of a pattern of cooperation proven over many decades, and convinced that by strengthening and expanding this partnership on an equal footing they will greatly contribute to continued stability, as well as to political and economic progress in Europe and in the world;

– aware of their shared responsibility, not only to further common interests but also to face transnational challenges affecting the well-being of all mankind;

– bearing in mind the accelerating process by which the European Community is acquiring its own identity in economic and monetary matters, in foreign policy and in the domain of security;

– determined further to strengthen transatlantic solidarity, through the variety of their international relations;

– have decided to endow their relationship with long-term perspectives.

Common goals

The United States of America and the European Community and its Member States solemnly reaffirm their determination further to strengthen their partnership in order to:

– support democracy, the rule of law and respect for human rights and individual liberty, and promote prosperity and social progress world-wide;

– safeguard peace and promote international security, by cooperating with other nations against aggression and coercion, by contributing to the settlement of conflicts in the world and by reinforcing the role of the United Nations and other international organizations;

– pursue policies aimed at achieving a sound world economy marked by sustained economic growth with low inflation, a high level of employment, equitable social conditions, in a framework of international stability;

– promote market principles, reject protectionism and expand, strengthen and further open the multilateral trading system;

– carry out their resolve to help developing countries by all appropriate means in their efforts towards political and economic reforms;

– provide adequate support, in cooperation with other states and organizations, to the nations of Eastern and Central Europe undertaking economic and political reforms and encourage their participation in the multilateral institutions of international trade and finance.

Principles of US–EC partnership

To achieve their common goals, the European Community and its Member States and the United States of America will inform and consult each other on important matters of common interest, both political and economic, with a view to bringing their positions as close as possible, without prejudice to their respective independence. In appropriate international bodies, in particular, they will seek close cooperation.

The EC–US partnership will, moreover, greatly benefit from the mutual knowledge and understanding acquired through regular consultations as described in this Declaration.

Economic cooperation

Both sides recognize the importance of strengthening the multilateral trading system. They will support further steps towards liberalization, transparency, and the implementation of GATT and OECD principles concerning both trade in goods and services and investment.

They will further develop their dialogue, which is already underway, on other matters such as technical and non-tariff barriers to industrial and agricultural trade, services, competition policy, transportation policy, standards, telecommunications, high technology and other relevant areas.

Education, scientific and cultural cooperation

The partnership between the European Community and its Member States on the one hand, and the United States on the other, will be based on continuous efforts to strengthen mutual cooperation in various other fields which directly affect the present and future well-being of their citizens, such as exchanges and joint projects in science and technology, including, inter alia, research in medicine, environment protection, pollution prevention, energy, space, high-energy physics, and the safety of nuclear and other installations, as well as in education and culture, including academic and youth exchanges.

Transnational challenges

The United States of America and the European Community and its Member States will fulfil their responsibility to address transnational challenges, in the interest of their own peoples and of the rest of the world. In particular, they will join their efforts in the following fields:

– combatting and preventing terrorism;

– putting an end to the illegal production, trafficking and consumption of narcotics and related criminal activities, such as the laundering of money;

– cooperating in the fight against international crime;

– protecting the environment, both internationally and domestically, by integrating environmental and economic goals;

– preventing the proliferation of nuclear armaments, chemical and biological weapons, and missile technology.

Institutional framework for consultation

Both sides agree that a framework is required for regular and intensive consultation. They will make full use of and further strengthen existing procedures, including those established by the President of the European Council and the President of the United States on 27th February 1990, namely:

– bi-annual consultations to be arranged in the United States and in Europe between, on the one side, the President of the European Council and the President of the Commission, and on the other side, the President of the United States;

– bi-annual consultations between the European Community Foreign Ministers, with the Commission, and the US Secretary of State, alternately on either side of the Atlantic;

– ad hoc consultations between the Presidency Foreign Minister or the Troika and the US Secretary of State;

– bi-annual consultations between the Commission and the US Government at Cabinet level;

– briefings, as currently exist, by the Presidency to US Representatives on European political cooperation (EPC) meetings at the Ministerial level.

Both sides are resolved to develop and deepen these procedures for consultation so as to reflect the evolution of the European Community and of its relationship with the United States.

They welcome the actions taken by the European Parliament and the Congress of the United States in order to improve their dialogue and thereby bring closer together the peoples on both sides of the Atlantic.

Document 4a/25   The New Transatlantic Agenda, Signed at the EU–US Summit, Madrid, 3 December 1995

We, the United States of America and the European Union, affirm our conviction that the ties which bind our people are as strong today as they have been for the past half century. For over 50 years, the transatlantic partnership has been the leading force for peace and prosperity for ourselves and for the world. Together, we helped transform adversaries into allies and dictatorships into democracies. Together, we built institutions and patterns of cooperation that ensured our security and economic strength. These were epic achievements.

Today we face new challenges at home and abroad. To meet them, we must further strengthen and adapt the partnership that has served us so well. Domestic challenges are not an excuse to turn inward; we can learn from each other's experiences and build new transatlantic bridges. We must first of all seize the opportunity presented by Europe's historic transformation to consolidate democracy and free-market economies throughout the continent.

We share a common strategic vision of Europe's future security. Together, we have charted a course for ensuring continuing peace in Europe into the next century. We are committed to the construction of a new European security architecture in which the North Atlantic Treaty Organization, the European Union, the Western European Union, the Organization for Security and Cooperation in Europe and the Council of Europe have complementary and mutually reinforcing roles to play.

We reaffirm the indivisibility of transatlantic security. NATO remains, for its members, the centrepiece of transatlantic security, providing the indispensable link between North America and Europe. Further adaptation of the Alliance's political and military structures to reflect both the full spectrum of its roles and the development of the emerging European security and defence identity will strengthen the European pillar of the Alliance.

As to the accession of new members to NATO and to the EU, these processes, autonomous but complementary, should contribute significantly to the extension of security, stability and prosperity in the whole of Europe. Furthering the work of Partnership for Peace and the North Atlantic Cooperation Council and establishing a security partnership between NATO and Russia and between NATO and Ukraine will lead to unprecedented cooperation on security issues.

We are strengthening the OSCE so that it can fulfil its potential to prevent destabilizing regional conflicts and advance the prospect of peace, security, prosperity, and democracy for all.

Increasingly, our common security is further enhanced by strengthening and reaffirming the ties between the European Union and the United States within the existing network of relationships which join us together.

Our economic relationship sustains our security and increases our prosperity. We share the largest two-way trade and investment relationship in the world.

We bear a special responsibility to lead multilateral efforts toward a more open world system of trade and investment. Our cooperation has made possible every global trade agreement, from the Kennedy Round to the Uruguay Round. Through the G7, we work to stimulate global growth. And at the Organization for Economic Cooperation and Development, we are developing strategies to overcome structural unemployment and adapt to demographic change.

We are determined to create a new transatlantic marketplace, which will expand trade and investment opportunities and multiply jobs on both sides of the Atlantic. This initiative will also contribute to the dynamism of the global economy.

At the threshold of a new century, there is a new world to shape – full of opportunities but with challenges no less critical than those faced by previous generations. These challenges can be met and opportunities fully realized only by the whole international community working together. We will work with others bilaterally, at the United Nations and in other multilateral fora.

We are determined to reinforce our political and economic partnership as a powerful force for good in the world. To this end, we will build on the extensive consultations established by the 1990 Transatlantic Declaration and the conclusions of our June 1995 Summit and move to common action.

Today we adopt a new transatlantic agenda based on a framework for action with four major goals:
– promoting peace and stability, democracy and development around the world. Together, we will work for an increasingly stable and prosperous Europe: foster democracy and economic reform in Central and Eastern Europe as well as in Russia, Ukraine and other new independent States; secure peace in the Middle East; advance human rights; promote non-proliferation and cooperate on development and humanitarian assistance:
– responding to global challenges. Together, we will fight international crime, drug-trafficking and terrorism; address the needs of refugees and displaced persons; protect the environment and combat disease;
– contributing to the expansion of world trade and closer economic relations. Together, we will strengthen the multilateral trading system and take concrete, practical steps to promote closer economic relations between us;
– building bridges across the Atlantic. Together, we will work with our business people, scientists, educators and others to improve communication and to ensure that future generations remain as committed as we are to developing a full and equal partnership.

. . .

I. Promoting peace and stability, democracy and development around the world

. . .

We will work towards a resolution of the Cyprus question taking into account the prospective accession of Cyprus to the European Union. We will support the UN Secretary General's Mission of Good Offices and encourage dialogue between and with the Cypriot communities.

We reaffirm our commitment to the achievement of a just, lasting and comprehensive peace in the Middle East. We will build on the recent successes in the peace process, including the bold steps taken by Jordan and Israel, through concerted efforts to support agreements already concluded and to expand the circle of peace. Noting the important milestone reached with the signing of the Israeli-Palestinian Interim Agreement, we will play an active role at the Conference for Economic Assistance to the Palestinians, will support the Palestinian elections and will work ambitiously to improve the access we both give to products from the West Bank and the Gaza Strip. We will encourage and support the regional parties in implementing the conclusions of the Amman Summit. We will also continue our efforts to promote peace between Israel, Lebanon and Syria. We will actively seek the dismantling of the Arab boycott of Israel.

We pledge to work together more closely in our preventive and crisis diplomacy; to respond effectively to humanitarian emergencies; to promote sustainable development and the building of democratic societies; and to support human rights.

We have agreed to coordinate, cooperate and act jointly in development and humanitarian assistance activities. To this end, we will establish a high-level consultative group to review progress of existing efforts, to assess policies and priorities and to identify projects and regions for the further strengthening of cooperation.

We will increase cooperation in developing a blueprint for UN economic and social reform. We will cooperate to find urgently needed solutions to the financial crisis of the UN system. We are determined to keep our commitments, including our financial obligations. At the same time, the UN must direct its resources to the highest priorities and must reform in order to meet its fundamental goals.

We will provide support to the Korean Peninsula Energy Development Organization (KEDO), underscoring our shared desire to resolve important proliferation challenges throughout the world.

II. Responding to global challenges

We are determined to take new steps in our common battle against the scourges of international crime, drug trafficking and terrorism. We commit ourselves to active, practical cooperation between the US and the future European Police Office, Europol. We will jointly support and contribute to ongoing training programmes and institutions for crime-fighting officials in Central and Eastern Europe, Russia, Ukraine, other new independent States and other parts of the globe.

We will work together to strengthen multilateral efforts to protect the global environment and to develop environmental policy strategies for sustainable worldwide growth. We will coordinate our negotiating positions on major global environmental issues, such as climate change, ozone layer depletion, persistent organic pollutants, desertification and erosion and contaminated soils. We are undertaking coordinated initiatives to disseminate environmental technologies and to reduce the public health risks from hazardous substances, in particular from exposure to lead. We will strengthen our bilateral cooperation on chemicals, biotechnology and air pollution issues.

We are committed to develop and implement an effective global early warning system and response network for new and re-emerging communicable diseases such as AIDS and the Ebola virus, and to increase training and professional exchanges in this area. Together, we call on other nations to join us in more effectively combating such diseases.

III. Contributing to the expansion of world trade and closer economic relations

We have a special responsibility to strengthen the multilateral trading system, to support the World Trade Organization, and to lead the way in opening markets to trade and investment.

. . .

(b) Middle East and Mediterranean

Middle East peace process

Despite the fact that the Member States have found it difficult to reach agreement with respect to the Middle East, several important Community/Union initiatives have been launched. Since the beginning of EPC, the Member States' positions have moved closer together, an example of the gradual formation of a *communauté de vue* and occasionally of a *communauté d'action*. But the EU remains peripheral to the ongoing peace process, and lacks the weight of the predominant US role in the region.

Before EPC was set up, the Member States had clearly differing stances on the conflict in the Middle East. They were very divided over the 1967 Six Day War: Germany was officially neutral but committed to Israel, France supported the Arabs, Italy was divided but supported Israel, and the Netherlands supported Israel. Two subjects were dealt with at the first EPC ministerial meeting in November 1970: the CSCE and the Middle East. France in particular pushed for consideration of the Middle East; it wanted the other Member States to come round to supporting its pro-Arab position. But in 1970 the Member States could not reach agreement on a public document on the Middle East.

Then came the October 1973 war and the subsequent OPEC oil embargo on the United States and the Netherlands. The immediate reactions to the Egyptian and Syrian attack on Israel came not from EPC but from separate Member States – and were varied. Only on 13 October did the member states (now the Nine) jointly call for ceasefire and negotiations on the basis of UN Resolution 242. Following the imposition of the oil embargo, the Nine were galvanized into action. On 6 November, they agreed on a common declaration (document 4b/1), which, most significantly, refers to the legitimate rights of Palestinians.

The show of unity by the Nine then prompted the unannounced arrival of a delegation of Arab foreign ministers at a summit of the Community heads of state in Copenhagen, 14–15 December 1973. The Arab ministers wanted to propose a dialogue and cooperation with the Community. The Copenhagen summit reaffirmed its 6 November position, and agreed to enter into a dialogue with the Arab countries on economic issues (including energy supplies).

The Arab League wanted to use Europe against the United States and to obtain political support from the Nine in return for stable energy supplies. The Nine, however, did not want to discuss the Arab–Israeli conflict, given the obvious problems that this would cause inside EPC and with the United States. Although the Euro-Arab dialogue, which got off to a start in mid-1975, took place within the EPC framework, it concentrated on economic, technical and trade cooperation.

The European Council meeting in London, 29–30 June 1977, went further towards the French position. Its statement on the Arab–Israeli dispute (document 4b/2) affirmed that a solution to the conflict should take into account the need for a Palestinian homeland.

The embryonic EPC policy, however, was soon overtaken by the Camp David peace process, which began after Egyptian President Anwar Sadat visited Jerusalem in November 1977. The peace process was bilateral, with the United States acting as the most important arbiter, and not the more-encompassing international conference sought by the Community Member States. Egypt was expelled from the Arab League following the Camp David accords and the Egyptian–Israeli peace treaty of March 1979, which led to the suspension of the Euro-Arab dialogue.* The Nine greeted the treaty with a noticeable lack of enthusiasm (document 4b/3).

The Camp David process predictably became bogged down over the question of Palestinian autonomy, which spurred the Nine to consider launching another initiative. The Venice European Council, 12–13 June 1980, issued a declaration on the Middle East, which went further than previous EPC declarations on the Palestinian issue, but was still toned down because of heavy US pressure. The Venice Declaration (document 4b/4) recognized the Palestinians' right to self-determination and stated that the Palestine Liberation Organization (PLO) had to be associated with the peace negotiations. The Luxembourg foreign minister, Gaston Thorn, then tried to garner support for the Venice Declaration. Gradually the Europeans were identifying themselves with an even-handed approach (they insisted on Israel's right to security) and this distinguished them from the United States.

The new Reagan Administration, in office from January 1981, was resolutely opposed to a European initiative outside the Camp David process; the Thatcher government in the UK agreed. With Mitterrand in office from May 1981, France was also more favourable to Israel, and less favourable to a European initiative. Under US pressure, four Member States (France, Italy, the Netherlands and the UK) agreed to participate in a multinational force to monitor Israeli withdrawal from Sinai, part of the Camp David process (document 4b/5). The United States was insistent that this should be seen as an EPC action. However, the shuttle diplomacy begun after Venice, in an attempt to broker a solution to the Palestinian question, seen as crucial by the Europeans, was continued by the Dutch and British presidencies of 1981. Eventually, Mitterrand and his foreign minister Cheysson also came back into line. But there were limits to EPC's leverage, and its role was supplanted in August 1981 by an initiative taken by King Fahd of Saudi Arabia.

The Israeli invasion of Lebanon on 6 June 1982 (document 4b/6) put an end to the Venice phase of EPC activism in the Middle East. Israel rejected the Ten's attempt to bring about a ceasefire. The Commission (later supported by the Council) then postponed the signing of a new financial protocol with Israel (eventually signed in June 1983), but no further measures were taken.

Over the next few years, no progress was made in the peace process. The Member States repeated their previous positions, but could not agree to do more (documents 4b/7, 4b/8 and 4b/9). The Community did, however, take action to favour the Palestinians (last paragraph of document 4b/7; last three paragraphs of document 4b/9), and became gradually more critical of Israeli intransigence. In February 1987, the Twelve called for an

---

*   The dialogue did not fully start again until 1989.

international peace conference on the Arab–Israeli conflict (document 4b/7), well before the United States pushed a similar idea in the aftermath of the 1991 Gulf War.

The Gulf War provided the United States with an opportunity to relaunch the peace process. The Community and its Member States were reduced to supporting the US initiative and making it clear that they wanted to participate in the peace conference, which opened in October 1991 in Madrid. But the Community's role in the peace process was limited to the economic arena, although the Community and the Member States repeatedly reiterated their willingness to be even further involved (document 4b/10). Israel vetoed the EC/EPC's participation in the political negotiations. Instead, the Community chaired the regional economic development working group.

The most important breakthrough, the Oslo agreement between Israel and the PLO (initialled in August 1993, signed in Washington DC in September), was concluded outside the peace conference framework. The Community and the Member States welcomed the agreement, and pledged immediate aid for the Palestinian Authority (document 4b/11). The Union has become the largest donor to the Occupied Territories.

The Brussels European Council, 10–11 December 1993, decided that one of the first CFSP joint actions would be in support of the peace process. The joint action, adopted in April 1994 (document 4b/12), indicated that the EU would continue to provide substantial assistance to the Occupied Territories, contribute to the creation of a Palestinian Police Force, and send observers to the elections in the Occupied Territories (held in January 1996).

Israel and the Palestinian Authority were included in the Euro-Mediterranean Conference, which first met in Barcelona in November 1995 (see document 46/54). As part of the EU's renewed Mediterranean policy, special association agreements would be negotiated and concluded with several 'third parties', including Israel and the Palestinian Authority (document 4b/13).

The EU never successfully managed to attain a political role to balance its primarily economic role. In October 1996, France, Italy and Spain urged the Dublin European Council to request a role in the peace process on an equal standing with the United States. The proposal went nowhere, given the reluctance of other Member States to agree to it, Israeli hostility and American bemusement. Instead, in November, the Council appointed a special envoy to the peace process (document 4b/14). Although France in particular, and Yasser Arafat himself, continued to call for a greater political role for the EU, the EU was unable to translate its economic power into political influence.

To some extent, given the dangers and difficulties of the dispute, the EU had resigned itself to playing a supporting role to the United States, as document 4b/15 reveals very clearly. Special Envoy Moratinos was active behind the scenes, and was generally well received, but the headlines were taken by visits from the US Secretary of State or *coups de théatre* such as President Clinton's brokering of the Wye River Memorandum in October 1998 (document 4b/16). The last lines of the EU's reaction, however, pointedly refers to the importance of a sound economy for the Palestinian people. An economy implies a state, and the EU was closely involved in Palestinian development, political as well as economic. Thus at the Berlin European Council meeting of 24–25 March 1999 (document 4b/17), at the end of a series of familiar exhortations, the Heads of State and Government looked forward to the 'early fulfilment' of the Palestinian 'right' to statehood 'on the basis of existing agreements'. Accompanying informal signals suggested that the EU would be ready to recognize a Palestinian state twelve months hence. This was designed to pressurize the intransigent Netanyahu government, which had been creating ostentatious difficulties over a Palestinian office in Jerusalem. Israeli opinion, however, has always been hostile and reactive to any instances of European pressure, and it was more by luck than judgement that the subsequent elections in May led to Netanyahu's defeat and his replacement by Barak, who had announced his determination both to withdraw from Lebanon and to negotiate seriously with the Palestinians.

Document 4b/1   Statement by the Nine Foreign Ministers on the situation in the Middle East, Brussels, 6 November 1973

The Nine Governments of the European Community have continued their exchange of views on the situation in the Middle East. While emphasizing that the views set out below are only a first contribution on their part to the search for a comprehensive solution to the problem, they have agreed on the following:

1.
They strongly urge that the forces of both sides in the Middle East conflict should return immediately to the positions they occupied on 22 October in accordance with Resolutions 339 and 340 of the Security Council. They believe that a return to these positions will facilitate a solution to other pressing problems concerning prisoners-of-war and the Egyptian Third Army.

2.
They have the firm hope that, following the adoption by the Security Council of Resolution No. 338 of 22 October, negotiations will at last begin for the restoration in the Middle East of a just and lasting peace through the application of Security Council Resolution No. 242 in all of its parts. They declare themselves ready to do all in their power to contribute to that peace. They believe that those negotiations must take place in the framework of the United Nations. They recall that the Charter has entrusted to the Security Council the principal responsibility for international peace and security. The Council and the Secretary-General have a special rôle to play in the making and keeping of peace through the application of Council Resolutions Nos. 242 and 338.

3.
They consider that a peace agreement should be based particularly on the following points:
I.   the inadmissibility of the acquisition of territory by force;
II.   the need for Israel to end the territorial occupation which it has maintained since the conflict of 1967;
III.   respect for the sovereignty, territorial integrity and independence of every State in the area and their right to live in peace within secure and recognized boundaries;
IV.   recognition that in the establishment of a just and lasting peace account must be taken of the legitimate rights of the Palestinians.

4.
They recall that according to Resolution No. 242 the peace settlement must be the object of international guarantee. They consider that such guarantees must be reinforced, among other means, by the despatch of peace-keeping forces to the

demilitarized zones envisaged in Articles 2 (c) of Resolution No. 242. They are agreed that such guarantees are of primary importance in settling the overall situation in the Middle East in conformity with Resolution No. 242, to which the Council refers in Resolution No. 338. They reserve the right to make proposals in this connexion.

5.
They recall on this occasion the ties of all kinds which have long linked them to the littoral States of the south and east of the Mediterranean. In this connexion they reaffirm the terms of the Declaration of the Paris Summit of 21 October 1972 and recall that the Community has decided, in the framework of a global and balanced approach, to negotiate agreements with those countries.

Document 4b/2 Statement by the European Council on the Middle East, London, 29 June 1977

1.
At the present critical stage in the Middle East, the Nine welcome all efforts now being made to bring to an end the tragic conflict there. They emphasize the crucial interest which they see in early and successful negotiations towards a just and lasting peace. They call on all the parties concerned to agree urgently to participate in such negotiations in a constructive and realistic spirit; at this juncture in particular all parties should refrain from statements or policies which could constitute an obstacle to the pursuit of peace.

. . .

3.
The Nine have affirmed their belief that a solution to the conflict in the Middle East will be possible only if the legitimate right of the Palestinian people to give effective expression to its national identity is translated into fact, which would take into account the need for a homeland for the Palestinian people. They consider that the representatives of the parties to the conflict including the Palestinian people, must participate in the negotiations in an appropriate manner to be worked out in consultation between all the parties concerned. In the context of an overall settlement, Israel must be ready to recognize the legitimate rights of the Palestinian people; equally, the Arab side must be ready to recognize the right of Israel to live in peace within secure and recognized boundaries. It is not through the acquisition of territory by force that the security of the states of the region can be assured; but it must be based on commitments to peace exchanged between all the parties concerned with a view to establishing truly peaceful relations.

4.
The Nine believe that the peace negotiations must be resumed urgently, with the aim of agreeing and implementing a comprehensive, just and lasting settlement of the conflict. They remain ready to contribute to the extent the parties wish in finding a settlement and in putting it into effect. They are also ready to consider participating in guarantees in the framework of the United Nations.

Document 4b/3   Statement by the Nine Foreign Ministers on the Egyptian–
Israeli Peace Treaty, Paris, 26 March 1979

Following their declaration of 19 September 1978 the nine member states of the
European Community have followed with the greatest attention the negotiations
which have resulted in the signature of the agreements between Egypt and Israel.
They are fully appreciative of the will for peace which has led President Carter to
engage himself personally in these negotiations, as well as of the efforts made by
President Sadat and Prime Minister Begin. While a difficult road remains to be
trodden before Security Council Resolution 242 is implemented in all its aspects
and on all fronts, the Nine consider that the treaty constitutes a correct application
of the principles of that resolution to Egyptian/Israeli relations.

They recall, however, that as they indicated in their declaration of 29 June 1977,
the establishment of a just and lasting peace in the Middle East can only take place
within the framework of a comprehensive settlement. Such a settlement must be
based on Security Council Resolutions 242 and 338, and must translate into fact
the right of the Palestinian people to a homeland.

In this context they take due note of the will expressed by the signatories in the
treaty to consider this not as a separate peace but as a first step in the direction of
a comprehensive settlement designed to bring to an end thirty years of hostility and
mistrust.

They hope that this will, to which they attach particular importance, can be given
practical form soon in a comprehensive agreement in which all the parties
concerned, including the representatives of the Palestinian people, would participate and to which the international community could give its endorsement.

The Nine express the hope that all the parties concerned will avoid any statement
or action which will impede the search for peace, such as the Israeli policy of settlements in the occupied territories.

Document 4b/4   Declaration by the European Council on the Situation in the
Middle East (Venice Declaration), Venice, 12–13 June 1980

1.

The Heads of State and Government and the Ministers for Foreign Affairs held a
comprehensive exchange of views on all aspects of the present situation in the Middle
East, including the state of negotiations resulting from the agreements signed
between Egypt and Israel in March 1979. They agreed that growing tensions
affecting this region constitute a serious danger and render a comprehensive solution to the Israeli-Arab conflict more necessary and pressing than ever.

2.

The nine member States of the European Community consider that the tradition-
alities and common interests which link Europe to the Middle East oblige them to
play a special rôle and now require them to work in a more concrete way towards
peace.

3.

In this regard, the nine countries of the Community base themselves on Security

Council resolutions 242 (1967) and 338 (1973) and the positions which they have expressed on several occasions, notably in their declarations of 29 June 1977, 19 September 1978, 26 March and 18 June 1979, as well as in the speech made on their behalf on 25 September 1979 by the Minister for Foreign Affairs of Ireland at the thirty-fourth session of the General Assembly of the United Nations.

4.
On the bases thus set out, the time has come to promote the recognition and implementation of the two principles universally accepted by the international community: the right to existence and to security of all the States in the region, including Israel, and justice for all the peoples, which implies the recognition of the legitimate rights of the Palestinian people.

5.
All of the countries in the region are entitled to live in peace within secure, recognized and guaranteed borders. The necessary guarantees for a peace settlement should be provided by the United Nations through a decision of the Security Council and, if necessary, on the basis of other mutually agreed procedures. The Nine declare that they are prepared to participate within the framework of a comprehensive settlement, in a system of concrete and binding international guarantees, including on the ground.

6.
A just solution must finally be found to the Palestinian problem, which is not simply one of refugees. The Palestinian people, which is conscious of existing as such, must be placed in a position, by an appropriate process defined within the framework of the comprehensive peace settlement, to exercise fully its right to self-determination.

7.
The achievement of these objectives requires the involvement and support of all the parties concerned in the peace settlement which the Nine are endeavouring to promote in keeping with the principles formulated in the declaration referred to above. These principles must be respected by all the parties concerned, and thus by the Palestinian people, and by the PLO, which will have to be associated with negotiations.

8.
The Nine recognize the special importance of the rôle played by the question of Jerusalem for all the parties concerned. The Nine stress that they will not accept any unilateral initiative designed to change the status of Jerusalem and that any agreement on the city's status should guarantee freedom of access for everyone to the holy places.

9.
The Nine stress the need for Israel to put an end to the territorial occupation which it has maintained since the conflict of 1967, as it has done for part of Sinai. They are deeply convinced that the Israeli settlements constitute a serious obstacle to the peace process in the Middle East. The Nine consider that these settlements, as well as modifications in population and property in the occupied Arab territories, are illegal under international law.

10.

Concerned as they are to put an end to violence, the Nine consider that only the renunciation of force and the threatened use of force by all the parties can create a climate of confidence in the region and constitute a basic element for a comprehensive settlement of the conflict in the Middle East.

11.

The Nine have decided to make the necessary contacts with all the parties concerned. The object of these contacts will be to ascertain the position of the various parties with respect to the principles set out in this declaration and, in the light of the results of this consultation process, to determine the form which an initiative on their part could take.

Document 4b/5   Conclusions of the European Council on the Middle East, Brussels, 29–30 March 1982

The European Council discussed developments in the Middle East.

Deeply concerned by the grave events taking place in the West Bank, the European Council appealed urgently for an end to the dangerous cycle of violence and repression. It particularly denounced measures imposed on the Palestinian population such as the dismissal of democratically elected Mayors by the Israeli authorities, as well as the violations of the liberties and rights of the inhabitants of these territories which followed the measures taken by Israel with regard to the Golan Heights, and which could only damage the prospects for peace.

Concerned at the continuing clashes in the Lebanon, the European Council urged all the parties involved to renounce the use of force and to assure conditions for the respect of the full sovereignty and territorial integrity of the country.

It furthermore reaffirmed the wish of the Ten, expressed on many occasions, to contribute to the achievement of a just and lasting peace in the Middle East.

The participation of four Member States of the European Community in the Multinational Force and Observers in Sinai (MFO) was a positive contribution in the context of the forthcoming completion, on 25 April, of the Israeli withdrawal from Sinai.

Document 4b/6   Statement by the Ten Foreign Ministers on the Situation in Lebanon, Bonn, 9 June 1982

The Member States of the European Community vigorously condemn the new Israeli invasion of Lebanon.

Like the bombardments which preceded it and which caused intolerably high loss of human life, this action cannot be justified. It constitutes a flagrant violation of international law and of the most basic humanitarian principles. Furthermore it compromises the efforts to achieve a peaceful settlement of the problems of the Middle East and creates the imminent danger of a generalised conflict.

The Ten reaffirm the important they attach to the independence, sovereignty, territorial integrity and national unity of Lebanon, which are indispensable for peace in the region.

The Ten strongly support the appeals made by the Secretary General of the United Nations. They urgently call on all the parties concerned to act in accordance with Security Council Resolutions 508 and 509, and in particular on Israel to withdraw all its forces immediately and unconditionally from the Lebanon and to place the United Nations Interim Forces in Lebanon (UNIFIL) in a position to accomplish its mission without hindrance. Should Israel continue to refuse compliance with the above resolutions the Ten will examine the possibilities for future action.

The objective of the Ten is to work for a Lebanon free from the cycle of violence which they have repeatedly condemned in the past. This cannot be dissociated from the establishment of a global, just and lasting peace in the region. They are ready to assist in bringing the parties concerned to accept measures intended to lower the level of tension, reestablish confidence and facilitate a negotiated solution.

The Ten will urgently examine within the institutions of the Community the use of the means at the disposal of the Community to give aid to the victims of these events.

Document 4b/7   Declaration by the Twelve Foreign Ministers on the Middle East, Brussels, 23 February 1987

1. The Member States of the European Community have particularly important political, historical, geographical, economic, religious, cultural and human links with the countries and peoples of the Middle East. They cannot therefore adopt a passive attitude towards a region which is so close to them nor remain indifferent to the grave problems besetting it. The repercussions of these problems affect the Twelve in many ways.

2. At the present time, tension and conflict in the Near and Middle East are continuing and worsening. The civilian population is suffering more and more without any prospect of peace. The Twelve would like to reiterate their profound conviction that the search for peace in the Near and Middle East remains a fundamental objective. They are profoundly concerned at the absence of progress in finding a solution to the Israeli-Arab Conflict.

3. Consequently, they have a direct interest in the search for negotiated solutions to bring just, global and lasting peace to the region and good relations between neighbours, and to allow the economic, social and cultural development which has been too long neglected. They have stated the principles on which solutions should be based on several occasions, in particular in their Venice Declaration.

4. Accordingly, the Twelve would like to state that they are in favour of an international peace conference to be held under the auspices of the United Nations with the participation of the parties concerned and of any party able to make a direct and positive contribution to the restoration and maintenance of peace and to the region's economic and social development. The Twelve believe this conference should provide a suitable framework for the necessary negotiations between the parties directly concerned.

5. For their part, the Twelve would be prepared to play their part with respect to such a conference and will endeavour to make an active contribution, both through

the President-in-Office and individually, to bringing the positions of the parties concerned closer to one another with a view to such a conference being convened. In the meantime, the Twelve request the parties concerned to avoid any action likely to worsen the situation or complicate and delay the search for peace.

6. Without prejudging future political solutions, the Twelve wish to see an improvement in the living conditions of the inhabitants of the occupied territories, particularly regarding their economic, social, cultural and administrative affairs. The Community has already decided to grant aid to the Palestinian population of the occupied territories and to allow certain products from those territories preferential access to the Community market.

Document 4b/8   Declaration by the European Council on the Middle East, Madrid, 26–27 June 1989

The European Council has examined the situation in the Middle East conflict in the light of recent events and of contacts undertaken over several months by the Presidency and the 'troika' with the parties concerned, and it has drawn the following conclusions:

The policy of the Twelve on the Middle East conflict is defined in the Venice Declaration of 13 June 1980 and subsequent declarations. It consists in upholding the right to security of all States in the region, including Israel, that is to say, to live within secure, recognized and guaranteed frontiers, and in upholding justice for all the peoples of the region, which includes recognition of the legitimate rights of the Palestinian people, including their right to self-determination with all that this implies.

The Twelve consider that these objectives should be achieved by peaceful means in the framework of an international peace conference under the auspices of the United Nations, as the appropriate forum for the direct negotiations between the parties concerned, with a view to a comprehensive, just and lasting settlement.

The European Council is also of the view that the PLO should participate in this process.

It expresses its support for every effort by the permanent members of the Security Council of the United Nations to bring the parties closer together, create a climate of confidence between them, and facilitate in this way the convening of the international peace conference.

The Community and its Member State have demonstrated their readiness to participate actively in the search for a negotiated solution to the conflict, and to cooperate fully in the economic and social development of the people of the region.

The European Council expressed its satisfaction regarding the policy of contacts with all the parties undertaken by the Presidency and the 'troika', and has decided to pursue it.

The European Council welcomes the support given by the Extraordinary Summit Meeting of the Arab League, held in Casablanca, to the decisions of the Palestinian

National Council in Algiers involving acceptance of Security Council Resolutions 242 and 338, which resulted in the recognition of Israel's right to exist, as well as the renunciation of terrorism.

It also welcomes the efforts undertaken by the United States in their contacts with the parties directly concerned and particularly the dialogue entered into with the PLO.

Advantage should be taken of these favourable circumstances to engender a spirit of tolerance and peace with a view to entering resolutely on the path of negotiations.

The European Council deplores the continuing deterioration of the situation in the Occupied Territories and the constant increase in the number of dead and wounded and the suffering of the population.

It appeals urgently to the Israeli authorities to put an end to repressive measures, to implement Resolutions 605, 607 and 608 of the Security Council and to respect the provisions of the Geneva Convention on the Protection of Civilian Populations in Times of War. They appeal in particular for the reopening of educational facilities in the West Bank.

On the basis of the positions of principle of the Twelve, the European Council welcomes the proposals for elections in the Occupied Territories as a contribution to the peace process, provided that the elections are set in the context of a process towards a comprehensive, just and lasting settlement of the conflict, that the elections take place in the Occupied Territories including East Jerusalem, under adequate guarantees of freedom, and that no solution is excluded and the final negotiation takes place on the basis of Resolutions 242 and 338 of the Security Council of the United Nation, based on the principle of 'land for peace'.

The European Council launches a solemn appeal to the parties concerned to seize the opportunity to achieve peace. Respect by each of the parties for the legitimate rights of the other should facilitate the normalizing of relations between all the countries of the region. The European Council calls upon the Arab countries to establish normal relations of peace and cooperation with Israel and asks that country in turn to recognize the right of the Palestinian people to exercise self-determination.

Document 4b/9   Declaration by the European Council on the Middle East, Dublin, 25–26 June 1990

. . .

The European Council is concerned that, by making territorial compromise ever more difficult, Israel's settlement policy in the Occupied Territories presents a growing obstacle to peace in the region. Reiterating that Jewish settlements in the territories occupied by Israel since 1967, including East Jerusalem, are illegal under international law, it calls earnestly on the Government of Israel not to permit settlements there. The European Council recognises and supports the right of Soviet

Jews to emigrate to Israel and elsewhere. It is, however, firmly of the view that this right must not be implemented at the expense of the rights of the Palestinians in the Occupied Territories.

Recent events underline once again that the status quo in the Occupied Territories is untenable. The lamentable position concerning the observance of human rights in the Occupied Territories has led the Community and its member States to set out repeatedly their concern. They are resolved to step up their already significant support for the protection of the human rights of the population of the Occupied Territories.

In the present situation, and particularly with regard to the protection of the population, the U.N., too, can and should play a useful role. The European Council supports such a role of the U.N.

The European Council refers to the obligation on Parties to the Geneva Convention Relative to the Protection of Civilian Persons in Time of War to respect and to ensure respect for its provisions. The Twelve have repeatedly called on Israel to adhere to its obligations towards the Palestinian population in the territory under its occupation which is protected by that Convention. They have observed that it has notably failed to do so in a number of important areas. Concerned that the human rights of the population of the Occupied Territories continue to be inadequately protected, the European Council calls for further action, in accordance with the Convention, to ensure that protection.

The European Council has reviewed the range of actions taken on the basis of the Strasbourg Declaration in order to arrest the deterioration of the economic and social situation in the Occupied Territories and to help to preserve the future of Palestinian society. It notes with satisfaction the significant increase of Community aid, particularly in the 1990 program of direct aid which is ready for adoption. It confirms its determination to double direct Community aid by 1992.

The European Council also expresses its satisfaction with the growth in exports of agricultural produce from the Occupied Territories to the Community. It invites the Community Institutions to take appropriate action for a rapid further improvement of the conditions of access to the Community market for Palestinian products and to examine further possibilities for increasing trade between the Community and the Occupied Territories.

As an expression of the importance which the European Council attaches to facilitating the speedy and efficient implementation of the Community's expanding program for the benefit of the population of the Occupied Territories, the Commission is invited to appoint a representative to the Occupied Territories for this purpose at an early date.

Document 4b/10   Statement on the Middle East Peace Process, European Political Cooperation, 10 October 1991

The Community and its member States reaffirm their full support for the Middle East peace initiative promoted by the United States and the USSR. They welcome the agreement in principle of all the parties to the dispute to the approach proposed by the US Secretary of State Mr Baker. In this respect they also welcome the positive attitude of the Palestine National Council. They hope that this emerging consensus will open the way to an early resolution of the problem of an authentic Palestinian representation. They do not believe that any formula on this issue can be held to prejudice negotiations on substantive issues such as the status of Jerusalem.

The Community and its member States continue to attach importance to the adoption by both sides of confidence-building measures designed to create the right climate for successful negotiations. They underline the importance they attach to a suspension of Israeli settlement activity in the Occupied Territories including East Jerusalem, and welcome the willingness of Arab States to freeze the trade boycott of Israel in return for this.

They reaffirm their strong disapproval of the "Zionism is Racism Resolution passed by the United Nations General Assembly which they believe should be consigned to oblivion.

While reaffirming their well-known positions of principle, the Community and its member States confirm their determination to give all possible support to efforts to convene a Middle East Peace Conference and their determination to play an active role as a full participant in such a Conference alongside the co-sponsors.

They believe that an unprecedented opportunity to create peace between Israel and the Arabs now exists and they call on all parties to show the flexibility and imagination necessary to grasp this.

Document 4b/11   Declaration on the Middle East Peace Process, European Political Cooperation, 13 September 1993

The European Community and its member States pay tribute to the vision and courage of the Israeli and Palestinian leaders who signed this historic agreement which represents a positive breakthrough in the peace process.

The European Community and its member States offer their continuing political support and readiness to participate in further international arrangements arising in connection with implementation of the agreement.

Stressing the fact that the Community and its member States are already the largest net contributor to the Occupied Territories, the Community and its member States announce their intention to continue to be a substantive contributor. The European Community is ready to offer a package of immediate aid of 20 mecu and to discuss medium term aid with Palestinian institutions as they are formed.

The European Community and its member States reiterate their commitment to a comprehensive peace and hope that progress will be accomplished in other bilateral negotiations and in the multilateral talks on future cooperation; as a chairman of the Regional Economic Development working group the European Community and its member States are prepared to contribute to all forms of regional economic cooperation.

Document 4b/12   Joint Action by the Council of the European Union Adopted on the Basis of Article J.3 of the Treaty on European Union in Support of the Middle East Peace Process, Luxembourg, 19 April 1994 (94/276/CFSP)

THE COUNCIL OF THE EUROPEAN UNION

Having regard to the Treaty on European Union and in particular Articles J (3) and J (11) thereof,

Having regard to the general guidelines issued by the European Council of 29 October 1993,

Having regard to the framework for joint action agreed by the European Council on 10 and 11 December 1993,

Considering Article C of the Treaty on European Union,

HAS DECIDED AS FOLLOWS:

Article 1

(a) The European Union, in order to work for the conclusion of a comprehensive peace in the Middle East based on the relevant United Nations Security Council resolutions, will:

  – participate in international arrangements agreed by the parties to guarantee peace in the context of the process begun in Madrid.
  – use its influence to encourage all the parties to support the peace process unconditionally on the basis of the invitations to the Madrid Conference and work for the strengthening of democracy and respect for human rights,
  – make its contribution to defining the future shape of relations between the regional parties in the context of the Arms Control and Regional Security Working Group.

(b) The European Union will:

  – develop its role in the ad hoc Liaison Committee responsible for the coordination of international aid to the Occupied Territories,
  – maintain its leading role in the regional economic development working group (REDWG) and develop its participation in other multilateral groups,
  – consider additional ways in which it might contribute towards the development of the region.

(c) The European Union will:

  – pursue confidence building measures which it has submitted to the parties,
  – pursue *démarches* to the Arab States with the aim of securing an end to the boycott of Israel,
  – closely follow the future of Israeli settlements throughout the Occupied Territories and pursue *démarches* to Israel about this issue.

Article 2

In accordance with the relevant Community procedures the Council will examine proposals that the Commission will make:
- for the rapid implementation of programmes of assistance for the development of the Occupied Territories and a Palestinian operating budget, in close consultation with the Palestinians and equally close coordination with other donors.
- to provide aid in the framework of existing guidelines to the other parties to the bilateral negotiations as they progress substantially towards peace.

Article 3

In order to contribute activity and urgently to the creation of a Palestinian Police Force:

(a) The European Union will provide assistance.

(b) The Presidency in close cooperation with the Commission will facilitate coordination through an exchange of information between Member States on their bilateral assistance.

(c) Funds for a maximum amount of ECU 10 million available from the Community budget will be used as a matter of urgency for the provision of assistance for the creation of a Palestinian Police Force.

Article 4

The European Union will, at the request of the parties, participate in the protection of the Palestinian people through a temporary international presence in the Occupied Territories, as called for in Security Council resolution 904 (1994).

Operation arrangements and financing arising from this article will be the subject of a separate and specific Council decision.

Article 5

At the request of the parties, the European Union will implement a coordinated programme of assistance in preparing for and observing the elections in the Occupied Territories foreshadowed by the Declaration of Principles of 13 September 1993. Precise operational arrangements and financing will be the subject of a separate Council decision once agreement has been reached between Israel and the PLO on arrangements for the elections. The European Parliament will be invited to participate in those arrangements.

Article 6

The European Union confirms its willingness to take further operational decisions in the field of this joint action, in accordance with developments in the peace process.

Article 7

This Decision shall take effect on today's date.

Document 4b/13   Conclusions by the General Affairs Council on the Middle
East Peace Process, 2 October 1995

The Council of the European Union:

- aware of the historic importance of the Interim Agreement signed between Israel and the PLO on 28 September 1995;
- convinced that it is necessary to contribute towards the success of that Agreement, and that economic and social development is a key factor for achieving just and lasting peace;
- resolved to strengthen cooperation by the Union, as the leading donor, with the Territories covered by the peace agreements;
- convinced that the peoples in the region must be the prime beneficiaries of peace,

1. invites the Commission to begin exploratory talks with the Palestinian Authority with a view to the conclusion of a Euro-Mediterranean Association Agreement as soon as circumstances permit;

2. restates its desire to conclude as soon as possible the Euro-Mediterranean Association Agreements which the Commission is in the process of negotiating with the countries of the region;

3. invites the Commission to take the necessary measures to enable the Territories covered by the peace agreements to benefit from increased aid in accordance with the conclusions of the Cannes European Council;

4. calls upon the European Investment Bank to speed up the commitment, at the earliest opportunity, of ECU 250 million in the form of appropriations for projects to develop the Territories covered by the peace agreements;

5. confirms that there will be observation of the elections to the Palestinian Council and that the international operation for observing these elections will be coordinated. To that end, the Council and the Commission have set up the European Electoral Unit which is already fully operational, since all its members have already been appointed and an ECU 10 million budget has been assigned to it;

6. agrees to prepare an International Ministerial Conference on economic assistance to the Palestinian people. The aim of the Conference will be to consider economic and trade requirements, technical assistance and ways of promoting economic and social development in the Territories covered by the peace agreements. The Conference will take place after agreement on revision of the tripartite action plan and on a new development strategy;

. . .

Document 4b/14   Joint Action by the Council of the European Union
Adopted on the Basis of J.3 in Relation to the Nomination
of an EU Special Envoy for the Middle East Peace Process,
25 November 1996 (96/676/CFSP)

THE COUNCIL OF THE EUROPEAN UNION

Having regard to the Treaty on European Union and, in particular, Articles J.3
and J.11 thereof,

Having regard to the declaration adopted by the European Council held in Florence
on 21 and 22 June 1996,

Whereas the Council declaration adopted on 1 October 1996 stated the readiness
of the European Union to play an active part in promoting the peace process,
commensurate with its interests in the region, and on the basis of its major contribution to the peace process so far;

Whereas on 28 October the Council adopted conclusions regarding the appointment of an EU special envoy for the Middle East peace process and taking account
of all international efforts under way in support of that process.

HAS ADOPTED THE FOLLOWING JOINT ACTION:

Article 1

Mr Miguel Angel Moratinos is appointed as EU special envoy for the Middle East
peace process.

The EU special envoy is appointed for a period of one year, subject to review after
six months of mandate, including administrative and financial aspects.

Article 2

The mandate of the EU Special Envoy will be:

–   to establish and maintain close contact with all the parties to the peace process,
    other countries of the region, the United States and other interested countries,
    as well as relevant international organizations, in order to work with them in
    strengthening the peace process,

–   to observe peace negotiations between the parties, and to be ready to offer the
    European Union's advice and good offices should the parties request this,

–   to contribute where requested to the implementation of international agreements
    reached between parties, and to engage with them diplomatically in the event
    of non-compliance with the terms of these agreements,

–   to engage constructively with signatories to agreements within the framework of
    the peace process in order to promote compliance with the basic norms of democ-
    racy, including respect for human rights and the rule of law,

–   to report to the Council's bodies on the possibilities for European Union inter-
    vention in the peace process, and on the best way of pursuing European Union

initiatives and ongoing Middle East peace process-related European Union business including the political aspects of relevant European Union development projects,

– to monitor actions by either side which might prejudice the outcome of the permanent status negotiations.

The EU special envoy will be guided by, and report under the authority of the Presidency to the Council on a regular basis, and as the need arises. The tasks of the envoy will be without prejudice to the role of the Commission which will be fully associated in these tasks.

Article 3

1.   In order to cover the costs related to the mission of the EU special envoy, a cum of ECU 2,137 million shall be charged to the general budget of the European Communities. This sum shall be available to finance the EU special envoy expenditure with effect from the date of adoption of the Joint Action.

2.   The expenditure financed by the amount stipulated in paragraph 1 shall be managed in accordance with the European Community procedures and rules applicable to the budget.

3.   The European Union will finance the infrastructure and current expenditure of the EU special envoy, including his salary and the cost of the supporting staff. The Member States and the Community may propose the secondment of staff to work with the EU special envoy. The remuneration of personnel which might be detached by a Member State, the Commission or another Community institution to the EU special envoy shall be covered respectively by the Member State concerned, the Commission or the other Community institutions.

4.   The Council notes that the Presidency, Commission and/or Member States as appropriate will provide logistical support in the region.

5.   The privileges, immunities and further guarantees necessary for the completion and smooth functioning of the mission of the EU special envoy and the members of his staff shall be defined with the parties. The Member States and the Commission shall grant all necessary support to such effect.

. . .

Document 4b/15   Press Statement on the Middle East Peace Process, Brussels and London, 7 May 1998

The EU welcomes the US effort in the London talks, and supports the proposals they have put forward. It also welcomes President Arafat's acceptance of these proposals. It regrets that it was not possible to reach final agreement on the proposals in London, and encourages the Government of Israel to respond positively to them in order to restore momentum in the Peace Process and facilitate the resumption of Final Status talks.

The EU offered its assistance to the parties in facilitating the discussions in London, and will continue to do all it can to help carry the process forward, in support of US efforts.

Document 4b/16   Press Statement on the Middle East Peace Process, Luxembourg and Vienna, 26 October 1998

The European Union warmly welcomes the signature in Washington on 23 October of the Wye River Memorandum between Prime Minister Benjamin Netanyahu and Chairman Yasser Arafat. The European Union congratulates Prime Minister Netanyahu and Chairman Arafat for their courage and sense of responsibility, and pays tribute to the important contribution of President Clinton and Secretary of State Albright to this successful outcome, as also to the personal support lent by King Hussein of Jordan. This breakthrough opens the door to the early resumption of the negotiations on Permanent Status as foreseen in the Oslo Accords, as well as to the implementation of outstanding commitments under the Interim Agreement.

The European Union welcomes this forward movement in the peace process and looks forward to the speedy implementation of the Agreement. It recognises that this will require a sustained political commitment by the parties and the determination to resist extremists and others wanting to frustrate progress towards peace.

The European Union now calls on the parties to complete negotiations as soon as possible on those remaining issues under the Interim Agreement still not settled, to start negotiations without delay on final status and meanwhile to avoid all unilateral acts which could prejudice the final outcome, thus building confidence which is essential for a lasting peace in the region. It attaches importance also to the early revival of the Syrian and Lebanese Tracks in order to arrive at a comprehensive settlement among all parties in the conflict.

The European Union reiterates its firm commitment to a just and comprehensive settlement in the Middle East based on the Madrid and Oslo Accords. It welcomes the continuing positive contribution being made by EU Special Envoy Ambassador Moratinos. The European Union has much to offer to the success of the peace process and is determined to continue playing its full part, enhancing it in all its aspects. Furthermore, recognising the importance of a sound economy to social and political stability among the Palestinian people, the European Union will continue its considerable economic and technical assistance and looks to Israel to meet its responsibilities in promoting conditions for economic development.

Document 4b/17 Conclusions of the European Council in Berlin, 24–25 March 1999

. . .

Middle East peace process

The Heads of State and Government of the European Union reaffirm their support for a negotiated settlement in the Middle East, to reflect the principles of 'land for peace' and ensure the security both collective and individual of the Israeli and Palestinian peoples. In this context, the European Union welcomes the decision by the Palestinian National Union and associated bodies to reaffirm the nullification of the provisions in the Palestinian National Charter which called for the destruction of Israel and to reaffirm their commitment to recognize and live in peace with Israel. However, the European Union remains concerned at the current deadlock in the peace process and calls upon the parties to implement fully and immediately the Wye River Memorandum.

The European Union also calls upon the parties to reaffirm their commitments to the basic principles established within the framework of Madrid, Oslo and subsequent agreements, in accordance with UNSC Resolutions 242 and 338. It urges the parties to agree on an extension of the transitional period established by the Oslo agreements.

The European Union calls in particular for an early resumption of final status negotiations in the coming months on an accelerated basis, and for these to be brought to a prompt conclusion and not prolonged indefinitely. The European Union believes that it should be possible to conclude the negotiations within a target period of one year. It expresses its readiness to work to facilitate an early conclusion to the negotiations.

The European Union urges both parties to refrain from activities which prejudge the outcome of those final status negotiations and from any activity contrary to international law, including all settlement activity, and to fight incitement and violence.

The European Union reaffirms the continuing and unqualified Palestinian right to self-determination including the option of a state and looks forward to the early fulfilment of this right. It appeals to the parties to strive in good faith for a negotiated solution on the basis of the existing agreements, without prejudice to this right, which is not subject to any veto. The European Union is convinced that the creation of a democratic, viable and peaceful sovereign Palestinian State on the basis of existing agreements and through negotiations would be the best guarantee of Israel's security and Israel's acceptance as an equal partner in the region. The European Union declares its readiness to consider the recognition of a Palestinian State in due course in accordance with the basic principles referred to above.

The European Union also calls for an early resumption of negotiations on the Syrian and Lebanese tracks of the Middle East peace process, leading to the implementation of UNSCRs 242, 338 and 425.

. . .

Iran

On 4 November 1979, Iranian student revolutionaries seized the US embassy in Tehran and began holding 63 hostages. On 12 November, the United States put a boycott on imports of Iranian oil; two days later, it froze Iranian assets in the United States. On 20 November, the Nine called for the release of the hostages; ten days later, the European Council repeated the message (document 4b/18).

The United States was pressuring the West Europeans to impose sanctions on Iran, as the Soviet Union had vetoed UN sanctions, but no EC Member State was completely in favour of sanctions. On 9 April 1980, the United States threatened military action against Iran if the allies did not impose sanctions. On 10 April, the Nine foreign ministers stalled on a response, until after a démarche was to be made. The démarche proving ineffective, the foreign ministers announced on 22 April that they had decided to impose sanctions (to be implemented nationally) on Iran (document 4b/19).* This was not enough to fore-stall the (abortive) US attempt to free the hostages by military action, on 24 April. The sanctions were confirmed on 17–18 May (document 4b/20). The crisis only ended when the hostages were released' after Algerian mediation, on the day of Ronald Reagan's inauguration as US President, 20 January 1981.

Relations with the United States over Iran have continued to be strained. After the hostage crisis, American sanctions continued and pressure on the Europeans to follow suit increased with the perception of Tehran's involvement in international terrorism. The Europeans took a neutral position in the Iran–Iraq War of 1980–8, but the fatwa against Salman Rushdie in 1989 led to collective protests. During the 1990s, the Europeans walked a tightrope between American pressure to isolate Iran and the policy launched at the December 1992 Edinburgh European Council: a critical dialogue with the Iranian govern-ment (document 4b/21). In April 1997, however, the EU suspended the dialogue after a German court found that the Iranian regime had ordered the 1992 assassination of four Iranian opposition members in Berlin (the Mykonos case), and the Presidency invited the Member States to recall their ambassadors from Iran. On 29 April, the Council gave the green light to the return of the ambassadors (document 4b/22), but because Iran refused to allow the German ambassador to enter the country, no EU Member State sent its ambassador back straight away. Following the election of a more reform-minded president in Iran, the EU decided to send its ambassadors back to Tehran in November 1997.

Document 4b/18   Statement by the European Council on Iran, Dublin, 30 November 1979

1.
The Heads of the State or Government and the Foreign Ministers of the Nine, meeting in the European Council, considered the grave situation created by the occupation of the Embassy of the United States in Tehran and the holding of members of its staff as hostages in flagrant breach of international law.

---

*   They had not yet reached the point at which the Member States would agree to impose sanc-tions on the basis of a EPC decision. This would first occur in the case of the sanctions on the Soviet Union in March 1982.

2.

The European Council strongly reaffirmed the statement which was issued by the Foreign Ministers of the Nine at their meeting of 20 November in Brussels. It is fundamental that diplomatic missions should be protected. The failure to uphold this principle and the taking of hostages to exert pressure on Governments are totally unacceptable. It is the duty of all Governments to oppose energetically such a breach of international law.

3.

The Nine Member States of the European Community fully respect the independence of Iran and the right of the Iranian people to determine their own future. They are conscious of the importance which the Iranian people attach to the changes which have taken place in their country. But in the same measure as they respect the rights of Iran they call on Iran to respect fully the rights of others and to observe the established principles that govern relations between States. Respect for these principles is essential to the effort to secure order and justice in international relations which is in the interest of all States including Iran.

4.

The Governments of the Nine, supported by public opinion in their countries, expressed in particular by the European Parliament, solemnly appeal to Iran to respect these fundamental rights and duties so long established in international law. They urge most strongly that the Iranian authorities take action immediately to release the hostages in complete safety and allow them to return to their own country.

Document 4b/19   Declaration by the Nine Foreign Ministers on the Question of the American Hostages Detained at the American Embassy at Tehran, Luxembourg, 22 April 1980

1.

The Foreign Ministers of the nine Member States of the European Community Meeting in Luxembourg on 22 April discussed the implications of the recent events in Iran in the light of the reports by their Ambassadors following the démarche to the President of Iran decided upon by the Foreign Ministers at their meeting in Lisbon on 10 April.

2.

The Foreign Ministers expressed the solidarity of the Nine with the Government and people of the United States at this time of trial.

3.

While welcoming the visit by the ICRC to the hostages on 14 April and noting the assurances given by President Bani Sadr as to the living conditions of the hostages, the Foreign Ministers expressed their profound regret that the Iranian Government has been unable to give precise assurances about the date and methods by which the hostages would be released. The Iranian Government continues to ignore the clear call of the UN Security Council and the International Court of Justice to bring to an end a flagrant violation of international law and release the hostages.

4.

Since the hostages were first detained the Nine, fully respecting the independence of Iran and the right of the Iranian people to determine their own future, have insisted that they must be released. The fact that after six months they are still detained, despite the efforts of the Nine and the clear condemnation by the Community of Nations, is intolerable from a humanitarian and legal point of view.

5.

The Foreign Ministers of the Nine, deeply concerned that a continuation of this situation may endanger international peace and security, have decided to seek immediate legislation where necessary in their National Parliaments to impose sanctions against Iran in accordance with the Security Council Resolution on Iran of 10 January 1980, which was vetoed, and in accordance with the rules of international law. They believe that these legislative processes should be completed by 17 May, date of the Foreign Ministers' Meeting in Naples. If by that time there has not been any decisive progress leading to the release of the hostages, they will proceed immediately to the common application of the sanctions. Steps will be taken within the Community in order that the implementation of the measures decided upon should not obstruct the proper functioning of the Common Market. The Ministers consider that, as of now and pending the entry into force of the measures mentioned above, no new export or services contract with persons or organizations in Iran should be concluded.

6.

The Foreign Ministers decided meanwhile to put into effect without delay the following measures, to the extent that they are not already in force:
(I)   reduction in Embassy Staffs in Teheran;
(II)   a reduction in the number of Diplomats accredited by the Government of Iran in their countries;
(III) the reintroduction, where not already in force, of a visa system for Iranian Nationals travelling to Member Countries of the Nine;
(IV)   the withholding of permission for the sale or export of arms or defence-related equipment to Iran.

7.

The Foreign Ministers instructed their Ambassadors to return to Tehran in the interval in order to convey the present decision to the Iranian Government, to follow the situation, and to undertake all possible efforts to alleviate and improve the living conditions of the hostages pending their release. They expressed the hope that the Iranian authorities would act along the lines suggested in this Statement.

8.

The Foreign Ministers of the Nine, believing that this situation should be a matter of concern to the whole international community, call upon other Governments to associate themselves with these decisions.

9.

The Foreign Ministers decided immediately to contact the Government of the United States through the Presidency and to inform it of the decisions taken by them.

Document 4b/20 Declaration by the Nine Foreign Ministers on Iran, Naples, 17–18 May 1980

. . .

1.

The Foreign Ministers of the nine Member States of the European Community, meeting at Naples on 17 and 18 May, re-examined in accordance with their declaration of 22 April the situation resulting from the detention of the American hostages in Iran, an act constituting a flagrant violation of international law.

2.

The Ministers reviewed the information emanating from Iran. While noting certain developments which could contribute to the release of the hostages, in particular the completion of the second round of parliamentary elections and the forthcoming convocation of the Majlis, they had to conclude that there had been no significant progress towards the release of the hostages since 22 April.

3.

They therefore decided to apply, in concert and without delay, the measures provided for in the draft Security Council resolution of 10 January. In particular they agreed that all contracts concluded after 4 November 1979 would be suspended. They will remain in close consultation in accordance with Article 224 of the Treaty of Rome.

. . .

Document 4b/21 Conclusions of the European Council on Iran, Edinburgh, 12 December 1992

Given Iran's importance in the region, the European Council reaffirms its belief that a dialogue should be maintained with the Iranian Government. This should be a critical dialogue which reflects concern about Iranian behaviour and calls for improvement in a number of areas, particularly human rights, the death sentence pronounced by a Fatwa of Ayatollah Khomaini against the author Salman Rushdie, which is contrary to international law, and terrorism. Improvement in these areas will be important in determining the extent to which closer relations and confidence can be developed.

The European Council accepts the right of countries to acquire the means to defend themselves, but is concerned that Iran's arms procurement should not pose a threat to regional stability.

In view of the fundamental importance of the Middle East Peace Process, the European Council also expresses the wish that Iran will take a constructive approach here.

Document 4b/22   Declaration by the Council of the European Union on Iran, Luxembourg, 29 April 1997

The Council had an extensive discussion on European Union relations with Iran, in the light of the Mykonos case. It reaffirmed the Presidency's declaration of 10 April 1997. It reiterated that the European Union has always wanted a constructive relationship with Iran, as expressed in the declaration of Edinburgh of 1992. However progress can only be made if the Iranian authorities respect the norms of international law and refrain from acts of terrorism, including against Iranian citizens living abroad' and cooperate in preventing such acts.

It called on Iran to abide by its commitments under international agreements, including those concerning the non-proliferation of weapons of mass destruction, as well as those concerning human rights. It urged Iran to ratify the Chemical Weapons Convention.

The Council, determined to fight against terrorism in all its forms, regardless of its perpetrators or motives, agreed on the following:

–   confirmation that under the present circumstances there is no basis for the continuation of the Critical Dialogue between the European Union and Iran;

–   the suspension of official bilateral Ministerial visits to or from Iran under the present circumstances.

–   confirmation of the established policy of European Union Member States not to supply arms to Iran;

–   cooperation to ensure that visas are not granted to Iranians with intelligence and security functions.

–   concentration in excluding Iranian intelligence personnel from European Union Member States.

The Council decided to keep the relationship with Iran under close review and instructed the Political Committee accordingly. Member States will instruct their Ambassadors, after their return to Teheran, to contribute in a coordinated way to the continual appraisal by the Council of the relationship.

Bulgaria, the Czech Republic, Estonia, Hungary, Iceland, Latvia, Lithuania, Norway, Poland, Romania, Slovakia and Slovenia align themselves with this declaration.

The EU has had to step particularly carefully over Iran, because of the considerable uncertainty over that country's intentions, and divided internal politics. The following answer to a parliamentary question about a reported build-up of arms, both conventional and chemical-biological, on the part of Syria, Iraq and Iran, is factual and even-handed (document 4b/23). It does, however, give hints of a favourable view of a changing Iran, and in 1998 the determination to support the elements of reform, which seemed finally to be gaining the upper hand over the clergy, became more evident (document 4b/24). It was something of a relief for European diplomats to be able to side with their Iranian counterparts against the extremism of the Taliban movement in Afghanistan.

Document 4b/23   Answer to a Written Question (E-2854/97) from Mr Van
der Waal (I-EDN) in the European Parliament, on the
Acquisition of Arms by Syrian, Iraq and Iran, 26 November
1997

The honourable Member's attention is drawn to the fact that, following the 1991
Gulf War, Iraq is subject to a UN sanctions regime aiming at full dismantlement
of the mass destruction capability built up by that country before the war.

The Council is concerned about the effects on regional security of Iran's arms
procurement and development activities. It raises these concerns with countries from
which Iran is known to be trying to achieve technology and know-how which could
enable it to develop a mass destruction capability. Until the discontinuation of the
EU–Iran Critical Dialogue following the verdict in the so-called 'Mykonos Trial' in
Berlin earlier this year, the Council also raised these questions with Iran itself.

. . .

The EU Member States are [therefore] committed, both by international legally-
binding instruments and political undertakings and by the European Union
Regulation and Joint Action, to apply the strictest controls to all exports of arms
and dual-use goods.

As to the countries mentioned by the honourable Member, Syria, Iraq and Iran
are parties to the Nuclear Non-Proliferation Treaty. Iran has signed the
Comprehensive Nuclear Test Ban Treaty.

Iran is in the process of ratifying the Chemical Weapons Convention.

Document 4b/24   Press Statement on Afghanistan/Iran, Brussels and Vienna,
11 September 1998

The EU has learned with dismay of the killing of Iranian diplomats during recent
fighting at Mazar-i-Sharif in Northern Afghanistan, and expresses its condolences
to the bereaved families and to the Government and people of the Islamic Republic
of Iran.

The EU condemns these inhuman acts and the violation of the Vienna Diplomatic
and Consular Conventions. The EU calls for an urgent investigation into these
crimes and a consequent indictment of those responsible. The EU calls on the
Taliban for full cooperation to ensure the release and safe return of remaining diplomats and other Iranian nationals still missing in Afghanistan. The EU notes the
statement of the Taliban that the bodies will be returned to Iran and the perpetrators brought to justice.

Terrorism: Libya and Syria, 1986

In December 1985, terrorists attacked the airports at Rome and Vienna. Italy then
demanded an EPC discussion on terrorism, which happened on 27 January 1986, to build

on the technical cooperation which had been taking place between experts since the mid-1970s. The foreign ministers agreed to intensify their cooperation in several areas, including airport security and visa policies. The Twelve would not export arms to countries implicated in supporting terrorism (document 4b/25). The United States, however, was demanding that the West European states single out Libya as responsible for terrorism in Europe, and impose sanctions on it. The United States was also considering a military strike against Libya. The Twelve resisted the US demands, unwilling to impose sanctions on or to support the use of force against Libya, until a Berlin discothèque was bombed and several American and allied service personnel were killed. On 14 April 1986, the foreign ministers condemned Libya, and imposed diplomatic (but not economic) sanctions (document 4b/26). But most Member States were also concerned that the United States would act militarily, and the statement urges restraint on all sides (paragraph 11). The EPC statement came too late to influence US policy: as the Community foreign ministers were meeting, the United States launched a punitive raid on Libya, without informing the Member States – with the exception of the UK, which had allowed American bombers to fly from US bases in England. The European Parliament demanded to know whether the UK foreign minister had informed his colleagues about the imminent US military action: in a testy exchange with several Members of the European Parliament (MEPs), Council President Hans van den Broek admitted that the US action had not been discussed during the meeting (document 4b/27). Not only had EPC been unable to influence the United States, but also the Member States were now split over how to respond to the US policy.

Syria also became a focus for European discussions about terrorism. In April 1986, a bomb was discovered in the luggage of a passenger bound for Tel Aviv from London Heathrow airport. Syria was suspected of being involved. In October, a UK court found the passenger's boyfriend (Nezar Hindawi) guilty of placing the bomb; the UK then broke off diplomatic relations with Syria and pressed the other Eleven for support. On 10 November 1986, the Member States agreed to impose diplomatic sanctions on Syria over the Hindawi affair (document 4b/28), but could not agree on stronger measures, despite (or perhaps because of) pressure from Mrs Thatcher's UK Presidency. Greece dissociated itself from the statement, but applied the measures in practice.

Document 4b/25   Statement by the Twelve Foreign Ministers on the Combating of International Terrorism, Brussels, 27 January 1986

1.   The Twelve reaffirm their strong condemnation of the recent terrorist attacks at Rome and Vienna airports, which are the latest outrages in the persistent phenomenon of international terrorism. They deeply deplore the loss of innocent lives. The Twelve condemn all forms of international terrorism, the perpetrators, accomplices and instigators as well as governments that support them. They condemn statements emanating from any quarter expressing support for terrorist attacks. Such terrorist attacks can never be justified and do not serve whatever political cause the perpetrators claim to be assisting.

2.   The Twelve express their strong concern about the tension that has developed in the Mediterranean. They reaffirm their support for urgent progress in the search for a just, lasting and comprehensive solution by peaceful means of the problems of the region and their readiness to play a part in efforts towards that end.

The Twelve express the wish to cooperate with all States, including those in the region, to deny terrorists support, cover or refuge.

They are ready to embark on a dialogue in the most appropriate manner with the countries of the region on the problem of international terrorism and the need to tackle its roots.

States that favour or protect terrorists cannot expect indulgence nor can they expect to have normal relations with the Twelve.

The Twelve will study in what way they can jointly clarify responsibilities for terrorist acts. They call upon all countries which are supporting or have been accused of supporting terrorism to renounce such support.

3.   The Twelve welcome the strong and unequivocal condemnation of all acts of international terrorism recently expressed by the Security Council and the General Assembly of the United Nations.

4.   The Twelve reiterate their determination and commitment to combat international terrorism in all its forms. They have reviewed and increased their security arrangements and cooperation in an effort to prevent further terrorist acts. In this respect they welcome and fully support the resolution of the European Parliament of 16 January 1986 in which the representatives of the European peoples condemned in the strongest terms these barbaric acts of terrorism and asked Ministers to step up consultations and cooperation on anti-terrorist measures and public security.

5.   The Twelve recall their previous decisions and efforts to curb these outrages, in particular:

i)   the agreement of September 1984 on a set of principles to increase cooperation against international terrorism, including the need for a joint response in the event of a serious terrorist attack involving the abuse of diplomatic immunity.

ii)   the recommendation dealing with the hijacking of aircraft adopted by the Ministers of the Interior and Justice in June 1985.

iii)   the decision of July 1985 to increase cooperation on aviation security.

Experts of the Twelve have continued to meet on numerous occasions during the last months to strengthen their cooperation and to elaborate common measures.

6.   The Twelve have now decided to intensify these efforts and to promote common action, particularly in the following areas, both to improve their own defences against terrorism and to discourage those who support it:

i)   security at airports, ports and railway stations;

ii)   control by Member States of persons entering or leaving the Community and circulating in it;

iii)   visa policies with respect to the problem of terrorism;

iv)   abuse of diplomatic immunity.

They have decided to establish a permanent working body with a precise mandate, within the European political cooperation, which will monitor and give impetus to the implementation of the above-mentioned measures.

7.   Furthermore, in addition to restrictions they already apply, the Twelve decided not to export arms or other military equipment to countries which are clearly implicated in supporting terrorism.

The Twelve have, in addition, decided to examine jointly with special care national measures designed to prevent the export of arms or other military equipment from being diverted for terrorist purposes.

8.   The Twelve will do everything within their power in order to avoid their nationals and industry seeking any commercial advantage from measures in reaction to terrorist attacks and other terrorist activities.

9.   The Twelve will keep the problems of international terrorism under constant review and take appropriate additional measures whenever the situation requires it.

Document 4b/26   Statement by the Twelve Foreign Ministers on International Terrorism and the Crisis in the Mediterranean, The Hague, 14 April 1986

1.   The Twelve are gravely concerned by the increased tension in the Mediterranean created by the recent acts of terrorism. They met today to concert common action against this scourge.

2.   They consider that States clearly implicated in supporting terrorism should be induced to renounce such support and to respect the rules of international law. They call upon Libya to act accordingly.

3.   The Twelve are convinced that terrorist attacks do not serve whatever political cause the perpetrators claim to be furthering. Outrages like the ones recently perpetrated on the TWA aircraft and in a discothèque in Berlin can never be justified. The Twelve vigorously condemn these outrages, deeply deplore the loss of innocent life involved and express their sympathy with the victims and their families.

4.   They also reject the unacceptable threats made by Libyan leaders against the Member States, which deliberately encourage recourse to acts of violence and directly threaten Europe. Any action of this sort will meet with a vigorous and appropriate response on the part of the Twelve.

5.   The Twelve have decided to act according to the following lines regarding Libya and, where necessary, regarding other States clearly implicated in supporting terrorism:

i)   restrictions on the freedom of movement of diplomatic and consular personnel;

ii)   reduction of the staff of diplomatic and consular missions;

iii)   stricter visa requirements and procedures.

6.   In conformity with their declaration of 27 January 1986 they reaffirm that no arms or other military equipment will be exported to Libya. They will continue to do everything within their power in order to ensure that their nationals and industry do not seek any commercial advantage from measures in reaction to terrorist attacks and other terrorist activities. They reserve the right to consider whether further measures may need to be taken.

No country which lends support to terrorism can expect to maintain normal relations with them.

7.   They have instructed the experts concerned immediately to identify appropriate measures to be taken by the Twelve, in particular, security measures, the application of international conventions on diplomatic and consular privileges and immunities and the safety of civil aviation. The experts' report will be considered at the ministerial meeting to be held next week.

8.   The Twelve are increasing their cooperation with other States in the field of intelligence, the improvement of security measures and, generally, to prevent acts of terrorism.

9.   In order to contribute to eliminating international terrorism, the Twelve will use their joint influence in contacts with Libya and, where necessary, with other States concerned.

10.   They have decided to inform the Arab States and the League of Arab States about their conclusions and to invite them to analyse jointly and urgently the issue of international terrorism.

11.   Finally and in order to enable the achievement of a political solution, avoiding further escalation of military tension in the region with all the inherent dangers, the Twelve underline the need for restraint on all sides.

Document 4b/27   Excerpts from Dutch Presidency's Answers to Oral Parliamentary Questions Concerning the Crisis in the Gulf of Sidra, Strasbourg, 16 April 1986

In the light of the recent hostilities between the United States and Libya, what steps have the Ministers taken or do they intend to take with a view to establishing a policy of consultation and peace in the Mediterranean so as to prevent an escalation in the current armed conflict?

Mr Van den Broek, President-in-Office of the Foreign Ministers:

. . .

Not least, the declaration issued last Monday evening by the Twelve emphasized the need for moderation on both sides, so as to prevent any further escalation of the military tension in the region, with all its attendant dangers. The United States nevertheless felt obliged despite the European appeal, to take direct military action against Libya on Monday. It must be acknowledged that tension in the region has been heightened by that action. The Presidency then decided at short notice to hold a further meeting of Foreign Ministers, a meeting that has now been fixed to take place tomorrow alongside the OECD meeting in Paris, to consider the new situation that has been created. . . .

As the Honourable Member rightly points out, the military operation by the United States took place after the meeting of the Twelve had opened. I have just indicated that consultation to review the situation in the light of the more recent development that came to light early on Tuesday morning still has to take place and that the Ministers will be meeting for that purpose tomorrow.

As to the Honourable Member's more specific question concerning European Ministers' knowledge of the American action, I can in any event inform him that the American action as such was not specifically discussed during consultations on Monday in The Hague. It was of course the case that the meeting had been called at such short notice by the Presidency because tension in the area was obviously mounting and the possibility of military intervention could not be ruled out.

It goes without saying that, if there were Ministers present at that consultation, which – I repeat – took place prior to the military intervention, who were in possession of any relevant information, no such sensitive information formed any part of advance talks among the Twelve.

. . .

Mr Van den Broek: I have as yet received no information from Mr Genscher concerning his talks with Mr Shultz. As to the information to which the Honourable Member refers – it was translated as 'Does proof exist?', so that I have not quite understood the question – if the question is: 'Was there advance information?', in other words the same question as that put by Mr Mattina – I can answer that, as the Honourable Member is aware, the American President, in advance of the military intervention, sent a special ambassador round a number of European capital cities. No communication has been forwarded to us by the governments concerned regarding the talks that were held with the American special representative.

. . .

I have already stated that the fact that an emergency meeting was called at all was already an indication in itself that developments were taking place that at the very least made it necessary to be ready to countenance the possibility of military intervention. As I understood yesterday, on the basis among other things of contacts with my British counterparts, the final decision – I don't mean on preparations, but the decision on military intervention itself – was not taken until the very day when the Twelve were meeting. It would be wrong to see a connection between the two things; it was simply a question of timing. The Ministers, while they could not have been in possession of concrete information concerning the final decisions on military intervention, nevertheless recognized the gravity of the situation, and it was against precisely that background that they drafted their declaration, in particular its concluding paragraph – to which I have already referred – urging moderation and self-restraint in order to forestall escalation.

. . .

I think that in my capacity as EPC President-in-Office I need have no reservations in stating here that the policy of the Twelve in situations of this kind is continually directed to considering how political solutions can be secured. The Honourable Member also referred in this connection to the Palestinian question. She is very well aware of the efforts of the Twelve, and this applies also to the recent past, in seeking to put forward proposals aimed at securing peaceful solutions to the Middle East conflict, and in that connection any attempt to impose a solution by military force can never be considered as a first option. Preference will naturally always be given to political solutions. . . .

Document 4b/28   Press Statement by the Presidency on Terrorism, London, 10 November 1986

1. Following on from our discussion on 27 October of Syrian involvement in the Hindawi case, we have all agreed that further joint action is essential to protect our citizens from any possible repetition of such acts of terrorism.

2. No-one should be in any doubt about our unanimous condemnation of international terrorism and our resolve to curb terrorism in all its forms. We wish to send Syria the clearest possible message that what has happened is absolutely unacceptable.

3. We stand firmly by the commitments in previous statements and have therefore decided that the following additional action is required. In the present circumstances:

- we shall not authorize new arms sales to Syria;

- we shall suspend high-level visits to or from Syria;

- we shall each review the activities of Syrian Diplomatic and Consular missions accredited in our country and apply appropriate measures;

- we shall each review and tighten security precautions surrounding the operations of Syrianair.

4. Our Embassies in Damascus were instructed to make representations to the Syrian authorities. The Syrian Government have delivered their reply. As far as the facts are concerned, this adds nothing to what was considered by the court which found Hindawi guilty, and to what the Embassies have presented to the Syrian authorities.

5. We shall continue to employ all the political means available to us in order to persuade the Syrian authorities to translate into concrete action their stated condemnation of international terrorism. In particular, we call on them to end all forms of support for those groups which have been clearly involved in terrorist acts and to deny them all facilities.

6. Our actions have a specific purpose. We look to the Syrian authorities for a constructive response. We have close and important links with all the countries of the Middle East which we remain determined to develop and strengthen. In this respect, we recall the proposals the Twelve have made to give a new impetus to the Euro-Arab dialogue, and the importance attached to this is the recent communication dated 6 November from the Secretary-General of the Arab League. We strongly reaffirm our commitment to contribute in every way we can to the search for just and lasting solutions to the region's problems.

7. We shall follow developments closely and shall remain in regular contact on all these issues within the framework of European Political Co-operation.

Iran–Iraq War

During the Iran–Iraq war, Iraq used poison gas against its own citizens (namely Kurds) and against Iran. On 27 March 1984, the Ten expressed distress at reports of these atrocities (document 4b/29). On 9 April 1984, the Ten discussed the question of chemical weapons exports and asked Coreper to look at the issue. But there was no majority for Community implementation of export controls on chemicals; France feared that this would open the way for an extension of Community involvement into arms control and disarmament issues, which, insofar as they escaped national jurisdiction, were for EPC (in practice, however, the restriction on the export of material which might form chemical weapons in 1982 had been one of the first uses of article 113 to implement an EPC decision on sanctions). On 25 February 1986, the Twelve condemned the violations of laws on the use of chemical weapons. On 18 April, the Twelve called for a international chemical weapons ban (document 4b/30).*

---

*   January 1989, there were growing suspicions that Libya was manufacturing chemical weapons, and that German firms had helped to build the factory. Germany then pressed for Community export controls, which were adopted on 20 February. The implementing regulation strongly emphasized EPC's role.

As a result of the Iran–Iraq War, navigation in the Gulf was threatened by mines. On 20 August 1987, the WEU Council met to discuss the situation. France, the UK, Italy, the Netherlands and Belgium decided to coordinate minesweeping activities, under the rubric of the WEU. This contributed to the relaunching of the WEU (see documents 3/1 and 3/2) and is the first indication that the WEU was being seen as a potential 'military arm' by Community Member States.

Document 4b/29 Statement by the European Council on the Iran–Iraq Conflict, Brussels, 27 March 1984

The Heads of State or of Government emphasize the gravity of the risks which continued warfare between Iraq and Iran poses for the region of the Gulf, for the entire Middle East, and for international peace and stability.

Recent developments have increased the sufferings of the peoples of both countries and could open the way to new and dangerous escalation in the intensity and spread of the conflict.

The Ten wish to record their distress at the allegations of the use of chemical weapons. They hope that light will be shed on the matter as a result of the United Nations enquiry. They recall their unqualified condemnation of any use of such weapons.

The Ten call on the parties to comply with the principles and provisions of humanitarian international law in armed conflicts.

The Ten hope that each of the parties will finally agree to comply with the Security Council resolutions and heed the numerous appeals addressed to them by the international community. They hope that the parties will co-operate in the search for a peaceful solution, honourable for them both.

They hope that the United Nations Secretary-General will intensify his efforts for the restoration of peace and are ready to lend him their support to this end.

Document 4b/30 Statement by the Twelve Foreign Ministers on the Use of Chemical Weapons in the Iran–Iraq War, The Hague, 18 April 1986

1. The twelve Member States of the European Community recall the earlier report of the Secretary-General of the United Nations to the effect that in the war between Iraq and Iran chemical weapons had been used. The Twelve have condemned without qualification any use of chemical weapons and they expressed the earnest hope that they would not be used again in this or any other conflict. However, the recent report of the mission of specialists dispatched by the Secretary-General (S/17911) concludes that chemical weapons on many occasions have been used by Iraqi forces against Iranian forces, most recently in the course of the present Iranian offensive into Iraqi territory.

2. The Twelve have taken note of this report with great concern. Accordingly they emphasized the importance of the declaration of the Security Council of the United Nations of 21 March 1986, and they strongly condemn the use of chemical weapons mentioned therein. They reiterate that they attach the greatest importance to the strict compliance with the provisions of the Geneva Protocol of 1925.

3.   The Twelve remain convinced that every effort should be made to work out a world-wide treaty that will completely ban chemical weapons, as this is the only effective long-term solution.

4.   The Twelve are deeply concerned about the extended conflict between Iraq and Iran. They make reference to their declaration of 25 February: calling once more upon the two sides to respect the territorial integrity of all States and stressing the urgent need for both countries to strenuously work for an early peaceful settlement of the conflict on the basis of Security Council resolution 582.

The Gulf War

On 2 August 1990, Iraq invaded Kuwait. The EPC/Community's reaction was very swift, especially in comparison to past such emergencies. An EPC condemnation of the invasion was issued the same day (document 4b/31). On 4 August, the Community and its Member States announced an embargo on oil imports from Iraq and Kuwait, an arms embargo, the freezing of Iraqi assets and the suspension of the generalized system of preferences for the two countries (document 4b/32). Following the 6 August UN Security Council decision to impose a wider embargo, the Community measures had to be strengthened. The Council imposed sanctions on 8 August. On 7 September, the Community and its Member States agreed to extend financial assistance to the countries most affected by the implementation of the embargo on Iraq: Egypt, Jordan and Turkey. However, the Member States then disagreed over how to divide up their contribution. Only on 4 December was the final decision to adopt Community measures taken.

On 21 August, the WEU decided to coordinate the efforts of its Member States present in the Gulf (document 4b/33). Several Member States sent troops to Saudi Arabia and other Gulf countries, but the extent of participation varied.

Throughout the autumn of 1990, Iraq was holding hostage the many foreign nationals who had been in Iraq or Kuwait at the time of the invasion. At the extraordinary European Council in Rome, of 27–28 October, the heads of state or government declared that no Community Member State would negotiate with Iraq for the release of the hostages. This stance was reaffirmed by the foreign ministers on 12 November (document 4b/34). However, several 'unofficial' visits by former high-ranking European politicians (Brandt, Cheysson and Heath) as well as parliamentarians were then undertaken, followed by the release of the hostages of the same nationality as the visiting politician. In early December, Iraq announced that all the hostages would be freed before 15 January.

On 29 November, the UN Security Council issued an ultimatum to Iraq: UN Member States would be authorized to use force against Iraq if it did not comply with Security Council resolutions by 15 January 1991. The European Council, meeting in Rome on 14/15 December, gave its total support for the UN ultimatum. In early January 1991, the Community and its Member States launched a diplomatic initiative to try to convince Iraq to back down and thus avoid a war. On 4 January, the foreign ministers proposed a meeting between the troika and Iraqi Foreign Minister Tarek Aziz (document 4b/35), but Aziz turned down the offer (document 4b/36). On 14 January, France unilaterally proposed a six-point peace plan, which was, however, rejected by the UN Security Council.

On 17 January, the air war began. On the same day, European foreign ministers expressed their regret that the use of force was necessary. At the same time, they renewed their support for the convening of an international conference on the Middle East (Saddam

Hussein had also linked the Palestinian question and an overall Middle East peace settlement to a resolution of the Gulf crisis). British, French and Italian forces took part in the war, under US operational control. On 19 February, the foreign ministers met to discuss efforts to be made after the war to stabilize the region (document 4b/37).

On 24 February, the land offensive began; on 27 February, Iraq accepted the twelve UN Security Council resolutions on the crisis, and a day later, US President George Bush announced the suspension of the offensive. The Community and its Member States welcomed the suspension of military operations (document 4b/38).

Following the end of the war, Saddam Hussein severely repressed the Kurds in the north of the country, and the Shiites in the south. On 3 April, the Twelve condemned the repression. On 8 April, on a British initiative, the European Council proposed the creation of protection zones (or 'safe havens') for the Kurds in Iraq, under UN auspices (document 4b/39). The United States was initially reluctant but the protection zones were set up by late April, and US, British and French forces were deployed to protect the Kurdish population in the zones.

Document 4b/31   Statement by the Community and its Member States on the Invasion of Kuwait by Iraq, Rome and Brussels, 2 August 1990

The Community and its Member States have followed with apprehension during the last weeks the increase in tension in the dispute between Iraq and some Arab countries. They have welcomed the diplomatic efforts that Arab countries and the Arab League itself were deploying and refrained from any stance and initiative in order to preserve such initiatives from any interference.

Following the breakdown of talks held in Jeddah under Arab auspices, the Community and its Member States are now gravely concerned at the latest developments in the dispute and in particular at the military aggression carried out by Iraq against Kuwait, not only a hostile action to a neighbour country, but also a dangerous threat to peace and stability in the region.

The Community and its Member States strongly condemn the use of force by a Member State of the UN against the territorial integrity of another State; this constitutes a breach of the UN Charter and an unacceptable means to solve international difference. They therefore fully support the resolution adopted today by the Security Council.

The Community and its Member States call upon all governments to condemn this unjustified use of force and to work for an early re-establishment of the conditions for the immediate resumption of peaceful negotiations. In this light they ask for an immediate withdrawal of Iraqi forces from Kuwait territory.

The Community and its Member States maintain the matter under review and are ready to take into consideration further initiatives.

Document 4b/32   Statement by the Community and its Member States on the Invasion of Kuwait by Iraq, Rome and Brussels, 4 August 1990

The Community and its Member States reiterate their unreserved condemnation of the brutal Iraqi invasion of Kuwait and their demand for an immediate and unconditional withdrawal of Iraqi forces from the territory of Kuwait, already expressed in their statement of 2 August.

They consider groundless and unacceptable the reasons provided by the Iraqi Government to justify the military aggression against Kuwait, and they will refrain from any act which may be considered as implicit recognition of authorities imposed in Kuwait by the invaders.

In order to safeguard the interests of the legitimate Government of Kuwait they have decided to take steps to protect all assets belonging directly or indirectly to the State of Kuwait.

The Community and its Member States confirm their full support for UN Security Council Resolution 660 and call on Iraq to comply with the provisions of that resolution. If the Iraqi authorities fail so to comply, the Community and its Member States will work for, support and implement a Security Council resolution to introduce mandatory and comprehensive sanctions.

As of now, they have decided to adopt the following:
(i)   an embargo on oil imports from Iraq and Kuwait;
(ii) appropriate measures aimed at freezing Iraqi assets in the territory of Member States;
(iii) an embargo on sales of arms and other military equipment to Iraq;
(iv) the suspension of any cooperation in the military sphere with Iraq;
(v)   the suspension of technical and scientific cooperation with Iraq;
(vi) the suspension of the application to Iraq of the system of generalized preferences.

The Community and its Member States reiterate their firm conviction that disputes between States should be settled by peaceful means, and are prepared to participate in any effort to defuse the tension in the area.

They are in close contact with the governments of several Arab countries and follow with the utmost attention the discussion within the Arab League and the Gulf Cooperation Council. They hope that Arab initiatives will contribute to the restoration of international legality and of the legitimate Government of Kuwait. The Community and its Member States are ready to lend their full support to such initiatives and to efforts to resolve by negotiations the differences between the States concerned.

The Community and its Member States are carefully monitoring the situation of EC nationals in Iraq and in Kuwait. They maintain strict coordination in order to guarantee their safety.

Document 4b/33   Communiqué by the Western European Union Council of Ministers, Paris, 21 August 1990

1. The Foreign and Defence Ministers of WEU met on 21 August 1990 to discuss the situation in the Gulf caused by the Iraqi invasion and then the annexation of Kuwait. . . .

2. The Ministers of the WEU member States repeat their unreserved condemnation of the invasion and annexation of Kuwait by Iraq and call on Iraq to

comply immediately and unconditionally with UN Security Council Resolution 660 and all necessary steps to comply with the embargo of Iraq in accordance with UN Security Council Resolution 661 and to render it effective. They call on the Security Council to take any further useful measures to this end.

...

7. Ministers welcome the measures being taken by member States in support of UN Security Council Resolution 661 and in response to the requests for assistance from States in the Gulf region, with the aim of obliging Iraq unconditionally to withdraw its troops from Kuwaiti territory and restore Kuwait's sovereignty.

8. They have decided closely to coordinate their operations in the area aimed at implementing and enforcing the measures mentioned in paragraph 7, as well as any further measures the Security Council may adopt, also assuring, by common agreement, the protection of their forces. Building on the experience acquired, including the consultation mechanisms during the Gulf operations in 1987 and 1988, they have instructed an ad hoc group of Foreign and Defence Ministry representatives to ensure the most effective coordination in capitals and in the region. This should cover among other things overall operational concepts and specific guidelines for coordination between forces in the region, including areas of operation, sharing of tasks, logistical support and exchange of intelligence. Contact points are being nominated in the Ministries of Defence to assist with cooperation at the practical/technical level and, as an immediate step, to prepare for a meeting of Chiefs of Defence Staff to be held in the next few days.

9. Ministers emphasise that coordination within WEU should also facilitate cooperation with other countries deploying forces in the region, including those of the United States.

...

Document 4b/34 Statement by the European Community and its Member States on the Gulf Crisis, Rome and Brussels, 12 November 1990

The Ministers discussed the initiatives of the Community and its Member States to try to find a solution to the problem of the foreign nationals held in Iraq and Kuwait. They reaffirmed the position by the Community and its Member States in the Rome European Council and repeated in their relevant statements. That position is based on total solidarity to secure freedom for all foreign nationals held in Iraq and Kuwait, condemnation of Iraq's unscrupulous use of those nationals for the sole purpose of trying to divide the international community, determination not to send representatives of their governments, in any capacity whatsoever, to negotiate with Iraq for the release of the foreign nationals and to discourage others from so doing. The Ministers accordingly agreed that any action by the Twelve should have the objective of securing the release of all hostages. They ruled out any negotiations on the matter between their governments and Iraq. In the context of implementing the principles set out in the declaration by the Rome European Council, the Ministers decided that the Community and its Member States would take vigorous action through representations to a large number of countries and groups of countries to persuade them to press the Iraqi authorities along the same lines. The first of those approaches was made by the Ministers themselves to their colleagues in the Maghreb Arab Union during today's meeting in Brussels.

Document 4b/35   Press Statement by the Presidency on the Gulf Crisis, Extraordinary European Political Cooperation (Ministerial) Meeting, Luxembourg, 4 January 1991

In accordance with the positions adopted by the Community and its member States since the beginning of the crisis, Ministers reiterate their firm commitment in favour of the full and unconditional implementation of the relevant resolutions of the UN Security Council. Should this happen, the Twelve consider that Iraq should receive the assurance not to be subject to a military intervention. They consequently recall that the entire responsibility for war or peace rests with the Iraqi government alone, as is spelled out in Resolution 678 of the UN Security Council.

Any initiative tending to promote partial solutions, or to establish a link between the full implementation of the resolutions of the UN Security Council and other problems is unacceptable.

Reaffirming their attachment to a peaceful solution in the full respect of the relevant resolutions of the UN Security Council, the Community and its member States welcome the agreement reached on a meeting between the American Secretary of State, Mr James Baker, and the Iraqi Minister of Foreign Affairs, Mr Tarek Aziz.

In accordance with the Declaration adopted by the European Council in Rome on 15 December 1990, Ministers have asked the Presidency to invite the Iraqi Foreign Minister to a meeting with the Troika in Luxembourg on January 10th. The Presidency will remain in close consultation with the United States, the Arab countries concerned and the Presidency of the Movement of the Non-Aligned, to prepare the two meetings.

In the spirit of the foregoing, and as soon as the present crisis will have been settled peacefully and in full respect of the resolutions of the UN Security Council, the Community and its Member States reaffirm their commitment to contribute actively to a settlement of the other problems of the region and establish a situation of security, stability and development there.

Document 4b/36   Declaration by the Twelve Foreign Ministers on the Gulf, Brussels, 14 January 1991

. . .

Through the Presidency statement of 4 January 1991, the Twelve had clearly indicated that if the resolutions of the Security Council were fully and unconditionally implemented, Iraq should receive the assurance that it would not be subject to a military intervention.

In the same statement, the Twelve had also clearly reaffirmed their commitment to contribute actively to the settlement of the other problems of the region and to establish their situation of security, stability and development, as soon as the Gulf crisis is resolved.

On the occasion of the Rome European Council on 15 December 1990, the European Community and its member States had indicated that they remained completely in favour of the convening of an international peace conference on the Middle East at the appropriate moment.

It is a fact that unfortunately must be acknowledged that the readiness thus displayed to contribute to a peaceful solution of the crisis opening the way to an equitable settlement of all the other problems of the region has not, up to this point, received a response from the Iraqi authorities.

In the face of the continued refusal of the Iraqi authorities to implement the resolutions of the Security Council and in the absence of any signal in this sense, the European Community and its member States regret to have to conclude that the conditions for a new European initiative do not exist as of this moment.

Nevertheless, the invitation to Mr Tarek Aziz to meet the Ministerial Troika remains on the table.

The European Community and its Member States are conscious of having done everything that was possible to find a peaceful exit from the crisis. They remain determined to explore all possibilities for the preservation of peace in the respect of international legality. In this context, they request Arab countries and organisations to continue to devote every effort to bringing the Iraqi authorities to understand that it is in the interest of Iraq, as of the whole Arab world, that it should abide by the resolutions of the Security Council.

Ministers have asked the Presidency to stay in close contact with all parties concerned.

Ministers and their Political Directors will remain in permanent touch in the coming days to follow the course of the crisis and take any necessary decisions.

Document 4b/37   Declaration by the Twelve Foreign Ministers on the Gulf
Crisis, Brussels, 19 February 1991

. . .

The Community and its member States believe that the Arab/Israeli conflict and
the Palestinian question are fundamental sources of instability in the region. They
consider that the international community should make renewed efforts urgently to
achieve a comprehensive, just and lasting solution. They continue to believe that a
properly structured international conference at an appropriate time will provide a
suitable framework for negotiations. Such a conference will require a serious preparation. They will actively promote the search for a peaceful settlement through
dialogue with and between all concerned parties.

Regarding the situation in Lebanon, they express their strong support for the full
implementation of the Taif agreement as the means to achieve national reconciliation in a Lebanon free of all foreign troops.

The Community and its member States endorse the view expressed in the Cairo
meeting about the importance of efforts by the Arabs themselves to foster greater
economic and social development, respecting the principle of sovereignty over
economic resources. The Community and its member States share this perspective
and stand ready, in full respect of this principle and in a spirit of mutual solidarity,
to develop their cooperation with the countries of the region. Their immediate priorities are to ensure the early implementation of their new Mediterranean policy and
the rapid disbursement of their aid for the three countries most directly affected by
the economic consequences of the Gulf crisis.

The Community and its member States are aware of the need for a comprehensive approach to all the problems of the Mediterranean, Middle East and Gulf
region. In this connection, they are willing to explore the modalities for launching
a process aimed at establishing a set of rules and principles in the field of security,
economic cooperation, human rights and cultural exchanges.

Document 4b/38   Statement by the European Community and the Member
States on the Gulf, Brussels, 28 February 1991

The Community and its member States welcome the suspension of military operations in the Gulf.

The Community and its member States are greatly satisfied that Kuwait has recovered its freedom and that international legality has been restored. They express
their gratitude to all states which committed forces to the cause of ensuring respect
for the resolutions of the Security Council of the United Nations.

They pay their respects to all those who have lost their lives in this conflict.

They note Iraq's acceptance of the twelve resolutions of the Security Council of
the United Nations and express the hope that its Government will rapidly accept
the conditions put forth by the coalition.

It is now the task of the Security Council of the United Nations to define the necessary arrangements to put an end to the conflict.

As they stated on the day on which military operations began, the Community and its member States reaffirm their commitment to contribute to bringing about for all the peoples of the region, in dignity and security, a future of peace, stability and development in a context of social justice and regional economic solidarity.

To this end, they will make a major effort to develop an overall approach with regard to the region, bearing at one and the same time on security questions, political problems, and economic cooperation.

Document 4b/39   Decision of the Informal Meeting of the European Council, Luxembourg, 8 April 1991

The Council decided to provide ECU 150 million of humanitarian aid for the Kurdish and other refugees in the region. ECU 100 million of this sum would come from the Community budget, supplementing the allocations already made, with the remaining ECU 50 million coming from Member State budgets. The Commission would coordinate the aid.

The Council expressed its support for the move to establish in Iraq a United Nations protected zone for minorities and backed the Commission's proposals for economic cooperation between the Community and the Middle East. With regard to political matters, it emphasized the irreplaceable role of the United Nations and again called on Iraq to implement immediately UN Security Council Resolution 687.

It pointed out the three conditions needed for peace and stability in the region: a solution to the Arab–Israeli conflict and the Palestinian question, greater democratic legitimacy of governments, and economic development with reduced disparities in income levels. Also discussed were Lebanon and Cyprus and the convening of a conference on security and cooperation in the Mediterranean.

In its consideration of economic issues, the Council examined the situation with regard to emergency measures, the implementation of policies agreed upon and new spheres of activity for the future, notably within the context of relations with the Arab Maghreb Union, Israel and Iran.

Iraq

Iraq continued to be a problem for the European Union no less than for the United States after the end of the Gulf War, as the result of Saddam Hussein's unremittingly brutal actions. Only a few examples can be canvassed here, but they indicate the interconnectedness of policy towards Iraq with that towards the whole Middle East region, and in particular with Turkey, an embarrassing applicant for membership of the EU but a staunch ally inside NATO. The EU was alarmed at the way the Kurdish problem, involving the territory of three states, had the potential to cause a further war, and was willing to criticize Turkey as well as Iraq (documents 4b/40 and 41). There was no doubt, however, that Iraq was the main focus of concern. No Member State has tended to argue that Saddam Hussein is a man to do business with, as Italy used to in relation to Colonel Gaddafi. On the other hand, as document 4b/42 shows, the EU was torn between an orthodox attachment to the sovereignty of Iraq, independent of its current leadership, and a wish to intervene for humanitarian reasons, in particular by supporting 'a Kurdish enclave in northern Iraq'. This dilemma anticipated that which was to come over Kosovo and it epitomizes the kinds of problems that a foreign policy based on democratic values, like that of the EU, increasingly faces.

By contrast the hostility towards Iraq's chemical weapons programme arose from more conventional foreign policy concerns, even if they too raised the issue of preventive intervention (documents 4b/43 and 44). The EU as a whole went along with the tough Anglo-American line in the UN Security Council, which envisaged and ultimately led to bombing raids in punishment for non-compliance, but there was no disguising the lack of enthusiasm felt in some Member States for this policy.

Document 4b/40   Press Statement on the Turkish Intervention in Northern Iraq, Brussels and Paris, 5 April 1995

During its visit to Ankara on 23 March, the ministerial troika expressed its concern at Turkey's intervention in northern Iraq and the risks incurred by civilians, particularly refugees. It asked for that operation to be brought swiftly to an end. It took note of the assurances given by the Turkish authorities as to the limited duration of the military intervention in northern Iraq and the protection of the civilian population.

In the light of recent statements and official contacts with certain members of the Turkish Government concerning the extension and objectives of the operation, the European Union once more expresses its grave concern, reaffirms the need for strict respect for human rights and international humanitarian law, and calls for the early withdrawal of Turkish troops.

Iceland and Norway, as EFTA Member States, parties to the EEA, associate themselves with this statement.

Document 4b/41   Press Statement on the Withdrawal of Turkish Troops from Northern Iraq, Brussels and Paris, 9 May 1995

The European Union, which regards the stability and territorial integrity of the states of the region as a matter of importance, has noted with satisfaction the announcement of the total withdrawal of Turkish troops from northern Iraq, in accordance with the undertakings given by Turkey to the troika on 23 March. It hopes that Ankara will deal similarly with the other concerns voiced by the European Union in recent months concerning democracy and human rights, thus creating more favourable conditions for the bringing about of the desired rapprochement between the European Union and Turkey, with a view in particular to the implementation of the agreement on customs union.

Document 4b/42   Statement in the European Parliament on the Events in Iraq, 18 September 1996

Mr Mitchell, Irish President-in-Office of the Council: Mr President, I am aware that Members have been carefully watching events in Iraq. The conflict in northern Iraq has led to a serious humanitarian emergency and there is even the threat of further consequences, with the possibility of military action between Iraq and the United States.

We all know that for many years the Iraqi dictatorship has brought great suffering on its own people and on its neighbours. Abroad, its expansionist ambitions and seizure of Kuwait caused the Gulf War with all the huge suffering and destruction that entailed, and even now Iraq still continues to threaten the stability of the Gulf. At home, it has consistently and massively violated the human rights of its own population, in defiance of Security Council resolutions, as well as the international human rights instruments. In southern Iraq, the regime has devastated the lifestyle of the Marsh Arab people in an attempt to subject them to Baghdad's control. In the north its oppression of its Kurdish population in the aftermath of the Gulf War was so severe that the international community had to step in and set up safe havens to protect them from the regime.

As a result of the oppression of its own population, the international community felt obliged in the aftermath of the Gulf War to modify the basic rule in international relations of the inviolability of frontiers and to assume responsibility for ensuring, through the no-fly zones, that Saddam Hussein eased the pressure on his own population.

Unfortunately, despite this international protection, it did not prove possible to resolve the bitter and long-standing differences between the two main Kurdish parties of Iraq, the Kurdistan Democratic Party and the Patriotic Union of Kurdistan – after the Gulf War. For some reason, a temporary ceasefire in the hostilities between the two factions was established and certain confidence-building measures were agreed between them, but the fragile peace that existed through 1995 has recently given way to renewed hostilities.

The fighting between the factions and the general state of lawlessness in northern Iraq added to the existing pressures on the area's stability, and led to border incursions by both Turkey and Iran. Turkey argued that its incursions were justified on the grounds that elements of its own outlawed Kurdish Workers party, the PKK, have been availing themselves of their relative protection in northern Iraq to strike at Turkey. Iran for its part claimed that a subgroup of the KDP had been mounting attacks on its territory from northern Iraq.

The volatile situation has offered Saddam Hussein the opportunity and pretext for reasserting his influence over the whole of Iraq, which had been denied to him by the establishment of the safe havens. His incursion into the Kurdish areas upset the element of stability that Resolution 688 and the subsequently-established no-fly zone had brought about and led to last week's US missile attacks.

The situation in northern Iraq was discussed by EU Foreign Ministers at their informal meeting in Tralee on 7 and 8 September last. As it was an informal meeting there were, of course, no formal declarations, but I believe that on the basis of the Tralee discussion there is a broad measure of agreement among Member States on the central issues of the current conflict. I would list the areas of agreement as follows.

The Union is greatly concerned at the potential for large-scale deaths and economic and social disruption involved in incursions into northern Iraq by outside forces, including those of the Iraqi regime.

The Union attaches major importance to the sovereignty and territorial integrity of Iraq.

The Union remains in favour of the maintenance of a Kurdish enclave in northern Iraq.

There is agreement on the need for the continued existence of a no-fly zone in Iraq as a means of controlling the oppressive policies of the Iraqi Government against the people of Iraq.

The European Union is still willing to pursue contacts with the neighbouring countries in the region with a view to de-escalation of tensions in northern Iraq.

The Union wishes to ensure that steps are taken to relieve the suffering of the Iraqi civilian population, and of children in particular, through the implementation of Security Council Resolution 986, which would allow the sale of Iraqi oil to pay for food as soon as conditions permit.

The Union will continue to pursue these objectives in cooperation with the international community through all available channels.

. . .

[After the following debate, Mr Mitchell stated:] Mr President, first of all, I have noted the comments of the distinguished Members in the debate and I would like to assure the House that the European Union is fully committed to the search for a just, lasting and comprehensive peace in the Middle East in general. The European Council in Florence reaffirmed that the success of the Middle East peace process remains a fundamental interest of the Union. The challenge before the Union and the international community is to restore momentum and impetus to the process and we will continue to engage constructively with all the parties in the region in our efforts to support the peace process.

A number of speakers raised the question of the Union's response to the future of northern Iraq and the humanitarian situation of the Iraqi population. The Union has a number of clear objectives. These are: ensuring the continued safety of the Iraqi civilian population; the de-escalation of tensions in northern Iraq, principally through the withdrawal of Iraqi Government forces, as well as through support for dialogue between the Kurdish factions; the maintenance of the sovereignty and territorial integrity of all the states in the region, including Iraq; and ensuring that steps are taken to relieve the suffering of the Iraqi civilian population, and children in particular, through the implementation of UN Security Council Resolution 986, as I stated earlier, which would allow the sale of Iraqi oil to pay for food as soon as conditions permit.

The Union will continue to pursue these objectives through all channels. I would repeat, as Commissioner Marín has stated, that the Union, which has a long-standing commitment to alleviating the humanitarian plight of the population in northern Iraq, intends to respond to the current refugee emergency as generously as resources allow.

Document 4b/43   Press Statement on Security Council Resolution 1154 on Iraq, Brussels and London, 3 March 1998

The EU welcomes the unanimous adoption of Security Council Resolution (SCR) 1154 on 2 March.

This Resolution commends the initiative by the UN Secretary-General to secure commitments from the government of Iraq on compliance with its obligations under the relevant Resolutions and endorses the Memorandum of Understanding signed by the Deputy Prime Minister of Iraq and the UN Secretary-General on 23 February 1998.

The EU calls on the Iraqi authorities to comply fully with the Memorandum of Understanding and with the relevant Security Council Resolutions.

The EU notes that under the terms of SCR 1154 any violation by Iraq of its obligations would have the severest consequences. On the other hand, compliance by Iraq with its obligations, repeated in the Memorandum of Understanding, to accord immediate, unconditional and unrestricted access to the Special Commission and the IAEA would allow the Security Council to act in accordance with the relevant provisions of SCR 687 on the lifting of sanctions. The EU notes that, in accordance with its responsibility under the Charter, the Security Council will remain actively seized of the matter, in order to secure the implementation of this Resolution and to secure peace and security in the area.

The EU meanwhile remains determined to ensure that the arrangements for bringing increased humanitarian assistance to the Iraqi people under SCR 1153 are fully and effectively implemented.

Document 4b/44   Press Statement on Iraq, Brussels and Vienna, 11 November 1998

The European Union condemns as totally unacceptable Iraq's decision of 31 October to cease all cooperation with UNSCOM. The European Union supports the Security Council's response to that decision, SCR 1205 of 5 November. The European Union urges Iraq to resume full cooperation with UNSCOM and the IAEA immediately, and expresses its continued support for both organisations. The European Union also welcomes the fact that the Security Council has again expressed its readiness to hold a comprehensive review of Iraq's obligations once Iraq had resumed cooperation. The European Union expresses its strong hope that Iraq will do so soon and confirms its full support for the Secretary-General in his efforts to seek full implementation of the Memorandum of Understanding of 23 February 1998.

Meanwhile, the European Union will work together with all the neighbours of Iraq to seek the more effective enforcement of existing sanctions. Specifically, the Presidency (troika) will make contact with these countries to that end. At the same time, the European Union will work to continue to ensure more effective implementation of the oil for food programme and full Iraqi cooperation in preventing any unnecessary suffering for the Iraqi people.

Algeria

On 26 December 1991, the opposition parties, including the Islamic Salvation Front, won over 80 per cent of the vote in the first round of legislative elections in Algeria. The government then cancelled the second round of elections, set for 16 January, and on 9 February 1992 declared a state of emergency. The Community and its Member States expressed concern about the developments and urged a return to normal institutional life (documents 4b/45 and 46). But the response was fairly muted, and the Community continued to cooperate with the regime, even though the cancellation of the elections was a patently undemocratic move. The government proceeded to fight as dirty a war against the fundamentalists as the fundamentalists were fighting against the government. But among Community governments, there was even greater uneasiness about the possible consequences of a victory for Islamic fundamentalist parties, in a country so closely linked to France.

Algeria has had a trade and cooperation agreement with the Community since 1975: the Union has not suspended the agreement. The press releases reporting the results of the cooperation council that regularly reviews the agreement barely mention the carnage (document 4b/48). The Union has condemned the use of violence and expressed support for attempts to establish a dialogue between the various forces (documents 4b/47 and 50), but Algeria was still included in the Euro-Mediterranean partnership (see documents 4b/49 and 54). In June 1996, the Council approved the Commission's mandate to negotiate a Euro-Mediterranean association agreement with Algeria. For six years the EU was remarkably silent on the Algerian crisis, given its geographical proximity and the large loss of life. What has been ever more remarkable has been the fact that silence has attracted far less public criticism than the flawed but activist policy over Bosnia. Finally, in January 1998, a German and British initiative led to the EU's troika visiting Algeria on a ministerial mission to continue 'political dialogue'. This mission was treated brusquely by the Algerian government.

The use of carrot, in the form of the promised new association agreement (spun out, and still not signed), plus stick, in the form of a more critical line towards the government (document 4b/51), may have had some marginal effect in encouraging the small signs of an emerging compromise inside Algeria itself.

Document 4b/45 Statement by the European Community and its Member States on Algeria, Brussels, 23 January 1992

The Community and its member States have been following closely the recent developments in Algeria.

The Community and its member States express the strong hope that the Algerian authorities will undertake every possible effort for a return to normal institutional life so that peaceful political dialogue among all parties concerned will take place and the democratic process will pursue on a stable course.

Remaining deeply attached to the respect of human rights and fundamental freedoms, the Community and its member States will follow with great attention how the situation will develop in Algeria and how those principles will be implemented.

Document 4b/46 Declaration by the European Community and its Member States on Algeria, Brussels, 17 February 1992

The Community and its member States have been following the situation in Algeria with concern.

The Community and its member States reiterate their wish for Algeria to return to a normal institutional life and their encouragement to the High Committee of State to promote dialogue among all parties concerned. The Community and its member States strongly urge the Algerian authorities to pursue their publicly announced commitments, namely the social and economic reforms, the restructuring of public administration and the protection of fundamental freedoms.

The Community and its member States will support all efforts undertaken by the Algerian authorities to restore the democratic process. They hope that this transitional process will be attained with respect for human rights, tolerance and political pluralism.

The Community and its member States are willing to cooperate with the Algerian authorities in the economic recovery of their country, bearing in mind that compliance with the aforementioned principles will be important in the context of bilateral relations.

Document 4b/47 Statement by the Presidency on behalf of the European Union on Algeria, Brussels, 26 September 1994

The European Union reaffirms its willingness to support a policy of democratic development and economic restructuring in Algeria and condemns all forms of violence there. In this connection the European Union recalls the declaration made by the European Council in Corfu on 24 and 25 June 1994. The European Union welcomes the renewed efforts to promote political dialogue in Algeria. It calls upon those parties which have not yet taken part in the dialogue to do so, and encourages all sides to create the basis for the development of a democratic society.

The European Union particularly welcomes the measures taken by the Algerian government to involve the political leaders of the Islamist movement in the dialogue. It is imperative to make all possible efforts to achieve peaceful cooperation among all sides. Therefore the European Union calls upon all sides to cease all acts of violence immediately to allow a peaceful dialogue. It is necessary for all sides to participate with the aim of achieving political reconciliation and the restoration of stability so that normal life without the constant threat of terrorist violence may resume.

The European Union appeals to all Maghreb states to collaborate in the spirit of good neighbourliness to develop the economic prosperity of their citizens and the stability of the region.

The four acceding countries associate themselves with this statement.

Document 4b/48   Joint Press Release by the EC–Algeria Cooperation Council, Luxembourg, 9 October 1995

The EC–Algeria Cooperation Council held its fifth meeting at Ministerial level in Luxembourg on 2 October 1995 with Mr Javier SOLANA, Minister for Foreign Affairs of Spain and President-in-Office of the Council of the European Union in the Chair.

. . .

This meeting of the Cooperation Council enabled the Community and Algeria to take stock of their relations within the Cooperation Council and provided them with the opportunity of discussing political questions of mutual interest. Both parties stressed the importance they attached to cooperation between them and expressed the firm hope that their relations could develop in a way which would allow such cooperation to be intensified.

Both parties stressed the importance of peace, balance, stability, security and well-being for the Euro-Mediterranean area.

They rejected the use of violence as a means of political action and reaffirmed their attachment to the respect for human rights and fundamental freedoms.

The European Union reiterated its condemnation of terrorism and violence in all its forms. It reaffirmed that it was up to Algerians to find solutions to the crisis facing their country.

The European Union noted the decision of the Algerian Government to organize Presidential elections.

The European Union encouraged the Algerian Government to continue talks with all political forces which undertake to renounce violence in order to foster the democratic process.

The Cooperation Council welcomed Algeria's progress in the field of economic reforms and the agreements it has concluded with the international financial institutions, with the aim of consolidating a market economy capable, amongst other things, of promoting Algeria's development and building up its links with the European Union and its other partners in the Mediterranean.

The Council acknowledged that Algeria would be an eligible candidate in future for the major increase in total resources for Mediterranean cooperation proposed at the Cannes European Council. The Union reaffirmed its readiness to support an economic restructuring policy in Algeria. Algeria reaffirmed its determination to continue and develop its economic restructuring policy.

. . .

Document 4b/49 Statement in the European Parliament on EU Policy towards Algeria, 19 February 1997

Mr Patjin, Dutch president of the Council:

. . .

The speedy conclusion of an association agreement with Algeria may be a favourable political factor in that country's efforts to restore law and order and democracy. The Council thus hopes that the Commission will be able to bring the negotiations which have just started to a satisfactory conclusion within the near future. This association agreement will after all offer the European Union the chance of a structured political dialogue with Algeria and in the context of that we can raise the question of the Algerian Government's human rights policy with it.

. . . in the Council's view Algeria still deserves international trust and support, especially from the European Union, in its efforts to overcome this deep and serious crisis. It is not merely in the economic interest of both sides that this European support should still be forthcoming. It is also part of the spirit of political partnership which must inform our cooperation with Algeria. That spirit is evident in the Union's efforts towards an association agreement with Algeria. It reflects the desire of all of us for cooperation with the Mediterranean region as part of the so-called 'Barcelona process'. This desire for dialogue does not mean unconditional support. Quite the contrary, we are equipping ourselves with instruments which will enable us to be both critical and constructive.

. . . the Algerians must resolve the crisis themselves by means of a return to democratic national government and by continuing economic structural adjustments. And to this end the European Union gave Algeria 125 million ECU at the end of December 1996.

The European Commission recently appointed a new delegate to Algeria. Talks on the association agreement are ongoing. High-level political contacts are held regularly. The Europeans are standing by Algeria. Cooperation continues.

. . . The peoples of the European Union and Algeria are, if you like, 'condemned' to work together. For reasons of geography, for reasons of history and for social and humanitarian reasons. And from the European point of view we do that with total respect for the cultural and religious traditions of our North African friends and total repudiation of the fundamentalists' abuse of those traditions. The Council remains willing to work with the present Algerian Government provided we are convinced that it is working to restore democracy and better respect for human rights. We thus call on the Government to hold elections in 1997 and to make them open and free. For our part I repeat that the European Union is prepared, as part of its Mediterranean policy, to give structural aid on a long-term basis for the social and economic development of the Algerian people under a bilateral cooperation agreement.

Document 4b/50   Declaration by the Presidency on behalf of the European Union on the Massacres in Algeria, London, 5 January 1998

The Presidency is deeply concerned that the scale of violence in Algeria has increased dramatically since the beginning of Ramadan.

The Presidency deplores and condemns the recent appalling attacks in the north–west of the country. The terrorists must stop this mindless violence against innocent people. No motive can justify these atrocities.

The European Union supports and encourages all efforts of the Algerian authorities, within the rule of law and consistent with human rights, to protect their citizens from terrorism.

The EU will explore with the government of Algeria and NGOs ways and means of helping the victims of terrorism.

Document 4b/51   Answer to a Written Question in the European Parliament by the United Kingdom Presidency, 9 March 1998

At its meeting on 26 January 1998, the Council welcomed the Ministerial troika's visit to Algiers from 19 to 20 January 1998. That visit was an effective expression of the deep concern of the European Union at the situation in Algeria, of the strong sympathy of the peoples of the European Union with their Algerian neighbours, and of the hope that the suffering of the Algerian people should come quickly to an end. The Council strongly reiterated its condemnation of all acts of terrorism and indiscriminate violence.

The Council reaffirmed the strong commitment of the Union to remaining engaged on this issue. The visit of the troika should be regarded as a key step towards an extensive dialogue with the Algerian Government, begun with the visit of Foreign Minister Attaf to Luxembourg in November. This dialogue has taken on a new quality and urgency. Taking forward talks on the EU–Algeria Association Agreement would be instrumental in pursuing the dialogue.

Through this intensified expression of international concern and support, the Council hoped that the Algerian Government would be in a better position to engage in finding the solution to the terrorist problem.

The Council regretted that offers of humanitarian assistance have not been taken up, but agreed they remain on the table should the Algerian authorities see scope for a meaningful role for neighbourly assistance.

. . .

The Council called for greater transparency on the part of the Government of Algeria about the situation, in which terrorist groups continue to perpetrate cowardly and brutal attacks on innocent civilians. The Council regretted that the Algerian authorities have felt unable to provide unhindered access for international organizations, NGOs and the media. The Council hoped that the Algerian authorities would feel able to accept a visit by Representatives of the United Nations in the near future. The Council continues to urge the Algerian authorities to reconsider these points in the light not only of the EU's approach but also of the support which this approach has received internationally.

The strengthening of inclusive democratic institutions and of the role of the judiciary will help to isolate and undermine those who seek political change through violence. In this context the Council encouraged more frequent contact between Algerian and European parliamentarians. The forthcoming visit of the representatives of the European Parliament will be an important step in this regard.

The Council looked forward to a further meeting between the Algerian Foreign Minister and the Presidency to continue a broad dialogue. Within the scope of this dialogue, the Council reaffirmed the willingness of the Union and its Member States to discuss any concerns and proposals that the Algerian authorities might seek to bring to its attention, including the struggle against terrorism.

The Euro-Mediterranean Initiative

The civil war in Algeria and France's concerns about it were part of the reason why in 1994 the EU decided to strengthen its relations with the countries of the southern rim of the Mediterranean. In 1976–7, the Community had concluded trade and cooperation agreements with the countries of the Maghreb (Morocco, Algeria and Tunisia) and the Mashreq (Egypt, Israel, Jordan, Lebanon and Syria). In 1990, aid and trade concessions were increased. The Corfu European Council, 24–25 June 1994, requested that the Council and Commission reinforce the EU's global policy in the Mediterranean (document 4b/52) and agreed that the next phase of EU enlargement would include Cyprus and Malta. Political concerns about the vulnerable southern flank of the EU were now much more to the fore. The Essen European Council, 9–10 December 1994, further articulated the policy (document 4b/53). This process resulted in the Barcelona Euro-Mediterranean Conference, 27–28 November 1995, with 27 participants, including the Palestinian Authority (document 4b/54). The foreign ministers of the 27 participants are to meet periodically (initially within the first six months of 1997), as are other ministers, senior officials and experts, although the declaration does not set a schedule of lower-level meetings. Parliamentarians, regional and local authority representatives and 'social partners' are to be encouraged to make contacts. No set schedule for such meetings was set out, however. EU aid to the Mediterranean has been increased; a customs union agreement was finally concluded with Turkey (and entered into force on 31 December 1995); while new association agreements have been signed with Morocco, Tunisia and Israel, and an interim trade and cooperation agreement signed with the Palestinian Authority. However, the virtual halt to the Israeli–Palestinian peace process in 1997 had negative implications for the Euro-Mediterranean initiative. Several Arab countries (including Tunisia and Morocco) refused to allow Israel to attend multilateral meetings under the Euro-Mediterranean framework or even cancelled meetings (document 4b/58). On the other side of the coin, Libya was formally excluded but also given back-door forms of participation (document 4b/57).

Turkey and Cyprus have always represented particularly difficult problems for Europe, and since the decisions at Corfu (document 4b/55) and Cannes (document 4b/56) to open negotiations for Cypriot accession to the EU six months after the end of the IGC which was to culminate in the Treaty of Amsterdam, they have become entangled and compounded. The EU adopted a high-risk strategy (possibly in a fit of absence of mind) by opening up the possibility that the Cyprus will be allowed into the Union while both Turkey and the Turkish Republic of Northern Cyprus will be excluded – thus accepting the permanent division of the island. More recently, the EU has tried to lower the risks and the Greco-Turkish rapprochement of late 1999 has helped. The EU states confirmed Turkey's eligibility for membership at the Luxembourg summit of December 1997 (document 4b/59), and at the Helsinki Summit of December 1999, formally acknowledged it as an applicant state and included it in the pre-accession strategy (document 4b/61). But there is no realistic chance of Turkey being wholeheartedly encouraged to join. The reasons for this are the geopolitical problems of size and position rather more than the factors of religion and culture which most Turks believe to be the key obstacles. Human rights, however, are also an important obstacle, and the furore over the capture and trial of the Kurdish leader Abdullah Ocalan in 1999, which even soured Turkey's relations with its erstwhile supporter Italy, further brought this problem into the open.

If Cyprus in its existing form is given a fast-track into the EU this will at the least alienate Turkey seriously, and at most precipitate a further crisis. The EU is gambling that opening negotiations with Cyprus will help to unblock the stalemated negotiations on a final settlement between the island's two communities.

Document 4b/52   Conclusions of the European Council on Relations with the Mediterranean Countries, Corfu, 24–25 June 1994

The European council confirms the importance it attaches to the close links already existing with its Mediterranean partners and its wish to develop them still further so that the Mediterranean area may become an area of cooperation guaranteeing peace, security, stability and well-being.

The European Council welcomes the progress made in the negotiations under way with Israel for the conclusion of a new agreement with a wider scope of application than the 1975 agreements and providing for a closer relationship between the parties on the basis of reciprocity and common interest. It considers that this new agreement should be supplemented by a separate agreement on scientific and technological cooperation. It also asks the Council and the Commission to do their utmost to ensure that these two agreements may be completed before the end of the year.

The European Council considers that these new contractual links will be strengthened by the development of regional cooperation involving Israel and the Palestinian side.

The European Council notes with satisfaction the progress made in the negotiations with Morocco and Tunisia on new partnership agreements. It asks the Council and the Commission to do their utmost to ensure that negotiations are completed before the end of the year.

The European Council also welcomes the opening of exploratory conversations between the Commission and the Egyptian authorities on a new partnership agreement.

The European Council expresses the wish of the European Union to develop existing cooperation relations with the Mashreq countries, taking into account the specific situation of each country.

The European Council is following closely the situation in Algeria. It condemns all acts of terrorism and violations of human rights, both against Algerians and foreign citizens.

The European Council encourages the rigorous pursuit of the national dialogue and the process of structural reform which is essential for the liberalization of the Algerian economy and its better integration into the world economy. The European Council notes with approval the recent Ecofin decision to consider favourably a proposal for further assistance of the order of ECU 200 million, subject to Algeria's continuing implementation of its IMF programme and the position of the Loan Guarantee Fund. Given the particular importance of this issue, the European Council invites the Ecofin Council to examine a Commission proposal very soon.

The European Council hopes that the internal situation in Algeria will improve so that relations with Algeria can develop in the framework of this new approach based on partnership.

The European Council stresses the value for all Mediterranean partners of jointly examining political, economic and social problems to which solutions may be more effectively sought in the context of regional cooperation. The European Council has given a mandate to the Council to evaluate, together with the Commission, the global policy of the European Union in the Mediterranean region and possible initiatives to strengthen this policy in the short and medium term, bearing in mind the possibility of convening a conference attended by the European Union and its Mediterranean partners.

This evaluation should prepare the ground for decisions at the European Council in Essen.

Document 4b/53   Conclusions of the European Council on Mediterranean Policy, Essen, 9–10 December 1994

. . .

Furthermore the European Council welcomes the intention of the future Spanish Presidency to convene in the second half of 1995 a Euro-Mediterranean Ministerial Conference with the participation of all Mediterranean countries concerned and the intention of the French Presidency to give high priority to its intensive preparation. This Conference should allow an in-depth discussion of future relations between the Union and the Mediterranean countries, addressing all relevant political, economic, social and cultural issues.

The Conference should reach an agreement on a series of economic and political guidelines for Euro-Mediterranean cooperation into the next century and will establish a permanent and regular dialogue on all subjects of common interest.

The European Council expresses concern at the emergence of extremist and fundamentalist forces in a number of North African States. European Union policy must take account of these developments.

. . .

Document 4b/54   Barcelona Declaration and Work Programme Adopted at the Euro-Mediterranean Conference, Barcelona, 27–28 November 1995

[The participants] taking part in the Euro-Mediterranean Conference in Barcelona:
– stressing the strategic importance of the Mediterranean and moved by the will to give their future relations a new dimension, based on comprehensive cooperation and solidarity, in keeping with the privileged nature of the links forged by neighbourhood and history;
– aware that the new political, economic and social issues on both sides of the Mediterranean constitute common challenges calling for a coordinated overall response;
– resolved to establish to that end a multilateral and lasting framework of relations based on a spirit of partnership, with due regard for the characteristics, values and distinguishing features peculiar to each of the participants;
– regarding this multilateral framework as the counterpart to a strengthening of bilateral relations which it is important to safeguard, while laying stress on their specific nature;
– stressing that this Euro-Mediterranean initiative is not intended to replace the other activities and initiatives undertaken in the interests of the peace, stability and development of the region, but that it will contribute to their success; the participants support the realization of a just, comprehensive and lasting peace settlement in the Middle East based on the relevant United Nations Security Council resolutions and principles mentioned in the letter of invitation to the Madrid Middle East Peace Conference, including the principle of land for peace, with all that this implies;
– convinced that the general objective of turning the Mediterranean basin into an

area of dialogue, exchange and cooperation guaranteeing peace, stability and prosperity requires a strengthening of democracy and respect for human rights, sustainable and balanced economic and social development, measures to combat poverty and promotion of greater understanding between cultures, which are all essential aspects of partnership;

hereby agree to establish a comprehensive partnership among the participants – the Euro-Mediterranean partnership – through strengthened political dialogue on a regular basis, the development of economic and financial cooperation and greater emphasis on the social, cultural and human dimension, these being the three aspects of the Euro-Mediterranean partnership.

Political and security partnership: establishing a common area of peace and stability

The participants express their conviction that the peace, stability and security of the Mediterranean region are a common asset which they pledge to promote and strengthen by all means at their disposal. To this end they agree to conduct a strengthened political dialogue at regular intervals, based on observance of essential principles of international law, and reaffirm a number of common objectives in matters of internal and external stability.

In this spirit they undertake in the following Declaration of principles:
– to act in accordance with the United Nations Charter and the Universal Declaration of Human Rights, as well as other obligations under international law, in particular those arising out of regional and international instruments to which they are party;
– to develop the rule of law and democracy in their political systems, while recognizing in this framework the right of each of them to choose and freely develop its own political, socio-cultural, economic and judicial system;
– to respect human rights and fundamental freedoms and guarantee the effective legitimate exercise of such rights and freedoms, including freedom of expression, freedom of association for peaceful purposes and freedom of thought, conscience and religion, both individually and together with other members of the same group, without any discrimination on grounds of race, nationality, language, religion or sex;
– to give favourable consideration, through dialogue between the parties, to exchanges of information on matters relating to human rights, fundamental freedoms, racism and xenophobia;
– to respect and ensure respect for diversity and pluralism in their societies, promote tolerance between different groups in society and combat manifestations of intolerance, racism and xenophobia; the participants stress the importance of proper education in the matter of human rights and fundamental freedoms;
– to respect their sovereign equality and all rights inherent in their sovereignty, and fulfil in good faith the obligations they have assumed under international law;
– to respect the equal rights of peoples and their right to self-determination, acting at all times in conformity with the purposes and principles of the Charter of the United Nations and with the relevant norms of international law, including those relating to territorial integrity of States, as reflected in agreements between relevant parties;

– to refrain, in accordance with the rules of international law, from any direct or indirect intervention in the internal affairs of another partner;

– to respect the territorial integrity and unity of each of the other partners;

– to settle their disputes by peaceful means, call upon all participants to renounce recourse to the threat or use of force against the territorial integrity of another participant, including the acquisition of territory by force, and reaffirm the right to fully exercise sovereignty by legitimate means in accordance with the UN Charter and international law;

– to strengthen their cooperation in preventing and combating terrorism, in particular by ratifying and applying the international instruments they have signed, by acceding to such instruments and by taking any other appropriate measure;

– to fight together against the expansion and diversification of organized crime and combat the drugs problem in all its aspects;

– to promote regional security by acting *inter alia* in favour of nuclear, chemical and biological non-proliferation through adherence to and compliance with a combination of international and regional non-proliferation regimes, and arms control and disarmament agreements such as NPT, CWC, BWC, CTBT and/or regional arrangements such as weapons-free zones including their verification regimes, as well as by fulfilling in good faith their commitments under arms control, disarmament and non-proliferation conventions.

The parties shall pursue a mutually and effectively verifiable Middle East Zone free of weapons of mass destruction, nuclear, chemical and biological, and their delivery systems.

Furthermore the parties will:

– consider practical steps to prevent the proliferation of nuclear, chemical and biological weapons as well as excessive accumulation of conventional arms;

– refrain from developing military capacity beyond their legitimate defence requirements, at the same time reaffirming their resolve to achieve the same degree of security and mutual confidence with the lowest possible levels of troops and weaponry and adherence to CCW;

– promote conditions likely to develop good-neighbourly relations among themselves and support processes aimed at stability, security, prosperity and regional and subregional cooperation;

– consider any confidence and security-building measures that could be taken between the parties with a view to the creation of an 'area of peace and stability in the Mediterranean', including the long-term possibility of establishing a Euro-Mediterranean pact to that end.

Economic and financial partnership: creating an area of shared prosperity

The participants emphasize the importance they attach to sustainable and balanced economic and social development with a view to achieving their objective of creating an area of shared prosperity.

The partners acknowledge the difficulties that the question of debt can create for the economic development of the countries of the Mediterranean region. They agree, in view of the importance of their relations, to continue the dialogue in order to achieve progress in the competent fora.

Noting that the partners have to take up common challenges, albeit to varying degrees, the participants set themselves the following long-term objectives:
– acceleration of the pace of sustainable socio-economic development;
– improvement of the living conditions of their populations, increase in the employment level and reduction in the development gap in the Euro-Mediterranean region;
– encouragement of regional cooperation and integration.
With a view to achieving these objectives, the participants agree to establish an economic and financial partnership which, taking into account the different degrees of development, will be based on:
– the progressive establishment of a free-trade area;
– the implementation of appropriate economic cooperation and concerted action in the relevant areas;
– a substantial increase in the European Union's financial assistance to its partners.

. . .

Work Programme

. . .

II. Political and security partnership: establishing a common area of peace and stability

With a view to contributing to the objective of progressively creating a zone of peace, stability and security in the Mediterranean, senior officials will meet periodically, starting within the first quarter of 1996; they will:
– conduct a political dialogue to examine the most appropriate means and methods of implementing the principles adopted by the Barcelona Declaration, and
– submit practical proposals in due time for the next Euro-Mediterranean Meeting of Foreign Ministers.

Foreign policy institutes in the Euro-Mediterranean region will be encouraged to establish a network for more intensive cooperation which could become operational as of 1996.

III. Economic and financial partnership: creating an area of shared prosperity
. . .

Establishment of a Euro-Mediterranean free-trade area

The establishment of a free-trade area in accordance with the principles contained in the Barcelona Declaration is an essential element of the Euro-Mediterranean partnership.

Cooperation will focus on practical measures to facilitate the establishment of free trade as well as its consequences, including:

– harmonizing rules and procedures in the customs field, with a view in particular to the progressive introduction of cumulation of origin; in the meantime, favourable consideration will be given, where appropriate, to finding *ad hoc* solutions in particular cases;
– harmonization of standards, including meetings arranged by the European Standards Organizations;
– elimination of unwarranted technical barriers to trade in agricultural products and adoption of relevant measures related to plant-health and veterinary rules as well as other legislation on foodstuffs;
– cooperation among statistics organizations with a view to providing reliable data on a harmonized basis;
– possibilities for regional and subregional cooperation (without prejudice to initiatives taken in other existing fora).

. . .

Document 4b/55   Conclusions of the European Council on Cyprus and Malta, Corfu, 24–25 June 1994

The European Council welcomes the significant progress made regarding the application by Cyprus and Malta for accession to the European Union and considers that an essential stage in the preparation process could be regarded as completed.

The European Council asks the Council and the Commission to do their utmost to ensure that the negotiations with Malta and Cyprus with a view to the conclusion of the fourth financial protocols, intended in particular to support the efforts of Malta and Cyprus towards integration into the European Union, are brought to a rapid conclusion.

The European Council notes that in these conditions the next phase of enlargement of the Union will involve Cyprus and Malta.

The European Council, recalling relevant decisions of the Council of 4 October 1993, 18 April 1994 and 13 June 1994, reaffirms that any solution of the Cyprus problem must respect the sovereignty, independence, territorial integrity and unity of the country, in accordance with the relevant United Nations resolutions and high-level agreements.

. . .

Concerning Turkey, the European Council notes the convening of the EC-Turkey Association Council to deal in particular with the achievement of the Customs Union foreseen in the Association Agreement of 1964.

Document 4b/56   Conclusions of the European Council on Relations with the Associated Countries of Central and Eastern Europe, Cyprus and Malta, Cannes, 26–27 June 1995

The participants in the European Council met the Heads of State and of Government and Ministers for Foreign Affairs of the associated countries of Central and Eastern Europe, including the Baltic States, as well as Cyprus and Malta. They held a wide-ranging exchange of views on various topical matters. They also made an initial, favourable assessment of the structured dialogue and of progress in implementing the pre-accession strategy. In this connection, a suitable forum for encouraging and pooling experience will need to be set up.

The European Council reaffirms that negotiations on the accession of Malta and Cyprus to the Union will begin on the basis of Commission proposals, six months after the conclusion of the 1996 Intergovernmental Conference and taking the outcome of that Conference into account. It stresses the importance it attaches to preparing the accession of the associated countries to the Union and approves the Council conclusions on the White Paper on integrating those countries into the internal market and the Council report on implementing the strategy of preparing for accession. It invites the Commission to report back to its next meeting on progress in implementing the White Paper and on the studies and analyses requested at Essen. The success of the Conference on Stability in Europe (held in Paris on 20 and 21 March 1995) will help bring the countries of Central and Eastern Europe and the European Union closer together. The European Council calls on the countries concerned and on all the parties to implement the agreements and arrangements in the Stability Pact, which has now been entrusted to the OSCE, and calls on the countries concerned to work for the practical improvement of good-neighbourly relations in Europe.

. . .

Document 4b/57   Answer by the Italian Presidency to an Oral Question in the European Parliament (H-978/95) from Ms Izquierdo Rojo on Libya and the Mediterranean, 17 January 1996

Question:

Will the Italian Presidency take steps to open up any kind of prospects for links with Libya as part of the new Euro-Mediterranean policy?

Answer

. . .

The Presidency believes this is a useful initiative with good potential for positive development. Libya was not invited to Barcelona because its relationships with the European Union are not of the same nature as those of the above mentioned countries.

The Presidency cannot ignore the diplomatic climate create by the Lockerbie affair. The Security Council of the United Nations has adopted two resolutions imposing sanctions against Libya. Such sanctions include an air embargo, the suspension of arms supplies as well as the curtailing of diplomatic relationships, measures which have been subsequently extended also to the funds and the financial resources to which the Libyan Government could have access abroad.

Obviously, the European Union and its Member States comply with the provisions of the Security Council.

On the other hand, the Presidency believes it is appropriate to draw the attention of the honourable colleague to the fact that the participants at the Barcelona Conference wanted to establish, through the Conference itself, the basis for a process open to further developments.

As a matter of fact, both the Arab countries of the Maghreb Union and the League of Arab States, represented by their respective General Secretaries, have taken part in the Conference as special envoys and the work schedule envisages that, subject to the agreement of all the participants, other countries or organizations will be able to join future scheduled activities.

Document 4b/58   Answer by the Irish Presidency to a Written Question in the European Parliament (E-1993/96) from Mr Méndez de Vigo (PPE), 29 November 1996

Question:

The meeting between the ministerial troika of the EU Council and foreign ministers of third countries from around the Mediterranean, which should have been held on 17 June 1996, was cancelled, apparently because many of the Mediterranean countries which had been invited had not confirmed that they would send representatives of appropriate political standing. It has been suggested in some of the media that the Italian Presidency had not made sufficient preparations for the meeting.

Can the Council say why the meeting was cancelled? . . .

Answer:

At the initiative of the Italian Presidency, all the Member States of the EU confirmed that they would be ready to participate in a ministerial meeting in Rome on 17 June with the Mediterranean third countries as part of the process of following up the Barcelona Conference. As to the participation of the Mediterranean partner countries, which had themselves reacted favourably to the idea of a ministerial meeting, soundings were taken and their interest in such a meeting was confirmed. On the day before the meeting was due to take place, a meeting of Foreign Affairs Ministers was convened in Cairo at the last minute to prepare for the Arab Summit planned for the next few days. Holding these two meetings at the same time would have made a satisfactory and appropriate level of ministerial attendance impossible and it was therefore thought preferable to cancel the Rome meeting. . . .

Document 4b/59 Conclusions of the European Council on a European Strategy for Turkey, Luxembourg, 12–13 December 1997*

. . .

A European strategy for Turkey

31. The Council confirms Turkey's eligibility for accession to the European Union. Turkey will be judged on the basis of the same criteria as the other applicant States. While the political and economic conditions allowing accession negotiations to be envisaged are not satisfied, the European Council considers that it is nevertheless important for a strategy to be drawn up to prepare Turkey for accession by bringing it closer to the European Union in every field.

32. This strategy should consist in:
   • development of the possibilities afforded by the Ankara Agreement;
   • intensification of the Customs Union;
   • implementation of financial cooperation;
   • approximation of laws and adoption of the Union acquis;
   • participation, to be decided case by case, in certain programmes and in certain agencies provided for in paragraphs 19 and 21.

33. The strategy will be reviewed by the Association Council in particular on the basis of Article 28 of the Association Agreement in the light of the Copenhagen criteria and the Council's position of 29 April 1997.

34. In addition, participation in the European Conference will enable the Member States of the European Union and Turkey to step up their dialogue and cooperation in areas of common interest.

35. The European Council recalls that strengthening Turkey's links with the European Union also depends on that country's pursuit of the political and economic reforms on which it has embarked, including the alignment of human rights standards and practices on those in force in the European Union; respect for and protection of minorities; the establishment of satisfactory and stable relations between Greece and Turkey; the settlement of disputes, in particular by legal process, including the International Court of Justice; and support for negotiations under the aegis of the UN on a political settlement in Cyprus on the basis of the relevant UN Security Council Resolutions.

36. The European Council endorses the guidelines that emerged from the General Affairs Council of 24 November 1997 on future relations between the Union and Turkey and asks the Commission to submit suitable proposals.

---

* See also document 4a/17.

Document 4b/60   Conclusions of the European Council in Helsinki, 11 December 1999 (Enlargement)

See Appendix

The War in the Former Yugoslavia

By the spring of 1991, the Yugoslav Federation was clearly in danger of disintegrating, as Slovenia and Croatia asserted their desire for independence. Outsiders, including the European Community and its Member States, feared the consequences of a breakup and urged the six republics to stay together (document 4b/61). War, however, broke out in June 1991. In the first year of the conflict, the Community/EPC tried to negotiate a solution. That it failed to do so is not necessarily solely the fault of the Community and its Member States – for the UN (which gradually took over the management of the crisis) also proved incapable of doing so. States could not decide whether this was a case requiring enforcement measures against identified guilty parties or one in which neutral mediation and interposition were more appropriate; the actions of the international community reflected this confusion. Only when the United States finally stepped in, with a heavy dose of realpolitik, to impose a solution after war-weariness had set in, did the conflict end in the Dayton Accords of November 1995.

The Community, EPC and later the Union have produced an enormous number of declarations, common positions and joint actions dealing with the conflict in Yugoslavia. Particularly in 1991, the Twelve discussed the war almost continuously: in addition to regularly scheduled EPC meetings, the foreign ministers held several extraordinary and informal meetings, and meetings at the margins of other gatherings. Only some of the key documents can be reproduced here, and they are grouped under two headings: mediation and diplomatic recognition.

(a) Mediation

As hostilities commenced in Slovenia and Croatia, the European Council met for its regularly scheduled summit, on 28–29 June 1991. On the first day of the summit, the European Council sent the troika of the Italian, Luxembourg and Dutch foreign ministers to Belgrade and Zagreb to secure a three-point plan. Their apparent success in doing so was welcomed by the European Council (document 4b/62). But this was just the first of several such visits, and the first of many ceasefires negotiated that were subsequently (often immediately) violated.

On 5 July, an emergency EPC meeting imposed an arms embargo on Yugoslavia,* and suspended the financial protocols to the 1980 EC–Yugoslav trade and cooperation agreement, which would have provided ECU 730 million in loans for 1991–5. The ministers also discussed the possibility of sending observers to Yugoslavia (document 4b/63).

On 7 July, the troika (now composed of the Luxembourg, Dutch and Portuguese foreign ministers) met with Slovenian, Croatian and federal presidency representatives, on the

---

*   The UN Security Council then imposed an arms embargo on Yugoslavia on 25 September.

island of Brioni in the Adriatic. Slovenia and Croatia agreed to suspend the implementa-tion of their declarations of independence for three months. The federal presidency then withdrew the JNA (Yugoslav People's Army) from Slovenia on 18 July, ending the war there. War continued, however, in Croatia.

The European Community Monitoring Mission (ECMM) was set up on 10 July to monitor the implementation of the Brioni agreement. The monitors (some 200 of them) came from the Member States, the Commission, and third states such as Poland, Czechoslovakia and Hungary; the mission was paid for by national governments rather than through EC funds. The ECMM was initially deployed in Slovenia; it did not arrive in Croatia until 5 September because Serbia objected to its presence there. Monitors were posted in Bosnia from the spring of 1992, but remained in the more secure areas. The ECMM also moni-tored the former Yugoslavia's borders with Albania, Bulgaria and Hungary to try to prevent the spread of the conflict.

On 27 August 1991, at another extraordinary EPC meeting, the foreign ministers agreed to convene a peace conference and establish an arbitration procedure (document 4b/64). The Twelve also clearly implicated Serbia in the war (paragraph one). As a result, Serbia no longer viewed the Community/EPC as an impartial negotiator, though this was a role the Community/EPC still tried to play.

The EC-sponsored peace conference opened in The Hague on 7 September, with Lord Carrington as chair. The Twelve foreign ministers, the Commission, the Yugoslav prime minister and the presidents of the six republics attended it. The principles the Twelve considered to be crucial for a solution to the crisis were clearly spelled out at the extra-ordinary EPC meeting on 19 September, including the importance of respecting the rights of minorities, such as the Serbs in Croatia (document 4b/65).

At the same meeting on 19 September, a WEU intervention force was proposed, by the Netherlands, France and Germany. The British were opposed to sending in forces, fearing another quagmire like that in Northern Ireland. The ministers could only agree that the WEU should study ways of strengthening the ECMM (document 4b/65). On 30 September, a WEU study group proposed several possible plans for intervening in the crisis, including sending a peacekeeping force, but neither EPC nor WEU ministers could reach agreement on WEU intervention. Instead, on 12 November 1991, the Twelve asked the UN Security Council to consider sending a peacekeeping force to Croatia.

Frustrated with the lack of progress in the peace conference, on 6 October the Twelve threatened to impose sanctions against those parties that did not contribute to the peace process, and held out the promise of diplomatic recognition. Initially, the threats seemed to have an effect: on 18 October, the peace conference agreed on a plan for Yugoslavia which provided for an association of independent republics and measures to protect minori-ties. But Serbia then rejected the plan, and a subsequent revised plan was submitted on 31 October.

On 8 November, the Community and its Member States imposed sanctions on Yugoslavia, including the termination of the 1980 trade and cooperation agreement and the suspension of aid (document 4b/66). On 2 December, compensatory positive measures were approved for the republics of Bosnia-Herzegovina, Macedonia, Slovenia and Croatia. Although the Twelve discussed imposing sanctions on Croatia, over its role in the war in Bosnia and its actions against the Serbs in Croatia, they never did do so, due mainly to German opposition.

In spring 1992, the potential for widespread violence in Bosnia-Herzegovina was becoming increasingly clear, and diplomatic attention turned to trying to prevent it. On 18

March, under Community/EPC auspices, the leaders of the three main ethnic groups in Bosnia (Muslims, Croats and Serbs) signed an agreement providing for the division of the republic into three autonomous units. But within days, the agreement had been interpreted differently by the parties and violence had spread (document 4b/67). In late March 1992, Lord Carrington convened a separate peace conference on Bosnia-Herzegovina.

By this stage, the United Nations had become increasingly involved in the Yugoslav crisis: a UN special envoy, Cyrus Vance, managed to secure a ceasefire in Croatia on 2 January 1992, and a UN peacekeeping force (UNPROFOR) was established in February 1992 in Croatia and extended to Bosnia in June.

As the fighting in Bosnia raged, the international community gradually came to identify Serbia and its ally, Montenegro (united in the Federal Republic of Yugoslavia), as the main instigator of the conflict. On 27 May 1992, the Community imposed a trade embargo on the Federal Republic of Yugoslavia; on 30 May, the UN Security Council imposed even tougher sanctions on Serbia/Montenegro, including an oil embargo.

Along with the increasingly tough measures on Serbia/Montenegro came UN authorization to use force, albeit for limited purposes such as enforcing the no-fly zone over Bosnia. Because of its greater capabilities, NATO took the lead in implementing these decisions; the WEU played a very limited part. From August 1992, WEU and NATO naval forces jointly monitored the Adriatic to ensure compliance with Security Council resolutions in Operation Sharp Guard. In June 1993, the two forces were combined under NATO command. From April 1993, the WEU helped Bulgaria, Hungary and Romania to enforce the arms and trade embargoes on the Danube River. But more robust action was clearly beyond the WEU's capabilities.

In July 1992, UN Secretary-General Boutros Boutros-Ghali criticized the EC/EPC's conduct of peace negotiations: the Community/EPC had asked the UN to supervise all heavy weapons under a ceasefire agreement reached in the peace talks, in which the UN had not participated (though the ceasefire never went into effect). The Twelve then invited the UN to co-chair the negotiations, and in August 1992, the International Conference on the Former Yugoslavia (ICFY) was established. Its chairmen were first Lord Carrington, then Lord Owen, and Carl Bildt for the EC/EPC, and Cyrus Vance and then Thorvald Stoltenberg for the UN.

Increasingly, the Community/EPC was playing less of a role in the international search for a solution, although it was one of the largest donors of humanitarian aid (ECU 1.6 billion between 1991 and 1995). Within the EC/EPC framework, the Member States were limited to declaring their concern and condemnation, as at the Lisbon (document 4b/68) and Edinburgh European Councils. One of the first CFSP joint actions, taken on 8 November 1993, supported the convoying of humanitarian aid to Bosnia-Herzegovina, but provided no means for ensuring that aid was delivered (document 4b/70).

In October 1992, Vance and Owen submitted a peace plan providing for a Bosnia divided into seven to ten autonomous provinces. Approval of the plan became a primary objective for the Community/EPC, which threatened several times to isolate completely Serbia and the Bosnian Serbs if it was not accepted (document 4b/69). In April and May 1993, sanctions were tightened on Serbia and the Bosnian Serbs. But the Vance–Owen plan was never accepted, nor was any later ICFY plan.

The United States harshly criticized the Community/EPC's handling of the crisis. Only in February 1993 did the new Clinton Administration grudgingly express support for the Vance–Owen plan. The United States, while still refusing to contribute soldiers to

UNPROFOR, then pushed for the lifting of the arms embargo and the launching of air strikes on Bosnian Serb targets. The West European states were opposed as this would endanger their troops serving on the ground (at the time, 4,000 French and 2,400 British soldiers were serving in Bosnia) and would risk escalating the conflict. The transatlantic dispute over the 'lift and strike' option was to continue for the duration of the conflict.

Eventually, the UN also bowed out of the negotiating process. The ICFY was supplanted by the 'great powers': a Contact Group consisting of Russia, the United States, France, the UK and Germany was formed in April 1994. Furthermore, US mediation resulted in the 18 March 1994 agreement for a federation between the Bosnian government and Bosnian Croats, which put an end to large-scale fighting between them.

Under the agreement, the EU was asked to administer the city of Mostar, site of some of the most intense fighting between Bosnians and Croats, and still a city divided along ethnic lines. On 16 May 1994, the EU Council amended a CFSP joint action on aid to Bosnia so as to set up the administration of Mostar (document 4b/71). The EU administration was formally established on 23 July 1994, with an initial mandate for two years. The aim was to overcome the ethnic division between Croats and Bosnians through a process of reconstruction and political and social reunification, thus creating the conditions for a single, multi-ethnic city administration. The WEU contributed a small police mission, to help train and integrate the Muslim and Croat police forces. This was the first time the WEU had been used to back up a CFSP decision, although the WEU never provided the entire contingent of police officers envisaged (154 rather than 182).

The EU administration was not a protectorate, and lacked the mandate, resources and will to enforce cooperation between the two sides. While the EU contributed significantly to reconstruction efforts (providing ECU 144 million in aid), it did not succeed in unifying Mostar given the hostility between the two sides. In February 1996, the Bosnian Croats violently refused a proposal to set up a neutral central zone in the city; the EU's Administrator, Hans Koschnick, even came under attack. When the Contact Group agreed to decrease the size of the central zone, Koschnick resigned in protest at the concession to Croat violence. He was replaced by Ricard Perez Casado.

The EU administration lasted until July 1996. Elections were held, with several delays, on 30 June 1996, resulting in victory for nationalist parties on both sides. On 15 July 1996, the EU decided to send a special envoy (Sir Martin Garrod) to Mostar to phase out the administration (document 4b/72). The EU continued to experience problems in convincing the Croats to participate in the unified city administration.

In summer 1995, a rapid reaction force was created, mainly by France and the UK, to try to respond to Serb threats against UNPROFOR personnel. But the marked increase in the UN/NATO military activity in Bosnia in the summer of 1995 was merely noted by the European Council. US involvement eventually resulted in the Dayton peace plan, signed in Paris in December 1995. The United States helped establish the conditions that made the agreement possible: it stood back while Croatia expelled the Krajina Serbs and then led the bombing of Bosnian Serb targets in the summer of 1995, which weakened that side. US agreement to deploy troops in Bosnia-Herzegovina helped ensure the success of the agreement. The Union participated in the implementation of the plan, on the 'civil' side (document 4b/73) – although many European states have participated in I-FOR and S-FOR. Follow-up decisions were taken on 2 February and 26 October 1998.

Document 4b/61   Declaration by the Informal European Political Cooperation Ministerial Meeting on Yugoslavia, Château de
Senningen, 26 March 1991

The Community and its member States follow with the greatest concern the situation in Yugoslavia. They encourage the efforts underway to resolve the constitutional crisis in the country by way of dialogue and appeal to all parties concerned to refrain from the use of force and to respect fully human rights and democratic principles in conformity with the Charter of Paris on the new Europe.

The Community and its member States, recalling their previous declarations, are convinced that the process of moving Yugoslav society in the direction of democratic reforms satisfactory to all Yugoslavia should be based on the results of a political dialogue between all parties concerned. Such a process will enable the full development of the cooperation which already exists between the Community and the Federal authorities. In the view of the Twelve, a united and democratic Yugoslavia stands the best chance to integrate itself in the new Europe.

Document 4b/62   Statement by the European Council on the Situation in
Yugoslavia, Luxembourg, 28–29 June 1991

The European Council examined the course of developments in Yugoslavia. It heard a report from the ministerial Troika on its return from Belgrade and Zagreb, and expressed satisfaction at the results of this mission. However, the European Council remains concerned about the situation in this country and requests the relevant organs of European cooperation to remain seized of this situation and follow developments closely.

It took note of the fact that Luxembourg has invoked the emergency mechanism in the CSCE framework in view of the extreme gravity of the situation in Yugoslavia.

Document 4b/63   Declaration on the Situation in Yugoslavia, Extraordinary
European Political Cooperation Ministerial Meeting, The
Hague, 5 July 1991

. . .

The Community and its member States welcome the fact that the collegiate Presidency has been able to meet following the elections of its President and Vice-president. They express the hope that the Presidency will now be able to play its full role in the negotiations on the future of Yugoslavia. It will not be able to do so unless it exerts full political and constitutional control over the Yugoslav People's Army.

The Community and its member States welcome [the fact] that in this context the recently established CSCE Emergency Mechanism has been able to meet for the first time, and they endorse its conclusions. In conformity with these, and having been requested to do so by the Yugoslav authorities, they have decided to organize a mission to help stabilize a cease-fire and to monitor the implementation of the two remaining elements of the agreement reached between the Yugoslav parties with the contribution of the Community and its member States. In this context, they decided to send at short notice a Troïka of high officials to Yugoslavia to establish the necessary practical arrangements. They are also prepared to contribute to the CSCE mission of good offices to facilitate the political dialogue among the parties concerned.

In view of the present situation in Yugoslavia, the Community and its member States decided upon an embargo on armaments and military equipments applicable to the whole of Yugoslavia. They launch an urgent appeal to other countries to follow this example. The Community and its member States also decided to suspend the second and third financial protocol with Yugoslavia. But they express the hope that a normalisation of the situation will permit them to put into effect as soon as possible the financial protocols so as to contribute to the indispensable economic recovery of the country.

Document 4b/64   Declaration of Yugoslavia, European Political Cooperation Extraordinary Ministerial Meeting, Brussels, 27 August 1991

The European Community and its member States are dismayed at the increasing violence in Croatia. They remind those responsible for the violence of their determination never to recognise changes of frontiers which have not been brought about by peaceful means and by agreement. It is a deeply misguided policy on the part of the Serbian irregulars to try to solve the problems they expect to encounter in a new constitutional order through military means. It is even more disconcerting that it can no longer be denied that elements of the Yugoslav People's Army are lending their active support to the Serbian side. The Community and its member States call on the Federal Presidency to put an immediate end to this illegal use of the forces under its command.

The Community and its member States will never accept a policy of fait accompli. They are determined not to recognise changes of borders by force and will encourage others not to do so either.

Territorial conquests, not recognised by the international community, will never produce the kind of legitimate protection sought by all in the new Yugoslavia. Such protection can be brought about only by negotiations based on the principle of the fullest protection of the rights of all, wherever they may live in Yugoslavia.

The European Community and its member States call on Serbia to lift its objection to the extension of the activities of their Monitor Mission in Croatia. Recent events have shown that without a comprehensive and effective cease-fire and impartial foreign monitors the situation in Yugoslavia cannot be sufficiently stabilised to allow for productive negotiations to be held.

In view of the deteriorating situation in Yugoslavia the European Community and its member States have asked the Presidency to request the Chairman of the CSCE

Committee of Senior Officials to advance the additional meeting of that Committee, agreed on during its second emergency meeting on 9 August 1991, to early September.

The Community and its member States cannot stand idly by as the bloodshed in Croatia increases day by day. An agreement on the monitoring of the cease-fire and its maintenance should allow the Community and its member States to convene a peace conference and establish an arbitration procedure.

. . .

Document 4b/65   Declaration on Yugoslavia, European Political Cooperation Extraordinary Ministerial Meeting, The Hague, 19
September 1991

. . .

The Community and its member States have long recognised that a new situation exists in Yugoslavia. They consider it self-evident that this calls for new relation-ships and structures. They reiterate that is entirely up to all people living in Yugoslavia to determine their own future. The Community and its member States will accept any outcome that is the result of negotiations conducted in good faith.

. . .

The Community and its member States wish to reiterate once again the basic prin-ciples they have subscribed to from the very beginning

- the unacceptability of the use of force;
- the unacceptability of any change of borders by force which they are determined not to recognize;
- respect for the rights of all who live in Yugoslavia, including minorities;
- the need to take account of all legitimate concerns and aspirations.

The Community and its member States call on all parties concerned to refrain from any political or military action which might undermine the Conference on Yugoslavia. The continuing violence in particular puts the continuation of the Conference at risk.

The Community and its member States regret that the EC monitor mission is no longer able to perform its task in full. They therefore welcome that the WEU explores ways in which the activities of the monitors could be supported so as to make their work a more effective contribution to the peace-keeping effort. It is their understanding that no military intervention is contemplated and that, before a rein-forced monitor mission were established, a cease-fire would have to be agreed with a prospect of holding and that all Yugoslav parties would have expressed their agree-ment.

The Community and its member States would wish to have the opportunity to examine and endorse the conclusions of the study. They also intend to seek the support of the nations of the CSCE and, through the UN Security Council, the international community as a whole.

Document 4b/66   Declaration on Yugoslavia, Extraordinary European Political Cooperation Ministerial Meeting, Rome, 8 November 1991

The European Community and its member States held an extraordinary Ministerial meeting in Rome today, 8 November 1991, to asses the Yugoslav crisis. They took note of the evaluation presented by Lord Carrington of the 8th plenary session of the Yugoslav Conference which took place in The Hague on 5 November.

They were deeply concerned at the fact that the fighting and indiscriminate bloodshed continued in spite of repeated cease-fire commitments. In this respect, they drew attention to the unacceptable threats and use of force against the population of Dubrovnik. Moreover, commitments for deblocking of barracks and withdrawal of JNA forces, to which parties subscribed on 18 October in The Hague and were reaffirmed on 5 November, have not been complied with. They reiterate that the use of force and a policy of *fait accompli* to achieve changes of borders is illusory and will never be recognized by the Community and its member States.

The Community and its member States also noted with great concern that the basic elements of the proposals on behalf of the Twelve put forward by Lord Carrington, aimed at a comprehensive political situation, have not been supported by all the parties. As a consequence, the negotiating process has been put in jeopardy.

In the light of the seriousness of the situation, the Community and its member States have decided to take the following measures:
- immediate suspension of the application of the trade and cooperation Agreement with Yugoslavia and a decision to terminate the same Agreement,
- restoration of the quantitative limits for textiles,
- removal of Yugoslavia from the list of beneficiaries of the General System of Preferences,
- formal suspension of benefits under the Phare programme. Yugoslavia has not been invited to take part in the next Ministerial meeting of G-24 on 11 November 1991.

. . .

The Community and its member States decided that positive compensatory measures will be applied vis-à-vis parties which do cooperate in a peaceful way towards a comprehensive political solution on the basis of the EC proposals.

. . .

In this respect they recall that the prospect of recognition of the independence of those Republics wishing it, can only be envisaged in the framework of an overall settlement, that includes adequate guarantees for the protection of human rights and rights of national or ethnic groups. They urge parties concerned to prepare forthwith legal provisions to this end.

. . .

Document 4b/67   Statement on Bosnia-Herzegovina, European Political Cooperation, Brussels, 11 April 1992

The Community and its member States wish to express their deepest concern about the security situation in Bosnia and Hercegovina and appeal to all parties for an immediate cease-fire. They reiterate the absolute need for all parties to abide to the Statement of Principles agreed in Sarajevo on March 18th, 1992, and call upon them to reach a peaceful and negotiated solution within the framework of the talks on constitutional arrangements for Bosnia and Hercegovina held under the auspices of the EC Peace Conference.

The Community and its member States reaffirm that they strongly uphold the principle of the territorial integrity of the Republic of Bosnia and Hercegovina as the unquestionable foundation of any constitutional order. They wish to make clear that violations of this principle will not be tolerated and will certainly affect the future relations of those responsible with the Community.

The Community and its member States urge all military and para-military forces operating in Bosnia and Hercegovina to refrain from any actions which violate the sovereignty of the Republic or undermine the ongoing peace process. In this respect, they specifically call upon Serbian and Croatian Governments to exercise all their undoubted influence to end the interference in the affairs of an independent Republic and to condemn publically and unreservedly the use of force in Bosnia and Hercegovina.

Document 4b/68   Declaration by the European Council on Former Yugoslavia, Lisbon, 26–27 June 1992

The European Council strongly condemns the continuing violence which has ravaged the territory of the former Yugoslavia for over a year, resulting in an appalling loss of life and a desperate humanitarian situation, in particular in Bosnia-Hercegovina. Although all parties have contributed, in their own way, to the present state of affairs, by far the greatest share of the responsibility falls on the Serbian leadership and the Yugoslav army controlled by it. The Community and its Member States stress again the need for full application of the sanctions stipulated by the UN Security Council.

With regard to Kosovo, the European Council expects the Serbian leadership to refrain from further repression and to engage in serious dialogue with representatives of this territory. The European Council reminds the inhabitants of Kosovo that their legitimate quest for autonomy should be dealt with in the framework of the Conference on Yugoslavia. It stresses the need to immediately dispatch observers to Kosovo as well as to neighbouring countries in order to prevent the use of violence and with a view to contributing to the restoration of confidence. The Community and its Member States call upon the CSCE to take the necessary steps to that effect and stand ready, as far as they are concerned, to take part in such a mission.

The European Council reiterates the position taken by the Community and its Member States in Guimaraes on the request of the former Yugoslav Republic of Macedonia to be recognized as an independent State (see document 4b/76). It expresses its readiness to recognize that republic within its existing borders according to their Declaration on 16 December 1991 under a name which does not include the term Macedonia. It furthermore considers the borders of this republic as inviolable and guaranteed in accordance with the principles of the UN Charter and the Charter of Paris.

The European Community and its Member States will not recognize the new federal entity comprising Serbia and Montenegro as the successor State of the former Yugoslavia until the moment that decision has been taken by the qualified international institutions. They have decided to demand the suspension of the delegation of Yugoslavia in the proceedings at the CSCE and other international forums and organizations.

The European Council states its determination to help the people of the former Yugoslavia in their quest for a peaceful future in Europe and reiterates that the EC Conference on Yugoslavia chaired by Lord Carrington is the only forum capable of ensuring a durable and equitable solution to the outstanding problems of the former Yugoslavia, including constitutional arrangements for Bosnia-Hercegovina. The European Council urges all parties involved in the peace process to participate fully and without further delay in the negotiations sponsored by the Conference.

Document 4b/69   Declaration on the Former Yugoslavia, European Political Cooperation, Brussels, 13 January 1993

The European Community and its member States met in Paris on 13 January 1993 to discuss the present state of the negotiations in Geneva under the International Conference on the former Yugoslavia. They heard a report on this matter from Lord Owen.

The Ministers expressed their firm support to the efforts of the Conference and the two co-Chairmen. The proposals for a political solution to the situation in Bosnia-Herzegovina tabled in Geneva represent the only possibility for a peaceful outcome.

The Ministers expressed their unequivocal demand that the Bosnian Serbs accept the proposed constitutional framework for Bosnia-Herzegovina and the document on military arrangements without any conditions whatsoever within the next 6 days.

If this will not be the case, the European Community and its member States will ask the Security Council of the United Nations to consider measures needed to be taken accordingly. Time is running out and no more delaying tactics will be tolerated.

While the negotiating process gives some hope for positive progress, the military actions and aggressions by the Bosnian Serbs continue to inflict immense human suffering on the population of Bosnia-Herzegovnia, most notably its Muslim inhabitants.

The Ministers stressed the need for an International Criminal Court and expressed their readiness to support this issue at the United Nations.

The European Community and its member States will ask the Security Council of the United Nations to complete its consideration on enforcement of the UNSCR 781 ("no-fly zone").

The European Community and its member States consider it of the utmost importance to strictly implement the agreed sanctions towards Serbia and Montenegro. The leaders of those republics must use all their undoubted influence on the leaders of the Bosnian Serbs to make them understand that by their present acts of violence and unspeakable brutality towards the population of Bosnia-Herzegovnia they are dooming themselves and the "Federal Republic of Yugoslavia" to total international isolation with the gravest consequences for a very long time to come.

The European Community and its member States will remain actively seized of the matter. Preparatory work on further measures leading to total isolation will start immediately, and Ministers will reconvene if the present hope for a negotiated settlement in Geneva is not fulfilled.

Document 4b/70   Joint Action of the Council of the European Union Decided on the Basis of Article J.3 of the Treaty on European Union on Support for the Convoying of Humanitarian Aid in Bosnia and Herzegovina, 8 November 1993 (93/603/ CFSP)

THE COUNCIL OF THE EUROPEAN UNION

Having regard to the Treaty on European Union, and in particular Article J.3 thereof,

Having regard to the general guidelines of the European Council meeting on 29 October 1993 adopting the search for a negotiated and lasting solution to the conflict in former Yugoslavia and the convoying of humanitarian aid in Bosnia and Herzegovina as an area of joint action,

HAS DECIDED AS FOLLOWS:

1.   The European Union will step up its efforts to assist the suffering populations in Bosnia and Herzegovina. To that end, it is willing to:
     – increase its contribution towards the resources placed at the disposal of the HCR;
     – support the convoying of international aid, in particular through the identification, restoration and preservation of priority routes.

2. The Presidency shall be responsible for contacting the co-Chairmen of the London Conference Steering Committee, the HCR and the Unprofor with a view to identifying priority routes, in particular to Sarajevo, and studying the conditions for, and ways and means of reopening the airports at Tuzla and Mostar.

3. The Presidency and the Commission, assisted by the ECMM and the ECTF, will draw up a report on aid convoying requirements in close liaison with the HCR and Unprofor. The role and possible strengthening of the ECMM and the ECTF will be evaluated in this context.

4. On the basis of that report, the Council will adopt the budget necessary to finance the requirements thus defined. It will decide on the amount to be charged to the Community budget, taking account of available national contributions. The budgetary procedure provided for by the Treaty establishing the European Community will apply with regard to the amount charged to the Community budget.

   At the same time, the Presidency will approach third countries with a view to obtaining from them additional contributions for the humanitarian action in Bosnia and Herzegovina.

5. Lord Owen, together with Mr T. Stoltenberg and in cooperation with the Presidency, the HCR and Unprofor, shall be responsible for bringing all the parties to the conflict in Bosnia and Herzegovina together at short notice in order to obtain their firm and specific commitment, in particular at local level, to the preservation of priority routes, as identified.

6. All appropriate means will be put in hand to support the convoying of humanitarian aid via priority routes, in accordance with the relevant Security Council Resolutions.

7. The Member States of the Union will do everything possible to strengthen their participation in Unprofor, particularly in the area of logistical support and engineering. The Presidency will be responsible for studying, in close liaison with the United Nations Secretary-General, ways and means of obtaining additional third country contributions to Unprofor.

8. The Commission shall be associated in full with the tasks entrusted to the Presidency in accordance with Article J.5 (3) of the Treaty.

. . .

Document 4b/71   Decision by the Council of the European Union to Adopt and Extend the Application of Decision 93/603/CFSP Concerning the Joint Action Decided on by the Council on the Basis of Article J.3 of the Treaty on European Union on Support for the Convoying of Humanitarian Aid in Bosnia and Herzegovina, 16 May 1994 (94/308/CFSP)

THE COUNCIL OF THE EUROPEAN UNION,

Having regard to the Treaty on European Union, and in particular Articles J.3 (3) and J.11 thereof,

Having regard to Council Decision 93/603/CFSP of 8 November 1993 concerning the joint action decided on by the Council on the basis of Article J.3 of the Treaty on European Union on support for the convoying of humanitarian aid in Bosnia and Herzegovina,

Having regard to Council Decision 93/729/CFSP of 20 December 1993 supplementing that joint action,

Having regard to Decision 94/158/CFSP of 7 March 1994 extending the application of Decision 93/603/CFSP,

HAS DECIDED AS FOLLOWS:

1. In view of developments in the situation in Bosnia and Herzegovina the joint action provided for in the above Decisions is hereby adapted so that up to ECU 32 million of the budget of ECU 48,3 million set by Decision 93/729/CFSP may also be used to provide initial support for the administration of the town of Mostar by the European Union.

2. The administration of this support action and in particular of the financial resources available for that purpose within the limits laid down shall be carried out as follows.

    The administrator shall assess the requirements and the means necessary for their financing and shall communicate those particulars to the Presidency.

    On the basis of those particulars the Presidency, assisted by an advisory working party composed of representatives of the Member States and in association with the Commission, shall issue guidelines, determine what measures are needed to meet those requirements and decide to release the amounts necessary to finance them one tranche at a time.

    The administrator shall carry out those measures and report regularly to the Presidency, which shall inform the Working Party.

3. The Member States' shares of the ECU 24,15 million to be contributed by them in accordance with this Decision, ECU 17 million of which shall be allocated to the administration of Mostar, shall be determined by means of the GNP scale.

The Member States' contributions shall be paid into an account opened in the administrator's name.

The Court of Auditors is invited to audit the administrator's accounts.

. . .

Document 4b/72   Joint Action Adopted by the Council on the Basis of Article J.3 of the Treaty on European Union, on the Nomination of a Special Envoy of the European Union in the City of Mostar, 15 July 1996 (96/442/CFSP)

THE COUNCIL OF THE EUROPEAN UNION,

Having regard to the Treaty on European Union, and in particular Articles J.3 and J.11 thereof,

Having regard to the general guidelines given by the European Council meeting in Corfu on 24 and 25 June 1994,

Whereas the European Council meeting in Florence on 21 and 22 June 1996 has underlined the importance it attached to the electoral process in Mostar and to the need for genuine commitment of the newly elected leadership to the reunification of the town;

Whereas, with the satisfactory holding of the local elections on 30 June 1996 in Mostar, the necessary basis for the establishment of a single, multi-ethnic and lasting administration as set out in Decision 94/790/CFSP is now in place; whereas the European Union Administration of Mostar (EUAM) is to end on 22 July 1996, as provided for in Article 4(1) of the Memorandum of Understanding signed in Geneva on 5 July 1994;

Whereas, in order to consolidate the achievements of the EUAM and prepare the phasing out of its activities, and in order to ensure the rapid integration of Mostar into the overall structure for peace implementation in Bosnia and Herzegovina, a European Union presence in the town remains necessary under a different form; whereas on 18 February the local parties formulated a request to that effect; whereas such a presence may be ensured through the appointment of a European Union Special Envoy;

Whereas, during the transfer of responsibilities from the European Union Administrator to the local authorities of Mostar, transitional measures may be necessary in order to facilitate full establishment of the newly elected unified local administration.

HAS ADOPTED THIS JOINT ACTION:

Article 1

Scope

1.   The European Union notes that, according to Article 4(1) of the Memorandum of Understanding, the EUAM ends on 22 July 1996.

2.   In order to ensure the gradual transfer of the responsibilities exercised by the European Union representatives to the newly elected unified local administration, and, consequently, to ensure the objective of the phasing out of the EUAM over a period ending as soon as possible after 23 July 1996, and, in any case, not later than 31 December 1998,* the European Union hereby appoints Sir Martin Garrod as its Special Envoy in Mostar. In addition, the action of the Special Envoy shall have as its objective to ensure the rapid integration of Mostar into the overall structures for peace implementation in Bosnia and Herzegovina.

3.   The European Union notes that the provisions of the Memorandum of Understanding remain in force and apply, *mutatis mutandis*, to the new form of the European Union presence in the town, with the exception of the provisions that are directly linked to the task of the EUAM.

Article 2

Mandate of the Special Envoy

Acting under the authority of the Presidency and in association with the Commission, and with a view to consolidation of the results achieved so far under the Memorandum of Understanding, as well as in accordance with the Rome Agreement of 18 February 1996, the Special Envoy shall have the task of promoting:

– the stabilization and strengthening of the newly elected unified administration of the town of Mostar,

– freedom of movement,

– the return to their homes in Mostar of refugees and displaced persons,

– the completion of the reconstruction projects still under way,

– the protection of human rights,

– the consolidation of a unified and effective law enforcement system,

– the implementation of the arrangements envisaged under Article 5.

. . .

Article 6

Financing of a Western European Union contingent

The tasks of the Western European Union police element as set out in Article 13 of the Memorandum of Understanding having been completed, the European Union, on the basis of the conditions agreed for the period of the EUAM, and subject to practical arrangements with the local parties, is prepared, if necessary, to finance a continuing presence in Mostar of a limited Western European Union contingent tending towards advice and training. Such financing shall be granted from the budget of the European Union Special Envoy and shall be limited to the period referred to in Article 1 (2).

. . .

---

*   This should read 31 December 1996.

Document 4b/73 Joint Action Adopted by the Council of the European Union on the Basis of Article J.3 of the Treaty on European Union on the Participation of the European Union in the Implementing Structures of the Peace Plan for Bosnia and Herzegovina, 19 December 1995 (95/545/CFSP)

On 11 December 1995 the Council adopted – by means of the written procedure – the joint action on the participation of the Union in the implementing structures of the peace plan for Bosnia and Herzegovina:

1. The European Union will make its contribution to the implementation of the Peace Plan for Bosnia and Herzegovina, both in the monitoring process and by bearing part of the expenditure essential to ensure the proper execution of the mission of the High Representative appointed at the London Conference on 8 and 9 December 1995, in the context of a fair distribution of the burden with the other donors.

2. In association with the Commission, the Presidency will express the position of the European Union within the coordination bodies established by the London Conference. Other Member States participating in these bodies will support the common positions of such bodies.
    Furthermore, the Council notes that the positions to be taken by the European Communities will be expressed by the Commission.

3. The Presidency will establish the necessary contacts with the High Representative, in particular to determine the arrangements for the submission by the latter to the Council of the European Union of the regular reports provided for in Article II(1)(f) of Annex 10 to the Peace Plan.

4. In order to cover the contribution of the European Union to operational expenses in connection with the High Representative's mission, a maximum amount of ECU 10 million is hereby charged to the general budget of the European Communities for 1995. The management of expenditure will be subject to the procedures and rules of the Community applying to budget matters.

5. The European Union will contribute to the financing of the infrastructure and curtrent expenditure of the High Representative, including his salary and the cost of the supporting staff, with the proviso that the salaries of staff seconded by a Member State or by the Commission to the High Representative will be paid by that Member State or the Commission respectively. The Member States and the Commission may propose the secondment of staff to work with the High Representative.

    The European Union's contribution to the budget of the High Representative will take account of the proportion of staff from its Member States and from the Commission in the total number of staff working for the High Representative belonging to the equivalent of category "A" as defined in the Staff Regulations of Officials of the European Communities.

6.   This joint action shall enter into force on the day of its adoption and shall apply until 31 December 1996.

7.   This joint action shall be published in the Official Journal.

The War in the former Yugoslavia

(b) Diplomatic recognition

The Twelve have notably been in disarray over the recognition issue, right from the start of the crisis. These disagreements are the clearest manifestation of confusion and discord over a common approach to the Yugoslav war. From the outbreak of war in June 1991, Germany (and large swathes of German public opinion) supported 'self-determination' for Slovenia and Croatia. Recognition of those two republics was opposed particularly by the UK, Greece, Spain and, initially, France. Throughout the autumn of 1991, the EPC position was that recognition would be envisaged only in the framework of an overall peace settlement. Frustrated with the lack of consensus on the recognition issue, Germany indicated in early December 1991 that it would recognize Slovenia and Croatia by Christmas, even in the face of objections from Lord Carrington, the UN Secretary-General and other Member States, that the move would exacerbate the conflict.

On 16 December, after a ten-hour debate, the Twelve foreign ministers agreed to recognize the independence of the Yugoslav republics on 15 January 1992, according to certain criteria. An arbitration commission (chaired by Robert Badinter) was to decide whether the republics met the conditions (document 4b/74). The next day, however, German Foreign Minister Hans-Dietrich Genscher announced that Germany would recognize Slovenia and Croatia regardless of the Badinter commission's findings; Germany then officially recognized the two republics on 23 December. This left the other Member States in a bind: to maintain the appearance of unity, they would have to follow suit. On 14 January, the Badinter commission recommended recognizing Slovenia and Macedonia and reserving judgement on Croatia and Bosnia-Herzegovina. But given the German *fait accompli,* the Community/EPC recognized Slovenia and Croatia on 15 January.

The Badinter commission recommended that Bosnia hold an internationally monitored referendum before it was recognized. The referendum was held 29 February–1 March, and resulted in a clear majority for independence, but it was boycotted by most Bosnian Serbs. On 7 April 1992, the Community recognized Bosnia-Herzegovina (document 4b/75).

According to the Badinter commission, Macedonia met the conditions for recognition. But Greece refused to recognize that republic unless it changed its name, which was considered an indication of territorial claims on the Greek province of Macedonia. The Twelve essentially backed Greece, declaring that they would recognize Macedonia only under a name acceptable to all the parties (documents 4b/68 and 76). The December 1992 European Council, however, extended aid to the republic (document 4b/77).

In April 1993, the republic joined the UN under the compromise name of the 'Former Yugoslav Republic of Macedonia' (FYROM). In December 1993, Denmark, France, Germany, Italy, the Netherlands and the UK recognized FYROM, over Greece's objections. In February 1994, Greece effectively imposed a blockade on FYROM; the Commission, and other Member States, denounced the Greek move and the Commission announced that it considered the action illegal because it blocked trade between

FYROM and other Member States and would pursue action in the European Court of Justice.

The Community/EPC refused to recognize the Federal Republic of Yugoslavia (Serbia/Montenegro) until 9 April 1996 (document 4b/78), after the Dayton Accords had ended the war.

Document 4b/74   Declaration on Yugoslavia, Extraordinary European Political Cooperation Ministerial Meeting, Brussels,16 December 1991*

The European Community and its member States discussed the situation in Yugoslavia in the light of their guidelines on the recognition of new states in Eastern Europe and in the Soviet Union. They adopted a common position with regard to the recognition of Yugoslav Republics. In this connection they concluded the following:

The Community and its member States agree to recognise the independence of all the Yugoslav Republics fulfilling all the conditions set out below. The implementation of this decision will take place on January 15, 1992.

They are therefore inviting all Yugoslav Republics to state by 23 December whether:

– they wish to be recognised as independent States;

– they accept the commitments contained in the above-mentioned guidelines;

– they accept the provisions laid down in the draft Convention – especially those in Chapter II on human rights and rights of national or ethnic groups – under consideration by the Conference on Yugoslavia;

– they continue to support the continuation of the Conference on Yugoslavia.

The applications of those Republics which reply positively will be submitted through the Chair of the Conference to the Arbitration Commission for advice before the implementation date.

In the meantime, the Community and its member States request the UN Secretary General and the UN Security Council to continue their efforts to establish an effective cease-fire and promote a peaceful and negotiated outcome to the conflict. They continue to attach the greatest importance to the early deployment of a UN peace-keeping force referred to in UN Security Council Resolution 724.

The Community and its member States also require a Yugoslav Republic to commit itself, prior to recognition, to adopt constitutional and political guarantees ensuring that it has no territorial claims towards a neighbouring Community State and that it will conduct no hostile propaganda activities versus a neighbouring Community State, including the use of a denomination which implies territorial claims.

---

*   See also document 4a/21

Document 4b/75   Declaration on Yugoslavia, European Political Cooperation, Brussels, 6 April 1992

The Community and its member States have decided to recognise as from 7 April 1992 the Republic of Bosnia-Hercegovina. The measures implementing this decision will be taken nationally in accordance with international practice.

The Community and its member States have also decided to extend to the Republic of Serbia the benefit of positive measures similar to those granted to the other republics on 2 December 1991 and 10 January 1992. The Presidency, the Commission and the Chairman of the Conference on Yugoslavia are asked to discuss with the authorities of Serbia the modalities for the implementation of this decision, in accordance with principles agreed among the Community and its member States.

The Community and its member States also heard a report from the Presidency about its efforts to reach a solution on the issue of the recognition of another republic. They expect these efforts to produce results soon.

Document 4b/76   Declaration on the Former Yugoslav Republic of Macedonia, Informal Meeting of Ministers for Foreign Affairs, Guimaraes, 1–2 May 1992*

The European Community and its member States, gathered in an informal ministerial meeting at Guimaraes on 1 and 2 May 1992, had an indepth discussion on the request of the former Yugoslav Republic of Macedonia to be recognised as an independent State.

They are willing to recognise that State as a sovereign and independent State, within its existing borders, and under a name that can be accepted by all parties concerned.

They expressed their high appreciation for the efforts of the Presidency, which included the preparation of a global package.

The Community and its member States look forward to establishing with the authorities of Skopje a fruitful cooperative relationship aimed at the promotion of meaningful cooperation, capable of improving political stability and economic progress in the area. Simultaneously, they urge the parties directly involved to continue to do their utmost to resolve the pending questions on the basis of the Presidency's package.

Document 4b/77   Declaration by the European Council on the Former Yugoslav Republic of Macedonia, Edinburgh, 12 December 1992

The European Council examined its policy on recognition of the former Yugoslav Republic of Macedonia in the context of the Lisbon Declaration and in the light

---

*   See also document 4b/68

of the report by the Presidency's Special Representative. It invites Foreign Ministers to remain seized of this question.

The European Council welcomes United Nations Security Council Resolution 795 authorising the United Nations Secretary General to establish an UNPROFOR presence in the Republic.

The European Council recalls its Declaration at Birmingham on the need to prevent this Republic from bearing the unintended consequences of UN sanctions. In this context the European Council underlines the importance of providing access to funding from the international financial institutions and of the regular and properly monitored supply of oil.

The European Council agrees that in addition the Community should make available to the former Yugoslav Republic of Macedonia a substantial package of economic assistance. It welcomed the intention of the Commission to earmark 50 mecu of humanitarian and technical assistance to the former Yugoslav Republic of Macedonia. Member States also agree to provide a matching amount from their own resources.

Document 4b/78 Declaration by the Presidency on Behalf of the European Union on Recognition by EU Member States of the Federal Republic of Yugoslavia, Brussels, 9 April 1996

On behalf of the European Union, the Presidency expresses appreciation for the agreement signed yesterday by the FRY and the FYROM authorities to the effect of settling their bilateral relations and exchanging diplomatic representatives at ambassadorial level. This development, which was considered important by the European Union, represents a substantial contribution to peace and stability in the region of former Yugoslavia and opens the way to recognition by the member States, in accordance with their respective procedures, of the Federal Republic of Yugoslavia as one of the successor States to the Socialist Federal Republic of Yugoslavia.

The European Union will welcome further steps by the Federal Republic of Yugoslavia leading the country to the full normalization of its relations with the international community.

The European Union considers that hereafter the development of good relations with the Federal Republic of Yugoslavia and of its position within the international community will depend on a constructive approach by the FRY to the following:

– mutual recognition among all the States of the former Yugoslavia, including between the Republic of Croatia and the Federal Republic of Yugoslavia. The EU urges the Federal Republic of Yugoslavia and the Republic of Croatia to overcome all remaining obstacles to the mutual recognition and full normalization of relations without delay;

– progress in the fulfilment of the commitments made in the Paris Peace Agreement, including cooperation with the International Tribunal;

- agreement among all the States of the former Yugoslavia on succession issues;

- full cooperation in implementing the basic agreement on Eastern Slavonia, and

- full respect for human rights, minority rights and the right to return of all refugees and displaced persons and the granting of a large degree of autonomy for Kosovo within the FRY.

The European Union places a particular emphasis on human rights and rights of national and ethnic groups. It recalls the Federal Republic of Yugoslavia's commitments made in the Paris Peace Agreement and its agreement at the London Peace Implementation Conference to the continuation of the Working Group on ethnic and national minorities and communities with its present terms of reference. This Group's mandate is to recommend initiatives for resolving ethnic questions in the former Yugoslavia on the basis of agreed principles concerning human rights and rights of national and ethnic groups. The European Union understands that the commitments in the Paris Peace Agreement and the acceptance of the continuation of this Group by the Federal Republic of Yugoslavia entail acceptance of these principles. This understanding is communicated to the Federal Republic of Yugoslavia and progress in implementing these principles will be carefully monitored.

Albania

Albania had been a source of concern to the Union since the end of the Cold War. Its poverty and history of isolation meant a difficult transition process, quite apart from the potential flashpoint of the neighbouring Serbian province of Kosovo, where an Albanian majority was denied basic rights. In the event, Albania became a crisis quite suddenly in March 1997, when the collapse of pyramid savings schemes led to anti-government rioting and what seemed like incipient civil war. Neither the EU nor the WEU proved able to act (documents 4b/79 and 80), despite urgent calls for them to do so, largely because the British and to a lesser extent the French felt unable to take on a major new commitment on top of their deployment in Bosnia. Moreover the obvious option of an injection of funds to restore the confidence of those who had lost their savings foundered on fears about precedents and the likely siphoning off of aid by the criminal gangs which were running large parts of Albanian society. Almost to their own surprise the Italian government, spurred on by fears of a major Albanian refugee exodus, then took the initiative to put together a 'coalition of the willing' – a multinational force under the auspices of the OSCE and the UN. This stayed in Albania from April to August 1997, and succeeded in restoring calm if not good government. The episode therefore demonstrated the failure of European foreign policy *strictu sensu* but its success in the sense of a flexible system capable of *ad hoc* solutions.

Over the succeeding two years Albania became ever more dependent on EU support, political and technical, and in proportion to the worsening of the crisis in Kosovo. When war eventually broke out in 1999 and Kosovar refugees poured out into the neighbouring states, Albania became a *de facto* international protectorate, with NATO playing the prime role, but the EU also important and aware of its long-term responsibilities. As the idea of the Stability Pact for South-Eastern Europe demonstrated (see document 4b/93) the EU was being forced into defining Albania and its neighbours less as an irritating distraction and more as an area of vital interest deserving support (document 4b/82).

Document 4b/79   Declaration by the Presidency on behalf of the European Union on Albania, Brussels, 17 March 1997

Ministers discussed at Apeldoorn on 15 and 16 March the grave situation in Albania. Welcoming the initiatives of the OSCE, they heard a report on the mission to the area on 14 March led by Mr Vranitzky, personal envoy of the OSCE Chairman-in-Office, with EU participation. They noted the request of the new Albanian government to the EU for external assistance.

In their discussion Ministers took note of the following elements.

- The EU is strongly committed to helping Albania to restore civilian structures and law and order.

- The need for the Albanians to accept responsibility for rebuilding their country and society and thus to enable the EU to help them.

- The Commission is ready to provide immediate humanitarian assistance as soon as conditions are sufficiently secure to assure its delivery.

- The Union which has already provided substantial economic and financial assistance to Albania, is ready to resume such assistance in collaboration with the International Financial Institutions once sufficient stability is restored.

- external assistance is needed immediately for the restoration of security in and around Tirana. Among the Member States there was readiness to send an Advisory Mission in the civilian as well as police and military fields. In this context consideration will be given to the needs of the mission for protection and communication.

- Consultations should take place in New York on the need for a UN Security Council Resolution.

- Further steps will be coordinated with the OSCE as well as the Council of Europe.

The Presidency will send, as a matter of urgency, a high level mission to Tirana comprising also representatives of the OSCE, the Commission and Albania's EU neighbours, Greece and Italy. Its aim is to discuss with the Albanian government ways in which the EU can best help to achieve the above elements and to make recommendations to the Presidency. The mission will also examine the protection need of the Advisory Mission.

Document 4b/80   Statement on the Situation in Albania in the European Parliament, 9 April 1997

Mr Patjin, Dutch President-in-Office of the Council:

Madam President, I am happy to respond to parliament's request for a statement on Albania . . .

Although definitive decisions are still needed in a number of areas, it seems likely that the activities of the international community will in any event include the following three elements: firstly, humanitarian aid with the European Union playing the leading role, together with a reinforcement of Albania's police capacity, possibly with the European Union playing a coordinating role together with the Council of Europe. Structural aid will also involve close cooperation with the IMF and World Bank.

Secondly, the more political part: elections, human rights, greater democracy. In this area the OSCE will play an important part in close co-operation with the Council of Europe.

Thirdly, a multinational protection force to which a number of countries will contribute troops. This multinational force, which the UN Security Council has meantime approved, is headed by Italy and will provide escorts for humanitarian aid and ensure the safety of international bodies working in Albania. There will be close liaison between the force commander and the OSCE representative in Tirana.

The European Union and OSCE will be consulting more closely and taking final decisions on the mandate and structure of the advisory mission. But I will touch on a number of aspects of specific aid provision and possible instruments through which it may be given. The first need is for law and order and proper policing. The preparatory mission found that the Albanian authorities need material support and more particularly with a view to the longer term they need advice and training. To obtain a better idea of training and advice requirements it would be a good idea for the advisory mission to include a team of 20 or so police officials. The preparatory mission's report says that the police framework envisaged should be a joint effort by the European Union and the Western European Union in coopera-tion with the Council of Europe. In addition to advising, the police team can also work in a supervisory capacity in four police districts of Tirana, with the collection of information also forming part of the requirements. The police team will also make specific recommendations on how the Albanian police can be helped in the short and medium term.

In conclusion, it must be obvious that given the complex problems in Albania the European Union is faced with a major challenge. It is equally obvious that aid cannot come from the European Union alone. Given this background it is most important that the Union should work at all levels with other institutions such as the OSCE and Council of Europe and that the efforts made should be properly coordinated. It is essential that these efforts should complement each other. Only if the work of cooperation is structured in this way can the international commu-nity give the best possible help in solving the crisis in Albania.

. . .

[After the following debate, Mr Patjin stated:] Madam President, you will appreciate that it is not easy to respond to the points raised by twenty different honourable Members, many of whom have quite rightly demonstrated their own particular concern and emotion at the developments in Albania. I understand those emotions because sometimes my blood runs cold when I see a European neighbour descending into a state of such anarchy and self-destruction. I think we are all extremely engaged by this and deplore it deeply.

Reacting to the main points raised by honourable Members, I can pick out three questions which are raised repeatedly. The first is: did we see this coming and did we react adequately? The second question: when the total collapse began in February / March, did the European Union react adequately then? And the third question: ought we not to intervene with a far more robust military response than is being prepared at the moment?

That is rather the thrust of the questions I am hearing.

As regards the first question, I would suggest that it is easy to be wise after the event. It is of course easy to look back and say, we did that wrong and we should have seen it coming. But we did not. A lot of systematic work was done last year. To start with, those wretched elections of May 1996 were carefully monitored by an OSCE mission. A report on them severely criticized the elections and recommended that they be re-run in a number of districts. The Council of the European Union took a clear political position on this, to the effect that if the OSCE report was not complied with the Council would not be prepared to pursue either contractual links or further economic cooperation for the development of relations with the Albanian Government.

At that time diplomatic ties were the only instrument open to the European Union. I should remind you that in the autumn local elections were held which were monitored by the Council of Europe and in the view of the Council of Europe they were fair. At that time the political assessment was that Albania had again turned a corner and was moving towards normal democratic conditions, so that some of the pressure had eased. After the winter it became apparent that a lot more was going on and then things really began to unravel in February / March, sparked off by the familiar problems of pyramid investment, perhaps, but of course the roots of the problem are broader and deeper.

The crisis in Albania, Madam President, is not a civil war. In Albania it is not one ethnic group fighting the other and we do not have one traditionally established political group refusing to allow another one its place in the sun; what we have is the complete collapse of a social and economic system, a total loss of authority on the part of the government in power, both nationally and regionally.

Faced with this, we in the Council asked ourselves the first question: we have to do something, but where do we start?

The place to start, ladies and gentlemen, is with the restoration of some degree of order and authority, because otherwise nothing can be done. So first we needed to establish contact with the interlocutors in the field: President Berisha, the political parties, the other people in authority. With this in mind the OSCE very promptly dispatched its envoy, Dr Vranitsky, to Albania and the Council sent its President, Mr van Mierlo. They endeavoured to secure an agreement amongst all the political groups involved, with two principal elements; firstly, immediate measures to restore public order and a minimum of public order and, secondly, the introduction of a joint political process leading to the restoration of normal political and democratic relations. That agreement was concluded, and as a result the Fino Government was formed which is now trying to make its mark. Those who say: we should not have sat on the fence, we should have told the President to step down, are forgetting the first priority, namely to restore a minimum of public order, because as things were nothing at all could be started. So that is the way we chose not to go. When we hear it said in this House 'you should not have done that', I think that the House, or some members of it, fail to recognize what the first priority is, namely to restore order.

The third question, and I am picking up here on a number of the comments made, is whether the European Union ought not to have acted more forcefully. Fast, and with military means, etc. My response to that is this. The European Union is not a military organization. The European Union has no mandate in military matters, has no mandate for defence policy. In the interinstitutional framework we are thus talking about something which is inappropriate.

. . .

I am particularly glad to see that a number of countries have formed a coalition of the willing – not as an initiative of the European Union, because it has no authority for that, the Council has no military authority – backed by a declaration of empowerment in a resolution of the Security Council to provide a multinational protection force. This is now being carefully put together. That means the definition of its remit, deployment, structure and cooperation on the one hand and the very complex question of the command structures and the rules of engagement on the other hand. All these things have to be very carefully considered, because as several honourable Members have said, the situation is still uncertain. The security position is precarious and unless we proceed with the utmost caution and plan carefully, cooperating as far as possible with the Albanian authorities which are willing to cooperate and also to lend their good offices to enable this police, military force to play its part, I think we can expect serious disappointment from the use of military resources.

Document 4b/81   Conclusions by the General Affairs Council on Albania, Luxembourg, 2–3 June 1997

The Council welcomed the decision by the Albanian authorities to hold elections on 29 June and looked to all political parties to participate fully in them and to honour their results. The Council emphasized that the primary responsibility for the future of the country lies with the Albanian people. It called on the international community to support the electoral process notably by making available the necessary number of observers.

The Council adopted a Common Position (see main elements below) under Article J.2. of the Treaty, defining the EU's overall action in Albania. The Union will help Albania, within the coordinating framework of the OSCE, to promote the democratic process, a return to political stability and internal security and the holding of free and fair elections. It will continue to support economic reforms and to provide humanitarian aid as needed in accordance with the conditions developed in its regional approach.

The Council took note of the information given by Italy and the Commission respectively on the international Ministerial conference in Rome planned for after the elections and on the proposed Donors Conference together with the IMF once the new Albanian Government has embarked on an economic programme supported by the IMF.

Common Position (adopted without debate)

As already indicated above, the Common Position provides that the EU shall help Albania, within the coordinating framework of the OSCE, through its own action and presence on the ground, to promote the democratic process, the return to political stability and internal security as well as the holding of free and fair elections. It will continue to support economic reforms and to provide humanitarian aid as needed in accordance with the conditions developed in its regional approach.

The Council notes, in particular, that the Commission, on behalf of the EC,

- is responding to the immediate needs of the Albanian people through the European Community Humanitarian Office;

- is considering focusing **PHARE** assistance on areas directly related to the consolidation of democracy, the relaunching of economic activity and the strengthening of public administration;

- is coordinating with International Financial Institutions the provision of financial assistance;

- is ready to contribute to the initiative of WEU and the Council of Europe aimed at the reestablishment of a viable police force;

- is ready to support the election assistance and monitoring activities of the OSCE.

The Union is ready to assist in the holding of early free and fair parliamentary elections, in particular through monitoring. It attaches special importance to the role of free Albanian media in the pre-election information effort. In this context, the Union shall decide as soon as possible on the arrangements for its contribution.

Furthermore, the EU is ready to consider the convening, at an appropriate time and under appropriate circumstances, of an international conference on Albania at which international financial institutions, the OSCE, the United Nations as well as third countries will be invited to participate.

Document 4b/82   Statement by the German Presidency after a Meeting with the Foreign Ministers of States from the Balkan Region affected by Events in Kosovo, 8 April 1999

As a follow-up to the meeting held by the EU Troika in Petersberg (Königswinter) on 1 April 1999, the EU Foreign Ministers, the EU Commission and ECHO met with the Foreign Ministers of Albania, Bosnia and Herzegovina, Bulgaria, Croatia, the Former Yugoslav Republic of Macedonia, Hungary, Romania, Slovenia and Turkey and the UN High Commissioner for Refugees, the OSCE CiO, NATO, the Council of Europe, the WEU, the IMF, the IBRD, the EBRD and the EIB. They assessed the implications of the Kosovo crisis on regional stability. The countries of the region were briefed on EU initiatives to assist the Kosovo deportees and the countries who host them.

All participants noted with satisfaction that rapid action had been taken to implement the measures agreed upon during the Petersberg Conference. Progress was being made on meeting the immediate aid needs of deportees, including by airlift. NATO was contributing to the aid effort. Close cooperation between states and organizations involved in the effort was being made more effective, including through coordination on the ground in Tirana and Skopje. The European Commission was reinforcing its Kosovo Crisis Team and had announced the release of further substantial humanitarian and financial aid resources. Special meetings of the EU Council of Ministers and other high level meetings had been held to keep the process moving forward with all urgency.

The Presidency expressed the EU's deepest appreciation to those countries in the region, primarily Albania and FYROM who, together with Montenegro, bear the brunt of Milosevic's criminal and irresponsible policies. The EU is fully aware of the magnitude of the challenges that these countries are facing politically, economically and socially. The General Affairs Council has pledged substantial assistance to those countries which participate in alleviating the burden in the spirit of regional solidarity and cooperation.

The EU attaches great importance to cooperation both with and among the countries in the region. European stability and prosperity cannot be dissociated from developments in the countries in South East Europe. Their political stability and economic well-being will be assured. The EU will continue to stand firmly beside them, both politically and in terms of economic and financial assistance.

As the EU pledged at Petersberg, it has moved swiftly to make available substantial assistance to the countries affected, both collectively and bilaterally. The Commission outlined the new EU assistance package of 250 MEURO which complements the substantial assistance already made available. This package consists of up to 150 MEURO for humanitarian purposes and 100 MEURO in the form of refugee-related support for the most affected countries to cover expenses related to hosting the Kosovo refugees. This is in addition to the bilateral assistance provided by the EU Member States. All participants in the meeting warmly welcomed the Commission's swift and effective response to the needs of the refugees and of the countries of the region.

Kosovo

It did not take a sophisticated forward planning unit to discern that the next outbreak of the Balkan crisis of the 1990s would be over Kosovo. Indeed Greece in particular warned of the dangers, and the EU was aware from at least 1996 that it might soon have to focus its energies on Kosovo (document 4b/83). Slobodan Milosevic pursued an intense campaign to reduce the autonomy of the region and to use its historic associations with Serbian nationalism for his own ends. In 1997–8 the EU was at least able to monitor events closely and communicate its concerns to Belgrade, while assembling a diplomatic coalition of the associated countries behind them (document 4b/84; the advantages of giving support, in terms coming closer to the EU, hardly needed to be spelt out to them). By March 1998 the policy of coordinated pressure on Belgrade was fully out in the open, including an arms embargo, and it is notable that the United Kingdom was willing and able to speak on behalf of all fifteen Member States in the UN Security Council (document 4b/85). The EU favoured 'a large degree of autonomy' for Kosovo, but not independence (as that could have secessionist implications for all kinds of states, including Spain). It also demanded restraint from the Kosovo Liberation Army (KLA).

By June 1998 the European Council was threatening further measures against Yugoslavia, including a ban on Yugoslav airliners travelling back and forth to EU cities (document 4b/86). It turned out that several countries, including the UK Presidency, were unwilling to go forward with this on the grounds that it broke existing contracts, but the level of threats was clearly being ratcheted up. On the other hand, as in 1992, the EU was quickly reaching the limits of its independent capability and began regularly to associate itself with the activities of other states and groupings, such as NATO, the Contact Group and the OSCE (document 4b/87). Moroever when the EU did try to expand the range of its actions, by requesting data from the WEU Satellite Centre, it ran into the old problem of opposition to a military profile, in this case from Denmark (document 4b/88). It was striking later on, in 1999, how Denmark left these reservations behind in its commitment to a humanitarian cause. In the end, all the 'anti-military' Member States signed up to the Cologne Summit's agreement to give the EU a defence arm (documents 2/24 and 3/18).

After the failure of the Rambouillet conference to resolve the crisis in January 1999, events moved rapidly. Forced into a corner, the EU states realized that they could not allow the repetition of massacres like that at Srebrenica in 1995, let alone anything like the Holocaust. Thus came the strong moral line warning of 'crimes against humanity' and the 'personal accountability' of Yugoslavia's leaders (document 4b/89). In practice, of course, the EU had to sit back and watch NATO take the military lead, albeit with important and sometimes surprising contributions from individual European states like France and Denmark. Collectively, however, they were reduced to relatively minor matters like the appointment of a Special Envoy to Kosovo (document 4b/90; Mr Petritsch's post was terminated on 29 July 1999).

As the prospect of peace finally approached the EU's civilian powers brought it back into centre stage, and the incoming EU President, Martti Ahtisaari, played an important role in mediating Serb withdrawal from Kosovo (document 4b/91). The EU was also the prime candidate to organize its own idea, taken up by the United Nations, of a Stability Pact for South-Eastern Europe, despite the long-term and burdensome nature of the likely commitments (documents 4b/92 and 93). Individual leaders, like Tony Blair of Britain in Bucharest, had not been above dropping broad hints about an accelerated path to EU entry for states which cooperated in the war. Either this was disingenuousness which will backfire, or it was irresponsible policy-making on the run when the problems even of the next round of enlargement have hardly been resolved. Almost without noticing it, the EU has been drawn in to a new role as the protector and stabilizer of South-East Europe, a burden which it may struggle to live up to, economically and politically.

Document 4b/83   Answer by the Irish Presidency to an Oral Question in the European Parliament (H-784/96) from Mr Posselt on the Situation in Kosovo, 23 October 1996

As the honourable Member knows, the Council has on many occasions expressed its deep concern at the situation in Kosovo. Indeed, it closely follows the developments in that region in order to contribute to a lasting solution of the problems emerging in this area where, as elsewhere in former Yugoslavia, risks of confrontation on the ground still exist.

More recently, at its session of 1 October the Council has welcomed the progress on educational issues which has been made in talks between the Belgrade authorities and the Albanian community in Kosovo, as a first step towards a comprehensive dialogue on the status of the region. It urged early implementation of the measures agreed upon and recalled the EU position – stated in the 9 April EU declaration – that a large degree of autonomy must be granted to the region within the Federal Republic of Yugoslavia.

The Council urged the Belgrade authorities to adopt a constructive approach with regard to the activities of the Working Group on regional issues acting under the responsibility of the High Representative, which in the Council's view remains the most appropriate forum for dialogue and negotiations on the matter.

The Council is convinced that an increased international presence in Kosovo can contribute to reducing tensions. An international presence would therefore be another positive factor in the context of finding an acceptable solution for the status of Kosovo within the FRY. To this end, the Council envisages establishing an EU presence in Kosovo, and FRY's cooperation in this question is a crucial factor in determining the Union's attitude towards the FRY.

Document 4b/84   Press Statement on the Trial of Kosovo Albanians Sentenced for Acts of Terrorism, 20 December 1997

The European Union is continuing to monitor closely the situation in Kosovo. The instability in Kosovo and underlying risk of violence have serious implications for regional stability. The European Union reaffirms that it cannot tolerate the use of force, by any party whatsoever, for political ends.

Following the recent trial in Pristina of Kosovo Albanians sentenced for acts of terrorism, the European Union would strongly emphasise once more the importance it attaches to respect for the rule of law and human rights.

It is seriously concerned at allegations that the individuals just sentenced made their confessions under torture.

The European Union trusts the appeal brought against the judgment of 16 December by the lawyers for the defence attached to the Serbian Supreme Court will be conducted completely independently and with due regard for the requirements of the rule of law.

The associated countries Bulgaria, Estonia, Hungary, Latvia, Lithuania, Poland, Romania, Slovakia, Slovenia, the Czech Republic, the associated country Cyprus and the EFTA countries, members of the European Economic Area, align themselves with this declaration.

Document 4b/85   Statement in the UN Security Council by the UK Presidency on Kosovo, 31 March 1998

The European Union is deeply concerned at the threat to regional peace and security posed by the situation in Kosovo. The international community must send a clear message to the FRY and Serbian authorities that the excessive violence by military police units, involving deaths and injury among the civilian population, is unacceptable. Equally, we condemn unreservedly all terrorist acts and call on those supplying financial support, arms or training to cease doing so. We urge both sides to engage immediately in genuine – and unconditional – dialogue, including the participation of an outside representative.

The Union fully supports the statement made by the Contact Group Foreign Ministers in Bonn on 25 March. It endorses their assessment that while some positive developments have occurred, notably the deal on implementation of the Education Agreement, progress has not been sufficient to meet the requirements set out by the meeting of Contact Group Foreign Ministers in London on 9 March. The European Union has nominated Mr Felipe González as European Union Special Representative with a view to enhancing the effectiveness of the European Union's contribution to resolving the problems in the Federal Republic of Yugoslavia, including Kosovo, and strongly supports the mission by Mr González as Personal Envoy of the OSCE Chairman-in-Office for the Federal Republic of Yugoslavia.

The European Union believes that pressure must be maintained to bring the Belgrade authorities to the negotiating table. That means implementing forthwith the measures agreed at the London Contact Group meeting.

Against this background, the European Union strongly supports the resolution before the Council. The Union already has a comprehensive arms embargo in place against the countries of the former Yugoslavia. We wish to see all other member states taking an equally stringent position. The resolution is an expression of the international community's rejection of the policy of violence, whether carried out by military police or terrorists.

It is essential also that the international response to the crisis is a united and coherent one. We know to our cost from the early days of the Bosnian war that international divisions undermine our efforts. Agreeing the resolution before us today sends a powerful signal to the authorities in Belgrade that the international community is united in its desire to see real progress on Kosovo and is monitoring events there closely. Neighbouring states have already expressed concern that further turmoil in Kosovo might spread instability beyond the Federal Republic of Yugoslavia's borders. We owe it to them to take a firm line.

Mr President, the European Union favours granting a large degree of autonomy to Kosovo within the Federal Republic of Yugoslavia. This must include meaningful self-administration for the local population. But the key is getting both sides to talk – and we will support a settlement on Kosovo's status reached by mutual agreement.

Document 4b/86   Statement by the European Council on Kosovo, Cardiff, 15 June 1998

The European Council condemns in the strongest terms the use of indiscriminate violence by the FRY and the Serbian security forces to impose the Belgrade Government's political terms. No state which uses brutal military repression against its own citizens can expect to find a place in the modern Europe. President Milosevic bears a heavy personal responsibility.

The crisis constitutes a serious threat to regional stability and requires a strong and united international response. The European Council calls for immediate action from President Milosevic in four areas, in particular:

- to stop all operations by the security forces affecting the civilian population and to withdraw security units used for civilian repression;

- to enable effective and continuous international monitoring in Kosovo;

- to facilitate the full return to their homes of refugees and displaced persons and unimpeded access for humanitarian organisations; and

- to make rapid progress in the political dialogue with the Kosovo Albanian leadership.

The European Council stresses the importance of President Milosevic taking advantage of his meeting with President Yeltsin in Moscow on 16 June, which it welcomes, to announce progress on the above steps and to commit Belgrade to their implementation in full.

Unless these four steps are taken without delay, a much stronger response, of a qualitatively different order, will be required from the international community to deal with the increased threat to regional peace and security. The European Council welcomed the acceleration of work in international security organisations on a full range of options, including those which may require an authorisation by the UN Security Council under Chapter VII of the UN Charter.

Given the gravity of the situation, the European Council has agreed to supplement measures already being implemented against the FRY and Serbian Governments by taking steps to impose a ban on flights by Yugoslav carriers between the FRY and EU Member States.

A solution to the problem of Kosovo's status can only be found through a vigorous political process. The European Council calls urgently on both sides to return to the negotiating table, with international involvement, to agree confidence-building measures and to define a new status for Kosovo. The European Union remains firmly opposed to independence. It continues to support a special status, including a large degree of autonomy for Kosovo, within the Federal Republic of Yugoslavia.

If any early reduction of tensions is to be achieved, an immediate cessation of violence will be required as well from the Kosovo Albanian side. While commending the commitment of Dr Rugova to a peaceful solution in Kosovo, the European Council calls on the Kosovo Albanian leadership to state clearly its rejection of violent attacks and acts of terrorism. The European Union will play its part in stopping the flow of money and weapons to Kosovo Albanian armed groups. The European Council calls on neighbouring states, whose security is a vital factor for the European Union, to ensure that their territory is not used in support of Kosovo Albanian armed activity.

Document 4b/87   Press Statement on a Comprehensive Approach to Kosovo, 27 October 1998

The EU remains gravely concerned at the situation is Kosovo, in particular regarding the plight of the civilian population, refugees and displaced persons. Tens of thousands of people may still be without permanent shelter in Kosovo as winter approaches. The EU will continue to engage substantial resources towards alleviating this plight.

The EU fully supports the agreements signed in Belgrade on 16 October 1998 between the FRY and the OSCE, and on 15 October 1998 between the FRY and NATO through negotiations mandated by the Contact Group on the basis of relevant SCRs, as an important step towards a political solution to the Kosovo crisis. It welcomed UN Security Council Resolution 1203 of 24 October conferring the authority of the UN on the demand for full and immediate compliance by all parties concerned with these agreements, the unilateral commitments and UNSCRs 1160 and 1199. The focus is now on full and immediate compliance, by all Parties concerned.

Although some progress has been made, the FRY is still not respecting the provisions of UNSCR 1199, in particular with regard to the withdrawal of security forces to their positions prior to March 1998. The EU calls on all parties, and in particular on President Milosevic, to live up to their obligations and commitments, to refrain from further acts of violence in the region and to engage in immediate political negotiations. It welcomes the statement of Ibrahim Rugova on 22 October in response to the efforts of the EU Special Envoy Petritsch calling on the armed Kosovo Albanian groups to refrain from action which could be used as a provocation for new attacks by Serb / Yugoslav security forces, and expressing his support for the Milosevic-Holbrooke Agreement. The need remains for pressure to be maintained to ensure compliance and to prevent a return to violence and repression. In this respect the EU will take the necessary steps to enhance the effective implementation of its own sanctions.

The EU pledges its full support for the OSCE and for the Kosovo Verification Mission, to which Member States will contribute very substantially in personnel and resources. It commends the efforts of Poland, as chair-in-office of the OSCE, and Norway in this respect. Clear and effective lines of responsibility within the KVM are essential. The substantial overall European contribution to the KVM should be fully reflected in the positions of responsibility to be filled by EU nationals. The Presidency has conveyed this point to the OSCE Chairman-in-Office. Financial provisions should be based on the principle of equitable burden-sharing and on established OSCE procedures.

The EU welcomes the ECMM plans to considerably and quickly increase its presence in Kosovo in order to facilitate the early start of KVM. The ECMM should maintain a liaison presence in KVM HQs in Pristina for reporting purposes.

The effectiveness and security of the OSCE KVM mission are paramount concerns. The EU expects President Milosevic and those responsible in the Kosovo Albanian community to ensure the safety of the verifiers and international humanitarian personnel. The EU supports the provision of a rapid reaction capability.

The EU also supports NATO's Air Verification Mission, and would welcome the participation of Russia and other non-NATO countries. Good coordination between air and ground verification are essential in verifying compliance.

It is urgent for the Parties to start real negotiations on the future status of Kosovo. President Milosevic must stand by his unilateral statement, which is a constitutive element in his overall agreement with Ambassador Holbrooke. The Kosovo Albanian leadership must engage in serious dialogue without preconditions, and with the widest possible representation in its negotiating team. The EU as a major factor in the stability of the Balkans will continue its efforts to restore peace in Kosovo. As part of these efforts, the EU will remain actively involved in supporting the negotiating process, notably through the activity of the EU Special Envoy, Ambassador Petritsch, on the basis of the US proposals as amended and endorsed by the Contact Group and the EU.

The EU is already contributing very substantially in Kosovo, and is prepared to continue contributing, not least in the framework of the KVM. The Commission is already urgently analysing all possibilities in the different fields of assistance to Kosovo. Member States will provide substantial assistance directly and through UN agencies, international organizations and NGOs. EU Member States are ready, in accordance with EU priorities, to make available additional financial resources to support the OSCE KVM mission and EC and Member States will consider this for humanitarian programmes. The EU will address the issues of refugee return, winterization and reconstruction, within a plan of action, on the basis of the assessment by the Belgrade and Geneva working groups on humanitarian issues.

The EU will consider ways in which it can contribute, under the right conditions, to implementing confidence-building measures among the various communities in Kosovo and to further civil society building, including community support for the implementation of the Education Agreement.

The Council has invited the Commission and competent Council bodies to prepare further proposals within this comprehensive approach for early presentation to the General Affairs Council.

Document 4b/88 Council Decision on the Monitoring of the Situation in Kosovo and Related Declaration by the Danish Delegation, 13 November 1998

COUNCIL DECISION

of 13 November 1998

adopted on the basis of Article J.4(2) of the Treaty on European Union, on the monitoring of the situation in Kosovo

(98/646/CFSP)

THE COUNCIL OF THE EUROPEAN UNION,

Having regard to the Treaty on European Union, and in particular Article J.4(2) thereof,

Having regard to the Declaration (No 30) on Western European Union included in the Final Act signed upon the adoption of the Treaty,

Whereas the Council adopted a declaration on 26 October 1998 defining a comprehensive approach to Kosovo including full support by the European Union to the agreements signed in Belgrade on 16 October 1998 between the Federal Republic of Yugoslavia (FRY) and the OSCE and on 15 October 1998 between the FRY and NATO, full support for the OSCE and for the Kosovo Verification Mission, as well as the European Union's readiness to contribute to the assistance to refugees and displaced persons;

Whereas the European Union action as defined above requires a precise knowledge of the situation on the ground in Kosovo; whereas such knowledge would be facilitated by information resulting from the interpretation of space imagery;

Whereas the Western European Union (WEU) Satellite Center has, among its missions, the supply of 'information resulting from the interpretation of space imagery', inter alia, for general security surveillance, including general surveillance of areas of interest for the WEU on the basis of a mandate of the Council and support for treaty verification;

Whereas under these conditions the European Union should have recourse to the WEU,

HAS ADOPTED THIS DECISION:

Article 1

The European Union requests the WEU to provide relevant information made available by the WEU Satellite Center concerning:

– the state of the implementation of the agreements signed in Belgrade on 16 October 1998 between the FRY and the OSCE and on 15 October 1998 between the FRY and NATO,

and

– the situation of refugees and displaced persons and of the infrastructure in this respect with a view for the European Union to contribute to the monitoring necessary for the overall success of the OSCE and NATO relevant missions.

Article 2

This Decision shall be notified to the WEU in accordance with the conclusions adopted by the Council on 14 May 1996 on the transmission to the WEU of documents of the European Union.

Article 3

This decision shall enter into force on the date of its adoption.

. . .

Declaration by the Danish delegation

In accordance with section C of the Decision adopted at the European Council in Edinburgh on 11 and 12 December 1992, Denmark does not participate in the elaboration and the implementation of decisions and actions of the Union which have defence implications.

The Danish Government has decided that Denmark will not participate in the Council Decision on the basis of Article J.4(2) on the monitoring of the situation in Kosovo.

In accordance with the Edinburgh Decision, Denmark will not prevent the development of closer cooperation between Member States in this area. Accordingly, the position indicated above does not prevent the adoption of the Council Decision.

Document 4b/89   Conclusions of the European Council Meeting in Berlin, 24–25 March 1999

The European Council is deeply concerned about the failure of the mediation efforts undertaken by Ambassador Holbrooke and the three Rambouillet Process negotiators, Ambassadors Hill, Majorski and Petritsch with the President of the Federal Republic of Yugoslavia, Slobodan Milosevic. The common objective of these efforts was to persuade the Federal Republic of Yugoslavia to accept a ceasefire in the Kosovo and a political solution to the Kosovo conflict, in order to stop a humanitarian catastrophe in Kosovo.

Over one quarter of a million of Kosovars are now homeless because of the repression carried out by Belgrade's security forces. 65,000 have been driven from their homes in the last month, 25,000 since the peace talks broke down in Paris last Friday. While the Kosovo Albanians signed the Rambouillet Accords, Belgrade's forces poured into Kosovo to start a new offensive. Since the outbreak of hostilities in Kosovo in March 1998 around 440,000 people, more than one fifth of the population of Kosovo, have fled or been displaced. There are new victims every day. The civilian population is the target of the hostilities.

. . .

On the threshold of the 21st century, Europe cannot tolerate a humanitarian catastrophe in its midst. It cannot be permitted that, in the middle of Europe, the predominant population of Kosovo is collectively deprived of its rights and subjected to grave human rights abuses. We, the countries of the European Union, are under a moral obligation to ensure that indiscriminate behaviour and violence, which became tangible in the massacre at Racak in January 1999, are not repeated. We have a duty to ensure the return to their homes of the hundreds of thousands of refugees and displaced persons. Aggression must not be rewarded. An aggressor must know that he will have to pay a high price. That is the lesson to be learnt from the 20th century.

Nor will the international community tolerate crimes against humanity. Those now persisting with the conflict in Kosovo should not forget that the mandate of The Hague Tribunal covers Kosovo. They and their leaders will be held personally accountable for their actions.

In the final analysis, we are responsible for securing peace and cooperation in the region. This is the way to guarantee our fundamental European values, i.e. respect for human rights and the rights of minorities, international law, democratic institutions and the inviolability of borders.

Our policy is neither directed against the Yugoslav or Serb population nor against the Federal Republic of Yugoslavia or the Republic of Serbia. It is directed against the irresponsible Yugoslav leadership under President Milosevic. It is directed against security forces cynically and brutally fighting a part of their own population. We want to put an end to these outrages. President Milosevic must stop Serb aggression in Kosovo and sign the Rambouillet Accords, which include a NATO-led implementation force to provide stability.

We urge the Yugoslav leadership under President Milosevic to summon up the courage at this juncture to change radically its own policy. It is not yet too late to stop the internal repression and to accept the international community's mediation efforts. The international community's only objective is to find a political future for Kosovo, on the basis of the sovereignty and territorial integrity of the Federal Republic of Yugoslavia, which does justice to the concerns and aspirations of all the people in Kosovo.

The Kosovo Albanians showed their commitment to a peaceful solution by signing the Rambouillet Accords. It is vital that they now show maximum restraint.

We underline that it is not our aim to keep the Federal Republic of Yugoslavia in its self-imposed isolation in Europe and the world. On the contrary, we would like to end the isolation of the Federal Republic of Yugoslavia in Europe. But for this to happen, Milosevic must choose the path of peace in Kosovo and the path of reform and democratisation, including freedom of the media in the whole of Yugoslavia.

Statement by the European Council on Kosovo

The European Council in its declaration earlier today set out the efforts which the international community had made to avoid the need for military intervention. We urged the Yugoslav leadership under President Milosevic to summon up the courage at this juncture to change radically its own policy. Now the North Atlantic Alliance is taking action against military targets in the Federal Republic of Yugoslavia in order to put an end to the humanitarian catastrophe in Kosovo.

The Federal Republic of Yugoslavia is now facing the severest consequences, about which it was repeatedly warned, of its failure to work with the international community for a peaceful settlement of the Kosovo crisis. President Milosevic must now take full responsibility for what is happening. It is up to him to stop the military action by immediately stopping his aggression in Kosovo and by accepting the Rambouillet Accords.

Document 4b/90　Joint Action Adopted by the Council on the Basis of Article J.3 of the Treaty of European Union in Relation to the Nomination of an EU Special Envoy for Kosovo, 30 March 1999 (99/239/CFSP)

. . .

Article 1

1. The EU special Envoy to Kosovo, Mr Wolfgang Petritsch, hereinafter referred to as the 'EU Special Envoy', appointed on 5 October 1998 to act on the spot for the European Union under the direction of the Presidency and in close coordination with the EU Special Representative for the FRY, shall continue to play an important role to further European Union policy in Kosovo.

2. To this effect, he shall be provided with the human and logistical resources needed to carry out his functions.

3. The EU Special Envoy shall be guided by, and report under, the authority of the Presidency to the Council on a regular basis, and as the need arises. The Commission shall be fully associated.

Article 2

1. In order to cover costs related to the mission of the EU Special Envoy, a sum of up to EUR 510,000 shall be charged to the general budget of the European Communities.

2. The expenditure financed by the amount stipulated in paragraph 1 shall be managed in accordance with the Community procedures and rules applicable to the budget.

3. The European Union will finance the infrastructure and current expenditure of the office of the EU Special Envoy, including allowances and the cost of support staff not covered by secondment. Member States and EU institutions may propose the secondment of staff to work with the EU Special Envoy. The remuneration of personnel who might be seconded by a Member State, or a European Union institution to the EU Special Envoy shall be covered respectively by the Member State or the European Union institution concerned.

4. The Council notes that the Presidency, Commission and/or Member States, as appropriate, will provide logistical support in the region.

Document 4b/91 Declaration of the European Union on Kosovo (Press Statement), 31 May 1999

1. The International Community continues to exert strong pressure on the Belgrade authorities to reverse their course of action in Kosovo and accept its demands for a political solution. The Council reaffirmed the EU's full support for the efforts, including a possible mission to Belgrade in the coming days, by the President of Finland, Martti Ahtisaari, on behalf of the EU, in close cooperation with the United States, Russia and the United Nations. In this regard, the Council expects Belgrade to translate its reported statements into a firm, unambiguous and verifiable commitment to accept the G8 principles and a UNSC resolution. The Presidency will remain in close contact with President Ahtisaari with a view to his attending the European Council in Cologne.

2. The Council welcomed the strong endorsement by the international community of the Stability Pact for South-East Europe and the result of the Petersberg Conference of 27 May. Work should now be carried forward urgently to clear remaining open issues among participants. The EU looks forward to an early Ministerial meeting to adopt the Stability Pact, and welcomed the Presidency's preparations for it.

Document 4b/92 Council Joint Action Concerning the Installation of the Structures of the United Nations Mission in Kosovo (UNMIK), 29 July 1999

COUNCIL JOINT ACTION

of 29 July 1999

concerning the installation of the structures of the United Nations Mission in Kosovo (UNMIK)

(1999/522/CFSP)

THE COUNCIL OF THE EUROPEAN UNION,

Having regard to the Treaty on European Union, and in particular Article 14 thereof,

Whereas:

(1) United Nations Security Council Resolution 1244 (1999) of 10 June 1999 establishes the principle of organisation of the civil administration in Kosovo (UNMIK), headed by a Special Representative of the United Nations Secretary-General;

(2) The Special Representative of the United Nations Secretary-General will be assisted in his duties by four Deputy Special Representatives, each responsible for one major component of the United Nations Mission;

(3) The United Nations Secretary-General wished to entrust the task of economic reconstruction, rehabilitation and development of Kosovo to the European Union; on 19 July 1999 the Council welcomed the rapid deployment of the fourth UNMIK component and the UN Secretary-General's appointment of Mr Dixon as Deputy Special Representative on 2 July 1999,

HAS ADOPTED THIS JOINT ACTION:

Article 1

The European Union shall ensure the installation of the UNMIK component which it has been made responsible for and notes the UN Secretary-General's appointment of Mr Joly Dixon as head of that component.

Article 2

1. The financial reference amount to cover the cost of the task referred to in Article 1 shall be EUR 910 000 for the period to 31 December 1999.

2. The amount referred to in paragraph 1 is intended to finance the infrastructure and current expenditure of the UNMIK component entrusted to the European Union, including the travel and subsistence expenses and daily allowances of seconded staff and the salaries of local staff.

3. Member States and institutions of the European Union may propose the secondment of staff to the UNMIK component entrusted to the Union. The remuneration of staff so seconded shall be covered by the Member State or institution concerned respectively.

Article 3

This Joint Action shall apply from 2 July to 31 December 1999.

. . .

Document 4b/93   Common Position Adopted by the Council on the Basis of Article 15 of the Treaty on European Union, concerning a Stability Pact for South-Eastern Europe, 17 May 1999

Having regard to the Treaty on European Union, and in particular Article 15 thereof;

Whereas:

(1) on 8 and 26 April 1999 the Council adopted conclusions concerning South-Eastern Europe;

(2) a political solution to the Kosovo crisis must be embedded in a determined effort geared towards stabilising the region as a whole;

(3) a Stability Pact for South-Eastern Europe should be prepared;

(4) such a Stability Pact should be founded on the UN Charter, the principles and commitments of the OSCE, and the relevant treaties and conventions of the Council of Europe, in particular the European Convention on Human Rights;

(5) the European Union should play the leading role in the Stability Pact, the OSCE has a key role to play in fostering security and stability, and the Stability Pact should be developed and implemented in close association with the OSCE;

(6) the European Union, within the framework of the regional approach and beyond, is already active in strengthening democratic and economic institutions in the region through a number of well established programmes;

(7) the European Union will draw the region closer to the perspective of full integration of these countries into its structures through a new kind of contractual relationship, taking into account the individual situation of each country, with a perspective of European Union membership on the basis of the Treaty of Amsterdam and once the Copenhagen criteria have been met;

(8) the Federal Republic of Yugoslavia should be invited to participate in such a Stability Pact once it has met the necessary conditions,

HAS ADOPTED THIS COMMON POSITION:

Article 1

1. The European Union will play the leading role in establishing a Stability Pact for South-Eastern Europe.

2. The aim of this Stability Pact is to help ensure cooperation among its participants towards comprehensive measures for the long-term stabilisation, security, democratisation, and economic reconstruction and development of the region, and for the establishment of durable good-neighbourly relations among and between them, and with the international community.

3. The European Union will work to ensure the creation among the participants themselves of a 'South-Eastern Europe Regional Table' to carry forwards the Stability Pact.

Article 2

1. In order to further the objectives stated in Article 1 the European Union will convene a conference on South-Eastern Europe.

2. The conference will take place at the level of Foreign Ministers, if possible no later than the end of July 1999. The conference will be held using the Royaumont format (excluding the Federal Republic of Yugoslavia until it has met the conditions of the international community for its participation). In addition, representatives of Canada, Japan, EBRD, EIB, IMF, WB, OECD, UN, NATO, WEU, UNHCR, as well as representatives of regional initiatives will also participate at the conference.

3. The conference will be prepared at a meeting in Königswinter (Petersberg) on 27 May 1999 at the level of senior officials, in the format set out in paragraph 2. With a view to this, work for this conference will be carried forward urgently.

Article 3

1. The European Union will actively support the countries in the region in achieving the objectives on the Stability Pact.

2. The European Union will undertake together with international donors to organise a donors / reconstruction conference for South-Eastern Europe.

Article 4

This Common Position shall take effect on the date of its adoption.

. . .

(c) **Europe's global reach**

Africa

Southern Africa

Quite apart from traditional European interests in Africa, the breakup of the Portuguese empire (1974–5) and the resultant concern about growing Soviet influence in southern Africa, prompted EPC to pay attention to the region. Civil war broke out in Angola soon after its independence from Portugal, and several external powers (including South Africa, the Soviet Union and Cuba) intervened. The Member States initially agreed to recognize jointly the *de facto* government of the Popular Movement for the Liberation of Angola, which was backed by the Soviet Union. But on 17 February 1976, France unilaterally announced its recognition of the government. On 23 February, the Member States issued a more general declaration setting out their policy towards southern Africa (document 4c/1).

In Rhodesia, a former British colony where the white minority had initially declared independence in 1965, civil war broke out and became increasingly serious in the mid-1970s. As a new Member State, Britain was glad to have the support of its new partners, while very much taking the lead itself in attempting to reach a settlement based on majority rule (documents 4c/2 and 3).

Document 4c/1 Statement by the Nine Foreign Ministers on the Situation in Southern Africa, Luxembourg, 23 February 1976

1.
The Foreign Ministers of the nine countries of the Community, meeting in Luxembourg and recalling the decisions which they took in respect of the People's Republic of Angola, examined problems arising in this region of Africa.

2.
The Ministers have very closely and with great concern followed the development of the conflict in Angola which has caused so much suffering and loss of life and so seriously damaged the economy. They call for peace to be re-established which is necessary for the reconstruction and development of the country.

3.
They believe that the people of Angola should decide on their own destiny. In view of this, they greatly appreciated the efforts of the OAU to find an African solution to the difficulties and refrained from anything likely to harm their success. From this point of view they condemned all external military intervention and fervently hoped that it would be very quickly stopped. In the interests of the prosperity of the region they hope that peaceful and constructive co-operation can be established which presupposes good neighbourly relations between the African States which are part of it.

4.
The Ministers confirmed the basic positions of the nine Member States of the Community:
– Willingness of the Nine to co-operate insofar as the African States wish them to do so and rejection of any action by any State aimed at setting up a sphere of influence in Africa;
– Respect for the independence of all African States and the right of the latter to determine their national policy quite independently and without foreign interference;
– Support for the OAU's attempts to promote African co-operation;
– Right of self-determination and independence of the Rhodesian and Namibian peoples;
– Condemnation of the policy of apartheid in South Africa.

Document 4c/2 Statement by the European Council on Rhodesia, Luxembourg, 2 April 1976

The nine countries of the European Community reaffirm the principles set out in the ministerial statement of 23 February 1976 and in particular the right of the Rhodesian people to self-determination and independence. They therefore deplore the fact that recent events have made a peaceful transfer of power to the majority more difficult in Rhodesia.
The Nine vigorously support the objectives laid down by the British Government on 22 March and the efforts it is making to achieve them.

They appeal solemnly to the Rhodesian minority, which at present is opposing a system of majority rule, to accept a rapid and peaceful transition to such a system. They confirm that they will continue to apply strictly the Security Council decisions concerning Rhodesia.

Document 4c/3   Statement by the Nine Foreign Ministers on Zimbabwe, Rome, 18 April 1980

On Zimbabwe's entry into the community of nations as an independent and sovereign State the Member Countries of the European Community extend their most cordial congratulations to the people and the Government of the new State, adding the sincere wish that Zimbabwe will be able to set out on the road of economic and social progress in a climate of national reconciliation.

This historic event, which is the result of co-operation among all Rhodesian parties, the persistent efforts of the British Government and the constructive attitude of the neighbouring countries, is the materialization of the hopes expressed in the statement issued by the Nine on 20 November 1979.

The countries of the Community declare their readiness to contribute to the economic and social progress of Zimbabwe both bilaterally and within the framework of the Lomé Convention if the new State decides to participate in it. They hope that Zimbabwe's example of the peaceful settlement of conflicts for the benefit of the nations of the region will lead to the solution of the problems still existing in southern Africa.

South Africa

In the 1970s, the Member States regularly condemned apartheid (as in document 4c/1), but were less able to agree on active measures. Some Member States wanted to take a tough stance, others were concerned about their economic interests in Africa's richest state. Three Member States in particular (the UK, Portugal and West Germany) opposed sanctions. The compromise first reached was the September 1977 Code of Conduct for EC firms operating in South Africa. The Code was not legally binding and at most 200,000 workers benefited from the guidelines urging desegregation and higher levels of pay for black workers. Black workers were to be free to join or form trade unions, and company funds could be used to provide social welfare measures such as housing, transport and medical insurance.

The Community/EPC position became increasingly untenable after violence broke out in South Africa in 1984–5, and the government declared a state of emergency on 22 July 1985. The US Congress took a hard line and imposed sanctions. On 10 September 1985, following a troika visit to South Africa, the Ten agreed to harmonize their positions on a series of negative measures and to take positive measures to help the black population (document 4c/4). However, the UK did not agree to the negative measures until 25 September, and then on condition that the measures would be implemented on a national basis.

On 3–4 February 1986, the Twelve held a ministerial meeting with the Frontline States, a grouping of Southern African countries designed to counter South Africa's armed incursions into their territory. The ministers agreed to consider further measures against South Africa should the situation not improve (paragraph 8, document 4c/5).

In June 1986, the European Council discussed additional restrictive measures, but could only agree to consult with other industrial countries about further measures (document 4c/6). UK Foreign Secretary and Council President Sir Geoffrey Howe visited South Africa in July, but the ANC representatives refused to meet him because the UK was considered responsible for the European Council's failure to agree on sanctions. The UK then changed its position and agreed to Community sanctions. On 16 September, the Community imposed some restrictive measures (document 4c/7), but these affected only 3.5 per cent of EC–South African trade. Coal exports and airline flights were notably left untouched.

The December 1989 European Council welcomed the cautious steps that President F.W. De Klerk had taken in the direction of liberalization, but decided to maintain pressure on South Africa until certain conditions had been met. After the release of Nelson Mandela in February 1990, the Twelve clashed over the possible lifting of sanctions. Most Member States felt that liberalization had not proceeded far enough, but the UK decided that a positive signal had to be sent and unilaterally decided to end the suspension of direct investments in South Africa. The Dublin European Council in June 1990 indicated that the negative measures would be relaxed as the process of change continued and agreed to increase Community aid to the victims of apartheid (document 4c/8). The Rome European Council in December 1990 lifted the ban on new investments (document 4c/9). The final sanctions were lifted in November 1993.

In 1992, the Member States agreed to send an EC observer team to try to defuse potential conflicts during the transition to multiracial democracy. One of the first CFSP Joint Actions was to send observers to help prepare and monitor the elections in April 1994 (document 4c/10). That same month, an aid package was extended to the new South African government (document 4c/11). In April 1997, South Africa acceded to the Lomé convention (the framework for cooperation between the European Union and 70 African, Caribbean and Pacific states). South Africa will not take part, however, in the Lomé trading arrangements nor will it benefit from financial resources under the convention; instead, a bilateral free trade agreement was negotiated in 1999, in the midst of intense disagreements between the parties over South Africa's access to the EU market.

Document 4c/4 Press Statement by the Ten Foreign Ministers on South Africa, Luxembourg, 10 September 1985

The Ministers of the Ten, Spain and Portugal heard the report of the European mission which visited South Africa from 30 August to 1 September 1985.

They noted with satisfaction that this mission had been able to carry out its task, which was to express to the South African Government the grave concern of the Ten, Spain and Portugal at the lack of any specific steps towards abolishing apartheid and at the resulting deterioration of the situation.

The European delegation called for the lifting of the state of emergency, the immediate and unconditional release of Mr. Nelson Mandela and the other political prisoners, an end to detention without trial and forced relocation, a firm commitment by the South African Government to end apartheid and to dismantle discriminatory legislation, particularly the pass laws and the Group Areas Act, and lastly real negotiations with the true representatives of the South African people, including those currently in prison.

The European delegation had very useful discussions with representatives of the churches and trade unions, leading businessmen, journalists and leaders of the Progressive Federal Party (PFP), INKATHA and the Azanian People's Organization (AZAPO).

To supplement these contacts, on 10 September the President-in-Office of the Council and the Member of the Commission responsible for external relations met representatives of the African National Congress (ANC).

It was on the basis of the information gathered in this way that the Ministers today discussed the policies to be pursued towards South Africa, in particular measures to be taken which should be immediate and harmonized.

The Ten, together with Spain and Portugal, noted that the situation had continued to deteriorate dramatically since their Helsinki meeting.

With regard to the views expressed to the European delegation by the South African authorities on 1 September, the Ministers wish to point out that the objective of the Ten, Spain and Portugal, is the complete abolition of apartheid as a whole and not just of certain components of the system. There can be no such thing as a good and a bad apartheid. They consider that all the citizens of South Africa should enjoy equal rights and that the protection of the minorities must be ensured. To achieve these objectives a genuine dialogue with the representatives of the black population is necessary.

They will therefore pursue their efforts until this has been achieved.

The conclusions which emerge from the visit of the three Foreign Ministers and today's discussions can be summarized in two points.

1. The Ten, together with Spain and Portugal, take note of the declaration of the South African Government and expect of it that it take specific steps.
2. Meanwhile they will maintain their pressure on South Africa.

The Ten and Spain and Portugal have decided to harmonize their attitudes on the following measures:

Restrictive measures

– A rigorously controlled embargo on exports of arms and para-military equipment to the RSA.
– A rigorously controlled embargo on imports of arms and para-military equipment from the RSA.
– Refusal to co-operate in the military sphere.
– Recall of military attachés accredited to the RSA, and refusal to grant accreditation to military attachés from the RSA.
– Discouraging of cultural and scientific events except where these contribute towards the ending of apartheid or have no possible role in supporting it; and freezing of official contacts and international agreements in the sporting and security spheres.
– Cessation of oil exports to the RSA.
– Cessation of exports of sensitive equipment destined for the police and armed forces of the RSA.
– Prohibition of all new collaboration in the nuclear sector.

Positive measures
- Code of conduct: adaptation, reinforcement and publicity.
- Programmes of assistance to non-violent anti-apartheid organisations, particularly to the churches.
- Programmes to assist the education of the non-white community, including grants for study at the universities in the countries originating the programmes.
- Intensification of contacts with the non-white community in the political, trade union, business, cultural, scientific and sporting sectors, etc.
- Programmes to assist the SADCC and the Front-Line States.
- Programme to increase awareness among the citizens of Member States resident in the RSA.

The question of other measures, including sanctions, remains. As the Ten, together with Spain and Portugal, stated on 22 July of this year, they may have to re-examine their attitude in the absence of significant progress within a reasonable period, and they will assess the situation regularly.

In addition, the departments responsible have been asked to examine the possibility of increasing social and educational assistance from the European Community to the non-white population and to political refugees.

Lastly, the Ministers wish once again to express their grave concern at the spread of violence and the increasing number of casualties in South Africa.

They see these developments as confirmation of the fears and warnings they have been expressing for so long.

There is an urgent need for the South African Government finally to take measures of the kind called for by the European delegation, in order to create a new political climate by opening up a prospect of profound, peaceful change.

Document 4c/5　Communiqué of the Meeting of the Foreign Ministers of the Frontline States and of the Member States of the European Community, Lusaka, 3–4 February 1986

1. The Foreign Ministers of the Frontline States* and those of the Member States of the European Community as well as a member of the Commission of the European Communities met in Lusaka, Zambia, on 3 and 4 February 1986 to consider the situation in Southern Africa.

2. The meeting was held in an atmosphere of cordiality and complete trust and understanding.

3. The Ministers examined the general situation prevailing in the sub-region. In particular, they reviewed recent developments and the current situation in South Africa and discussed such issues as the policies to be followed vis-à-vis South Africa aimed at contributing to the abolition of apartheid and thereby facilitating a peaceful solution in South Africa; the relations between the Republic of South Africa and other States in the region; and the question of the independence of Namibia.

. . .

---

*　Angola, Botswana, Mozambique, Tanzania, Zambia and Zimbabwe.

7. Concerning the policies to be followed vis-à-vis the Republic of South Africa aimed at contributing to the abolition of apartheid, the Ministers considered a wide range of options. They stressed the importance of continuing international pressure on the Government of South Africa to bring about the abolition of apartheid through peaceful means, in the interest of peace and stability in South Africa itself and in the region.

8. They agreed that the measures against South Africa announced by the EC, the Commonwealth, the Nordic countries, the United States of America and other governments and organizations are very important. In the event that all these various measures fail to achieve the desired results, the Ministers agreed that further measures should be considered.

9. Regarding relations between the Republic of South Africa and other Southern African States, they noted that the dismantling of apartheid would significantly contribute to the peaceful co-existence of all the States in the region. The Ministers condemned the military acts of aggression and destabilization perpetrated by South Africa against the neighbouring States in the region. In this connection they demanded the complete withdrawal of all South African troops from Angola. They deplored the loss of human life and destruction of property resulting from these actions on the part of South Africa. They recognized the fact that these actions cannot bring peace to the region; on the contrary, they endanger the peace and stability of the region.

10. The Ministers equally condemned South Africa's policy of destabilization in all its manifestations, including the use of any direct or indirect armed actions in neighbouring States, in particular Angola and Mozambique. In this regard they agreed to deny perpetrators of such actions any assistance or support.

11. In relation to Namibia, the Ministers condemned South Africa's continuing illegal occupation of that international territory and the stalemate in efforts aimed at securing its independence within the framework of the United Nations independence plan for Namibia. In this connection, they re-affirmed the centrality and relevance of United Nations Security Council resolution 435 (1978) which to date represents the only valid basis for a peaceful solution of the question of the independence of Namibia. They called for the implementation of this resolution without further delay. In this connection, the Ministers rejected attempts to delay Namibia's independence by linking it to the withdrawal of Cuban troops from Angola.

12. In this connection, the Ministers considered as null and void the so-called interim administration in Namibia which was set-up contrary to resolution 435, and appealed to all countries to desist from giving it any form of assistance.

13. The Ministers re-affirmed the commitment of their respective countries to work towards the abolition of apartheid in South Africa and to promote efforts aimed at bringing about independence for Namibia.

. . .

Document 4c/6   Conclusions of the European Council on South Africa, The Hague, 27 June 1986

1. The European Council is gravely concerned about the rapid deterioration of the situation and the increasing levels of violence in South Africa. The reimposition of the State of Emergency and the indiscriminate arrest of thousands of South Africans can only further delay the start of a genuine national dialogue on South Africa's future, which is so urgently needed if a peaceful solution of the country's problems is to be found. Furthermore, extensive censorship has been imposed on the media. The European Council believes that the present policies of the South African Government can only lead to increasing repression, polarization and bloodshed.

2. Against this background, the European Council has re-examined the Twelve's policy towards South Africa. It reaffirms that the main goal of this policy is the total abolition of apartheid. To support the process of non-violent change in South Africa and to emphasize their deep concern about the recent course of events, the Heads of State and Government have decided to take additional action.

3. The European Council has declared itself in favour of a concerted European programme of assistance to the victims of apartheid . . .

5. In the meantime in the next three months the Community will enter into consultations with the other industrialized countries on further measures which might be needed, covering in particular a ban on new investments, the import of coal, iron, steel and gold coins from South Africa.

6. The European Council decided to ask the future UK Presidency Foreign Minister to visit southern Africa, in a further effort to establish conditions in which the necessary dialogue can commence.

Document 4c/7   Statement by the Twelve Foreign Ministers on South Africa, Brussels, 16 September 1986

1. The Foreign Ministers of the Twelve reviewed their policy towards South Africa in the light of decisions adopted at The Hague European Council on 26/27 June. They heard a report from Sir Geoffrey Howe on the mission to the region which he undertook at the request of Heads of State and Government.

2. Ministers expressed their grave concern that the situation in South Africa appeared to have entered a new phase of increased tension under the State of Emergency. They shared the widespread anxiety within the Member States over reports of the conditions in which some detainees are being held. They once again condemned the practice of detention without trial. They called for the release of all people so detained under the State of Emergency, which they wished to see brought to an end.

3. The Ministers underlined the importance they attached to the strengthening and more effective co-ordination of the positive measures being taken to assist the victims of apartheid both by Member States and by the Community itself. They noted that the draft Community Budget for 1987 forwarded to the European Parliament by

the Council on 10 September contained an increased provision for the Community programme, with particular emphasis on training.

4. Ministers reaffirmed the urgent need for a genuine national dialogue, across lines of colour, politics and religion. They deplored the fact that the South African Government was not yet prepared to take the steps necessary to make this possible. Two steps in particular were identified at The Hague:
- the unconditional release of Nelson Mandela and other political prisoners;
- the lifting of the ban on the African National Congress, the Pan-Africanist Congress of Azania, and other political parties.

They undertook to work towards a programme of political action designed to promote the achievement of these objectives.

5. In view of the South African Government's failure to respond and after consultation with other industrialized countries, Ministers decided that the Twelve should now proceed to adopt a package of restrictive measures on the lines envisaged at The Hague. This consists of bans on new investment and on the import of iron, steel and gold coins from South Africa. On implementation, they took an immediate decision to suspend imports of iron and steel in the framework of the ECSC Council with effect from 27 September. Ministers also decided to ban the import of gold coins originating in South Africa and new investments in that country, without prejudice to the means of implementation of these measures which will be the subject of further examination by the Committee of Permanent Representatives and the Political Committee.

6. Most partners were also willing to implement a ban on the import of coal from South Africa if a consensus on this could be achieved. On this question, the Presidency will continue to seek consensus on the basis of the statement made by The Hague European Council.

Document 4c/8   Declaration by the European Council on Southern Africa, Dublin, 25–26 June 1990

The European Council welcomes the important changes that have taken place in Southern Africa since it met in Strasbourg.

The European Council warmly welcomes the successful conclusion of the process of bringing Namibia to independence with a constitution based on multi-party democracy and human rights. The European Community and its member States will continue to give aid and support to the people of Namibia as they build their new country, in particular in the framework of the new Lomé Convention. They welcome the talks which have taken place between the Angola Government and UNITA under Portuguese auspices. They look forward to the resolution of the conflict in Angola and also of that in Mozambique through dialogue.

The European Council greatly welcomes the significant changes that have taken place in South Africa in recent months: the release of Nelson Mandela and of other political prisoners; the unbanning of political organizations; the substantial lifting of the state of emergency; the commitment by the Government to abolish the apartheid system and to create a democratic and non-racial South Africa, and its willingness to enter into negotiations on the future of South Africa with the representatives of the majority.

. . .

Through the program of positive measures, the Community has, for a number of years, been providing assistance to the victims of apartheid. In the light of the recent developments in South Africa and as a strong signal of political support to those disadvantaged by apartheid and of the will to contribute to a new socio-economic balance, the Community intends to increase the funds being made available under its program and to adapt the program to the needs of the new situation, including those connected with the return and settlement of exiles. It welcomes the positive attitude being displayed by all parties, including the new South African Government, to such programs.

At its meeting in Strasbourg in December last, the European Council decided that the Community and its member States would maintain the pressure that they exert on the South African authorities in order to promote the profound and irreversible changes which they have repeatedly stood for. The European Council affirms its willingness to consider a gradual relaxation of this pressure when there is further clear evidence that the process of change already initiated continues in the direction called for at Strasbourg.

Document 4c/9   Declaration by the European Council on South Africa, Rome, 14–15 December 1990

The Community and its member States have consistently followed developments in South Africa with the greatest attention and have given a favourable reception to the initiatives which have been taken to bring about the abolition of apartheid and the establishment of a united, non-racial, and democratic South Africa. They have already expressed approval of the results of the talks between the Government and the ANC, in particular those of the Pretoria meeting in August which opened the way to the negotiation of a new Constitution.

They deplore the phase of serious violence through which South Africa is passing which may endanger these developments. They welcome, however, further indications serving to confirm that the process of change already begun is going ahead in the direction advocated by the Strasbourg European Council. They have decided to continue to encourage this process.

Against this background, the European Council has decided that as soon as legislative action is taken by the South African government to repeal the Group Areas Act and the Land Acts, the Community and its member States will proceed to an easing of the set of measures adopted in 1986.

As of now, so as to contribute to combatting unemployment and improving the economic and social situation in South Africa, and to encourage the movement underway aimed at the complete abolition of apartheid, the European Council has decided to lift the ban on new investments.

At the same time, the Community and its member States, with the objective of sending a clear signal of political support to the victims of apartheid, and intending to contribute to a new economic and social balance in South Africa, have agreed to strengthen the programme of positive measures and to adapt it to the requirements of the new situation, including requirements related to the return and resettlement of the exiles.

The Community and its member States hope in this way to be able to contribute to the speeding up of the process underway through sending to all the parties involved in negotiation a concrete sign of support for the establishment of a new South Africa, united, non-racial, and democratic, and capable of resuming the place which it deserves in the international community.

Document 4c/10   Joint Action Adopted by the Council of the European Union on the Basis of Article J.3 of the Treaty on European Union Concerning Support for the Transition towards a Democratic and Multi-Racial South Africa, 6 December 1993 (93/678/CFSP)

THE COUNCIL OF THE EUROPEAN UNION,

Having regard to the Treaty on European Union, and in particular Article J.3 thereof,

Having regard to the general guidelines issued by the European Council on 29 October 1993 which take up as an area for joint action support for the transition towards multi-racial democracy in South Africa through a coordinated programme of assistance in preparing for the elections and monitoring them, and through the creation of an appropriate cooperation framework to consolidate the economic and social foundations of this transition,

HAS DECIDED AS FOLLOWS:

Article 1

The European Union shall implement a coordinated programme of assistance in preparing for the elections taking place in South Africa on 27 April 1994 and monitoring them, on the basis of the following factors:

1.   assistance in preparing for the elections will cover the provision of advice, technical assistance and training, continued support for non-partisan voter education, and the provision of a substantial number of European observers as part of an overall international effort coordinated by the United Nations;

2.   the establishment at this stage of a 'European Electoral Unit' in South Africa in accordance with the procedures set out in the Annex.

Article 2

The operation expenditure incurred in implementing the coordinated programme referred to in Article 1 shall be charged to the Community budget (special programme).

However the salaries and travel expenses to and from South Africa of those monitoring the elections shall be charged to the Member States which send them.

Article 3

The Council will set in motion an internal debate on setting up an appropriate cooperation framework to consolidate the economic and social foundations of the democratic and multi-racial transition and will examine any proposals that the Commission may make to that end both for the immediate period of transition and for the longer term.

. . .

Document 4c/11 Declaration of the European Union on South Africa, Brussels, 6 May 1994

The European Union warmly welcomes the holding of the first democratic elections in South Africa and congratulates all the people of South Africa and its leaders on this historic occasion.

The European Union is ready to support the efforts of the new government to accomplish the goal of leading the country to a democratic and non-racial society in which the respect of Human Rights, the respect of the rights of minorities, the rule of law, promotion of social justice and the elimination of all forms of discrimination will prevail.

Furthermore, the European Union recalls its ministerial decision of 19 April 1994, in which it pledged for a package of immediate measures for the new South Africa. These measures will focus on a dialogue centred on important sectors of the new South Africa, as trade, economic co-operation and development co-operation, in order to support addressing the immediate needs and aspirations of the South Africans. These measures will be coupled with the beginning of a political dialogue, in order to enhance and consolidate the democratic institutions upon which the new South African society will build its future.

The European Union rejoices for the new era in which South Africa has officially entered. The European Union is confident that this era will be characterised by adherence to commitments made during the negotiating process and urges the South Africans to continue to find solutions through dialogue and peaceful means.

The European Union expresses the hope that the new South African government will do its utmost to address the legitimate aspirations of all South Africans, who have dreamt and fought for this day, and whom it now represents.

The Great Lakes Region

In the mid-1990s, conflicts between the Hutu and Tutsi ethnic communities in the Great Lakes region of Africa (and particularly Rwanda and Burundi) prompted great international concern, partly because of the horrifying extent of the violence and partly because global television coverage of the suffering prompted public demands for governments to 'do something'. The widespread violence and genocide that occurred in Rwanda from April 1994 onwards was strongly condemned by the EU (documents 4c/12 and 13). The UN Security Council could not agree to reinforce the small UN mission already present in Rwanda (given the unfortunate precedent of Somalia); France then decided to intervene unilaterally, in June 1994. The Security Council authorized the French-led mission, although there were concerns that France was intervening to protect the Rwandan government against the rebel forces of the Rwandese Patriotic Front (RPF), which in July 1994 came to power. This was, however, too little too late. The French mission was withdrawn in August 1994, and the UN Assistance Mission for Rwanda took over. The EU had supported the operation, and the WEU had offered to help coordinate the contributions of Member States to it (document 4c/14). As time went on the inadequacies of European intervention, both national and collective, became more apparent, and the tragic slaughter left a stain on the EU's reputation.

The genocide and civil war prompted a massive refugee crisis. In October 1994, the EU approved a CFSP common position which set out its objectives towards Rwanda, which included providing humanitarian aid for the refugees (document 4c/15). This completely missed the point, since the refugees included many of those responsible for the genocide.

The spread of violence in neighbouring Burundi also generated EU concern. In March 1995, it set out its objectives (document 4c/16) and adopted a common position. A year later, the EU appointed a special envoy (Aldo Ajello) to the Great Lakes Region, to try to help peace efforts (document 4c/17).

Zaire periodically threatened to send the Rwandan refugees back to Rwanda, because it claimed that rebel groups were operating out of the refugee camps. In late 1996, a crisis loomed, as chaos and revolt spread throughout eastern Zaire. The EU adopted a Joint Action aimed at helping the refugees to return, and asked the WEU to examine how it could help carry out the Joint Action (documents 4c/18 and 19). Denmark did not participate in the request to the WEU, in line with the agreement of the Edinburgh European Council (see document 2/19). But the Rwandan refugees began to return of their own accord, and the potential intervenors decided not to send troops to the region.

Document 4c/12   Declaration of the European Union on Rwanda, Brussels, 18 April 1994

The European Union notes with dismay that the widespread violence and atrocities are continuing and extending in Rwanda, where very many lives have been lost since 6 April 1994.

The violence and the resulting chaos prompted the forced evacuation of virtually all nationals of the international community present in Rwanda. As a result of the solidarity shown by Member States, it was possible to rescue those nationals in a satisfactory manner.

The European Union repeats its pressing call for Rwandese lives to be protected and urgently appeals to the opposing forces to bring the violence to an end and to resume negotiations on the basis of the principles in the Arusha agreement.*

It wishes to see appropriate humanitarian action organized in response to the human tragedy unfolding in the region and undertakes to play its part in such action.

Document 4c/13   Declaration of the European Union on Rwanda, Brussels, 16 May 1994

The European Union, recalling its declaration of 18 April 1994 on Rwanda, again appeals urgently to all parties to the conflict to bring an end to the genocide now taking place in the country.

The European Union expresses its full support for the United Nations' humanitarian efforts and in this context welcomes the resolution that is currently before the Security Council. The European Union looks forward to an urgent decision on measures which can be implemented soon.

The European Union welcomes the initiative of the United Nations High Commissioner on Human Rights to conduct a mission to both Rwanda and Burundi and supports the call for a special meeting of the UN Commission on Human Rights.

The European Union expresses its appreciation and support for the efforts of the OAU and to President Mwinyi of Tanzania for their initiatives in convening a regional conference, in which both the authorities of Rwanda and the RPF will be invited.

The European Union urges the two sides to agree on the need to respect the Arusha agreement, which, through the way of negotiation, offers the best available basis for national reconciliation. In this context the European Union supports the call for an early imposition of an arms embargo on Rwanda, and calls on all concerned to refrain from any action that is liable to exacerbate the situation.

The European Union is eager to increase its humanitarian aid whenever and where such aid can be brought to the populations that have suffered so cruelly from the violence. In this respect it will continue its immediate assistance to refugees in the neighbouring countries and will endeavour to equally assist the stricken populations within Rwanda, whenever conditions allow this.

The European Union has decided on 6 May 1994 to dispatch a Troika mission, on a Development Ministers level, to visit as soon as possible the countries neighbouring Rwanda, with a view to evaluating the humanitarian situation vis-à-vis the influx of the refugees.

---

*   The Arusha agreement was signed between the Government of Rwanda and the Rwanda Patriotic Front on 4 August 1993.

Document 4c/14   Conclusions of the European Council on Rwanda, Corfu, 24–25 June 1994

The European Council expresses its horror at the genocide taking place in Rwanda. Those responsible should be brought to justice. The European Council appeals urgently to all parties to the conflict to stop the wanton killing of civilians and to come back to the negotiating table to work for peace and security for all, on the basis of the Arusha Agreement.

It particularly welcomes the adoption of Security Council Resolution No 929 authorizing the establishment of a temporary operation, pending the arrival of the reinforced Unamir, to protect displaced persons, refugees, and civilians at risk in Rwanda. The European Council welcomes the 21 June 1994 decision of the Western European Union to support the efforts of its Member States which have expressed their willingness to contribute to this operation by ensuring the co-ordination of their contributions.

The European Council expresses its appreciation to the African countries, which have taken up the burden of so many refugees and are contributing to the political solution of the conflict. The European Union will for its part continue and increase its own humanitarian aid.

Document 4c/15   Common Position Adopted by the Council on the Basis of Article J.2 of the Treaty on European Union on the Objectives and Priorities of the European Union *vis-à-vis* Rwanda, 24 October 1994 (94/697/CFSP)

THE COUNCIL OF THE EUROPEAN UNION,

Having regard to the Treaty on European Union, and in particular Article J.2 thereof,

Taking note of the measures and programmes already undertaken by the Community to contribute to the Union's objectives and priorities towards Rwanda in the Framework of the ACP/EEC Conventions and of the Commission's intention to continue such action and to take appropriate steps in the context of the fourth ACP/EEC Convention,

HAS DECIDED AS FOLLOWS:

Article 1

The statement set out in the Annex hereto shall be adopted as an integral part of this common position.

. . .

OBJECTIVES AND PRIORITIES OF THE EUROPEAN UNION *VIS-À-VIS* RWANDA

Priority must be given to the return of refugees. Reconciliation, broadening of the new government's bases and the creation of essential conditions for the return are vital. The Council states its opinion that any aid should be disbursed progressively depending on the observed performance in these areas. International cooperation will have an important role to play in this process.

Objectives and priorities for the European Union are:

– to continue to provide humanitarian aid for refugees,

– to take short-term rehabilitation measures on a coordinated basis for Rwanda, especially in the most urgent fields of water and electricity, but also in education, health and housing, in order to create incentives for the return of refugees and for their successful reintegration,

– to resume progressively and under certain conditions development cooperation with Rwanda,

– to initiate coherent measures for the repair of economic, ecological and social damages in those countries bordering Rwanda, which have been particularly struck by the refugee crisis.

For all the measures and programmes close coordination between the Commission and the Member States is necessary.

The European Union further deems it important to increase as early as possible the number of human rights observers in Rwanda and emphasizes the importance of a rapid total deployment of Unamir forces, in order to assure protection against acts of revenge and persecution.

The European Union stresses the importance of bringing to justice those responsible for the grave violations of humanitarian law, including genocide. In this respect the European Union considers the establishment of an international tribunal as an essential element to stop a tradition of impunity and to prevent future violations of human rights.

The European Union underlines that within a long-term perspective such conflicts should be solved by Africa itself and recommends strengthening the OAU's capacities of preventing and solving regional conflicts.

The European Union also expresses its concern about the unstable political situation in Burundi, where acts of violence are increasing.

Document 4c/16   Declaration by the Presidency on behalf of the European Union's Objectives and Priorities Regarding Burundi, Brussels, 19 March 1995

The European Union's objectives and priorities regarding Burundi are to consolidate the process of national reconciliation and a return to normal democratic life, in particular by restoring the rule of law, and to promote the economic and social recovery of the country.

Following the appointment, by the President of the Republic of Burundi, of Mr Nduwayo as Prime Minister and the forming of a new Government, the European Union wishes them both every success in their task.

The European Union is however still concerned at the way the political situation is developing and the worsening of security conditions in Burundi. That concern prompted it to send a mission to Bujumbura on 10 and 11 February 1995.

The European Union is determined to give strong backing to the "Government Convention" concluded on 10 September 1994 with provisions forming the institutional framework for necessary national reconciliation, and would urge all political parties, military forces and sectors of civilian society to respect and implement it in a spirit of dialogue, moderation and compromise.

The European Union supports the action being taken in Burundi by the international community, and in particular by the United Nations Organization and the Organization of African Unity, and is resolved to step up the efforts which it is already making to help strengthen stability in Burundi.

The European Union is therefore prepared to:
- assist the Burundi Government in organizing a "national debate" of the kind provided for by the "Government Convention" with the participation of all sectors of the Burundi nation in order to consolidate national reconciliation and reconstruct democracy,
- help strengthen the action already being taken by the United Nations High Commissioner for Human Rights, inter alia by support to the sending of experts as provided for in the 1995/90 Resolution adopted on 8 March 1995 by the United Nations Commission for Human Rights,
- contribute to restoring the rule of law and strengthening the Burundi legal system, inter alia by giving help with the training of magistrates,
- in view of the role which could be played by an International Commission of Enquiry into the attempted coup in 1993 and the massacres which followed, the European Union hopes that the United Nations will be able to adopt a position quickly on the request submitted to it by the Burundi Authorities,
- it also pays tribute to the action taken by the OAU, which it hopes will be extended further and is prepared to support.

The European Union is convinced that the economic and social recovery of Burundi will facilitate a return to stability and its consolidation for the future, and it would like a round table of donors to be organized swiftly with the participation of international institutions and all countries which are friends of Burundi.

The European Union is also prepared to help implement and follow up the action plan adopted by the regional conference on assistance to refugees, returnees and displaced persons in the Great-Lake region held in Bujumbura from 15 to 17 February 1995.

By way of support for the Burundi Nation in its search for peaceful and democratic solutions, the European Union would encourage all partners to take any measures they deem necessary against extremist elements in Burundi in order to prevent them travelling abroad and receiving assistance.

The European Union is aware of the close links which exist between the various humanitarian and political problems facing the region and the considerable danger of destabilization which persists, calls for the organization of the conference on peace, security and stability desired by the United Nations Security Council and reiterates its strongest support for all forces in Burundi which are working towards peace, dialogue and national reconciliation.

Document 4c/17   Joint Action Adopted by the Council on the Basis of Article J.3 of the Treaty on European Union, in Relation to the Nomination of a Special Envoy for the African Great Lakes Region, 25 March 1996 (96/250/CFSP)

THE COUNCIL OF THE EUROPEAN UNION,

Having regard to the Treaty on European Union and, in particular, Articles J.3 and J.11 thereof,

Having regard to the conclusions of the European Council of 15 and 16 December 1995 in Madrid,

Having regard to the conclusions of the Council of 29 January and 26 and 27 February 1996,

HAS ADOPTED THE FOLLOWING JOINT ACTION:

Article 1

The Union shall pursue the following objectives with respect to the African Great Lakes Region and the countries of the region:

1. to assist these countries in resolving the crisis affecting their region; and

2. to support the efforts of the UN and the Organization of African Unity (OAU), as well as those of regional leaders and other parties, aimed at finding a lasting and comprehensive peaceful solution to the political, economic and humanitarian problems facing the region.

Article 2

To this end, the Special Envoy of the Union will support the efforts aimed at creating the conditions for solving the crisis, including the preparation for the holding of a Conference on Peace, Security and Stability in the Great Lakes Region, which is an important step in the process of finding a lasting and peaceful solution.

The Special Envoy will:

−   work in support of the efforts of the UN and of the OAU, which are striving to bring an end to the conflicts in the region, and of those African personalities who are assisting the two organizations;

- establish and maintain close contact with the Governments of the countries of the region, with other interested Governments and international organizations in order to identify measures which need to be taken towards solving the problems of the region;

- coordinate closely with the representatives of the UN and of the OAU in the region, which are responsible for the convening of the Conference;

- cooperate with regional leaders and other parties working towards the same objective; and

- where appropriate, establish contact with other parties who might have a role to play in achieving progress.

Article 3

The Special Envoy:

- is appointed for a period of six months, subject to review after three months of mandate, including the administrative and financial aspects;

- shall report every two months, or whenever necessary, to the Council or its designated instances;

- may be called to report orally on developments, whenever the need arises; and

- may make recommendations to the Council on measures which the Union might undertake to fulfil its objectives in the region.

Article 4

1. In order to cover the costs related to the mission of the Special Envoy, a sum of ECU 950 000 shall be charged to the general budget of the European Communities for 1996.

2. The expenditure financed by the amount stipulated in paragraph 1 shall be managed in accordance with the European Community procedures and rules applicable to the budget.

3. A sum of up to the amount specified in paragraph 1 shall be allocated to finance the infrastructure and current expenditure of the Special Envoy, including his salary and that of his support staff. The remuneration of personnel which a Member State or the Commission may detach to the Special Envoy will be covered respectively by the Member State concerned and the Commission. Member States and the Commission may propose the detachment of personnel to the Special Envoy.

4. The Council notes that the Commission intends to provide logistical support in the region.

5. The guarantees necessary for the completion and smooth functioning of the mission of the Special Envoy and the members of his staff shall be defined with the parties. The Member States and the Commission shall grant all necessary support to such effect.

Article 5

This Joint Action shall enter into force on the date of its adoption. It shall apply until 25 November 1996.

. . .

Document 4c/18   Joint Action Adopted by the Council on the Basis of Article J.3 of the Treaty on European Union on the African Great Lakes Region, 22 November 1996 (96/669/CFSP)

THE COUNCIL OF THE EUROPEAN UNION,

Having regard to the Treaty on European Union, and in particular Article J.3 thereof,

Having regard to the conclusions of the European Council meeting in Florence on 21 and 22 June 1996,

Having regard to the common position of 24 October 1994 on the objectives and priorities of the European Union *vis-à-vis* Rwanda,

Having regard to the declarations adopted at its meeting on 28 October 1996 and at the special meeting of the Ministers for Development Cooperation and Humanitarian Aid on 7 November 1996, devoted to the situation in eastern Zaire,

Whereas on 9 and 15 November 1996, respectively, the United Nations Security Council adopted Resolutions 1078 and 1080; whereas those Resolutions must be implemented;

Recognizing the importance of the contribution of the African States to resolving the crisis in the Great Lakes Region;

Whereas the European Union is already involved in the search for a solution to the crisis through the constructive action of its Special Envoy to the Great Lakes Region;

Whereas the European Union must integrate its efforts to resolve this crisis with the action undertaken by the international community in accordance with the relevant Security Council Resolutions;

Whereas the Council today adopted a concomitant Decision requesting the Western European Union to elaborate and implement the specific aspects of this joint action which have defence implications,

HEREBY ADOPTS THIS JOINT ACTION:

Article 1

The European Union supports the urgent implementation of the relevant United Nations Security Council Resolutions, with a view to enabling the delivery of humanitarian aid to eastern Zaire and facilitating the return by free consent of refugees to their country of origin and the return of displaced persons. The Community and its Member States will contribute to implementing those Resolutions in ways which they deem appropriate, and which they will coordinate in the manner set out in this Joint Action. The European Union reaffirms the priority which must be given to the return of the refugees to their country of origin and the need to overcome all obstacles to that end. It confirms its willingness to assist Rwanda to create the essential conditions for the return of the Rwandan refugees.

Article 2

In the context of support for United Nations coordination, the Council notes that the Commission will ensure coordination of the efforts of the Community and its Member States with a view to providing and delivering humanitarian aid to the refugees and displaced persons in eastern Zaire as a manner of urgency.

Article 3

Taking into account their voluntary contributions in humanitarian and military aid, the Member States will consult and cooperate within the Council on their voluntary contributions in support of African participation in the multinational force, in accordance with the relevant United Nations Security Council Resolutions.

Article 4

As regards the financing of the Community contribution to the objectives of this Joint Action, the Council notes that the Commission will examine the possibilities and make appropriate proposals.

Article 5

The European Union will intensify its efforts to restore stability in the Great Lakes Region, in particular by encouraging the setting up of democratic institutions and respect for human rights. It reaffirms that the holding of an international conference on peace, security and development in the Great Lakes Region, under the auspices of the United Nations and the Organization of African Unity, has a decisive role to play in finding a lasting settlement of the crisis in the region. It invites all the parties to redouble their efforts so that such a conference may be held.

. . .

Document 4c/19 Joint Action Adopted by the Council on the Basis of Article J.4(2) of the Treaty on European Union on the Elaboration and Implementation of a Joint Action by the Union in the Great Lakes Region, 22 November 1996 (96/670/CFSP)

THE COUNCIL OF THE EUROPEAN UNION,

. . .

Having regard to the Declaration on Western European Union (WEU), set out in the Final Act signed when the Treaty on European Union was adopted,

Whereas the Council today adopted on the basis of Article J.3 of the Treaty on European Union a Joint Action on the Great Lakes Region,

Whereas the implementation of this Joint Action has defence implications and may, in particular, require the use of military means; whereas, in these circumstances, use should be made of the Western European Union,

HAS DECIDED AS FOLLOWS:

Article 1

The European Union hereby requests the WEU to examine as a matter of urgency how it can, for its part, contribute to the optimum use of the operational resources available.

Article 2

This Decision is notified to the WEU in accordance with the conclusions adopted by the Council on 14 May 1996 on the forwarding of European Union documents to the WEU.

. . .

STATEMENT BY DENMARK

concerning the Council Decision on the implementation of the European Union Joint Action on the Great Lakes Region

In accordance with Section C of the Decision adopted at the European Council held in Edinburgh on 11 and 12 December 1992, Denmark does not participate in the elaboration and the implementation of decisions and actions of the Union which have defence implications.

The Danish Government has decided that Denmark does not participate in the Council Decision requesting the WEU to elaborate and implement the action of the Union in the Great Lakes Region.

In accordance with the Edinburgh decision Denmark will not prevent the development of closer cooperation between Member States in this area. Accordingly, the position indicated does not prevent the adoption of the Council Decision.

Nigeria

The political situation in Nigeria, one of the largest aid recipients under the Lomé convention, has caused the Community/Union considerable concern. In June 1993, the Nigerian military government annulled the Nigerian presidential elections, which had apparently been won by opposition candidate Moshood Abiola. The Community and its Member States then decided to impose several negative measures. The situation had not improved two years later, as the EU noted on 30 June 1995. The death sentences passed on Nigerian writer Ken Saro-Wiwa and eight others were criticized by the EU on 9 November 1995.

Saro-Wiwa was executed anyway the next day. The EU then imposed further negative measures (documents 4c/20 and 21). Sanctions did not affect Nigeria's most important export, oil, given the economic interests of several Member States. But eventually international isolation appeared to work, as the military regime agreed to hand over power to a democratically elected government. In October 1998, the Council lifted most of the sanctions; in June 1999, the Community resumed development cooperation with Nigeria – after the democratically elected president, Olusegun Obasanjo, took office.

Document 4c/20   Common Position Adopted by the Council of the European Union on the Basis of Article J.2 of the Treaty on European Union on Nigeria, 20 November 1995 (95/515/CFSP)

1. The Council strongly condemns the executions, on 10 November, of Mr Ken Saro-Wiwa and his eight co-defendants. This constituted a clear failure by Nigeria to honour its commitment to human rights, as it stems from a number of international instruments to which Nigeria is a party.

2. The European Union condemns the human-rights abuses perpetrated by the military regime, including capital punishment and harsh prison sentences, implemented after flawed judicial process and without granting the possibility of recourse to a higher court. In this context, it expresses its particular concern at the detention without trial of political figures and the suspension of *habeas corpus*.

3. The European Union recalls its deep concern at the annulment in June 1993 of elections that were considered free and fair and the subsequent installation of a new military dictatorship. It notes that the military regime has yet to demonstrate convincingly its intention to return to civilian democratic rule within a credible and rapid time-frame and

(a) reaffirms the following measures adopted in 1993:
   - suspension of military cooperation,
   - visa restrictions for members of the military or the security forces, and their families,
   - suspension of visits of members of the military,
   - restrictions on the movement of all military personnel of Nigerian diplomatic missions,
   - cancellation of training courses for all Nigerian military personnel,
   - suspension of all high-level visits that are not indispensable to and from Nigeria;

(b) introduces the following, additional measures:
   (i) visa restrictions on members of the Provisional Ruling Council and the Federal Executive Committee and their families;
   (ii) an embargo on arms, munitions and military equipment (1).

(1)   The aforementioned embargo covers weapons designed to kill and their ammunition, weapon platforms, non-weapon platforms and ancillary equipment. The embargo also covers spare parts, repairs, maintenance and transfer of military technology. Contracts entered into prior to the date of entry into force of the embargo are not affected by this Common Position.

4. Development cooperation with Nigeria is suspended. Exceptions may be made for projects and programmes in support of human rights and democracy as well as those concentrating on poverty alleviation and, in particular, the provision of basic needs for the poorest section of the population, in the context of decentralized cooperation through local civilian authorities and non-governmental organizations.

5. This Common Position will be monitored by the Council, to which the Presidency and the Commission will report regularly, and will be reviewed in the light of developments in Nigeria. Further measures are under examination.

6. This Common Position shall take effect on 20 November 1995.

. . .

Document 4c/21   Common Position Defined by the Council of the European Union on the Basis of Article J.2 of the Treaty on European Union on Nigeria, 4 December 1995 (95/544/CFSP)

THE COUNCIL OF THE EUROPEAN UNION,

Having regard to the Treaty on European Union, and in particular Article J.2 thereof,

HAS DEFINED THE FOLLOWING COMMON POSITION:

1. In addition to the common position adopted by the Council on 20 November 1995 and the measures contained therein, the Council decides to take the following further measures:
   - Member States will take, in accordance with national law, such measures as are appropriate in the context of their own immigration procedures to ensure that members of the Nigerian Provisional Ruling Council and the Federal Executive Council, members of the Nigerian military and security forces and their families in possession of long-term visas are not admitted,
   - expulsion of all military personnel attached to the diplomatic representations of Nigeria in Member States of the European Union, and withdrawal of all military personnel attached to diplomatic representations of Member States of the European Union in Nigeria,
   - interruption of all contacts in the field of sports through denial of visas to official delegations and national teams.

2. Furthermore, the European Union will actively pursue:
   (a) the adoption of a resolution on Nigeria at the 50th United Nations General Assembly; and
   (b) the inclusion of the situation in Nigeria on the agenda of the Commission on Human Rights.

3. This common position will be monitored by the Council, to which the Presidency and the Commission will regularly report. Further measures will be considered, including sanctions, if specific steps are not taken by the Nigerian authorities:

(i)   towards an early transition to democracy; and

(ii) to ensure full respect of human rights and the rule of law.

4.   This common position shall take effect on 4 December 1995 for a renewable
period of six months in the light of the considerations in paragraph 3 above.

. . .

Democracy and conflict resolution

The tragic events of the 1990s in Africa – from the breakdown of government in Somalia to genocide in Rwanda – led the Community/Union increasingly to emphasize democracy and the protection of human rights in its relations with African states. At the Copenhagen European Council in June 1993, the foreign ministers issued a declaration on Africa (document 4c/22), stressing their concern for the respect of human rights and democratic principles on the continent. The document also contained conclusions on a number of African countries: it welcomed progress towards democracy in South Africa, expressed concern over the continuing civil wars in Sudan and Liberia, urged progress to be made in the peace processes in Angola and Mozambique, condemned the attack on Pakistani UN soldiers serving in Somalia, and denounced the halt to democratization in Zaire and Nigeria.

Issues of peacekeeping and conflict resolution also naturally rose to the fore, yet Western states were less and less willing to intervene in internal conflicts, particularly after the disaster-prone intervention in Somalia. The Union thus decided to help build the Organization of African Unity's capabilities for peacekeeping and conflict resolution. In December 1995, the Council declared that it would support OAU efforts in preventive diplomacy and peacekeeping: the EU would help develop early warning systems (by exchanging information and training experts), organize seminars on preventive diplomacy, and consider supporting OAU peacekeeping missions via the WEU. In early June 1997, the Council issued another statement on conflict prevention in Africa (document 4c/23), emphasizing the need to address the roots of conflict (particularly socio-economic) and pledging help to develop African peacekeeping and preventive diplomacy capabilities. In May 1998, the Council approved a common position on human rights, democratic principles, rule of law and good governance in Africa, which is notable also because it pledges coherence in EU external policy: the CFSP and the Community's aid programmes are clearly linked (document 4c/24). Progress in implementing the common position is reviewed regularly; in May 1999, the General Affairs Council reviewed the EU's activities in Africa over the previous six months. These included support for elections in several countries (including Nigeria and Mozambique), presentations of démarches to several governments (including Zimbabwe's), the imposition of an arms embargo on Ethiopia and Eritrea, and the reconsideration of development cooperation with Niger after a military coup there.

Document 4c/22   Conclusions of the Twelve Foreign Ministers on Africa,
Copenhagen, 21–22 June 1993

Foreign Ministers, meeting on the occasion of the European Council in Copenhagen
on 21 and 22 June 1993, agreed on the following conclusions:

Africa

Europe is Africa's major partner, politically, economically, and with regard to development cooperation. The European Council underlined the importance of a continued cooperation based on solidarity.

In 1993 the Community and its Member States have taken a number of steps towards deeper and wider cooperation with Africa. The European Council stressed the importance of further expansion of cooperation in democratization, peaceful development and development assistance.

The Community and its Member States are committed to supporting the democratization process which is gaining momentum in Africa, including support for good governance, sound economic management and respect for human rights. The European Council recalled the resolution adopted by the Council (Development) on 28 November 1991 on human rights, democracy and development.*

The Community and its Member States have engaged themselves actively in supporting the election process in a number of African countries. They will continue their efforts to coordinate this assistance to ensure that all African countries in a transitional process towards democracy are offered the necessary support and attention.

The successful referendum on the independence of Eritrea after 30 years of civil war has raised hopes that conflicts in Africa can be solved in a peaceful manner.

The European Council welcomed the increasing engagement by African countries in solving crises and armed conflicts, as seen recently in a number of cases. The European Council also hoped that Heads of State of OAU at their forthcoming Cairo summit will address the important question of conflict prevention and resolution. A useful contact with the OAU was established during the visit to Copenhagen in June of the Secretary General of this organization.

The Community and its Member States have further strengthened development cooperation with Africa. The Lomé Convention forms an important element in this cooperation. Effectiveness and speed in the implementation of the European Development Fund is increasing to the benefit of all parties.

Development Ministers have agreed on a special rehabilitation initiative for Africa. At least 100 million ecu will be allocated immediately to fast track rehabilitation programmes in selected sub-Saharan countries. The Council of Ministers is examining a further special rehabilitation programme for developing countries.

Document 4c/23   Conclusions by the General Affairs Council on the Prevention and Resolution of Conflicts in Africa, Luxembourg, 2–3 June 1997

1.   In adopting the Common Position on the prevention and resolution of conflicts in Africa, the Council recalled its conclusions of 4 December 1995 on "Preventive diplomacy, conflict resolution and peace-keeping in Africa", which were endorsed

---

*   See document 4c/36.

by the Madrid European Council. Preventive diplomacy, peace-keeping and the strengthening of international security are priority aims of the Common Foreign and Security Policy (CFSP). It recalled also the Commission's Communication on "The European Union and the issue of conflicts in Africa: conflict prevention and beyond" presented to the Council in March 1996. The latter sets out the parameters for a proactive, comprehensive and integrated approach and highlights the need to enhance peace-building capacities in Africa. The Council's conclusions of 4 December 1995, which underscored the primary role of the United Nations in the matter, were subsequently brought to the attention of the Organisation of African Unity, with whom the matter has been the subject of discussion.

. . .

6. The Community and the Member States will exchange information on their bilateral aid programmes in the realm of prevention and resolution of conflicts, with a view to leading to better coordination between the different programmes. Consideration will be given to identifying appropriate mechanisms to this end. The Community and the Member States will jointly undertake the identification of suitable measures for conflict prevention on a country-by-country basis whereby an adequate and coordinated combination of all instruments available should be considered in view of a comprehensive and integrated policy.

7. The Member States of the European Union, recognizing that the availability of arms in quantities exceeding needs for self-defence may be a factor contributing to situations of instability:
    – reaffirm their commitment to exercise utmost restraint with regard to arms exports, taking full account of the eight criteria for arms exports established by the European Council; and
    – will strengthen their efforts to prevent and combat illicit trafficking of arms, particularly of small arms.
    The Member States will study the possibility of taking further measures to restrain their citizens from acting as mercenaries in violent conflicts.

8. The Union will seek to facilitate African efforts. To this end, there should be better linkage between the EU's and African efforts. The EU will deepen the dialogue with the OAU and subregional organisations on concrete possibilities of support for their efforts in the fields of early warning, preventive diplomacy, peacekeeping, as well as awareness-raising concerning the importance of the respect for human rights, the rule of law, pluralist society, democratic institutions and practices, and of a culture of tolerance and peaceful existence. Civil society organisations, in particular women's organisations, can play an important role in this respect.

9. There is a need to identify and address the root causes of conflict. To this end, the European Union will seek to collate and analyse existing information on causes of conflict. The sources of this information can include international organisations, Member States and non-governmental organisations. The European Union's analysis can then be used to inform action by the Community, Member States and other actors. The EU will reinforce its efforts to close the gap between early warning, analysis and timely political action.

10. In striving to support African efforts, the Council stresses the importance of coordinating the EU'S actions with those of other members of the international community. In responding to an outbreak of violence, whether internal or inter-state, the EU will first and foremost encourage efforts to promote a peaceful settlement by the parties themselves, with appropriate assistance from the UN, OAU, sub-regional organisations or other intermediaries. Should such a response have defence implications, the EU will request the Western European Union (WEU) to elaborate and implement this initiative as regards these defense implications, in particular the use of military means, in accordance with the relevant Treaty provisions.

11. In implementing its Common Policy, the Council underlines the need to make maximum use of existing fora and resources.

. . .

Document 4c/24 Common Position on Human Rights, Democratic Prin-ciples, the Rule of Law and Good Governance in Africa, 25 May 1998 (98/350/CFSP)

COMMON POSITION

of 25 May 1998

defined by the Council on the basis of Article J.2 of the Treaty on European Union, concerning human rights, democratic principles, the rule of law and good gover-nance in Africa

(98/350/CFSP)

THE COUNCIL OF THE EUROPEAN UNION,

Having regard to the Treaty on European Union and in particular Article J.2 thereof,

Whereas under Article J.1(2) of the Treaty on European Union, one of the objec-tives of the Common Foreign and Security Policy is to develop and consolidate democracy and the rule of law, and respect for human rights and fundamental free-doms;

Whereas the Council and representatives of the Member States meeting in the Council adopted a resolution on human rights, democracy and development on 28 November 1991;

Whereas under Articles 4 and 5 of the Fourth ACP-EC Convention, signed at Lomé on 15 December 1989 as revised by the agreement signed in Mauritius on 4 November 1995, the work undertaken by the Community and its Member States in the framework of ACP/EC cooperation must take into account the human dimen-sion and is based on the respect of human rights, democratic principles, the rule of law and good governance;

Whereas under Article 3 of Common Position 97/356/CFSP on conflict prevention and resolution in Africa adopted on 2 June 1997, the Council notes that, in
accordance with the relevant procedures, steps will be taken to ensure coordination
of the efforts of the European Community and those of the Member States in development cooperation and the support for human rights, democracy, the rule of law
and good governance;

Whereas human rights are universal, indivisible, interdependent and intrinsically
linked,

HAS DEFINED THIS COMMON POSITION:

Article 1

The objective of the Union is to work in partnership with African countries to
promote respect for human rights, democratic principles, the rule of law and good
governance. This approach shall serve as a framework for the actions of the Member
States.

The aim of this common position is to contribute to the coherence of external
Union activities in Africa, including appropriate policy responses. The Union recognises that democratisation is a process which can be assisted by appropriate support
from the international community, including the Union, and that many African
countries have successfully introduced reforms in recent years which have improved
the ability of individuals to enjoy human rights and democratic processes.

Article 2

The Union fully recognises the right of sovereign states to establish their own
constitutional arrangements and to institute their own administrative structures
according to their history, culture, tradition and social and ethnic composition.
In this framework, the Union is committed to encourage and support the ongoing democratisation process in Africa on the basis of respect for the following
principles:

(a) protection of human rights (civil and political, and social, economic and cultural);

(b) respect of basic democratic principles, including:
–   the right to choose and change leaders in free and fair elections,
–   separation of legislative, executive and judicial powers,
–   guarantees of freedom of expression, information, association and political
organisation;

(c) the rule of law, which permits citizens to defend their rights and which implies
a legislative and judicial power giving full effect to human rights and fundamental
freedoms and a fair, accessible and independent judicial system;

(d) good governance, including the transparent and accountable management of
all a country's resources for the purposes of equitable and sustainable development.

Article 3

(a) When deciding policy towards individual countries, the Union shall take into account their points of departure and the direction and pace of change within them, as well as the policy commitments of the respective governments. The Union shall give high priority to a positive and constructive approach that encourages human rights, democratic principles, the rule of law and good governance.

(b The Union, working with both governments and civil society on the basis of partnership and cooperation, shall consider increasing its support for African countries in which positive changes have taken place and where the governments concerned are engaged in promoting positive change. Where changes are negative, the Union shall consider the appropriate responses that could help reverse those developments on the basis of the principles laid down in the resolution adopted on 28 November 1991.

Article 4

The Council notes that the Commission intends to direct its action towards achieving the objectives and the priorities of this common position, where appropriate, by pertinent Community measures.

Article 5

Union activities in implementation of this common position shall be reviewed on a six-monthly basis.

. . .

Latin America

The Falkland Islands War

On 1–2 April 1982, Argentina invaded the Falkland Islands, a British dependency. The Community and its Member States immediately declared their solidarity with the UK and condemned the invasion on 2 April (document 4c/25); the Commission also did so separately (document 4c/26). The UK imposed sanctions on Argentina on 6 April; the Ten followed suit on 10 April (document 4c/27). The Ten's reaction was stronger than that of the United States, which remained neutral until 30 April and the collapse of its peace initiative.

The UK sent a naval task-force to the South Atlantic. Within the Community/EPC, there was increasing concern about the outbreak of hostilities, which was not alleviated by the sinking on 2 May of the *General Belgrano* battlecruiser by a British submarine, with the loss of 368 lives. On 16 May, Ireland and Italy took advantage of the escape clause in article 224 of the EEC Treaty to withdraw from sanctions, although they agreed not to allow EC measures to be undermined. Denmark also withdrew because it objected to the use of Community instruments for political purposes, but replaced EC sanctions with its own, identical national measures. The sanctions were lifted on 22 June 1982, following the UK's military victory.

Document 4c/25   Declaration on the Falklands, European Political Cooperation, 2 April 1982

The Foreign Ministers of the Ten condemn the armed intervention in the Falkland
Islands by the Government of Argentina in defiance of the statement issued on 1
April by the President of the Security Council of the United Nations, which remains
seized of the question.

They urgently appeal to the Government of Argentina to withdraw its forces immediately and to adhere to the appeal of the United Nations Security Council to refrain
from the use of force and to continue the search for a diplomatic solution.

Document 4c/26   Statement by the European Community on the Falklands,
6 April 1982

The Commission of the European Communities condemns the armed intervention
of Argentina against a British territory linked to the Community, an intervention
committed in violation of international law and the rights of the inhabitants of the
Falkland Islands. The Commission expresses its solidarity with the United Kingdom.
It makes an urgent appeal to the Argentine Government to implement the resolution of the Security Council, calling on it to withdraw its troops from the Islands
and to continue seeking a diplomatic solution. It expresses the hope that the
Organization of American States will join its efforts to those of the United Nations
in order to ensure, by diplomatic means, that a solution based on law prevails.

Document 4c/27   Statement on the Falklands, European Political Cooperation, 10 April 1982

The Ten discussed the serious situation resulting from Argentina's invasion of the
Falkland Islands.

The Ten recall that, in their declaration of 2 April, they already condemned the
flagrant violation of international law represented by Argentina's actions.

The Ten remain deeply concerned about the further development of this crisis,
which jeopardizes international peace and security. They thus attach the greatest
importance to effective and immediate application of all points of Security Council
Resolution 502, i.e. the cessation of hostilities, the immediate withdrawal of all
Argentine forces from the Falkland Islands and the search for a diplomatic solution
by the Governments of Argentina and the United Kingdom.

With this in mind, and in a spirit of solidarity among the Member States of the
Community, the Ten have decided to adopt a series of measures against Argentina
which should be implemented as soon as possible.

The governments of the Ten have already decided to apply a total ban on exports
of arms and military equipment to Argentina.

They will also take the measures needed to prohibit all imports into the Community from Argentina.

Since these are economic measures, they will be taken in accordance with the relevant provisions of the Community Treaties.

Since the situation resulting from the invasion of the Falkland Islands by Argentine armed forces is a matter of serious concern for the whole of the international community, the Ten call on other governments to support their decisions so that Security Council Resolution 502 can be fully implemented as soon as possible.

Central America

In the early 1980s, the Ten's interest in Central America grew, partly because newly elected French President François Mitterrand was pushing for Community/EPC involvement in the region, and partly out of alarm at US policy there. The Reagan Administration seemed to be seeking a military solution to the simmering revolutions: it sponsored rebels in Nicaragua, and sent military aid to the right-wing government in El Salvador (which was fighting left-wing guerrillas). The Ten, by contrast, considered the cause of instability in Central America to be economic and social backwardness. Consequently, economic development and regional cooperation were seen as the best means to help stabilize the region. The European Council in March 1982 agreed to increase the Community's aid to Central America (document 4c/28). In January 1983, the Contadora Group (Mexico, Venezuela, Panama and Colombia) called for multilateral talks on Central America. The European Council in June 1983 declared its support for these efforts (document 4c/29).

In June 1984, Costa Rica proposed holding a conference of all the Community and Central American foreign ministers (including that of Nicaragua). The Ten accepted the invitation and the conference was held in September 1984 in San José, where, notably, every EC foreign minister showed up (bar Luxembourg) – a clear signal to Washington. The ministers agreed to continue their dialogue and to negotiate an economic cooperation agreement (document 4c/30). At the second meeting, in November 1985, the Community and the Central American countries signed a framework cooperation agreement and issued a declaration on political dialogue. This set up the San José process, which has continued, on both economic and political fronts, to the present. In 1999, the EU launched a high-profile initiative towards all of Latin America, with a summit between the EU and 48 Latin American and Caribbean countries, and a pledge to start trade talks with Mercosur (Brazil, Argentina, Paraguay and Uruguay).

Document 4c/28   Conclusions by the European Council on Central America, Brussels, 29–30 March 1982

The European Council discussed the situation in Central America. It expressed serious concern at the continued growth of tensions in the region. It welcomed with interest any initiative likely to put an end to violence and lead, through dialogue and respect for democratic norms and for human rights, to the restoration of peace in the region, while safeguarding national sovereignty and the wishes of the people. In this context it noted with interest the proposals made by a number of countries in the region.

Noting that the tensions and conflicts ravaging Central America frequently stemmed from the grave economic problems and social inequalities which had been aggravated by world economic conditions to the detriment of the poorest countries, the European Council believed that the international community could not remain indifferent to these evils. It welcomed the efforts currently being exerted to remedy them, and particularly hopes that the initiative of the Nassau Group will contribute to this in accordance with the principles set out above.

The Community and its Member States too had, in the past, provided substantial assistance to the region.

The European Council however agreed that the aid given by the Member States of the Community and by the Community itself for development in Central America and the Caribbean should be co-ordinated and increased within the limits of their possibilities.

The European Council instructed the Foreign Ministers to work out detailed arrangements for the provision of Community aid on the basis of proposals by the Commission.

Document 4c/29   Conclusions by the European Council on Central America, Stuttgart, 17–19 June 1983

The Heads of State and Government confirmed their close interest in developments in Central America. They are deeply concerned at the economic and social conditions in many parts of the region, at the tensions which these create, and at the widespread misery and bloodshed.

They are convinced that the problems of Central America cannot be solved by military means, but only by a political solution springing from the region itself and respecting the principles of non-interference and inviolability of frontiers. They, therefore, fully support the current initiative of the Contadora Group. They underlined the need for the establishment of democratic conditions and for the strict observance of human rights throughout the region.

They are ready to continue contributing to the further development in the area in order to promote progress towards stability.

Document 4c/30   Joint Communiqué of the Conference of Foreign Ministers of the European Community and its Member States, Portugal and Spain, the States of Central America and the Contadora States, San José, Costa Rica, 28–29 September 1984

. . .

3.   Inspired by a consciousness of their shared cultural heritage and of their common attachment to the ideals and values enshrined in the United Nations Charter, the participating countries have inaugurated through this conference a new

structure of political and economic dialogue between Europe and Central America. They are convinced that this dialogue, and the increased practical cooperation that it will engender, will reinforce the efforts of the countries of Central America themselves, with the support of the Contadora States, to bring an end to violence and instability in Central America and to promote social justice, economic development and respect for human rights and democratic liberties in that region.

4. A comprehensive discussion took place between the Ministers of the 10 Member States of the European Community and those of the Central American countries on the political, economic and cultural relations between them and agreements were reached on the future development of those relations. They have agreed that further meetings in this dialogue should take place at regular intervals. The level of such meetings, whether at ministerial or official level, will be determined in the light of circumstances. The Foreign Ministers of Spain and Portugal associated themselves with these agreements.

5. The Foreign Ministers exchanged views on current regional and international problems and developments, and in particular the situation in Central America. They expressed their preoccupation at the conditions and acts which gravely disturb the peace and security of the Central American region, and agreed on the necessity for the governments of the area to intensify negotiations which lead to mutual understanding and permanent stability.

6. The Ministers reaffirmed their commitment to the objectives of peace, democracy, security and economic and social development, and political stability in Central America, and were united in the view that the problems of that region cannot be solved by armed force, but only by political solutions springing from the region itself. In this conviction they affirmed their support for the pacification measures which are being developed in the Contadora process. They expressed their conviction that this process represents a genuinely regional initiative and the best opportunity to achieve a solution to the crisis through political undertakings aimed at the achievement of the aims set out in the 'Document of objectives' approved by all the governments of the region on 9 September 1983. They noted with satisfaction the progress achieved so far towards such a solution, and that the revised draft Contadora Act for Peace and Cooperation in Central America is a fundamental stage in the negotiating process for the attainment of peace in the region. They called on the States concerned to continue to make every effort to bring the Contadora process rapidly to final fruition through the signature of a comprehensive agreement which would bring peace to the region. They were agreed on the necessity for a practical commitment to the implementation of any such agreement by all the States in the region and all other countries which have interests there, and on the necessity for the verification and control of that implementation.

7. The European countries expressed their willingness to support, within their capabilities and if requested, the efforts of those States to which it falls to implement the provisions of any agreement.

8. The Ministers discussed the international economic situation and, in particular, economic and trade relations and cooperation between the European Community and Central America.

9.   The Ministers agreed that the current international economic situation should be regarded as particularly difficult. In this context, they underlined the problems concerning the external indebtedness of the developing countries and the wider economic, trade and social implications of continued indebtedness for those countries. Within this framework, the Central American Ministers stressed that, in present circumstances, debt servicing by the countries in Central America is even more burdensome given increased interest rates and deteriorating prices for those products which make up the bulk of their exports.

The Community Ministers and those of Portugal and Spain declared themselves ready to assist the countries of Central America, in the appropriate framework, in the pursuit of policies aimed at solving these problems.

10.   The Ministers expressed their determination to cooperate in the appropriate international forums with a view to improving the present international economic situation.

11.   An effective manner of contributing to the reduction of political tension in Central America would be to support the action intended to preserve the degree of economic interdependence existing between the countries of the region.

The Community Ministers recognized that the Central American region has a definite development potential through the process of integration and reaffirmed their willingness to support this through the further development of relations between the two regions.

In this connection, the Ministers looked forward to the accession of Portugal and Spain to the European Community and welcomed the contribution which they will make to the further strengthening of cooperation between the two regions.

12.   The European Ministers and those of the Central American isthmus declared themselves satisfied with the results already produced by their relations and agreed on the need to broaden and deepen these relations. They concentrated more particularly on the areas in which cooperation with the European Community has proved useful for the economic development of the group of Central American countries and where mutual cooperation should be strengthened (specific development projects, particularly agricultural and rural projects with a regional basis, regional integration, trade promotion and generalized preferences).

13.   The European and Central American Ministers, in looking ahead to the future, in the perspective of the development of mutual cooperation, recognized the existence of solid ground for cooperation activities, on the basis of equity, respect and mutual benefit, notably along the lines of the following paragraphs.

14.   The Community and Portugal and Spain and the group of Central American countries recognized the need to develop, extend and diversify their mutual trade to the fullest possible extent. In this connection the Ministers considered that the generalized system of preferences could be an appropriate means to encourage the growth of foreign trade and industrialization of the countries concerned. They agreed that the use of the system should be simplified and its benefits be extended.

The Community reaffirmed the importance it attaches to the fundamental objectives of the generalized preferences system and announced its intention, where the development and the application of the system is concerned, of taking into account the interest that will be shown by the Central American countries.

15.   Taking account of the importance of economic development for the countries of the Central American region, the Community will do everything possible, within the context of its present and future programmes in support of developing countries, towards the development of the region. These actions should be identified by common agreement, based on the priorities and objectives of the region and should be multilateral in character. The Community declared itself willing to exploit to the full the institutional infrastructure existing in the region.

In addition to aid given on a bilateral basis by Member States of the Community to the countries of the region, the Community will provide technical and financial assistance to Central America, in particular for agricultural, agro-industrial and rural projects. With the aim of promoting regional economic integration and the development of intra-regional trade, it is the intention of the Community to give priority assistance to projects of a regional nature and to help the countries of Central America and their regional institutions through sharing with them the Community's specific experience acquired in matters of integration.

For its part, the group of Central American countries declared itself ready to present specific projects in priority fields, which take into account, *inter-alia*, social welfare aspects.

By way of illustration, mention was made, with regard to projects, of the demands which were presented jointly by the countries of Central America to the international financial community in Brussels in September 1983.

The Central American Ministers emphasized the importance they attach to the reactivation of production and particularly of the production of goods traded within the Central American isthmus. For the purpose of the latter, financial support is required for the countries of the Central American isthmus, preferably through the Banco Centro-americano de Integración Económica (CABEI), so that that support will contribute to the reactivation of the industrial and agricultural sectors of the region.

It is the intention of the Community and of its Member States to give priority to the development of their assistance to regionally-oriented projects and to those of a social nature such as health programmes and those intended to relieve the situation of those who for one reason or another have been compelled to abandon their traditional homes.

16.   The Ministers on the two sides considered that economic cooperation represented an area of interest for future relations between the Community and the group of Central American countries. In this context, they mentioned specifically the promotion of business contacts between the two regional groupings, cooperation between public and private national financing instruments in the two regions, as well as scientific, technical and basic training, especially in research fields. The Community Ministers took note of the possibility offered by the CABEI Board of Governors to open its membership to countries outside the region.

In view of the important role assumed by foreign investments in the economic development of Central American countries, the Ministers agreed that the promotion and protection of European investments in Central America are in their mutual interest. In this connection, they stressed the need for an improved climate for investments in the region by appropriate measures of encouraging private investments.

17.   The Ministers of the European Community and those of Central America acknowledged the interest in strengthening and giving institutional form to their mutual relations. Acknowledging the importance of strengthening relations, they declared themselves ready to start discussions as soon as possible with a view to negotiating an inter-regional framework cooperation agreement. On the Community side, the agreement would be negotiated in accordance with its established procedures. Both sides considered that the conclusion of an agreement of this type would confirm the political will of both regions to extend and develop their relations and that it would also help to reinforce relations between the Community and Latin America as a whole.

18.   The Central American Ministers expressed the view that the appropriate inter-governmental forum for approving the main lines of a regional position as a mechanism for negotiation and follow-up in the economic sphere is the Central American Economic Council, with the participation of a representative from the Government of Panama.

The negotiating body, under the aegis of the Central American Economic Council, will be an *ad hoc* group composed of delegates from every government. This body will act in coordination with the Group of Heads of Mission of the countries of the Central American isthmus (GRUCA) with headquarters in Brussels. The SIECA will support the mechanism for negotiation and follow-up and will seek the collaboration of other institutions connected with Central American integration and other regional and international bodies in accordance with the circumstances.

19.   The Ministers expressed their conviction that this meeting constitutes a first step in a process which will effectively increase existing cooperation between Central America and Europe.

. . .

Asia

ASEAN

The Association of South-East Asian Nations (ASEAN), created in 1967, sought contacts with the Community/ EPC during the 1970s. West German Foreign Minister Hans-Dietrich Genscher, a long-time supporter of regional cooperation, suggested a joint ministerial meeting. In November 1978, the first EC–ASEAN ministerial meeting was held (document 4c/31). An economic cooperation agreement was signed in March 1980, on the occasion of another ministerial meeting (document 4c/32), but the political dialogue has been the heart of EC/EU–ASEAN relations.

Document 4c/31 Joint Declaration of the Community–ASEAN Foreign Ministers' Conference, Brussels, 20–21 November 1978

The ASEAN Foreign Ministers and the Foreign Ministers of the Member States of the European Community exchanged views on current regional and international issues and developments. They reaffirmed their commitment to world peace, international cooperation and understanding, economic development and social justice. The discussions took place in a spirit of friendliness and understanding.

The Foreign Ministers of the Member States of the European Community welcomed the favourable development of ASEAN as a regional organization committed to economic growth, social progress and cultural development. They recognized ASEAN as a factor of stability and balance which contributes to the maintenance of peace in South-East Asia.

The Foreign Ministers of the Member States of the European Community reaffirmed their support for ASEAN's efforts to achieve self-reliance, progress and stability on the basis of economic, social and cultural cooperation.

The Foreign Ministers of the Member States of ASEAN recognized the work of European integration and the role played by the Europe of the Nine as a factor of economic and political stability and as an element of balance in international relations. They welcomed the outward-looking character of this integration exemplified by the desire of the Member States to cooperate with ASEAN.

The Foreign Ministers of the Member States of the European Community and ASEAN underlined the importance which they attach to the pursuance and development of relations and reaffirmed their common will to broaden the scope of their cooperation on the basis of equality, respect and mutual benefit. They also agreed that this cooperation should serve their people by promoting greater prosperity, social justice and human rights.

. . .

The Community recognized that ASEAN is a developing region and agreed that cooperation between ASEAN and the Community should be expanded in such a manner as to contribute to ASEAN's efforts in enhancing its self-reliance and economic resilience. The two sides noted that the work of the ASEAN-Commission Joint Study Group had strengthened relations between the two regional groupings. In this context, they noted the study on long-term cooperation between ASEAN and the Community which is currently in progress.

. . .

Against this background and that of the already prevailing economic cooperation between ASEAN and the Community, and in the light of the discussions which had taken place during the meeting, ASEAN and the Community agreed that it would be desirable to place the relations between the two groupings on a more formal footing and, to this end, it was agreed that exploratory discussions on the content of a possible cooperation agreement should shortly be started between the two sides.

. . .

Document 4c/32   Joint Statement, EC–ASEAN Ministerial Meeting, Kuala Lumpur, 7–8 March 1980

1.

On the occasion of the second ASEAN/EEC Ministerial Meeting in Kuala Lumpur on 7–8 March, 1980, the Foreign Ministers of the ASEAN Member States and the Foreign Ministers of the Member States of the European Community held informal meetings during which they conducted an intensive exchange of views on regional and international problems and developments since the meeting in Brussels in November 1978. They reaffirmed their commitment to world peace, international co-operation and understanding, economic development, social justice and human rights. They further emphasised the need for all States to observe strictly the following principles: respect for sovereignty, territorial integrity, and independence of States; non-resort to force or threat of the use of force and non-interference in the internal affairs of other States. They agreed that these principles are of vital importance to inter-state relations. The discussion took place in a spirit of great cordiality and mutual friendship.

2.

The Foreign Ministers of the ASEAN Member States and the Foreign Ministers of the Member States of the European Community, having analysed current international developments, expressed deep concern over the emergence of new and dangerous sources of tension, at a time when no solutions have been found for other serious difficulties already posing formidable problems. They noted that the tension and the difficulties are focused mainly in regions of the Third World where a climate of peace and international co-operation is indispensable to the achievement of progress in the economic and social fields. They urged the international community, especially the United Nations and its Secretary-General, to work actively for the resolution of problems in accordance with the principles of the United Nations Charter.

3.

The Foreign Ministers of the ASEAN Member States and the Foreign Ministers of the Member States of the European Community expressed great concern over open armed interventions by foreign powers against two non-aligned countries in Asia, namely the continuing Vietnamese intervention in Kampuchea and the Soviet military intervention in Afghanistan. They strongly deplored the armed interventions against these two countries, which have as a common denominator the imposition of will on small independent states by foreign powers through the use of force in open violation of international law, thereby threatening international peace and security. They called for an early implementation of United Nations General Assembly Resolutions No. 34/22 of 14 November 1979 and No. ES-6/2 of 14 January 1980 including total withdrawal of foreign forces from Kampuchea and Afghanistan.

4.

The Foreign Ministers of the ASEAN Member States and the Foreign Ministers of the Member States of the European Community deplored the denial of self-determination to the peoples of Kampuchea and of Afghanistan who should be allowed to decide their political future without foreign interference, coercion or intimidation. They further expressed their deep concern for the suffering of the Kampuchean and Afghan peoples, who have been forced to leave their countries on account of external aggression and for whom material assistance is now essential for their survival.

5.
The Foreign Ministers of the ASEAN Member States and the Foreign Ministers of the Member States of the European Community, taking into consideration the results of the meeting of Nine in Rome on February 19, 1980 and of the Islamic Conference of Foreign Ministers in Islamabad on January 27–29, 1980, appealed to all states to respect the sovereignty, territorial integrity, political independence and non-aligned character of Afghanistan. In that context they took the view that the crisis could be overcome constructively through the emergence of a neutral and non-aligned Afghanistan, outside competition among the powers.

6.
The Foreign Ministers of the ASEAN Member States and the Foreign Ministers of the Member States of the European Community noted with deep concern that the peoples in the Indochinese Peninsula, after many years of war and suffering, have yet to find peace and that this dangerous situation may be aggravated and spread to neighbouring countries. They agreed that peace and stability in South East Asia are essential. However, this and the establishment of friendly and co-operative relations among all the states of the region depend upon a political solution to the Kampuchean question on the basis of the withdrawal of foreign forces from Kampuchea, and self-determination for the Kampuchean people. They called for the early establishment of an independent and neutral Kampuchea with a genuinely representative government, free of all foreign military presence and maintaining friendly and peaceful relations with all countries in the region. They also emphasized the necessity of strict observance of non-interference in all forms in the internal affairs of states in South East Asia. They strongly urge the parties concerned and all states which can bring influence to bear on them, to exert utmost efforts in order to avert the possible spill-over of hostilities into neighbouring ASEAN countries and widening the area of conflict.

. . .

Burma/Myanmar

Relations with ASEAN in the 1990s have been strained by two issues: the Indonesian annexation of East Timor (which actually took place in 1975) and the enlargement of ASEAN to include Burma/Myanmar. Since the massacre of protesters in Dili, East Timor, in November 1991, Portugal (the former colonial power in East Timor) has blocked the conclusion of a new EU–ASEAN cooperation agreement. With democratic elections in Indonesia and movement towards independence for East Timor in 1999, the EU's relations with ASEAN could settle down. But events remain unpredictable. Moreover Burma/Myanmar remains a problem. The EU has imposed diplomatic sanctions and an arms embargo on Burma/Myanmar over its lack of democracy (document 4c/33) and cut off its tariff preferences under the generalized system of preferences because of the wide-spread use of forced labour in the country. ASEAN's decision to allow Burma/Myanmar to join the organization was not welcomed with enthusiasm in the EU (document 4c/34). Burma/ Myanmar would not be allowed to accede to the EC–ASEAN cooperation agreement or participate in the Asia–Europe meeting (ASEM)*. By mid-1999, a high-level EU–ASEAN ministerial meeting had been postponed for over two years because EU Member States refused to sit at the same table as Burmese representatives.

Document 4c/33   Common Position Defined by the Council of the European Union on the Basis of Article J.2 of the Treaty on European Union on Burma/Myanmar, 28 October 1996 (96/635/CFSP)

THE COUNCIL OF THE EUROPEAN UNION,

Having regard to the Treaty on European Union, and in particular Article J.2 thereof,

HAS DEFINED THE FOLLOWING COMMON POSITION:

1.   The European Union, considering the recent discussions with Burma/Myanmar at meetings in Jakarta and New York, is disappointed at the unwillingness of the State Law and Order Restoration Council (Slorc) to enter into a meaningful dialogue with it. The European Union reaffirms its determination to resume such dialogue at any time.

2.   The European Union is concerned at the absence of progress towards democratisation and at the continuing violation of human rights in Burma/Myanmar. It deplores, in particular, the practice of torture, summary and arbitrary executions, forced labour, abuse of women, political arrests, forced displacement of the population and restrictions on the fundamental rights of freedom of speech, movement and assembly. It condemns the detentions in May and September 1996 of members and supporters of the National League for Democracy (NLD). It calls for the immediate and unconditional release of all detained political prisoners. The NLD and other legitimate political parties, including those from ethnic minorities, should be allowed to pursue freely their normal activities. It calls on the Slorc to enter into meaningful dialogue with pro-democracy groups with a view to bringing about national reconciliation.

. . .

5.   With a view to promoting progress towards democratisation and securing the immediate and unconditional release of detained political prisoners, the European Union:

(a)   reaffirms the following measures already adopted:
   (i) expulsion of all military personnel attached to the diplomatic representations of Burma/Myanmar in Member States of the European Union and withdrawal of all military personnel attached to diplomatic representations of the Member States of the European Union in Burma/Myanmar;

---

*   The Asia–Europe biennial summits began in 1996 at Bangkok. They are attended by the EU-15, Japan, China, South Korea and ASEAN (minus Laos and Myanmar).

(ii) an embargo on arms, munitions and military equipment (^{1}) and suspension of non humanitarian aid or development programmes. Exceptions may be made for projects and programmes in support of human rights and democracy as well as those concentrating on poverty alleviation and, in particular, the provision of basic needs for the poorest section of the population, in the context of decentralized cooperation through local civilian authorities and Non-Governmental Organisations;

(b) introduces the following, additional measures:
(i) ban on entry visas for senior members of the Slorc and their families;
(ii) ban on entry visas for senior members of the military or the security forces who formulate, implement or benefit from policies that impede Burma/Myanmar's transition to democracy, and their families; and
(iii) suspension of high-level bilateral governmental (Ministers and Officials at the level of political director and above) visits to Burma/Myanmar.

6.   The implementation of this common position will be monitored by the Council, to which the Presidency and the Commission will regularly report, and will be reviewed in the light of developments in Burma/Myanmar. Further measures may need to be considered. In the case of a substantial improvement of the overall situation in Burma/Myanmar, not only the suspension of the aforementioned measures, but also the gradual resumption of cooperation with Burma/Myanmar will be considered, after careful assessment of developments by the Council.

7.   This Common Position shall take effect on 29 October 1996 for a renewable six months period.

. . .

Document 4c/34   Conclusions by the General Affairs Council on Burma/Myanmar, Luxembourg, 26 June 1997

The Council discussed the implications for the EU of the accession in particular of Burma/Myanmar to ASEAN.

The Council underlined that the deteriorating human rights situation in Burma/Myanmar is a matter of serious concern to the EU. On several occasions the EU has reiterated its concern at development in Burma/Myanmar. Most recently, on 30 May, the EU issued a declaration on the anniversary of the 1990 elections in which the SLORC-regime is urged to release the people detained on that occasion and to engage in a serious dialogue with the pro-democracy groups. Furthermore, the Council called on the SLORC to accept a visit to Burma/Myanmar by the UN special rapporteur at an early date.

(^{1}) The aforementioned embargo covers weapons designed to kill and their ammunition, weapon platforms, non-weapon platforms and ancillary equipment. The embargo also covers spare parts, repairs, maintenance and transfer of military technology. Contracts entered into prior to the date of entry into force of the embargo are not affected by this common position.

The Council stressed the importance they attach to the strengthening and deepening of EU–ASEAN relations in accordance with the conclusions of the EU–ASEAN Ministerial Meeting in Singapore in February 1997.

The Council confirmed the EU's commitment to the EU-ASEAN dialogue including on human rights and democratic principles. It expects membership of ASEAN to contribute to the promotion of these values in Burma. It agreed that the opportunity of the EU–ASEAN dialogue should be used to discuss the situation in Burma/Myanmar.

Bearing in mind that the current circumstances, reflected in the prolongation of the EU Common Position for another period of six months, preclude starting negotiations on the possible accession of Burma/Myanmar to the EC–ASEAN Cooperation Agreement, the Council considers that the presence of Burma/Myanmar at the forthcoming ARF/PMC Ministerial Meetings does not prejudge in any way its participation as observer at the upcoming EU–ASEAN Joint Cooperation Committee in November 1997 and other meetings in the institutional EU–ASEAN framework.

The Council reaffirmed that membership of Burma/Myanmar of ASEAN does not automatically imply membership of ASEM.

On the subject of possible additional measures against Burma/Myanmar, the Council agreed to look into this matter again in September in the light of the ARF/PMC Ministerial Meetings and the future developments in Burma/Myanmar.

Relations with Japan

The weakest side of the 'triangle' between the United States, Europe and Japan is that between Europe and Japan. An attempt to strengthen the relationship was made on 18 July 1991, with a joint Community–Japanese declaration (document 4c/35). The declaration is similar to the two declarations issued in November 1990, between the Community and the United States (see document 4a/24) and the Community and Canada. It has led to somewhat regular meetings between EU and Japanese representatives, but has not enjoyed a high profile.

Document 4c/35   Joint Declaration on EC–Japan Relations, The Hague, 18 July 1991

Preamble

The European Community and its Member States on the one part and Japan on the other part,

conscious of their common attachment to freedom, democracy, the rule of law and human rights;

affirming their common attachment to market principles, the promotion of free trade and the development of a prosperous and sound world economy;

recalling their increasingly close ties and acknowledging growing worldwide interdependence and, consequently, the need for heightened international cooperation;

affirming their common interest in security, peace and stability of the world;

aware of the importance of deepening their dialogue in order to make a joint contribution towards safeguarding peace in the world, setting up a just and stable international order in accordance with the principles and purposes of the United Nations Charter and taking up the global challenges that the international community has to face;

mindful of the accelerated process whereby the European Community is acquiring its own identity in the economic and monetary sphere, in foreign policy and in the field of security;

have decided to intensify their dialogue and to strengthen their cooperation and partnership in order that the challenges of the future may be met.

General principles of dialogue and of cooperation

The European Community and its Member States and Japan will firmly endeavour to inform and consult each other on major international issues, which are of common interest to both parties, be they political, economic, scientific, cultural or other. They will strive, whenever appropriate, to coordinate their positions. They will strengthen their cooperation and exchange of information both between the two parties and within international organizations.

Both parties will likewise consult together on the international situation and on regional matters with a view, in particular, to joining their efforts to bring about an easing of tensions and to ensure respect for human rights.

Objectives of dialogue and cooperation

The two parties will set out to explore together areas of possible cooperation, including where appropriate common diplomatic action. They will endeavour to strengthen their cooperation in a fair and harmonious way in all areas of their relations taken as a whole, in particular with respect to the following:

promoting negotiated solutions to international or regional tensions and the strengthening of the United Nations and other international organizations;

supporting social systems based on freedom, democracy, the rule of law, human rights and market economy;

enhancing policy consultation and, wherever possible, policy coordination on the international issues which might affect world peace and stability, including international security matters such as the non-proliferation of nuclear, chemical and biological weapons, the non-proliferation of missile technology and the international transfer of conventional weapons;

pursuing cooperation aimed at achieving a sound development of the world economy and trade, particularly in further strengthening the open multilateral trading system, by rejecting protectionism and recourse to unilateral measures and by implementing GATT and OECD principles concerning trade and investment;

pursuing their resolve for equitable access to their respective markets and removing obstacles, whether structural or other, impeding the expansion of trade and investment, on the basis of comparable opportunities;

strengthening their dialogue and cooperation on various aspects of multifaceted relations between both parties in such areas as trade, investment, industrial cooperation, advanced technology, energy, employment, social affairs and competition rules;

supporting the efforts of developing countries, in particular the poorest among them, to achieve sustained development and political and economic progress, along with fostering respect for human rights as a major factor in genuine development, with due regard for the objectives set by international organizations;

joining their efforts in meeting transnational challenges, such as the issue of environment, the conservation of resources and energy, terrorism, international crime and drugs and related criminal activity, in particular the laundering of the proceeds of crime;

strengthening cooperation and, where appropriate, promoting joint projects in the field of science and technology with a view to contributing to the promotion of scientific knowledge which is essential for the future prosperity of all mankind;

developing academic, cultural and youth exchange programmes aiming to increase knowledge and improve understanding between their respective peoples;

supporting, in cooperation with other States or organizations, Central and Eastern European countries engaged in political and economic reforms aimed at stabilizing their economies and promoting their full integration into the world economy;

cooperating, in relation with the countries of the Asia-Pacific region, for the promotion of peace, stability and prosperity of the region.

Framework for dialogue and consultation

Both parties are committed to engage in continuous dialogue to give substance to this declaration. To this end, in addition to the full use of all existing regular consultation mechanisms, both parties have decided to strengthen their mechanisms for consultation and substantial cooperation on global and bilateral issues:

(i)   especially they have decided to hold annual consultations in Europe or in Japan between, on the one hand, the President of the European Council and the President of the Commission and, on the other, the Japanese Prime Minister;

(ii)   an annual meeting continues to be held between the Commission and the Japanese Government at ministerial level;

(iii)   six-monthly consultations continue to be held between the Foreign Ministers of the Community and the Member of the Commission responsible for external relations (troika) and the Japanese Foreign Minister;

(iv)   the representatives of Japan are briefed by the Presidency of European political cooperation following ministerial political cooperation meetings, and Japan informs the representatives of the Community of the Japanese Government's foreign policy.

In order to give substance to this declaration, both parties will make use of the existing and above-mentioned forums with a view to regularly reviewing its implementation and to provide a permanent stimulus to the development of EC-Japan relations.

Human rights

Before the end of the Cold War, human rights were not a major consideration in the Community's foreign relations. EPC issued many declarations condemning human rights violations, but the Community/EPC rarely backed up the declaratory diplomacy with action. Concerns about human rights and democracy did impede the development of the Community's relations with Greece, Portugal and Spain, but the Community and the Member States maintained trade ties and detente with their neighbours in Eastern Europe as a way of encouraging liberalization (as the row over the gas pipeline illustrated). The Community's development aid was supposed to be non-political, although an exception had to be made in order to respond to the atrocities of Idi Amin in Uganda. But even that response proved to be rather mild: in 1977, the Community decided only that aid was not to be used to sustain the Ugandan regime. Limited sanctions were imposed on South Africa in 1985 and 1986, and sanctions were imposed against China following the Tiananmen Square events in 1989.

After democratic movements spread in Eastern Europe, the Community incorporated political conditionality into its external relations (see Section 4a). In June 1991, the European Council issued a declaration on human rights, stressing their indivisibility. Human rights considerations were made an explicit part of the Community's development policy with the November 1991 declaration on human rights, democracy, and development (document 4c/36). The possibility of including 'human rights clauses' in agreements with third countries was envisaged, and in May 1995 the Council decided that all EC agreements (including the Lomé convention) would state that respect for human rights and democratic principles are essential elements of the agreements; if they are violated, the EC could take appropriate action. While the EU has not been very consistent in applying conditionality (hesitating to cut off links with important commercial partners, for example), it has nonetheless developed a far-reaching human rights policy by the standards of other actors and of its own past. This should be evident in many of the documents throughout this book. The protection of human rights in third countries is also to be one of the factors that Member States consider before issuing arms exports licenses, under the 1998 Code of Conduct on Conventional Arms Exports, agreed within the CFSP framework (document 4c/37). On 10 December 1998, the fiftieth anniversary of the Universal Declaration of Human Rights, the Union issued a declaration which highlights the importance of human rights in the EU's external relations and lists further measures which could be implemented (document 4c/38).

Document 4c/36   Resolution of the Council and of the Member States Meeting in the Council on Human Rights, Democracy and Development, 28 November 1991

1. The Council recalls the European Council Resolution of 29 June 1991 which stated that respect for human rights, the rule of law and the existence of political

institutions which are effective, accountable and enjoy democratic legitimacy are the basis for equitable development. It also recalls the 1986 Declaration of Foreign Ministers of the Community on Human Rights (21 July 1986) and reaffirms that respecting, promoting and safeguarding human rights is an essential part of international relations and one of the cornerstones of European cooperation as well as of relations between the Community and its Member States and other countries. In this regard it stresses its attachment to the principles of representative democracy, of the rule of law, of social justice and of respect for human rights.

2.   The Council shares the analysis contained in the Commission's communication of 25 March 1991 and acknowledges that human rights have a universal nature and it is the duty of all States to promote them. At the same time, human rights and democracy form part of a larger set of requirements in order to achieve balanced and sustainable development. In this context, account should be taken of the issue of good governance as well as of military spending.

The Council considers it important that the Community and its Member States should have a common approach aimed at promoting human rights and democracy in developing countries. Such an approach would improve the cohesion and consistency of initiatives taken in this field. The objective of the present resolution is to formulate concrete guidelines, procedures and lines of action.

3.   The Community and its Member States recognize the necessity of a consistent approach towards human rights, democracy and development in their cooperation with developing countries. Development cooperation is based on the central place of the individual and has, therefore, in essence to be designed with a view to promoting – in parallel with economic and social rights – civil and political liberties by means of representative democratic rule that is based on respect for human rights. They endorse, on the basis of these principles, the following approaches, instruments and activities.

4.   The Community and its Member States will give high priority to a positive approach that stimulates respect for human rights and encourages democracy. An open and constructive dialogue between them and the governments of developing countries can make a very important contribution to the promotion of human rights and democracy. Various initiatives can be undertaken, for example, through active support for:
• countries which are attempting to institute democracy and improve their human rights performance;
• the holding of elections, the setting-up of new democratic institutions and the strengthening of the rule of law;
• the strengthening of the judiciary, the administration of justice, crime prevention and the treatment of offenders;
• promoting the role of NGOs and other institutions which are necessary for a pluralist society;
• the adoption of a decentralized approach to cooperation;
• ensuring equal opportunities for all.

At the request of the Commission or one of the Member States, the possibility of increased assistance to developing countries in which substantive positive changes in human rights and democracy have taken place will be examined.

5.   The Council stresses the importance of good governance. While sovereign States have the right to institute their own administrative structures and establish their own constitutional arrangements, equitable development can only effectively and sustainably be achieved if a number of general principles of government are adhered to: sensible economic and social policies, democratic decision-making, adequate governmental transparency and financial accountability, creation of a market-friendly environment for development, measures to combat corruption, as well as respect for the rule of law, human rights, and freedom of the press and expression. The Community and Member States will support the efforts of developing countries to advance good governance and these principles will be central in their existing or new development cooperation relationships.

6.   While, in general, a positive and constructive approach should receive priority, in the event of grave and persistent human violations or the serious interruption of democratic processes, the Community and its Member States will consider appropriate responses in the light of the circumstances, guided by objective and equitable criteria. Such measures, which will be graduated according to the gravity of each case, could include confidential or public *démarches* as well as changes in the content or channels of cooperation programmes and the deferment of necessary signatures or decisions in the cooperation process or, when necessary, the suspension of cooperation with the States concerned.

The Member States and the Commission will exchange immediate information concerning such measures and consider joint approaches in reaction to violations. They will be informed in such cases through the EPC communications network and particular cases may be further discussed within the Council framework.

7.   The Community's response to violations of human rights will avoid penalizing the population for governmental actions. Rather than simply discontinuing development cooperation, the Community and the Member States may adjust cooperation activities with a view to ensuring that development aid benefits more directly the poorest sections of the population in the country, for example through non-governmental or informal networks, while at the same time establishing a certain distance *vis-à-vis* the government concerned. Such adjustment will focus on the choice of partners of projects and of the type of cooperation programmes. In all cases, however, humanitarian and emergency aid, which directly benefit vulnerable populations, will continue to be made available.

8.   The Council welcomes the efforts undertaken in recent years by developing countries to move towards democracy. It is recognized that governments have to build the political, economic and social structures to support democracy and that this is a gradual process which will sometimes take a relatively long period. The Community and its Member States will support the process and hold regular informal exchanges of views on the best possible course of action in order to achieve lasting results as speedily as possible.

9.   The Council attaches very great importance to the question of military spending. Excessive military expenditure not only reduces the funds available for other purposes, but violations of international law, as well as often being meant and used for purposes of internal repression and denial of universally recognized human rights.

Moreover, in a period in which donor countries are engaged in a process leading to levels of armament not exceeding sufficiency levels, development cooperation with governments which maintain much larger military structures than needed will become difficult to justify. In the dialogue with their partners in developing countries, the Community and its Member States will stress the negative effects of excessive military spending on the development process. They will consider adopting concrete measures in their cooperation in order to encourage developing countries to reduce their military expenditure, which is often excessive in relation to their legitimate security needs, and simultaneously to implement development projects of an economic and social nature, with particular emphasis on the education and health sectors. With this in mind, they may consider increasing support for countries which achieve substantial reductions in their military expenditure, or reducing support for countries which fail to do so. The Council recognizes the need for restraint and transparency in the transfer of conventional weapons to developing countries. It will further examine the question of military spending by developing countries along these lines. The Community and its Member States will request countries with which development cooperation relationships are maintained to cooperate voluntarily with the new UN register of arms transfers.

10.   The Community and its Member States will explicitly introduce the consideration of human rights as an element of their relations with developing countries; human rights clauses will be inserted in future cooperation agreements. Regular discussions on human rights and democracy will be held, within the framework of development cooperation, with the aim of seeking improvements.

In order to facilitate timely support by the Community for initiatives in developing countries aiming at the promotion of respect for human rights and the encouragement of democracy and good governance it is intended to expand resources devoted to these ends within the overall allocations available for development. Sound activities in Third World countries promoting human rights and democracy, both by government and by non-governmental entities, will be eligible for financial support. The Community and its Member States undertake in addition to integrate the promotion of respect for human rights and the advancement of democracy in their future cooperation programmes.

The Commission will transmit an annual report to the Council on the implementation of this resolution.

In addition to the consultations and meetings which can be convened as stipulated in paragraphs 4, 5 and 6, a meeting will be held annually by representatives of the Commission and Member States to consider policies and specific lines of action to further enhance respect for human rights and establishment of representative democratic rule.

Document 4c/37   EU Code of Conduct on Arms Exports

See Appendix

Document 4c/38 Declaration of the European Union on the Occasion of the Fiftieth Anniversary of the Universal Declaration on Human Rights, Vienna, 10 December 1998

On the occasion of the 50th Anniversary of the adoption of the Universal Declaration of Human Rights, the Union recalls the primary importance that it attaches to this Declaration. It constitutes the foundation for national, regional and global policies to advance and ensure human dignity world-wide.

The universality and indivisibility of human rights and the responsibility for their protection and promotion, together with the promotion of pluralistic democracy and effective guarantees for the rule of law, constitute essential objectives for the European Union as a union of shared values and serve as a fundamental basis for our action.

. . .

III. The European Union, which is founded on the principles of liberty, democracy, respect for human rights and fundamental freedoms and the rule of law, shares the values in which the Declaration is rooted. It is conscious of the need to promote human rights in its own countries. Both internally and externally, respect for human rights as proclaimed in the Universal Declaration is one of the essential components of the activities of the Union. In their activities, the institutions of the Union respect human rights as guaranteed by the European Convention on the Protection of Human Rights and Fundamental Freedoms and as resulting from the constitutional traditions common to the Member States, under the control of the Court of Justice of the European Communities. Equally, Member States are bound by the European Convention and their actions are submitted to the supervision of the European Court of Human Rights. With the entry into force of the Treaty of Amsterdam, respect for human rights and fundamental freedoms will be a condition for accession to the European Union, and a serious and persistent breach of these rights may lead to the suspension of rights of a Member State.

Moreover, the Amsterdam Treaty will further strengthen the commitment to safeguard and promote human rights and fundamental freedoms, especially by measures against discrimination in a wide range of fields including by strengthening the possibilities of ensuring equal opportunities for men and women. Furthermore, aware of the European Social Charter and the Community Charter on Basic Social Rights of Workers, it defines aims in the field of basic social rights. The European Union in its co-operation in the field of justice and security will also be guided by its respect for human rights.

Respect for human rights and fundamental freedoms is also one of the objectives of the Union's Common Foreign and Security Policy as well as of its development co-operation. The Union pursues this goal both in its bilateral relations with third countries and in the framework of the United Nations and other multilateral fora, in particular the Organisation for Security and Co-operation in Europe, and the Council of Europe.

In pursuit of its policy of promoting human rights in all parts of the world, the Union regularly raises human rights questions in its dialogue with third countries, as an important and legitimate part of this dialogue, and in demarches as well as declarations.

The European Community has included in the agreements it concludes a clause which makes respect for human rights, in particular as contained in the Universal Declaration on Human Rights, an essential element for its agreement to be bound. The Union thus assumes its responsibility for the promotion and protection of human rights as a legitimate concern of the international community, while reaffirming that this protection and promotion remain the primary responsibility of each and every government.

The Union expresses its preoccupation about recent incidents of racism and xenophobia, both within the Union and throughout the world, and will work actively towards achieving meaningful results at the World Conference on Racism. A range of practical measures complement the Union's efforts in these fields; the Union wishes to highlight, in this context, notably the activities of the Vienna Monitoring Centre on Racism and Xenophobia.

The Union has decided this year to reinforce its efforts for the universal abolition of the death penalty as a strongly held policy agreed by the EU. Where the death penalty still exists, the Union calls for its use to be restricted, and demands that it be carried out only in accordance with international safeguards. The Union is also pressing, where relevant, for moratoria to be introduced.

The Union accords high importance to supporting efforts for the promotion of democracy, respect for human rights, the rule of law, and good governance. The Union therefore provides support for a wide range of projects and programmes in these fields throughout the world.

The Union and its Member States are committed to co-operating with international human rights mechanisms at the global and regional levels. The Union actively supports the action of the UN High Commissioner for Human Rights and her activities, especially at the field level. The Union encourages the efforts by the UN Secretary General towards better integrating human rights into the broad range of UN activities.

The Union particularly welcomes the adoption of the Statue of a permanent International Criminal Court to try the most serious crimes and violations of humanitarian law of concern to the international community and calls for an early ratification of this statute.

IV.   These policies must be continued and, where necessary, strengthened and improved. In this regard, it is important that the Union reinforce its capacity to achieve its objectives on the protection and promotion of human rights and fundamental freedoms. In this context, the Union is determined to ensure respect for human rights in all its actions. In particular the Union will consider concrete measures such as:

1)   enhance the capacity to jointly assess the human rights situation in the world by closer co-ordination and otherwise ensure that all pertinent means for action are available within the framework of the Union, including through the possible publication of an annual EU human rights report;

2)   further develop cooperation in the field of human rights, such as education and training activities, in coordination with other relevant organisations, and ensure the continuation of the Human Rights Masters Programme organised by fifteen European universities;

3)   reflect on the usefulness of convening a periodic human rights discussion forum with the participation of EU institutions as well as representatives of academic institutions and NGOs;

4)   strengthen the capacities to respond to international operational requirements in the field of human rights and democratisation, such as through the possible establishment of a common roster of European human rights and democracy experts, for human rights field operations and electoral assistance and monitoring;

5)   foster the development and consolidation of democracy and the rule of law and respect for human rights and fundamental freedoms in third countries, in particular through working towards the earliest possible adoption of the draft regulations, currently under consideration in the EU framework, on the implementation of co-operation operations;

6)   ensure all means to achieve the coherent realisation of these goals, including through the consideration of strengthening relevant EU structures.

Appendix

Document 3/19   Conclusions of the European Council in Helsinki, 10–11 December 1999 (ESDP).

Common European Policy on Security and Defence

25.   The European Council adopts the two Presidency progress reports (see Annex IV) on developing the Union's military and non-military crisis management capability as part of a strengthened common European policy on security and defence.

26.   The Union will contribute to international peace and security in accordance with the principles of the United Nations Charter. The Union recognises the primary responsibility of the United Nations Security Council for the maintenance of international peace and security.

27.   The European Council underlines its determination to develop an autonomous capacity to take decisions and, where NATO as a whole is not engaged, to launch and conduct EU-led military operations in response to international crises. This process will avoid unnecessary duplication and does not imply the creation of a European army.

28.   Building on the guidelines established at the Cologne European Council and on the basis of the Presidency's reports, the European Council has agreed in particular the following:

– cooperating voluntarily in EU-led operations, Member States must be able, by 2003, to deploy within 60 days and sustain for at least 1 year military forces of up to 50,000–60,000 persons capable of the full range of Petersberg tasks;

– new political and military bodies and structures will be established within the Council to enable the Union to ensure the necessary political guidance and strategic direction to such operations, while respecting the single institutional framework;

– modalities will be developed for full consultation, cooperation and transparency between the EU and NATO, taking into account the needs of all EU Member States;

– appropriate arrangements will be defined that would allow, while respecting the Union's decision-making autonomy, non-EU European NATO members and other interested States to contribute to EU military crisis management;

– a non-military crisis management mechanism will be established to coordinate and make more effective the various civilian means and resources, in parallel with the military ones, at the disposal of the Union and the Member States.

29. The European Council asks the incoming Presidency, together with the Secretary-General/High Representative, to carry work forward in the General Affairs Council on all aspects of the reports as a matter of priority, including conflict prevention and a committee for civilian crisis management. The incoming Presidency is invited to draw up a first progress report to the Lisbon European Council and an overall report to be presented to the Feira European Council containing appropriate recommendations and proposals, as well as an indication of whether or not Treaty amendment is judged necessary. The General Affairs Council is invited to begin implementing these decisions by establishing as of March 2000 the agreed interim bodies and arrangements within the Council, in accordance with the current Treaty provisions.

. . .

ANNEX 1 TO ANNEX IV

PRESIDENCY PROGRESS REPORT TO THE HELSINKI EUROPEAN COUNCIL ON STRENGTHENING THE COMMON EUROPEAN POLICY ON SECURITY AND DEFENCE

Introduction

Recalling the guiding principles agreed at Cologne, the European Union should be able to assume its responsibilities for the full range of conflict prevention and crisis management tasks defined in the EU Treaty, the Petersberg tasks.

The European Union should have the autonomous capacity to take decisions and, where NATO as a whole is not engaged, to launch and then to conduct EU-led military operations in response to international crises in support of the Common Foreign and Security Policy (CFSP). The action by the Union will be conducted in accordance with the principles of the UN Charter and the principles and objectives of the OSCE Charter for European Security. The Union recognises the primary responsibility of the United Nations Security Council for the maintenance of international peace and security.

For this purpose, the following has been agreed:

A common European headline goal will be adopted for readily deployable military capabilities and collective capability goals in the fields of command and control, intelligence and strategic transport will be developed rapidly, to be achieved through voluntary co-ordinated national and multinational efforts, for carrying out the full range of Petersberg tasks.

New political and military bodies will be established within the Council to enable the Union to take decisions on EU-led Petersberg operations and to ensure, under the authority of the Council, the necessary political control and strategic direction of such operations.

Principles for cooperation with non-EU European NATO members and other European partners in EU-led military crisis management will be agreed, without prejudice to the Union's decision-making autonomy.

Determination to carry out Petersberg tasks will require Member States to improve national and multinational military capabilities, which will at the same time, as appropriate, strengthen the capabilities of NATO and enhance the effectiveness of the Partnership for Peace (PfP) in promoting European security.

In presenting this report, the Presidency has taken note of the fact that Denmark has recalled Protocol no 5 to the Amsterdam Treaty on the position of Denmark.

Military capabilities for Petersberg tasks

Member States recall their commitment made at Cologne and their determination to give the EU appropriate capabilities, without unnecessary duplication, to be able to undertake the full range of Petersberg tasks in support of the CFSP. Such capabilities will enable them to conduct effective EU-led operations as well as playing, for those involved, their full role in NATO and NATO-led operations. More effective European military capabilities will be developed on the basis of the existing national, bi-national and multinational capabilities, which will be assembled for EU-led crisis management operations carried out with or without recourse to NATO assets and capabilities. Particular attention will be devoted to the capabilities necessary to ensure effective performance in crisis management: deployability, sustainability, interoperability, flexibility, mobility, survivability and command and control, taking account of the results of the WEU audit of assets and capabilities and their implications for EU-led operations.

To develop European capabilities, Member States have set themselves the headline goal: by the year 2003, cooperating together voluntarily, they will be able to deploy rapidly and then sustain forces capable of the full range of Petersberg tasks as set out in the Amsterdam Treaty, including the most demanding, in operations up to corps level (up to 15 brigades or 50,000–60,000 persons). These forces should be militarily self-sustaining with the necessary command, control and intelligence capabilities, logistics, other combat support services and additionally, as appropriate, air and naval elements. Member States should be able to deploy in full at this level within 60 days, and within this to provide smaller rapid response elements available and deployable at very high readiness. They must be able to sustain such a deployment for at least one year. This will require an additional pool of deployable units (and supporting elements) at lower readiness to provide replacements for the initial forces.

Member States have also decided to develop rapidly collective capability goals in the fields of command and control, intelligence and strategic transport, areas also identified by the WEU audit. They welcome in this respect decisions already announced by certain Member States which go in that direction:

- to develop and coordinate monitoring and early warning military means;
- to open existing joint national headquarters to officers coming from other Member States;
- to reinforce the rapid reaction capabilities of existing European multinational forces;
- to prepare the establishment of a European air transport command;
- to increase the number of readily deployable troops;
- to enhance strategic sea lift capacity.

The General Affairs Council, with the participation of Defence Ministers, will elaborate the headline and capability goals. It will develop a method of consultation through which these goals can be met and maintained, and through which national contributions reflecting Member States' political will and commitment towards these goals can be defined by each Member State, with a regular review of progress made. In addition, Member States would use existing defence planning procedures, including, as appropriate, those available in NATO and the Planning and Review Process (PARP) of the PfP. These objectives and those arising, for those countries concerned, from NATO's Defence Capabilities Initiative (DCI) will be mutually reinforcing.

The European NATO members who are not EU Member States, and other countries who are candidates for accession to the European Union will be invited to contribute to this improvement of European military capabilities. This will enhance the effectiveness of EU-led military operations and will, for those countries concerned, contribute directly to the effectiveness and vitality of the European pillar of the NATO.

Member States welcome the recent progress made towards the restructuring of European defence industries, which constitutes an important step forward. This contributes to strengthening the European industrial and technological defence base. Such developments call for increased efforts to seek further progress in the harmonisation of military requirements and the planning and procurement of arms, as Member States consider appropriate.

Decision-making

The Council decides upon policy relevant to Union involvement in all phases and aspects of crisis management, including decisions to carry out Petersberg tasks in accordance with Article 23 of the EU Treaty. Taken within the single institutional framework, decisions will respect European Community competences and ensure inter-pillar coherence in conformity with Article 3 of the EU Treaty.

All Member States are entitled to participate fully and on an equal footing in all decisions and deliberations of the Council and Council bodies on EU-led operations. The commitment of national assets by Member States to such operations will be based on their sovereign decision. Member States will participate in the ad hoc committee of contributors in accordance with the conditions provided for by paragraph 24.

Defence Ministers will be involved in the common European security and defence policy (CESDP); when the General Affairs Council discusses matters related to the CESDP, Defence Ministers as appropriate will participate to provide guidance on defence matters.

The following new *permanent* political and military bodies will be established within the Council:

a) – *A standing Political and Security Committee (PSC)* in Brussels will be composed of national representatives of senior/ambassadorial level. The PSC will deal with all aspects of the CFSP, including the CESDP, in accordance with the provisions of the EU Treaty and without prejudice to Community competence. In the case of a military crisis management operation, the PSC will exercise, under the authority of the Council, the political control and strategic direction of the operation. For that purpose, appropriate procedures will be adopted in order to allow effective and urgent decision taking. The PSC will also forward guidelines to the Military Committee.

b) – *The Military Committee (MC)* will be composed on the Chiefs of Defence, represented by their military delegates. The MC will meet at the level of the Chiefs of Defence as and when necessary. This committee will give military advice and make recommendations to the PSC, as well as provide military direction to the Military Staff. The Chairman of the MC will attend meetings of the Council when decisions with defence implications are to be taken.

c) – *The Military Staff (MS)* within the Council structures will provide military expertise and support to the CESDP, including the conduct of EU-led military crisis management operations. The Military Staff will perform early warning, situation assessment and strategic planning for Petersberg tasks including identification of European national and multinational forces.

As an *interim* measure, the following bodies will be set up within the Council as of March 2000:

a) – Fully respecting the Treaty provisions, the Council will establish a standing interim political and security committee at senior/ambassadorial level tasked to take forward under the guidance of the Political Committee the follow up of the Helsinki European Council by preparing recommendations on the future functioning of the CESDP and to deal with CFSP affairs on a day-to-day basis in close contacts with the SG/HR.

b) – An interim body of military representatives of Member States' Chiefs of Defence is established to give military advice as required to the interim political and security committee.

c) – The Council Secretariat will be strengthened by military experts seconded from Member States in order to assist in the work on the CESDP and to form the nucleus of the future Military Staff.

The Secretary General/High Representative (SG/HR), in assisting the Council, has a key contribution to make to the efficiency and consistency of the CFSP and the development of the common security and defence policy. In conformity with the

EU Treaty, the SG/HR will contribute to the formulation, preparation and implementation of policy decisions.

In the interim period, the SH/HR, Secretary General of the WEU, should make full use of WEU assets for the purpose of advising the Council under Article 17 of the EU Treaty.

Consultation and cooperation with non-EU countries and with NATO

The Union will ensure the necessary dialogue, consultation and cooperation with NATO and its non-EU members, other countries who are candidates for accession to the EU as well as other prospective partners in EU-led crisis management, with full respect for the decision-making autonomy of the EU and the single institutional framework of the Union.

With European NATO members who are not members of the EU and other countries who are candidates for accession to the EU, appropriate structures will be established for dialogue and information on issues related to security and defence policy and crisis management. In the event of a crisis, these structures will serve for consultation in the period leading up to a decision of the Council.

Upon a decision by the Council to launch an operation, the non-EU European NATO members will participate if they so wish, in the event of an operation requiring recourse to NATO assets and capabilities. They will, on a decision by the Council, be invited to take part in operations where the EU does not use NATO assets.

Other countries who are candidates for accession to the EU may also be invited by the Council to take part in EU-led operations once the Council has decided to launch such an operation.

Russia, Ukraine and other European States engaged in political dialogue with the Union and other interested States may be invited to take part in the EU-led operations.

All the States that have confirmed their participation in an EU-led operation by deploying significant military forces will have the same rights and obligations as the EU participating Member States in the day-to-day conduct of such an operation.

In the case of an EU-led operation, an ad-hoc committee of contributors will be set up for the day-to-day conduct of the operation. All EU Member States are entitled to attend the ad-hoc committee, whether or not they are participating in the operation, while only contributing States will take part in the day-to-day conduct of the operation.

The decision to end an operation will be taken by the Council after consultation between the participating states within the committee of contributors.

Modalities for full consultation, cooperation and transparency between the EU and NATO will be developed. Initially, relations will be developed on an informal basis, through contacts between the SG/HR for CFSP and the Secretary General of NATO.

Follow-up for the Portuguese Presidency

The Portuguese Presidency is invited, together with the Secretary General/High Representative, to carry toward the work within the General Affairs Council on strengthening the common European security and defence policy. The Portuguese Presidency is also invited to report to the European Council in Feira on the progress made, including:

a) – recommendations on the institutional development of the new permanent political and military bodies related to the CESDP within the EU, taking into account the paper on "Military bodies in the European Union and the planning and conduct of EU-led operations" and other contributions made;

b) – proposals on appropriate arrangements to be concluded by the Council on modalities of consultation and/or participation that will allow the third States concerned to contribute to EU military crisis management.

c) – proposals on principles for consultation with NATO on military issues and recommendations on developing modalities for EU/NATO relations, to permit co-operation on the appropriate military response to a crisis, as set out in Washington and at Cologne;

d) – an indication of whether or not Treaty amendment is judged necessary.

. . .

ANNEX 2 to ANNEX IV

Presidency Report on Non-Military Crisis Management of the European Union

The Presidency was mandated by the European Council in Cologne to continue the work on all aspects of security including the enhancement and better coordination of the Union's and the Member States' non-military crisis response tools. Developments inter alia in Kosovo have for their part underlined the importance of this task. To this end, a thorough discussion has been carried out within the Council instances.

Work listing all available resources of the Member States and the Union has been initiated and has led to inventories of the tools available to the Union and to Member States, which are contained respectively in doc. 11044/99 REV 1 for the Union and in doc. 12323/99 for the Member States.

The inventories which have been drawn up clearly show that Member States, the Union, or both have accumulated considerable experience or have considerable resources in a number of areas such as civilian police, humanitarian assistance, administrative and legal rehabilitation, search and rescue, electoral and human rights monitoring, etc. This inventory should be pursued further. Regular updating will be necessary to better identify lacunae as well as strongpoints.

In order to be able to respond more rapidly and more effectively to emerging crisis situations, the Union needs to strengthen the responsiveness and efficiency of its resources and tools, as well as their synergy.

It is therefore appropriate to draw up an Action Plan which would show the way ahead and indicate the steps the Union has to undertake to develop a rapid reaction capability in the field of crisis management using non-military instruments.

ACTION PLAN

A. The Union should aim at:

– strengthening the synergy and responsiveness of national, collective and NGO resources in order to avoid duplication and improve performance, while maintaining the flexibility of each contributor to decide on the deployment of assets and capabilities in a particular crisis, or via a particular channel;

– enhancing and facilitating the EU's contributions to, and activities within, other organisations, such as the UN and the OSCE whenever one of them is the lead organisation in a particular crisis, as well as EU autonomous actions;

– ensuring inter-pillar coherence.

B. To that end:

Member States and the Union should develop a rapid reaction capability by defining a framework and modalities, as well as by pre-identifying personnel, material and financial resources that could be used in response to a request of a lead agency like the UN or the OSCE, or, where appropriate, in autonomous EU actions.

An inventory of national and collective resources should be pursued to give an overview of resources that could be marshalled within such a rapid reaction framework. In this process Member States and the EU institutions could, if they wish, highlight sectors in which they find that they have acknowledged expertise.

A database should be set up to maintain and share information on the pre-identified assets,. capabilities and expertise within all areas relevant to non-military crisis management. The availability and quality of these assets would need to be clearly defined.

A study should be carried out, taking into account lessons learned, to define concrete targets for the EU Member States' collective non-military response to international crises (e.g. the ability to deploy at short notice and sustain for a defined period a set number of civilian police as a contribution to civpol missions; to deploy a combined search and rescue capability of up to 200 people within twenty-four hours). This work should be taken forward by the Portuguese Presidency together with the SG/HR.

The inventory, the database project and the study should help identify areas of relative strength and weakness and could promote improved trading standards, sharing of experience and best practice, as well as bilateral or multilateral projects between Member States (e.g. 'pairing' one Member State's helicopter lift with a specialist medical team from another).

A coordinating mechanism, fully interacting with the Commission services, should be set up at the Council Secretariat. It would run the database project and the different capabilities initiatives. In particular crises, depending on the EU's role, it may set up an ad hoc centre to coordinate the effectivenss of EU Member States' contributions. This should be a lean, efficient, non-bureaucratic structure permitting close interaction with the Commission (ECHO in particular).

In establishing a rapid reaction capability urgent consideration will be given to developing civil police capabilities.

Rapid financing mechanisms such as the creation by the Commission of a Rapid Reaction Fund should be set up to allow the acceleration of the provision of finance to support EU activities, to contribute to operations run by other international organisations and to fund NGO activities, as appropriate.

DECISION-MAKING AND IMPLEMENTATION

The Union should develop a comprehensive approach with a view to marshalling national and collective non-military instruments within the time limits called for by the situation on the ground.

For the coordination of civilian crisis management tools, the co-ordinating mechanism for a civilian crisis management will be established. This mechanism, which will be of inter-pillar nature, will provide expert advice in support of the management of crises. Decision-making and implementation of non-military crisis management tools under the first pillar will remain subject to institutions and procedures of the EC Treaty.

As an interim practice, this work to develop the co-ordinating mechanism for civilian crisis management may draw on experts from the Member States.

If appropriate, the Union will lay down general guidelines ensuring inter-pillar coherence and setting out the means which should be made available. Arrangements for rapid financing mechanisms for a prompt response to crisis situations could be devised in this context.

Document 4b/60   Conclusions of the European Council in Helsinki, 11 December 1999 (Enlargement)

. . .

I PREPARING FOR ENLARGEMENT

The enlargement process

3. The European Council confirms the importance of the enlargement process launched in Luxembourg in December 1997 for the stability and prosperity of the entire European continent. An efficient and credible enlargement process must be sustained.

4. The European Council reaffirms the inclusive nature of the accession process, which now comprises 13 candidate States within a single framework. The candidate States are participating in the accession process on an equal footing. They must share the values and objectives of the European Union as set out in the Treaties. In this respect the European Council stresses the principle of peaceful settlement of disputes in accordance with the United Nations Charter and urges candidate States to make every effort to resolve any outstanding border disputes and other related issues. Failing this they should within a reasonable time bring the dispute to the International Court of Justice. The European Council will review the situation relating to any outstanding disputes, in particular concerning the repercussions on the accession process and in order to promote their settlement through the International Court of Justice, at the latest by the end of 2004. Moreover, the European Council recalls that compliance with the political criteria laid down at the Copenhagen European Council is a prerequisite for the opening of accession negotiations and that compliance with all the Copenhagen criteria is the basis for accession to the Union.

. . .

8. The European Council notes with satisfaction the substantive work undertaken and progress which has been achieved in accession negotiations with Cyprus, Hungary, Poland, Estonia, the Czech Republic and Slovenia.

9. (a) The European Council welcomes the launch of the talks aiming at a comprehensive settlement of the Cyprus problem on 3 December in New York and expresses its strong support for the UN Secretary-General's efforts to bring the process to a successful conclusion.

(b) The European Council underlines that a political settlement will facilitate the accession of Cyprus to the European Union. If no settlement has been reached by the completion of accession negotiations, the Council's decision on accession will be made without the above being a precondition. In this the Council will take account of all relevant factors.

. . .

12. The European Council welcomes recent positive developments in Turkey as noted in the Commission's progress report, as well as its intention to continue its reforms towards complying with the Copenhagen criteria. Turkey is a candidate State destined to join the Union on the basis of the same criteria as applied to the other candidate States. Building on the existing European strategy, Turkey, like other candidate States, will benefit from a pre-accession strategy to stimulate and support its reforms. This will include enhanced political dialogue, with emphasis on progressing towards fulfilling the political criteria for accession with particular reference to the issue of human rights, as well as on the issues referred to in paragraphs 4 and 9(a). Turkey will also have the opportunity to participate in Community programmes and agencies and in meetings between candidate States and the Union in the context of the accession process. An accession partnership will be drawn up on the basis of previous European Council conclusions while containing priorities on which accession preparations must concentrate in the light of the political and economic criteria and the obligations of a Member State, combined with a national programme for the adoption of the acquis. Appropriate monitoring mechanisms

will be established. With a view to intensifying the harmonisation of Turkey's legislation and practice with the acquis, the Commission is invited to prepare a process of analytical examination of the acquis. The European Council asks the Commission to present a single framework for coordinating all sources of European Union financial assistance for pre-accession.

Document 4c/37   EU Code on Arms Exports, Council Statement, 25 May 1998, Brussels

EU CODE OF CONDUCT ON ARMS EXPORTS*

Council Statement, 25 May 1998.

The Council of the European Union.

BUILDING on the Common Criteria agreed at the Luxembourg and Lisbon European Councils in 1991 and 1992, [EPC Bulletin, Docs 91/196 and 92/253.]

RECOGNISING the special responsibility of arms exporting states,

DETERMINED to set high common standards which should be regarded as the minimum for the management of, and restraint in, conventional arms transfers by all EU Member States, and to strengthen the exchange of relevant information with a view to achieving greater transparency,

DETERMINED to prevent the export of equipment which might be used for internal repression or international aggression, or contribute to regional instability,

WISHING within the framework of the CFSP to reinforce their cooperation and to promote their convergence in the field of conventional arms exports,

NOTING complementary measures taken by the EU against illicit transfers, in the form of the EU Programme for Preventing and Combating Illicit Trafficking in Conventional Arms,

ACKNOWLEDGING the wish of EU Member States to maintain a defence industry as part of their industrial base as well as their defence effort,

RECOGNISING that states have a right to transfer the means of self-defence, consistent with the right of self-defence recognised by the UN Charter,

have adopted the following Code of Conduct and operative provisions:

CRITERION ONE

Respect for the international commitments of EU Member States, in particular the sanctions decreed by the UN Security Council and those decreed by the Community, agreements on non-proliferation and other subjects, as well as other international obligations.

---

*   Text in which political agreement was reached. The text was formally adopted on 8 June 1998

An export licence should be refused if approval would be inconsistent with, inter alia:

a) the international obligations of Member States and their commitments to enforce UN, OSCE and EU arms embargoes;

b) the international obligations of Member States under the Nuclear Non-Proliferation Treaty, the Biological and Toxin Weapons Convention and the Chemical Weapons Convention;

c) their commitments in the frameworks of the Australia Group, the Missile Technology Control Regime, the Nuclear Suppliers Group and the Wassenaar Arrangement;

d) their commitment not to export any form of anti-personnel landmine.

CRITERION TWO

The respect of human rights in the country of final destination

Having assessed the recipient country's attitude towards relevant principles established by international human rights instruments, Member States will:

a) not issue an export licence if there is a clear risk that the proposed export might be used for internal repression;

b) exercise special caution and vigilance in issuing licences, on a case-by-case basis and taking account of the nature of the equipment, to countries where serious violations of human rights have been established by the competent bodies of the UN, the Council of Europe or by the EU.

For these purposes, equipment which might be used for internal repression will include, inter alia, equipment where there is evidence of the use of this or similar equipment for internal repression by the proposed end-user, or where there is reason to believe that the equipment will be diverted from its stated end-use or end-user and used for internal repression. In line with operative paragraph 1 of this Code, the nature of the equipment will be considered carefully, particularly if it is intended for internal security purposes.

Internal repression includes, inter alia, torture and other cruel, inhuman and degrading treatment or punishment, summary or arbitrary executions, disappearances, arbitrary detentions and other major violations of human rights and fundamental freedoms as set out in relevant international human rights instruments, including the Universal Declaration on Human Rights and the International Covenant on Civil and Political Rights.

CRITERION THREE

The internal situation in the country of final destination, as a function of the existence of tensions or armed conflicts.

Member States will not allow exports which would provoke or prolong armed conflicts or aggravate existing tensions or conflicts in the country of final destination.

CRITERION FOUR

Preservation of regional peace, security and stability

Member States will not issue an export licence if there is a clear risk that the intended recipient would use the proposed export aggressively against another country or to assert by force a territorial claim.

When considering these risks, EU Member States will take into account inter alia:

a) the existence or likelihood of armed conflict between the recipient and another country;

b) a claim against the territory of a neighbouring country which the recipient has in the past tried or threatened to pursue by means of force;

c) whether the equipment would be likely to be used other than for the legitimate national security and defence of the recipient;

d) the need not to affect adversely regional stability in any significant way.

CRITERION FIVE

The national security of the Member States and of territories whose external relations are the responsbility of a Member State, as well as that of friendly and allied countries

Member States will take into account:

a) the potential effect of the proposed export on their defence and security interests and those of friends, allies and other Member States, while recognising that this factor cannot affect consideration of the criteria on respect of human rights and on regional peace, security and stability;

b) the risk of use of the goods concerned against their forces or those of friends, allies or other Member States;

c) the risk of reverse engineering or unintended technology transfer.

CRITERION SIX

The behaviour of the buyer country with regard to the international community, as regards in particular to its attitude to terrorism, the nature of its alliances and respect for international law

Member States will take into account inter alia the record of the buyer country with regard to:

a) its support or encouragement of terrorism and international organised crime;

b) its compliance with its international commitments, in particular on the non-use of force, including under international humanitarian law applicable to international and non-international conflicts;

c) its commitment to non-proliferation and other areas of arms control and disarmament, in particular the signature, ratification and implementation of relevant arms control and disarmament conventions referred to in sub-para b) of Criterion One.

CRITERION SEVEN

The existence of a risk that the equipment will be diverted within the buyer country or re-exported under undesirable conditions

In assessing the impact of the proposed export on the importing country and the risk that exported goods might be diverted to an undesirable end-user, the following will be considered:

a) the legitimate defence and domestic security interests of the recipient country, including any involvement in UN or other peace-keeping activity;

b) the technical capability of the recipient country to use the equipment;

c) the capability of the recipient country to exert effective export controls;

d) the risk of the arms being re-exported or diverted to terrorist organisations (anti-terrorist equipment would need particularly careful consideration in this context).

CRITERION EIGHT

The compatability of the arms exports with the technical and economic capacity of the recipient country, taking into account the desirability that states should achieve their legitimate needs of security and defence with the least diversion for armaments of human and economic resources

Member States will take into account, in the light of information from relevant sources such as UNDP, World Bank, IMF and OECD reports, whether the proposed export would seriously hamper the sustainable development of the recipient country. They will consider in this context the recipient country's relative levels of military and social expenditure, taking into account also any EU or bilateral aid.

OPERATIVE PROVISIONS

1. Each EU Member State will assess export licence applications for military equipment made to it on a case-by-case basis against the provisions of the Code of Conduct.

2. This Code will not infringe on the right of Member States to operate more restrictive national policies.

3. EU Member States will circulate through diplomatic channels details of licences refused in accordance with the Code of Conduct for military equipment together with an explanation of why the licence has been refused. The details to be notified are set out in the form of a draft pro-forma at Annex A. Before any Member State grants a licence which has been denied by another Member State or States for an essentially

identical transaction within the last three years, it will first consult the Member State or States which issued the denial(s). If following consultations, the Member State nevertheless decides to grant a licence, it will notify the Member State or States issuing the denial(s), giving a detailed explanation of its reasoning.

4. The decision to transfer or deny the transfer of any item of military equipment will remain at the national discretion of each Member State. A denial of a licence is understood to take place when the member state has refused to authorise the actual sale or physical export of the item of military equipment concerned, where a sale would otherwise have come about, or the conclusion of the relevant contract.

For these purposes, a notifiable denial may, in accordance with national procedures, include denial of permission to start negotiations or a negative response to a formal initial enquiry about a specific order.

EU Member States will keep such denials and consultations confidential and not to use them for commercial advantage.

EU Member States will work for the early adoption of a common list of military equipment covered by the Code, based on similar national and international lists. Until then, the Code will operate on the basis of national control lists incorporating where appropriate elements from relevant international lists.

The criteria in this Code and the consultation procedure provided for by paragraph 3 of the operative provisions will also apply to dual-use goods as specified in Annex 1 of Council Decision 94/942/CFSP as amended, where there are grounds for believing that the end-user of such goods will be the armed forces or internal security forces or similar entities in the recipient country.

In order to maximise the efficiency of this Code, EU Member States will work within the framework of the CFSP to reinforce their cooperation and to promote their convergence in the field of conventional arms exports.

Each EU Member State will circulate to other EU Partners in confidence an annual report on its defence exports and on its implementation of the Code. These reports will be discussed at an annual meeting held within the framework of the CFSP. The meeting will also review the operation of the Code, identify any improvements which need to be made and submit to the Council a consolidated report, based on contributions from Member States.

EU Member States will, as appropriate, assess jointly through the CFSP framework the situation of potential or actual recipients of arms exports from EU Member States, in the light of the principles and criteria of the Code of Conduct.

It is recognised that Member States, where appropriate, may also take into account the effect of proposed exports on their economic, social, commercial and industrial interests, but that these factors will not affect the application of the above criteria.

EU Member States will use their best endeavours to encourage other arms exporting states to subscribe to the principles of this Code of Conduct.

This Code of Conduct and the operative provisions will replace any previous elaboration of the 1991 and 1992 Common Criteria.

ANNEX to the Code of Conduct on arms exports

('Pro forma' for notification of refused licences)

. . . . . . (name of Member State) has the honour to inform partners of the following denial under the EU Code of Conduct:

Destination Country: . . . .

Short description of equipment, including quantity and where appropriate, technical specifications: . . . .

Proposed consignee: . . . .

Proposed end-user (if different): . . . .

Reason for refusal: . . . .

Date of denial: . . . .

Other decisions

List of commonly used abbreviations

Note: We have included here only those abbreviations that appear frequently throughout the book. Abbreviations that appear more rarely are not listed here – they are usually explained in full at the start of the relevant document.

ACP	African, Caribbean and Pacific countries
ANC	African National Congress
APEC	Asia-Pacific Economic Cooperation
ASEAN	Association of South-East Asian Nations
ASEM	Asia-Europe (summit) meetings
CCP	Common Commercial Policy
CEECs	Central and East European Countries
CESDP	Common European Security and Defence Policy
CFE	Conventional Forces in Europe (treaty)
CFSP	Common Foreign and Security Policy
CIS	Commonwealth of Independent States
CJTF	Combined Joint Task Force
CMEA	Council for Mutual Economic Assistance
Coreper	Committee of Permanent Representatives
COREU	*Correspondance européenne* telex network
CSCE	Conference on Security and Co-operation in Europe
CWC	Chemical Weapons Convention
EAPC	Euro-Atlantic Partnership Council
EBRD	European Bank for Reconstruction and Development
EC	European Community
ECHO	European Community Humanitarian Office
ECJ	European Court of Justice
ECMM	European Community Monitoring Mission
Ecofin	Council of Economic and Finance Ministers
ECSC	European Coal and Steel Community
EDC	European Defence Community
EEC	European Economic Community
EFTA	European Free Trade Association
EIB	European Investment Bank

EMS	European Monetary System
EMU	Economic and Monetary Union
EP	European Parliament
EPC	European Political Cooperation
ESDI	European Security and Defence Identity
EU	European Union
EUAM	European Union Administration of Mostar
FAWEU	Forces Answerable to the Western European Union
FRY	Federal Republic of Yugoslavia
FYROM	Former Yugoslavia Republic of Macedonia
GATT	General Agreement on Tariffs and Trade
GCC	Gulf Cooperation Council
GSP	Generalised System of Preferences
IAEA	International Atomic Energy Authority
IBRD	International Bank for Reconstruction and Development (World Bank)
ICFY	International Conference on the Former Yugoslavia
ICJ	International Court of Justice
IEPG	Independent European Programme Group
IFOR	Implementation Force (Bosnia-Herzegovina)
IGC	Intergovernmental Conference
IFI	International Financial Institution
IMF	International Monetary Fund
JNA	Yugoslav National Army
KLA	Kosovo Liberation Army
KVM	Kosovo Verification Mission
MFO	Multinational Force and Observers in Sinai
NAC	North Atlantic Council
NACC	North Atlantic Cooperation Council
NATO	North Atlantic Treaty Organisation
NPT	Nuclear Non-Proliferation Treaty
OAU	Organisation of African Unity
OECD	Organisation for Economic Cooperation and Development
OPEC	Organisation of Petroleum Exporting Countries
OSCE	Organisation for Security and Cooperation in Europe
PARP	Planning and Review Process (within NATO's Partnership for Peace)
PCA	Partnership and Cooperation Agreement
PfP	Partnership for Peace (NATO)

PHARE	Poland/Hungary: Assistance for the Reconstruction of the Economy
PLO	Palestinian Liberation Organisation
QMV	qualified majority voting
RPF	Rwandan Patriotic Front
SADCC	Southern African Development Coordination Conference
SEA	Single European Act
SFOR	Stabilisation Force (Bosnia-Herzegovina)
START	Strategic Armed Forces Reduction Treaty
TACIS	Technical Assistance to the Commonwealth of Independent States
TEC	Treaty of the European Community
TEU	Treaty of European Union
UN	United Nations
UNCTAD	United Nations Conference on Trade and Development
UNHCR	United Nations High Commissioner for Refugees
UNITA	National Union for the Total Independence of Angola
UNMIK	United Nations Mission in Kosovo
UNPROFOR	United Nations Protection Force (former Yugoslavia)
UNSCOM	United Nations Special Commission (Iraq)
UNSCR	United Nations Security Council Resolution
USSR	Union of Soviet Socialist Republics
WB	World Bank
WEU	Western European Union
WMD	weapons of mass destruction
WTO	World Trade Organisation

Index